# The MAILBOX®

The Education Center®

The Idea Magazine For Teachers®

INTERMEDIATE®

# 2000–2001 YEARBOOK



**Becky S. Andrews, Editor**
**Scott Lyons, Project Manager**

**The Education Center, Inc.**
**Greensboro, North Carolina**

*The Mailbox*® 2000–2001 Intermediate Yearbook

Founding Editor in Chief: Margaret Michel
Senior Editor: Becky S. Andrews
Associate Editor: Peggy W. Hambright
Executive Director, Magazine Publishing: Katharine P. S. Brower
Editorial and Freelance Management: Karen A. Brudnak
Curriculum Director: Karen P. Shelton
Editorial Training: Irving P. Crump
Contributing Editors: Irving P. Crump, Cayce Guiliano, Deborah T. Kalwat, Debra Liverman, Scott Lyons
Copy Editors: Gina Farago, Karen Brewer Grossman, Karen L. Huffman, Amy Kirtley, Debbie Shoffner
Traffic Manager: Lisa K. Pitts
Graphic Services Coordinator: Teresa R. Davidson
Staff Artists: Pam Crane, Nick Greenwood, Rebecca Saunders (SENIOR ARTISTS); Theresa Lewis Goode, Clevell Harris, Sheila Krill, Mary Lester, Clint Moore, Kimberly Richard, Greg D. Rieves, Barry Slate, Donna K. Teal
Cover Artist: Lois Axeman
Typesetters: Lynette Maxwell, Mark Rainey
Editorial Assistants: Terrie Head, Melissa B. Montanez, Hope Rodgers, Jan E. Witcher
Librarian: Dorothy C. McKinney

ISBN 1-56234-455-2
ISSN 1088-5552



Printed in the United States of America.

The Education Center, Inc.
P.O. Box 9753
Greensboro, NC 27429-0753

# Contents

# Teacher Resource Ideas

# A "Fín-tastic" First Day

## Our Readers' Favorite Activities for the First Day of School

Fishin' around for some new ways to make the first day of school extra special? With the following "fin-tastic" ideas from our readers, your kids will be back in the swim of things in no time!

### First-Day Envelopes

Keep kids busy on the first morning of school with this easy idea. Use colorful stickers to decorate a large manila envelope (or a lunch-sized paper bag) for each child. Stuff the envelopes with the items shown and place them on students' desktops. Not only can the activities buy you time for completing first-day tasks, but students can use the envelopes at the end of the day to take home important forms and information.

- a back-to-school puzzle
- a new, sharpened pencil
- a box of crayons
- an interesting picture to color
- a welcome letter from you (Make a note in your planbook for the last week of school to have this year's students write the letters for next year's class.)
- a nutritious snack, such as a box of raisins or a baggie of trail mix

Garlene Turner, Mildred Dean Elementary
Butler, KY

### Me Boxes

Find out all about your new students with this first-day homework assignment. One week before school begins, send each child a note welcoming him to your class. In the note, ask him to decorate the outside of a shoebox with words or pictures that represent his personal qualities, the things he values, and the people he loves. Inside the box, have him place three items that are special to him. Then, on the first day of school, divide students into groups to share their boxes with one another.

Shawn L. Parkhurst, Canadian Academy
Kobe, Japan

### Getting-Acquainted Letters

It's a familiar first-day dilemma: parents who arrive with their kids want to chat with you, but students are also waiting at their desks for something to do. Say "so long!" to such a scenario with this getting-acquainted activity. First, write a three-paragraph letter about yourself to place on each student's desk along with a sheet of colorful stationery and a new pencil. In the first paragraph of the letter, tell about your family and hobbies. In the second paragraph, share what you did during the summer. In the third paragraph, state your goals for the year. Conclude the letter by asking each student to answer it (in the same three-paragraph format) using the stationery and new pencil.

Shawn L. Parkhurst

I am a boy with light brown hair and brown eyes who likes to ride horses. I love pepperoni pizza, strawberry ice cream, and the chocolate chip cookies that my mom makes. I have a dog named Checkers and a cat named Claws.

## Guess Who?

Help students take a closer look at their new classmates with this first-day writing activity. Review the qualities of good descriptive writing. Then have each student cut out a copy of the pattern on page 11. Direct the child to write a description of himself on the pattern (without including his name); then have him write his name on the back. Arrange the magnifying glasses and a copy of your class roster on a bulletin board titled "Can You Guess Who's in [name of teacher]'s Class?" During free time, have students try to match the names and descriptions. On Back-to-School Night, challenge parents to guess which magnifying glass describes their child!

Michelle Trubitz—Grs. 5 & 6, Brookside Upper Elementary
Westwood, NJ

## Big Rules

Make expectations crystal clear on the first day with this surefire activity. In advance, write each of your class rules on a different sheet of poster board. (Keep the list to three to five general rules; see the sample list below.) On the first day, ask each student to list rules that she thinks are important on index cards (one per card). Next, introduce your rules by displaying the posters. In turn, have each child read one of her rules aloud. Discuss with students how the rule fits under one of your "big" rules. Then have that student tape her card to the appropriate poster. After all the cards have been shared, pair students and assign each twosome a different big rule. Each pair's job is to design a poster that shows how the student cards explain their assigned rule more clearly. Display the students' posters next to yours. Then, when disciplining a child later in the year, point to the posters as a reminder of the rules that everyone agreed on.

Teena Andersen—Grs. 4–6, Hadar Public School, Pilger, NE

Treat others with kindness.
No name-calling.
No teasing.
Don't hurt a person's feelings.


**Sample rules:**
- Treat others with kindness.
- Always do your best work.
- Be a responsible member of this class.

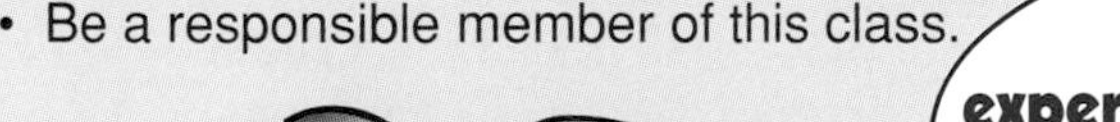

**I like science experiments and recess, but I don't care for pop quizzes!**

Pam Crane

## A Few of My Favorite (and Least Favorite) Things

Share your expectations for the school year with this fun brainstorming activity. First, have students brainstorm a list of the things they like best about school: activities they enjoy, topics they like learning about, kinds of tests they prefer, etc. Next, ask students to name things that they don't like. After this list is complete, turn the tables by sharing *your* favorite things, such as students who raise their hands before speaking and kind attitudes toward others. Also share your least favorite things, such as impolite or disruptive behavior. Suggest that you'll try to avoid the things students dislike *if* they'll avoid yours. Then make a pact, agreeing to make this a pleasant year for everyone!

Jaimie K. Hudson, Pace, FL

## Classmate Crossword

Help students learn how to spell one another's names correctly with this fun first-day activity. First, let each child have the fun of writing his name on the chalkboard. Then give each student a sheet of half-inch graph paper on which to create a crossword puzzle that includes all of his classmates' names. Now that spells *fun!*

Jennifer Balogh-Joiner—Gr. 4
Franklin Elementary, Franklin, NJ

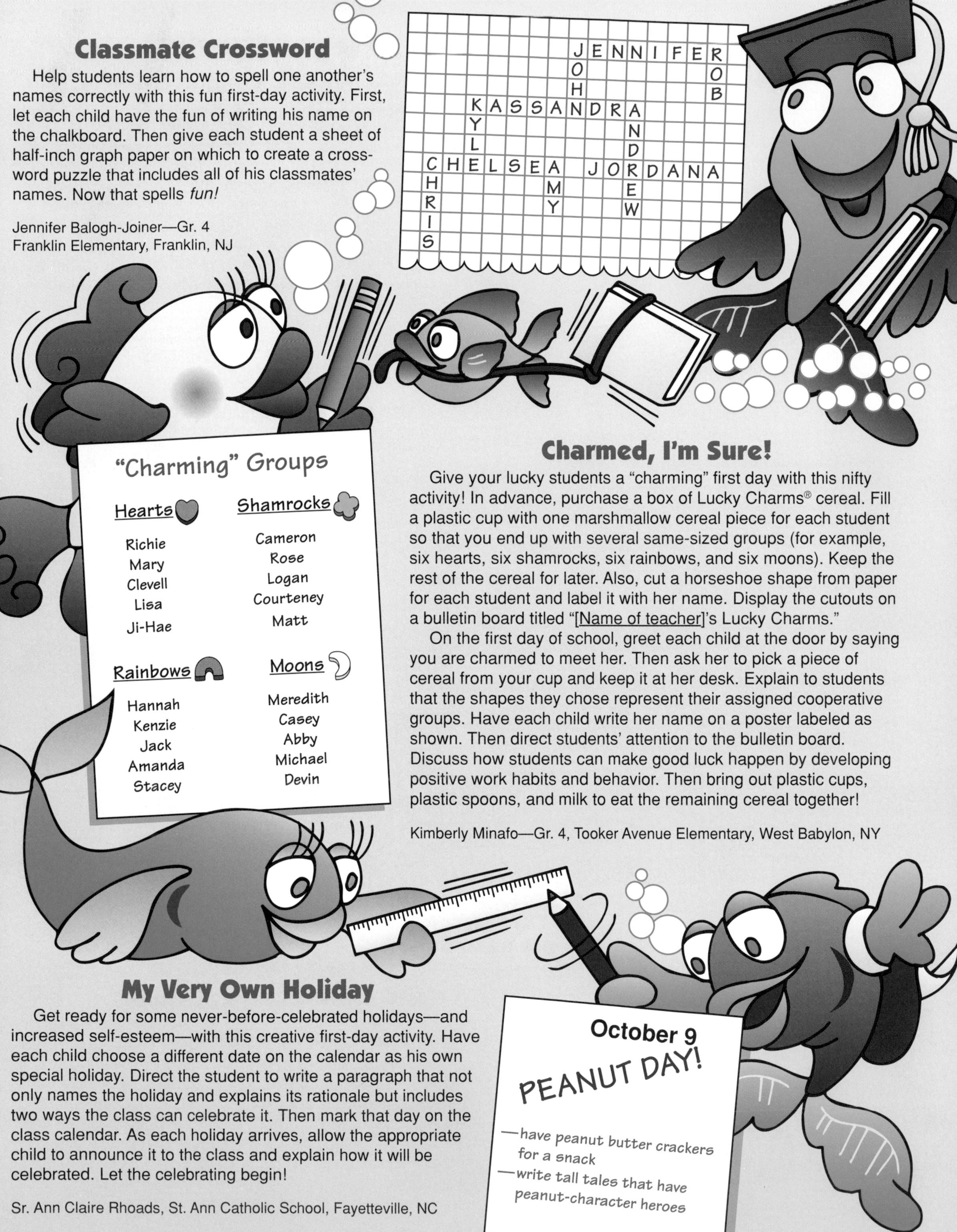

JENNIFER
ROB
JOHN
KASSANDRA
KYLE
ANDREW
CHELSEA
AMY
JORDANA
CHRIS
"Charming" Groups
Hearts
Richie
Mary
Clevell
Lisa
Ji-Hae
Shamrocks
Cameron
Rose
Logan
Courteney
Matt
Rainbows
Hannah
Kenzie
Jack
Amanda
Stacey
Moons
Meredith
Casey
Abby
Michael
Devin
October 9
PEANUT DAY!
—have peanut butter crackers for a snack
—write tall tales that have peanut-character heroes


## Charmed, I'm Sure!

Give your lucky students a "charming" first day with this nifty activity! In advance, purchase a box of Lucky Charms® cereal. Fill a plastic cup with one marshmallow cereal piece for each student so that you end up with several same-sized groups (for example, six hearts, six shamrocks, six rainbows, and six moons). Keep the rest of the cereal for later. Also, cut a horseshoe shape from paper for each student and label it with her name. Display the cutouts on a bulletin board titled "[Name of teacher]'s Lucky Charms."

On the first day of school, greet each child at the door by saying you are charmed to meet her. Then ask her to pick a piece of cereal from your cup and keep it at her desk. Explain to students that the shapes they chose represent their assigned cooperative groups. Have each child write her name on a poster labeled as shown. Then direct students' attention to the bulletin board. Discuss how students can make good luck happen by developing positive work habits and behavior. Then bring out plastic cups, plastic spoons, and milk to eat the remaining cereal together!

Kimberly Minafo—Gr. 4, Tooker Avenue Elementary, West Babylon, NY

## My Very Own Holiday

Get ready for some never-before-celebrated holidays—and increased self-esteem—with this creative first-day activity. Have each child choose a different date on the calendar as his own special holiday. Direct the student to write a paragraph that not only names the holiday and explains its rationale but includes two ways the class can celebrate it. Then mark that day on the class calendar. As each holiday arrives, allow the appropriate child to announce it to the class and explain how it will be celebrated. Let the celebrating begin!

Sr. Ann Claire Rhoads, St. Ann Catholic School, Fayetteville, NC

## A Sweet Way of Getting to Know You

Treat students to a sweet way of getting to know one another with this activity. Give each child a small bag of M&M's® or Skittles® candy. Direct him to reach into his bag without looking and remove one piece of candy. Have students holding the same color of candy form a group. In turn, ask each group member to introduce himself and then share one interesting fact about himself. Repeat until each child has met all his classmates.

Cathy Ogg, Happy Valley Elementary, Carter County, TN

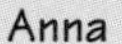

## Bio-Poem Project

Get the scoop on your new students with a winning first-day poetry project. Use the form on the right to model the writing of a bio-poem about yourself. Then have each child follow the form to write a similar poem about herself. Finally, guide students through the steps provided to display their poems in a unique way.

**Materials for each student:**
wire clothes hanger, bent into an oval shape
large sheet of skin-colored tissue paper
glue
scissors
various art materials (colorful paper scraps, yarn, fabric, buttons, etc.)
pair of paper hands and arms

**Steps:**

1. Cut the tissue paper in half.
2. Apply glue to the rim of the hanger. Place the glued rim facedown on one of the tissue paper halves.
3. Apply glue to the other side of the hanger. Press the remaining tissue paper to the rim. Allow to dry overnight.
4. Trim the extra paper from the outside edge of the hanger.
5. Turn the hanger so that its hook is at the top. Decorate the oval with art materials to resemble your face.
6. Glue paper hands and arms to each side of the oval to hold your poem.

Kim Clasquin—Gr. 4, Garrett Elementary
Hazelwood, MO

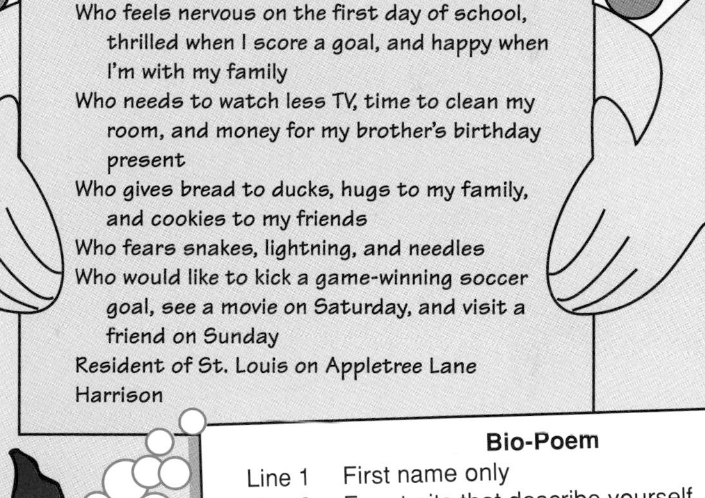

Anna
Spunky, artistic, athletic, bright
Sister of Andy
Lover of theme parks, board games, and soccer
Who feels nervous on the first day of school, thrilled when I score a goal, and happy when I'm with my family
Who needs to watch less TV, time to clean my room, and money for my brother's birthday present
Who gives bread to ducks, hugs to my family, and cookies to my friends
Who fears snakes, lightning, and needles
Who would like to kick a game-winning soccer goal, see a movie on Saturday, and visit a friend on Sunday
Resident of St. Louis on Appletree Lane
Harrison

**Bio-Poem**

| | |
|---|---|
| Line 1 | First name only |
| Line 2 | Four traits that describe yourself |
| Line 3 | Brother/sister of...(or son/daughter of) |
| Line 4 | Lover of...(three people or ideas) |
| Line 5 | Who feels...(three things) |
| Line 6 | Who needs...(three things) |
| Line 7 | Who gives...(three things) |
| Line 8 | Who fears...(three things) |
| Line 9 | Who would like to...(three things) |
| Line 10 | Resident of...(your city) on (your street) |
| Line 11 | Last name only |

## A Letter to Me

Start the new year—and end it—with this simple self-esteem booster. On the first day of school, have each student write a letter to himself expressing his goals for the year and listing ten positive things about himself. Collect the letters. On the last day of school, return each letter, to which you've added a note congratulating its owner for the goals he reached during the school year. A letter-perfect start, a letter-perfect ending!

Sr. Ann Claire Rhoads, St. Ann Catholic School, Fayetteville, NC

## Getting-to-Know-You Graphs

Get to know your class with a first-day graphing activity that really stacks up! In advance, label each of several sheets of graph paper with a topic, such as "Number of Siblings," "Favorite Color," "Type of Pet," etc. Label each graph's axes appropriately. Post the graphs on a bulletin board titled "[Grade level taught] Graders Really Stack Up!" On the first day of school, provide each student with enough small stickers so that he can place one on each graph. When students are finished, have the class help you evaluate the data on the resulting bar graphs.

Kimberly Minafo—Gr. 4, Tooker Avenue Elementary
West Babylon, NY

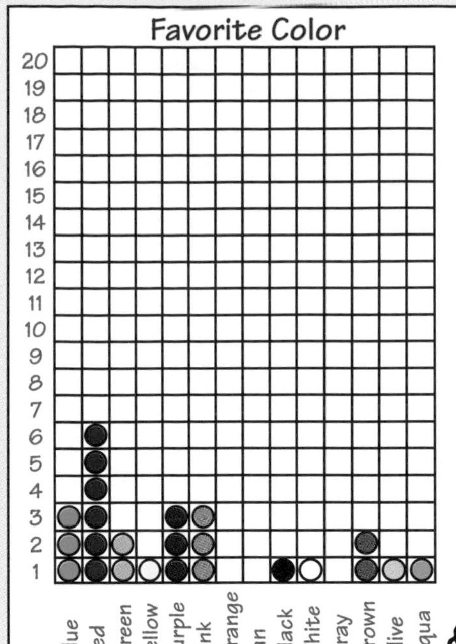

This Year I Want to...
...join 4-H club.
...read 25 new books.
...learn about tornadoes.
...learn about dinosaurs.
...make honor roll.
H
H
H
H
Jane


## A Hands-Down Favorite

Learn what your students want to accomplish this year with a first-day activity that's sure to be a hands-down favorite! Have each child trace her hand on a sheet of paper. Direct her to write "This Year I Want to…" at the top of the paper. On each finger of the tracing, have her write something she wants to learn or accomplish during the school year. Then have her personalize the tracing with colorful drawings that illustrate some of her favorite things. Display students' completed papers on a bulletin board. Then send them home with the students' first batch of graded papers. What a "hand-y" way for you—and parents—to learn about your kids' goals!

Tammie M. Guidry—Gr. 5, Iota Elementary, Iota, LA

## Missing-Piece Puzzles

Use this hands-on activity on the first day to show students how important it is to cooperate with others and ask for help. In advance, cut a variety of pictures from old magazines (one picture per student). Laminate the pictures; then cut each one into several puzzle pieces. Put all the pieces of a picture inside a plastic resealable bag; then take out one piece and place it in a bag that holds a different puzzle. Continue in this manner until each bag contains a puzzle with one missing piece and one piece that does not belong.

On the first day of school, give each student a bag of puzzle pieces to assemble. When a child discovers that a piece of his puzzle is missing and the extra piece doesn't work, suggest that he ask his classmates for help. Then watch as students happily complete their puzzles with a little help from their friends!

Barbara Samuels, Riverview School, Denville, NJ

## Pattern

Use with "Guess Who?"
on page 7.

# High-Flyin' Homework Hints

Make homework a breeze for everyone with these high-flyin', practical ideas from our readers!

## HOT Tickets

When spring fever hits—or a big holiday is approaching—minds turn anywhere but to homework! Increase the motivation to complete homework with this simple solution. Make copies of the "HOT Ticket" (Homework on Time) pattern on page 276 on neon orange paper. Each time a student completes his homework and turns it in on time, let him fill out a ticket and place it in a special container. At the end of the week, draw one or more tickets; then award a special prize to each lucky winner. Want to work a little math practice into this incentive? On Friday morning, announce the number of tickets in the container; then have each student determine the probability of his name being drawn, based on the number of tickets he earned during the week.

Joy Allen & Marcia Crouch—Gr. 4, Sam Houston Elementary, Bryan, TX

HOT TICKET

Homework on Time

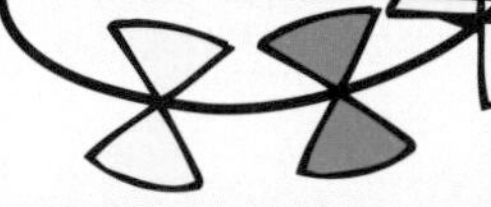


name

## Homework Club Card

Want to increase students' motivation for doing homework? Then join the club—the Homework Club, that is! Make a class supply of the Homework Club Card pattern on page 276. Explain to the class that you understand that circumstances occasionally make it difficult to complete homework. Then distribute the homework cards, each of which entitles its owner to one free homework pass per month, plus one additional "FREE" space to use any month. When a student wants to use a pass, he brings the card to you; then you punch a hole in the appropriate month's space (or the "FREE" space). In the beginning, students will probably rush to use the cards right away. But gradually they'll learn the advantages of saving the pass for emergencies, such as when an assignment is accidentally left at home or forgotten.

Joy Allen & Marcia Crouch

## When Parents Help

Just because a student makes 100 percent on a homework assignment doesn't necessarily mean that she understood a concept. At the beginning of the year, ask parents to sign the top of any homework assignment they needed to help their children with. If a parent's signature is across the top of an assignment, it will signal to you that the student needs extra help on that skill.

Joan Cuba—Gr. 5, Pleviak School, Lake Villa, IL

Name
Homework Diary
Date
Assignment
I didn't turn in this assignment because
Check when turned in
Date
Assignment
I didn't turn in this assignment because
Check when turned in
Date
Assignment
I didn't turn in this assignment because
Check when turned in
Date
Assignment
I didn't turn in this assignment because
Check when turned in

## Homework Diary

Keep track of missed assignments—and emphasize students' responsibility to complete them—with the help of an inexpensive three-ring binder. Make a class supply of the form on page 15. Label a page for each student; then punch holes in the page and place it in the binder. When a student misses an assignment, have her fill out an entry on her binder page. Then, if a student or parent questions whether an assignment was turned in, you'll have an explanation of what happened in the student's own handwriting. Use the binder to monitor make-up work by checking the box on the form when the missing assignment is turned in.

Loraine Moore—Gr. 5, Pearl Prep School, Arcadia, CA

## Homework Bucket

Teachers aren't the only ones who need a helping hand where homework is concerned—parents do too! In a letter sent home at the beginning of the year, suggest to parents that they fill an inexpensive bucket, plastic bin, or basket with the following items: special homework pencils and pens, a stapler, paper clips, colored pencils, page markers, sticky notes, highlighters, and any other office supplies that the child might like. Have the parents stipulate that the supplies can *only* be used for completing homework. Students will love having their own "offices" to work from at home.

Janet Bavonese—Gr. 4, Perrine Baptist Academy, Miami, FL

Megan's Homework Bucket

## Dialing for Homework

If you've got a phone in your classroom, here's a simple idea that makes informing parents about homework assignments a breeze. Purchase an inexpensive answering machine for your class phone. At the end of each day, record the day's homework assignments on the machine. Parents and students can then call after school to make sure that all assignments have been completed. Absent students can also call to find out the work they've missed. For fun, let students take turns recording the message. Or challenge small groups of students to design flyers and business cards advertising your homework hot line to parents.

Paul Chilson—Gr. 5, East Jackson Memorial School, Jackson, MI

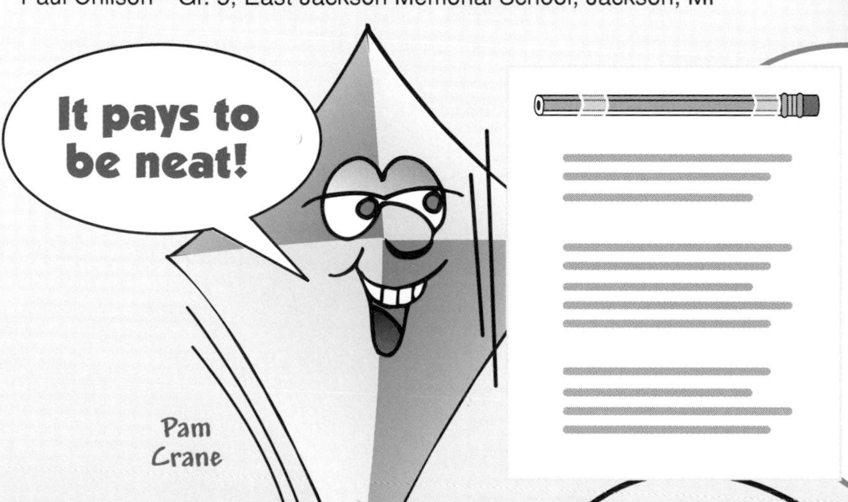
It pays to be neat!
Pam Crane

## Pencil Prizes

Surprise students who work hard to turn in neatly done assignments with this inexpensive incentive. Tape a new pencil to a tidy homework paper before passing it back to its owner. Students will appreciate being recognized for completing legible work, even if there are mistakes on the assignment.

Patricia E. Dancho—Gr. 6
Apollo-Ridge Middle School, Spring Church, PA

## Hooray for Homework!

Students who shout "Hooray for homework"? It could happen with this monthly motivator. At the end of each month, hold an awards ceremony to honor students who turned in all of their homework assignments. Present each deserving student with a special certificate that entitles her to skip homework one night during the upcoming month. Did someone just say "Hooray"?

Kirsten Sasaki—Gr. 6, Copiague Middle School, Copiague, NY

## "Gimme" One of Three, Please!

If you've got lots of kids and lots of papers to grade, it's often easy to be in the dark about whether a student was absent or just didn't do an assignment. Solve this challenge by asking each student to hand in one of the following each time you collect a homework assignment:

- the homework assignment
- a sheet of paper labeled with the student's name, the date, the assignment name, and the phrase "I was absent on [the date the student missed school]."
- a sheet of paper labeled with the student's name, the date, the assignment name, and the phrase "I did not complete [name of assignment]."

File any "I did not complete..." papers to use during student and parent conferences.

Patricia E. Dancho—Gr. 6, Apollo-Ridge Middle School
Spring Church, PA

Homework Certificate
Hooray!
I've Got to Hand It to You!
You've done a great job this week with your assignments. Thanks for keeping up with your homework.
You deserve a hand!
I OWE MY TEACHER THESE ASSIGNMENTS:
Spelling:
Reading:
Math:
Science:
Social Studies:
Writing:
Other:
Please do the above homework as soon as possible.
Date:

## Handy Homework Helper

Turn a bulletin board into a tool that keeps track of missing assignments and rewards students for responsible homework habits. For each student, cut the front from a manila file folder as shown. Staple the folder to a bulletin board along the sides to form a pocket; then label the folder with the student's name. Also make a supply of forms similar to the two shown on yellow and blue paper.

If a student is absent, place copies of the assignments he missed in his pocket. If a student owes you an assignment, fill out a yellow form and place it in his pocket to remind both him and you that he owes work. Slip a completed blue form into the pocket of any student who turned in all assignments for the week. How handy!

Carol Jorgensen, Lena Elementary, Lena, WI

## Homework Organizer

Avoid the paper chase that homework can sometimes create with this tip. Type a class list and make copies. Each time you collect homework, place a copy of the list atop the papers. Then follow these steps:

1. Cross out the names of students who turned in the assignment.
2. Highlight the names of students who didn't turn in the assignment.
3. Paper-clip the list to the top of the papers.
4. Label the list with grades as you assess the work.
5. Transfer the grades to your gradebook.

Keep the list until Friday so you can refer to it when informing students about who owes work for the week.

Jennifer Peterman—Gr. 6, Eli Whitney Elementary, Stratford, CT

Name ____________________

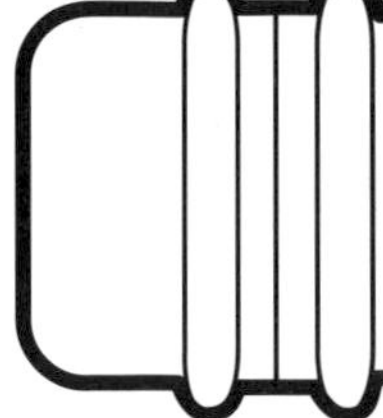

# Homework

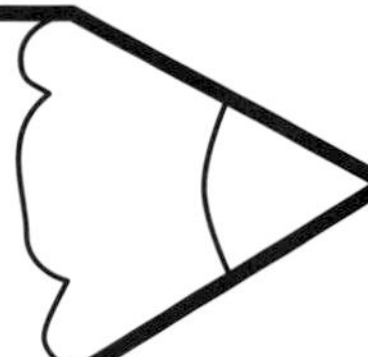

# Diary

Date ____________________ Check when turned in ☐

Assignment ____________________

I didn't turn in this assignment because ____________________

---

Date ____________________ Check when turned in ☐

Assignment ____________________

I didn't turn in this assignment because ____________________

---

Date ____________________ Check when turned in ☐

Assignment ____________________

I didn't turn in this assignment because ____________________

---

Date ____________________ Check when turned in ☐

Assignment ____________________

I didn't turn in this assignment because ____________________



**Note to the teacher:** Use with "Homework Diary" on page 13.

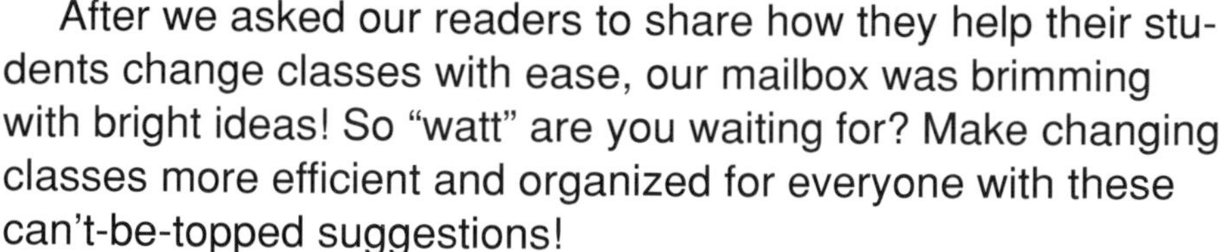


After we asked our readers to share how they help their students change classes with ease, our mailbox was brimming with bright ideas! So "watt" are you waiting for? Make changing classes more efficient and organized for everyone with these can't-be-topped suggestions!

## Wipe-Off Organizers

With this handy tip, you and the other teachers on your team may never hear "What do I need today?" again! Hang a small dry-erase board outside each classroom. In the morning, have each teacher list the items students will need to bring with them to her class that day. So that students don't congregate around the board before class, also write the list on the board inside the classroom.

Michelle Zakula
St. Roman Catholic School
Milwaukee, WI

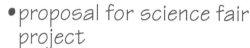

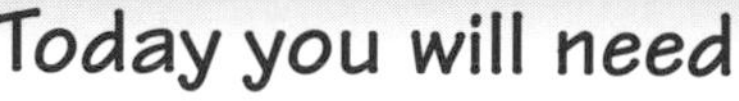


- proposal for science fair project
- permission slip for Dec. 2 field trip
- pencil
- science journal

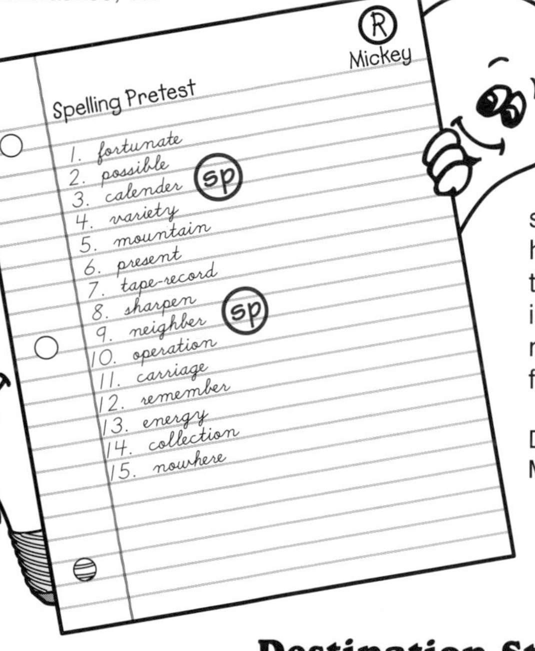

R
Mickey
Spelling Pretest
1. fortunate
2. possible
3. calender sp
4. variety
5. mountain
6. present
7. tape-record
8. sharpen
9. neighber sp
10. operation
11. carriage
12. remember
13. energy
14. collection
15. nowhere


## Returning Student Papers

Here's a hassle-free way to return graded papers to students who have several different teachers. Require that each student write the initial of his homeroom teacher's last name at the top of each assignment and then circle the letter. If you have more than one teacher in your group with the same initial, ask students to include the second (or an additional) letter of the name as well. In just a glance, you'll know where to send graded papers for filing or sending home.

Donna Viola—Grs. 4–5
McPherson, KS

## Destination Station

Do your students all go in different directions when they change classes? Help everyone know exactly where he's supposed to go and when with this simple strategy. At the start of the year, make a large chart that lists each student's destination for each day and class period of the week (see the illustration). Post the chart near your classroom door so it can be seen clearly by everyone. This chart not only helps you locate a student in a glance, but it also can indicate the best times to schedule makeup tests.

Georgina Cole-McCarthy—Gr. 6
Bennie Dover Jackson Middle School
New London, CT

**Destination Code**
R=Mr. Rashad, M=Mrs. Miller, S=Mrs. Smithon, P=Mr. Peters, B=Band, Re=Resource Room, L=Library

| | M-1 | M-2 | T-1 | T-2 | W-1 | W-2 | Th-1 | Th-2 | F-1 | F-2 |
|---|---|---|---|---|---|---|---|---|---|---|
| Bobby | P | P | M | M | P | B | M | M | P | Re |
| Claire | S | S | R | L | S | S | R | R | S | B |
| | | | | | | | | | | |
| | | | | | | | | | | |
| | | | | | | | | | | |
| | | | | | | | | | | |
| | | | | | | | | | | |
| | | | | | | | | | | |

## This Way, Please!

If your classroom has two doors, try this traffic control tip. Label one door as the entrance into your room; label the other door as the exit. Each morning place hints about the upcoming class around the entrance door. Decorate the exit with reminders about assignments, tests, and other important information. This simple idea will save tons of time that's often lost during the transition.

Julie Alarie—Gr. 6
Essex Middle School
Essex, VT

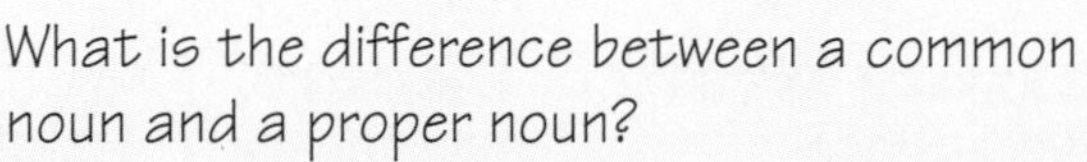

What is the difference between a common noun and a proper noun?
What are the plural spellings of these words: *child, bus, brush?*
What is the plural possessive spelling for the noun *man?*


## Three to Get Ready

Now that the kids are in your room, how do you calm them down quickly so you can all get to work? Prior to class, write three review questions on a transparency. As students enter the room, turn on the overhead projector to display the questions. Direct students to begin answering the questions in their journals as soon as they get settled. At the end of each six-week period, give each student who answered the questions and turns in a neat and well-organized journal an extra 100-percent test grade or other treat or privilege. In just one easy activity, you'll boost writing skills, review class material, and get students focused on the class period ahead.

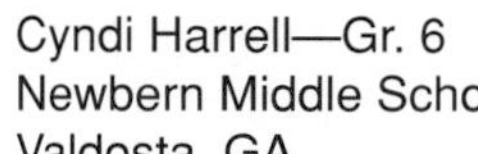

Cyndi Harrell—Gr. 6
Newbern Middle School
Valdosta, GA

## Once Upon a New Class...

Here's another no-fuss way to settle down your students after they've entered your room. After everyone has been seated, start the new class by reading aloud from a favorite children's novel for several minutes. This simple technique not only calms the class, but it also motivates reading and introduces students to some great literature.

Susan Keller and Jackie Fort—Gr. 5
Plumb Elementary
Clearwater, FL

## Listen Up!

Settle down students who are lined up to switch classes with this fun activity. Say the chant shown, with students repeating each line after you. When you get to the fourth line, announce a category related to a topic being studied, such as nouns, state capitals, multiplication facts, etc. When you get to the last line, announce the name of a student. Then have that child name an item in the stated category. In turn, each classmate standing in line with him must name a different item with no repeats. Great listening practice, plus a terrific way to review!

Mary Skelly
Salem Central School
Salem, NY

**Listen Up!**

*(Students repeat each line after teacher chants it.)*

Listen up!
Everyone!
Going to name
Some [fill in with a category: states, proper nouns, multiplication facts, etc.].
One apiece,
No repeats,
No hesitation,
Just concentration,
Starting with...
[Student's name].

## Organizing Graded Papers

When your kids change classes, getting graded papers filed and sent home can be an organizational challenge. To avoid a frustrating paper chase, purchase an inexpensive plastic crate for each homeroom class. Place a hanging file folder in the crate for each student. Then file graded papers inside the folders. When a second teacher wants to file her papers in your homeroom students' folders, just send her the crate.

Sharon Longton and Lisa Edwards—Gr. 4
Stovall Academy
Houston, TX

## Community Calendar

It's every kid's (and parent's) worst nightmare: two tests or projects scheduled on the same date. Sidestep this hazard of changing classes with a simple solution. Each month post a large calendar outside your students' classrooms. Have each teacher use a different color of marker to label the calendar with all tests and projects due in her class that month. With this tip, teachers can avoid assigning multiple tests and projects on the same dates. The calendar will also help students and visiting parents keep up-to-date as well.

Michelle Zakula
St. Roman Catholic School
Milwaukee, WI

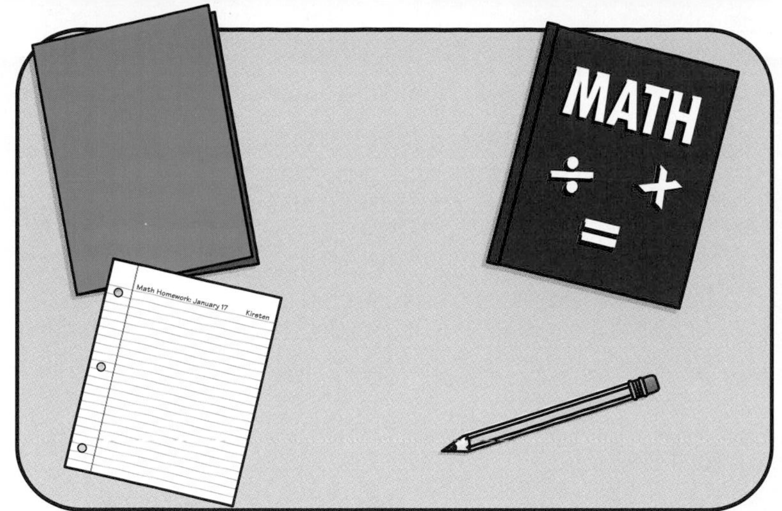


## Four Corners

When a new class enters your room, make sure supplies come with them with this idea. After everyone is seated, call out "Four corners!" Then have each student place his folder on the top left corner of his desk, his textbook on the top right corner, his pencil in the bottom right, and his homework in the bottom left. Scan the room to see who is prepared. In just a few short weeks, students will automatically remember this "four corners" reminder and bring their materials to class.

Mary Skelly
Salem Central School
Salem, NY

## Road to Success

Send your students on a road trip that leads to responsible behavior with this cool contest. Use chalk to draw a dotted line down the middle of several sheets of black construction paper. Then mount the papers on a wall, as shown, to resemble a road. Using the chalk, mark at least 30 "miles" on the road as shown. Next, create a car template like the pattern shown. Label one cutout car for each of your classes.

When the display is ready, announce to students that each class will try to earn miles so that its car can travel down the Road to Success. Classes can earn up to five miles a day for each of the following:

- Everyone enters and exits the room quietly.
- Everyone has all needed materials for class.
- Everyone completed the homework assignment.
- Everyone is seated and ready by [designate the time].
- The teacher doesn't have to stop teaching to address poor behavior.

At the end of the grading period, recognize the class whose car traveled the farthest with a reward of the students' choice (see the suggested list).

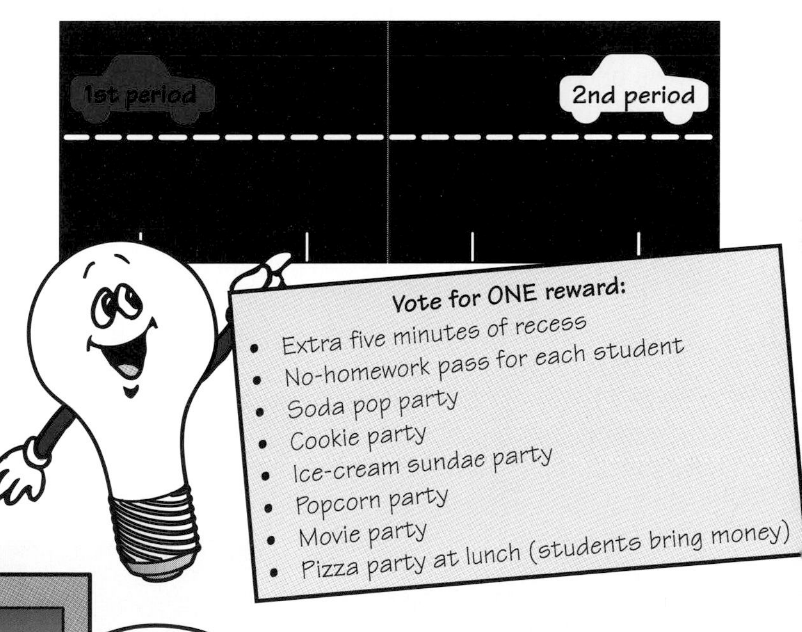

1st period
2nd period
Vote for ONE reward:
• Extra five minutes of recess
• No-homework pass for each student
• Soda pop party
• Cookie party
• Ice-cream sundae party
• Popcorn party
• Movie party
• Pizza party at lunch (students bring money)


Sue Calaway—Gr. 5
Jack Hayes School
Monroe, LA

Today you will need:
• Last night's homework
• Number cards
• Calculator
• Pencil
• Scrap paper

## Materials Needed

With this easy-to-do tip, you won't waste another minute of valuable teaching time answering "What do we need today?" Before your new class arrives, list on the board the materials needed for that period. When students sit down, they'll know exactly what items to get out. Plus you'll be helping students learn important organizational skills.

Susan Keller and Jackie Fort—Gr. 5
Plumb Elementary
Clearwater, FL

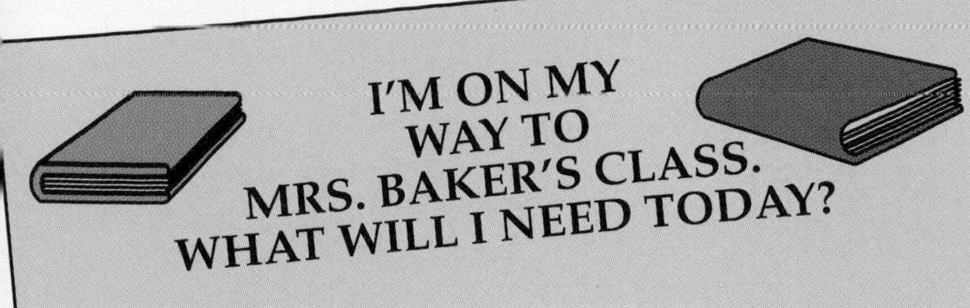

I'M ON MY
WAY TO
MRS. BAKER'S CLASS.
WHAT WILL I NEED TODAY?
• Five-subject notebook • Vocabulary cards and box
• LA book • Pleasure reading book • Notes or forms for
the teacher • My snack • Pencils • Paper
• Homework • Project • Junior Great Book
• Literature book • Assignments to hand in • Other...


## Supplies Reminder Card

Students who travel between classrooms seem bound to forget something different every day. To save the time spent retrieving supplies, give each student a copy of a card like the one shown. On the card, list the supplies that students coming to your class will need. Laminate the cards; then have each child tape a copy onto his notebook. The only things students will leave behind now are their forgetful habits!

Marcia Worth-Baker
Gould School
North Caldwell, NJ

## Teachers on the Move

If having students change classes doesn't seem to be working, why not do the switching instead of your kids? When it's time to change classes, have the teachers swap classrooms, leaving the students ready to get to work at their own desks. Use a rolling cart to transport teacher's manuals and materials back and forth with ease. This simple solution translates into calmer students who aren't tempted to bother someone else's desk and personal supplies.

Jane Hutchison—Gr. 4
Tom Joy Elementary
Nashville, TN

## Color Us Organized!

Help students get organized to change classes with this colorful tip. At the start of the new year, ask each student to bring a supply of different-colored pocket folders to school. Designate one color for each subject, for example, the red folder for math, the blue folder for social studies, and the green folder for science. When a student is getting ready to change classes, she'll know immediately which folder to take with her. Extend the color coordination by having students place colored dot stickers that match their folders on their composition notebooks.

Mary Skelly
Salem Central School
Salem, NY

# Classroom Displays

Lock up a sensational school year with this student-made display! Post an enlarged copy of the locker character shown. Have each student fill in the rim of a lock pattern (page 34) with her own combination for unlocking a great year. Then have her label the lock with her name and lightly color it. All locked up!

Michelle Trubitz—Grs. 5–6, Brookside Upper Elementary, Westwood, NJ

For a year that's sure to shape up nicely, "tri" this motivational display! Give each student a large equilateral triangle cut from colorful paper. Have the child decorate his cutout to illustrate a way he can "tri" to succeed this year. Mount the drawings on a bulletin board as shown to create one giant triangle. Not enough student triangles to complete the large one? Just ask several kids to decorate more than one triangle. Or if you have more student triangles than you need, use the extras to decorate the corners of the display.

Andrea Troisi
LaSalle Middle School
Niagara Falls, NY

# DISPLAYS

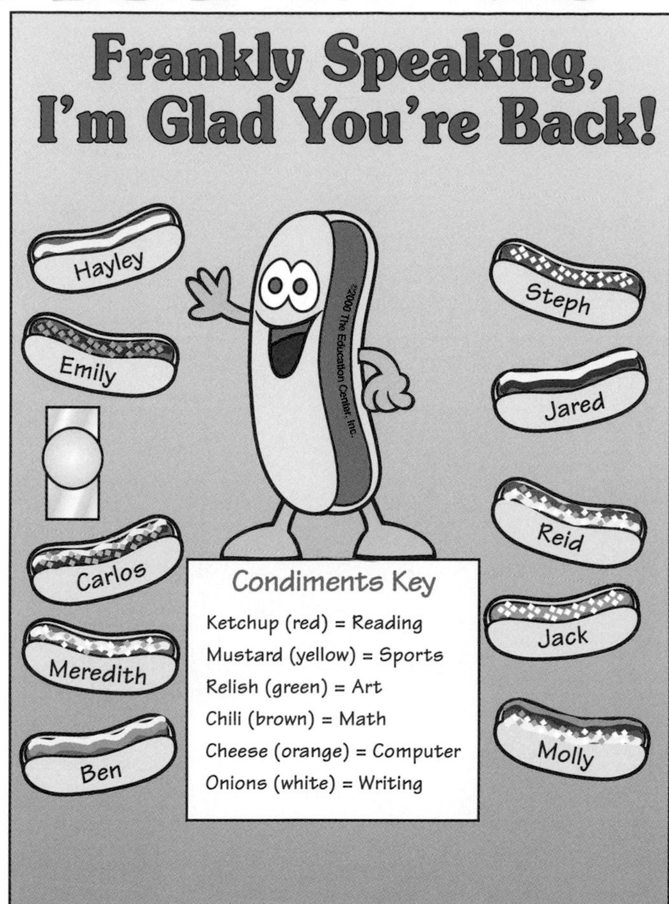

Frankly Speaking, I'm Glad You're Back!
Hayley
Emily
Carlos
Meredith
Ben
Steph
Jared
Reid
Jack
Molly
©2000 The Education Center, Inc.
Condiments Key
Ketchup (red) = Reading
Mustard (yellow) = Sports
Relish (green) = Art
Chili (brown) = Math
Cheese (orange) = Computer
Onions (white) = Writing


Welcome students back with this "hot-doggity" door display! Post an enlarged copy of the character shown on your classroom door. On the first day of school, have each student label a hot dog pattern (page 34) with his name; then have him decorate it using crayons and the Condiments Key shown to indicate some of his favorite things. Post the hot dogs and a key on your door for a display that's frankly fantastic!

adapted from an idea by Donna DeRosa—Gr. 4
Good Shepherd Academy
Nutley, NJ

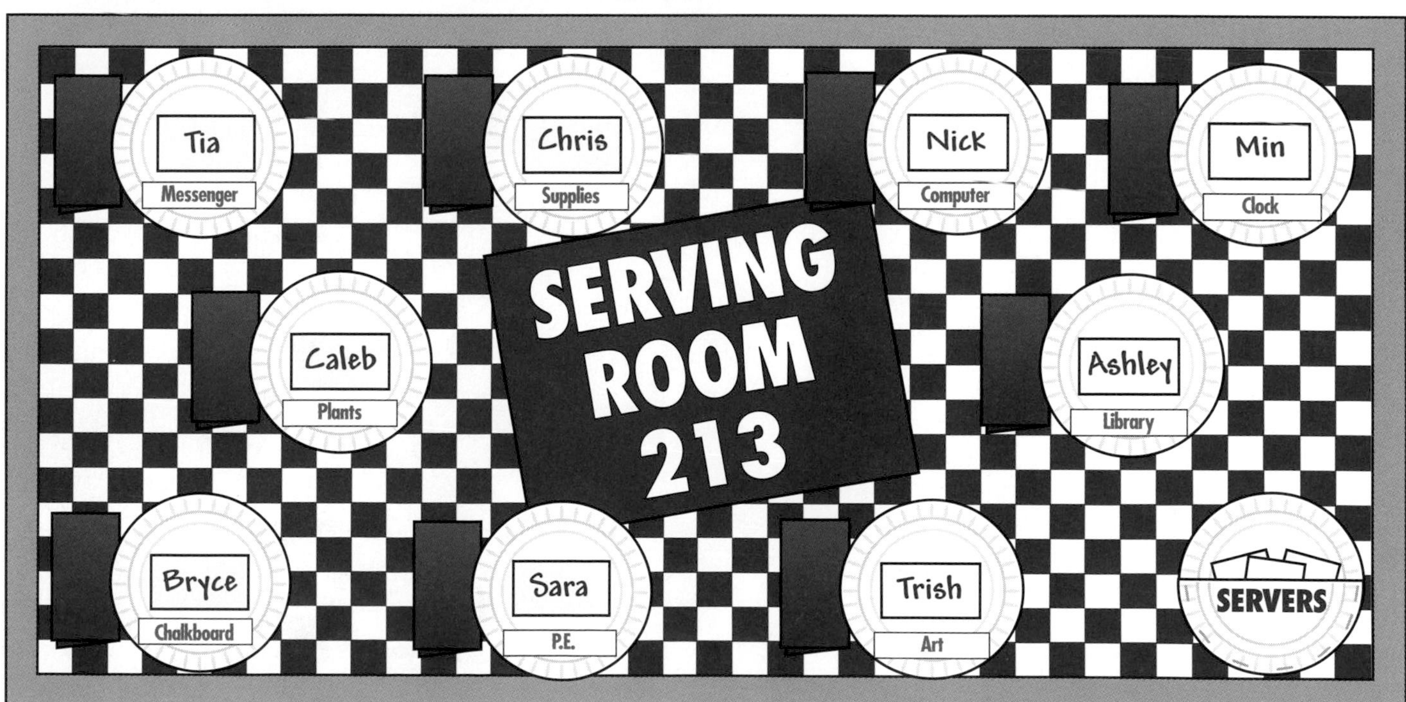


Assign classroom jobs in a jiffy with this display. Cover a board with a vinyl tablecloth. Add napkins and paper plates labeled with your classroom jobs as shown. Also label an index card for each student. To assign a job, pin a student's card to a plate. Store unused cards in a paper plate pocket stapled to the board as shown.

Donna G. Pawloski—Gr. 4, Primos Elementary, Primos, PA

# CLASSROOM

## PUZZLE PATCH

To plant a patch of vocabulary review, have each student cut out a paper pumpkin and add a cutout face that includes a toothy grin. Direct the student to label the teeth with the scrambled letters of a vocabulary word from a current unit. Number and post the pumpkins. Then have students unscramble the words, check their work with an answer key, and use the words in fall writing assignments.

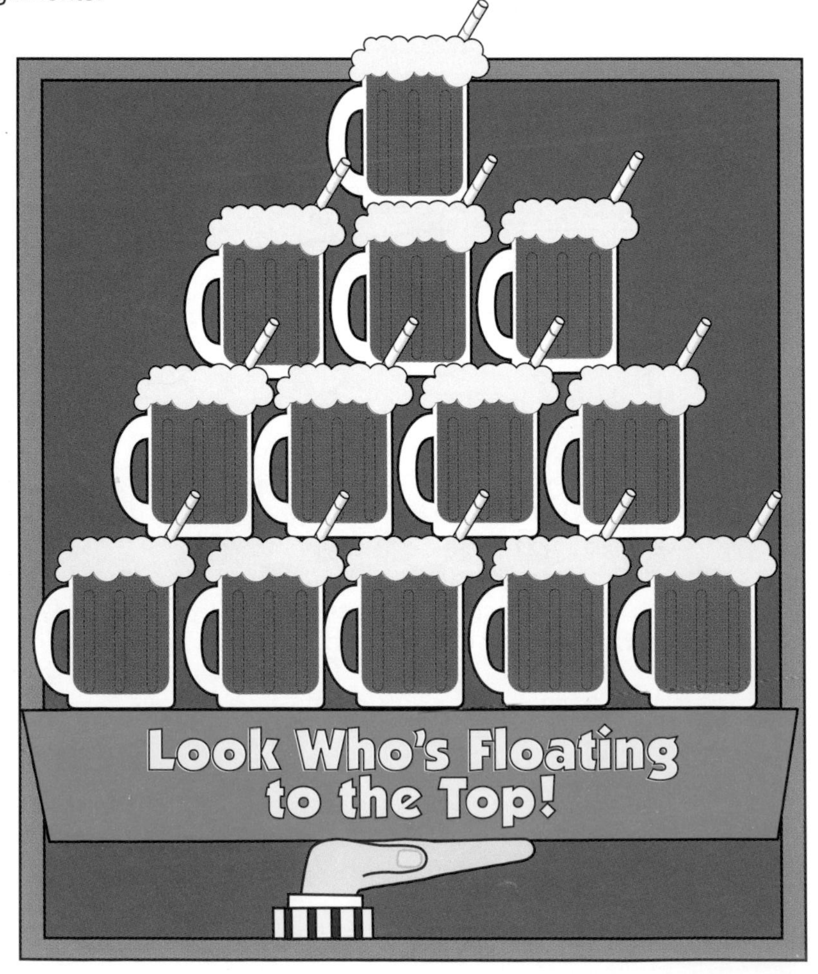
Look Who's Floating to the Top!

Say cheers to your class's hard work with this frosty display. Make the hand/tray shown and mount it on a bulletin board. Also make and have students color a supply of the float pattern on page 35. Tape a drinking straw behind each float. Each time your class meets a predetermined goal, staple a float to the tray. When the floats reach the top of the board, celebrate with a root beer or ice-cream float party.

**Back-to-school variation:** Label a float for each of your new students. Change the title of the display to "Look Who's Floating to the Top of [your grade] Grade!"

adapted from an idea by Colleen Dabney
Williamsburg-JCC Public Schools
Williamsburg, VA

# DISPLAYS

Room 5: Where Math Rules!

Send the message that math rules your roost with this multipurpose display. Each student labels a 2" x 12" strip of yellow paper to resemble a ruler. After adding cutout features, the student posts the ruler on the board. Add to the display students' math papers, puzzles or word problems to solve, current event articles pertaining to math, or other math-related items.

Count your blessings this November with the help of a fruitful door display! Enlarge and color the cornucopia pattern on page 35 and post it on your classroom door. Have each student label a purple circle cutout with something he is "grape-ful" for; then mount the grapes and cutout leaves on the door as shown. Invite other classes to get into the act by adding their own grapes to the display.

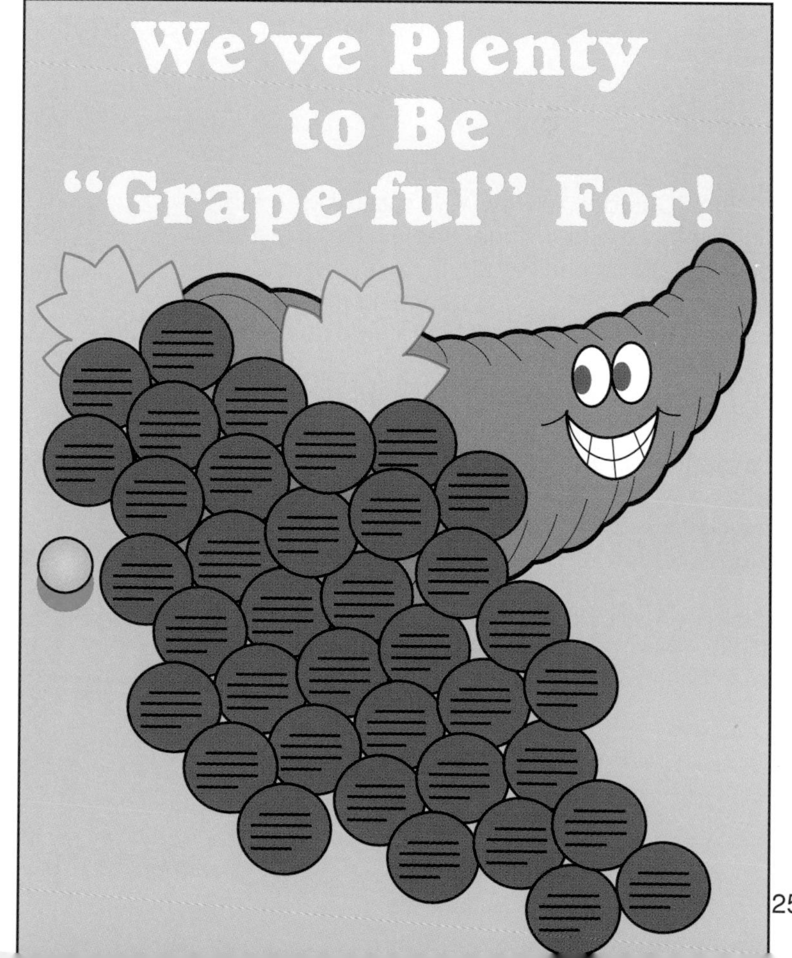

We've Plenty
to Be
"Grape-ful" For!

# CLASSROOM

'Tis the season to be reading according to this bright display! After mounting a large tree cutout on a bulletin board, copy the light pattern on page 36 onto colorful construction paper to make a class supply. Have each child use a black pen or marker to label a pattern with his name, the title of his book, and the book's highlights. Then staple the lights and some shiny metallic cord or tinsel to the board.

Jane Krier—Gr. 4, Byron Elementary, Byron, MN

Say "Can do!" to New Year's goals with this unique three-dimensional display. Copy the label on page 36 for each student. On the left side of the label, the child writes one thing that she cannot yet do and a target date (expiration date) for meeting her goal. On the right side, the student writes her goal as if she had already accomplished it (see the example). Then she colors the label and glues it on a can. Use Sticky-Tac to attach the cans—"cannot yet" side facing out—to the board. When a student meets a goal, let her turn her can around. Can do!

Kimberly A. Minafo—Gr. 4
Tooker Avenue School
West Babylon, NY

# DISPLAYS

When the weather outside is frightful, have small groups of students create frosty friends that are downright delightful! Display the creations in a hallway. Then have each child write an original story about his group's snowy pal.

**Materials per group:** a 2' x 4' piece of white bulletin board paper with corners rounded, a 12" x 30" piece of black bulletin board paper, one 4" x 5" sheet of orange construction paper, one 12" x 18" sheet of colorful construction paper, a ruler, scissors, glue, chalk

**Steps:**

1. Cut the black paper as shown to create a hat. Glue the hat to the top of the white paper. Save the black scraps for Step 3.
2. Cut a nose out of the orange paper; glue it to the snowman's head.
3. Cut eyes, a mouth, and buttons from the black paper scraps. Glue them to the snowman.
4. Cut the colorful sheet of paper in half lengthwise. Glue the two pieces to the snowman, as shown, to create a scarf. Fringe the end of the scarf.
5. As a group, write a name for your snowman in chalk on the scarf. Add details to the hat and scarf with the chalk.

Patricia A. Wisniewski—Gr. 4
St. Joseph School
Batavia, NY

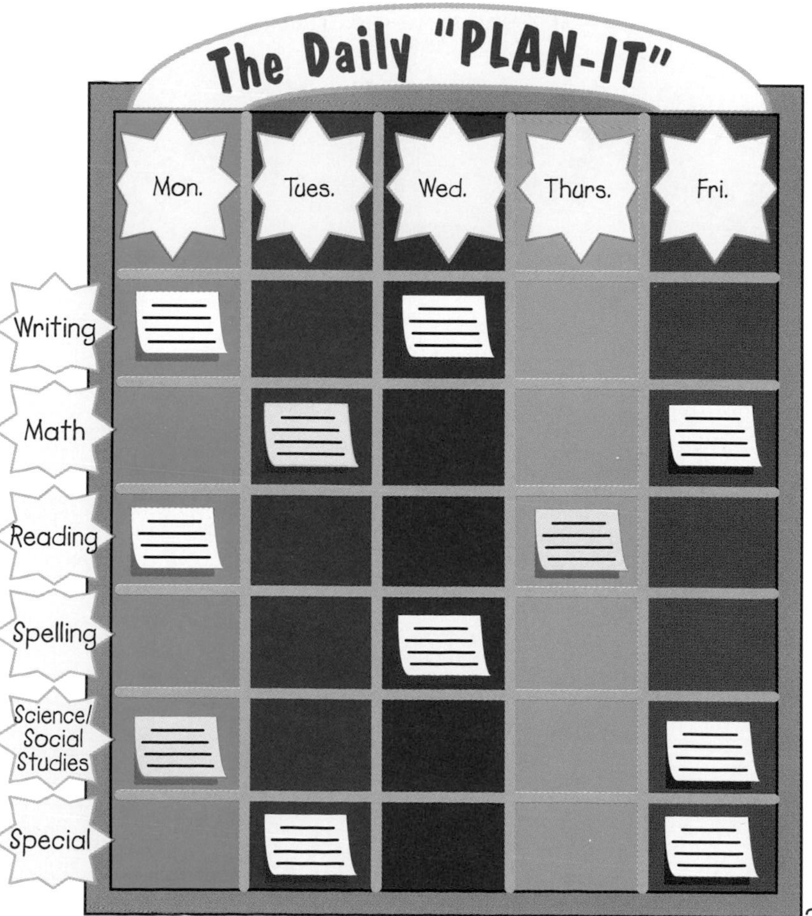


Organize your class in a flash with this giant weekly calendar. Use different colors of construction paper to create a grid labeled with subject areas and days of the week as shown. During the week, write assignments, reminders, and other important information on self-sticking notes to place on the grid.

Kimberly A. Minafo—Gr. 4
Tooker Avenue School
West Babylon, NY

# CLASSROOM

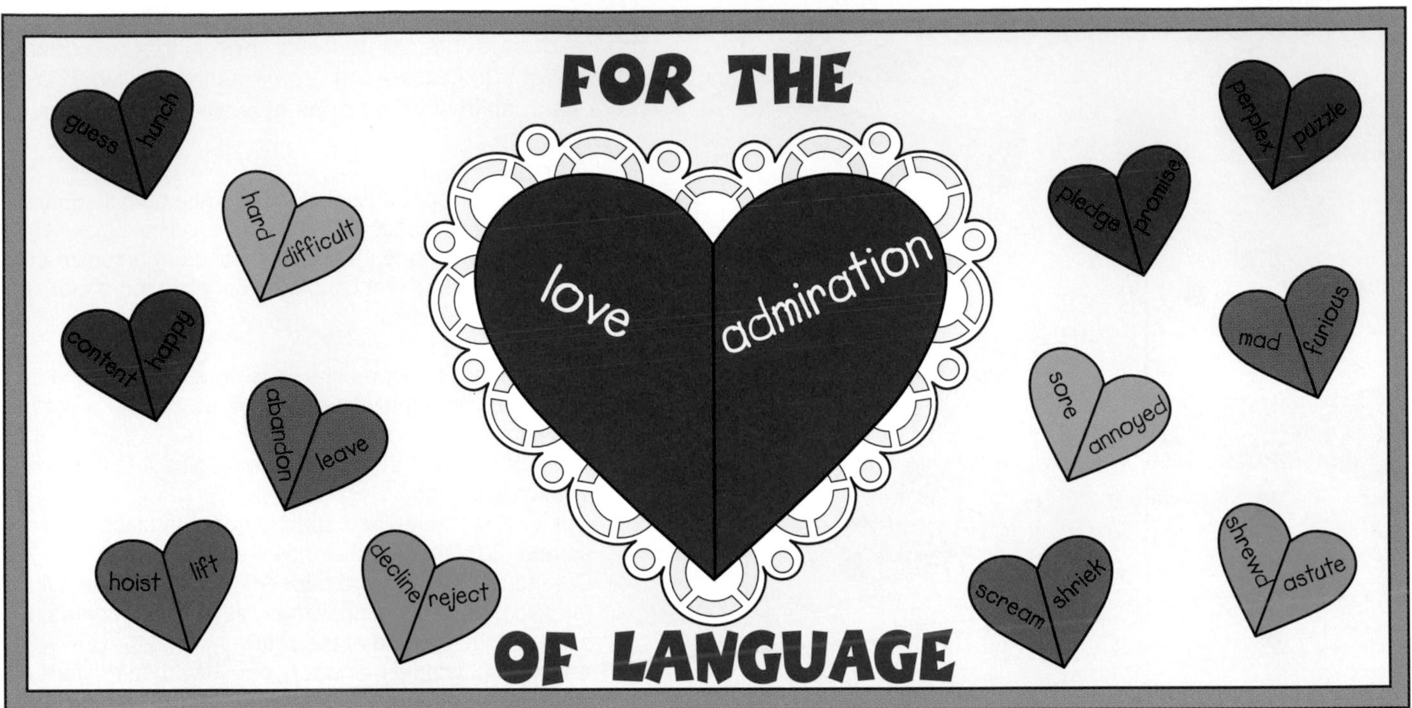


For a vocabulary display that "heart-ly" takes any time to make, have each student label half of a cutout heart with a vocabulary word from the book he's currently reading. Have him use a thesaurus to label the other half with a synonym for the word. Challenge small groups to determine different ways to sort the display's words. Or have students alphabetize the words or use them in sentences that give context clues about their meanings.

Kimberly A. Minafo—Gr. 4, Tooker Avenue School, West Babylon, NY

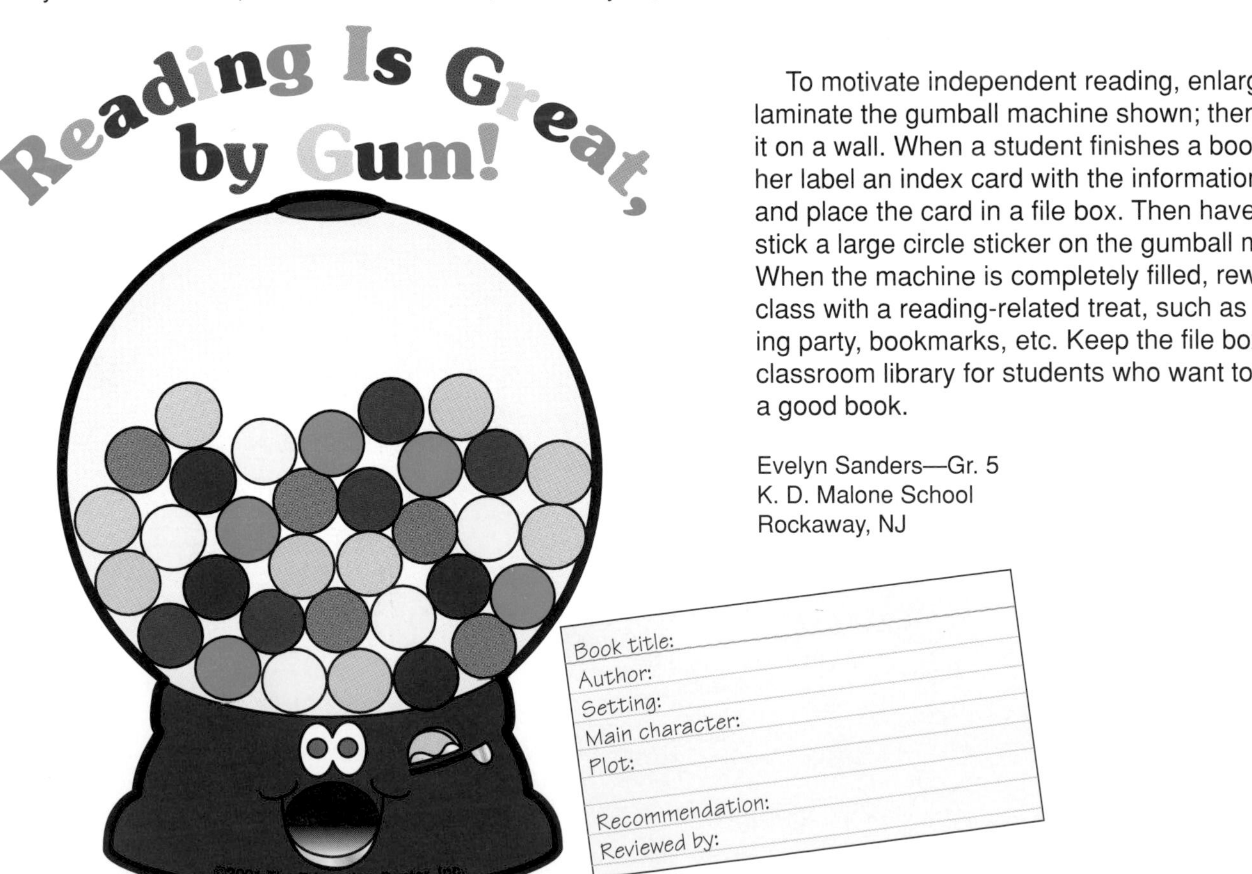


To motivate independent reading, enlarge and laminate the gumball machine shown; then mount it on a wall. When a student finishes a book, have her label an index card with the information shown and place the card in a file box. Then have her stick a large circle sticker on the gumball machine. When the machine is completely filled, reward the class with a reading-related treat, such as a reading party, bookmarks, etc. Keep the file box in your classroom library for students who want to "chews" a good book.

Evelyn Sanders—Gr. 5
K. D. Malone School
Rockaway, NJ

# DISPLAYS

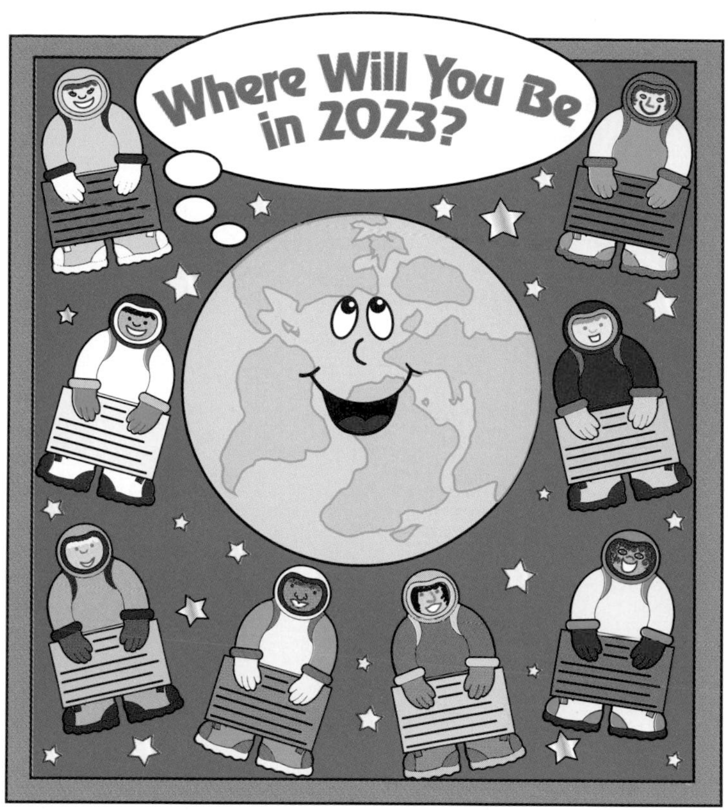


Where will *you* be in 2023? Pose this futuristic question on a display that's truly out of this world! Make a class supply of page 37; then have each student complete the page as directed. After each child shares his project, post the astronauts around a cutout globe as shown. Add shiny, self-sticking stars to the display. To extend this activity, have students write narrative stories about their lives in the future.

Julie Alarie—Gr. 6
Essex Middle School
Essex, VT

Find out what your students really think with this easy-to-adapt display. Mount an enlarged copy of the ink bottle and title shown. Tack several sheets of poster board—each labeled with a thought-provoking question—to the display (making sure students can easily reach them). Place a supply of fine-tipped markers nearby so students can write their responses on the posters. Change the posters frequently to keep interest high.

Kimberly A. Minafo—Gr. 4, Tooker Avenue School, West Babylon, NY

# CLASSROOM

Fishing for a creative way to display student work? Help your class brainstorm a list of praise words and phrases. Have each child write one praise on a colorful fish pattern (page 38); then have him decorate the cutout with art materials. Use each fish to embellish your students' papers as shown.

Evelyn Mason, Locust Valley Middle School, Locust Valley, NY

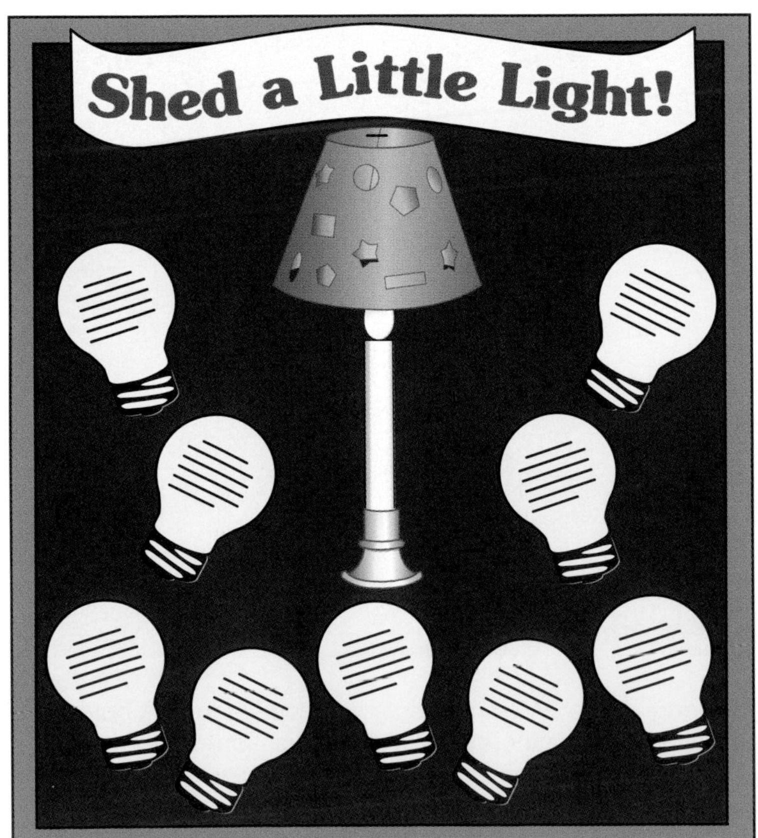


Shed a little light on your students' bright ideas and ignite their writing skills with this one-of-a-kind display. Use clear packing tape to attach a battery-powered candle to a bulletin board. Cut small shapes in a 1' x 2' strip of bulletin board paper. After rolling the paper into a lampshade shape and taping the edges together, trim the shade where necessary and staple it to the board above the candle. Add yellow paper lightbulbs (pattern on page 38) that are labeled with curriculum-related writing prompts or questions. Tell students that they are invited to write about the topics *only* when the light is turned on.

Kimberly A. Minafo—Gr. 4
Tooker Avenue School
West Babylon, NY

Use with the bulletin boards on pages 22 and 23.

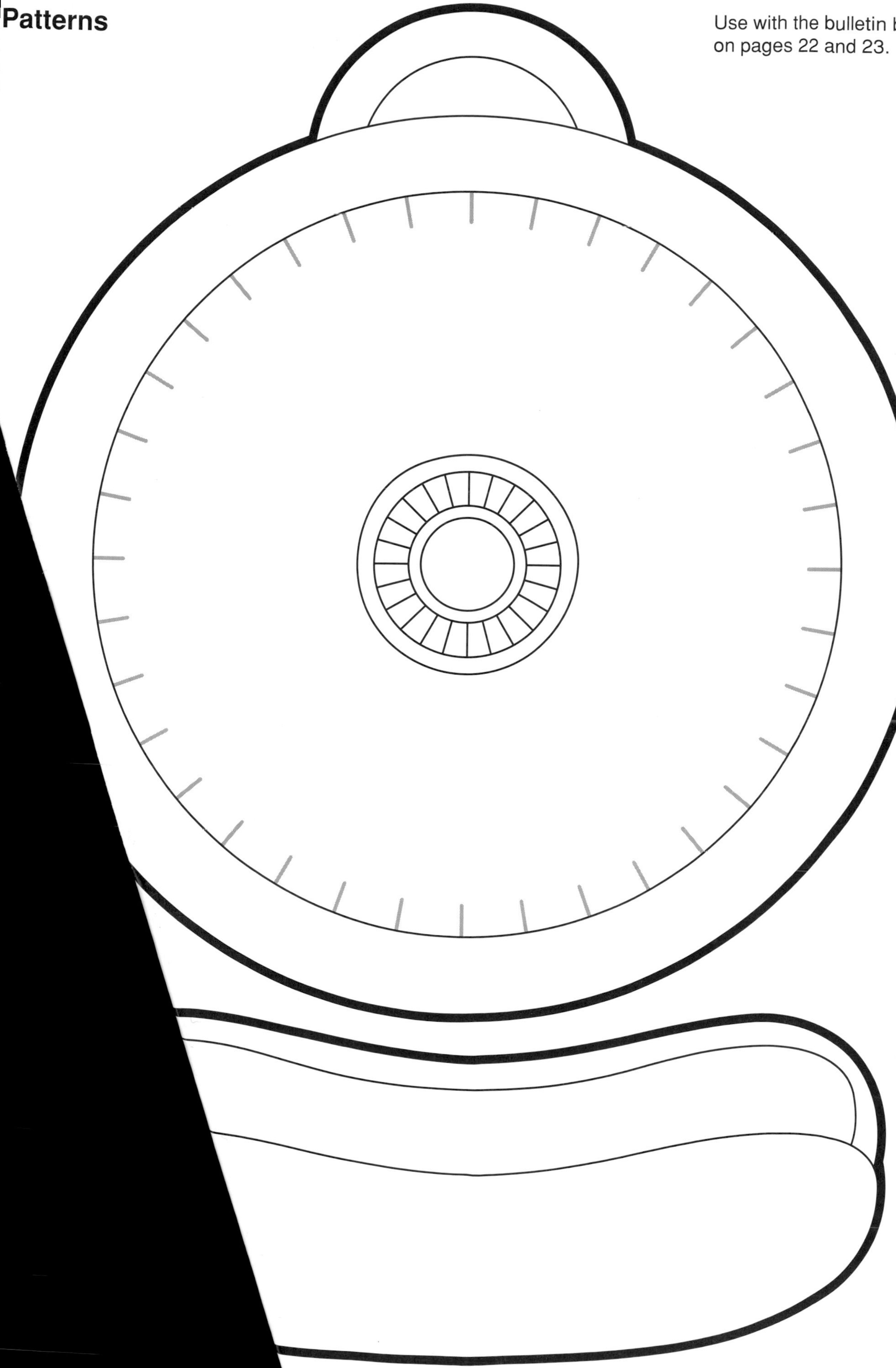

# DISPLAYS

If your students feel alienated from skills taught earlier in the year, help them get ready for testing day with this star-studded display. Enlarge the alien pattern on page 39 to post onto the board. Label cutout stars (pattern on page 39) with review questions; then write the answers on the backs. Hang each star from the board with a length of black yarn. Students check their answers by flipping the cutouts.

Darby Anne Herlong—Gr. 6, Lugoff Elgin Middle School, Lugoff, SC

Cultivate an interest in reading with a sunny class challenge! First, mount a large sun cutout on the board, using yellow chalk to add rays as shown. Cut a supply of hearts from construction paper in the colors listed below. When a student reads a book and completes a short review of it, give him a heart cutout colored according to the Heart Key. Have him label the heart with the book's title and author and his name. Then have the student staple his heart onto the board above the sun. When the class fills the horizon with a predetermined number of hearts, celebrate with a book-related reward, such as a book swap party, bookmark-making session, or other reading-related treat.

Colleen Dabney, Williamsburg–JCC Public Schools
Williamsburg, VA

**Heart Key**
*blue* = Realistic Fiction
*green* = Nonfiction
*red* = Humor
*yellow* = Mystery
*orange* = Fantasy or Science Fiction
*purple* = Historical Fiction
*pink* = Poetry

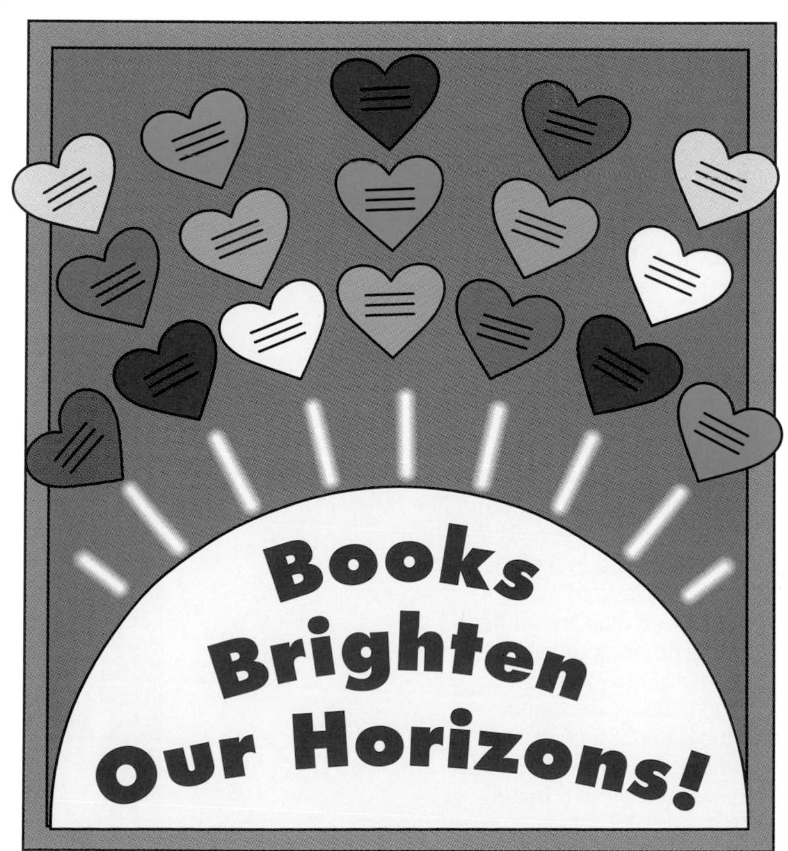

# CLASSROOM DISPLAYS

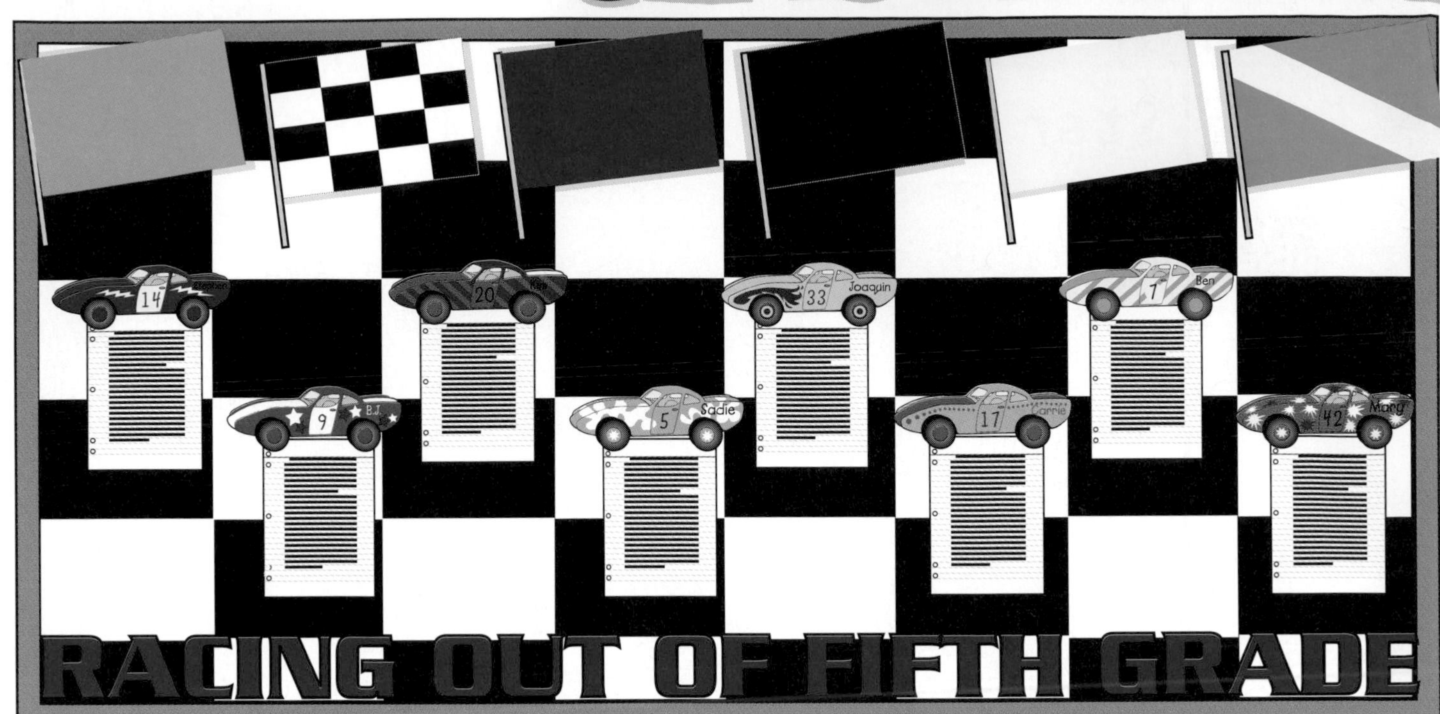


If motivation begins to flag during the final lap of school, rev up everyone's engine with this display! Cover a bulletin board with alternating sheets of black and white paper. Add paper flags as shown to represent those used in real automobile races. Then have each student color, personalize, and cut out a car pattern (page 40) to post on the board with an excellent paper.

Deanna M. Wyrick—Gr. 4, Aboite Elementary, Ft. Wayne, IN

Reminisce about the year that's about to end with this fine-feathered display! Follow the steps below to make the owl character. Place markers near the display; then invite students to write about their favorite memories directly on the background paper. What a hoot!

Colleen Dabney
Williamsburg-JCC Public Schools
Williamsburg, VA

**To make the owl:** Cut two same-sized paper squares, one brown and one white. Trim the white square as shown and use markers to add eyes. Glue a small orange triangle to the back of the white piece to make a beak. Then glue the white piece and beak to the brown square. Tape a small black pipe cleaner to the back of a black triangle. Glue the triangle to the top of the owl's head.

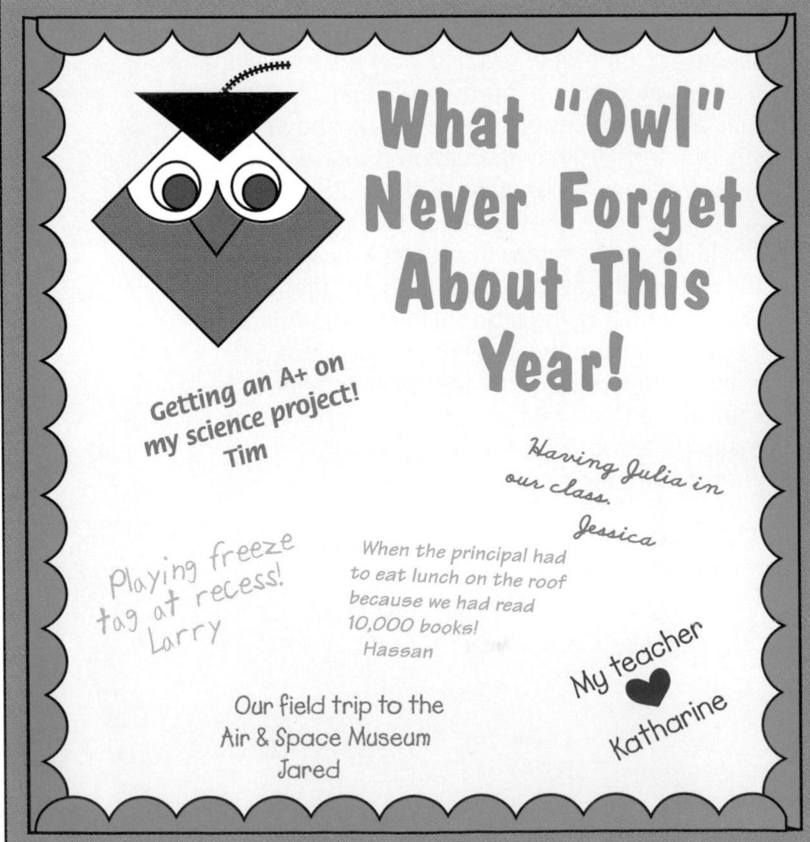

What "Owl" Never Forget About This Year!
Getting an A+ on my science project! Tim
Having Julia in our class. Jessica
Playing freeze tag at recess! Larry
When the principal had to eat lunch on the roof because we had read 10,000 books! Hassan
Our field trip to the Air & Space Museum Jared
My teacher ♥ Katharine


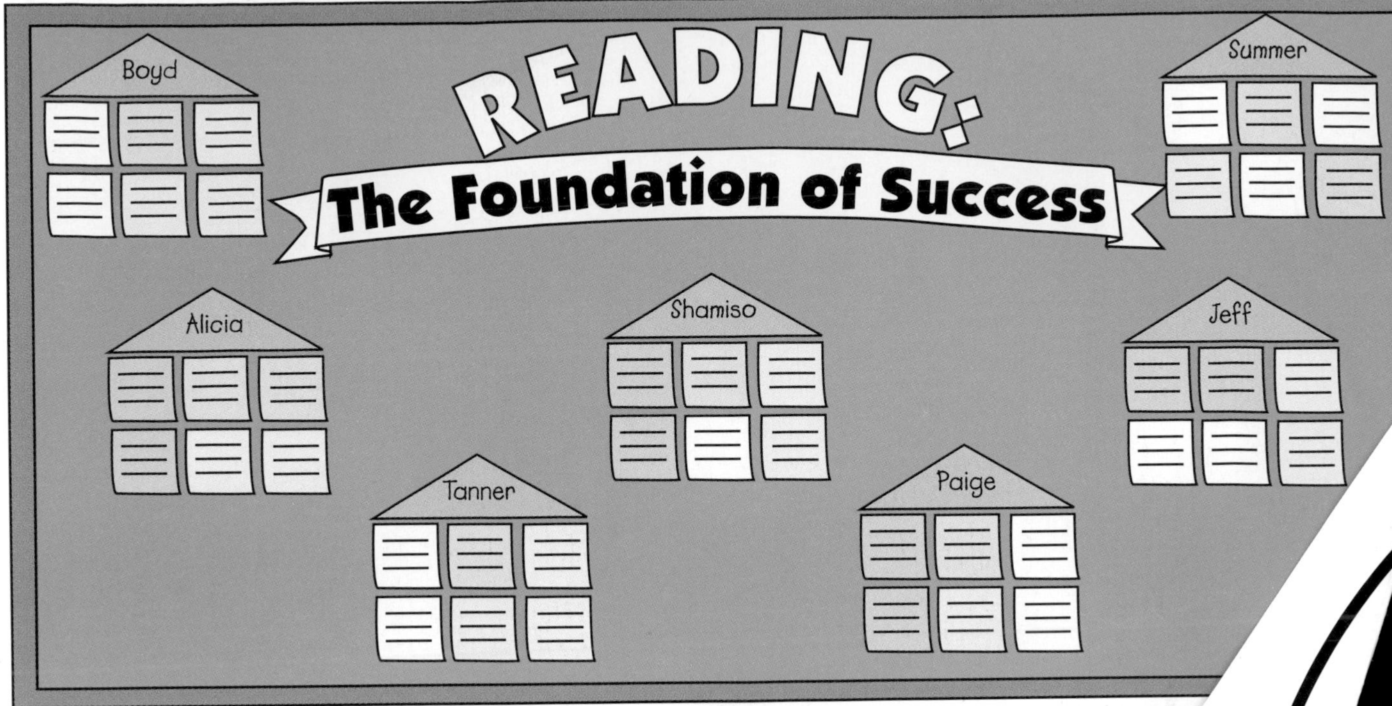


Help students identify story elements with this homey display! Have each child label a paper ro
name and post it on a bulletin board. When a student finishes a book, he labels six self-adhesiv
mation about the book, including its title and author, characters, setting, theme, plot, and his f
sticks the six notes under his roof. Students will love "remodeling" their houses each time th

Kimberly Minafo—Gr. 4, Tooker Avenue School, West Babylon, NY

Enlist the help of your smart cookies to make an end-of-the-year bulletin board that doubles as a back-to-school display. Have each student label a fortune cookie cutout (pattern on page 40) with her name. Then have her staple the cutout to the board along with a white paper strip that she's labeled with advice for next year's students. Use the display again in August to welcome your new class.

Colleen Dabney
Williamsburg-JCC Public Schools
Williamsburg, VA

Use with the displays on pages 24 and 25.

## Patterns

Use the label pattern with "Can Do!" on page 26.

Glue this edge to can first.

**CAN**

Bottled at the Factory of Hard Work

**CANNOT**
**yet...**

Expiration date: ______

Use the light pattern with "Books Make Us Bright!" on page 26.

Name____________________ Following directions, critical thinking

# Where Will You Be in 2023?

The future is sure to hold many changes and surprises. What do you think your life will be like in the year 2023? Think about this question; then follow these steps:

1. Cut out the spacesuit and gloves.
2. Draw and color a picture of your face in the visor.
3. Glue the gloves on the spacesuit where indicated.
4. Label an index card with the information shown on the spacesuit.
5. Glue the index card under the gloves as shown.
6. Use colored pencils or markers to add details to your suit.

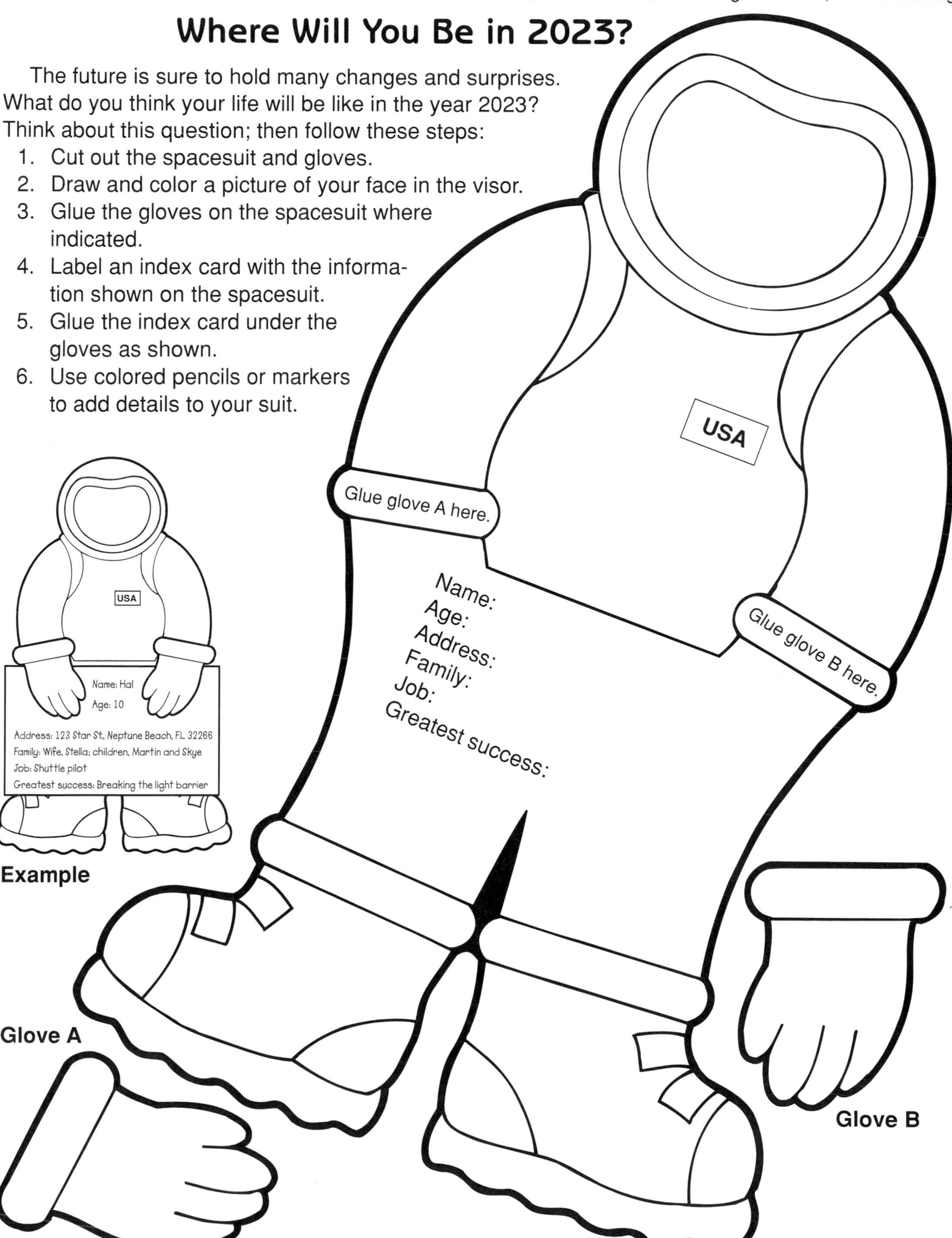




**Note to the teacher:** Use with the display on page 29. Provide each student with a copy of this page, a 3" x 5" index card, glue, scissors, and colored pencils or markers.

## Patterns

Use with the displays on page 30.

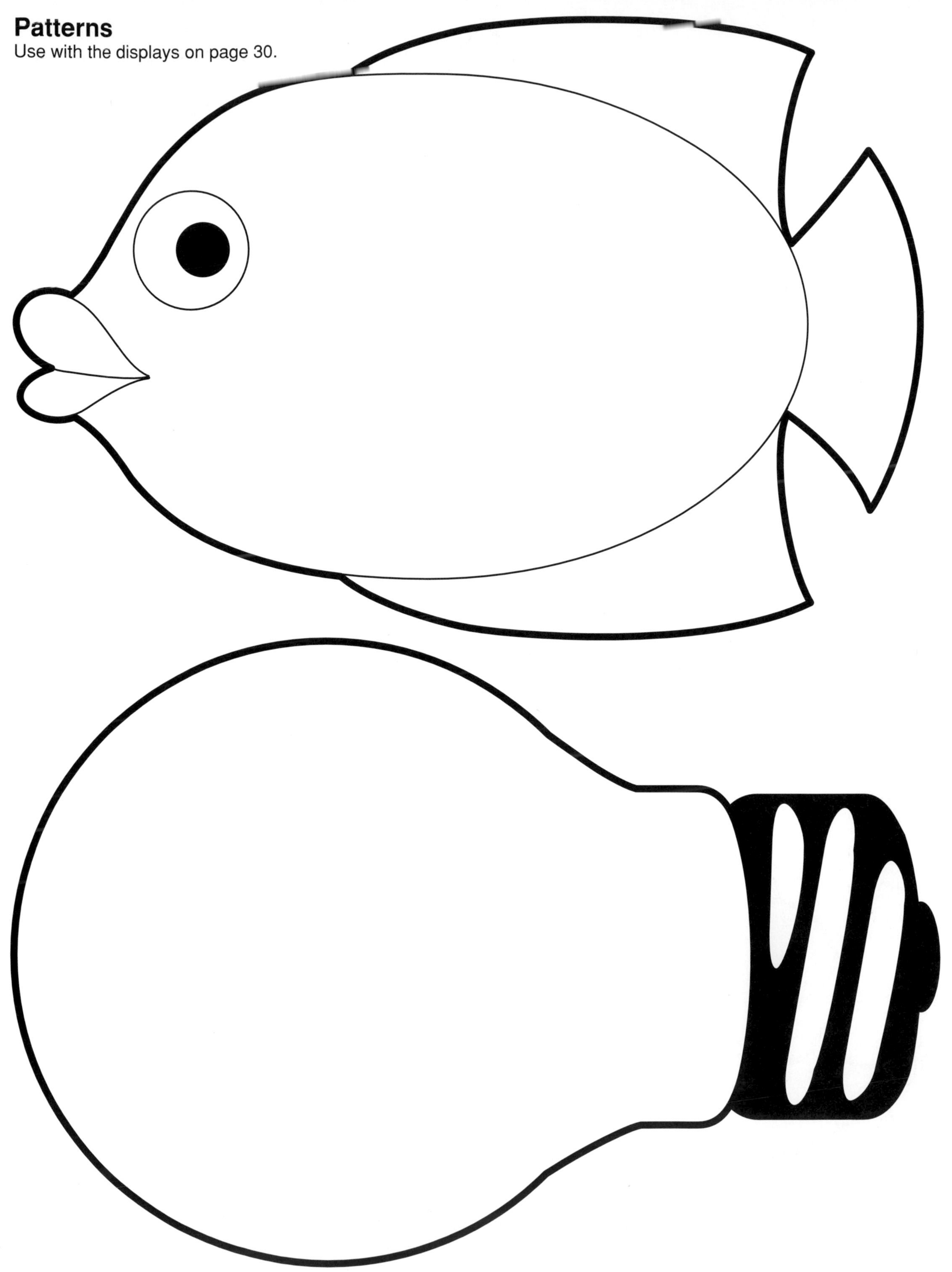

Use with the display on page 31.

## Patterns

Use the car pattern with the bulletin board on page 32.
Use the fortune cookie pattern with the bulletin board on page 33.

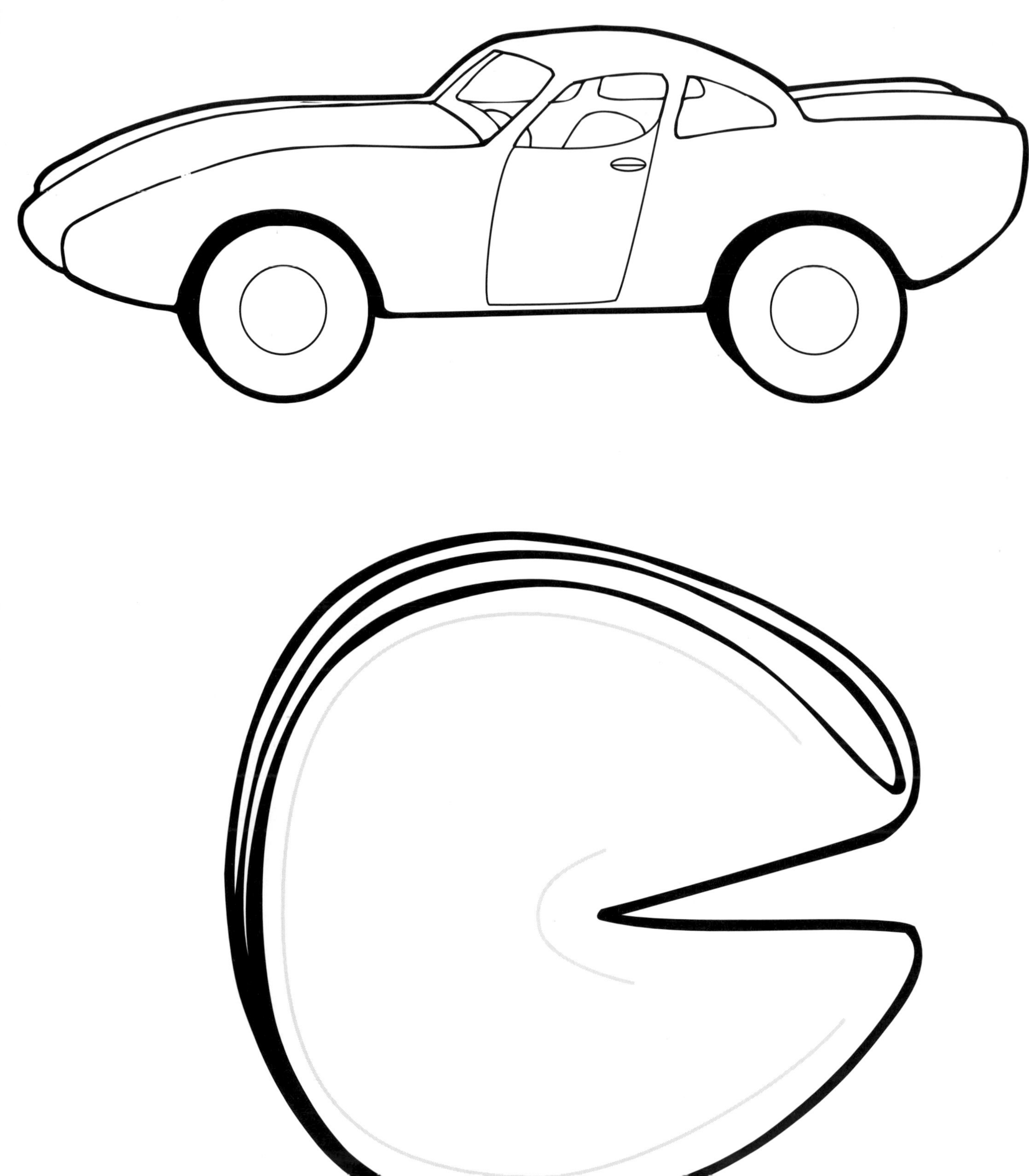

# Art Across the Curriculum

# ACROSS THE CURRICULUM

## Language Arts: Sentence Collages

Turn abstract art into a creatively concrete review of sentence types! Ask each student to cut eight to ten small pictures from old magazines. Have him position the cutouts on construction paper to create an abstract collage. Next, direct the student to glue his cutouts in place and trade the collage with a classmate's. Then have each child write four sentences about his partner's artwork—an exclamatory, an imperative, a declarative, and an interrogative—on the back of the collage. After students return the collages to their owners, have each child share his artwork and his classmate's sentences with the class. Post the finished collages on a bulletin board; then challenge students to write other sentences during free time to earn extra credit points.

**Exclamatory:** Don't step on the cat!
**Imperative:** Please eat the ice cream and strawberries.
**Declarative:** The butterfly is flitting around the flowers.
**Interrogative:** Why is the Statue of Liberty holding a cookbook?

Beth Gress
Granville, OH

## Science: Fossil Paperweight

Send students on a fun archaeological dig without ever leaving the classroom!

**Materials for each student:**
- plaster of paris
- water
- plastic laundry detergent scoop
- bowl and craft stick for mixing plaster
- acrylic paints
- paintbrush
- tiny shells (or plastic beads)
- metal spoon

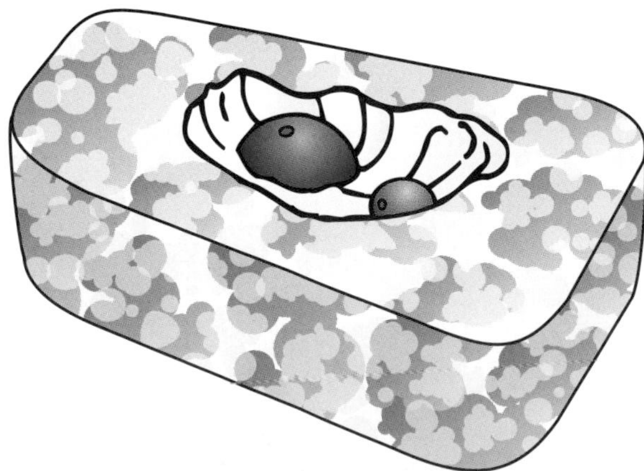

**Steps:**
1. Mix the plaster of paris and water according to package directions.
2. Pour the mixture into the plastic laundry scoop until it is half full.
3. Place a few shells or beads atop this mixture in the center of the scoop.
4. Add more plaster of paris to the scoop until it is full. Allow the mixture to dry overnight.
5. Remove the hardened plaster from the scoop. Using the spoon (either end), find the hidden items by carefully digging into the center of the plaster to create a hollow opening. Dig just until the items are visible without digging them loose.
6. Paint the paperweight with colorful designs.

Colleen Dabney
Williamsburg—JCC Public Schools
Williamsburg, VA

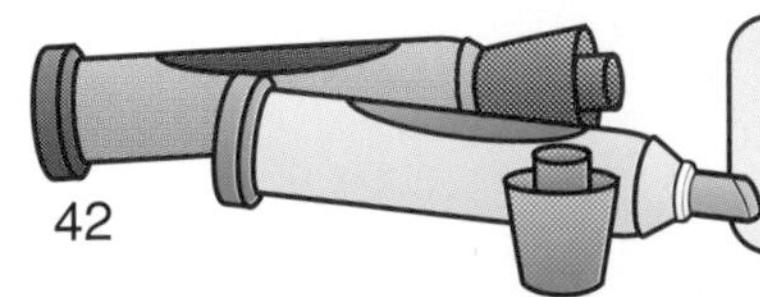

If you often ask students to make posters for projects, then help them do it successfully with the terrific list of **poster-making guidelines** on page 48.

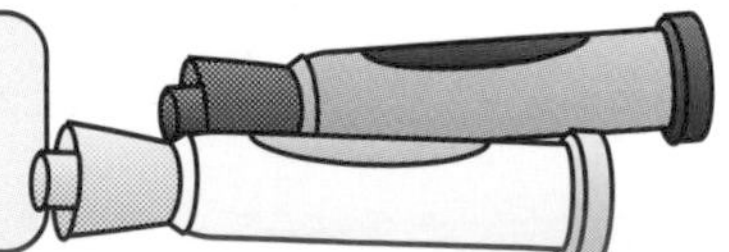

## Social Studies: Art for Peace Program

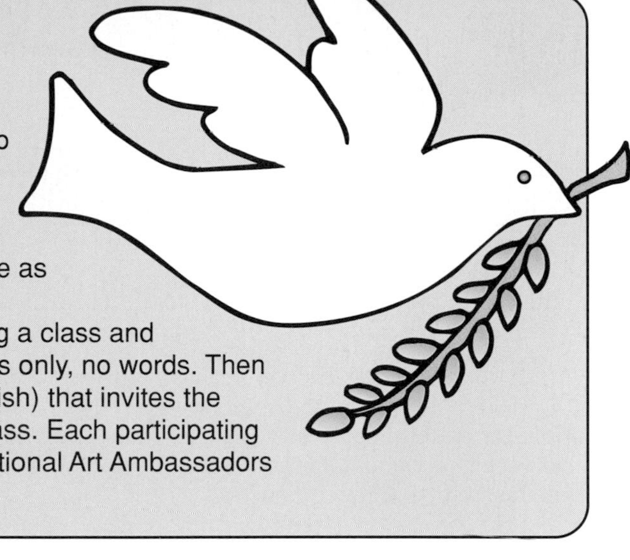

Inspire students to contribute to world peace by participating in the Students' Art for Peace program. This program invites students around the world to use the universal language of art to create and share illustrations of their ideas about world peace. Just go to **www.art-for-peace.org** to get information about this free program and to download the teacher's guide. To request the name and address of a class of schoolchildren the same age as yours in another country, email the program's headquarters at artpeaceman@aol.com, or fax at (941) 746-9886. After receiving a class and address, have your students create peace pictures using images only, no words. Then mail the pictures, along with a brief friendship message (in English) that invites the students there to send their own peace pictures back to your class. Each participating class will receive a certificate identifying the students as International Art Ambassadors for Peace. *(Information current as of 2/2000.)*

## Math: Practice Pals

Math practice is always more fun when done with a pal, right? So guide each student through the steps below to create a math buddy that provides plenty of math practice. Or make these cute creepy-crawlies for a class of younger students.

**Materials for each student:**

colorful sock
fiberfill (or cotton)
stapler
4 rubber bands
two 8" clear straws, cut in half
two 12" green pipe cleaners, cut in half
one 12" red pipe cleaner, cut in half
two 1" x 12" strips of colorful construction paper, laminated
scissors
pencil
wipe-off marker
construction paper scraps
glue

**Steps:**

1. Stuff the sock with fiberfill. Staple the open end closed.
2. Wrap rubber bands around the sock in four places to represent a segmented body.
3. Use the pencil to make a pair of holes on the bottom center of segments 2–5.
4. Push one piece of straw through each pair of holes. Insert a length of green pipe cleaner into each straw so that about one inch extends beyond the straw at both ends.
5. Cut the laminated paper strips into 16 same-sized rectangles.
6. Use the wipe-off marker to program eight rectangles with math problems. Program their answers on the other eight rectangles.
7. Staple a pair of rectangles on each pipe cleaner end—problem faceup and answer facedown—so that the pipe cleaner is sandwiched between them.
8. Use the pencil to make two holes in the top of the first segment. Push one red pipe cleaner into each hole to make antennae.
9. Glue paper eyes and a mouth to the first segment.
10. Trade pals with a partner and solve each other's problems. To check, flip the pal's feet.
11. To change the problems, just wipe your pal's feet clean and reprogram them with a wipe-off marker.

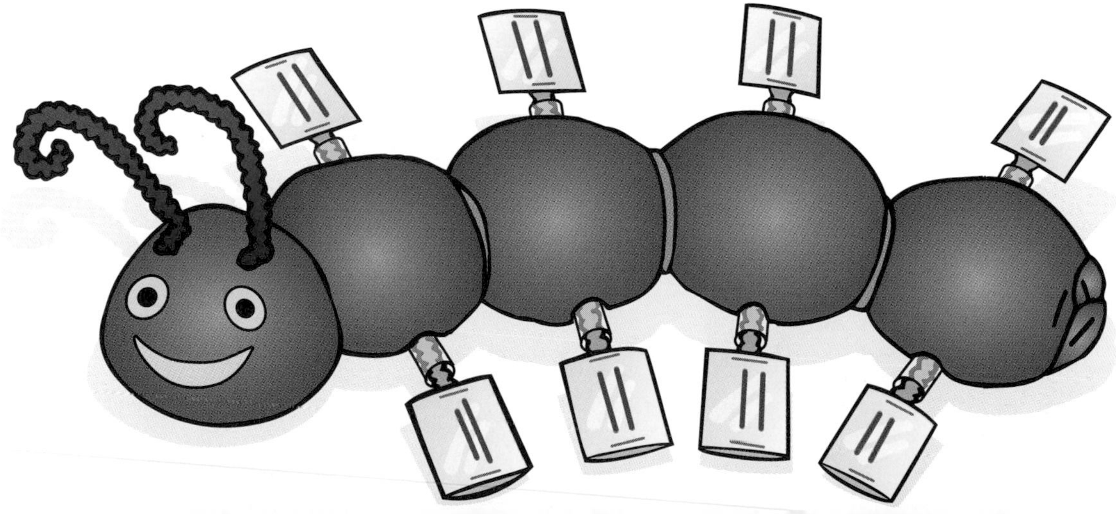

# ACROSS THE CURRICULUM

## Language Arts: Totally "Tee-rific"!

Looking for a simple but totally "tee-rific" activity to practice expressive- or descriptive-writing skills? You've found it! Have each student write about a day that was so great he'd live it all over again in a heartbeat. Then guide the student through the steps below to create a unique self-portrait to glue onto his story. Be sure to include these nifty projects on your open house bulletin board!

**Materials for each child:** 7" x 9" piece of white paper towel; a ruler; a spring-type clothespin (optional); scissors; glue; 9" x 12" sheet of construction paper; crayons, markers, or colored pencils
**Materials for the class:** paper towels, water, food coloring, plastic cups (one for each different food coloring used)

**Steps:**

1. Put several drops of red food coloring into a cup along with a few drops of water. (The less water used, the darker the color.) Repeat for the remaining colors.
2. Fold the paper towel piece several times into squares, rectangles, and triangles until it is about 2" x 2".
3. Dip each corner of the folded paper towel into a different cup for five seconds. If desired, use a clothespin to hold the paper towel while dipping it.
4. Blot the folded paper towel on clean paper towels. Then unfold it and allow to dry on another paper towel.
5. Cut a T-shirt shape from the dried paper towel and glue it to the construction paper.
6. Draw a picture of yourself wearing the T-shirt as shown. Cut out the picture and glue it to the final copy of your story.

Beth Gress, Harrison, OH

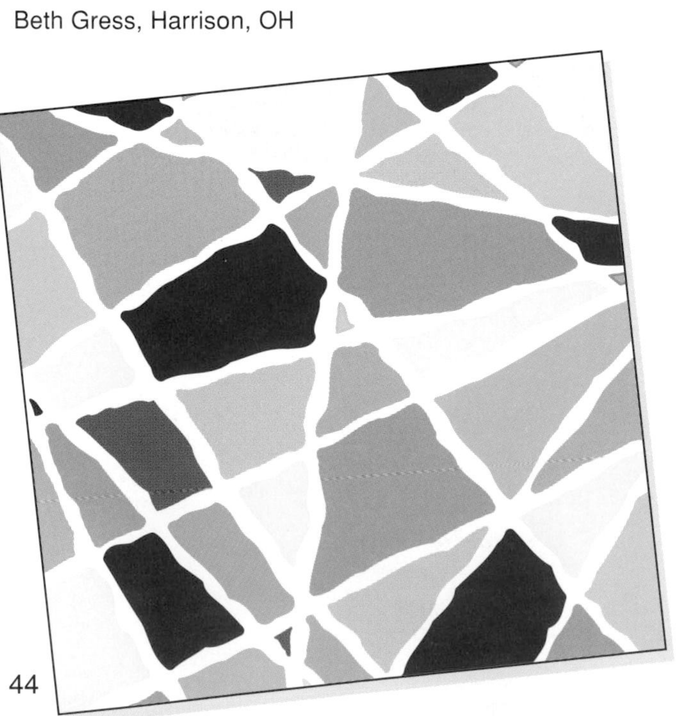

## Math: Intersecting-Lines Design

Turn a review of intersecting lines and polygons into a head-turning display! Give each student a 12-inch square of white construction paper, a ruler, and colored markers. Have the student draw intersecting lines on her paper to create a design of different-sized polygons. Direct her to color each polygon a different color; then have her trace the intersecting lines with a black marker or black (or white) Tulip Puffy® fabric paint. As students view the vivid artwork, challenge them to look not only for triangles and quadrilaterals, but also for pentagons, hexagons, and other polygons!

## Social Studies: **Prehistoric Cave Drawings**

Let students simulate the artwork prehistoric people created on cave walls 20,000 years ago with this exciting project. First, show students pictures of cave paintings from encyclopedias or other reference books. Explain that the paintings represent a form of early communication. Also point out that primitive artists used black, red, and yellow because these pigments came from natural materials that were readily available.

Next, give each child a 1' x 3' piece of brown butcher paper and three crayons: black, red, and yellow. Direct her to fold her paper two times to create four equal sections. After the student opens the paper, have her trace the fold lines with the black crayon. Then have her illustrate four important personal events—one per section—on the paper. Cover your classroom walls with the completed drawings to create a cavelike atmosphere. During a sharing time, ask each child to tell a story based on the four scenes in her artwork. Then challenge her classmates to identify the drawing that matches the tale.

Dana Sanders, Cartersville, GA

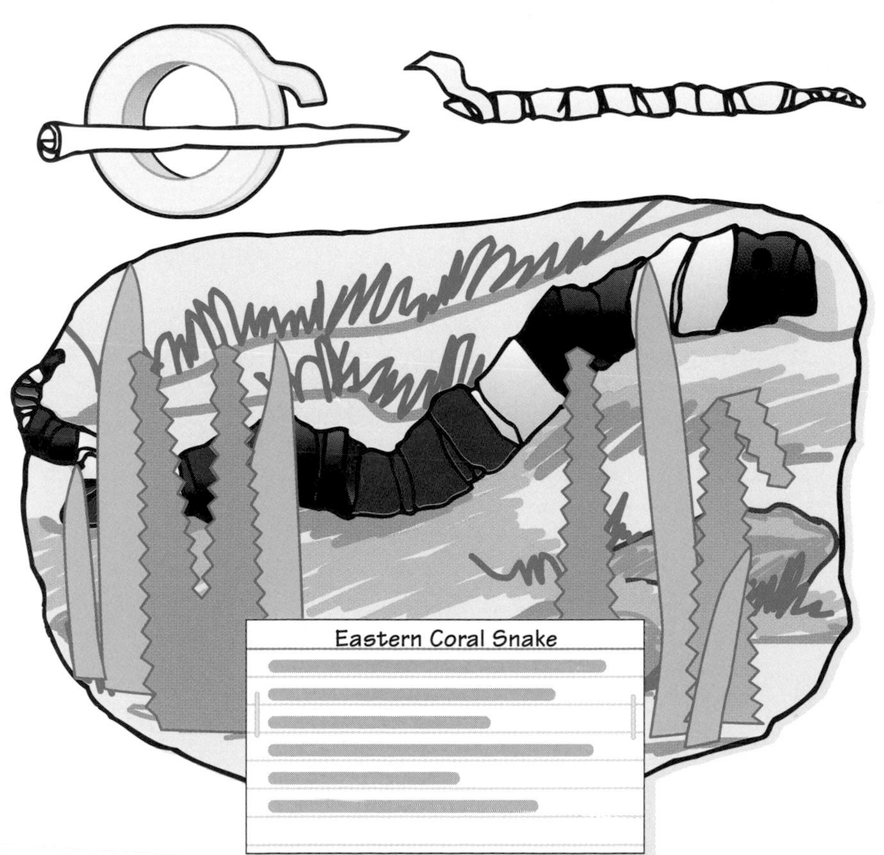


## Science: **Slithery Snakes**

Sssneak a little art into your science curriculum with this slithery project! Assign each child a different kind of snake to research. Have him list important facts about his snake on an index card. Next, have the student roll two paper towels tightly together to make a snake's body. Then have him wrap the body with one continuous piece of masking tape. After the student paints his model, have him staple it to a piece of oaktag that's been decorated with a background scene. To complete the project, have the student staple paper grass (try cutting it with pinking shears) and his fact card to the scene. Sssimply sssensational!

Joan M. Macey
Binghamton, NY

# Across the Curriculum

## Math: Wonderful Whirligigs

Let students demonstrate competence with a compass by making this colorful, fun toy! Have each student use her compass to draw a four-inch circle on cardboard; then have her cut out the circle and poke two holes a half inch apart in the center. After the student decorates her disc with colorful designs, have her thread a 40-inch length of string through the holes to make a loop and knot the ends together. To wind the toy, have the child hold one end of the string in each hand so the disc hangs between her hands and swing it around in the same direction many times. To whirl the toy, have her quickly pull both ends of the string and move her hands together and apart. If desired, have students review families of facts while whirling their toys. On the windup, they can say two addition or multiplication facts. On the whirl, they can say the corresponding subtraction or division facts. Let 'em whirl!

Colleen Dabney
Toano Middle School
Toano, VA

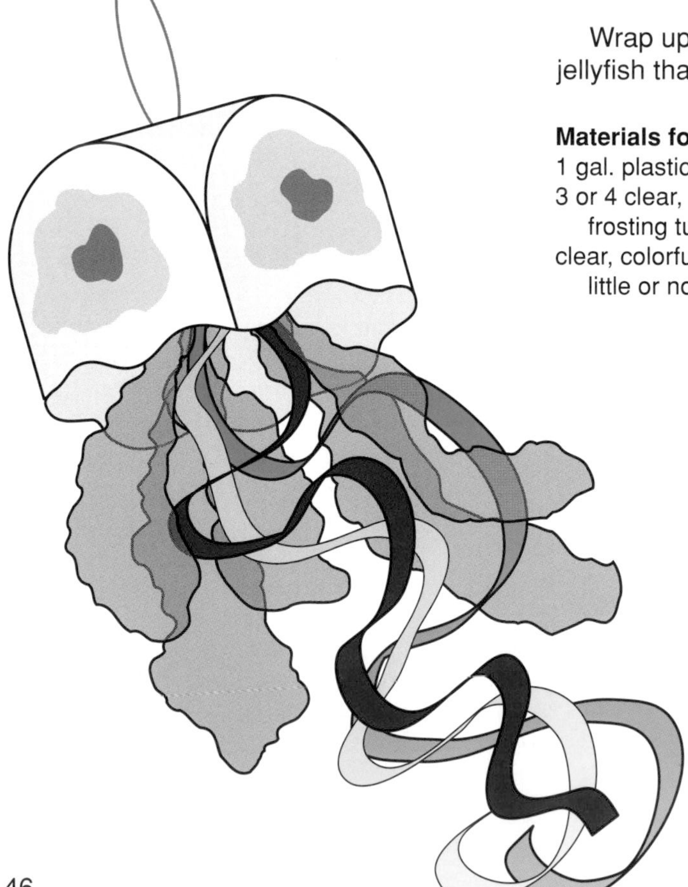

## Science: Water-Jug Jellyfish

Wrap up a unit on invertebrates by having students create a school of jellyfish that flutter in the breeze like windsocks!

**Materials for each student:**

- 1 gal. plastic water jug with label removed
- 3 or 4 clear, colorful plastic lids (from frosting tubs, cans of nuts, etc.)
- clear, colorful plastic shopping bag (with little or no lettering)
- 15" length of fishing line
- scissors
- metal compass
- permanent markers

**Steps:**

1. With your teacher's help, cut the jug in half horizontally. Trim the edge of the bottom half in a wavy pattern. Discard the top half.
2. With your teacher's help, use the sharp end of the compass to poke two holes a half inch apart in the center of the jug's bottom. Use markers to decorate the outside of the jug.
3. Cut the rims from the plastic lids. Then cut each plastic circle into a thin spiral.
4. Tear the plastic bags into five strips that are each approximately 3" x 15".
5. With your teacher's help, use the sharp end of the compass to poke a hole in the center of each spiral and at one end of each plastic strip.
6. Thread the fishing line through the holes in the spirals and strips. Then thread the ends of the fishing line through the jug's holes. Knot the ends together to make a loop and hang.

Christy Morejon—Grs. 1–8 Art
The Chapel School
Bronxville, NY

Little House in the Big Woods
by Laura Ingalls Wilder


## Language Arts: Name-Design Book Reports

What's in a name? Everything needed for a picture-perfect book report! Give each student art paper, a larger sheet of colorful construction paper, colored pencils or markers, and glue. Direct the student to create a name picture based on the letters in the name of her book's main character. Explain that each letter must represent a specific trait of the character or an event that involved him or her. Have the student mount her finished name portrait on the sheet of construction paper. When sharing time arrives, have each student explain why she designed each letter as she did.

Julie Alarie—Gr. 6
Essex Middle School
Essex, VT

## Social Studies: Gifts From the Heart

Enhance the study of any historical period or culture with a project that points to the contributions of some of its most famous people. Assign each student a person to research. Then have him follow the steps below to create a paper bust of the person to display on a bulletin board titled "Great Gifts of the [historical period or cultural group]."

**Materials for each student:**
one 7" x 9" piece of flesh-colored paper
one 9" x 12" sheet of flesh-colored paper
two 5" x 18" pieces of white construction paper
scissors
colored pencils or markers
glue
yarn and various other decorative craft materials
fine-tipped black marker

**Steps:**
1. Trim the 7" x 9" piece of paper to make an oval-shaped face.
2. Decorate the face to resemble the person you researched.
3. Decorate the 5" x 18" pieces as sleeves on clothing your person might wear.
4. Trace your own hands on the 9" x 12" sheet of paper. Cut out the tracings and glue one cutout to the end of each sleeve.
5. Glue the straight ends of the arms together, overlapping them slightly.
6. Glue the head (face forward) to the middle top of the undecorated side of the arms strip.
7. Fold the arms toward the middle so that the hands overlap.
8. Open the arms. In the space inside, write a brief paragraph describing the important contributions your person made to his culture or historical period.

Julie Alarie—Gr. 6

# Poster-Making Pointers

Use the poster-making guidelines below to create picture-perfect posters every time!

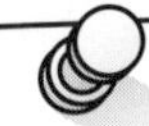

## Purpose

What is the purpose of your poster?

- to share information?
- to advertise?
- to persuade?

Be sure the content and design of your poster communicates the appropriate message.

## Rough Draft

What should your rough draft include?

- Make everything the actual size in the rough draft. Practice any free-hand drawing or lettering.
- Leave equal-sized margins around all four sides (one inch for a 14" x 22" poster).
- Leave a margin between each row of lettering.

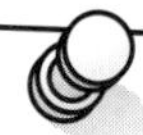

## Creativity

*What could make your poster different and eye-catching?*

- *a unique style of lettering*
- *3-D details*
- *a reversal of positive and negative spaces*
- *striking colors*
- *bold graphics*
- *textured surfaces*

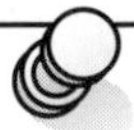

## Layout & Design

What should be included in your poster's design?

- Include a combination of text (words) and graphics (pictures).
- Arrange and size the lettering according to importance.
- Include appropriate graphics that represent the topic.
- Include a balance of positive and negative space.
- Make sure the overall design is balanced and attractive without being busy or cluttered.

## Lettering

What makes a poster's lettering stand out?

- Use letters that are neat and easy to read from a distance (minimum size for a 14" x 22" poster = one inch).
- Use large letters to communicate important information.
- Space letters uniformly (no crowding or overspacing).
- Use uniform colors within the same word or phrase (no writing each letter of a word with different colors).
- Use colors that contrast (for example, avoid yellow letters on a white poster).
- Keep the placement of lettering consistent within a section. Make it all either centered or aligned left.

## Final Draft

What are some tips for completing the final product?

- Use a pencil to lightly outline all drawings and lettering before applying any paint or markers.
- Use a ruler to draw straight lines.
- Cover the finished product to protect it and keep it neat.

# Language Arts Units

# Picture-Perfect

## Plurals and Possessives

When teaching plurals and possessives, you just can't avoid the rules—and all those wonderful *exceptions* to them! But help is on the way! Check out the following creative activities and reproducibles—all guaranteed to give students picture-perfect success with plurals and possessives!

*by Simone Lepine*

### Plurals: They're Everywhere!

There are more nouns in the English language than any other kind of word. So that means lots of noun plurals, too! Use the following ideas to help students master the spelling rules for noun plurals.

### Playing by the Rules

**Skills: Reviewing plural rules, making a study aid**

Kick off this study by laying down the rules—the rules about plural nouns, that is! Have each student stack three sheets of white paper, fold them in half from top to bottom, and then staple them along the fold. Next, have the student color and cut out the booklet cover art and page labels from a copy of page 53. Then have him glue the cover art to the front of his booklet and the labels onto the blank pages as shown. Encourage students to add words that match each rule to their booklets. And when students need to review how to write plural nouns, all they have to do is check out their rule books!

### Go Fish!

**Skill: Writing plural nouns**

Here's a new twist on a game that's been around for a while! First, give each student 24 index cards. Assign each student one noun from the list shown; then have her print the noun on each of her cards. When finished, have the student divide her cards into eight sets of three cards each. Collect one set of cards from each student to build a deck; then repeat seven more times to make eight decks in all. To play:

1. Divide students into eight groups. Give each group a deck of cards.
2. Instruct students to play Go Fish, building matches of *three* cards each instead of *two*.
3. At the end of a game, each player must write the plural of each word in a set that he has won.
4. Write the plurals on the chalkboard and have students check their work. The winner in each group is the student who wrote the most correct plural nouns.

**Noun List**

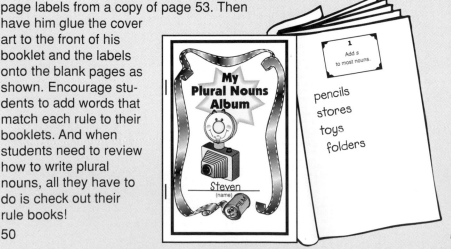

school, window, picture, farm, church, box, wish, waltz, cherry, fairy, story, penny, donkey, toy, key, tray, wife, knife, leaf, puff, safe, patio, rodeo, piano, solo, taco, deer, sheep, trout, moose, swine, man, woman, child, foot

## Possessing Possessives

Now that students know their plural nouns, possessives will be a cinch! Briefly review the apostrophe and how it's used in writing possessives. Also review and post the three rules shown. Then use the following ideas.

**Singular Possessive Nouns**
*Add apostrophe and* **s.**
*cats = cat's*
*Jesse = Jesse's*

**Plural Possessive Nouns**
*(that end with* **s***)*
*Add an apostrophe.*
*dogs = dogs' trees = trees'*

**Plural Possessive Nouns**
*(that don't end with* **s***)*
*Add apostrophe and* **s.**
*deer = deer's women = women's*

## And in This Corner...
### Skill: Determining plural noun spelling rules

Here's a game that's easy to prepare, takes little time to play, and is fun—what a deal! Label four sheets of poster board as shown. Place each poster in a different corner of the classroom. You'll also need a noun list (see pages 50 and 54–56). Have students count off one through four; then have each child stand by the poster that matches her number. To play:

1. Call out a singular noun.
2. As a class, decide which rule is used to make that noun plural.
3. Have students at that rule's poster return to their seats. (For example, if the word is *knife,* the students standing at poster #3 would sit.)
4. Direct each remaining student to go to a different corner.
5. Call out another singular noun and repeat Steps 2, 3, and 4.
6. Continue play until only one student is standing.

Challenge students by calling out a noun that doesn't follow any of the four rules, such as *moose* or *deer.* During these rounds, everyone remains in the game!

① **Add s.**

② **Change y to i. Add es.**

③ **Drop f or fe. Add ves.**

④ **Add es.**

## Picture This!
### Skill: Singular possessive nouns

Punctuating singular possessive nouns is simple, so review this skill with a creative game. First, make a master copy of the singular noun possessives shown. Then make a copy for each group of four to six students. Cut each group's copy into strips and put them in an envelope.

Next, divide the class into groups of four to six players each. Give each group an envelope, a sheet of lined paper, a pencil, and several sheets of drawing paper. Then divide each group into two teams. To play:

1. A player from Team 1 draws a slip from the envelope, reads it, and then illustrates the phrase on drawing paper.
2. The player's teammates have one minute to guess the phrase. A recorder writes it on the lined paper.
3. If the phrase is spelled and punctuated correctly, that team earns a point. If not, no point is earned.
4. If the team cannot guess the phrase in the allotted time, then the opposing team gets a turn with the same phrase. Or the opposing team may pass and draw a new phrase. The first phrase is set aside and not used again.
5. The team with the most points after a preset number of rounds is the winner.

| | |
|---|---|
| plane's wing | tree's bark |
| cat's food | lady's watch |
| chair's leg | watch's hands |
| book's pages | girl's skateboard |
| deer's antlers | boy's bookbag |
| mug's handle | bird's nest |
| sun's rays | pen's ink |
| fish's tank | alligator's snout |
| picture's frame | kite's tail |
| car's trunk | television's screen |

## Insiders Vs. Outsiders
### Skill: Singular and plural possessives

Get students moving with this activity! First, make one copy of page 56. Cut the two columns in half along the bold line; then cut out each card. Glue each pair's noun on one side of an index card and the sample sentence on the opposite side. Then follow these steps:

1. Divide the class into two equal teams named the Insiders and the Outsiders.
2. Have the Insiders form a circle facing outward. Have each Outsider face an Insider. (If the groups are uneven, join in the fun!)
3. Give each Insider a card. (You'll use about half of the cards for this first round.) Tell the Insiders to hold their cards so that the starred side faces them and the noun side faces the Outsiders.
4. On your signal, the Insider reads the bold word to the Outsider facing him. He then reads the sample sentence. The Outsider must spell the possessive form of the word within 30 seconds.
5. Tell the Outsiders to move one place to the right. Have the Insiders stand still, but pass their cards to their right. Now each Insider has a new partner and a new card.
6. Repeat Steps 4 and 5 until all the Outsiders return to their original partners.
7. Now have the circles switch places with each other. Take up the first set of cards, distribute the second set, and play another round.

## Share and Share Alike
### Skill: Writing shared possessives

Kids sometimes grumble about having to share things, but they won't mind sharing in this activity! Have each student think of a common noun that names a thing or place and write it on a slip of paper. Collect the slips and put them in a bag.

Next, ask three or four students to stand in a row at the front of the class. On the board, write their names in a series, such as "Jake, Roland, and Abby." Draw a slip of paper from the bag and announce the noun, such as "puppy." Ask the class how to write a possessive showing that these three students own the puppy. Then add an apostrophe and *s* to the last name in the series, and then the word *puppy:* "Jake, Roland, and Abby's puppy."

Now ask the students standing to choose classmates to take their places. Once the new group is lined up, have a volunteer choose a slip from the bag and read it aloud. Direct the rest of the students to write the possessive phrase on their papers as you did in the first example. Have students share what they wrote and how they punctuated it. Continue play until each student has had a turn up front.

## Booklet Cover Art

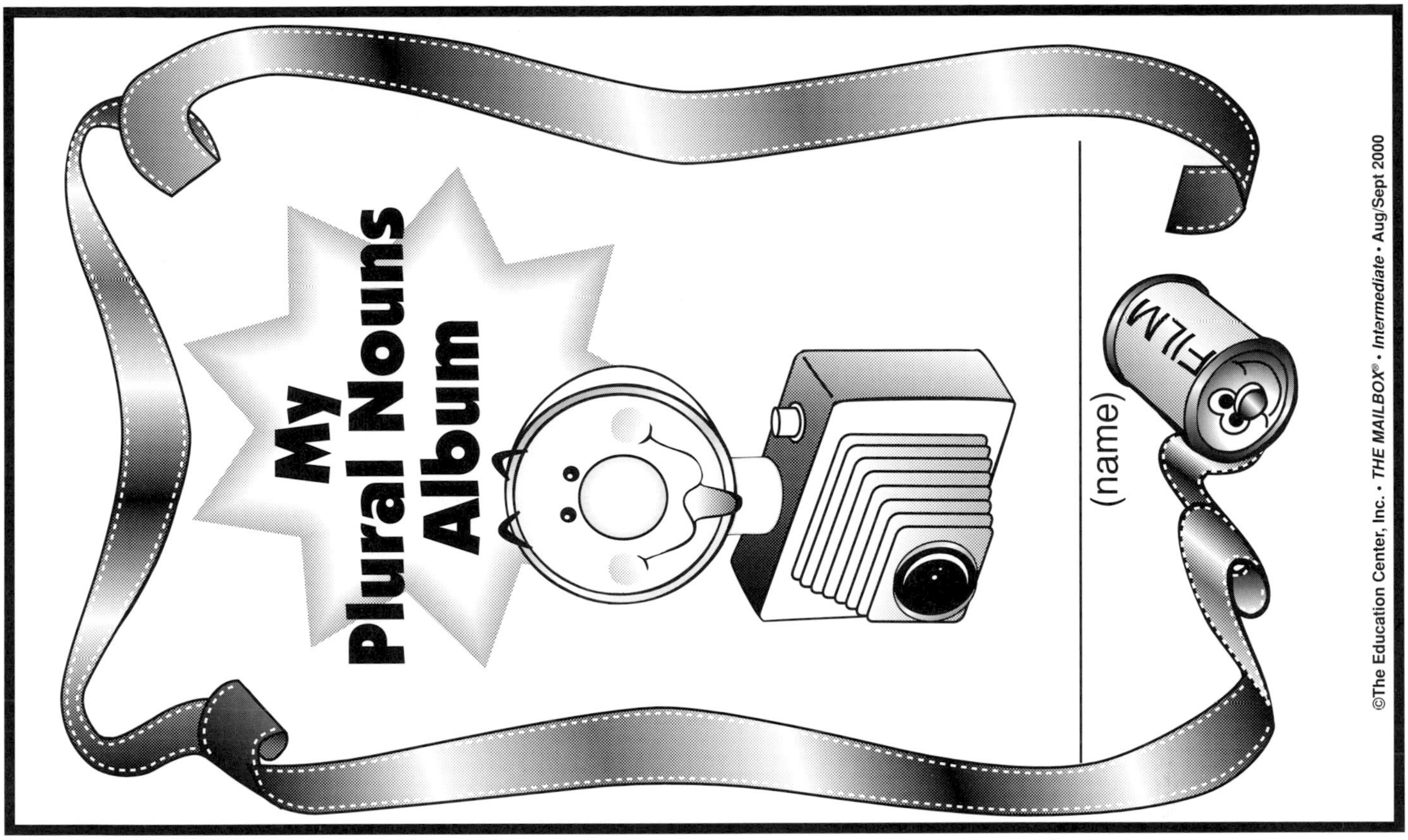

My Plural Nouns Album

FILM

(name)



## Booklet Page Labels

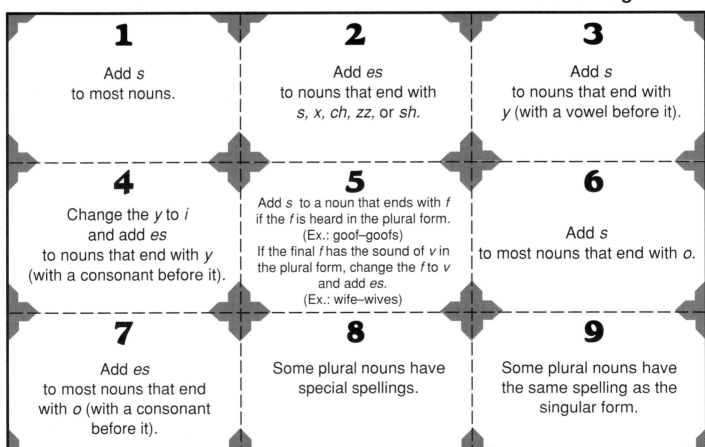

| | | |
|---|---|---|
| **1**<br>Add *s*<br>to most nouns. | **2**<br>Add *es*<br>to nouns that end with<br>*s, x, ch, zz,* or *sh.* | **3**<br>Add *s*<br>to nouns that end with<br>*y* (with a vowel before it). |
| **4**<br>Change the *y* to *i*<br>and add *es*<br>to nouns that end with *y*<br>(with a consonant before it). | **5**<br>Add *s* to a noun that ends with *f*<br>if the *f* is heard in the plural form.<br>(Ex.: goof–goofs)<br>If the final *f* has the sound of *v* in<br>the plural form, change the *f* to *v*<br>and add *es.*<br>(Ex.: wife–wives) | **6**<br>Add *s*<br>to most nouns that end with *o.* |
| **7**<br>Add *es*<br>to most nouns that end<br>with *o* (with a consonant<br>before it). | **8**<br>Some plural nouns have<br>special spellings. | **9**<br>Some plural nouns have<br>the same spelling as the<br>singular form. |



**Note to the teacher:** Use this page with "Playing by the Rules" on page 50.

Name ____________________ Irregular plural nouns

# Exceptional Exceptions

*We're mice!*

English is a funny language! We say two *houses,* but not two *mouses!* And if *teeth* is correct, shouldn't the plural of *booth* be *beeth?* You just have to learn some plural nouns that don't follow the rules!

Make your own flash cards to practice spelling these unusual plurals. You'll need 20 index cards, scissors, and glue. First, cut along the middle bold line. Then cut out each pair of words. Glue the singular form to one side of an index card and the plural form to the opposite side.

Work with a partner as you spell the noun plurals. You'll learn these rule breakers in no time!

| singular | plural | singular | plural |
|---|---|---|---|
| tooth | teeth | cactus | cacti |
| man | men | deer | deer |
| child | children | sheep | sheep |
| ox | oxen | trout | trout |
| foot | feet | moose | moose |
| goose | geese | bison | bison |
| die | dice | salmon | salmon |
| mouse | mice | radius | radii |
| axis | axes | oasis | oases |
| woman | women | crisis | crises |



**Note to the teacher:** For a variation, use these noun cards to make a matching game. Make one copy for each pair of students. Have the pair cut out each word and glue it onto a separate index card. Then have each pair lay the cards facedown in an 8 x 5 array and play Concentration.

Name________________________________________ Plural possessives

# The BIG Picture!

It's easy to show possession when a noun is singular. All you do is add an apostrophe and an *s.* But when the noun is plural, it's a little trickier! Review the two rules below for how to write plural possessive nouns. Then see if you can match the plural nouns in the photo with the nouns they possess. Write the correct possessive form of each word in a blank. The first one is done for you.

If a plural noun ends in *s,* just add an apostrophe.
cats = cats' waitresses = waitresses'
If a plural noun does not end in *s,* add an apostrophe and an *s.*
deer = deer's children = children's
trees
sheep
trout
countries
songs
radios
roofs
lions
teeth
geese
women
deer
houses
mice
moose
books
children
cowboys
~~bicycles~~
policemen

| | | | | | |
|---|---|---|---|---|---|
| 1. | *bicycles'* | wheels | 11. | ______________ | cheese |
| 2. | ______________ | cubs | 12. | ______________ | fawns |
| 3. | ______________ | gaggle | 13. | ______________ | calves |
| 4. | ______________ | dresses | 14. | ______________ | horses |
| 5. | ______________ | uniforms | 15. | ______________ | flags |
| 6. | ______________ | toys | 16. | ______________ | antennas |
| 7. | ______________ | pages | 17. | ______________ | mailboxes |
| 8. | ______________ | enamel | 18. | ______________ | stream |
| 9. | ______________ | branches | 19. | ______________ | lambs |
| 10. | ______________ | notes | 20. | ______________ | shingles |

**Bonus Box:** Write five sentences about your family. Include a possessive noun in each sentence. Try to include at least one plural possessive. Examples: My <u>dad's</u> name is Guy. Soccer is my <u>cousins'</u> favorite sport.

| | | | |
|---|---|---|---|
| 1<br>**toy** | ★ 1<br>The **toy's** part is missing. | 15<br>**piano** | ★ 15<br>Bob counted the **piano's** keys. |
| 2<br>**women** | ★ 2<br>The **women's** club met today. | 16<br>**men** | ★ 16<br>The **men's** team won! |
| 3<br>**kite** | ★ 3<br>A **kite's** tail hung from a tree. | 17<br>**road** | ★ 17<br>We drove to the **road's** end. |
| 4<br>**geese** | ★ 4<br>We heard the **geese's** honks. | 18<br>**children** | ★ 18<br>Mom directed the **children's** play. |
| 5<br>**chair** | ★ 5<br>The **chair's** leg is broken. | 19<br>**man** | ★ 19<br>Kim found a **man's** wallet. |
| 6<br>**sisters** | ★ 6<br>My two **sisters'** boyfriends visited us. | 20<br>**foxes** | ★ 20<br>The **foxes'** den was hidden. |
| 7<br>**tree** | ★ 7<br>We sat in the elm **tree's** shade. | 21<br>**map** | ★ 21<br>The information is in the **map's** key. |
| 8<br>**mice** | ★ 8<br>We found the **mice's** nest. | 22<br>**houses** | ★ 22<br>Five **houses'** roofs were blown off. |
| 9<br>**coat** | ★ 9<br>My **coat's** collar is torn. | 23<br>**mouse** | ★ 23<br>I see a **mouse's** footprints! |
| 10<br>**cities** | ★ 10<br>We found the **cities'** populations. | 24<br>**monkeys** | ★ 24<br>We heard the **monkeys'** chatter. |
| 11<br>**lady** | ★ 11<br>The **lady's** hat is stunning. | 25<br>**child** | ★ 25<br>Evan checked the **child's** work. |
| 12<br>**heroes** | ★ 12<br>The **heroes'** parade was thrilling! | 26<br>**elves** | ★ 26<br>The **elves'** work was done. |
| 13<br>**wolf** | ★ 13<br>A **wolf's** howl was heard. | 27<br>**hero** | ★ 27<br>Sally was given a **hero's** welcome. |
| 14<br>**pages** | ★ 14<br>The **pages'** numbers are all even. | 28<br>**puppies** | ★ 28<br>The **puppies'** tails wagged excitedly. |





**Note to the teacher:** See "Insiders Vs. Outsiders" on page 52 for information on using these game cards.

## Ideas for Building Students' Word Power

Pumping up your students' word power is a cinch with these vocabulary-enriching activities from our subscribers!

### Daily Word Building

**Skills: Learning new words, using a dictionary**

Boost students' vocabulary and dictionary skills with this daily activity. Each day have one student choose a word from the dictionary. Check the word to make sure that it's appropriate and that it's not a proper noun or an abbreviation. Then have the student copy his word on a large index card. On the back of the card, have the student write the word, its pronunciation and part of speech, a definition, and a sample sentence. Check the completed card and award bonus points for neatness and accuracy. Then have the student show his word to the class and give its pronunciation and part of speech. Direct classmates to ask yes or no questions to determine the word's meaning. If no one can guess the word's meaning, have the student who created the card share his sample sentence as a clue.

After about 20 word cards have been created, test students on the new words they've learned. You'll be amazed when you notice students using these new words!

Cheryl Crater—Gr. 5
South Wilmington Elementary
South Wilmington, IL

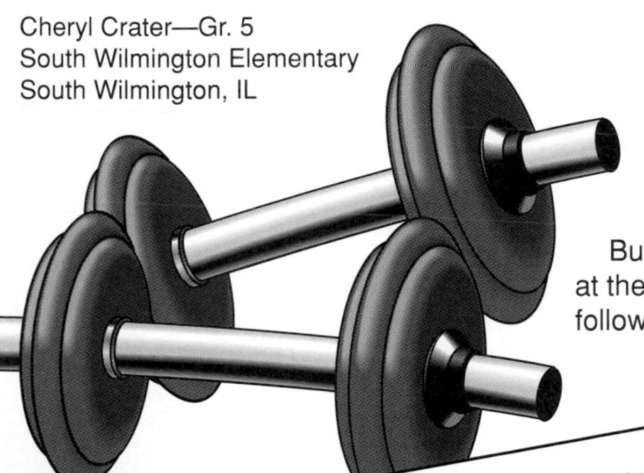

### Word Pyramids

**Skills: Using base words, prefixes, and suffixes**

Build students' knowledge of base words and affixes with the reproducible at the top of page 61. To complete a word pyramid, direct each student to follow these steps:

**Level 1:** Write a base word.
**Level 2:** Write two words. In the box on the left, write the base word with a prefix. In the box on the right, write the base word with a suffix.
**Level 3:** Write four words. In the two boxes on the left, use the prefix from level two with two new base words. In the two boxes on the right, use the suffix from level two with two new base words.
**Level 4:** Write two sentences. In the left box, write a sentence with one of the three new words on the left side of the pyramid. In the right box, write a sentence with one of the three new words on the right side of the pyramid.

To vary the activity, provide students with a word for either level two or three of the pyramid. Then have them complete the eight other sections of the pyramid.

Kimberly A. Minafo—Gr. 4
Tooker Avenue Elementary
West Babylon, NY

# Art or Spelling? Look Closely!

**Skill: Learning descriptive words**

A fun art activity is one way to help students use descriptive words! Select a page from a primary coloring book that has a large, simple picture and copy the page for your students. Instruct each student to place a sheet of duplicating paper over the picture as if he's going to trace it; then have him staple the two pages together to keep them aligned. Next, instead of tracing the image, have the student fill in the entire picture space on the sheet of duplicating paper with words that describe it (see the example). Have students use different colors of fine-tipped markers to write their words. When each student is finished, have him separate the two sheets, cut around his word picture, and attach it to a sheet of black background paper for display. Spelling or art? Yes!

Lisa Peterson—Gr. 4
Erwin, TN

# Bookmark It!

**Skill: Learning vocabulary during independent reading**

Here's an easy way for students to increase word power when reading independently. Provide each student with a copy of a bookmark like the one shown, or have students make their own. Have each student jot down on the bookmark any unknown words that she encounters while reading, plus the page numbers on which they first appear. After noting ten words, instruct the student to reread the passage that includes each word, write a definition of the word based on its context, identify the word's part of speech, and use the word in a sample sentence. Laminate completed bookmarks for students to collect or display on a reading bulletin board.

Shawn Parkhurst—Gr. 6
Canadian Academy
Kobe, Japan

# Word Butterflies

**Skill: Using precise vocabulary**

An overused word—such as *very, do, nice,* or *good*—sometimes needs to undergo a metamorphosis, just like a butterfly! Remind students to use more precise vocabulary in their writing with this fluttery display. First, cut out a supply of colorful butterfly bodies using the pattern on page 61. Write an overused word on each body. Then staple it, at the top only, to a bulletin board as shown. Add the title "Common Words Become Beautiful Butterflies." Also make several copies of the butterfly pattern at the bottom of page 61.

Whenever students identify two or more words that could replace an overused one listed on a butterfly body, have a volunteer write those words on the wings of a butterfly pattern and color the pattern. Then have the student slip the pattern beneath the appropriate butterfly body, staple the butterfly to the board, and then fold the wings on the dotted lines for a three-dimensional effect. Invite students to visit their butterfly word garden when writing, especially when they want to replace an old, tired word with a beguiling one!

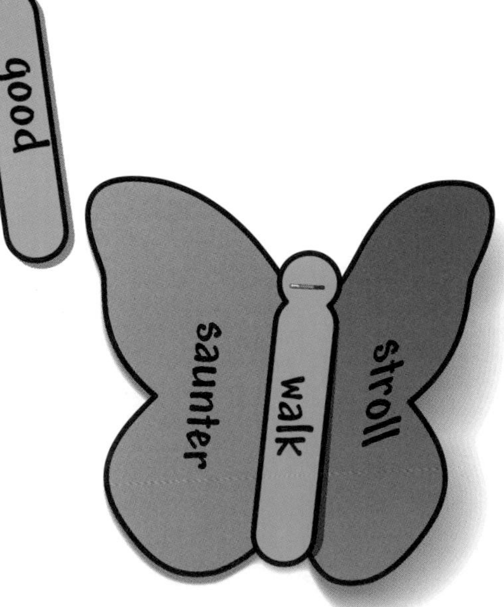


Kimberly A. Minafo—Gr. 4
Tooker Avenue Elementary
West Babylon, NY

## Will the Real Word Please Stand Up?

**Skills: Research, learning new words**

pummel

torsade

blipnik

Turn your students on to new vocabulary with this weekly challenge. Post three new words each week: two that are unfamiliar to students plus a third that you make up. Encourage students to use dictionaries and other reference materials to figure out which word is the phony one. Then, at the end of the week, pronounce the first word and ask those students who believe it's the phony one to stand up. Repeat with the other two words. After everyone has voted, reveal the fake word. Discuss the two real words and challenge students to use them in their writing and speaking. For fun, have students invent definitions and ways to use your made-up word!

Terry Healy—Gifted
Eugene Field Elementary
Manhattan, KS

## New Words Are in the Bag!

**Skills: Developing vocabulary, categorizing**

An old gym bag, an alarm clock, some index cards, and a supply of plastic resealable bags are all you need to make this fun vocabulary center. First, make several sets of word cards, with about ten cards per set. Include a set of common words, words from your current classroom novel, words related to a current topic you're studying, or words from current events. Put each set of cards in a resealable bag that you've labeled with the category name; then put all of the bags into the gym bag. Once every few days, set the alarm clock to go off in the middle of class. When it does, have students stop what they're doing; then invite a volunteer to reach into the gym bag and draw a bag. Discuss each word in this set by asking students for a definition, sample sentence, part of speech, etc. Or list the words on the board for students to alphabetize, use in a paragraph, or illustrate with simple drawings. Don't be alarmed when students beg you to set the clock!

Kimberly A. Minafo—Gr. 4
Tooker Avenue Elementary
West Babylon, NY

## ABC Lists

**Skill: Learning topic-related words**

Help students build vocabulary and stretch their critical-thinking skills with this activity that's as easy as A, B, C. First, have each student write the alphabet in one column on a sheet of paper. Then announce a category or topic, such as the unit you're currently studying or a topic in the news. Tell students that they are to list words that are related to the topic—one word beginning with each letter of the alphabet. For example, when studying the weather, help students get started with these words: *arctic, balmy, cold, drizzle, extreme, fog, gusty,* etc. Occasionally, announce a fun topic as well, such as sports, music, colors, animals, mall words, city words, etc. Easy!

Isobel L. Livingstone
Rahway, NJ

Name________________________________________________

# Anagrams Through the Alphabet
## (Well, almost!)

An *anagram* is a word or phrase made by rearranging the letters of another word or phrase. For example, the letters in the word *pots* can be anagrammed to make *stop, post, tops, spot,* and *opts.* And here's a neat phrase: *eleven plus two* can be anagrammed to make *twelve plus one*.

**Directions:** Anagram your way through the alphabet! Rearrange the letters in each word below; then write its anagram in the space provided. The first letter of each new word is given, and an example has been done for you. (Even Stretch Wordstrong couldn't think of an example that begins with the letter *x!* Can you?)

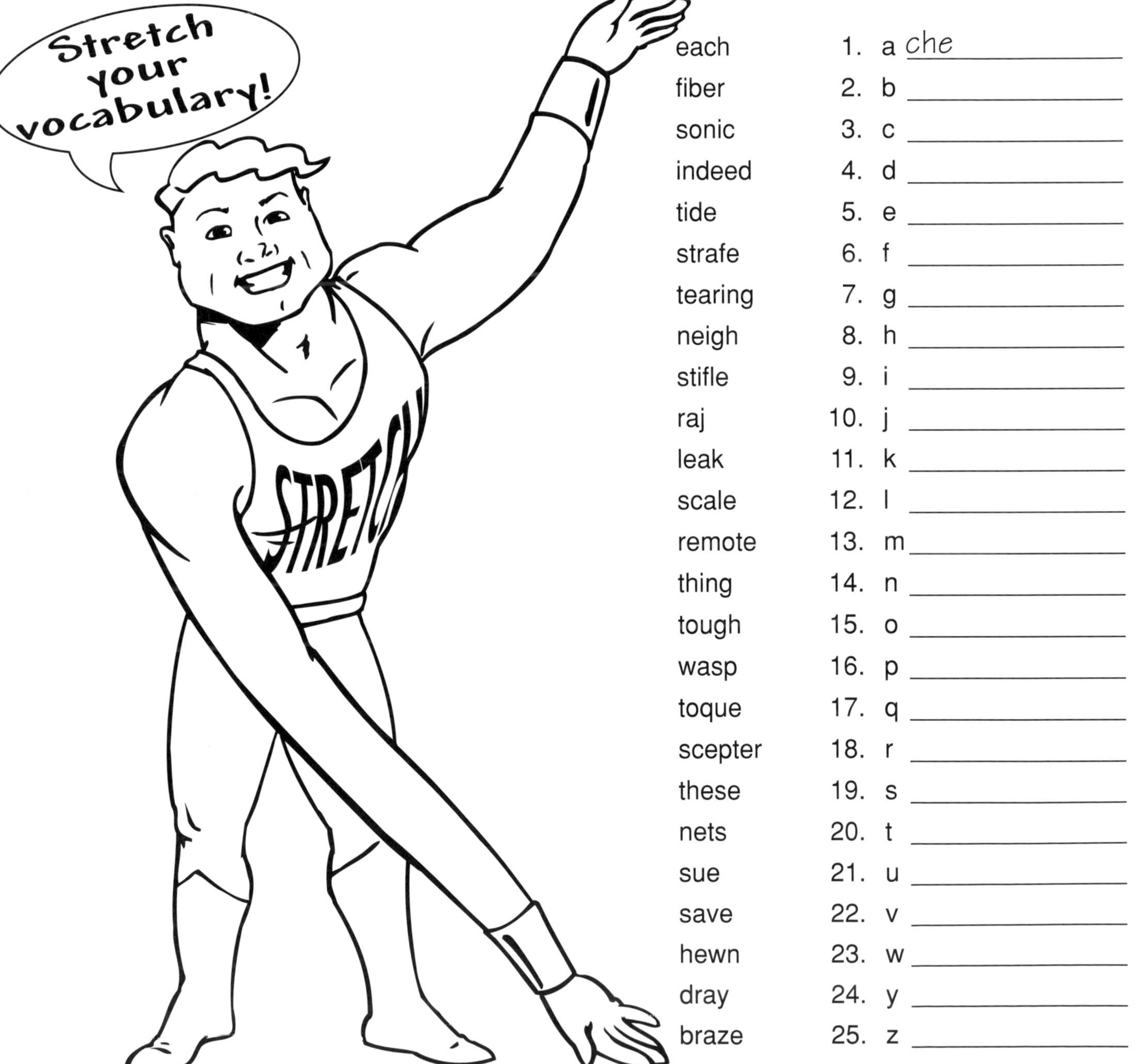
Stretch your vocabulary!
STRETCH

| | |
|---|---|
| each | 1. a che |
| fiber | 2. b ______ |
| sonic | 3. c ______ |
| indeed | 4. d ______ |
| tide | 5. e ______ |
| strafe | 6. f ______ |
| tearing | 7. g ______ |
| neigh | 8. h ______ |
| stifle | 9. i ______ |
| raj | 10. j ______ |
| leak | 11. k ______ |
| scale | 12. l ______ |
| remote | 13. m ______ |
| thing | 14. n ______ |
| tough | 15. o ______ |
| wasp | 16. p ______ |
| toque | 17. q ______ |
| scepter | 18. r ______ |
| these | 19. s ______ |
| nets | 20. t ______ |
| sue | 21. u ______ |
| save | 22. v ______ |
| hewn | 23. w ______ |
| dray | 24. y ______ |
| braze | 25. z ______ |

**Bonus Box:** Can you make at least three anagrams for each of the following words: *bates, tares, poser, seton?*

Name ________________________________ Base words, prefixes, suffixes

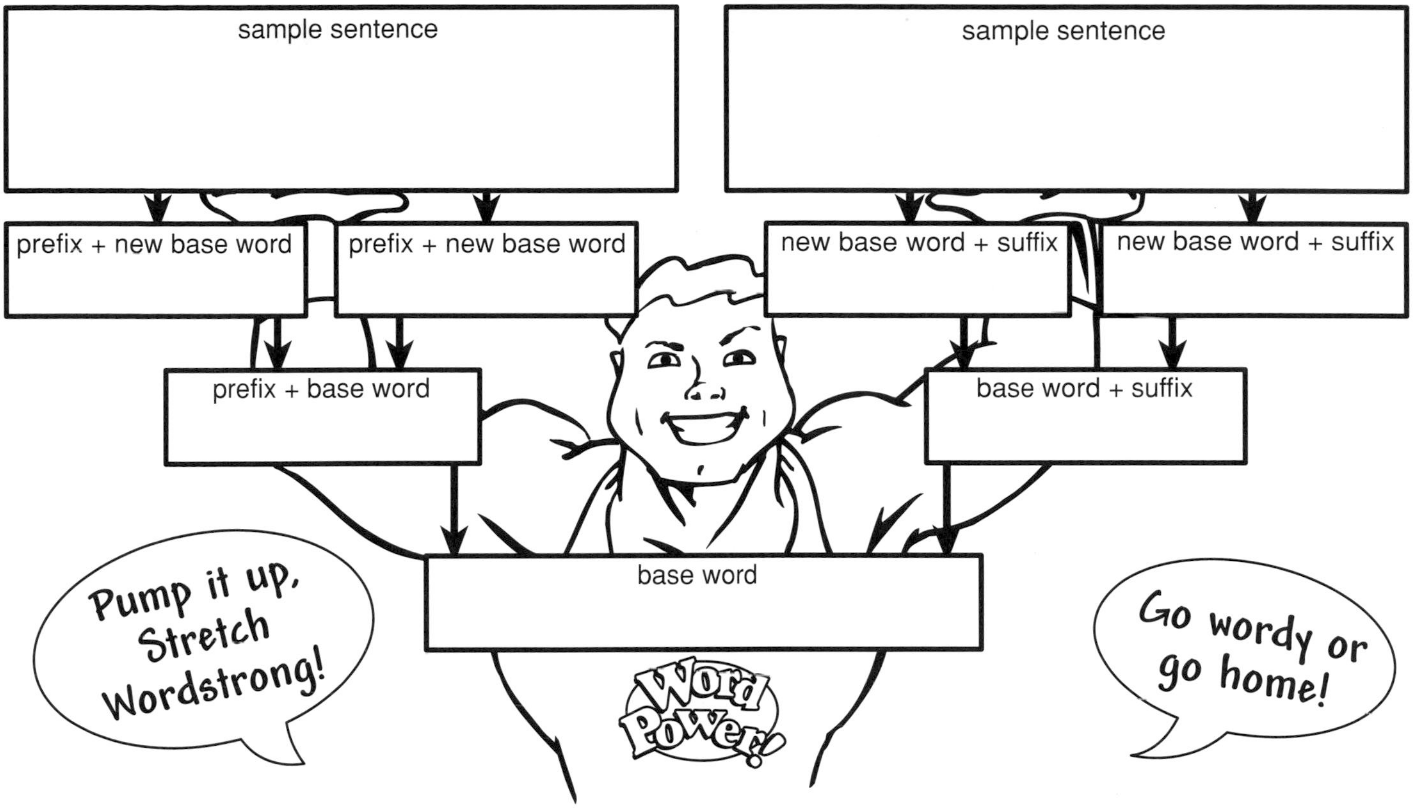

sample sentence

sample sentence

prefix + new base word

prefix + new base word

new base word + suffix

new base word + suffix

prefix + base word

base word + suffix

base word

Pump it up, Stretch Wordstrong!

Go wordy or go home!

Word Power!



**Note to the teacher:** Use with "Word Pyramids" on page 57.

## Patterns

Use with "Word Butterflies" on page 58.

**Butterfly Body Pattern**

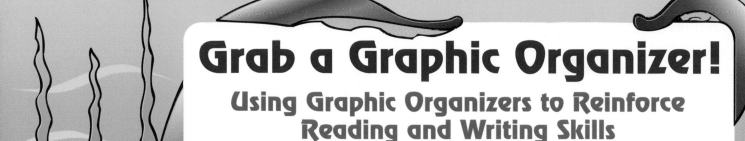

# Grab a Graphic Organizer!

## Using Graphic Organizers to Reinforce Reading and Writing Skills

Dive into the following "sea-sational" ideas and reproducibles on using graphic organizers to reinforce important reading and writing skills!

*by Simone Lepine*

## Story Elements Organizer

**Skills: Identifying story elements, writing a book summary**

Fill the pockets of these adaptable hands-on organizers with the literary elements that make up the stories your students read or want to write. To make the organizers, give each student four business envelopes, a file folder, scissors, and a glue stick. Then have her follow these steps:

1. Seal each envelope; then cut it in half as shown to create two small pockets. Label the pockets as shown.
2. Label the front of the file folder "My Story Elements Organizer." Add your name.
3. Open the folder; then glue the pockets inside in the order shown.
4. Slip a 3" x 5" index card inside each pocket.

Discuss the story elements listed on the pockets. Then read aloud a story or picture book and have each student fill out the cards in her organizer. Discuss the students' cards; then have each child use her cards to write a brief summary of the story. Collect the organizers to use again whenever you want students to practice identifying story elements. For another graphic organizer for identifying story elements, see the reproducible on page 65.

**Ways to adapt:**

- Have each student read a story independently and complete the cards for her organizer.
- Ask a student to complete her organizer so you can assess her comprehension of a story or as an alternative to a traditional book report.
- Have students use their folders to help them organize ideas for writing original fiction stories.

## Plot Peak

**Skill: Analyzing a plot**

Want to help students summarize and illustrate the plot of any story? Then take a "peak" at this idea! Display a transparency of page 66. Explain to students that a good story includes events that build suspense and lead to a climax, followed by falling action that leads to a resolution. If necessary, review the terms *introduction, rising action, climax, falling action,* and *resolution*. Next, discuss the events of a story students have recently read. On a sheet of chart paper or a blank transparency, model how to briefly summarize each story event. Then have students help you place the events in order on the transparency of page 66. Repeat with another story if necessary. After students seem comfortable with doing a plot diagram, have each child complete a copy of page 66 to analyze the plot of a story or book she has read.

**Ways to adapt:**

- Have each student use the graphic organizer on page 66 to plan a plot for an original story. Have each child discuss her plot diagram with a partner before starting the writing process.

# Character Charts

## Skills: Identifying and inferring character traits

All arrows point to this great graphic organizer that helps students analyze characters from books or develop interesting characters for their own stories. Give each student the following materials: a 12" x 18" sheet of construction paper, three small index cards, four circle stickers, scissors, and a marker. Have the student follow these steps to complete a character chart about herself:

1. In the center of the paper, draw a stick figure to represent yourself.
2. Draw four small arrows as shown. Place a circle sticker at the tip of each arrow.
3. Label each sticker with a positive character trait that you possess.
4. Cut each index card into four pieces to make 12 smaller cards.
5. Think of three examples, or evidences, to support each trait. Write each example on a card.
6. Attach the cards near the appropriate circles as shown. Draw a small arrow to connect each circle to each related card.

After each student shares her chart, provide additional materials so that she can create a similar one to analyze a character in the story or book she's reading.

**Ways to adapt:**

- Have each student make a chart to plan a character for an original story. Direct the student to label the four circles "Feelings," "Behavior," "Physical Traits," and "Personality Traits."

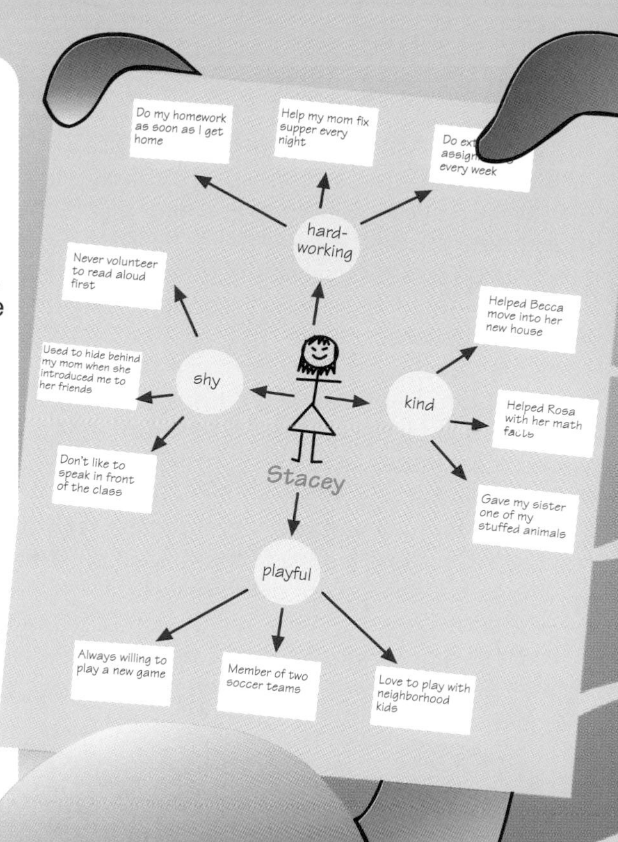


# "Van" Diagram

## Skill: Comparing and contrasting

If your students run out of gas when it comes to writing good comparisons, this fun version of the classic Venn diagram is sure to fill your tank! First, review with students how to use a Venn diagram to compare and contrast two items. Next, read aloud two different stories. Divide the class into two groups. Give each group a large sheet of bulletin board paper on which you've drawn the simple "van" diagram shown. Also give each group member a different colored marker. Direct each student, in turn, to write a similarity or difference between the two stories on her group's diagram. When each group agrees that its van is loaded and ready to go, post its diagram in the room. Then give groups time to examine the diagrams and make any changes or additions to their work. As an extension, have each student use the information on her group's organizer to write an essay that compares and contrasts the two stories.

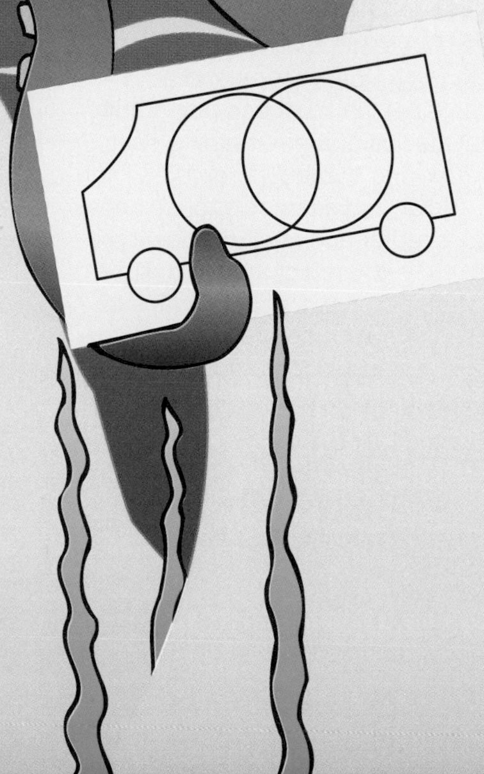

**Ways to adapt:**

- After reading two different stories, divide the class into four groups: Setting, Characters, Plot, Theme. Have each group complete a "van" diagram that compares and contrasts the stories based on its assigned element.
- Use this activity to have students compare/contrast two different characters in a book, or different forms of poetry, polygons, historical figures or time periods, etc.

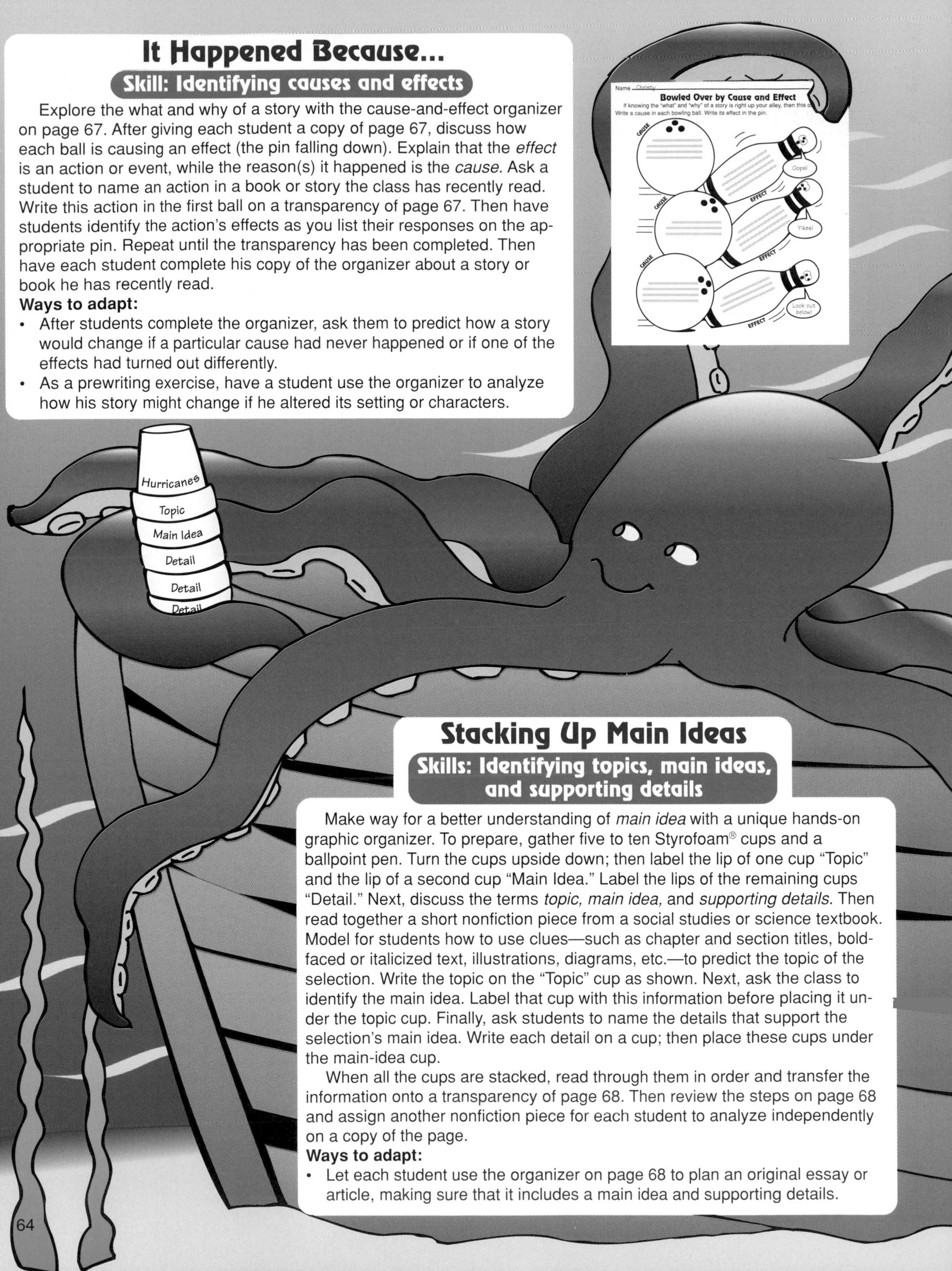


## It Happened Because...

### Skill: Identifying causes and effects

Explore the what and why of a story with the cause-and-effect organizer on page 67. After giving each student a copy of page 67, discuss how each ball is causing an effect (the pin falling down). Explain that the *effect* is an action or event, while the reason(s) it happened is the *cause*. Ask a student to name an action in a book or story the class has recently read. Write this action in the first ball on a transparency of page 67. Then have students identify the action's effects as you list their responses on the appropriate pin. Repeat until the transparency has been completed. Then have each student complete his copy of the organizer about a story or book he has recently read.

**Ways to adapt:**

- After students complete the organizer, ask them to predict how a story would change if a particular cause had never happened or if one of the effects had turned out differently.
- As a prewriting exercise, have a student use the organizer to analyze how his story might change if he altered its setting or characters.

## Stacking Up Main Ideas

### Skills: Identifying topics, main ideas, and supporting details

Make way for a better understanding of *main idea* with a unique hands-on graphic organizer. To prepare, gather five to ten Styrofoam® cups and a ballpoint pen. Turn the cups upside down; then label the lip of one cup "Topic" and the lip of a second cup "Main Idea." Label the lips of the remaining cups "Detail." Next, discuss the terms *topic, main idea,* and *supporting details*. Then read together a short nonfiction piece from a social studies or science textbook. Model for students how to use clues—such as chapter and section titles, boldfaced or italicized text, illustrations, diagrams, etc.—to predict the topic of the selection. Write the topic on the "Topic" cup as shown. Next, ask the class to identify the main idea. Label that cup with this information before placing it under the topic cup. Finally, ask students to name the details that support the selection's main idea. Write each detail on a cup; then place these cups under the main-idea cup.

When all the cups are stacked, read through them in order and transfer the information onto a transparency of page 68. Then review the steps on page 68 and assign another nonfiction piece for each student to analyze independently on a copy of the page.

**Ways to adapt:**

- Let each student use the organizer on page 68 to plan an original essay or article, making sure that it includes a main idea and supporting details.

Name ______________________________ 

# On the Road to a Super Story

Get ready to plan your next story using the graphic organizer below. Fill in each street section with information about its literary element. Then cut out the sections on the bold lines and glue them together in order to create a road. Use your "road map" to help you write a super story!

| | | |
|---|---|---|
| **Setting Street** | 1 | TAB |
| **Main Character Avenue** | 2 | TAB |
| **Problem Path** | 3 | TAB |
| **Resolution Route** | 4 | TAB |
| **Resolution Route (continued)** | 5 | TAB |
| **Dead End Road (ending)** | 6 | |



**Note to the teacher:** Provide students with scissors and glue. After each child completes the organizer, divide the class into groups. Have each student share his organizer and adjust his plans as needed before writing his story. Or have each student read a piece of literature and complete the organizer to identify the selection's story elements.

 Name________________________ 

# Plot Peak

Welcome to Plot Peak, where stories climb to dizzying heights and tireless climbers analyze plots without fear! On another sheet of paper, list and summarize the important events in your story or book. Then write the events on the diagram below.

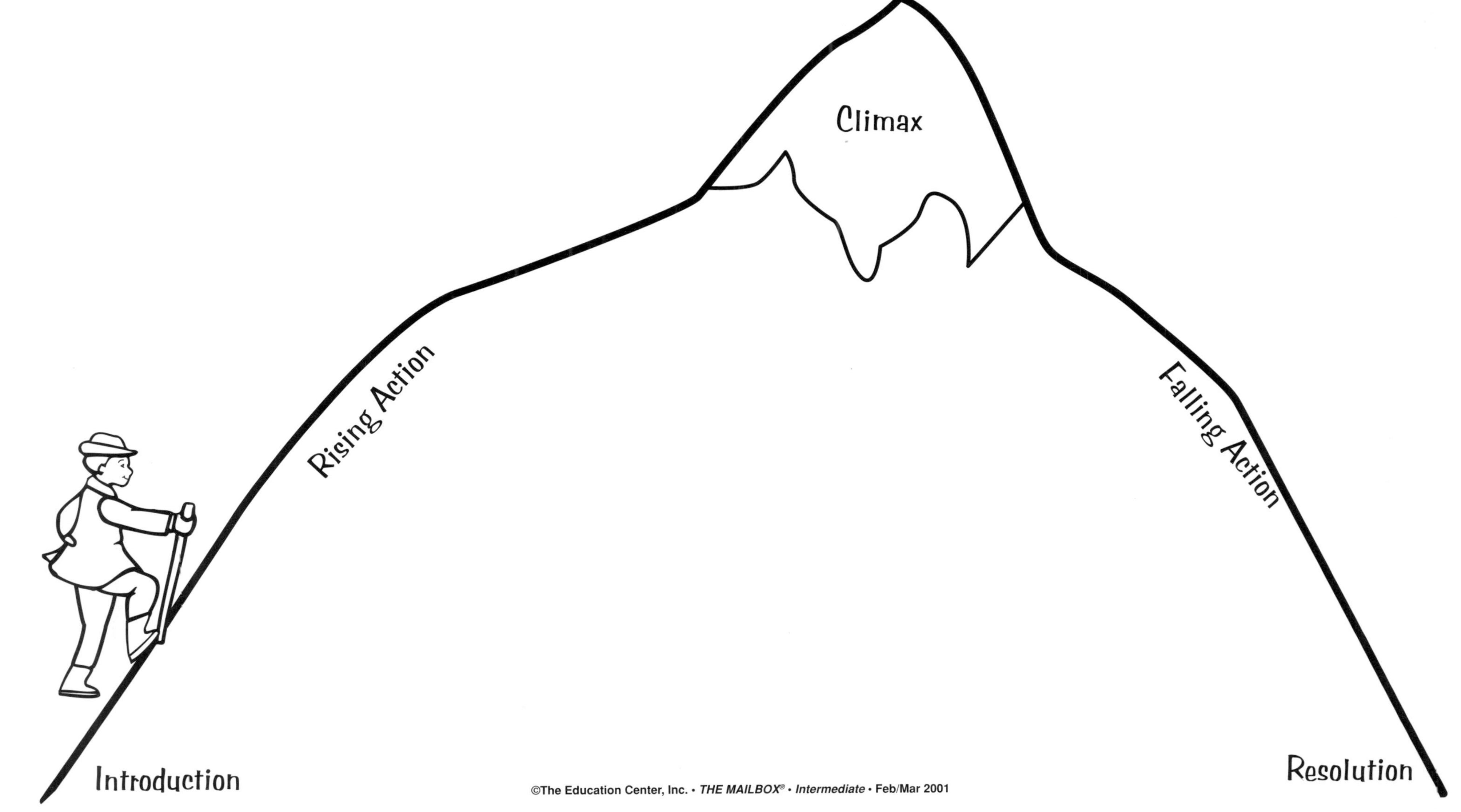




**Note to the teacher:** Use with "Plot Peak" on page 62.

# Bowled Over by Cause and Effect

If knowing the "what" and "why" of a story is right up your alley, then this organizer is for you! Write a cause in each bowling ball. Write its effect in the pin.

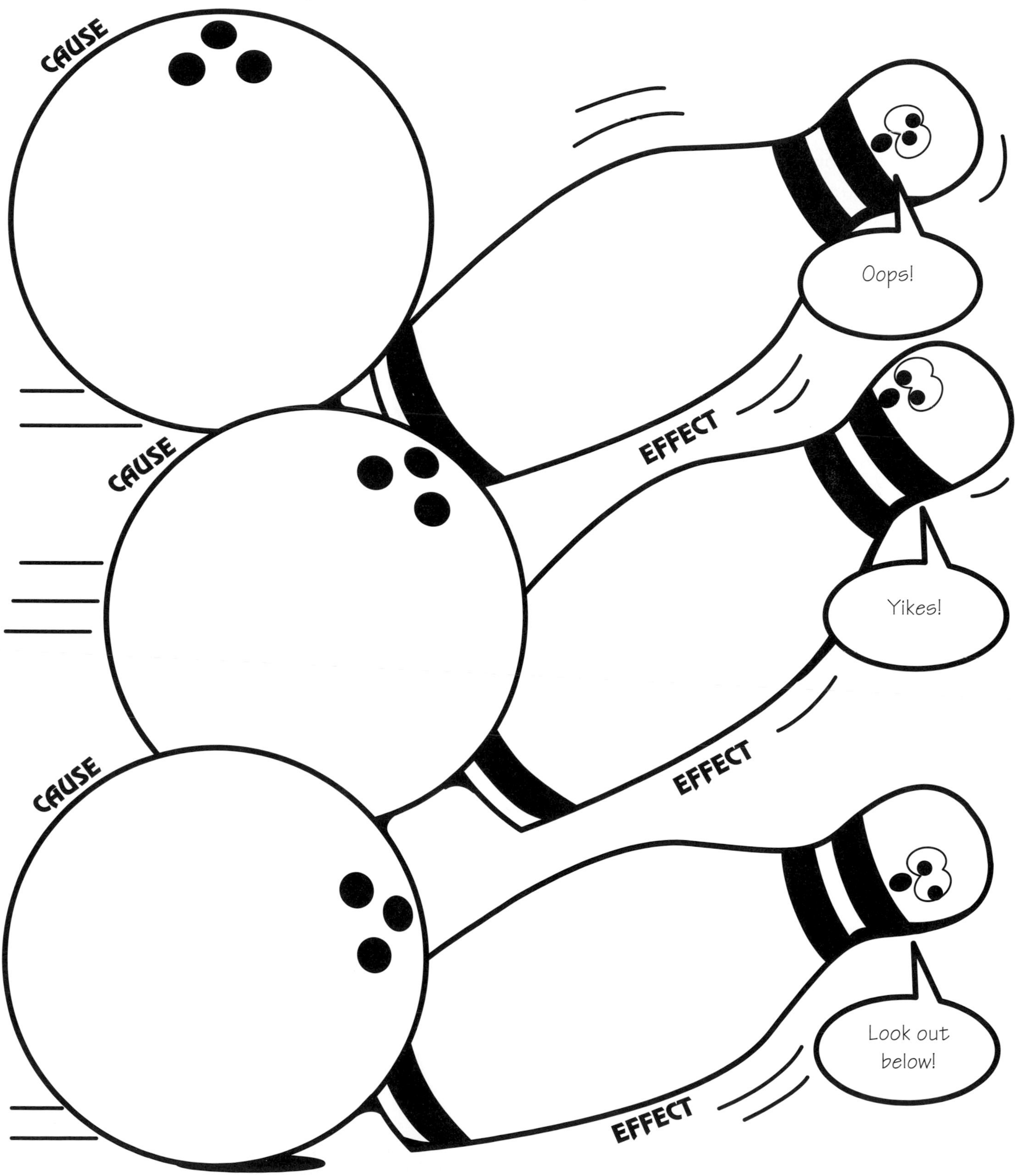




**Note to the teacher:** Use with "It Happened Because…" on page 64. Point out to students that a cause may have more than one effect, and that an effect may have several different causes.

Name_______________________________________________ 

# Good Writing Stacks Up!

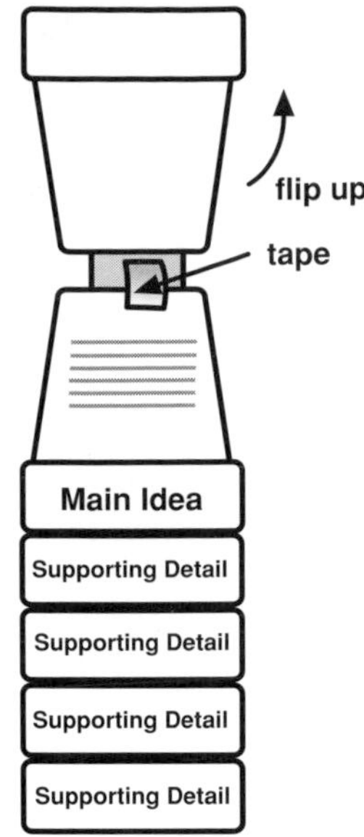


Make the main idea your cup of tea with the cool graphic organizer below!

**Directions:**

1. Fill in each cup with information about the selection you read.
2. Cut out the cups and the strip at the bottom of the page.
3. Use clear tape to attach the "Topic" cup to the top of the strip.
4. Tape the "Main Idea" cup below the "Topic" cup so that only the lip (the section that's labeled) shows. See the diagram.
5. Tape the supporting details to the strip in the same manner as in Step 4.
6. Meet with a classmate to compare your organizers.

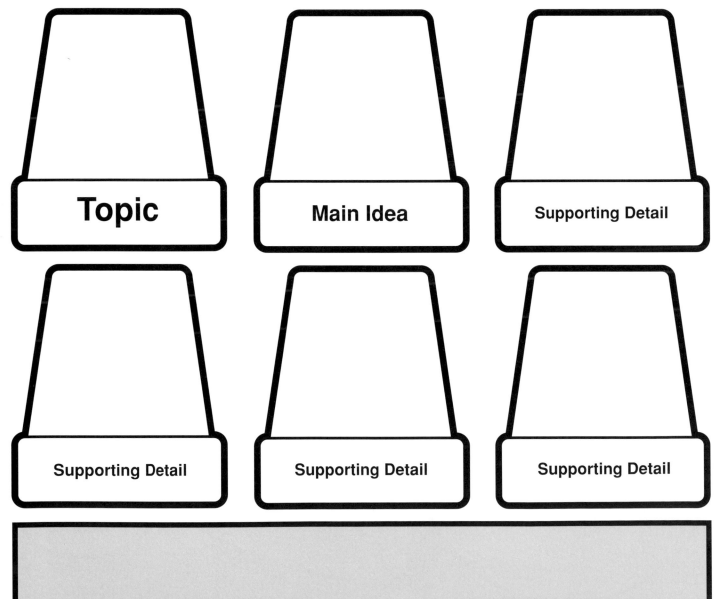

**Topic**

**Main Idea**

**Supporting Detail**

**Supporting Detail**

**Supporting Detail**

**Supporting Detail**



**Note to the teacher:** Use with "Stacking Up Main Ideas" on page 64. Provide students with scissors and transparent tape. If a reading selection has more than four supporting details, direct the student to trace one of the cups above onto a sheet of white paper to make additional cups.

# Make It Shine!

## Brightening Up Editing and Proofreading Skills

Polish editing and proofreading skills with these bright ideas and reproducibles—all guaranteed to make your students' writing shine!

*ideas by Pat Twohey, Smithfield, RI*

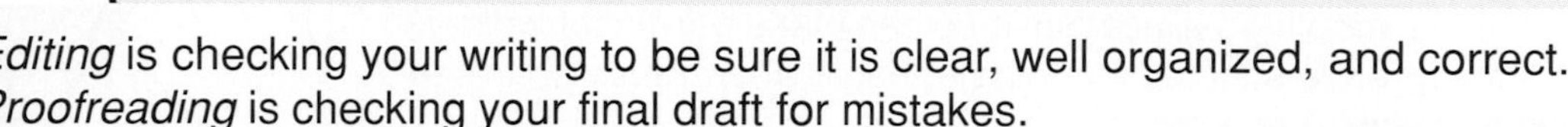

*Editing* is checking your writing to be sure it is clear, well organized, and correct. *Proofreading* is checking your final draft for mistakes.

**Editing Ideas**

### Packed With Verb Power

**Skill: Using specific action verbs**

Motivate students to invigorate their writing with vivid verbs using this power-packed group activity. Cut six simple battery shapes from construction paper as shown. Label each cutout with a different common verb (see the list below). Next, divide students into groups. Give each group a different cutout and a colorful marker. Allow each group five minutes to label its cutout with different powerful synonyms for the verb. Then have the groups swap cutouts. Continue until every group has added at least one verb to each cutout. Display the cutouts on a wall titled "A Power Pack of Verbs." Encourage students to refer to the display whenever they edit their written work. If students find additional synonyms while working on other assignments or while using a thesaurus, have them add the verbs to the cutouts.

**say** **walk** **see** **yell**
**run** **jump** **like** **go**

### Not Your Ordinary Nouns!

**Skill: Using specific nouns**

A good writer knows that *dalmatian* paints a much clearer picture than *dog.* Help students learn to use specific nouns in their writing with this fast-paced game. Direct each child to divide a sheet of paper into five columns and label each column with a different common noun selected by you (see the list below). To play, call out a letter, such as *D.* Allow students three minutes to write one specific noun that begins with the letter called in each column. Direct the student who finishes first to stand and say, "Be specific!" When the time limit is up, have students share their answers. Then let the student who was first to finish call out a letter to start the second round. Have students keep their game sheets in their writing folders to use as a handy reference the next time they need a specific noun or two.

| animal | plant | snack | place | game |
|---|---|---|---|---|
| dachshund | daisy | doughnut | dentist's office | darts |
| mouse | maple tree | milk chocolate | Maine | marbles |
| rooster | rose | raisins | Richmond | Ring Around the Rosie |
| | | | | |
| | | | | |
| | | | | |

**animal** **game** **book** **liquid**
**plant** **event** **vegetable** **song**
**snack** **person** **clothing** **country**
**place** **toy** **product** **movie**

spotted

The small dog ran down the street quickly.

## Colorful Editing

### Skill: Using specific adjectives and adverbs

Like bright paints on a white canvas, modifiers can turn a colorless piece of writing into a fun-to-read masterpiece. Provide each child with four colored pencils: red, blue, orange, and green. As the student edits her work, have her underline all nouns in blue, verbs in red, adjectives in orange, and adverbs in green. Then ask the child to determine whether adding more adjectives and adverbs would make her writing any easier to picture. If so, have her use the orange and green pencils to insert additional modifiers where needed. However, caution students against *overusing* modifiers, since doing so can make a piece of writing sound unnatural. Finally, have each editor hold her paper at arm's length to see if it provides a pleasing balance of color.

## Sentence-Starting Spinners

### Skill: Varying sentence beginnings

If you've ever read an essay in which every other sentence begins with *I,* then you know how this bad habit can make a piece of writing dull. To help students learn to write varied sentence beginnings, display a poster such as the one shown below and go over it with the class. Next, give each child an oaktag circle divided into fourths. Direct him to write "Sentences can start…" in the center of the circle and then to label its sections as shown.

Next, divide students into four teams. Give each team a sheet of lined paper and a paper clip. Direct one player on each team to spin a sentence starter on his circle as shown. Have the team then construct a sentence that begins with the indicated type of starter. After each group shares its work with the class, award one point for every correct sentence. Then select a different player on each team to spin and play another round. After several rounds, declare the team with the most points the winner.

Follow up by having each student use his spinner and a handful of paper clips when he is ready to edit his own writing. As he reads his written work, have him decide how each sentence begins; then have him slip a paper clip onto the spinner section that describes it. When done, one glance will tell the student if he's overusing one or more types of sentence beginnings.

### Four Ways to Start a Sentence

- ***With a Subject***
  George Washington was the first president of the United States.
  I wished I could just disappear!
- ***With a Modifier***
  Shyly, Erin introduced herself to her new piano teacher.
  Quickly, the boy stepped onto the escalator.
- ***With a Phrase***
  With a wide smile, Toby placed the gift into his grandmother's hands.
- ***With a Clause***
  When he was sure of the answer, Andy raised his hand.

Proofreading Ideas
Don
Katie
Matt
loud noise woke
A lowd noize wok me up.
looked
When I lookt out my
window what
winder, I saw wot had
happened motorcycle
happent. A motercycle had
crashed fence
crasht into our fince.


## A Rainbow of Proofreaders

### Skill: Spelling

Make the task of fixing spelling errors a colorful job with this bright idea. First, have each writer proofread his work for spelling errors, using his favorite color to circle words he thinks are misspelled. Direct him to use a dictionary to check and correct the spelling of each circled word. After the student has checked his work, have him ask a classmate to proofread it. Instruct this peer editor to write her name with a different color at the top of the paper and circle any misspelled words. When the author gets his paper back, have him make any corrections. (If the peer editor circled a correctly spelled word, have him place a check mark over it.) Then instruct the writer to ask another classmate to check his work using a third color. The pot of gold at the end of this rainbow? A piece of writing that's spelling-error free!

## Hole-Punch Punctuation

### Skill: Punctuation

Add some punch to proofreading for punctuation with this nifty activity! Enlarge the boxing glove template shown and glue it to a manila envelope. On an index card, list four different punctuation rules that you want students to focus on. Store the card in the envelope with a hole puncher; then place the envelope at a center. When a student is ready to proofread her rough draft for punctuation, she goes to the center, refers to the envelope's card, and proofreads for one of the rules listed. Then she punches a hole in the top of her paper. Four holes tells you that the child has proofread for all four rules. Periodically replace the card with a new one so students can practice proofreading for other punctuation rules.

Punching Out Punctuation XXX



SHINE A LOT

**Punctuation Checklist**

- Did you end each sentence with the correct punctuation mark?
- Did you use commas to separate items in a series?
  You can travel by car, bus, plane, or train.
- Did you place a comma between two independent clauses joined by and, but, or or?
  It was cloudy outside, but it did not rain.
- Did you place quotation marks around the exact words of each speaker?
  Sam said, "Let's go play soccer."
  "Okay," Pat replied. "Where do you want to go?"

## Capping Off Capitalization

### Skill: Capitalizing words

Tip your cap to better capitalization skills after students play this creative group game. Use a cap pattern like the one shown to make a cutout for each capitalization rule you want students to practice. Label each cutout with a different rule; then attach a piece of magnetic tape to the cutout's back. Next, stand the cutouts on the chalk tray and divide students into two teams. Write a sentence on the board that contains one or more capitalization errors. Have a player from Team 1 come to the board and position the appropriate cap above an incorrect word. Award one point for every error the player "caps" correctly. If he is incorrect, give Team 2 a chance to find and correct the mistake(s). As the game progresses, make the sentences more challenging. Then tip your cap to the winning team!

Name________________________________________

What's the right way to my spaceship?
Help!
I wanna go home!

# Bongo or Bust!

Meet Bee-Bop-Bing from the planet Bongo. He's having a hard time understanding our language. Words such as *their, they're,* and *there* and *to, too,* and *two* are just too confusing for him. Help Bee-Bop-Bing find his way back to his spaceship by coloring the path of boxes whose sentences use these confusing words correctly. Then, on the back of this page or another sheet of paper, rewrite the sentences in the eight uncolored boxes correctly.

| | | | | |
|---|---|---|---|---|
| | 1. Jason is planning to visit his friend Alan. | 2. They're going on a camping trip together. | 3. Andy and his friends ate at their favorite restaurant. | 4. Is he holding up two fingers or three? |
| 5. Put the glass down over their. | 6. Is that they're dog running down the street? | 7. There playing a soccer game at four o'clock. | 8. We want too bake five dozen cookies. | 9. Kendra will go there on her vacation. |
| 10. On Saturday, they're cleaning the garage. | 11. There are many different breeds of dogs. | 12. Their cat Snowball is completely white. | 13. Beth wants to compete in the swim meet. | 14. They're the best of friends. |
| 15. You can't help but laugh when they're telling jokes. | 16. Park your bicycle over their. | 17. We stopped at the twins' house too say hello. | 18. That team wants two win the basketball championship. | 19. They're coach is a nice guy. |
| 20. Look! There goes a shooting star! | 21. There must be at least 20 different colors in that shirt! | 22. Is it time to go? | 23. They're having tryouts for junior-league basketball next week. | |

You helped Bee-Bop-Bing find his spaceship!

**Bonus Box:** On another sheet of paper, write a short story about one of Bee-Bop-Bing's adventures on Earth. Use *their, there, they're, to, too,* and *two* correctly in your story. Then share your story with your classmates.

**Note to the teacher:** Each student will need a crayon or marker to complete this activity.

Name ____________________

# The Sentence Cleanup Crew

The Sentence Cleanup Crew is on the loose! These careful cleaners won't stop until every sentence is squeaky clean (contains no mistakes). Follow the directions to help this hard-scrubbing crew save the sentences below.

**Directions:** Read the box about sentence errors. Then write the number of each group of words below on a cloth to show the type of error it contains. On another sheet of paper, write each sentence correctly.

A **sentence fragment** is a group of words that is missing the subject or main verb, or that does not express a complete thought.
*Example:* Wants to go home. (The *subject* is missing.)
*Correction:* Brad wants to go home.

A **run-on sentence** is two sentences that are joined without a comma and a conjunction.
*Example:* I really liked the movie it had a surprise ending.
*Correction:* I really liked the movie. It had a surprise ending.
*Correction:* I really liked the movie, and it had a surprise ending.

A **rambling sentence** is several short sentences joined together by *and.*
*Example:* I got out of the car and the muddy pavement caused me to fall and my clothes got covered with mud.
*Correction:* I got out of the car. The muddy pavement caused me to fall. My clothes got covered with mud.

1. Shandra went to the basketball court and she played a game with Lianne and then they went to Shandra's house for something to eat.
2. The dog chased his tail he went around and around in a circle.
3. Went to the bowling alley with friends.
4. Jake's class went on a field trip they went to the aquarium.
5. Knew my friend Kayla from school.
6. The football game was tied and Eric kicked a field goal during the final quarter and his field goal won the game.
7. Ran to the store as fast as he could.
8. The computer is a good tool and it can help you get information for reports and computers can help you make charts and graphs.
9. Lee has a guinea pig and it is cute and the guinea pig has a funny name and Lee calls it Squeaky.
10. My cousin Sharon in my mother's chair.
11. Jon's grandmother is from Russia she speaks Russian to him all the time.
12. The bus driver got lost we were 20 minutes late getting to the museum.
13. Drove my brother and me to the skating rink.
14. The man on the bus.
15. Erica's sister stood in line for hours to get tickets to a rock concert she got third-row seats.

**Bonus Box:** On another sheet of paper, write a note to one of your parents explaining why your bedroom doesn't always need to be squeaky clean. Check the note to make sure it doesn't contain any sentence errors.

# Developing the Art of Persuasive Writing

If practice makes perfect, then this collection of creative ideas and reproducibles will help students produce great masterpieces of persuasive writing!

*ideas by Simone Lepine, Fayetteville, NY*

## Tricks of the (Persuasive) Trade

**Skills: Identifying persuasive techniques, making a frequency table**

Get started with an activity that helps students develop a knack for identifying the persuasive tactics used in ads. Have students bring in a variety of ads from magazines and newspapers. Copy the propaganda techniques below on a transparency or chart paper and discuss them with students. Explain that advertisers use these techniques to get messages across quickly in small amounts of space. Afterward, divide students into groups. Give each group several ads; then have it identify the techniques used in the ads and tally them in a frequency table as shown below. Next, have each group trade its ads with another group until every group has classified all the ads and recorded the frequencies in the last column. If desired, challenge each student to create a bar graph of the data. Then let students explore how much persuasive tactics have invaded their lives by having them complete copies of page 78 as directed.

- **Loaded Words:** Using words that appeal to the emotions, rather than facts. *The sporty new design of our cars will make you feel like a teenager again!*
- **Plain Folks Approach:** Using words that appeal to common people instead of the rich or privileged. *As a homemaker like you, I want a product like Easy Glow that makes my floors shine.*
- **Testimonial:** Using a famous person to endorse a product. *Michael Jordan uses it…so should you!*
- **Bandwagon:** Trying to persuade someone to join the group. *Don't be the last person in your neighborhood to get a Lawn Happy mower.*
- **Opinions as Facts:** Using the personal opinion of the speaker or writer as a fact. *Vita Vitamins is the best brand on the market.*
- **Unsupported Generalities:** Making bold claims and empty promises without supporting them with facts. *We are the best at what we do!*

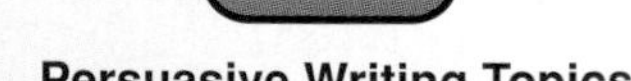

**Persuasive Writing Topics**

bicycle helmet laws
food choices in the school cafeteria
school uniforms
year-round schools
in-line skates vs. skateboards
holding parents responsible for poor student behavior
movie/compact disc rating systems
school on Saturdays
longer school days
chewing gum in school
learning a foreign language in school

| Technique | Tally | Frequency |
|---|---|---|
| Loaded Words | 卌 卌 卌 | 15 |
| Plain Folks Approach | 卌 | 5 |
| Testimonial | 卌 I | 6 |
| Bandwagon | 卌 卌 II | 12 |
| Opinions as Facts | 卌 卌 卌 II | 17 |
| Unsupported Generalities | 卌 II | 7 |

# Where Do You Stand?

If everyone thought alike, there would be no need for persuasive writing! Use the following duo of activities to show students that there are very few issues on which *everyone* agrees!

## No Fence Straddling!

**Skills: Defending a stance, writing a persuasive paragraph**

Target fence straddling with this activity that lets students practice taking a stand on an issue. Present an issue that affects students, such as "Should children be forced by law to wear helmets when riding a bike?" (See the topics on page 74 for other suggestions.) Have students who support the issue stand on one side of the room and those opposing it on the opposite side. Direct anyone who is undecided to stand in the middle of the room. Next, have the groups discuss among themselves why they believe their stance is the right one. Instruct the undecided group to discuss why it's unsure. (If there are no undecided students, debate the issue anyway. Later, present a different issue so students can experience how persuasion affects indecisive people.) Next, direct each group to list the reasons for its stand on chart paper. Then have a spokesperson from each group present his group's view to the class. After the presentations, require each fence straddler to join one side or the other and to explain to the class what influenced his decision. Conclude by having each student write a paragraph defending his stance. Display the paragraphs on a bulletin board titled "Here's Where We Stand!"

## Putting Opinions on the Line

**Skills: Writing a persuasive letter, speaking skills**

Vary the activity at the left with an idea that also targets speaking skills! After presenting an issue, have students stand in one line, with those who strongly agree making up one end of the line and those who strongly disagree making up the other end. Have those who are neither strongly for nor against the issue stand in the middle of the line. Then divide the line in half. Have the two smaller lines stand opposite one another so that a student strongly for the issue is across from one who strongly opposes it, and a child who weakly favors it is across from one who weakly opposes it. On your signal, ask each student to give the classmate opposite her a one-minute, uninterrupted explanation of the reasons for her stance. Afterward, have students in each line meet together to discuss what they heard and whether anyone was persuaded to change her stance. Follow up by having each student write a persuasive letter to a classmate who holds an opposite view in an attempt to sway that child's decision.

Undecided
Would I go to jail if I didn't wear a bike helmet?
Would a police officer give me a ticket?
If I wore the helmet and still got hurt, could I stop wearing it?
At what age would students be allowed to stop wearing helmets?

# Turkeys Rule, Bald Eagles Drool?

**Skill: Writing a persuasive paragraph**

After discussing the advertising techniques on page 74, let students practice writing with these tricks of the trade—and learn an interesting historical fact as well! Have each student complete a copy of page 79 as directed and share her writing with the class. Follow up by having each child use one or more of the tactics to write a persuasive paragraph expressing how she *really* feels about the turkey being the national symbol of the United States!

BEFORE IT'S TOO LATE...
SAVE OUR SEA LIFE!


# Letter to the Editor

**Skill: Writing a persuasive business letter**

The editorial pages of a newspaper serve as the perfect forum for citizens to voice their opinions and try to persuade others to share their views. Gather examples of letters to the editor from your local newspaper to share with the class. Then announce that each student will be writing her own letter to the editor! Help students generate a list of issues that are near and dear to their hearts, such as the value of building a community park for Frisbee® golf or upgrading the city's public swimming pool. Review with students the correct form of a business letter. Next, have each child select an issue and write a persuasive letter to the local editor expressing her personal stance on that topic. While students are working, staple several very large sheets of newsprint together to resemble a newspaper. When the letters are finished, glue them to the newspaper's pages as shown. Then display the paper on a bulletin board or table so students can read all about it!

# Catching the Public's Eye

**Skill: Writing and designing a persuasive poster**

Another ingredient to consider when persuading people to think or act in particular ways is visual appeal. Challenge students to use the techniques they've been learning about to create eye-catching public service posters about important issues. First, have each student select a topic he feels strongly about. Or suggest he choose one from the list below. Then have him use a persuasive technique from page 74 to help him write a message for his poster. If desired, have students give their posters a three-dimensional effect, such as stapling crumpled newspapers and plastic sandwich bags to antilitter posters or gluing plastic animals onto posters about saving endangered species. Display the completed posters throughout the school building or in local businesses to see how well they catch the public's eye!

**Public Service Topics**

- antidrugs
- antidrinking
- antismoking
- antilittering
- recycling
- saving endangered animals
- bicycle safety
- neighborhood watch program
- reducing water use
- reducing electricity use
- staying in school
- youth sports programs

Letters to the Editor
From Mrs. Layton's Class

Dogs make better pets than cats.
Math is easier than spelling.
Brothers are nicer than sisters.
Winter is more fun than summer.
Animals should be used for medical research.

## Two Sides to Every Argument

**Skills: Understanding different points of view, writing a persuasive paragraph**

It is just as important for students to understand *why* a person feels as he does about an issue as it is to understand *where* he stands on it. Having this information can make an argument for a particular stance even stronger or can be used to prove that one view is preferable to another. To help students experience an issue from a different perspective or point of view, explain what it means to play the *devil's advocate* (hold one view but represent another for argument's sake). To demonstrate, have a student who likes chocolate ice cream and one who likes vanilla come to the front of the room. Ask the student who prefers chocolate to give reasons why he likes vanilla; have the student who prefers vanilla give reasons why she likes chocolate. If students have trouble providing reasons, suggest an example such as "I like vanilla ice cream because it is *much* easier to wash out of clothes."

Follow up by assigning the class a topic from the list on the left. Have each student use the topic to complete a copy of page 80 as directed. Then have students share their paragraphs with the class. Or let each child read his paragraph to a classmate who holds an opposing view to see if he can change that student's mind!

## Trial by Jury

**Skill: Writing a persuasive argument**

A jury trial is the perfect setting for practicing persuasive tactics. Practice persuasive writing by having students role-play the parts of prosecutor and defender to determine if a well-known story character is guilty of a crime. First, inform students that Goldilocks is being brought to trial by the Bear family for breaking and entering and that *they* will play key roles in her trial. Pair students, assigning one partner the role of prosecutor and the other the role of defender. Explain that the prosecutor's job is to prove Goldilocks is guilty of the crime and that the defender's job is to prove her innocence. Help students gather evidence to build their cases by reading the story *Goldilocks and the Three Bears* aloud to the class. Then have each student write a persuasive paragraph that represents her role in the case. Remind students to support their arguments with facts.

When the paragraphs have been completed, staple the prosecutors' papers together and bind them in a folder. Do the same for the defenders' papers. Send both folders to another class, requesting that the students listen to the arguments of both sides and then render a verdict. While the jury is "out," you can bet your class will anxiously await the decision on Goldilocks's innocence or guilt!

Is Goldilocks Guilty?
VERDICT DUE TODAY!

Name ______________________________________________ 

# Tricks of the (Persuasive) Trade

Advertisers use many methods to get people to buy their products. Some of those tactics are listed below. Find an ad that represents each technique. Your ads can be from TV or radio commercials or from magazines or newspapers. Fill in the information for each ad in the box provided. Then mark an *X* on the scale to rate how effective you think that ad could be in persuading others to try the product.

### Loaded Words

Product: ____________________

Circle where you saw or heard the ad.
TV  Printed Ad  Radio

Rate how persuasive you think the ad is.

Not Persuasive  OK  Very Persuasive

### Plain Folks Approach

Product: ____________________

Circle where you saw or heard the ad.
TV  Printed Ad  Radio

Rate how persuasive you think the ad is.

Not Persuasive  OK  Very Persuasive

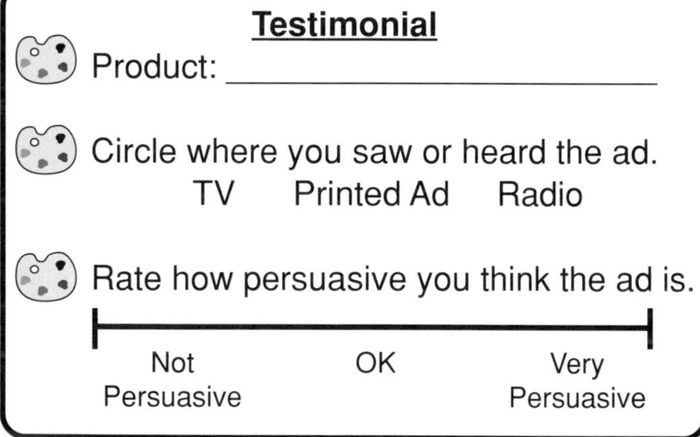

### Testimonial

Product: ____________________

Circle where you saw or heard the ad.
TV  Printed Ad  Radio

Rate how persuasive you think the ad is.

Not Persuasive  OK  Very Persuasive

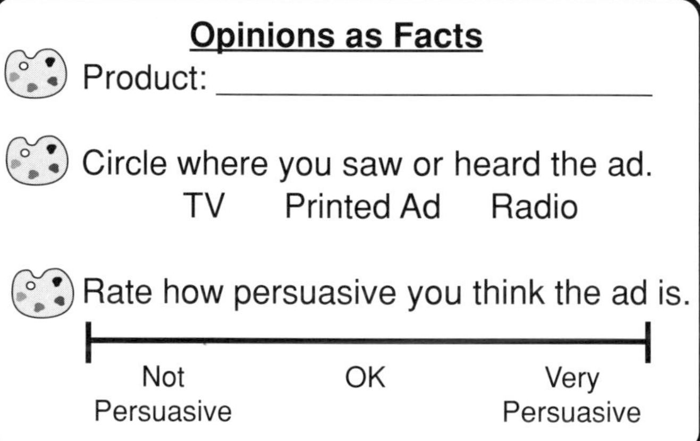

### Opinions as Facts

Product: ____________________

Circle where you saw or heard the ad.
TV  Printed Ad  Radio

Rate how persuasive you think the ad is.

Not Persuasive  OK  Very Persuasive

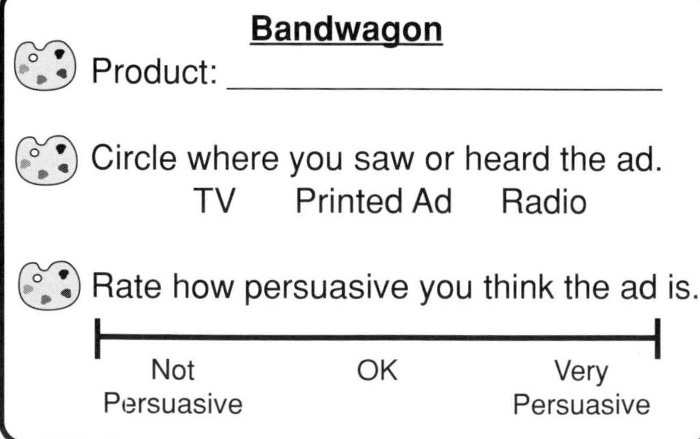

### Bandwagon

Product: ____________________

Circle where you saw or heard the ad.
TV  Printed Ad  Radio

Rate how persuasive you think the ad is.

Not Persuasive  OK  Very Persuasive

### Unsupported Generalities

Product: ____________________

Circle where you saw or heard the ad.
TV  Printed Ad  Radio

Rate how persuasive you think the ad is.

Not Persuasive  OK  Very Persuasive

**Bonus Box:** Choose one product listed above. On the back of this page, write a paragraph telling why you think that product's ad is or is not persuasive. Give examples from the ad to support your opinion.



 **Note to the teacher:** Use with "Tricks of the (Persuasive) Trade" on page 74.

Name________________________________ Writing a persuasive paragraph

# Turkeys Rule, Bald Eagles Drool?

Did you know that Benjamin Franklin was not in favor of choosing the bald eagle as America's national symbol? He preferred the turkey! Perhaps if Ben had used one of the techniques below, he could have convinced the U.S. Congress to see things his way. Go back in time to 1782 and see if you can help him change the vote!

**Directions:** Choose any two tactics listed in the box. Record the tactics on the lines below. Then write two persuasive paragraphs in favor of the turkey becoming the national symbol. Use one tactic and the paper at the left for one paragraph. Use the second tactic and the paper on the right for the second paragraph.

- **Loaded Words:** Using words that appeal to the emotions, rather than facts. *The sporty new design of our cars will make you feel like a teenager again!*
- **Plain Folks Approach:** Using words that appeal to common people instead of the rich or privileged. *As a homemaker like you, I want a product like Easy Glow that makes my floors shine.*
- **Testimonial:** Using a famous person to endorse a product. *Michael Jordan uses it...so should you!*
- **Bandwagon:** Trying to persuade someone to join the group. *Don't be the last person in your neighborhood to get a Lawn Happy mower.*
- **Opinions as Facts:** Using the personal opinion of the speaker or writer as a fact. *Vita Vitamins is the best brand on the market.*
- **Unsupported Generalities:** Making bold claims and empty promises without supporting them with facts. *We are the best at what we do!*

Tactic: ________________________________

Tactic: ________________________________



**Note to the teacher:** Use with "Turkeys Rule, Bald Eagles Drool?" on page 76.

# Two Sides to Every Argument

Have you ever heard your parent or a teacher say, "I need to hear both sides of the story before I can make a decision"? This is because there are usually two different points of view involved in any argument. Knowing each person's point of view is important when discussing or debating a topic.

On the paintbrush below, record the topic your teacher assigns. On the art palette, list reasons why people might be for and against this topic. Then, on the canvas, write a persuasive paragraph expressing *your* feelings and thoughts about the topic.

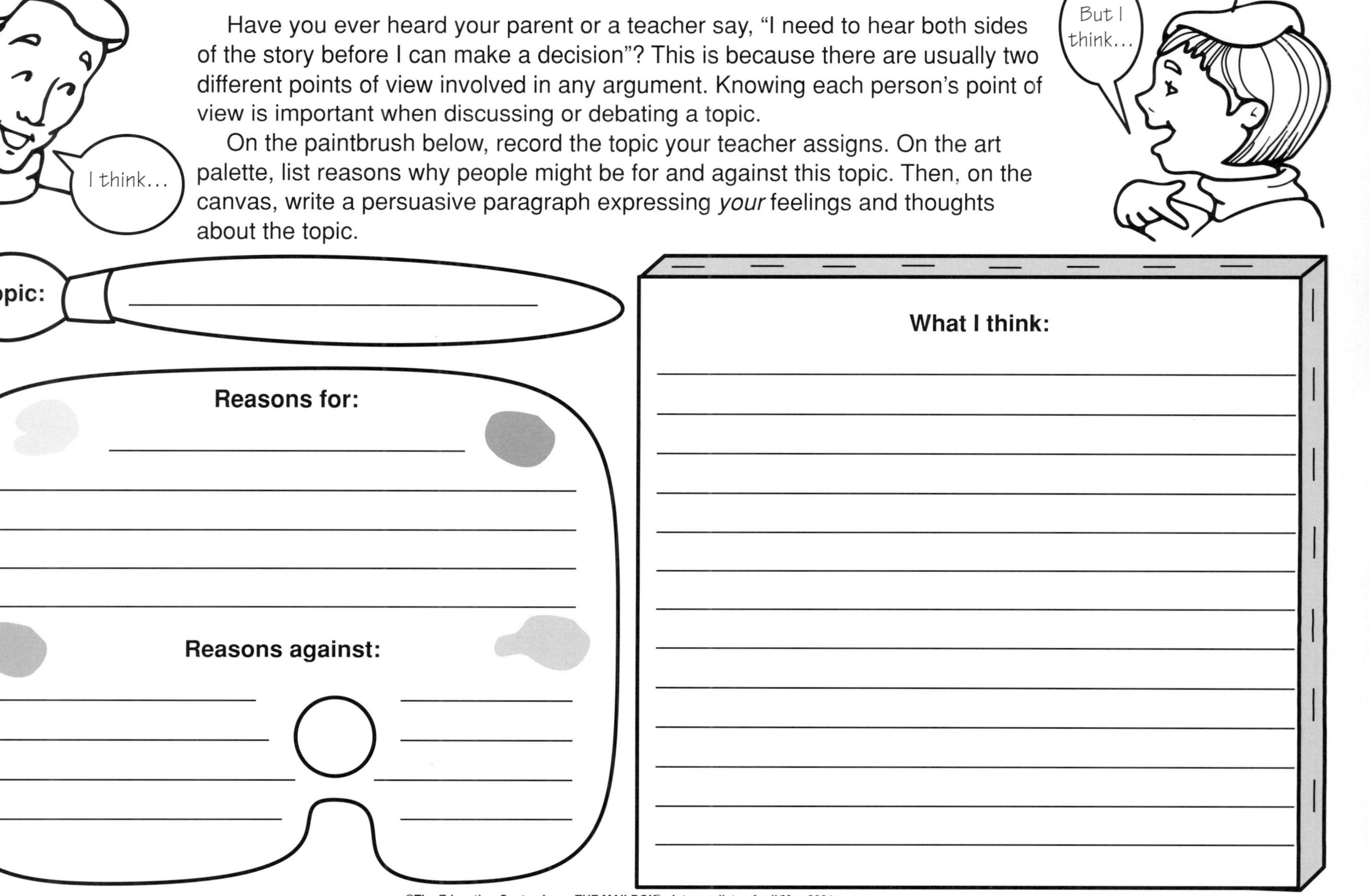




**Note to the teacher:** Use with "Two Sides to Every Argument" on page 77.

# THE HOW-TO PROJECT

**Think you can't interest students in reading nonfiction how-to books or get parents involved in your reading program? Bet you *can* with the following unbeatable project!**

*idea by Julie Alarie, Williston, VT*

## INTRODUCING THE PROJECT:

Tell students that they will be reading how-to books, nonfiction books that explain step-by-step how to do something. Share with students the steps that follow. Explain that parents and other adult volunteers will present a variety of how-to workshops on different topics for them to attend. Then announce that the project will culminate with each student becoming a full-fledged presenter himself!

## STEP 1:
### SEND A LETTER TO STUDENTS' FAMILIES

One month in advance, set the date you want the workshops to be held. Add this date, a date for returning the bottom portion of the letter, and your signature to a copy of the letter on page 83. Have each child take home a copy of this letter, which invites family members to participate. Then have the student return the bottom portion of the letter. Invite other faculty and staff members to participate as well. Plan to present a workshop yourself on how to do one of the following: study, take a test, proofread, make an outline, read a textbook, etc. Then compile a list of presenters, plus the supplies and equipment that will be needed.

## STEP 2:
### SEND A CONFIRMATION NOTE TO EACH VOLUNTEER

Send each volunteer a copy of the confirmation note on page 83, thanking him or her for agreeing to participate and verifying all the details.

## STEP 3:
### SELECT THE BOOKS

Have each student choose a how-to book from the library to read.

## STEP 4:
### CREATE A STUDENT SIGN-UP SHEET

Give each child a list similar to the one shown of all the workshops that have been planned. Briefly describe each workshop. Then have each student write a 1, 2, or 3 in the blank next to each workshop to indicate his first, second, and third choices.

**Workshop Sign-Up Sheet**

Choose the workshops you'd like to attend by writing a 1, 2, or 3 in the box next to your **first, second,** and **third** choices.

**I want to learn how to...**

___ use sign language to communicate
___ cook a tasty treat
___ play noncompetitive games
___ do a silk scarf painting
___ speak a little German
_3_ make greeting cards on the computer
___ make fabulous fabric book covers
_1_ make yummy microwave fudge
___ french braid hair with flair
___ do neat nails (We're talking fingers!)
___ swing dance—It's fun! It's fast!
___ make an awesome omelette
___ make chewy caramels
___ do origami
_2_ develop a knack for backpacking
___ create a miniature Guatemalan worry doll

# STEP 5:
## POST WORKSHOP SIGNS

Display a sign for each workshop. On each sign, list the workshop's title, date, time, and location, plus the presenter's name and the names of the participants.

# STEP 6:
## HOLD THE WORKSHOPS

Have students participate in the workshops. At the end of each workshop, have each presenter ask each participant to write three sentences explaining what he learned from the workshop. Collect the writings from the presenters before they leave.

# STEP 7:
## SEND THANK-YOU NOTES TO PRESENTERS

Review with students how to write a thank-you note. Then have each child write a note to the presenter of the workshop(s) he attended. To help students with their writing, post the sentence starters shown below.

Thank you very much for...
I was so surprised that...
I'll never forget...
Do you ever...?
Before you came, I didn't know that...
I really enjoyed...
My favorite part was...
I hope you can come again because...
I hope you remember your visit here as...
I never expected to...
Whenever I ______, I'll remember how you...
I liked what you said about...
It really impressed me when you said...
The best part of the workshop was...
I wonder...
Thanks again for...

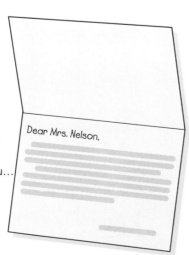


# STEP 8:
## HOLD STUDENT WORKSHOPS

Have each student present a brief workshop to demonstrate something he learned from reading a how-to book. To help him know what to include in his presentation, have him complete a copy of the planning web on page 84 as directed.

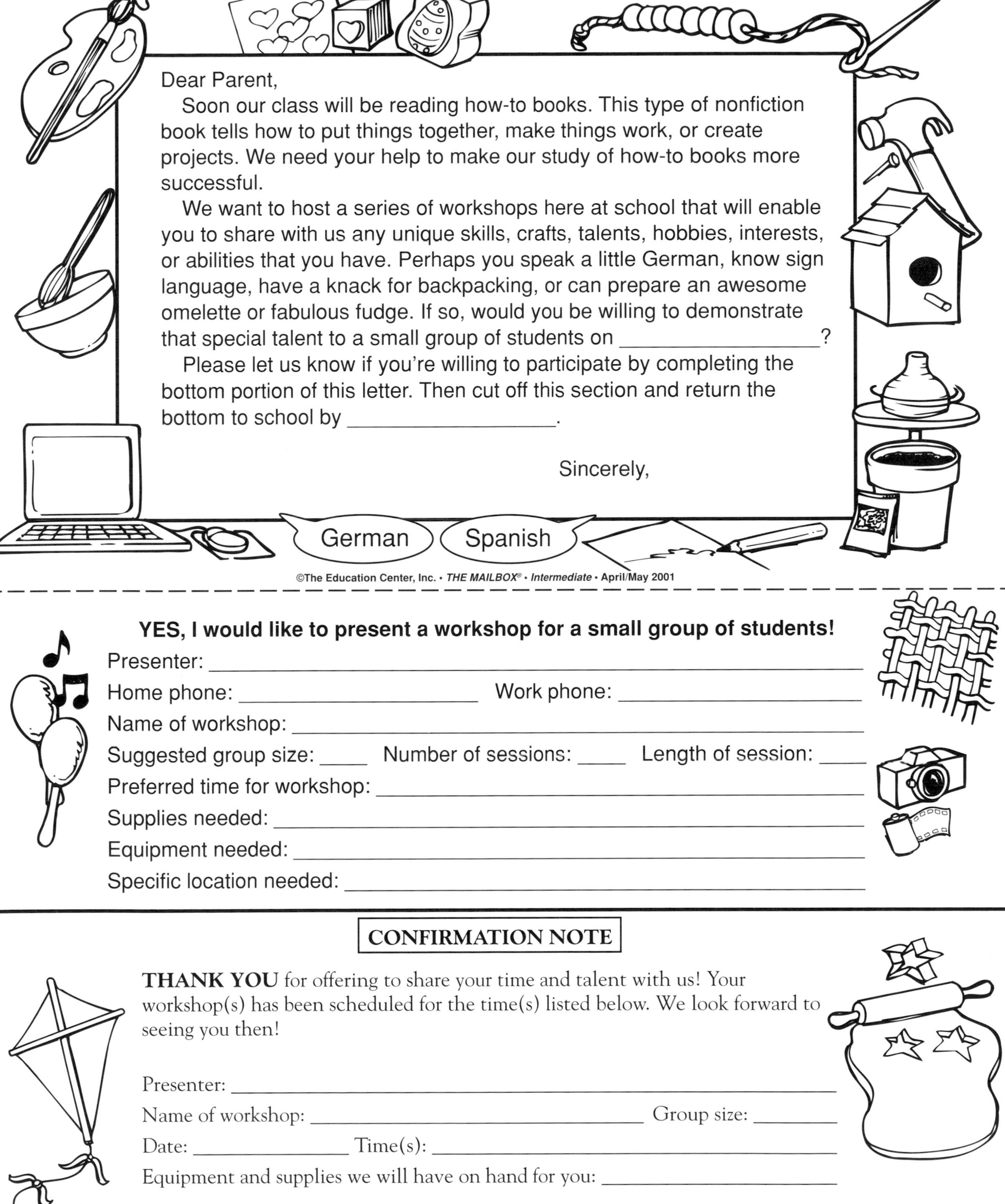

Dear Parent,

Soon our class will be reading how-to books. This type of nonfiction book tells how to put things together, make things work, or create projects. We need your help to make our study of how-to books more successful.

We want to host a series of workshops here at school that will enable you to share with us any unique skills, crafts, talents, hobbies, interests, or abilities that you have. Perhaps you speak a little German, know sign language, have a knack for backpacking, or can prepare an awesome omelette or fabulous fudge. If so, would you be willing to demonstrate that special talent to a small group of students on ________________?

Please let us know if you're willing to participate by completing the bottom portion of this letter. Then cut off this section and return the bottom to school by ________________.

Sincerely,





**YES, I would like to present a workshop for a small group of students!**

Presenter: ______________________________

Home phone: ______________ Work phone: ______________

Name of workshop: ______________________________

Suggested group size: ____ Number of sessions: ____ Length of session: ____

Preferred time for workshop: ______________________________

Supplies needed: ______________________________

Equipment needed: ______________________________

Specific location needed: ______________________________

## CONFIRMATION NOTE

**THANK YOU** for offering to share your time and talent with us! Your workshop(s) has been scheduled for the time(s) listed below. We look forward to seeing you then!

Presenter: ______________________________

Name of workshop: ______________________ Group size: ________

Date: ______________ Time(s): ______________________

Equipment and supplies we will have on hand for you: ______________________

______________________________



**Note to the teacher:** Use with "The How-To Project" on pages 81–82. Use the letter with Step 1 and the confirmation note with Step 2.

Name ____________________ Planning sheet

# Planning My How-To Presentation

**Directions:** Think of something you learned from your how-to book that you could demonstrate for the class. Then fill in the information below. Use the information to help you plan a brief demonstration of how to complete a task or project described in your book.

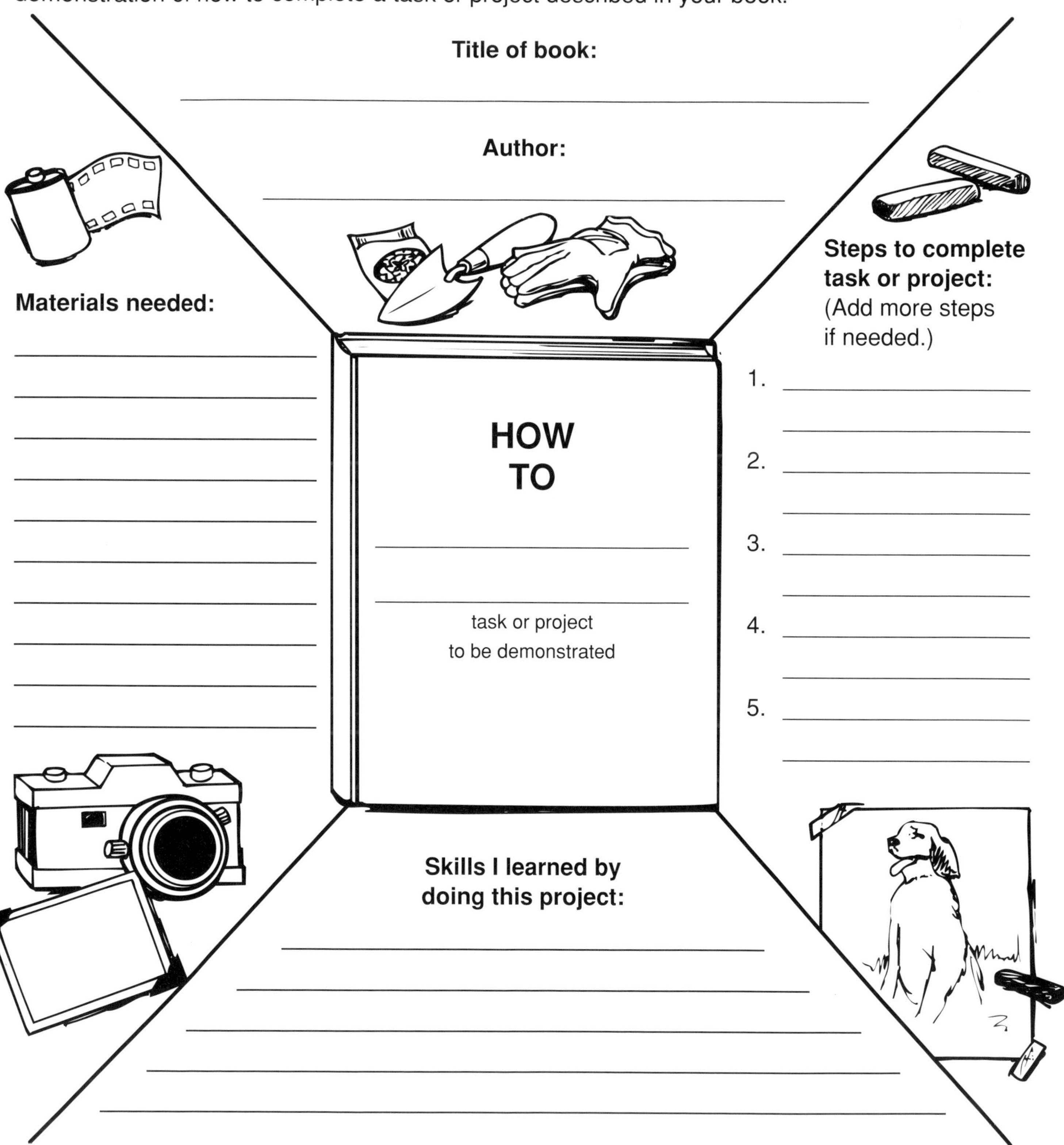

Title of book:
Author:
Materials needed:
Steps to complete task or project:
(Add more steps if needed.)
1.
2.
3.
4.
5.
HOW TO
task or project to be demonstrated
Skills I learned by doing this project:




 **Note to the teacher:** Use with Step 8 of "The How-To Project" on page 82.

# Word Analysis Workout

Exercise students' word analysis skills with exciting ideas, games, and reproducibles that add up to one wonderful workout!

*ideas by Lori Sammartino, Cranberry Township, PA*

## Flex Those Affixes!

**Skills: Prefixes, suffixes**

Start your workout with an exercise that firms students' understanding of prefixes and suffixes. Write a base word, such as *love,* on the board and circle it. Ask students to suggest different prefixes and suffixes that can be added to *love* to form new words. Record students' responses on the board as a word web. Then challenge students to use what they know about the meaning of each new word's prefix or suffix to compare the new word's meaning to that of the base word.

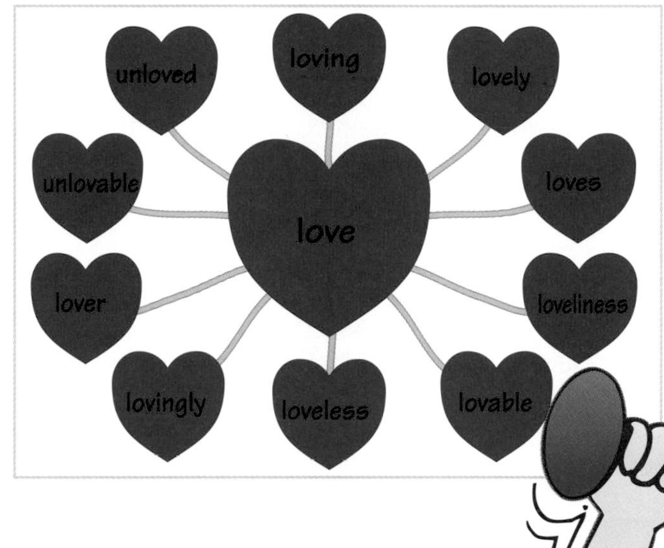


Next, pair students. Assign each pair a different base word from the list below and challenge the twosome to create a web of related words. Then have the pair illustrate its web in a creative way on a sheet of construction paper. After students share their webs, display the projects on a bulletin board titled "Wonderful Word Webs." For more practice with prefixes and suffixes, see the reproducible on page 89.

| | | |
|---|---|---|
| able | cheer | fix |
| move | open | call |
| like | read | happy |
| prove | enjoy | joy |
| wind | agree | draw |

## Compound Word Conditioning

**Skills: Compound words, creative thinking**

Focus your word analysis workout on compound words with this nifty guessing game. Have each student list ten compound words. Then have her divide each compound word into the two smaller words that form it. Next, explain to students that a *portmanteau* is a word that is formed by blending two words. For example, *chuckle* and *snort* blend to form *chortle.* Have each student blend the two words in each of her compound words to make a new portmanteau. When students are finished, direct each child to write and illustrate one of her new words on one side of a sheet of drawing paper. Have her label the back of the paper with the two words she blended together. Collect the drawings and divide students into two equal teams. Hold up one drawing at a time; then award one point to the first team to correctly identify the compound word that was used to create it. Ask the illustrator of the drawing being displayed not to participate in that round. Continue playing until all drawings have been displayed. Declare the team with more points the winner. For more practice with compound words, see the reproducible on page 88.

## Syllabication? No Sweat!

**Skill: Syllabication**

Get hearts a-pumping with a syllabication game that also practices dictionary skills. Provide a dictionary for each child. Cover the sides of a die with small stick-on labels cut to size; then label the die with the numerals *1, 2,* and *3* (using each numeral twice).

Next, divide students into two teams. Write a category—such as snack foods, animals, or ice-cream flavors—on the board. Have a player from Team A roll the die; then have him write a word on the board that is in the designated category and has the same number of syllables as the number rolled. For example, if the category is snack foods and a 2 is rolled, the player might write *popcorn* on the board. If the player needs help spelling the word, let his teammates use their dictionaries to help. Award one point for a correct answer. Give the player a chance to earn an additional point by dividing the word into syllables. Play until all students have had a turn. Then declare the team with more points the winner.

Here's a snack with two syllables!

## Abbreviation Meltdown

**Skill: Abbreviations**

Help students build abs (abbreviations) of steel with this "abs-olutely" awesome game! Have students brainstorm as many different abbreviations as they can as you list them on chart paper. Then hide this master list. Without using a text to help with spelling, have each child list any 20 abbreviations on her paper. Then bring out the master list and place it where only you can see it. Have students stand beside their desks.

To play, announce an abbreviation from the master list. Choose a student to write the abbreviation on the board. If she misspells it, allow her classmates to help her spell it correctly. Then direct students who listed that abbreviation on their papers to check its spelling with the one on the board. If they spelled the abbreviation correctly, have them cross it off their lists. If not, have them circle and correct the abbreviation before crossing it off their lists. Continue calling out abbreviations in random order. When a student has crossed off all 20 abbreviations on her list, have her sit down. Continue until only one child is standing. Have that student call out the abbreviation(s) remaining on her list to confirm that it has not been called. Then declare her the winner.

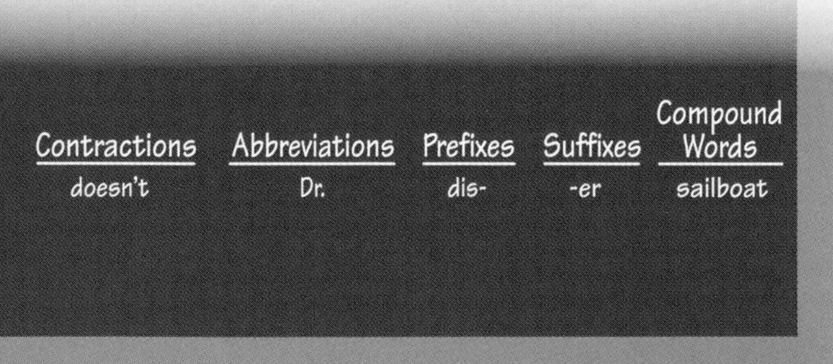

Dr. Baker doesn't dislike her sailboat even though it is an older model.


## Word Analysis Cooldown

**Skill: Reviewing word analysis skills**

Wrap up your word analysis workout with this creative-thinking game. Make a chart on the board as shown. Divide students into five groups; then assign each group a different topic from the chart. Next, give each group five minutes to brainstorm as many examples related to the topic as it can while its recorder lists them on paper. When time is up, have each group share one of its examples as you write it under the corresponding heading on the board. Then give each group a marker and a sheet of chart paper. Give each group three minutes to write one sentence that includes as many of the five items from the board as possible. At the end of the time limit, have each team share its sentence with the class. Award five points for using all five examples in the sentence, four points for using four examples, and so on. To start another round, have each team add a different example to the chart as before. After several rounds, declare the team with the most points the winner.

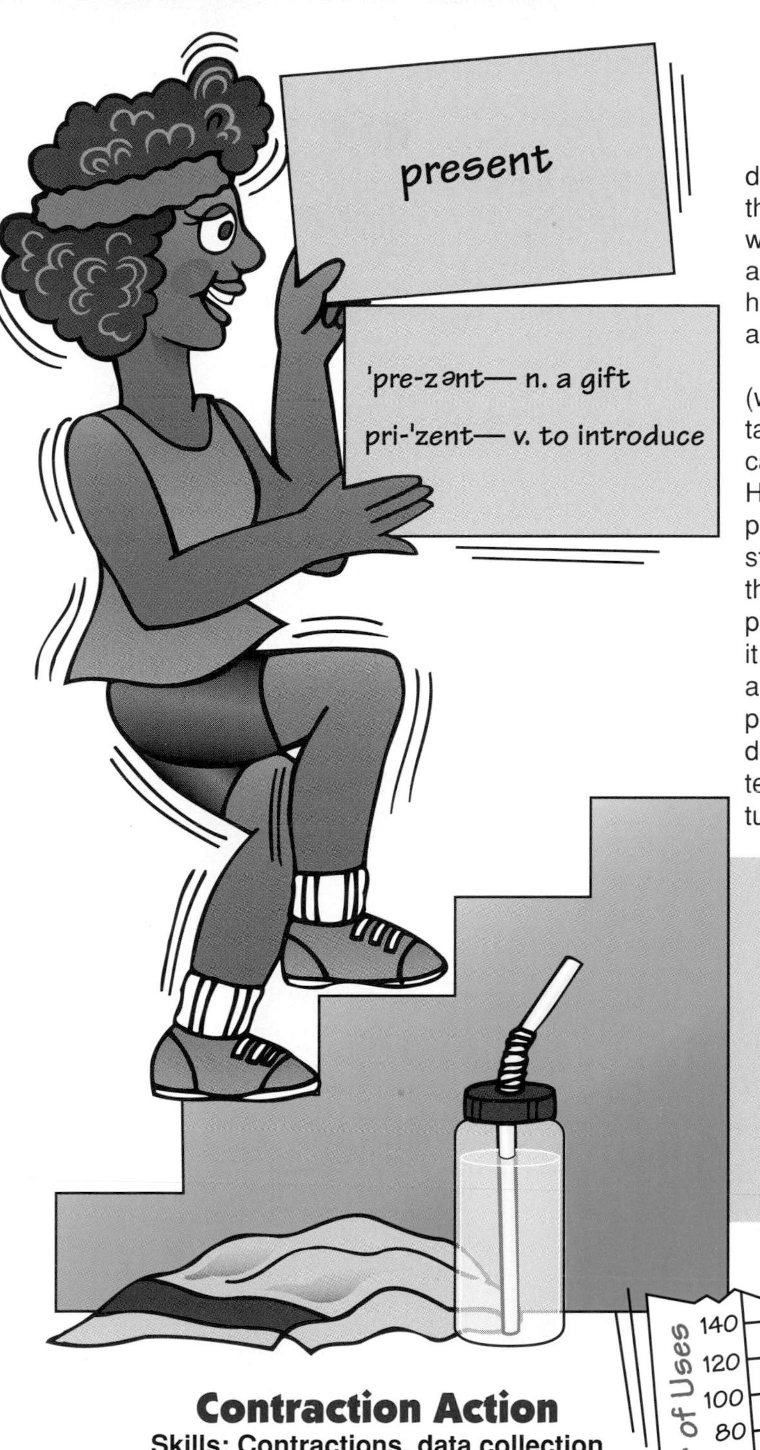


## Ready to Roll!

**Skills: Pronunciation, accentuation**

All you need for this fun word analysis game is a set of index cards, a toy car, and kids who like to have fun! Program the cards with the words shown (one per card). After reviewing with students how to use a pronunciation key, give each child a dictionary and one labeled card. On the back of the card, have the student write two different pronunciations of his word and a definition that matches each one.

Collect the cards and place them end to end on the floor (word up) to form a long, straight line. Affix a strip of masking tape to the floor in front of the first card. Then position a toy car behind this starting line and divide students into two teams. Have a player from Team A stand behind the starting line and push the car so that it rolls alongside the cards. When the car stops, direct the player to pick up the card closest to it (one that he did not label) and give it to you. Hold the card so the player can read the word; then have him pronounce and define it. Give his team one point if he pronounces the word correctly and another if he correctly defines it. Award two additional points if the player can provide the alternate pronunciation and definition. If a player answers incorrectly, give the opposing team a chance to answer. Play until every student has taken a turn. Then declare the team with more points the winner.

| | | | |
|---|---|---|---|
| present | suspect | produce | compact |
| separate | record | project | compress |
| perfect | desert | refuse | compound |
| minute | estimate | content | conflict |
| upset | convict | contest | abuse |
| address | digest | contract | graduate |
| rebel | duplicate | alternate | insert |
| object | progress | affix | relay |

## Contraction Action

**Skills: Contractions, data collection**

Concentrate on contractions with an activity that involves data collecting and more! Give each student a crayon and a newspaper section. Have students comb their newspaper sections for five minutes and circle every contraction they find no matter how many times it is repeated. When time is up, have students share the contractions they circled as you list them on the board. Use tally marks to track the number of times students circled each contraction. When the list has been completed, have each student copy it on his paper. Beside each contraction, direct the student to list the two words that formed it and the total number of times it was circled. Then have students study the data to find out which contraction(s) appeared most and least often. For even more exercise, have each student create a bar graph to display the data.

Name________________________________________________ Compound words, creative thinking

# Weighty Words

It's time to test your strength! How many (com)pounds can you bench-press? To lift the barbells at each station, complete Part One and Part Two below. Good luck!

**Part One:** The bar on each barbell below is labeled with a different compound word. Label the ends of each barbell with the two words that form the compound word on the bar. Use the four words in each station to list as many different compounds as you can on a sheet of paper. (It's okay to make nonsense words.) Then write a definition for each word.

**Station 1**

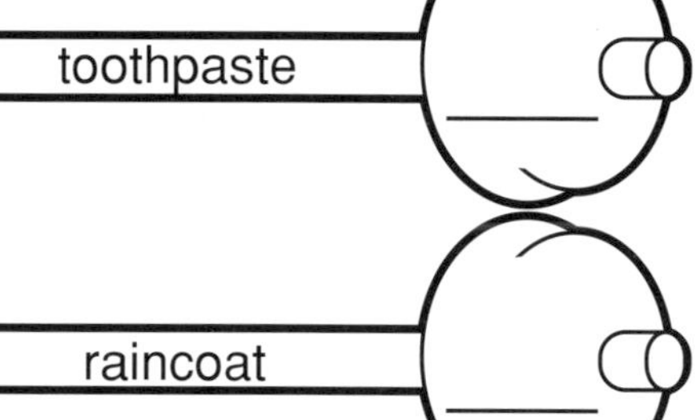

toothpaste

raincoat

**Station 2**

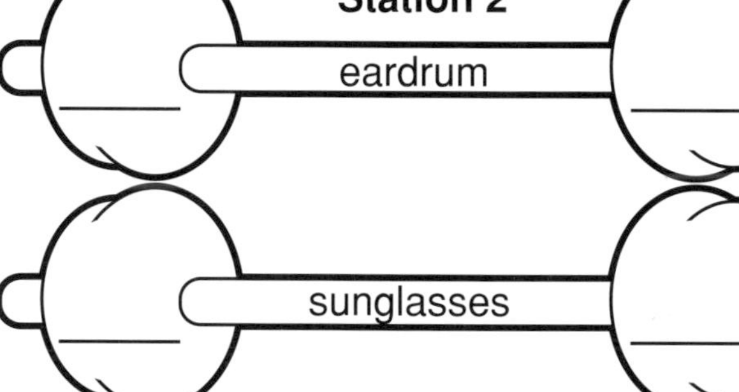

eardrum

sunglasses

**Station 3**

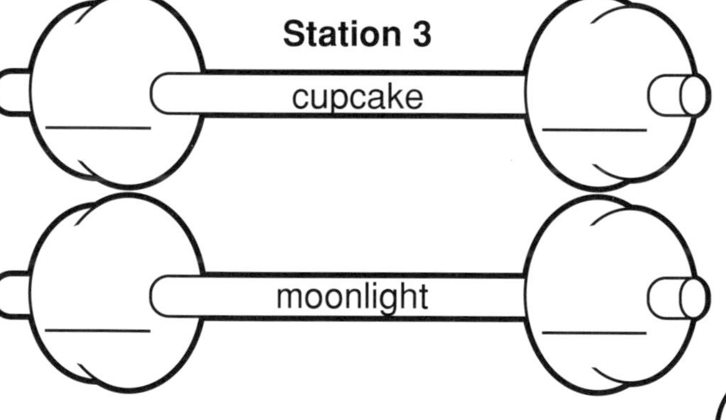

cupcake

moonlight

**Station 4**

bathtub

airplane

**Part Two:** Add a word to each word on the weights below to form as many different compound words as you can (only real words this time!). Write the words on your own paper.

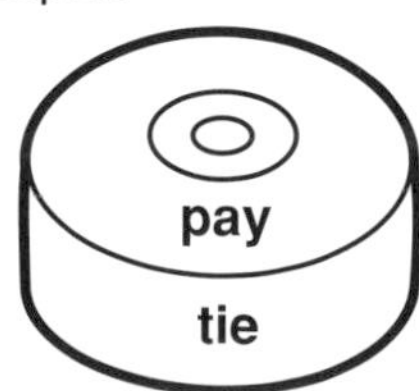


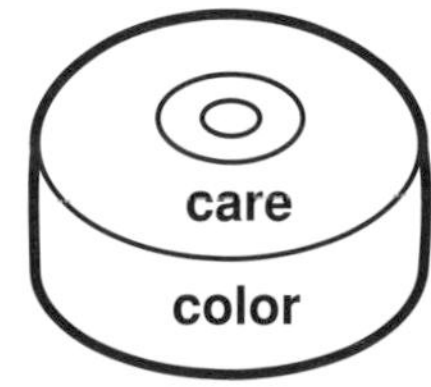


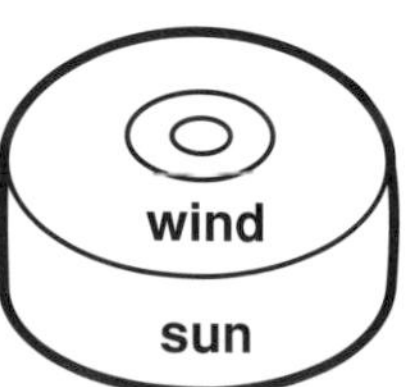




 **Note to the teacher:** Use with "Compound Word Conditioning" on page 85.

# Morpheme Mix-Up

Help! There's been a major mix-up at Woody's Word Analysis Workout Gym! Woody broke down several words into *morphemes.* (A *morpheme* is the smallest part of a word that has meaning.) But the morphemes got jumbled when a janitor tripped and fell against the table where they'd been sorted. Follow the steps below to help Woody organize everything again. Write your answers on the back of this page or on another sheet of paper.

What a mixed-up mess!

1. Guess the number of words that can be formed by using the prefixes, suffixes, and base words listed below.

| Prefixes | Suffixes | Base Words |
|---|---|---|
| un- | -ful | pay |
| re- | -less | tie |
| dis- | -ing | care |
| over- | -er | color |
| pre- | -y | wind |
| | | sun |

2. a. Add a prefix, a suffix, or both to each base word above to form as many words as you can.
   b. Sort the words into columns by prefix and suffix (put all words beginning with *un-* in one column, *re-* in a second column, etc.).
   c. What conclusions can you make about each column of words?

3. Read the questions below. First, define the boldfaced word in each question using what you know about the meaning of the prefix or suffix used. Then write a sentence that answers the question.

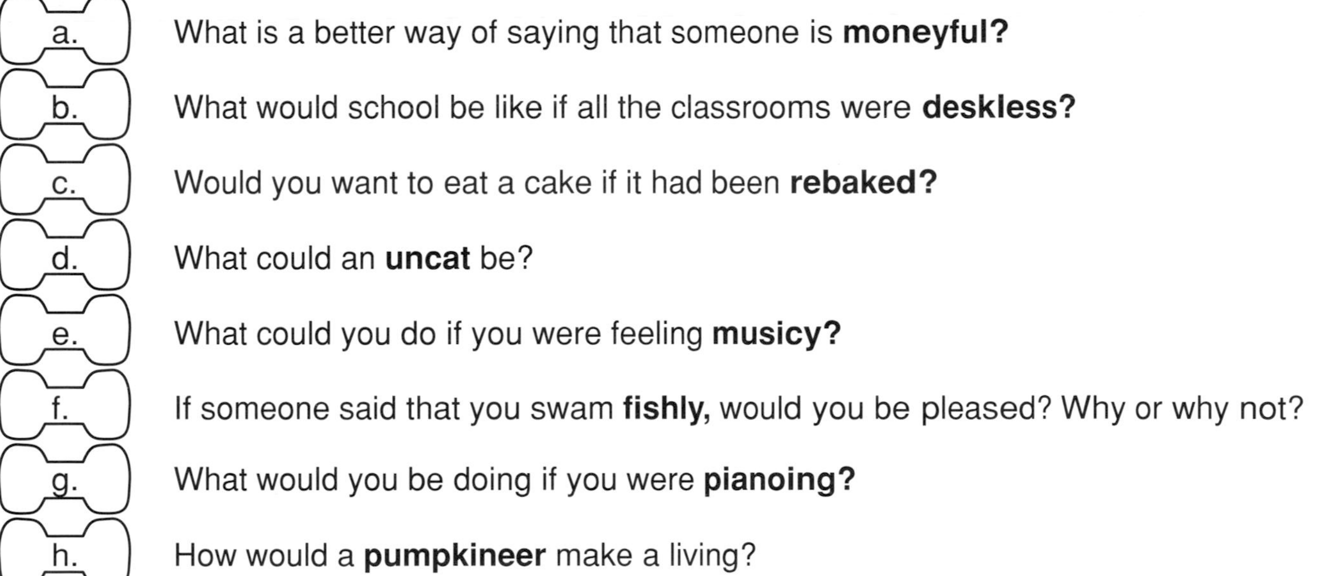

a. What is a better way of saying that someone is **moneyful?**

b. What would school be like if all the classrooms were **deskless?**

c. Would you want to eat a cake if it had been **rebaked?**

d. What could an **uncat** be?

e. What could you do if you were feeling **musicy?**

f. If someone said that you swam **fishly,** would you be pleased? Why or why not?

g. What would you be doing if you were **pianoing?**

h. How would a **pumpkineer** make a living?

**Bonus Box:** Write as many words as you can that contain the prefixes *non-* and *co-* and the suffixes *-ness* and *-ist.* List the words on the back of this page or on another sheet of paper.



**Note to the teacher:** Use with "Flex Those Affixes!" on page 85.

Name ____________________



# Word-Fraction Workout

The newest workout at Woody's Word Analysis Workout Gym lets exercisers test their strength at solving word fractions. The first part of the workout involves spelling a contraction and the two words that combine to form it. The second part involves spelling an abbreviation and the word it represents. Study the example below to get warmed up. Then see if you can complete all 15 repetitions of the workout. Good luck!

The last $^{2}/_{3}$ of *awe* + the last $^{1}/_{4}$ of *said* = we + 'd = we'd. The long form of this contraction is we would or we had.

## CONTRACTIONS

1. the first $^{2}/_{5}$ of *doves* + the last $^{1}/_{3}$ of *ran* + the first $^{1}/_{3}$ of *toe* = ___ ___ + ___ + ' ___ = ____________
   long form: ____________
2. the first $^{3}/_{5}$ of *youth* + the last $^{2}/_{4}$ of *dare* = ___ ___ ___ + ' ___ ___ = ____________
   long form: ____________
3. the first $^{1}/_{7}$ of *Ireland* + the first $^{1}/_{6}$ of *monkey* = ___ + ' ___ = ____________
   long form: ____________
4. the first $^{3}/_{4}$ of *then* + the last $^{1}/_{6}$ of *beauty* + the first $^{2}/_{3}$ of *red* = ___ ___ ___ + ___ + ' ___ ___ = ____________
   long form: ____________
5. the last $^{2}/_{3}$ of *the* + the first $^{1}/_{8}$ of *spelling* = ___ ___ + ' ___ = ____________
   long form: ____________
6. the first $^{3}/_{6}$ of *wonder* + the last $^{1}/_{5}$ of *heart* = ___ ___ ___ + ' ___ = ____________
   long form: ____________
7. the first $^{2}/_{7}$ of *company* + the first $^{1}/_{8}$ of *umbrella* + the last $^{2}/_{4}$ of *bald* + the last $^{2}/_{5}$ of *slant* = ___ ___ + ___ + ___ ___ + ___ ' ___ = ____________
   long form: ____________
8. the first $^{2}/_{6}$ of *island* + the first $^{1}/_{8}$ of *necklace* + the last $^{1}/_{6}$ of *ticket* = ___ ___ + ___ ' + ___ = ____________
   long form: ____________

## ABBREVIATIONS

9. the first $^{2}/_{7}$ of *Seattle* + the last $^{1}/_{3}$ of *pin* = ___ ___ + ___ = ____________
   long form: ____________
10. the first $^{1}/_{6}$ of *Monica* + the last $^{1}/_{5}$ of *tower* = ___ + ___ = ____________
    long form: ____________
11. the last $^{1}/_{5}$ of *peach* + the first $^{1}/_{6}$ of *rabbit* = ___ + ___ = ____________
    long form: ____________
12. the first $^{1}/_{8}$ of *Samantha* + the first $^{2}/_{9}$ of *epidermis* + the last $^{1}/_{7}$ of *blanket* = ___ + ___ ___ + ___ = ____________
    long form: ____________
13. the first $^{1}/_{10}$ of *Washington* + the first $^{2}/_{11}$ of *educational* = ___ + ___ ___ = ____________
    long form: ____________
14. the first $^{1}/_{5}$ of *quick* + the last $^{1}/_{10}$ of *investment* = ___ + ___ = ____________
    long form: ____________
15. the first $^{1}/_{10}$ of *buttermilk* + the last $^{1}/_{6}$ of *tunnel* + the first $^{1}/_{7}$ of *volcano* + the last $^{1}/_{5}$ of *bread* = ___ + ___ + ___ + ___ = ____________
    long form: ____________

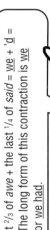

**Bonus Box:** On another sheet of paper, write six of your own word-fraction equations: three with contractions and three with abbreviations. Then trade papers with a classmate and try to solve each other's equations.

# MATH UNITS

## Hands-On Activities for Teaching Perimeter, Area, and Volume

Investigating perimeter, area, and volume has never been easier—especially with the following creative activities and reproducibles!

*by Irving P. Crump*

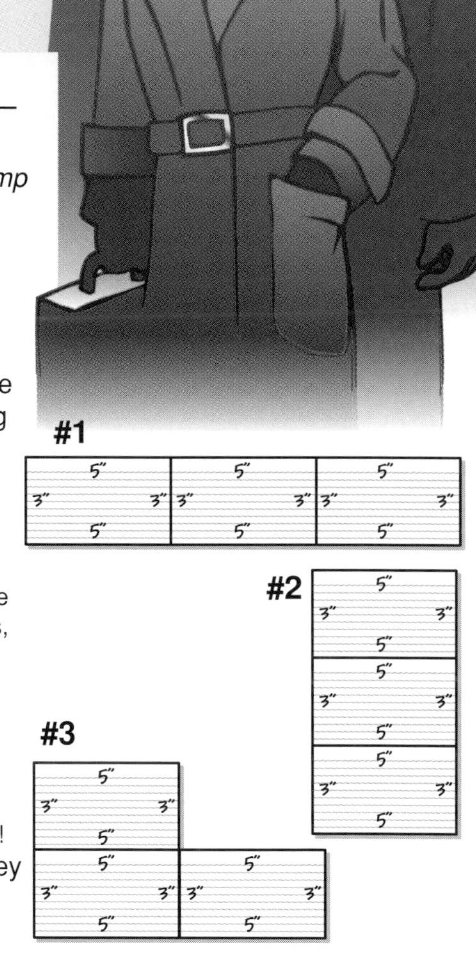

### A Card Mystery

**Skill: Comparing perimeter and area**

Do shapes with the same area also have equal perimeters? Have your junior detectives find out with this simple hands-on activity. Have each student label three 3" x 5" index cards with one card's dimensions. Then lead students in the following activities:

1. Review the formula for finding the perimeter of a rectangle: P = 2(L + W). Then direct each student to lay his cards on his desk end to end as shown. Have the child compute the perimeter of the shape. *(36 in.)* After reviewing how to find the area of a rectangle (A = L x W), have each student determine the shape's area. *(45 sq. in.)*
2. Have each student lay his cards on his desk as shown. Ask the class to determine the area of this shape. *(45 sq. in.)* Help students see that the total area of the three cards, regardless of how they're arranged, remains 45 square inches. Ask volunteers to predict whether the perimeter of the shape will be the same as when the cards were placed end to end. Then have each student compute this shape's perimeter. *(28 in.)*
3. Have each student lay his cards on his desk as shown. Ask students the area of this shape. *(45 sq. in.)* Then ask if the shape's perimeter will be 36 or 28 inches. Remind students that they must add the measures of all the sides of this shape to find its perimeter. Finally, have students compute the shape's perimeter—which is 32 inches!

Point out to students that although two or more shapes have the same area, they may not have the same perimeter.

#1

| 5" | 5" | 5" |
|---|---|---|
| 3" 3" | 3" 3" | 3" 3" |
| 5" | 5" | 5" |

#2

#3

### The Mystery Continues

**Skill: Comparing perimeter and area**

Do shapes with the same perimeter have the same area? To find out, give each student a copy of page 94. In Part 1, direct the student to draw a 4-cm square and three rectangles with the following dimensions: 1 cm x 7 cm, 2 cm x 6 cm, and 3 cm x 5 cm. Next, have students determine each shape's perimeter. *(16 cm)* Ask which shape is the largest. After students have shared their predictions, have them compute the area of each shape. *(The areas are 4 cm x 4 cm = 16 sq. cm, 1 cm x 7 cm = 7 sq. cm, 2 cm x 6 cm = 12 sq. cm, and 3 cm x 5 cm = 15 sq. cm. The largest shape is the square.)*

Extend this activity by having students complete Part 2 on the page. After students have drawn their shapes, have each child color the one he thinks has the greatest area. Then have students find the area of each shape. Help students see that although two or more shapes have the same perimeter, they may not have the same area.

# More Card Mysteries

**Skill: Computing area**

**Square:** Have each student fold down a corner of a 3" x 5" index card to the bottom edge and then cut along the intersection as shown. Then have him unfold this shape and identify it and its dimensions. *(a 3-in. square)* Review the formula for finding the area of a square (L x W or $s^2$); then have students find the shape's area. *(9 sq. in.)*

**Right triangle:** Have each student cut along the fold of her square to form two right triangles. Have her compare one triangle to the whole square. *(It's one-half of the square.)* Then ask students to predict the area of each triangle. *(Since each right triangle is one-half of the square, its area is one-half of the square's area, or 4 1/2 sq. in.)* Help students see why the formula for finding this triangle's area is A = 1/2 bh, or 1/2 x base x height.

**Any triangle:** Have each student fold a second index card in half, cut along a diagonal through both sides as shown, and then unfold the folded section to create three triangles. Have the student place the three pieces back together. Ask students to compare the area of the large triangle to the combined area of the two smaller triangles. *(The areas are equal.)* Ask students to compare the area of the large triangle to the area of the entire card. *(The area of the large triangle is half the area of the card.)* Have students determine the large triangle's height and base. *(h = 3 in.; b = 5 in.)* Then ask them how they can find the area of the large triangle. Lead students to see that to find the area of a triangle, one must multiply the base by the height and then halve it. By applying the formula A = 1/2bh to the large triangle, the students will get 7 1/2 sq. in. (1/2 x 5 x 3). Point out to students that the height and base of a triangle must be known in order to determine the triangle's area. The height and base of a triangle must be perpendicular to each other—they must form a right angle.

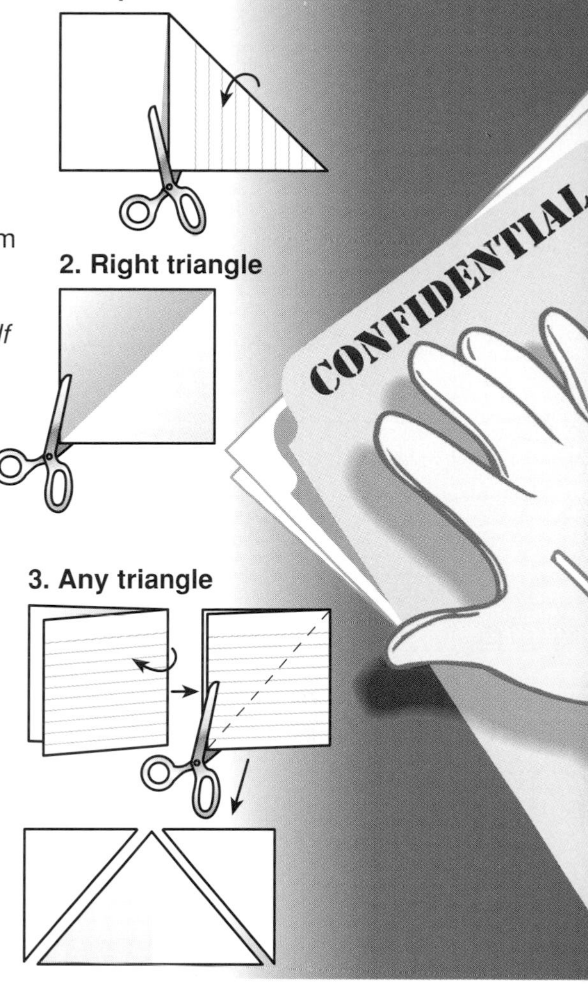

**Parallelogram:** Have each student flip one of the smaller triangles and then lay the two triangles side by side as shown to form a rectangle. Ask students if they can determine the dimensions of this rectangle. *(3 in. x 2 1/2 in. Remind students that one-half of 5 is 2 1/2.)* Then have them compute the area of this rectangle. *(7 1/2 sq. in.)* Next, have students place the two shapes together as shown to form a parallelogram. Ask students to predict the area of this parallelogram. *(It's the same as the rectangle: 7 1/2 sq. in.)* Ask if students can determine a formula for finding the area of a parallelogram. Help them discover that the area of a parallelogram is found by multiplying its base by its height. *(2 1/2 in. x 3 in.)* Remind students that, like triangles, the height is needed to find the area of a parallelogram. And, like triangles, the base and height must be perpendicular to each other.

Have students move the two small triangles to form a different parallelogram (see the illustration). Ask students to determine the area of this parallelogram. *(Since it's the same size as the original rectangle and the first parallelogram formed above, its area is 7 1/2 sq. in.)* Have students determine the base and height of this parallelogram; then apply the formula A = bh to find the area. *(b = 3 in. and h = 2 1/2 in., so the same area results: 7 1/2 sq. in.)*

Name________________________________________________

# The Case of Perimeter vs. Area

**Part 1:** Draw 1 square and 3 rectangles according to your teacher's directions.

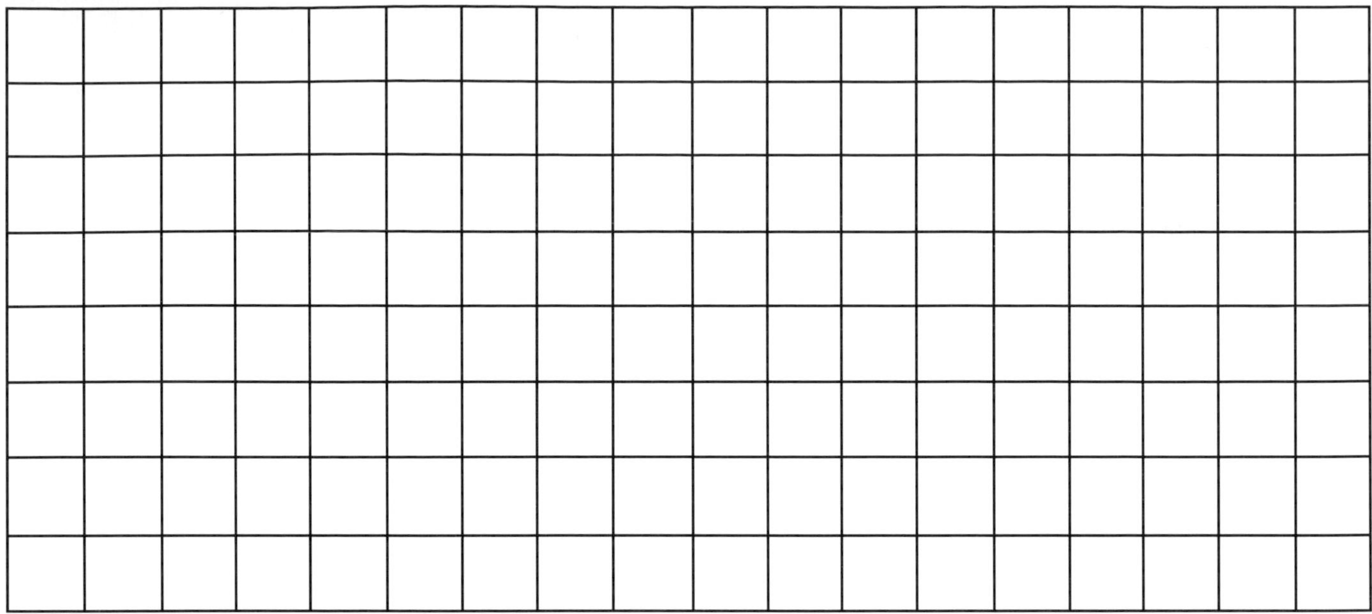

**Part 2:** Draw 1 square and 3 rectangles. Each shape must have a perimeter of 24 cm.



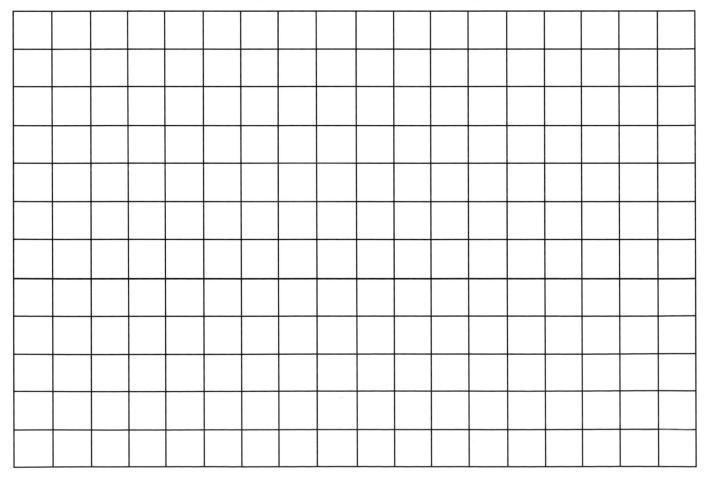

**Note to the teacher:** See "The Mystery Continues" on page 92 for information on using this page.

Name ______________________________ 

# The Scene of the Crime

It's a crime that happens nearly every day. But it won't make the headlines of your local newspaper. The diagram below shows the floor plan of the crime scene. Follow the directions below to identify the crime.

**Directions:**

The dimensions of some rooms in the diagram are not given. Use the number clues provided to help you determine the missing lengths and widths. Write them on the diagram. Then

1. Find the perimeter and area of each room. Show all of your work on another sheet of paper.
2. Match each room's letter to that room's perimeter and area listed in the chart.
3. When you're finished, you will identify the crime. Case closed!

L 48' x 6'

T 30' x 6'

N

G

36' x 6' K

I

42' x 6' M

E

L 18' x 12'

I 18' x 6'

I 12' x 8'

**The crime:**

| perimeter/area | letter |
|---|---|
| 84 ft./216 ft.$^2$ | |
| 40 ft./96 ft.$^2$ | |
| 60 ft./216 ft.$^2$ | |
| 108 ft./288 ft.$^2$ | |
| 48 ft./108 ft.$^2$ | |
| 36 ft./72 ft.$^2$ | |
| 84 ft./432 ft.$^2$ | |
| 84 ft./96 ft.$^2$ | |
| 72 ft./180 ft.$^2$ | |
| 72 ft./324 ft.$^2$ | |
| 96 ft./252 ft.$^2$ | |
| 44 ft./120 ft.$^2$ | |

**BONUS BOX:** Compute the perimeter and area of the entire building above.

Name____________________ Problem solving, logical thinking

# A Backlog of Cases

There's a backlog of cases that need to be investigated! Below are eight cases for you to solve. Are you up for the challenge? Use your knowledge of area and perimeter—and a little logical detective work—to solve each one. Write each answer on the file folder.

1. ________ This unusual rug is made up of five square sections, each the same size. The area of the entire rug is 80 square feet. What is the perimeter of the rug?

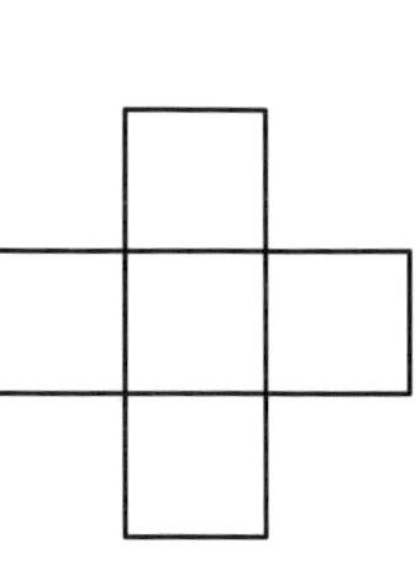

2. ________ This box of fencing will be used to enclose a rose garden. What is the area of the largest possible garden that the fence will go around? Sketch the garden in the space provided. Show its length and width.

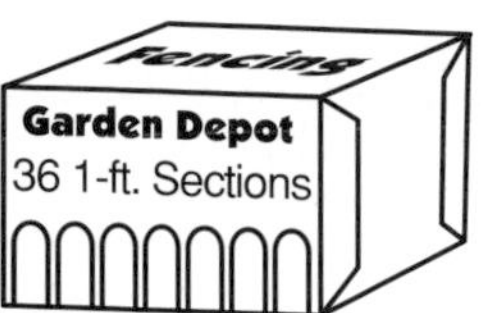


3. ________ How many 4" x 6" cards can be cut from the sheet of poster board?

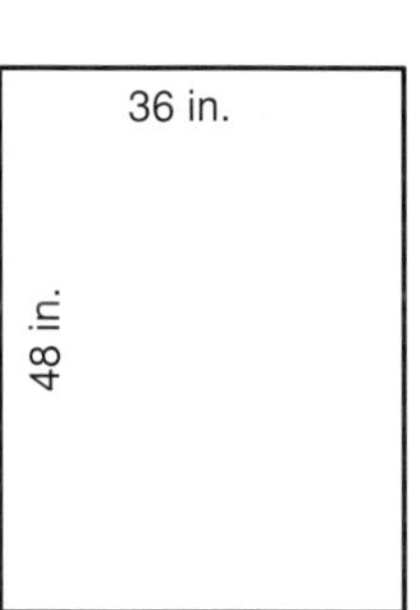


4. ________ A square sheet of drawing paper has an area of 400 square inches. It was cut in half to make two equal rectangles. What is the perimeter of each rectangle?

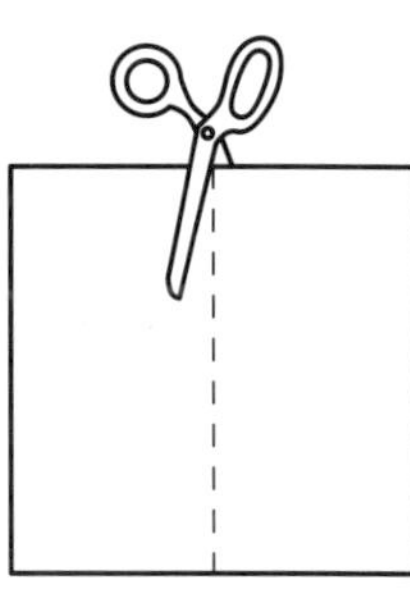

5. ________ The sidewalk around the pool is five feet wide. What is the total area of the sidewalk?

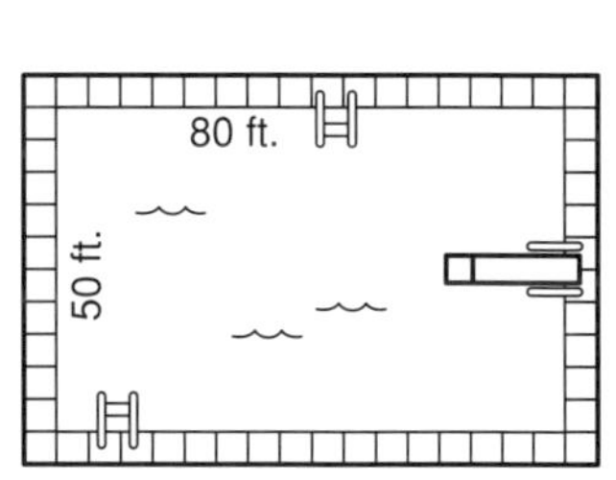


6. ________ A farmer divided her square garden into six equal rectangular sections. The area of the garden is 144 square yards. What is the perimeter of each section?

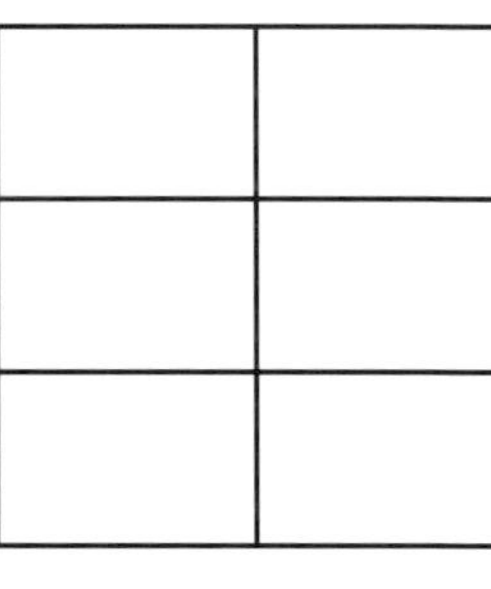

7. ________ The walkways that cut through and surround this garden are three feet wide. What is the area of the garden? (Hint: Cut out the garden.)

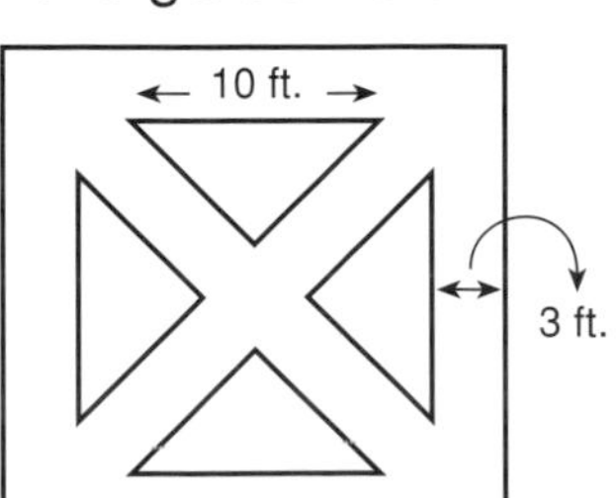


8. ________ ________ Cut out the square, two triangles, and parallelogram. Put them together to make a rectangle. What is the perimeter of the rectangle? What is its area?

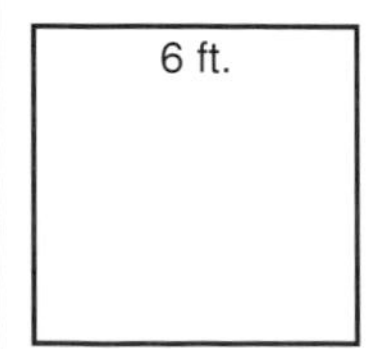

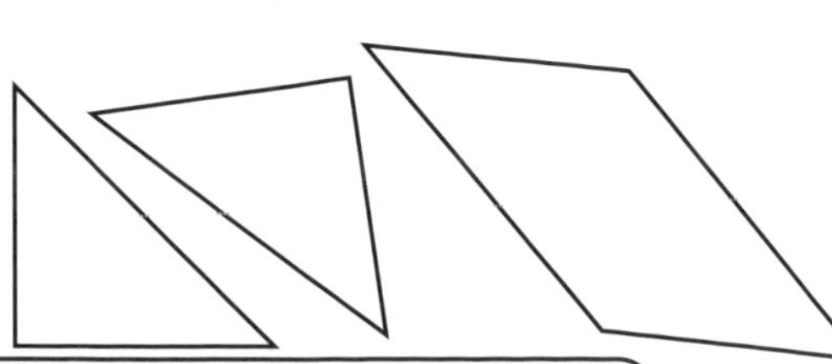


**Bonus Box:** On the back of this sheet, draw a square whose area and perimeter are the same.

Name ______________________________ Computing volume

# The Lineup

Can you spot the shape that was at the scene of the crime? First, fold your paper on the dashed line so that the answer box is hidden. Next, find the volume of each shape. When you're finished, check your work with a calculator.

To find out who was at the crime scene, unfold your paper. Write a check (√) on each shape whose answer is listed in the answer box. Then circle the shape that *does not* have a matching answer—that's the crook!

**Remember:** *Volume* is the number of cubic units needed to fill a container. To find the volume of a cube or a rectangular prism, multiply the length, the width, and the height. Example:

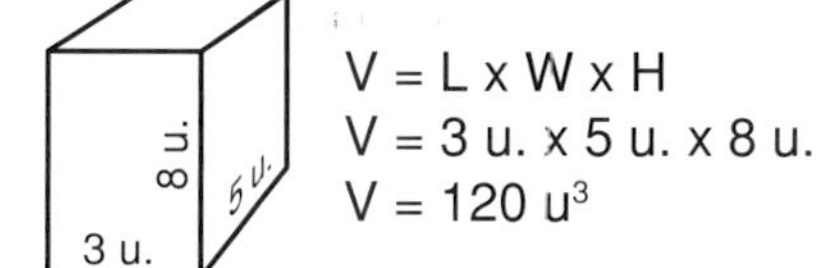


V = L x W x H
V = 3 u. x 5 u. x 8 u.
V = 120 u³

Volume is expressed in *cubic units* because it includes length, width, and height.

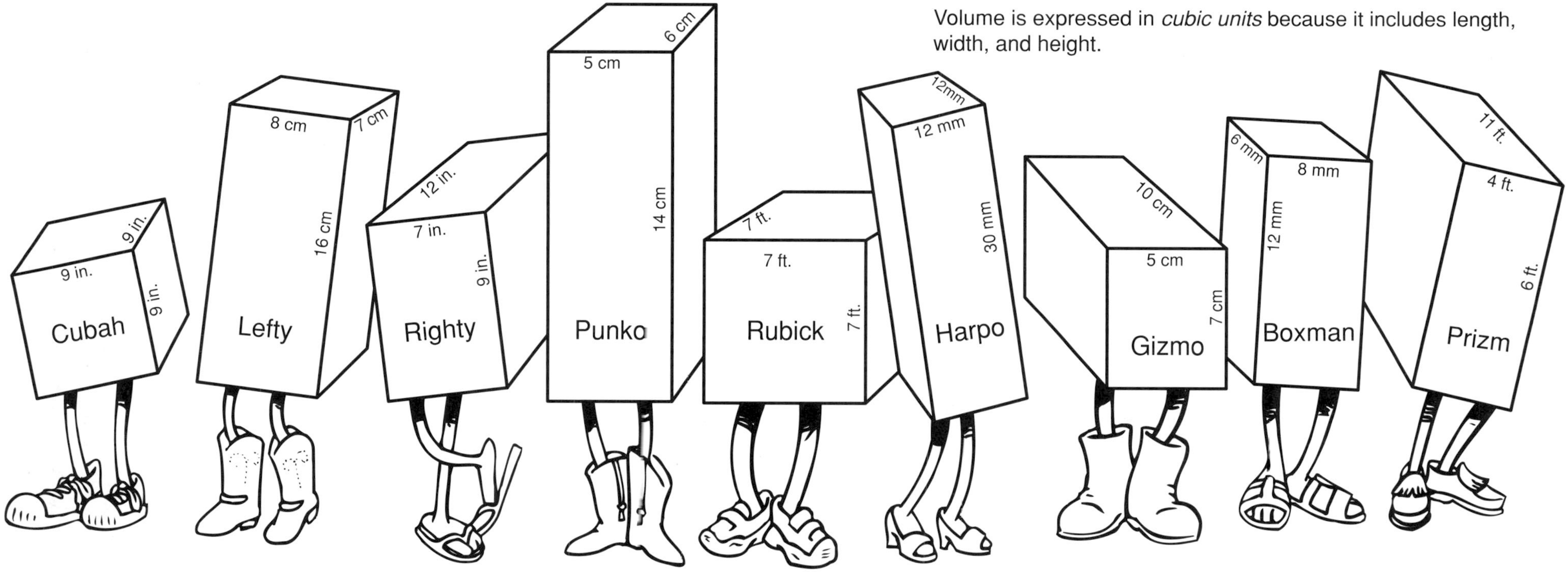

Cubah: 9 in., 9 in., 9 in.
Lefty: 8 cm, 7 cm, 16 cm
Righty: 7 in., 12 in., 9 in.
Punko: 5 cm, 6 cm, 14 cm
Rubick: 7 ft., 7 ft., 7 ft.
Harpo: 12 mm, 12mm, 30 mm
Gizmo: 10 cm, 5 cm, 7 cm
Boxman: 6 mm, 8 mm, 12 mm
Prizm: 11 ft., 4 ft., 6 ft.

V = ______ V = ______ V = ______ V = ______ V = ______ V = ______ V = ______ V = ______ V = ______

**Answer Box**

| | | | | | |
|---|---|---|---|---|---|
| 343 ft.³ | 896 cm³ | 27 in.³ | 576 mm³ | 4,320 mm³ | 720 mm³ |
| 350 mm³ | 264 ft.³ | 729 in.³ | 3,500 cm³ | 756 in.³ | 420 cm³ |

# Serving Up Circles

**Looking for ideas that deliver plenty of hands-on learning about circles? Then serve up these "pizza-riffic" activities and reproducibles!**

*by Lori Sammartino, Cranberry Township, PA*

## Any Way You Slice It

**Skills: Circle parts and attributes**

Introduce students to the basic parts and attributes of a circle with this pizza-slicing activity. First, ask students to identify a pizza's shape *(circle)*. Next, give each child a four-inch white paper circle (or have him use a compass to construct his own), scissors, a ruler, and crayons in the following colors: red, black, green, blue, orange, and purple. Guide students through the steps below in order. Then conclude by having students brainstorm real-life objects—other than pizzas!—that are circular or contain circular shapes. List students' responses on chart paper to use with "Concentric Pizzas" on page 101. Challenge students to add items to this list throughout the unit.

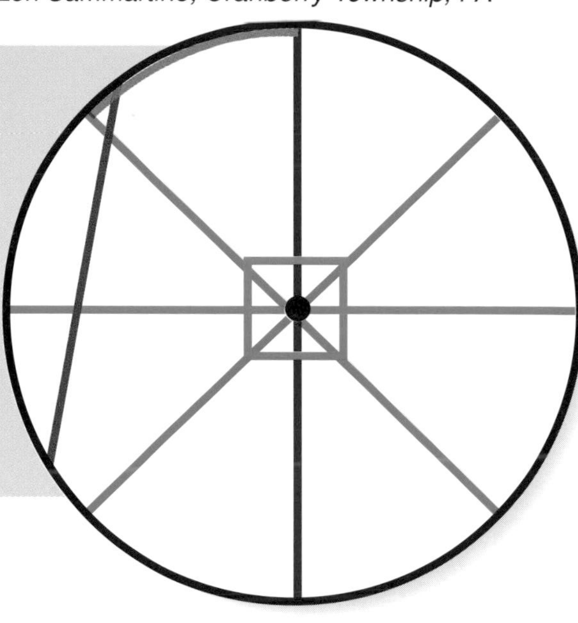

**Steps:**

1. **Circumference (the distance around the outside of a circle):** Use the black crayon to trace the outer edge of the circle.

2. **Diameter (any straight line that passes through the center of a circle):** Fold the circle in half. Unfold it. Use the red crayon to trace the fold line. Measure the diameter *(four inches)*.

3. **Center of circle (the point in the exact middle of the circle):** Refold the circle in half and fold it in half again to make fourths. Unfold it. Use the black crayon to mark the point where the fold lines intersect.

4. **Radius (the distance from the center of the circle to any point on the circumference of the circle):** Use the green crayon to trace the new fold line outward in each direction from the center. Measure each radius *(two inches)*. Identify the angles formed *(four right angles)* by marking them as shown. Calculate the total degrees in a circle *(4 x 90° = 360°)* and in a half circle *(180°)*. Fold the circle in fourths and then in half again to make eighths. Use the blue crayon to trace the new fold lines. Find the degrees in $^1/_8$ circle *(45°)*.

5. **Arc (any section of the circumference):** Use the orange crayon to trace $^1/_8$ of the circle. Determine if tracing $^1/_4$, $^3/_8$, $^1/_2$, $^5/_8$, $^3/_4$, or $^7/_8$ of the circle each represents an arc. *(yes)*

6. **Chord (a straight line that connects any two points on the circle):** Use the purple crayon to trace a line from one point on the circle to another without passing through the center.

If desired, extend the activity by having students use protractors to help them create two circles, one having six equal pieces (60° angles) and another with nine equal pieces (40° angles).

## Circular Stories

**Skills: Connecting math and literature, writing a review**

Connect reading and writing to your circles study with this well-rounded activity! Have your media specialist gather circle-related books, such as those suggested below. Encourage students to read as many of the books as they can. If desired, read several selections aloud to the class. Explain that some of the selections are written in a circular pattern in which events flow from one to the next, with the main character always ending up where he or she started. Point out that others feature circle-shaped characters or teach younger readers about circles. Then challenge each student to write a review about one of the following to share with the class: (1) a circular story, (2) a story that has a circle-shaped character, or (3) a story that teaches a concept about circles.

**Circular stories:**

*What Comes Around Goes Around* by Richard McGuire (Viking, 1995)

*Where the Wild Things Are* by Maurice Sendak (HarperTrophy, 1988)

*If You Give a Mouse a Cookie* by Laura Joffe Numeroff (Scholastic Inc., 1985)

*Circle Song* by Diana Engel (Cavendish Children's Books, 1999)

The Missing Piece by Shel Silverstein (HarperCollins Children's Books, 1976)

*Rosie's Walk* by Pat Hutchins (Aladdin Paperbacks, 1983)

**Books with circle characters:**

*Circle Dogs* by Kevin Henkes (Greenwillow Books, 1998)

*Rolie Polie Olie* by William Joyce (HarperCollins Children's Books, 1999)

**Books that teach circle concepts:**

*Sir Cumference and the First Round Table: A Math Adventure* by Cindy Neuschwander (Charlesbridge Publishing, Inc.; 1997)

*So Many Circles, So Many Squares* by Tana Hoban (Greenwillow Books, 1998)

*What Is Round?* by Rebecca Kai Dotlich (HarperFestival, 1999)

*Ed Emberley's Picture Pie: A Circle Drawing Book* (Little, Brown and Company; 1984)

## Discovering Pizza "Pi"

**Skill: Diameter and circumference**

Use this activity to help students discover that a circle's circumference is a little more than three times its diameter. Give each student a 12-inch length of string, a ruler, a calculator, and a copy of page 102 to complete as directed. When students have completed the sheet and its Bonus Box, check the answers together. Help students conclude that the numbers in the table's last column are all close to three. On the board, write *"pi* = 3.14." Explain that *pi* represents the relationship between a circle's circumference and its diameter (found by dividing the circumference by the diameter). Have students prove this by first using their string to measure the circumference of any circle on page 102 and then calculating the number of diameters needed to equal that length *(three)*. If desired, extend the activity by having students write an equation for finding circumference when only the diameter is known *(C = d x 3.14)*. Afterward, have each student use the formula to calculate the answers on page 102 and explain why the answers differ *(3.14 is a more exact number than 3)*.

## Pizza Estimations

**Skills: Estimating the area of a circle, constructing circles**

Practice estimating the area of circles with this nifty activity. Begin by drawing a circle on the board and asking students how they could determine its area. If no one suggests drawing square units, start drawing intersecting horizontal and vertical lines inside the circle. Guide students to conclude that they can count the square units to estimate the circle's area. Point out that some squares are partial units. Together, discuss strategies for simplifying the counting process *(adding whole units first and then partial units, or dividing the circle into four equal parts and multiplying the whole units in one quadrant by four)*. Then give each student a compass, several sheets of graph paper, and a copy of page 103 to complete as directed.

For more practice on finding circumference and diameter, give students a ruler and a length of string with which to measure the circles on page 103. For an extra challenge, have students use the formula $A = 3.14 \times r^2$ to calculate the actual area of each circle; then have them explain why the estimated and exact areas differ.

1 2 3
4 5
6

6 whole squares

about 2 partial squares

2 partial squares ÷ 2 = 1 sq. unit

6 whole units
+1 (partial squares ÷ 2)
7 units

7 units in one quadrant
x 4 quadrants
28 sq. units (estimated area)

This circle's area is about 28 square units.

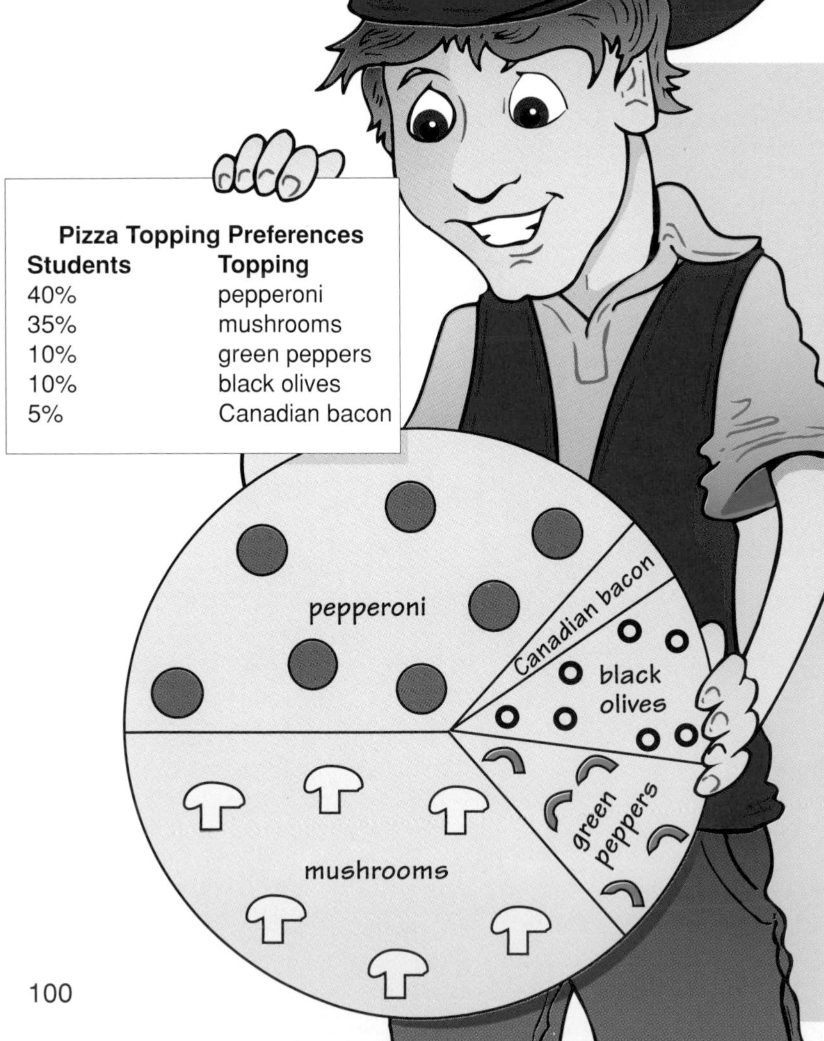


**Pizza Topping Preferences**

| Students | Topping |
|---|---|
| 40% | pepperoni |
| 35% | mushrooms |
| 10% | green peppers |
| 10% | black olives |
| 5% | Canadian bacon |

## Making a Pizza Pie Graph

**Skills: Calculating percent, using a compass and protractor**

Show students that constructing circle graphs can be as easy as pizza pie! In advance, copy the table shown onto the board or a transparency. Review with students that there are 360° in a circle, 180° in a half circle, and 90° in a quarter circle. Have student volunteers illustrate these amounts on the board by drawing circles that are 100% shaded, 50% shaded, and 25% shaded. Afterward, model how to calculate the degrees represented in a circle that is 20% shaded: 0.20 (the decimal equivalent of 20%) x 360° = 72°. Then construct a circle on the board. Use a protractor to measure a 72° angle in the circle and shade it in. Next, give each student a sheet of white paper, a compass, a protractor, and crayons or markers. Have each child construct on his paper a circle with a two-inch radius. Display the table; then challenge each student to follow the procedure you modeled to convert each percent in the table to degrees. After checking students' calculations (pepperoni = 144°, mushrooms = 126°, green peppers = 36°, black olives = 36°, and Canadian bacon = 18°), have each child construct and color a circle graph that represents the data.

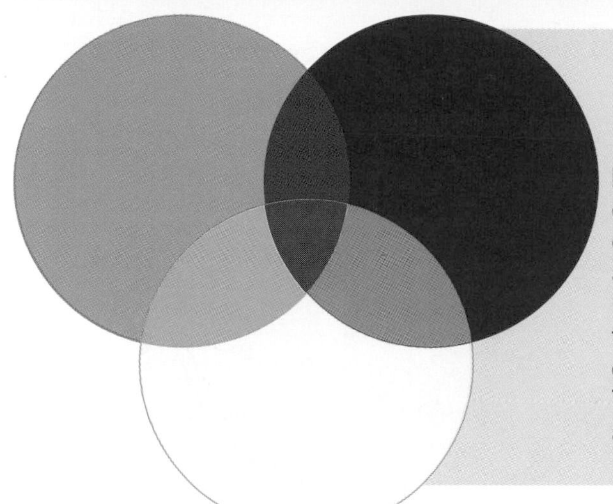

## Overlapping Pizzas

**Skill: Using overlapping circles to make comparisons**

Serve up a lesson on overlapping circles with the following hard-to-beat activity! Cut three circles from cellophane: one red, one yellow, and one blue. Overlap the blue and yellow circles and display them on an overhead projector. Point out the new color produced in the overlapping area *(green)*. Tell students it represents a combination of the two colors. Next, overlap the red and yellow circles (creating an orange area) and the blue and red circles (making a purple area). Finally, overlap all three circles as shown to create areas of orange, green, purple, and black. Then give each student a copy of page 104. Have students complete and check Part 1 together before completing Part 2 independently.

## Concentric Pizzas

**Skill: Constructing concentric circles**

Build your own concentric-circle pizzas with this circle-within-a-circle activity. On the board, draw a lollipop made of concentric circles as shown. Together, brainstorm other real-world items that suggest (or have) the shape of one circle within another, such as a bull's-eye, bagel, CD, etc. Have students also refer to the chart made in "Any Way You Slice It" on page 98 for other items that might represent concentric circles. Next, give each student a sheet of paper and a compass. Have her construct a circle having a three-inch radius. Inside that circle, have her construct a smaller circle with a two-inch radius; then have her create a circle with a one-inch radius inside the two-inch circle. After this practice, give each child scissors, glue, and three 9" x 12" sheets of construction paper (one tan, one red, and one yellow). Have her make an eight-inch tan circle, a seven-inch red circle, and a six-inch yellow circle. Then have her stack and glue the circles together to form the crust, sauce, and cheese layers of a pizza. From her scraps, have her cut out six different toppings and glue them on top of the cheese before delivering her concentric pizza to you to display!

## A Circular Celebration

**Skill: Identifying circular shapes**

Conclude your unit by having students create a colossal class mural of circular shapes! Have students cut out magazine pictures that represent different types of circles. Then have one small group of students at a time mount the cutouts on a bulletin board until it is filled with different-sized, overlapping, and concentric circles. Celebrate the project's completion by letting students munch on a variety of round-shaped snacks. What a circular celebration!

Name ______________________



# How Big Is Your Pizza "Pi"?

Discover a special relationship between a circle's circumference and its diameter by following the directions below.

**Directions:**

1. Use string to measure the distance around each pizza shown.
2. Place the string atop a ruler. Measure the string to the nearest half inch. Record the measurement in the "Circumference" column of the table.
3. Use a ruler to measure the diameter of each pizza. Record the measurement in the table.
4. Use a calculator to divide the circumference by the diameter. Record your answer in the table. *(Hint: $^1/_2$ inch = 0.50)*

| Pizza | Circumference | Diameter | Circumference ÷ Diameter |
|---|---|---|---|
| Pepperoni | | | |
| Black olive | | | |
| Cheese | | | |
| Anchovy | | | |
| Green pepper | | | |
| Mushroom | | | |

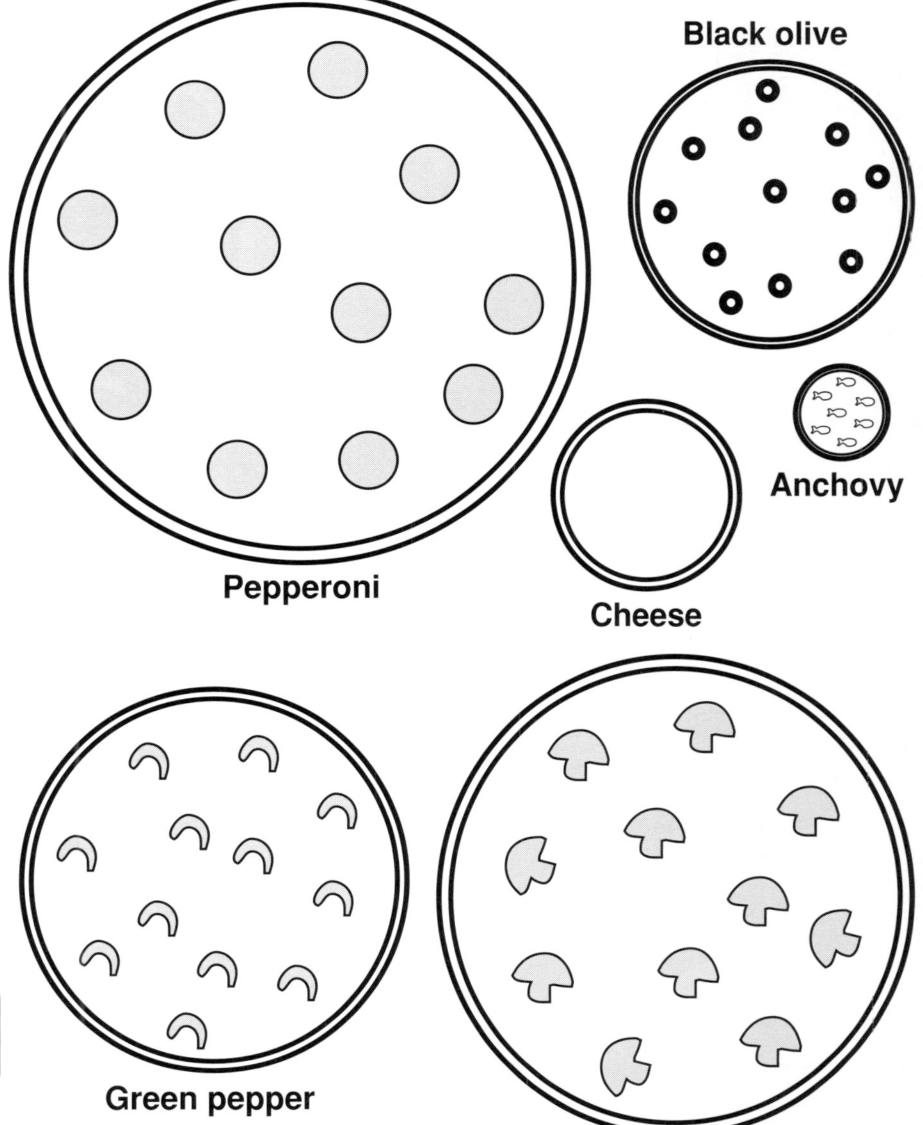


**Bonus Box:** On the back of this page, write a sentence explaining the relationship between circumference and diameter. Base your explanation on the numbers in the last column above.



**Note to the teacher:** Use with "Discovering Pizza 'Pi' " on page 99.

Name ______________________________ Estimating area, using a compass

# Peppi's Pizza Predicament

The pizza chefs at Peppi's Pizza Parlor are in a dilemma. They don't know how to estimate the area of the pizzas they've made! Help them out by following the directions below.

**Part 1:** For each circle, count all of the whole squares and all of the partial squares in the shaded area. Next, divide the number of partial squares by 2. If necessary, round the quotient to the nearest whole number. Then add the whole squares and the answer to *b* together. Finally, multiply the answer in *c* by 4 to find the estimated area of the circle.

1.

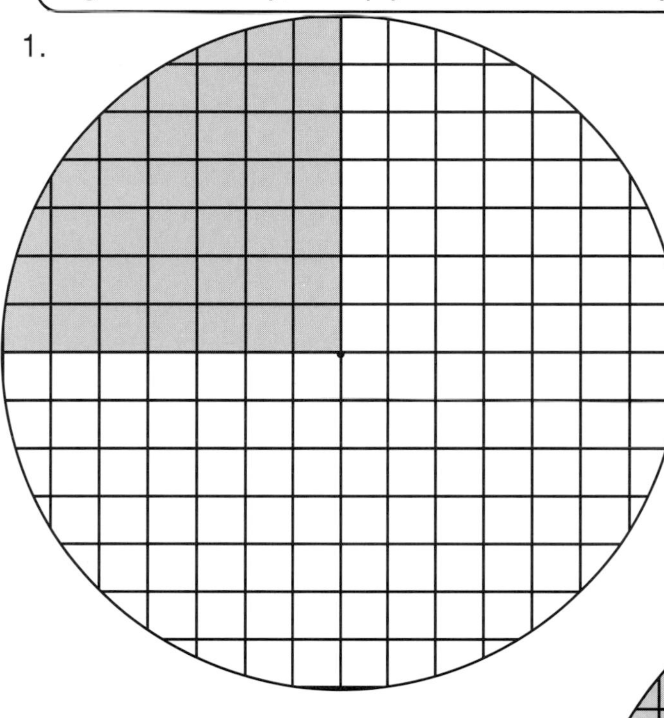

a. _____ whole squares
   _____ partial squares
b. partial squares ÷ 2 = _____ sq. units
c. whole squares + answer to *b* = _____ sq. units
d. estimated area = answer to *c* x 4 = _____ sq. units.

2.

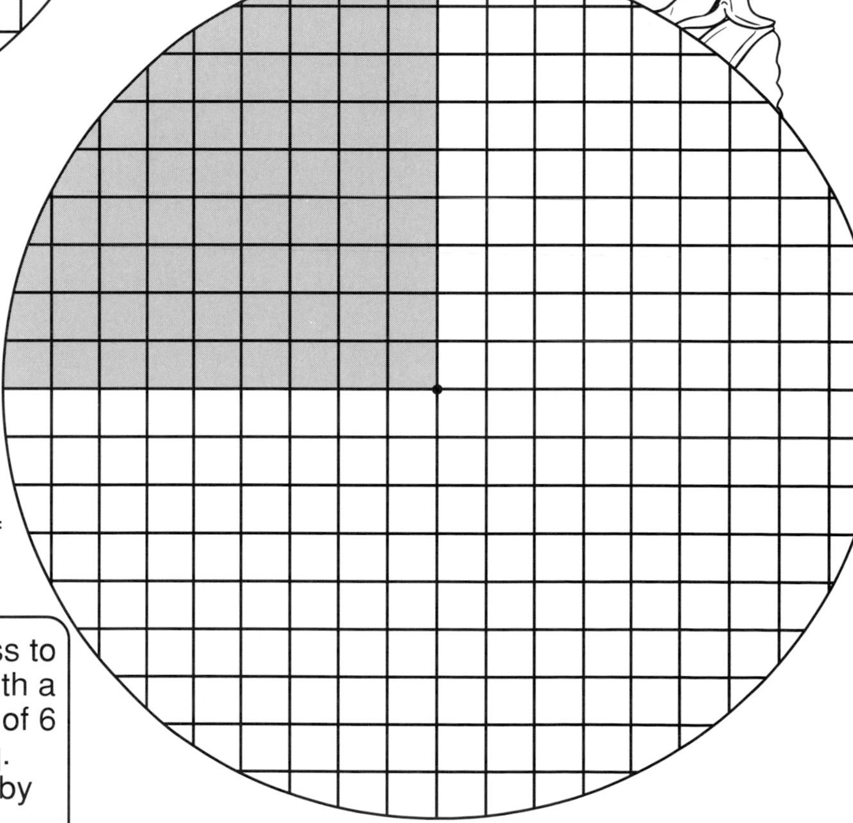

a. _____ whole squares
   _____ partial squares
b. partial squares ÷ 2 = _____ sq. units
c. whole squares + answer to *b* = _____ sq. units
d. estimated area = answer to *c* x 4 = _____ sq. units.

**Part 2:** On graph paper, use a compass to construct three different circles: one with a radius of 5 sq. units, one with a radius of 6 sq. units, and one with a radius of 3 sq. units. Estimate the area of each circle by counting its square units.

**BONUS BOX:** What method did you use to find the area of the circles you drew in Part 2? Explain your method on the back of this page.



**Note to the teacher:** Use with "Pizza Estimations" on page 100.

Name ______________________________ 

# Overlapping Pizzas

A marketing team for Peppi's Pizza Parlor has come up with a new concept. They want Peppi to create overlapping pizzas to start a new combination-pizza craze. So Peppi made the test samples below.

**Part 1:** Look carefully at the overlapping pizzas. Then answer the questions.

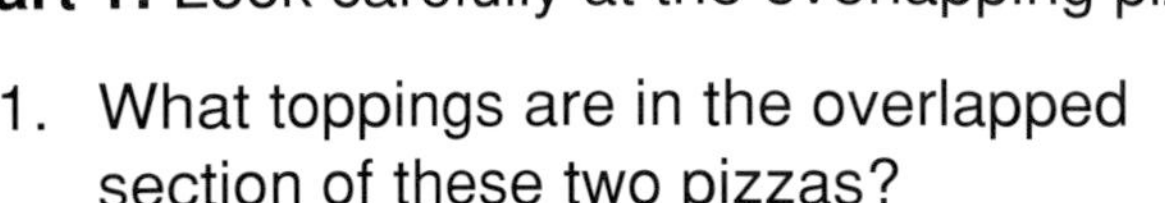

1. What toppings are in the overlapped section of these two pizzas? __________

______________________________

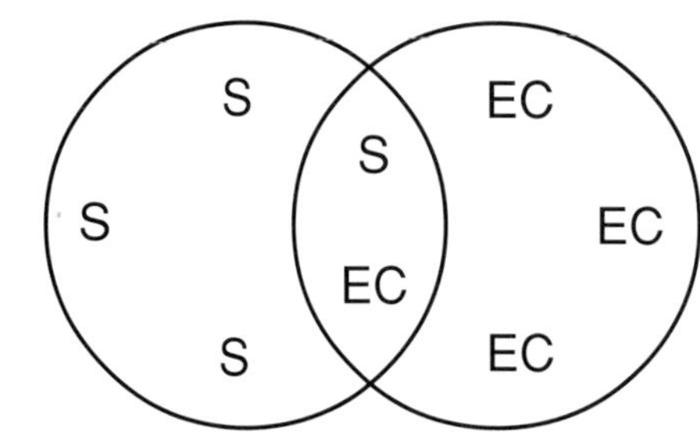


sausage = S     extra cheese = EC

2. How many different topping combinations are possible in these three overlapping pizzas? ________ List them. __________

______________________________

______________________________

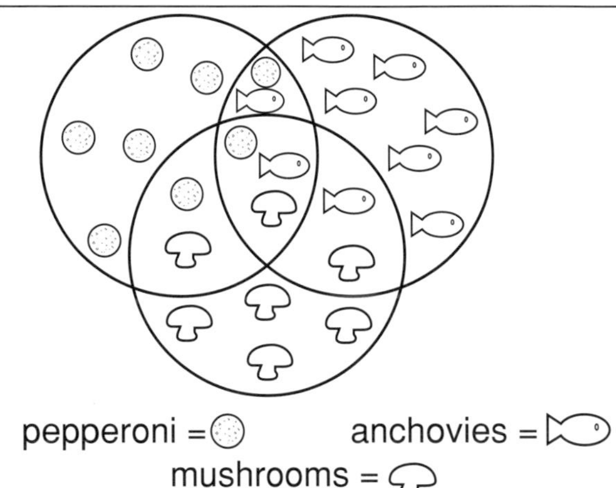

pepperoni = ◯     anchovies = (fish)
mushrooms = (mushroom)

**Part 2:** Now it's time to create overlapping pizzas of your own! Complete a key for each pizza. Include a symbol for each topping.

3. Use two different toppings to make this overlapping pizza. Cover one pizza with one topping and the second pizza with the second topping. What toppings are in the overlapped section? __________

______________________________

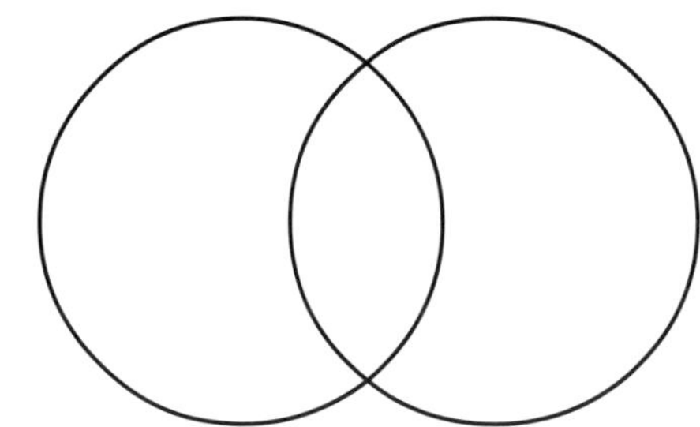

4. Use three different toppings to make this overlapping pizza. Cover one pizza with one topping, the second pizza with the second topping, and the third pizza with the third topping. How many different toppings are possible? ______ List them on the back of this page.

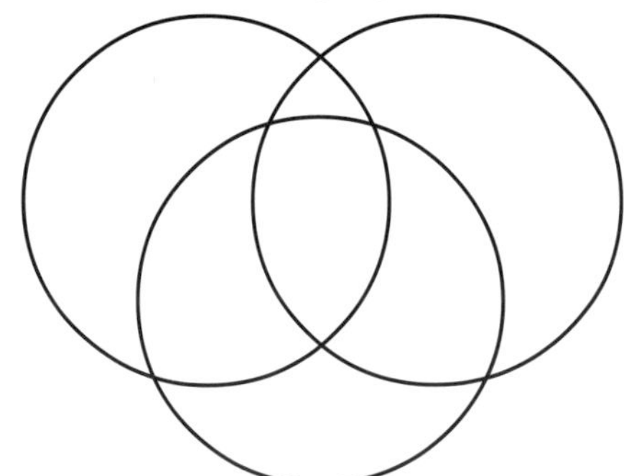



**Note to the teacher:** Use with "Overlapping Pizzas" on page 101. Each student will need a compass and crayons or colored pencils to complete the page.

# GEO-TREK...

## A Journey Into Real-World Geometry

Show students that geometry isn't just *out* of this world, but also smack-dab *in* it with the following ideas on geometric concepts in the real world!

*by Irving P. Crump*

### They're Golden!

**Skills: Rectangles, using ratio**

Are some rectangles more pleasing to look at than others? The ancient Greeks thought so! To find out what your students think, draw on a chalkboard four rectangles with these dimensions: 2" x 10", 10" x 16", 5" x 6", and 1" x 12". Ask students to vote on which rectangle they think is most pleasing to the eye. It will likely be the 10" x 16" one. Share with students that *golden rectangles* (ones with a length to width ratio of about 1.6 to 1) are more pleasing to the eye than other rectangles. Why? No one really knows.

Next, provide each student with a copy of the top half of page 107, which tells how to construct a golden rectangle. After students complete the activity, have them brainstorm examples of real-world rectangles as you list them on the board. (See the suggestions below.) Assign each pair of students one rectangle and ask if it is similar to the one on the reproducible. Then instruct the pair to measure the length and width of its assigned rectangle and use a calculator to determine if it is "golden." (Example: If the ratio of length to width is 30/16, divide both terms by 16 to get 1.9/1 or 1.9 to 1.) If the ratio of the rectangle's length to its width is approximately 1.6 to 1, then the rectangle is golden.

**Examples:** construction paper (different sizes), index card, notecard, credit card, driver's license, door, television, flag, desktop, sheet of notebook paper, sticky note, calculator face, wallet-sized photo, textbook, mouse pad, computer screen, magazine, newspaper page, dollar bill, postage stamp, envelope, business card, classroom poster, framed picture or photo, greeting card, license plate, brochure, postcard

### Flyin' High!

**Skill: Identifying geometry concepts**

The flag of the United States illustrates several geometric concepts. (See the illustration.) Share with students that the flag, however, is *not* a golden rectangle as described in "They're Golden!" The ratio of its length to its width is 1.9 to 1.

Many state flags and flags of other nations incorporate geometric concepts too. Assign each student a state or country from the list shown. Have the student research, draw, and color that state's or country's flag. Then have her list on an index card all of the geometric concepts that she can identify in the flag's design. After she shares her flag and geometry terms, instruct the student to attach the index card to the bottom of her drawing. Display the flags on a bulletin board titled "Flyin' High!"

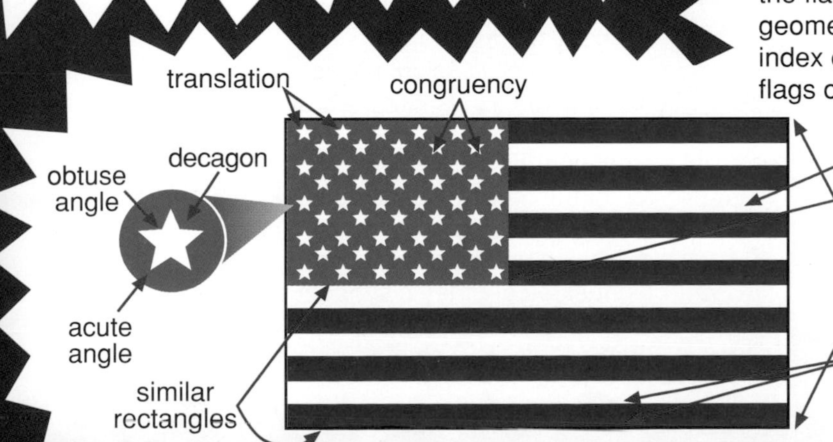


Alabama, Arizona, New Mexico, Colorado, Ohio, Georgia, Hawaii, Tennessee, Texas, Maryland, Mississippi, Puerto Rico, Grenada, Congo, Liberia, Tanzania, Canada, South Africa, Guyana, St. Lucia, Kuwait, Philippines, Denmark, Greece, United Kingdom, Israel, Jordan, Jamaica, Cuba

# Welcome to Geo-Village!

**Skills: Identifying geometry terms, making three-dimensional models**

Nowhere is geometry more evident in our world than in construction and architecture. Provide each student with a copy of page 109. Discuss the terms at the bottom of the page; then direct students to complete the activity as directed. Share with students that many of the terms listed are represented multiple times in the village.

After discussing page 109, divide students into six groups. Provide each group with a white sheet of poster board. Instruct each group to measure and draw a two-inch border around three sides of its poster board as shown below; then have the group color this border gray. Tell students that the border represents streets that surround three sides of a city block. Next, direct each group to use a variety of materials to create a three-dimensional model of a city block, with each structure facing the street. Students may also include items in the center of a block, such as a park, playground, or parking lot. Have students gather a variety of materials ahead of time (see below). As they work, have group members make a list identifying the geometric terms illustrated in its model.

When all six city blocks are completed, display them by laying the pieces of poster board together as shown. Have each group share its project by pointing out all of the examples of geometric terms.

**Materials:** clean, empty milk cartons (pint and 1/2-pint sizes); game pieces; cube tissue boxes; checkers; dominoes; construction paper; scissors; tape; dice; glue; different sizes of aluminum cans; straws; bottle caps; craft sticks; small paper cups; cardboard; small boxes

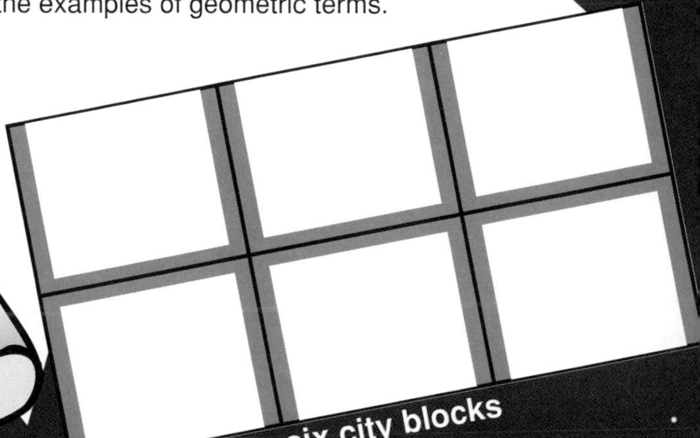

six city blocks

# Geo-Scavenger Hunt

**Skills: Finding examples of geometry terms, making an octahedron**

As a homework extension, send your students out in the world on a geo-scavenger hunt! Have each student find examples of items that illustrate eight geometry terms. (Choose from the list at the bottom of page 109 and these three-dimensional shapes: *cone, disk, cylinder, cube, rectangular prism, triangular prism,* and *sphere.*) Encourage students to look in their neighborhoods, homes, or yards. Have each student sketch and label his examples and bring the drawings to school the next day for discussion.

After the discussion, provide each student with a copy of page 108. Have him draw and label each item from his list on a triangle in the pattern. Make sure that the student turns the pattern so that the label (1–8) is at the top of the triangle that he is working on. After decorating his completed pattern, have each child follow the directions on the page to make an *octahedron*—an eight-sided geometric shape. For an eye-catching display, have each student place his completed octahedron on top of an empty plastic soda or water bottle.

Name ______________________________ Following directions

# Looking for Gold!

Can you make a golden rectangle? Just follow the steps on the right very carefully. You only need a pencil and a ruler.

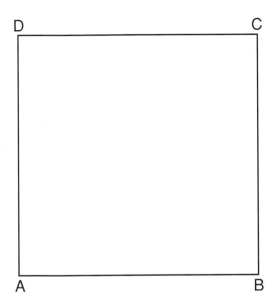

**Steps:**

1. Find the midpoint of $\overline{AB}$. Label it M.
2. Find the midpoint of $\overline{DC}$. Label it N.
3. Draw a straight line to connect M and C.
4. Measure $\overline{MC}$ and record the length. ____
5. Lay your ruler along $\overline{AB}$ with its end at point M.
6. Measure the length that you recorded in #4, making $\overline{MB}$ longer. Label the new endpoint E.
7. Lay your ruler along $\overline{DC}$ with its end at point N.
8. Measure the length that you recorded in #4, making $\overline{NC}$ longer. Label the new endpoint F.
9. Draw a straight line to connect E and F.
10. You did it! AEFD is a golden rectangle.



Name ______________________________ Puzzles, visual thinking

# A Puzzling Pair

**Puzzle 1**

How many squares do you see on the checkerboard? 64? 65? Not even close! (Hint: Be sure to count squares that are made up of smaller ones. For example, count all of the squares that are two small squares long and two small squares wide.)

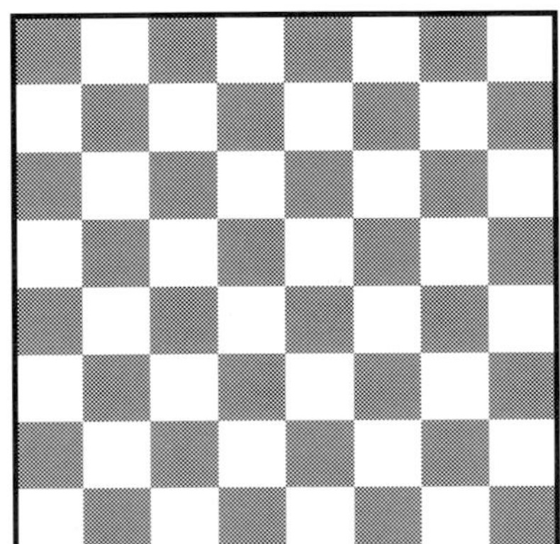

My answer: __________ squares

**Puzzle 2**

How many triangles do you see? Six? Seven? You got it—not even close! (Hint: Label each of the six small triangles with a letter. Then list each different triangle with a combination of letters.)

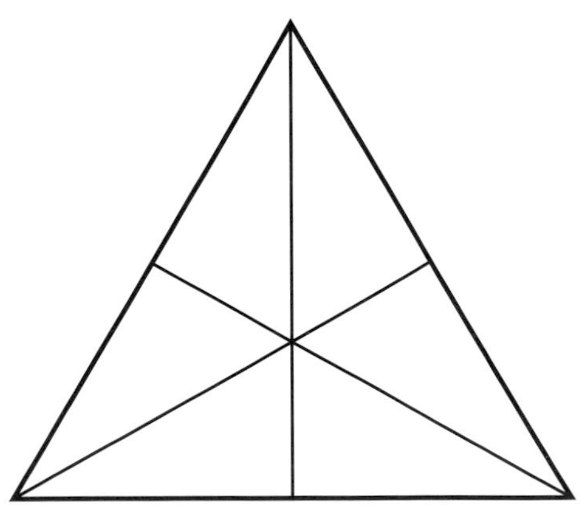

My answer: __________ triangles



**Note to the teacher:** Use the top half of this reproducible with "They're Golden!" on page 105. Provide each student with a ruler. Use the bottom half ("A Puzzling Pair") as a free-time challenge.

# Geo-Scavenger Hunt

Draw each scavenger hunt item on a triangle in the pattern. Each number is at the top of a triangle; be sure to turn the pattern so that the number is at the top when you draw. Then follow the steps below to make an octahedron.

1. Carefully cut out the pattern.
2. Turn the pattern over and fold up each tab (A–E).
3. Next, fold at each remaining dashed line, keeping the drawing to the outside.
4. Glue tab B under triangle 1. Hold the tab and triangle together until the glue dries.
5. Glue tab E under triangle 7. Hold the tab and triangle together until the glue dries.
6. Glue tab D to triangle 2, tab A to triangle 7, and tab C to triangle 6.
7. You've done it! You've made an *octahedron*—an eight-sided geometric shape.

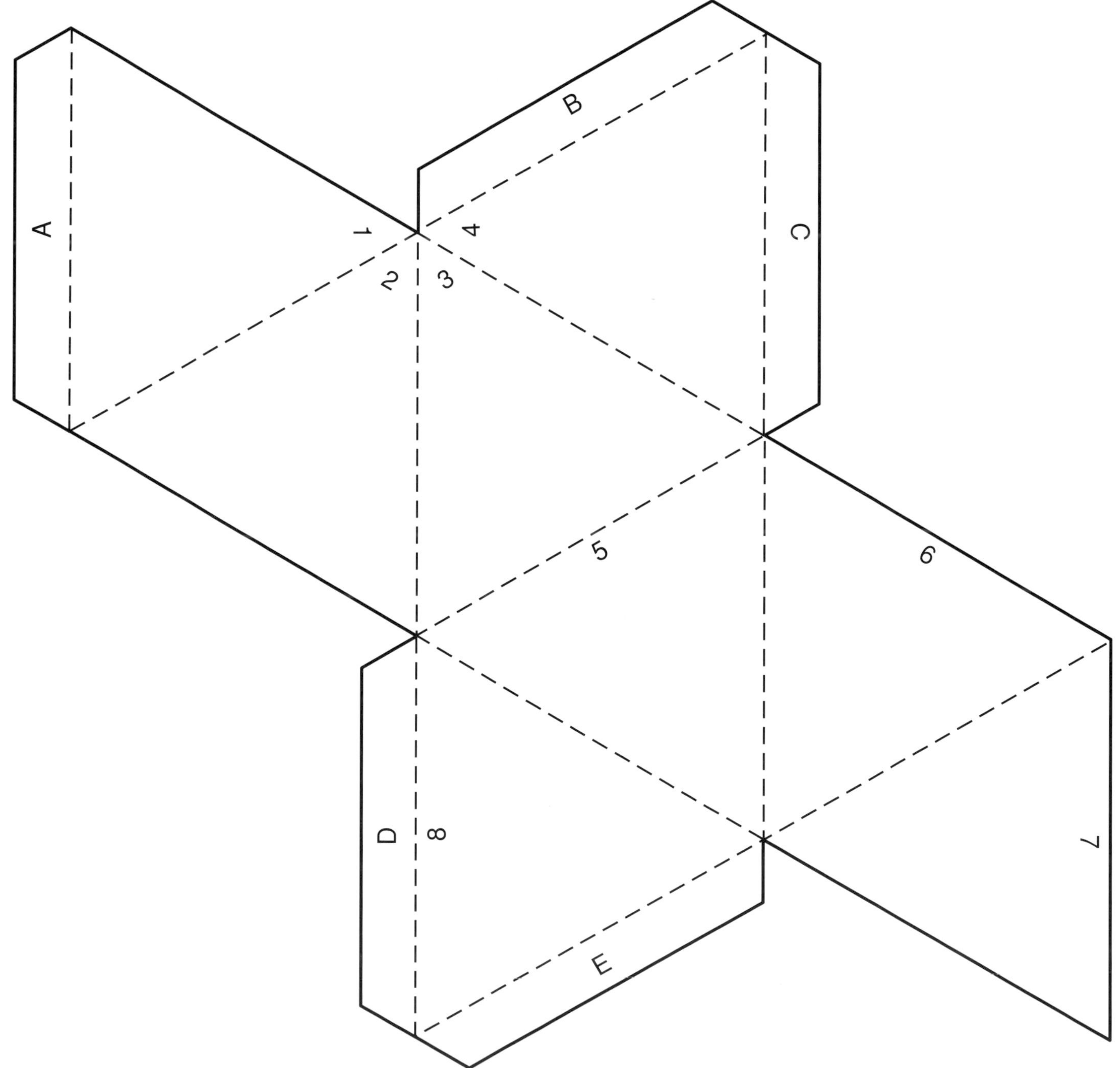




 **Note to the teacher:** Use this reproducible with "Geo-Scavenger Hunt" on page 106.

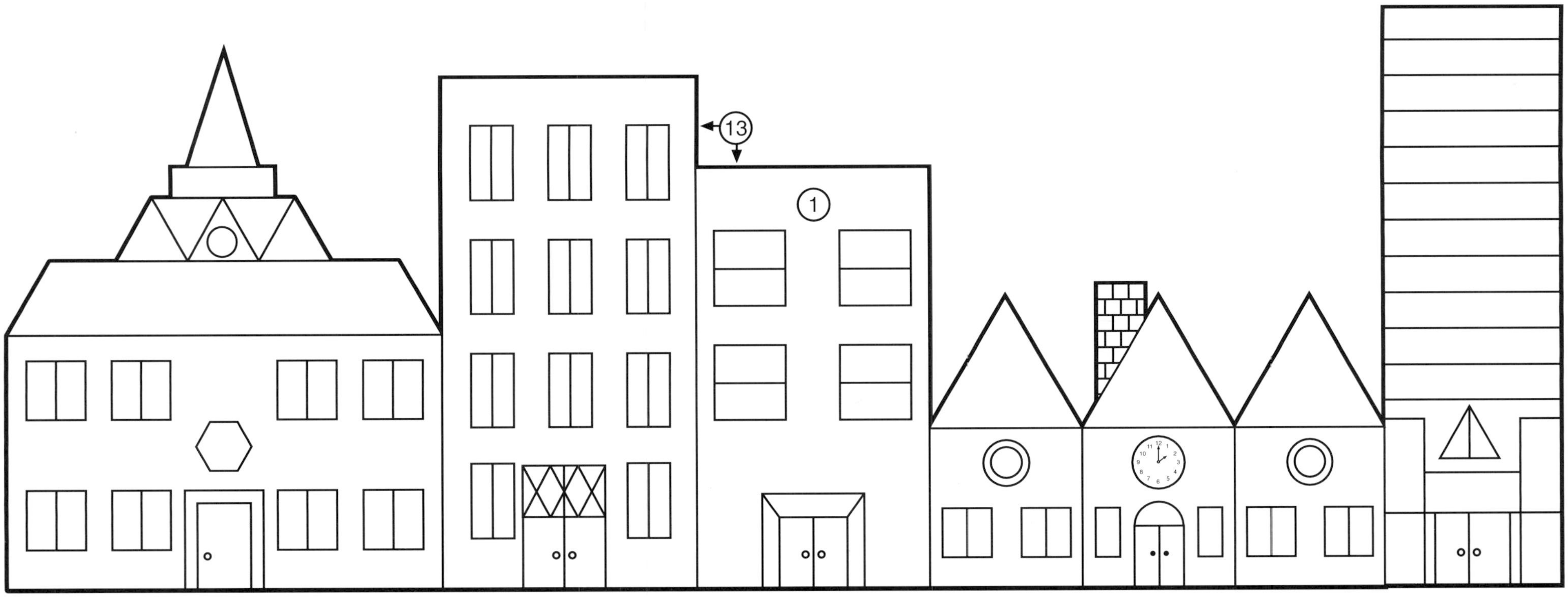

Name ______________________________ Geometry vocabulary

# Welcome to Geo-Village!

How many of the following geometry terms can you find illustrated in Geo-Village? Find at least one example of each term. Write the number in a circle; then draw an arrow to the part of the village where that word is illustrated. Two examples (1 and 13) have been done for you.

1. plane
2. point
3. line segment
4. right angle
5. acute angle
6. obtuse angle
7. line of symmetry
8. symmetric figure
9. congruent figures
10. vertex
11. diagonal
12. intersecting lines
13. perpendicular lines
14. parallel lines
15. square
16. rectangle
17. trapezoid
18. parallelogram
19. rhombus
20. scalene triangle
21. isosceles triangle
22. equilateral triangle
23. acute triangle
24. right triangle
25. circle
26. semicircle
27. pentagon
28. hexagon
29. octagon
30. translation (slide)
31. rotation (turn)
32. reflection (flip)

**Bonus Box:** *Congruent figures* have the same size and shape. *Similar figures* have the same shape. If two shapes are congruent, they are also similar. But two similar shapes may not be congruent. Find three pairs of similar shapes in Geo-Village. Label the pairs A, B, and C.

**Note to the teacher:** Use this reproducible with "Welcome to Geo-Village!" on page 106.

# Taking a Bite out of Algebra!

## Creative Teaching Suggestions for Introducing Algebra Concepts

Patterns, relations, and functions—oh my! Intermediate graders may not be familiar with these algebra terms, but they have already begun to think and talk algebraically. Help your students make the connection between arithmetic and algebra with the following creative teaching ideas and reproducibles.

*by Irving P. Crump*

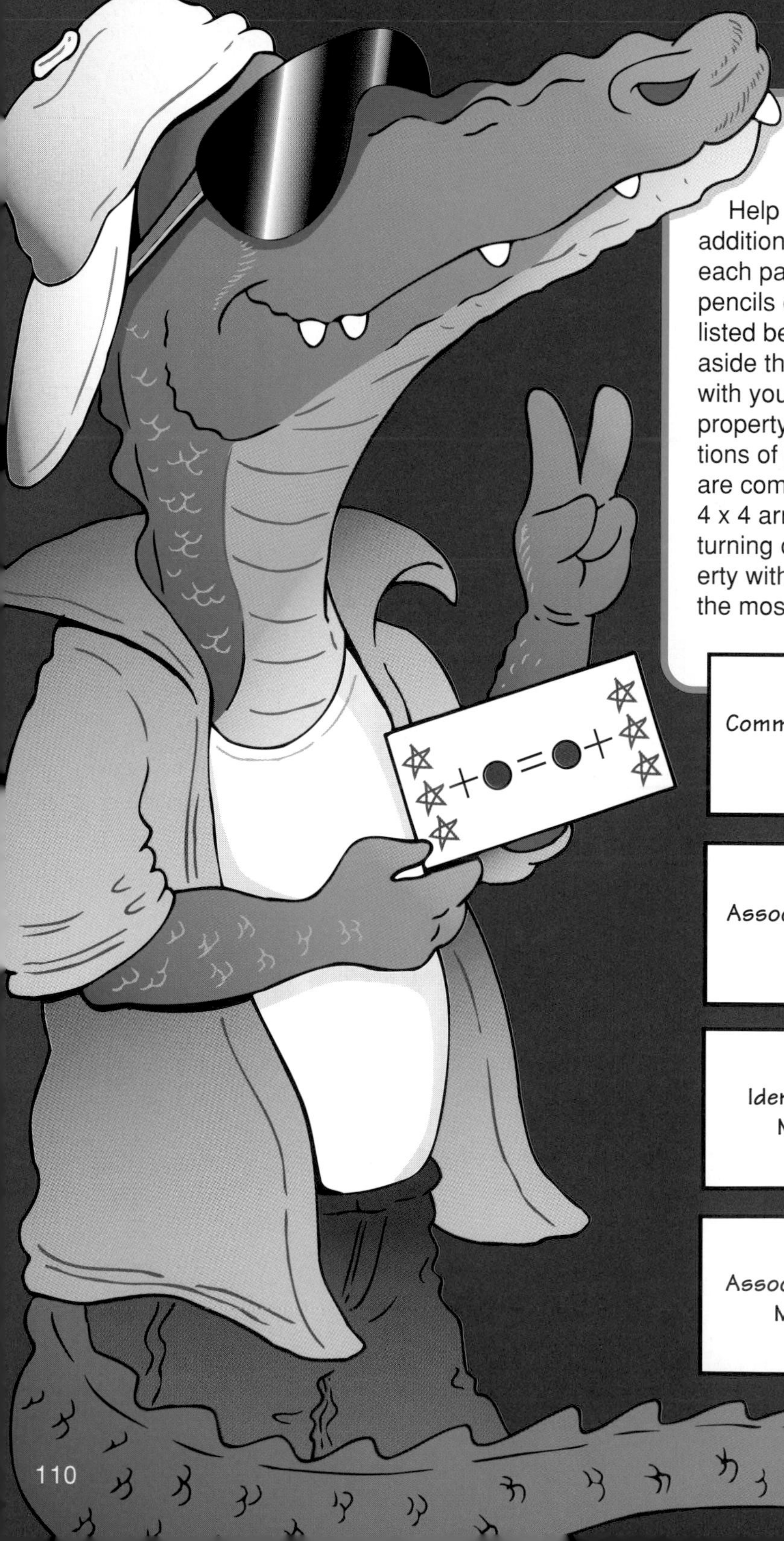

### Property Matches

**Skill: Understanding properties**

Help students better understand the special properties of addition and multiplication with this matching activity. Provide each pair of students with 16 large index cards and colored pencils or crayons. Instruct each pair to write each property listed below on a separate index card. Have students set aside the remaining eight cards. After reviewing the properties with your students, direct each twosome to illustrate each property on one of the eight remaining cards, using combinations of pictures, numbers, and symbols. When all 16 cards are completed, have each pair lay its cards upside down in a 4 x 4 array. Direct each twosome to play a matching game by turning over one pair of cards at a time, trying to match a property with its illustration. The winner is the player who makes the most correct matches.

| | |
|---|---|
| Commutative Property—Addition | Identity Property—Addition |
| Associative Property—Addition | Commutative Property—Multiplication |
| Identity Property—Multiplication | Property of Zero—Multiplication |
| Associative Property—Multiplication | Distributive Property |

## Input/Output Relay

**Skills: Basic operations, completing input/output tables**

Have students put on their algebraic thinking caps with this relay game! Begin by drawing two input/output tables like the one shown on opposite ends of the chalkboard. Next, divide the class into two teams, and have the first player from each team go to one of the tables on the board. Call out five numbers—such as 15, 18, 22, 41, and 36—for each player to write in the input column of his table. Remind students that an *input number* is the number that an operation rule is applied to, and that the *output number* is the result of that operation. Next, announce a rule, such as "add 13," for each player to write at the top of his table.

On a signal, the two players complete their tables by applying the rule to each number in the input column and writing the answer in the output column. When a student finishes, direct him to put down his chalk and turn around to face the class. With the class's assistance, check both players' tables. To score, award one point for each correct response, subtract a point for each incorrect response, and add a five-point bonus to the score of the student who correctly completed his table first. Continue play with other rules that are appropriate to use with the list of input numbers, such as "subtract 9" and "multiply by 2." Play additional rounds with new sets of input numbers and different rules.

| rule: | |
|---|---|
| input | output |
| | |
| | |
| | |
| | |
| | |

## Thinking in Reverse

**Skill: Inverse operations**

Understanding inverse operations and their relationships will help students when solving algebraic equations. After every student has had an opportunity to participate in the input/output relay above, continue with additional rounds in which students must determine the input numbers for a table. To play, provide a list of numbers for each player to write in the output column of his table, such as 48, 36, 12, 54, and 30. Next, call out the rule for each player to write at the top of his table, such as "times 6." Instruct each player to work in reverse to determine the input number that, when the rule is applied, results in the output number. Lead students to discover that to find each input number, they should perform the inverse operation. For example, students should *divide* by 6 since the rule is *times* six. Play and score the relay game as described in "Input/Output Relay" above.

To further extend this activity, provide one or both numbers for each row of an input/output table like the sample shown. Then direct the two players to complete the table by first determining the rule, then filling in the missing input and output numbers.

| rule: | |
|---|---|
| input | output |
| ? | 20 |
| ? | 26 |
| 10 | 22 |
| 30 | 42 |
| 19 | ? |

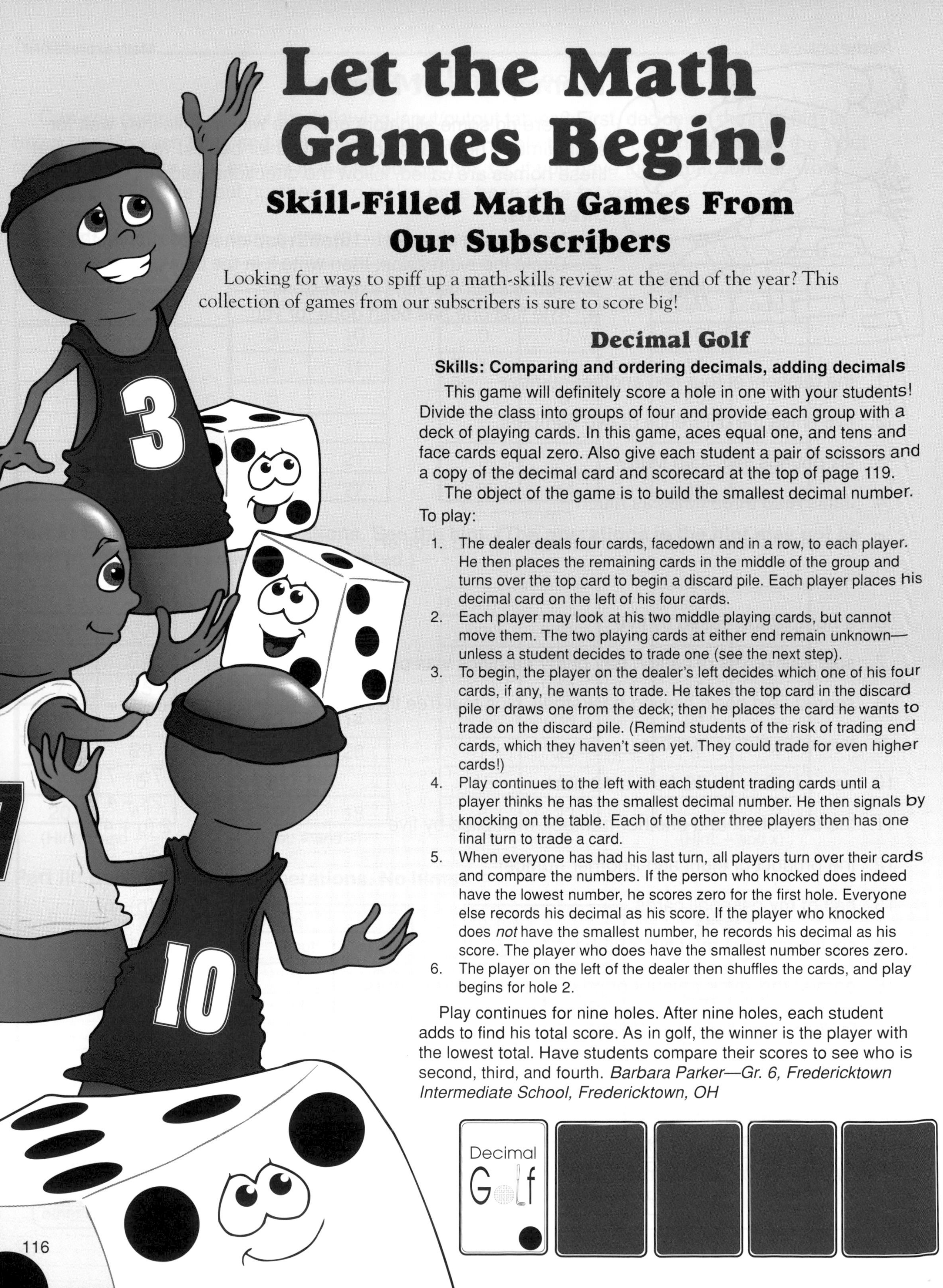


# Let the Math Games Begin!

## Skill-Filled Math Games From Our Subscribers

Looking for ways to spiff up a math-skills review at the end of the year? This collection of games from our subscribers is sure to score big!

### Decimal Golf

**Skills: Comparing and ordering decimals, adding decimals**

This game will definitely score a hole in one with your students! Divide the class into groups of four and provide each group with a deck of playing cards. In this game, aces equal one, and tens and face cards equal zero. Also give each student a pair of scissors and a copy of the decimal card and scorecard at the top of page 119.

The object of the game is to build the smallest decimal number.

To play:

1. The dealer deals four cards, facedown and in a row, to each player. He then places the remaining cards in the middle of the group and turns over the top card to begin a discard pile. Each player places his decimal card on the left of his four cards.
2. Each player may look at his two middle playing cards, but cannot move them. The two playing cards at either end remain unknown—unless a student decides to trade one (see the next step).
3. To begin, the player on the dealer's left decides which one of his four cards, if any, he wants to trade. He takes the top card in the discard pile or draws one from the deck; then he places the card he wants to trade on the discard pile. (Remind students of the risk of trading end cards, which they haven't seen yet. They could trade for even higher cards!)
4. Play continues to the left with each student trading cards until a player thinks he has the smallest decimal number. He then signals by knocking on the table. Each of the other three players then has one final turn to trade a card.
5. When everyone has had his last turn, all players turn over their cards and compare the numbers. If the person who knocked does indeed have the lowest number, he scores zero for the first hole. Everyone else records his decimal as his score. If the player who knocked does *not* have the smallest number, he records his decimal as his score. The player who does have the smallest number scores zero.
6. The player on the left of the dealer then shuffles the cards, and play begins for hole 2.

Play continues for nine holes. After nine holes, each student adds to find his total score. As in golf, the winner is the player with the lowest total. Have students compare their scores to see who is second, third, and fourth. *Barbara Parker—Gr. 6, Fredericktown Intermediate School, Fredericktown, OH*

| 3 | 9 | 7 | 4 | 6 | 2 |
|---|---|---|---|---|---|
| 8 | 2 | 6 | 8 | 1 | 4 |
| 6 | 7 | 4 | 3 | 5 | 9 |
| 7 | 6 | 9 | 1 | 7 | 1 |
| 5 | (3) | (8) | 2 | 5 | 3 |
| (1) | 2 | 5 | (4) | 8 | 9 |

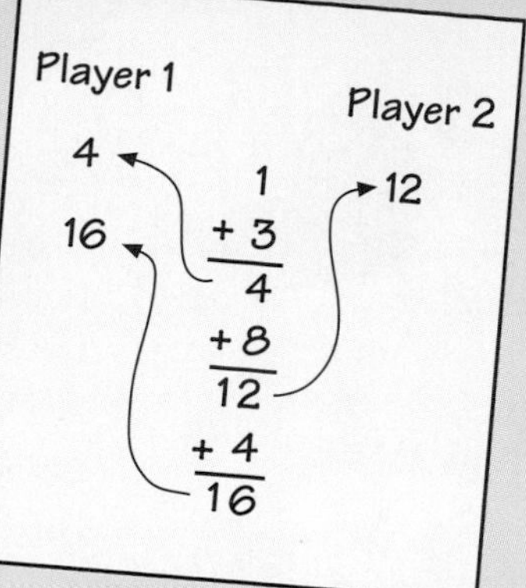


## The Fab Four Challenge

**Skills: Multiples, addition**

Have students face off for addition and multiplication practice with this nifty game for pairs. First, have each pair draw a 6 x 6 grid on a piece of paper. Direct a student in each pair to write "1" in each of four grid boxes. Have her partner write "2" in each of four remaining boxes. Then have students take turns writing four 3s, four 4s, four 5s, and so on until all 36 grid boxes are programmed with the numbers 1–9. To play:

1. Player 1 circles any corner number, draws a line connecting it to an adjacent or diagonal number, and circles that number. She then adds the two numbers and writes the sum on her paper as shown. This sum is the first addend in a running total. If the sum is a multiple of 4, she earns that number of points. (See the example: Player 1 circled 1 and 3, whose sum is 4. Since 4 is a multiple of 4, she earned 4 points. If she had instead circled 1 and 5, whose sum is *not* a multiple of 4, she would not have earned any points.)
2. Player 2 then draws a line connecting the last number circled by Player 1 to any uncircled adjacent or diagonal number and circles it. He should try to circle a number that, when added to the running total, results in a multiple of 4. (See the example: The running total is 4. Player 2 may circle 5, 7, 6, 9, 8, 5, or 2. He would earn points only if he circled 8, since 4 and 8 are the only numbers whose sum, 12, is a multiple of 4.)
3. The game continues with players taking turns connecting and circling numbers until all numbers in the grid have been circled. If no adjacent or diagonal numbers can be circled, a player can choose from any remaining unused numbers in the grid. The winner is the player with the most points at the end of the game.

Adapt this game by having students aim for multiples of other numbers, such as 5, 7, and 9. *Terry Healy—Grs. K–6 Gifted, Eugene Field Elementary, Manhattan, KS*

## What's It Worth?

**Skills: Place value, addition of large numbers**

To prepare this fun game of skill (and luck!), program a set of index cards with alphabet letters, one card per student. Next, write numbers on the board, one for each matching letter on a card. Include numbers up to the largest place value that your students have learned. Underline one digit in each number. To play:

1. Have the first player from Team 1 choose a letter card and go to the board.
2. The player circles the number on the board that matches the letter on her card. Then she reads the number aloud and announces the value of the underlined digit to the rest of the class. (Example: 91,892. "Ninety-one thousand eight hundred ninety-two. The value of 8 is 800.")
3. If she is correct, her team scores that number of points. (In the example in Step 2, the team would earn 91,892 points!)
4. Then the first player from Team 2 repeats Steps 1–2.

Each student keeps a running total of his team's points. The team with more points after all of the numbers on the board have been circled is the winner. *Leighton Rudd—Gr. 4, Bucklin Grade School, Bucklin, KS*

Starting Number
23
Target Range
3,000 – 3,100

Estimate 1: 42
23 x 42 = 966 Too low!
Estimate 2: 5
966 x 5 = 4,830 Too high!
Estimate 3: 0.8
4,830 x 0.8 = 3,864 Closer!
Estimate 4: 0.8
3,864 x 0.8 = 3,091.2 YES!

## Bull's Eye

**Skills: Estimation, using a calculator**

Need an activity to get your students on target with estimation? Try this challenging game! Write a starting number and target range on the board as shown. Have a student estimate a number that, when multiplied by the starting number, will result in a product within the target range. Have the student write his problem and answer on the board. If the student estimates too high or too low and the product misses the range, give another student a chance to estimate. Have this second student multiply the first student's product by a number to get a product within the target range. (If the first product is too high, remind the second student that he must multiply it by a decimal number in order to get closer to the target range.) Continue play until the range is reached. Then write a new target number and range on the board. Challenge the class to reach the new range in fewer estimates. *Marsha Schmus, Ypsilanti, MI*

## Target!

**Skills: Using coordinates, mental math**

This game, similar to Battleship®, provides lots of practice with using coordinates and mental math. Provide each student with a copy of the gameboard at the bottom of page 119. Instruct each student to use a marker to outline five "ships" in the grid, each consisting of adjacent boxes: one five-box ship, one four-box ship, and three three-box ships. Each ship must be either vertical or horizontal, and the ships cannot overlap.

To play, call out a pair of coordinates, such as (5, D), and have each student find the box at those coordinates. Next, give students a mental math problem to solve, such as "How many eggs are in four dozen?" Each student then writes her answer in that box. (Make a key on an extra copy of the grid.) Continue play until a student completely fills a ship with answers and calls out, "Target hit!" Check the student's answers. If she's correct, she scores the number of points equal to the size of the ship: either three, four, or five. If she has an incorrect answer, play continues. Play until all of a student's targets have been hit or time runs out (in which case, the player with the highest score wins). *Pat Forrester, Colorado Springs, CO*

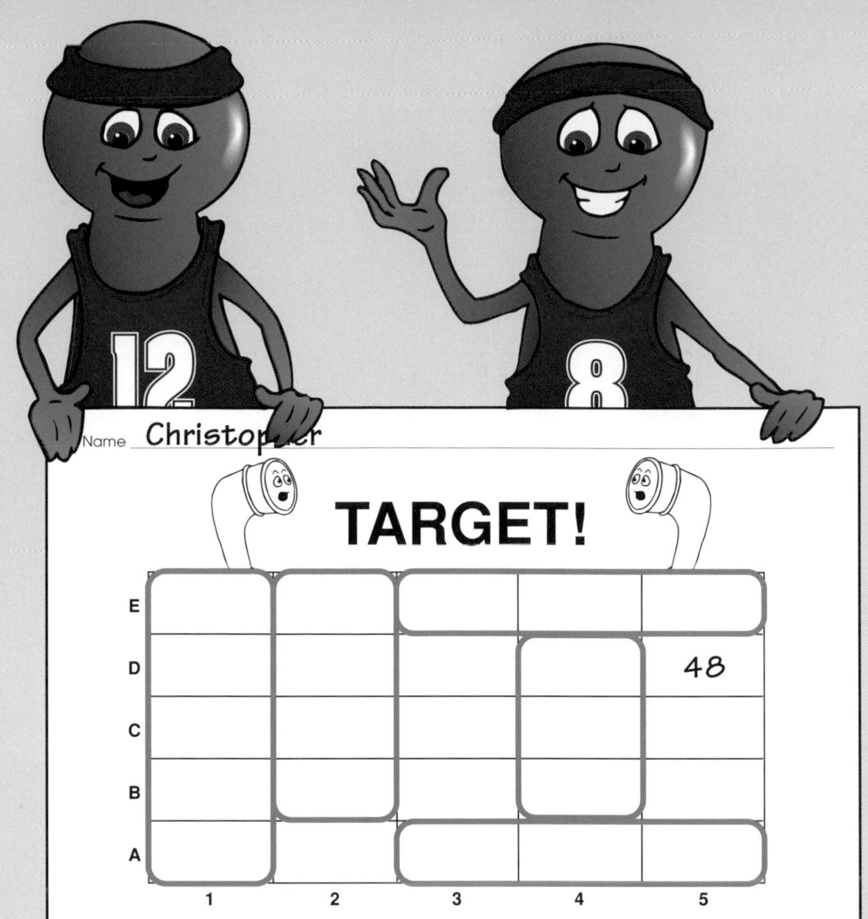

## Four Corners Math

**Skill: Review of any math skill**

Try this version of the popular game Four Corners to get your students up and moving—and doing math! To prepare, label the four corners of your classroom 1–4. Also label four index cards 1–4. To play:

1. Divide students into four teams. Have each team go to a corner.
2. Draw an index card and announce its number. The team standing in the matching corner plays the first round.
3. State a math problem for that team to solve. Allow the team about 20 seconds to solve it.
4. Call on one student in the team to give you the team's answer. If the answer is correct, each member of that team earns a point. If incorrect, no points are earned. Instruct each individual team member to keep up with the number of points he earns.
5. Next, tell every student to go to a different corner. (A team does not have to stay together. In fact, it's better if the teams split up.)
6. When everyone has moved to a different corner, mix up the four index cards. Then repeat Steps 2–5.

Continue play until you've called out a preset number of problems. Then direct all students to return to the corners at which they began the game. Have each team tally its final point total by adding all of the individual scores. Declare the team with the most points the winner. *Miriam A. Becker—Gr. 5, DuJardin School, Bloomingdale, IL*

## Decimal Card

Cut out the card below. Place it on the left of your four playing cards.

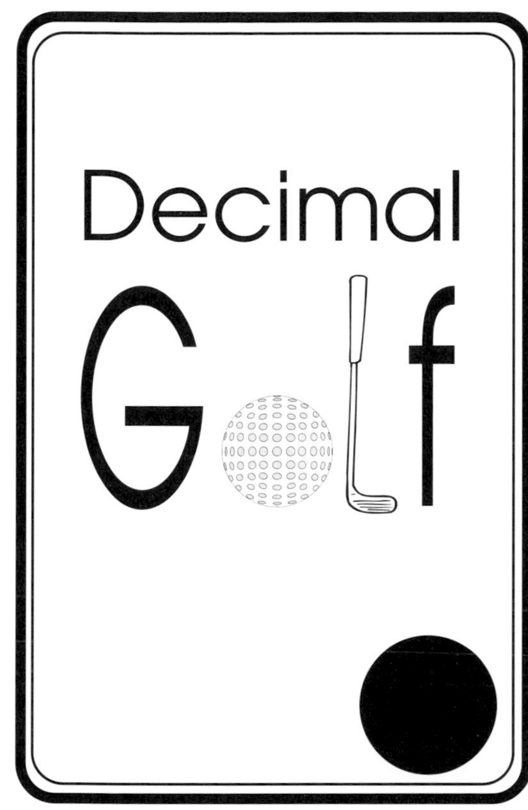


**Decimal Golf Scorecard**
Cut out the scorecard. Write your score for each hole in the blank provided.

Decimal Golf

**Remember!**
aces = 1
10s = 0
face cards = 0

Player: ______________________

| Hole | Score |
|---|---|
| #1 | ______ |
| #2 | ______ |
| #3 | ______ |
| #4 | ______ |
| #5 | ______ |
| #6 | ______ |
| #7 | ______ |
| #8 | ______ |
| #9 | ______ |
| Total score for nine holes: | ______ |



**Note to the teacher:** Use this half-page reproducible with "Decimal Golf" on page 116.

---

Name ______________________________

# TARGET!

| | | | | | |
|---|---|---|---|---|---|
| **E** | | | | | |
| **D** | | | | | |
| **C** | | | | | |
| **B** | | | | | |
| **A** | | | | | |
| | **1** | **2** | **3** | **4** | **5** |



**Note to the teacher:** Use this half-page reproducible with "Target!" on page 118.

Name ____________________



# Big Four

Challenge your classmates to a game of Big Four!

**Materials for two to four players:**

- calculators
- scratch paper and pencils
- scissors
- copy of this page for each player

**To prepare:**

1. Cut out the 24 game cards.
2. Spread out the number cards facedown.
3. Place all of the operation cards faceup.

**To play each game:**

1. Each player…
   - draws five number cards from her pile.
   - arranges the five number cards and the four operation cards—in any order— to make an equation. For example:

     | 6 | ÷ | 2 | x | 9 | + | 5 | – | 0 |

   - solves her equation and writes the answer on scratch paper.
2. Players check each other's answers.
3. If an answer is correct, the player records it on her scorecard. If the answer is incorrect, the player reworks the equation and records the correct answer.
4. Each player returns her number cards to the pile.
5. Play five rounds. Then add your answers for the five rounds to find your total for Game 1.

**Note:** Your answer may be a decimal number or a negative number.

| Game 1 | Game 2 |
|---|---|
| **Object: Find the largest possible answer.** | **Object: Find the smallest possible answer.** |
| Round 1: ________ | Round 1: ________ |
| Round 2: ________ | Round 2: ________ |
| Round 3: ________ | Round 3: ________ |
| Round 4: ________ | Round 4: ________ |
| Round 5: ________ | Round 5: ________ |
| Total for Game 1: ________ | Total for Game 2: ________ |

| 0 | 1 | 2 |
|---|---|---|
| 3 | 4 | 5 |
| 6 | 7 | 8 |
| 9 | 0 | 1 |
| 2 | 3 | 4 |
| 5 | 6 | 7 |
| 8 | 9 | + |
| – | x | ÷ |

 

Name ____________________ Game for two: adding and subtracting integers

# Down the Chute!

Luck...or skill? You decide when you challenge a partner to these integer games!

**Materials:** all aces, 2s, 3s, 4s, and 5s from a deck of playing cards

- Aces equal 1.
- All red cards are negative integers.
- All black cards are positive integers.

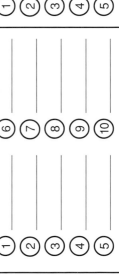

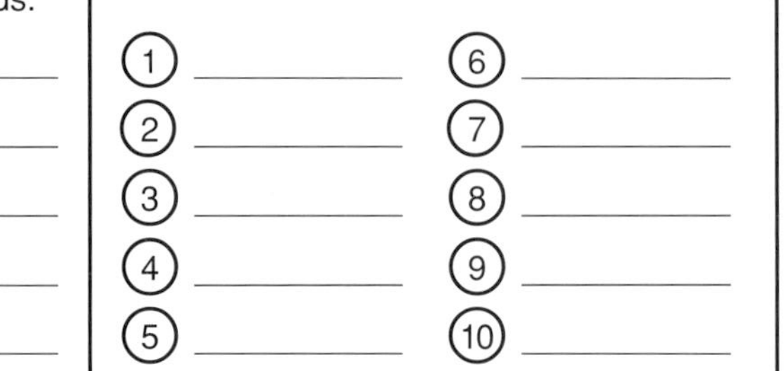


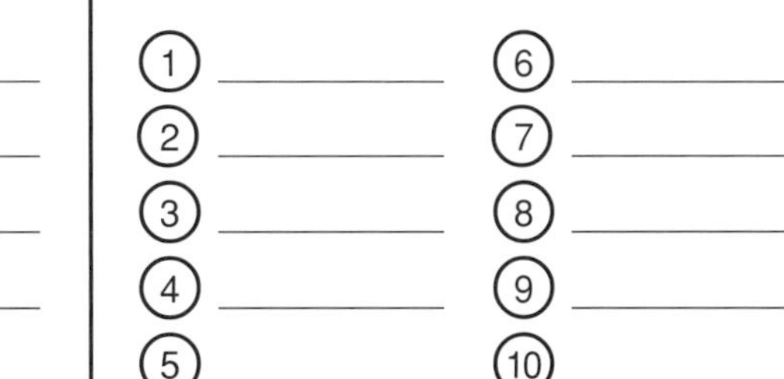

**How to play:**

1. Shuffle the cards and stack them facedown.
2. Player 1 draws the top card and lays it faceup in front of him.
3. Player 1 draws the next card and lays it faceup on the right of the first card.

## Game 1

4. Player 1 adds the two cards together and writes the answer in the blank below.
5. If the sum is
   - 0, score 10 points for Round 1
   - a positive integer, score 8 points
   - a negative integer, score 5 points
6. Player 2 then repeats Steps 2–5.
7. Play 10 rounds.
8. Add to find your total score.
9. The player with the higher score is the winner.

Note: After Round 5, reshuffle the cards.

(1) ______ (6) ______
(2) ______ (7) ______
(3) ______ (8) ______
(4) ______ (9) ______
(5) ______ (10) ______

Total: ______

## Game 2

4. Player 1 subtracts the second card from the first card and writes the answer in the blank below.
5. If the difference is
   - 0, score 5 points for Round 1
   - a positive integer, score 3 points
   - a negative integer, score 2 points
6. Player 2 then repeats Steps 2–5.
7. Play 10 rounds.
8. Add to find your total score.
9. The player with the lower score is the winner.

Note: After Round 5, reshuffle the cards.

(1) ______ (6) ______
(2) ______ (7) ______
(3) ______ (8) ______
(4) ______ (9) ______
(5) ______ (10) ______

Total: ______

## Game 3

4. Player 1 adds the two cards together and writes the answer in the blank below.
5. The sum is Player 1's score for Round 1.
6. Player 2 then repeats Steps 2–5.
7. Play 10 rounds.
8. Add to find your total score.
9. The player with the higher score is the winner.

Note: After Round 5, reshuffle the cards.

(1) ______ (6) ______
(2) ______ (7) ______
(3) ______ (8) ______
(4) ______ (9) ______
(5) ______ (10) ______

Total: ______

## Game 4

4. Player 1 subtracts the second card from the first card and writes the answer in the blank below.
5. The difference is Player 1's score for Round 1.
6. Player 2 then repeats Steps 2–5.
7. Play 10 rounds.
8. Add to find your total score.
9. The player with the lower score is the winner.

Note: After Round 5, reshuffle the cards.

(1) ______ (6) ______
(2) ______ (7) ______
(3) ______ (8) ______
(4) ______ (9) ______
(5) ______ (10) ______

Total: ______



**Note to the teacher:** Each student will need a copy of this sheet.

# Fired Up About Fractions

Looking for some hot ideas to help spark your students' understanding of basic fraction concepts? Check out the following creative activities and reproducibles. They're sure to add a little sizzle to your math lessons!

*by Irving P. Crump*

## Mmmm...Good Math!

**Skills: Fractions as parts of a whole, adding and subtracting like denominators**

Reinforce addition and subtraction of like fractions with this yummy idea! Provide each student with a Hershey's® milk chocolate bar (1.55 oz.) and a paper towel. Direct each student to unwrap her candy bar and place it on the towel. Tell students that the candy bar represents one whole and that it is divided into 12 equal parts. Ask them how many twelfths make up the whole bar *(12);* then write this equation on the chalkboard: $1 = {}^{12}/_{12}$. Next, have each student break her candy bar into individual pieces, place them in groups of 2, and illustrate the groups as shown on her paper. Ask how many groups are formed *(6)*. Tell students that each group represents $^1/_6$ of the whole bar; then ask how many sixths are in the entire bar *(6)*. Next, have each student place the pieces in groups of 3 and illustrate the groups. Ask how many groups are formed *(4);* then tell students that each group represents $^1/_4$ of the bar. Repeat with groups of 4 (for $^1/_3$) and 6 (for $^1/_2$).

Next, copy each problem shown on the board and have students use their candy bars to help them solve each one. Complete the activity by inviting students to eat their math manipulatives!

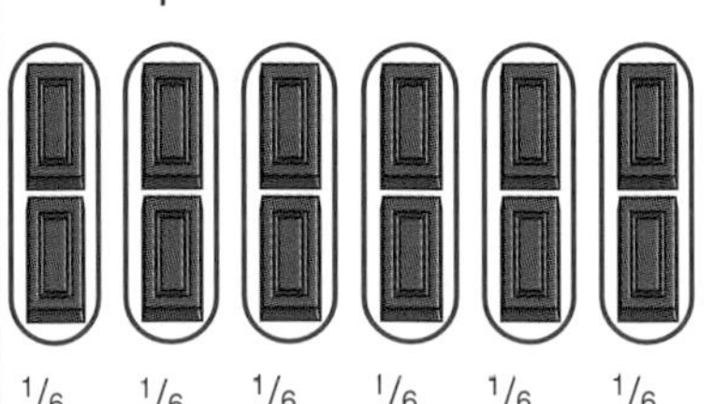


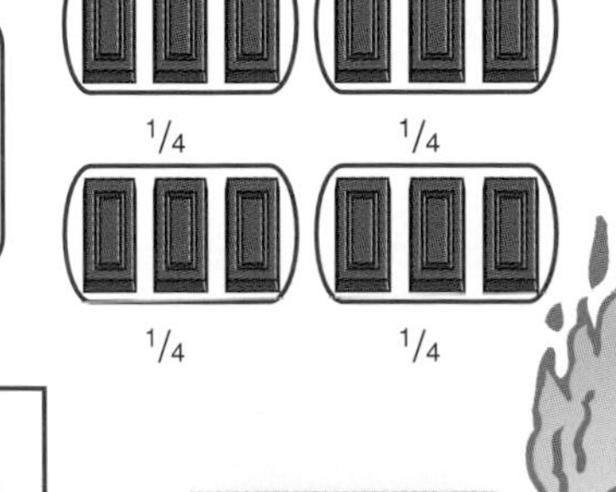


| | |
|---|---|
| $^7/_{12} + {}^4/_{12} =$ | $^1/_3 + {}^1/_3 =$ |
| $^1/_4 + {}^1/_4 =$ | $^1/_6 + {}^3/_6 =$ |
| $^5/_6 - {}^2/_6 =$ | $^3/_{12} + {}^2/_{12} =$ |
| $^5/_{12} - {}^3/_{12} =$ | $^2/_3 - {}^1/_3 =$ |

## In the Chips

**Skills: Fractions as parts of a set, addition and subtraction of unlike denominators**

Students often add and subtract fractions with unlike denominators—before finding the least common denominator. This activity helps students better understand why finding the least common denominator is necessary. Divide students into pairs and provide each pair with at least 40 chips (or paper squares) and six small sticky notes. Review with students how fractions are used to show parts of a set. Then have each pair count out 12 chips, label a sticky note "1 set," and place the sticky note under the set. Next, have the pair use chips to build and then label models showing the fractions $^1/_2$ (6 chips), $^1/_3$ (4 chips), $^1/_4$ (3 chips), $^1/_6$ (2 chips), and $^1/_{12}$ (1 chip). Ask, "If $^1/_3$ of the whole set of chips is 4, how many are in $^2/_3$? If $^1/_6$ of the set of chips is 2, how many are in $^5/_6$?" *(8, 10.)* Next, have the pairs use their remaining chips to solve the problems listed by combining or removing chips.

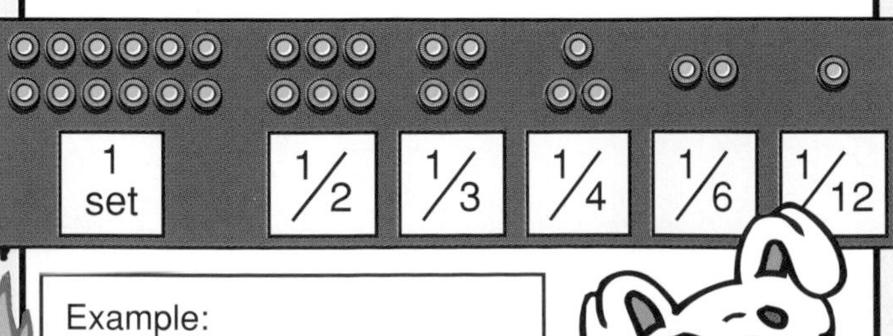


Example:
$^1/_2 + {}^1/_3 = {}^6/_{12} + {}^4/_{12} = {}^{10}/_{12} = {}^5/_6$

| | |
|---|---|
| $^1/_2 + {}^1/_4 =$ | $^2/_3 - {}^1/_6 =$ |
| $^1/_3 - {}^1/_{12} =$ | $^5/_{12} + {}^1/_3 =$ |
| $^1/_4 + {}^1/_6 =$ | $^3/_4 - {}^2/_3 =$ |

# A Picture Is Worth a Thousand Numbers

**Skill: Adding and subtracting like denominators**

This art project results in lots of visual reminders to help students remember how to add and subtract like denominators. Pair up students and provide each pair with two 9" x 6" sheets of drawing paper. Assign each pair a different denominator, such as 3, 4, 5, 6, 8, 9, 10, 12, 15, 16, 18, 20, etc. Have the students in each pair work together to illustrate an addition and a subtraction problem with fractions having their assigned denominator. Instruct each pair to include one problem that illustrates a fractional part of a whole and one that illustrates a fractional part of a set. Share the examples shown. Display students' completed drawings on a bulletin board or wall space titled "A Picture Is Worth a Thousand Numbers!"

# LCD...ASAP!

**Skill: Naming least common denominators**

Challenge students to think on their feet with this mental-math activity! First, draw the grid shown on the board. Next, divide students into two teams. Have the first player from each team go to the board and stand to one side of the grid. Give each player a piece of chalk.

To play, roll a pair of dice and announce the sum. Roll the dice a second time and announce that sum. (Roll again if the sum is the same as the first one.) The object of the game is to see which player at the board can first name the least common denominator of the two sums. The first player to call out the correct LCD is awarded five points. If the LCD is in the grid, she circles it and earns a five-point bonus. (If the LCD is a two- or three-digit number, its digits must be adjacent to each other vertically, horizontally, or diagonally.) If the player calls out an incorrect LCD, her opponent then gets a chance to name it and find it in the grid. Numbers in the grid can be circled more than once. Continue play until every student has had a turn or until a team reaches a predetermined total.

| | | | | |
|---|---|---|---|---|
| 1 | 0 | 8 | 2 | 2 |
| 1 | 2 | 4 | 5 | 7 |
| 0 | 5 | 1 | 0 | 5 |
| 5 | 8 | 0 | 6 | 9 |
| 4 | 4 | 3 | 3 | 9 |

# Pairing Up for Sums and Differences

**Skill: Adding and subtracting unlike denominators**

Students know that they can multiply two denominators together to determine a common denominator, but it may not be the *least* common denominator. Give students practice in finding LCDs—and adding and subtracting fractions with unlike denominators—with this fun movement activity.

Provide each student with an index card and a safety pin. Assign each student one of the fractions listed to write on his index card. (Two students may have the same fraction.) Have each student pin his card near his shoulder. On a signal, have each student pair up with a partner whose fraction has a different denominator. Direct the partners to add the two fractions shown on their index cards. While students are working, choose any two fractions with unlike denominators from the list, find their sum, and then write it on the board. When students finish their work, announce that any pair who has a sum that matches yours is to go to the board and show the work for arriving at that sum. After checking that pair's work, continue the game by having students choose new partners. Repeat the steps, alternating rounds of adding and subtracting.

1/2
1/3
2/3
1/4
3/4
3/5
4/5
1/6
5/6
2/7
5/7
3/8
7/8
5/9
3/10
7/10
7/12
11/12

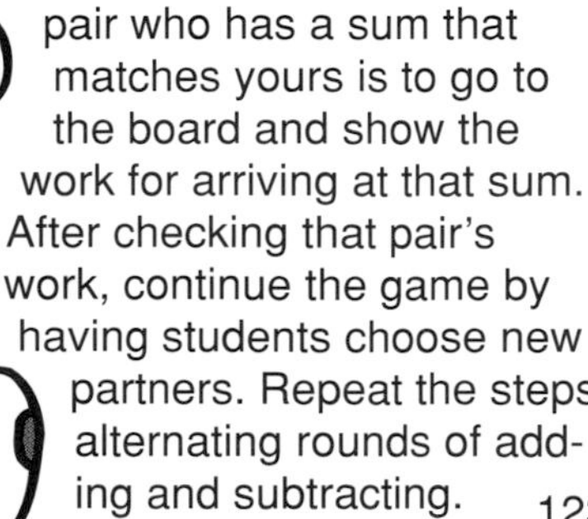

Name ____________________ Visual thinking

# Wild About Tiles

a 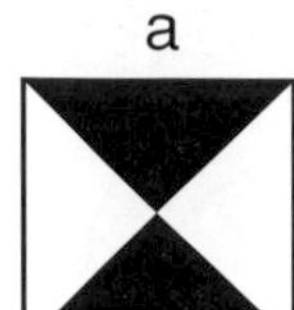 b 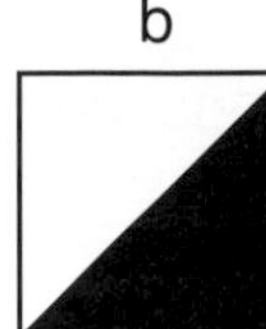 c  d 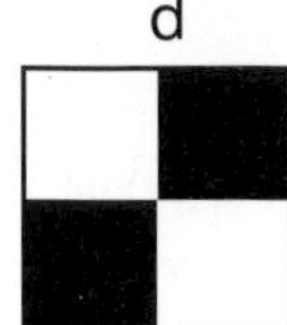 e  f 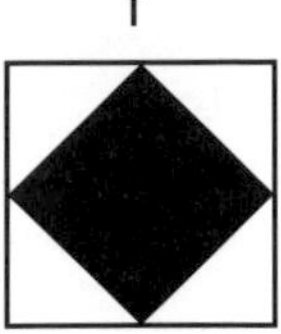 g 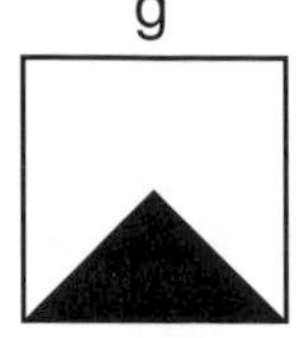 h 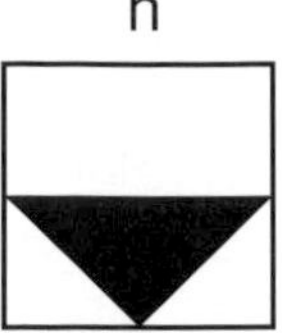

The tiles above were used to make each design shown below. Designs 1–3 are made up of 9 tiles each; designs 4 and 5 have 16 tiles each. First, decide which tiles were used to make each design; then decide how many copies of each tile were used. Finally, write a fraction to show the part of the design represented by each tile. Reduce each fraction to lowest terms.

The first one has been started for you.

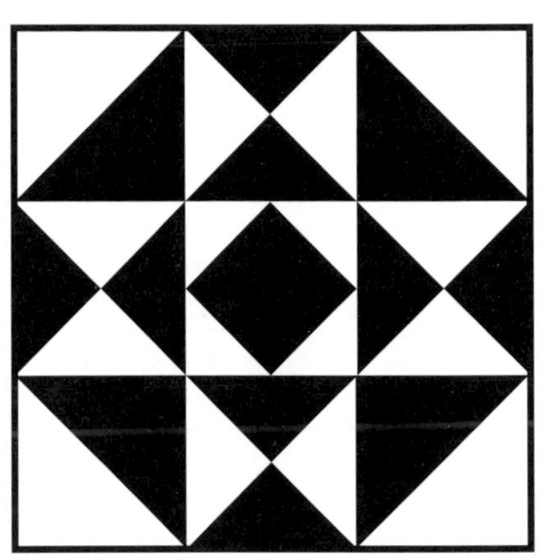

① __4__ of tile __C__ = __4/9__
____ of tile ____ = ____
____ of tile ____ = ____

② ____ of tile ____ = ____
____ of tile ____ = ____
____ of tile ____ = ____

③ ____ of tile ____ = ____
____ of tile ____ = ____
____ of tile ____ = ____

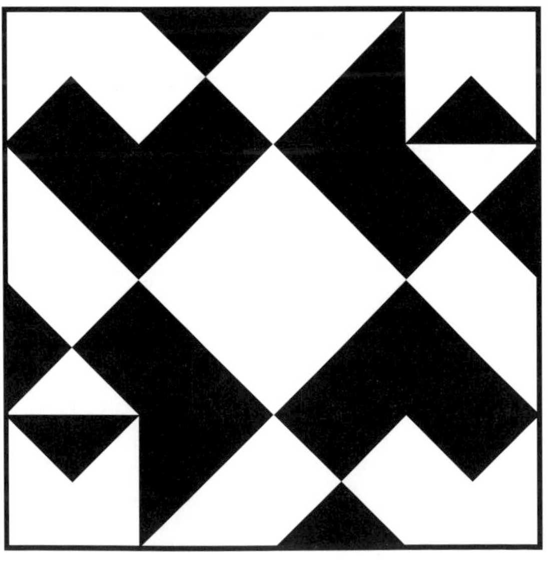

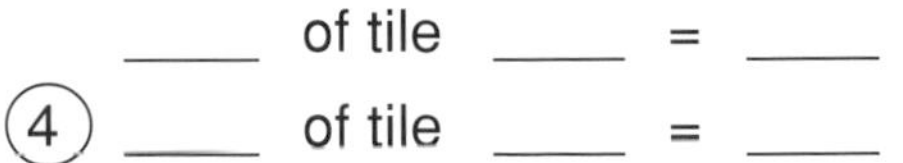

④ ____ of tile ____ = ____
____ of tile ____ = ____

⑤ ____ of tile ____ = ____
____ of tile ____ = ____
____ of tile ____ = ____

**Bonus Box:** Which tile was not included in any of the designs? Draw a 4 x 4 grid. Make a design on the grid that includes the tile that was not used.

Name________________________________________ Equivalent fractions, number sense

# Wacky Graphs

A group of fifth graders completed some surveys for a project. They created graphs on a computer to show their findings. But all of the titles and labels for the graphs disappeared!

Read each item below. Use number sense and equivalent fractions to help you match each item to its graph. The first one has been done for you.

a. 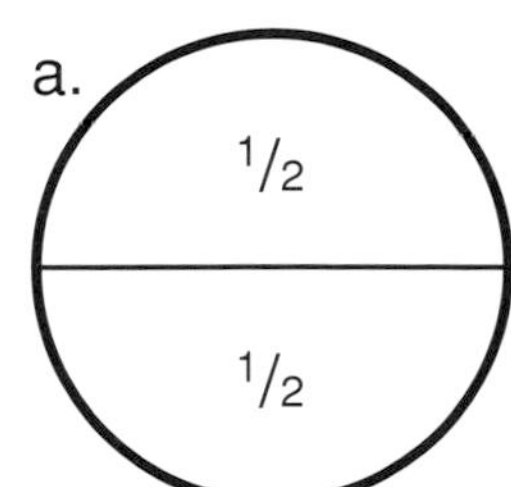


f. 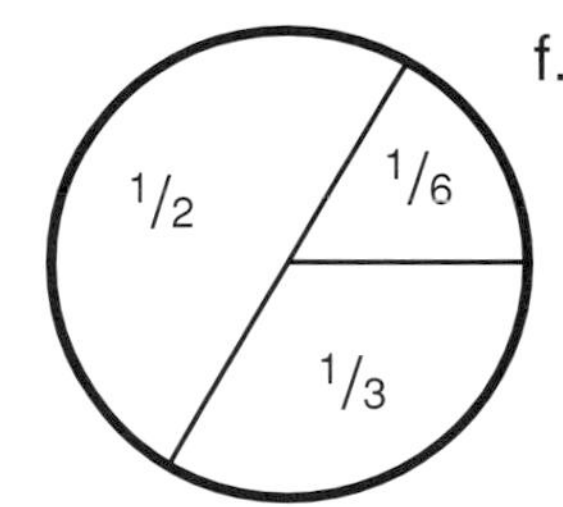


b. 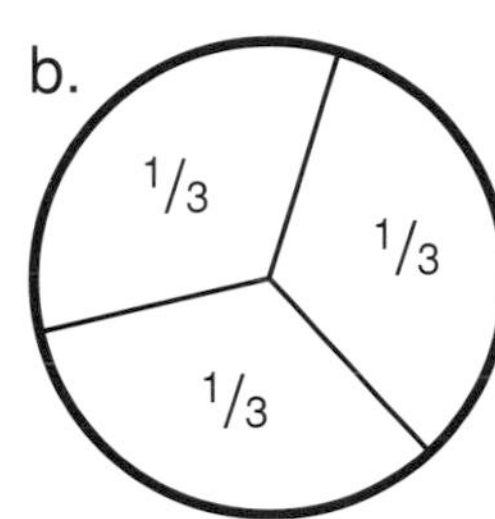


g. 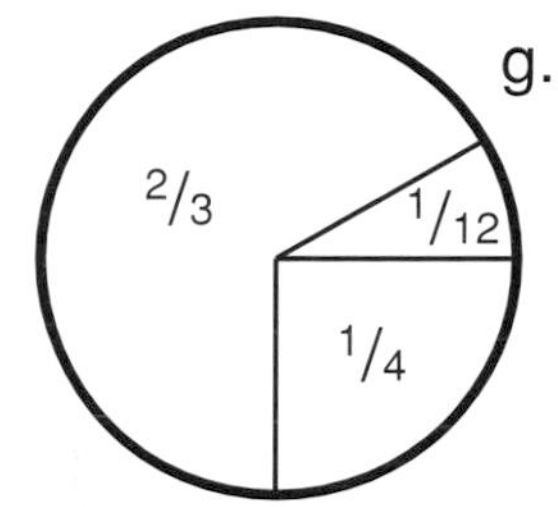


c. 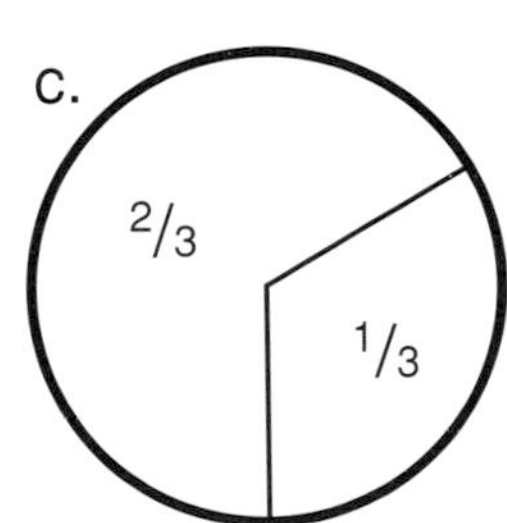


h. 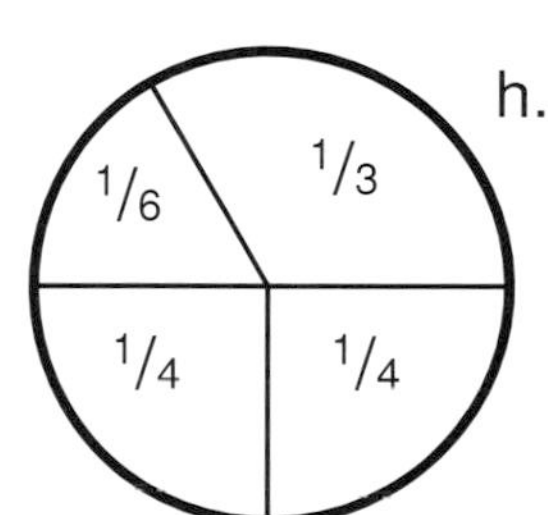


d. 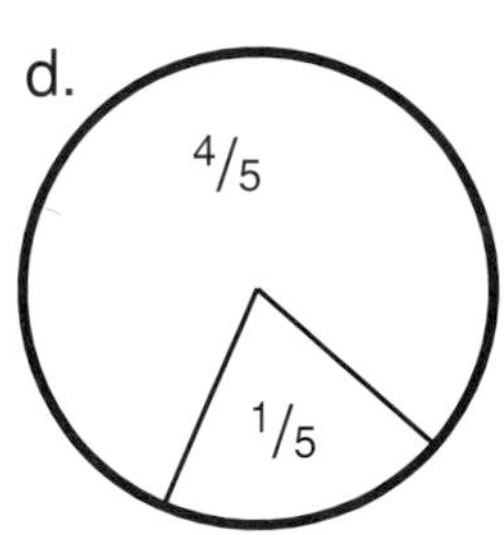


i. 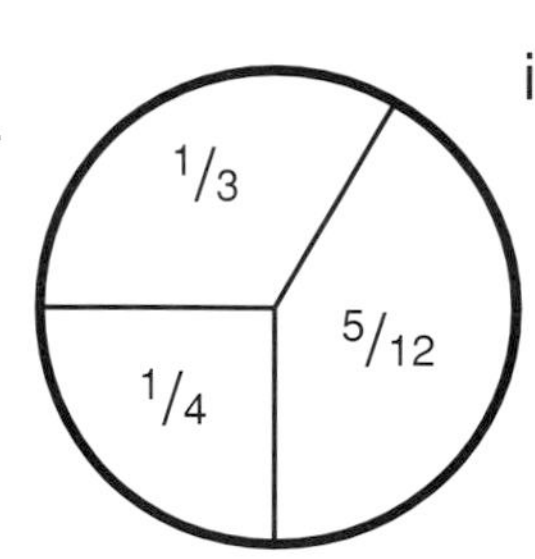


j. 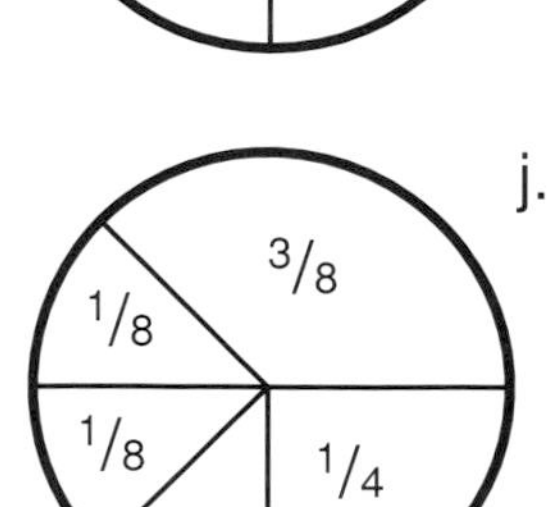


e. 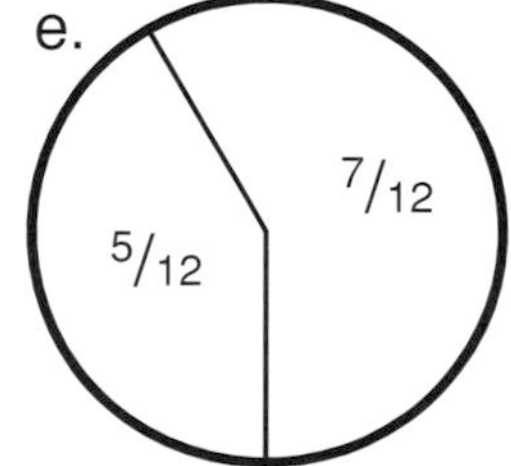

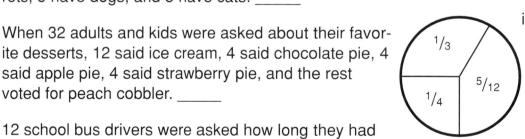

1. 24 adults were asked how often they read. 10 said they read every day. 14 said they read at least five days a week. ___e___
2. 20 students answered a question about a longer school year. 16 thought it would be a good idea; the others didn't! ______
3. 18 students were asked about their favorite music. 6 replied rap, 9 said pop, and 3 said country. ______
4. 28 kids were asked about their favorite pizza toppings. 14 like pepperoni, and 14 prefer cheese. ______
5. 48 adults were asked to name their favorite television news network. 20 said CNN, 16 replied CBS, and 12 said ABC. ______
6. Of the 30 students who were asked if they had ever eaten asparagus, 20 said no and the rest said yes. ______
7. 15 students were asked about their pets. 5 have ferrets, 5 have dogs, and 5 have cats. ______
8. When 32 adults and kids were asked about their favorite desserts, 12 said ice cream, 4 said chocolate pie, 4 said apple pie, 4 said strawberry pie, and the rest voted for peach cobbler. ______
9. 12 school bus drivers were asked how long they had been driving buses. 3 replied less than a year, 3 replied 1–3 years, 4 said 4–7 years, and 2 have been driving 8 years or more. ______
10. 36 fifth graders were asked to name their favorite sports. 24 answered soccer, 9 said basketball, and 3 replied baseball. ______

**BONUS BOX:** Take a look at the 7 different denominators in the graphs above. What is the least common denominator of those 7 numbers? (Hint: It has 3 digits!)

Name ____________________ 



# Magic Squares

These squares are all magical in some way. Just follow the directions for completing each set.

In each square, circle three fractions in a row that are in lowest terms.

1.

| | | |
|---|---|---|
| 6/9 | 6/18 | 11/22 |
| 3/7 | 4/5 | 9/10 |
| 5/15 | 3/9 | 2/4 |

2.

| | | |
|---|---|---|
| 6/9 | 5/9 | 2/3 |
| 5/10 | 1/9 | 3/15 |
| 7/8 | 4/8 | 6/8 |

3.

| | | |
|---|---|---|
| 12/15 | 6/7 | 3/5 |
| 7/21 | 11/14 | 17/20 |
| 10/16 | 14/18 | 4/9 |

In each square, circle three fractions in a row that are equivalent to each other.

4.

| | | |
|---|---|---|
| 8/10 | 3/5 | 1/2 |
| 4/5 | 12/20 | 2/3 |
| 5/20 | 6/10 | 10/12 |

5.

| | | |
|---|---|---|
| 5/6 | 10/18 | 2/3 |
| 6/9 | 9/12 | 3/4 |
| 3/4 | 12/16 | 6/8 |

6.

| | | |
|---|---|---|
| 1/2 | 2/4 | 3/9 |
| 10/18 | 10/20 | 4/10 |
| 3/6 | 3/5 | 6/12 |

Circle three fractions in a row that are equivalent to the following:

7. 4/5

| | | |
|---|---|---|
| 18/30 | 16/20 | 8/10 |
| 10/18 | 20/25 | 12/20 |
| 12/15 | 20/32 | 16/25 |

8. 2/3

| | | |
|---|---|---|
| 12/20 | 10/15 | 8/12 |
| 4/6 | 6/9 | 16/28 |
| 6/12 | 16/24 | 10/18 |

9. 5/6

| | | |
|---|---|---|
| 10/12 | 8/18 | 30/42 |
| 25/30 | 35/40 | 20/24 |
| 15/18 | 40/42 | 15/20 |

In each square, circle the fraction that is *not* equivalent to the other eight.

10.

| | | |
|---|---|---|
| 4/8 | 6/12 | 1/2 |
| 2/4 | 5/10 | 9/18 |
| 13/28 | 12/24 | 3/6 |

11.

| | | |
|---|---|---|
| 2/8 | 5/20 | 3/12 |
| 10/40 | 6/24 | 1/4 |
| 4/16 | 10/32 | 9/36 |

12.

| | | |
|---|---|---|
| 16/40 | 8/20 | 12/30 |
| 6/15 | 4/10 | 2/5 |
| 10/25 | 14/35 | 20/45 |

**BONUS BOX:** Make a 3 x 3 grid. Write each of the digits 1–9 in the grid so that the sum of the digits in each row (vertical, horizontal, and diagonal) is 15.

# Social Studies Units

# What's Up Down Under?

## Introducing Students to Australia

In September 2000, all eyes were on Sydney, Australia, as it hosted the Summer Olympic® Games. Help your kids learn about the land down under with the following creative activities.

*with ideas by Kelli Plaxco and Jennifer Munnerlyn*

### Moving to Oz

**Skills: Research skills, creative thinking**

Use this idea to make "Oz"—slang for *Australia*—an instant hot spot for your students. Request pamphlets on Australia from a local travel agent, use the Internet sites suggested below, or have various research materials on hand for students to review. Then read aloud *Alexander and the Terrible, Horrible, No Good, Very Bad Day* by Judith Viorst (Aladdin Paperbacks, 1987). In the story, Alexander has a bad day and decides that his life would be better if he moved to Australia. After reading the story, direct each student (or student pair) to make a travel brochure or poster aimed at convincing Alexander's mother to indeed let him move to Australia. Display the projects around the room during the unit to keep students in an Aussie frame of mind!

**Oz on the Internet:**
http://www.chateaudebrou.com/australie/english/indexva.htm
http://www.tourism.org.au
*(current as of 2-00)*

### Australia's "Oz-some" Animals

**Skills: Research skills, creative writing**

Head with your students to the Australian outback to learn about some of nature's most resilient and extraordinary animals. Begin by explaining to students that all native Australian mammals are either *monotremes* (mammals that lay eggs) or *marsupials* (mammals that give birth to embryos that develop in the mother's pouch). Direct each student to choose a monotreme or marsupial from the list below. Then let her research her mammal and complete one of the projects below. Set aside time for each student to present her Aussie animal to the class.

**Research Projects:** Each project should include information about what the animal looks like, where it lives, and how it behaves.

- Write a report from your animal's point of view.
- Pretend your animal is lost in Australia. Make a lost-and-found poster.
- Write a song about your animal. Use a familiar tune like "Row, Row, Row Your Boat."
- Give your animal an award. Design the award and describe why it should be presented to your animal.

**Monotremes:** platypus, spiny anteater
**Marsupials:** red kangaroo, banded anteater, cuscus, grey kangaroo, desert rat kangaroo, brush-tailed possum, banded hare, tree kangaroo, koala, Tasmanian devil, wombat, wallaby

**Australian Words**

*barbie* (n.): barbecue
*bickies* (n.): money
*bloke* (n.): man
*chalkie* (n.): teacher
*clobber* (n.): clothes
*cozzie* (n.): bathing suit
*flog* (v.): to sell
*jackaroo* (n.): cowboy
*lollies* (n.): candy
*mate* (n.): a person
*mozzies* (n.): mosquitoes
*postie* (n.): mail carrier
*rapt* (v.): delighted
*ripper* (adj.): good
*sheila* (n.): woman
*spunk* (adj.): attractive
*stickybeak* (n.): nosy person
*strine* (n.): slang
*tucker* (n.): food
*yakka* (n.): work

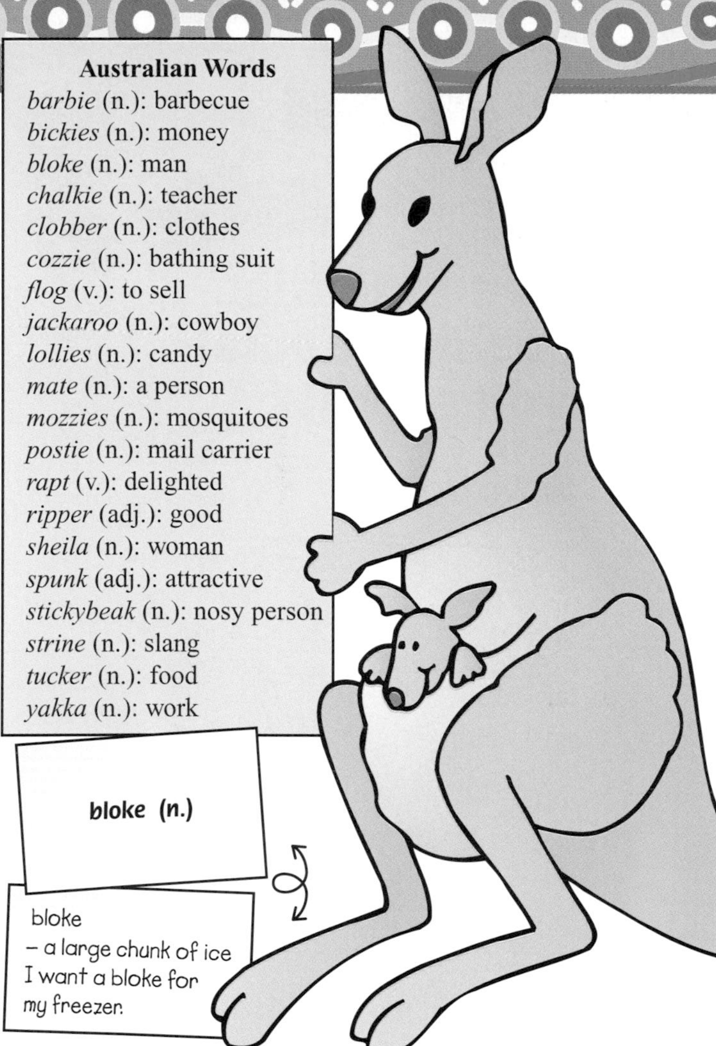

bloke (n.)
bloke
– a large chunk of ice
I want a bloke for
my freezer.


## EFOs (Early Flying Objects)

### Skill: Making a model

Thousands of years ago Australian Aborigines invented a hunting tool called a boomerang. This early throwing-stick could lift into the air like an airplane and return to its thrower due to the slight curve in its surface. Fly through your study of Australia by helping students make their own *bonzer* (that's Aussie for *great*) boomerangs! Instruct each student to glue an enlarged copy of the pattern shown to an 8" x 11" piece of tagboard; then have him cut it out. Next, have the child decorate the boomerang with markers or crayons before gently curving up its wings as shown. Allow each student to practice flying his boomerang in a large open area. Direct the student to hold his boomerang vertically between his thumb and index finger and spin it as he tosses it straight forward. To catch the boomerang, have the student clap it between his hands, as if catching a Frisbee® disc. As a follow-up activity, let each child make and test his own boomerang creations using different materials and designs. Many happy returns!

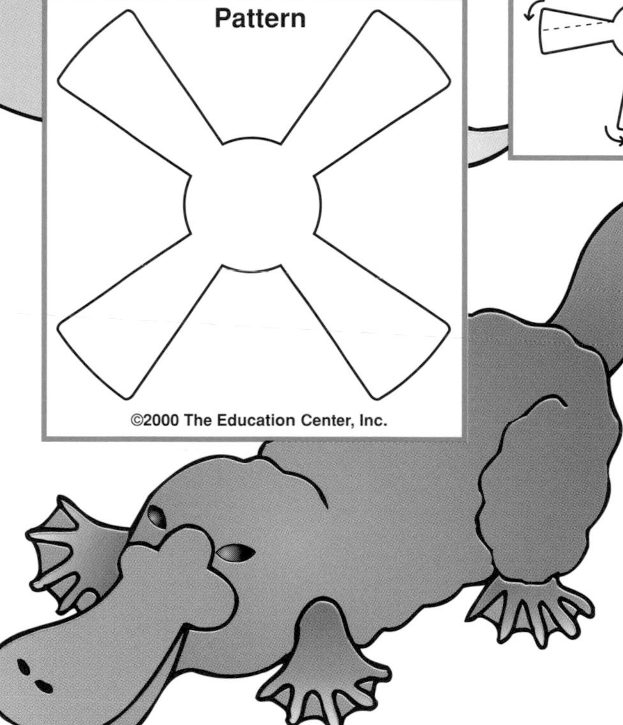


## Say What?

### Skills: Vocabulary, creative thinking

Use this *ripper* activity to make your young *blokes* and *sheilas* fluent in Aussie *strine!* Begin by progamming two sets of index cards with the Aussie words listed above (one word on each of two cards). On the backs of one set of cards, write the definition of each word. Next, pair students and give each pair a card labeled with a word only. Instruct the pair to use the part of speech to guess the word's meaning; then have the twosome label the card with a definition and a sample sentence as shown. Collect the cards and add them to the set you labeled earlier with the correct definitions.

To play, read aloud both definitions for one word and have students vote on the one they think is correct. (Direct each pair not to vote when its card is being read.) Keep track of the votes; then reward students whose definitions were voted on as correct with a small prize or treat.

## Awesome Aussie Reads

*Animal Dreaming: An Aboriginal Dreamtime Story* by Paul Morin (Silver Whistle, 1998)
*Australia* (Countries of the World) by Michael S. Dahl (Bridgestone Books, 1997)
*The Australian Outback and Its People* (People and Places) by Kate Darian-Smith (Thomson Learning, 1995)
*Down Under: Vanishing Cultures* by Jan Reynolds (Harcourt Brace Jovanovich, Publishers; 1992)
*Dreamtime: Aboriginal Stories* by Oodgeroo Noonuccal (Lothrop, Lee & Shepard Books; 1994)
*The Gift Stone* by Robyn Harbert Eversole (Alfred A. Knopf, Inc.; 1998)
*Tasmanian Devil: On Location* by Kathy Darling (Lothrop, Lee & Shepard Books; 1992)
*Where the Forest Meets the Sea* by Jeannie Baker (William Morrow & Company, Inc.; 1988)

On a Roll With Social Studies!
Creative Activities for Teaching Social Studies Skills


## Geography Bingo

**Skill: Identifying geographic locations**

Watch students' geography knowledge soar with this versatile game of bingo! To prepare, number the countries on a blank map of the continent you're currently studying. Include bodies of water and islands so that the total number is a multiple of five. Provide each student with a copy of the map. Then have him color each numbered location, making sure to use each color only five times (see the example).

Next, play a few practice rounds by calling out a location's name and its number. Have each student cover the place with a small scrap of white paper. When a student has covered five sections of the same color, he calls "Bingo!" Check by having the student state each number and its geographic name. Continue playing until several students win. Then have students clear their maps to begin a new game. This time, call out only the geographic names. Adapt this game to help students learn states and capitals or countries and their capitals.

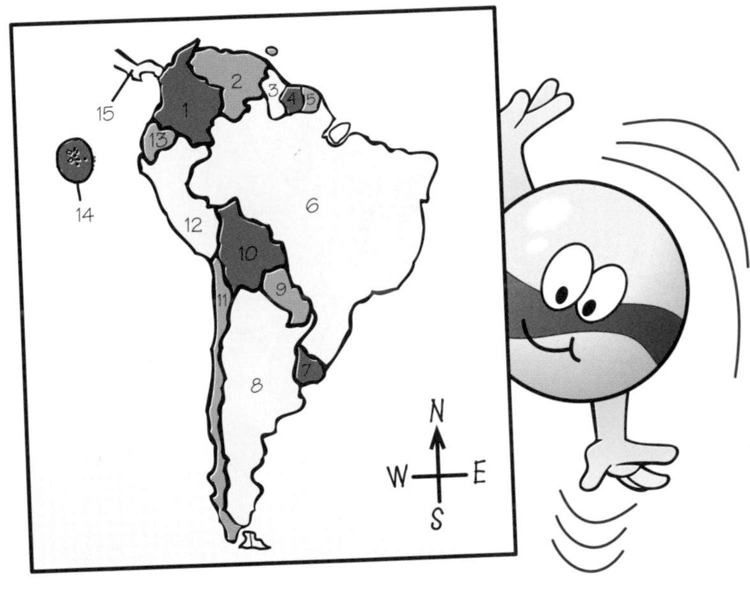


Denise Fischer—Gr. 6
Rio del Mar School
Aptos, CA

## Taxation Without Representation!

**Skill: Critical thinking**

What was taxation without representation *really* like? Try this simulation to help your students relate to an emotional event in our nation's history. Before studying the American Revolution, share with your students an official-looking (but fake!) letter stating that in one week the school lunch price will increase by one dollar. Tell students that you have no control over the situation; then ask how they feel about it. Students will likely get fired up and come up with ideas on how to fight the decision. Remind them they are *only* children; then the ideas will really start to fly! List their suggestions on the board and discuss the merit of each one. Once students have come up with several ideas, reveal that the letter isn't real. Further explain that you wanted to give them a better understanding of how the colonists felt when they learned they were going to be taxed. As a follow-up, have students design posters encouraging the colonists to stand up and fight for their rights.

Aimee Dunn—Gr. 4
Fairfield South Elementary
Fairfield, OH

## State Alphabet Book

**Skills: Creative thinking, art**

These alphabet books are the perfect culminating activity when studying your state (or a U.S. region or a country). First, have each student list a word or phrase that begins with each letter of the alphabet—and that is associated with or describes your state. Then, as a class, vote on the word for each letter that best represents your state. Next, divide students into groups and assign each group several letters and words. For each letter, have the group create a page for its word that includes a few descriptive sentences and an illustration. After all the pages are complete, bind them together to make "[Your state's] Alphabet Book."

C
ountry Music
Country music is a major industry and tourist attraction in Tennessee.


Cathy Ogg
Happy Valley Elementary
Elizabethton, TN

## Diggin' Archaeology

**Skills: Observation, making inferences**

Archaeologists make assumptions about items they discover—assumptions based on their own culture and background. Although these assumptions have to be made, students must understand that they are sometimes unreliable. Bring this concept to life with the following activity. Place several pocket-sized items (an old pen, small coins, a matchbook, an old watch, etc.) on a tray. Include at least one item that students may not readily recognize, such as an unusual tool. Tell students that the items were inside an old backpack found near the school and that the police have asked for help in determining who the owner might be. Next, divide students into groups and allow each group a few minutes to examine the items. Then have each group meet and collaboratively write a description of the person based on the items. Students will be surprised to discover that the groups may have very different ideas, even though they are all basing their assumptions on the same evidence. Not only does this brief activity give students a better understanding of the difficult tasks that archaeologists face, but it's also a great team-building exercise!

Dr. Donna M. McDougall
Kearny, AZ

## Parade of Historical Personalities

**Skills: Research, writing a report**

Make the famous people of any historical period come to life with this giant-sized project! Have each student select a historical figure from the time period you're studying; then have her research her person and write a brief report. Next, divide students into pairs. Give each pair two large sheets of white bulletin board paper. Instruct each student to trace her partner's body on a sheet of paper. Have students cut out their tracings. Then have them research the clothing of the time period and decorate their tracings to look like the people they have researched. Hang the completed cutouts and reports in a hallway to create a parade of historical personalities.

Sharon Seybold—Gr. 5
Loring Flemming Elementary
Blackwood, NJ

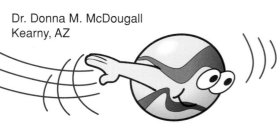

# Park It!

## ACTIVITIES ON UNITED STATES REGIONS AND NATIONAL PARKS

Looking for a new way to introduce your students to our nation's regions? Then pack your teaching bag of tricks with the following activities that highlight our spectacular national parks.

*with ideas by Simone Lepine*

### FAST FACTS ABOUT NATIONAL PARKS

- Currently the United States has 53 national parks, which are all part of the National Park System.
- The first national park in the world was Yellowstone National Park. Established in 1872, it covers over two million acres of land in Montana, Wyoming, and Idaho.
- A national park can only be created through an act of Congress.

## BACKPACK FAST FACTS

**Skills: Research, comparing and contrasting**

Review important research skills on your trek through our national parks with an activity that also sharpens comparing and contrasting skills. Assign each student two parks (in two different regions) from the list on page 136. Also give each child two copies of the graphic organizer on page 135. After each student has finished researching his parks and filling out both copies of page 135, have him glue one organizer to the front of a file folder and the other to the back. Then have him open the folder and draw a large Venn diagram inside. Finally, have the student compare and contrast his two parks and fill in his diagram. As an extension, challenge each student to use an atlas to plan a route between his two parks; then have him use the scale of miles to estimate the number of miles he would cover if he hiked from one to the other.

## UNPACKING MY BACKPACK

**Skill: Planning and giving an oral presentation**

Follow up the previous activity with a unique idea on how students can share what they learned about national parks. Have each student choose one of the two parks she researched in "Backpack Fast Facts." Then direct the student to pack her school backpack with items that represent information she learned about her park. (Provide spare backpacks for students who may need to use them. Also allow students to pack pictures or drawings as well as actual objects.) For example, a student who researched Rocky Mountain National Park might pack a sweater to represent the cold temperatures, an ice tray to represent the glaciers found there, and a plastic flower to represent the park's many wildflowers. Set aside time for each student to unpack her backpack in front of the class and share how each item relates to her park.

## MYSTERY PARK

**Skill: Identifying locations of U.S. regions, states, and national parks**

For another nifty activity to use after students have researched national parks, make one copy of page 136. Mask out the regions and list of parks on the boots; then make a class supply of the masked copy on tan construction paper. Have each student cut out his two boot patterns and label them as follows:

| | |
|---|---|
| front of boot 1: | three clues about a park he researched |
| back of boot 1: | name of the park written lightly in pencil |
| front of boot 2: | name of the park and the state(s) and region in which it is located |

Collect the boots. Then place the boots with clues in a shoebox labeled "CLUES" and the other boots in a shoebox labeled "PARKS." Set the boxes at a center and encourage students to try to pair the matching boots in their free time. Or use the boots in a game between two teams. To play, draw a PARKS boot and read aloud the park's name and the state in which it is located. If a player can identify the park's region, award his team one point. For a more challenging game, draw a CLUE boot and read it aloud. If a player can identify the name of the park, award his team one point. Award two extra points if the player can name the region and state(s) in which the park is located.

Grand Teton!
• Snake River runs through it
• Over 300,000 acres
• Named after highest mountain in park
Grand Teton National Park
Wyoming
West Region

## MAPPIN' IT OUT

**Skills: Reading a map, locating U.S. regions and states**

Map out a plan for practicing several important skills using the map skills reproducible on page 137. Review the U.S. regions and state postal abbreviations listed on page 136. Then give each student a copy of page 137 and crayons or colored pencils. After each child completes the page as directed, discuss the students' answers. Ask these questions: Which region has the most national parks on the map? Which region(s) has the least? Why do you think there are so many national parks in the West and so few in the Northeast? As an extension, divide the class into pairs. Give each twosome a copy of page 136. On this copy, have the students cross out the 14 parks listed on page 137. Then have them number the remaining parks 15–53. Finally, have the student pair label parks 15–53 by number on the map.

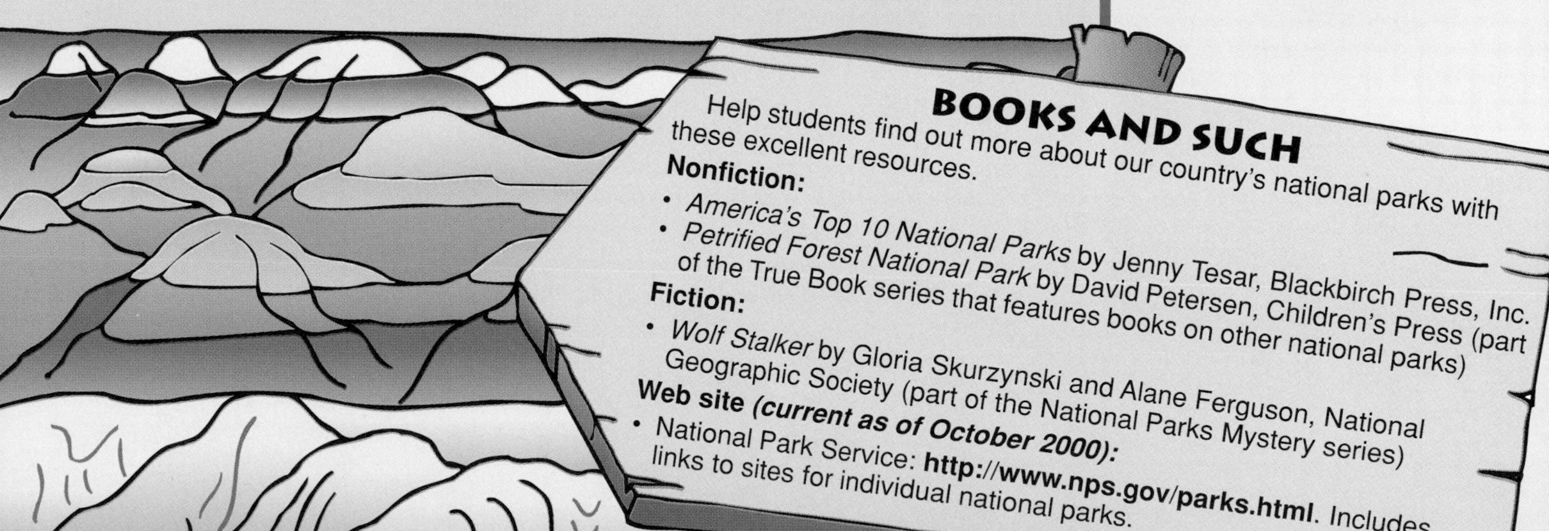

## BOOKS AND SUCH

Help students find out more about our country's national parks with these excellent resources.

**Nonfiction:**

- *America's Top 10 National Parks* by Jenny Tesar, Blackbirch Press, Inc.
- *Petrified Forest National Park* by David Petersen, Children's Press (part of the True Book series that features books on other national parks)

**Fiction:**

- *Wolf Stalker* by Gloria Skurzynski and Alane Ferguson, National Geographic Society (part of the National Parks Mystery series)

**Web site *(current as of October 2000)*:**

- National Park Service: **http://www.nps.gov/parks.html**. Includes links to sites for individual national parks.

# PARK TREASURE HUNT

**Skill: Reading for specific information**

Hunt for the amazing natural treasures found in our national parks with this bulletin board activity. In advance, write each item from list A on the right on a separate white index card. Write each item from list B on a separate colored card (excluding the italicized answer). Pin the cards on a bulletin board titled "Discover the Treasures!" Next, explain to students that our parks are home to many natural treasures. Read over the items listed on the white and colored cards; then assign each student one or more parks to research. As students read, they fill in the cards with information about the treasures. For example, if a student finds out that a glacier is in his park, he writes the park's name and location on the white card labeled "glaciers." If he discovers the identity of a park that matches a colored card, he writes the park's name and location on that card.

At the end of your unit, review the treasures on the board. Then discuss these questions: Which treasures did students find most interesting? Why is it important to protect and preserve these treasures? What might happen if these treasures weren't protected?

**List A** *(Write each on a white index card.):*
arches, geysers, prairies, volcanoes, deserts, islands, rivers, glaciers, Native American ruins, caves and/or caverns, petrified woods, mountains, craters, canyons, waterfalls, tundras

**List B** *(Write each on a colored index card, excluding the italicized answer.):*
world's tallest trees *(Redwood)*
world's largest gorge *(Grand Canyon)*
North America's highest mountain *(Mount McKinley in Denali National Park and Preserve)*
world's largest living thing *(Sequoia and Kings Canyon)*
world's first national park *(Yellowstone)*
deepest lake in the United States *(Crater Lake)*
largest U.S. national park *(Wrangell-St. Elias)*
lowest point in western hemisphere *(Death Valley)*
world's largest known cave network *(Mammoth Cave)*
highest waterfall in North America *(Yosemite)*

# PLACE THAT PARK!

**Skill: Identifying the locations of U.S. regions and national parks**

Play this fun game at the end of your unit to review the locations of U.S. regions and national parks.

Isle Royale National Park Michigan

Middle West

**To prepare:**

1. After referring to page 136, write each park and the state(s) in which it is located on a separate index card. These will be called park cards.
2. Write each region's name (see page 136) on a separate colored index card. These five cards will be called region cards.

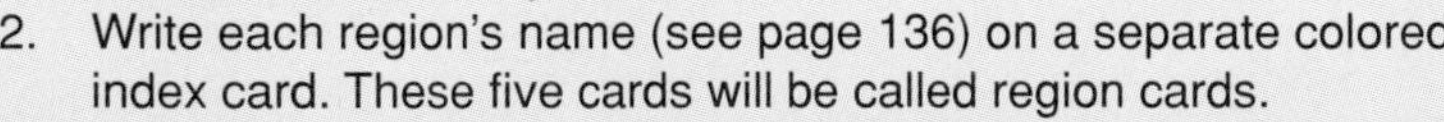

3. Write each of the five region names on a separate sheet of construction paper. Post these five sheets on your classroom walls.
4. Make a copy of your class list to use for keeping score.

**To play:**

1. Give each student a park card. Set the extras aside for the next round.
2. At your signal, have each student "park" himself under the sign that indicates the region in which his park is located. If desired, let students refer to the maps they completed in the "Mappin' It Out" activity on page 133.
3. Check to make sure that each student is in the correct region. Then draw and read aloud a region card. On a copy of your class list, award one point to each student in that region. Then return the card to its deck.
4. Draw one or two more region cards and award points as in Step 3.
5. To play round 2, collect everyone's park cards and set them aside. Give each student a new park card from the extras set aside earlier. Then repeat Steps 2–4.
6. At the end of several rounds, declare the student(s) with the most (or least) points the winner.

Name ______________________________________________

# BACKPACK FAST FACTS

Strap on your backpack and get ready to make your mark at a national park! Research one of our country's national parks and fill in the blanks below.

______________________________
park

______________________________
location

______________________________
U.S. region

Year established: ______________________

Area (in acres): ______________________

Important natural features: ______________________

______________________________________________

______________________________________________

______________________________________________

Animals: ______________________________________________

______________________________________________

Plants: ______________________________________________

______________________________________________

Climate: ______________________________________________

______________________________________________

Must-see attraction at park: ______________________________

______________________________________________

Cool fact: ______________________________________________

______________________________________________

______________________________________________

Researched by ______________________________



**Note to the teacher:** Use with "Backpack Fast Facts" on page 132.

# HIKING AROUND OUR NATIONAL PARKS

*(organized by region)*

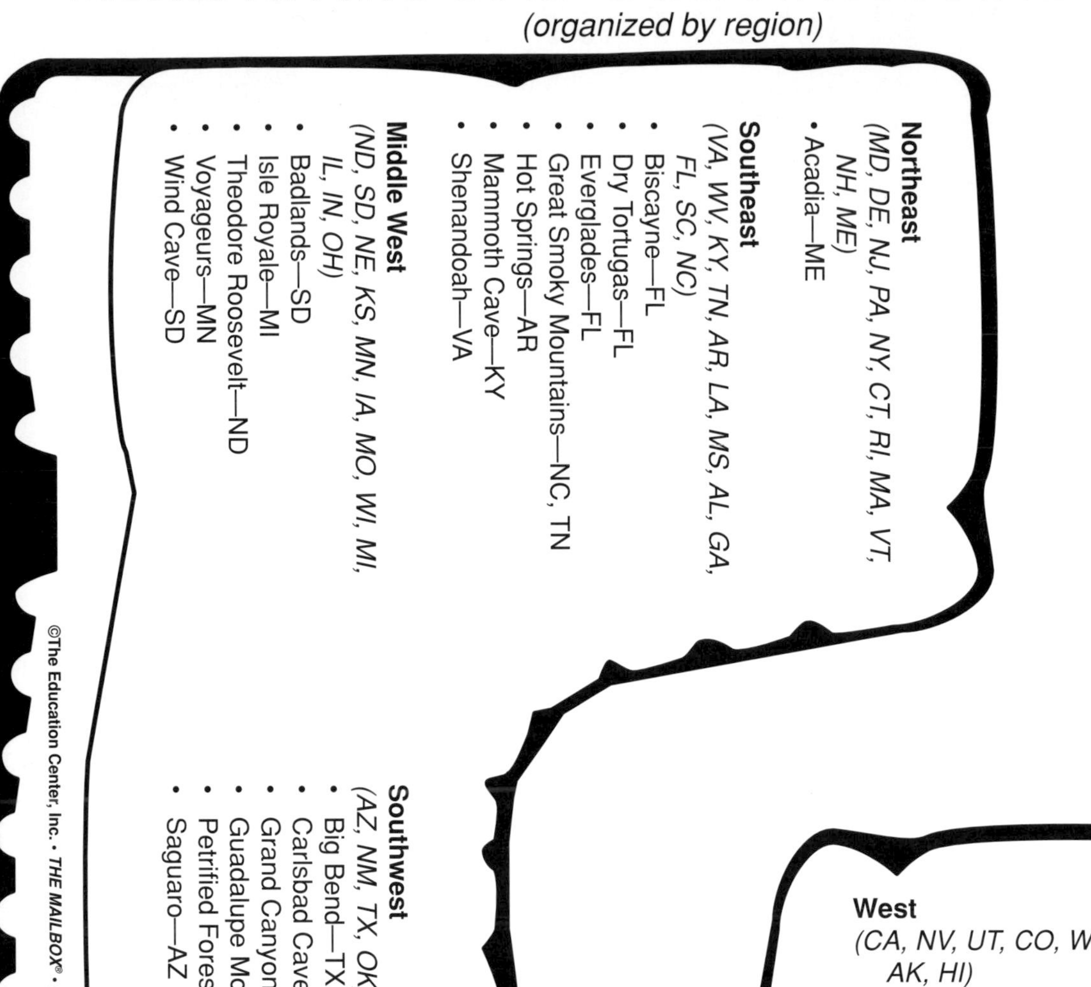

Northeast
(MD, DE, NJ, PA, NY, CT, RI, MA, VT, NH, ME)
• Acadia—ME
Southeast
(VA, WV, KY, TN, AR, LA, MS, AL, GA, FL, SC, NC)
• Biscayne—FL
• Dry Tortugas—FL
• Everglades—FL
• Great Smoky Mountains—NC, TN
• Hot Springs—AR
• Mammoth Cave—KY
• Shenandoah—VA
Middle West
(ND, SD, NE, KS, MN, IA, MO, WI, MI, IL, IN, OH)
• Badlands—SD
• Isle Royale—MI
• Theodore Roosevelt—ND
• Voyageurs—MN
• Wind Cave—SD


**Southwest**
*(AZ, NM, TX, OK)*
- Big Bend—TX
- Carlsbad Caverns—NM
- Grand Canyon—AZ
- Guadalupe Mountains—TX
- Petrified Forest—AZ
- Saguaro—AZ



**West**
*(CA, NV, UT, CO, WY, ID, OR, WA, MT, AK, HI)*
- Arches—UT
- Black Canyon of the Gunnison—CO
- Bryce Canyon—UT
- Canyonlands—UT
- Capitol Reef—UT
- Channel Islands—CA
- Crater Lake—OR
- Death Valley—CA, NV
- Denali—AK
- Gates of the Arctic—AK
- Glacier—MT
- Glacier Bay—AK
- Grand Teton—WY
- Great Basin—NV
- Haleakala—HI
- Hawaii Volcanoes—HI
- Joshua Tree—CA
- Katmai—AK
- Kenai Fjords—AK
- Kings Canyon—CA
- Kobuk Valley—AK
- Lake Clark—AK
- Lassen Volcanic—CA
- Mesa Verde—CO
- Mount Rainier—WA
- North Cascades—WA
- Olympic—WA
- Redwood—CA
- Rocky Mountain—CO
- Sequoia—CA
- Wrangell-St. Elias—AK
- Yellowstone—WY, ID, MT
- Yosemite—CA
- Zion—UT

©The Education Center, Inc. • *THE MAILBOX®* • *Intermediate* • April/May 2001

**Note to the teacher:** Use with "Backpack Fast Facts" on page 132, "Mystery Park" and "Mappin' It Out" on page 133, and "Place That Park!" on page 134.

Name______________________________ 

# PARK IT IN THE USA!

The numbers on the map show the locations of 14 national parks in the United States. Use the state abbreviations to match each number to the correct park. Write the numbers in the blanks. Then follow the directions in the box below.

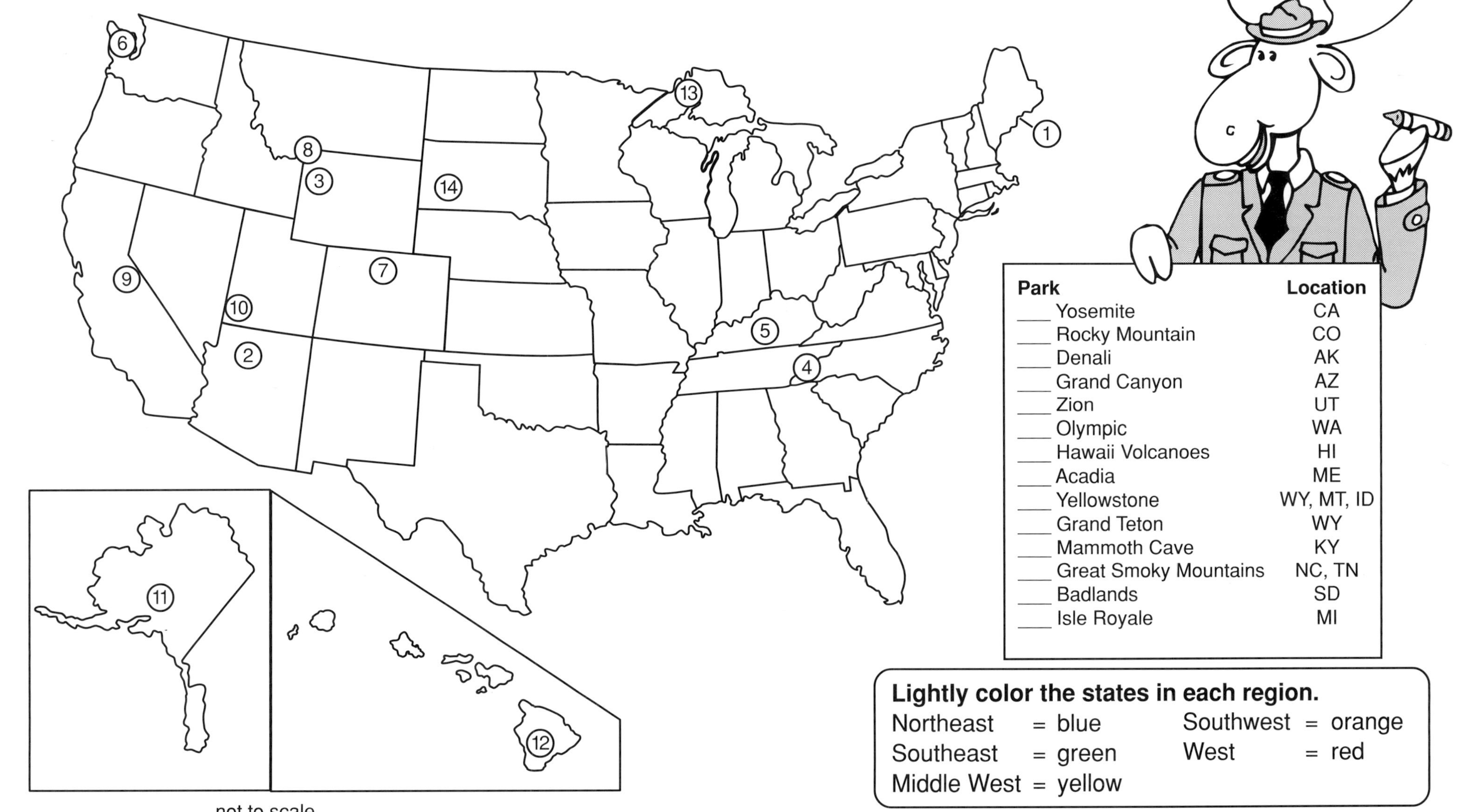


| Park | Location |
|---|---|
| ____ Yosemite | CA |
| ____ Rocky Mountain | CO |
| ____ Denali | AK |
| ____ Grand Canyon | AZ |
| ____ Zion | UT |
| ____ Olympic | WA |
| ____ Hawaii Volcanoes | HI |
| ____ Acadia | ME |
| ____ Yellowstone | WY, MT, ID |
| ____ Grand Teton | WY |
| ____ Mammoth Cave | KY |
| ____ Great Smoky Mountains | NC, TN |
| ____ Badlands | SD |
| ____ Isle Royale | MI |

**Lightly color the states in each region.**

Northeast = blue
Southeast = green
Middle West = yellow
Southwest = orange
West = red



**Note to the teacher:** Use with "Mappin' It Out" on page 133. Students will need crayons or colored pencils to complete this activity. Review state postal abbreviations before introducing the map to students. If desired, have students label the states with their abbreviations before having them complete the coloring activity in the box.

# Spotlighting RENAISSANCE Superstars

## Activities on Famous People of the Renaissance

Michelangelo, Galileo, Queen Elizabeth I, Shakespeare, da Vinci—was there ever a greater gathering of talent during any period of world history? Introduce students to the Renaissance with a skill-boosting study of the magnificent minds that marked this star-studded cultural movement.

*with ideas by Beth Gress*

### Renaissance Rundown

The Renaissance was a cultural movement that began in Italy during the early 1300s. It spread across Europe and ended about 1600. The word *Renaissance* comes from a Latin word that refers to the act of being reborn. The Renaissance represented a rebirth of interest in the cultures of ancient Greece and Rome. It also was marked by a revival of interest in learning. While scholars during the Middle Ages concentrated their studies on theology, Renaissance thinkers focused on the study of humanity and the achievements of different cultures, especially ancient Greece and Rome.

### What Is the Renaissance?

**Skills: Skimming, reading comprehension**

Introduce your Renaissance unit with this fun group challenge. Ask your media specialist to gather resources about the Renaissance (see the list below). Also staple a sheet of chart paper in the center of a bulletin board. Next, ask students, "What do you know about the Renaissance?" Record their answers on the chart paper. Then divide the class into groups. Give each group three index cards and several of the books gathered earlier. Challenge each group to browse through its books and label each of its cards with a true or false statement about the Renaissance. Direct the group to write *T* or *F* on the back of each card.

After groups have finished, play this guessing game. In turn, a group reads each of its statements and challenges classmates to guess whether it is true or false. At the end of the game, staple true cards to one side of the bulletin board and false ones to the other. Challenge students to add other cards to the display during the unit.

### Renaissance Resources

**Web Sites** *(current as of June 2000)*:

- Extensive list of outstanding Web sites and resources on the Renaissance: **http://www.history.evansville.net/renaissa.html**
- Great source of information on the Renaissance: **http://www.learner.org/exhibits/renaissance/**
- A virtual museum tour on the life and works of Leonardo da Vinci: **http://www.museoscienza.org/english/leonardo/default.htm**

**Books:**

- *The Renaissance* (See Through History series) by Tim Wood, Viking, 1993
- *Outrageous Women of the Renaissance* by Vicki Léon, John Wiley & Sons, Inc.; 1999
- *A Renaissance Town* (Inside Story series) by Jacqueline Morley, Peter Bedrick Books, 1996
- *The Renaissance: Artists and Writers* (Who and When? series), edited by Sarah Halliwell, Raintree Steck-Vaughn Publishers, 1998
- *Science in the Renaissance* (Science of the Past series) by Brendan January, Franklin Watts, Inc.; 1999

## Leonardo da Vinci: Renaissance Man

**Skills: Making predictions, listening, recalling details**

Artist, inventor, scientist, architect—they all describe the Renaissance's Leonardo da Vinci. To introduce students to this fascinating talent, write the term *Renaissance man* on the board. Ask students what they think the term means. List their responses on the board. Then read aloud Diane Stanley's picture book *Leonardo da Vinci* (William Morrow & Company, Inc.; 1996). After reading, ask students how they might revise their earlier definitions of Renaissance man. Then write the following on the board: "a person who has wide interests and is an expert in several areas." Discuss with students why da Vinci qualifies as a Renaissance man. Follow up by giving each child a copy of page 141, which includes several da Vinci–related projects for individuals or small groups. To dish up more details about da Vinci, visit this Web site that's straight from his hometown: http://www.leonet.it/comuni/vinci/ *(current as of June 2000)*.

## Johannes Gutenberg: Spreading Renaissance Ideas

**Skills: Persuasive, clarification, and descriptive writing**

A book that costs as much as a car? After posing this possibility, ask each student to guess the number of books in her home. Then ask her to think about how that number might change if each book were handmade. Explain that before the Renaissance books had to be handwritten, making them too expensive for everyone but the rich. Around 1450, a German named Johannes Gutenberg developed a new press that made printing much easier. Because books became more affordable and available, Renaissance ideas spread quickly through Europe.

Next, have each student choose one of the topics below to write about. Have the student glue her finished piece onto one side of a folded 12" x 18" sheet of construction paper. Staple the paper on a bulletin board as shown to resemble an open book. Title the display "Way to Go, Gutenberg!"

**Writing Topics:**
- Write a speech to nominate Johannes Gutenberg as Person of the Year.
- Explain why the printing press is one of the most important inventions of its century.
- Write a letter to the editor explaining why you support a new tax to pay for library funding.
- If you could only afford to own one book, which book would it be and why?
- Describe a library to a Renaissance person who has never seen one.
- What do you think is the most important book ever written? Why did you choose this book?
- Write a letter to your parents persuading them to give you a new-book allowance each month.

- Elizabeth was born to King Henry VIII and Anne Boleyn on September 7, 1533.
- As a baby, Elizabeth was moved to the country to be raised by a foster mother, Lady Bryan.
- When Elizabeth was only three, King Henry VIII had Anne Boleyn beheaded for treason.
- The day after Anne Boleyn was executed, Henry VIII married Jane Seymour.
- In 1537, Jane Seymour gave birth to Elizabeth's half-brother, Edward.
- When she was ten, Elizabeth was being tutored in Latin, Greek, French, and Italian.
- In 1547, Henry VIII died. Elizabeth's nine-year-old brother, Edward, became king.
- At the age of 15, King Edward VI caught tuberculosis and died.
- Elizabeth's older sister, Mary, became queen of England after the death of Edward VI and a nine-day reign by Lady Jane Grey.
- In November of 1558, Mary died and Elizabeth was crowned queen.
- In 1588, Elizabeth led the English navy in defeating the Spanish navy, the Armada.
- Elizabeth died in 1603 after reigning for 45 years.

## Queen Elizabeth I: A Renaissance Ruler

**Skills: Reading comprehension, critical thinking**

Learning about the life of an English monarch might sound boring to today's kids, but they'll change their tune after meeting England's Elizabeth I, whose life included intrigue, invasions, sibling rivalry, and beheadings...more than enough excitement for anyone! Introduce students to this famous Renaissance ruler with this reading comprehension activity. Divide the class into groups of three or four students each. Then give each group a copy of page 142, a sheet of construction paper, scissors, and a glue stick. After the group completes Part I as directed, have each student complete Part 2 on his own paper. Provide time for each student to share his answer to Part 2 with the other members of his group.

## William Shakespeare: Poet and Playwright

**Skills: Reading comprehension, vocabulary**

Introduce students to one of the Renaissance's most famous writers with the reproducible reading comprehension activity on page 143. For an up close look at Shakespeare's mysterious life, read aloud the picture book *Bard of Avon: The Story of William Shakespeare* by the award-winning team of Diane Stanley and Peter Vennema (William Morrow & Company, Inc.; 1992).

Galileo

Michelangelo

## Galileo and Michelangelo: Comparing Science and Art

**Skills: Researching a topic, comparing and contrasting**

One made controversial scientific discoveries. The other has been described by some as the greatest artist of all time. Introduce students to two Renaissance superstars with this skill-packed group activity. In advance, ask your media specialist for resources on Galileo and Michelangelo. Staple two large yellow star shapes, labeled as shown, onto a bulletin board titled "Two Renaissance Superstars."

Next, divide the class into two groups: one to research Galileo and the other Michelangelo. Give each group a copy of the questions shown. Provide time for each group to research the questions and then write the answer to each question inside one of its star's points. After each group shares its information, ask students the following questions: How were these two people alike? Different? How is the study of science similar to the study of art? How are science and art different? How might science be used by an artist? How might a scientist use art? Vary this activity by choosing two different Renaissance figures for students to research, compare, and contrast. Or have each student study a different Renaissance personality, write her information on a cutout star, and then display her star on a bulletin board.

**Research questions:**

- How did your person display his special talents as a child?
- What kind of training did he get in his field as a young person?
- What were his major accomplishments?
- What difficulties did he encounter?
- How would the world be different today if this person had never lived?

Name ______________________________ Student contract

# Leonardo da Vinci: The Renaissance Man

**Directions:** Read the project descriptions below. Complete _______ project(s) by this date: ______________________.

Leonardo da Vinci has been described as a real *Renaissance man.* A Renaissance man is someone who is interested in many different things and is an expert in several areas. Da Vinci was a painter, sculptor, military architect, engineer, naturalist, mathematician, and inventor. Think of someone you know who is good at many different things. Write a letter to Leonardo da Vinci that identifies and describes this person. In the letter, explain why this individual qualifies as a Renaissance person.

Leonardo's most famous painting is the *Mona Lisa*. It was one of da Vinci's favorite paintings. He kept it with him until he died. People all over the world recognize this portrait of a lady with a mysterious smile. In fact, it's been used in many advertisements for lots of different products. Design a magazine or newspaper ad that uses the *Mona Lisa* to help sell a product.

Leonardo da Vinci was a brilliant person, but he had a major problem. Once he planned a project, such as a painting, he often lost interest and would stop working on it. No one really knows why Leonardo did this. Research to find out about one of these unfinished projects. Then write a brief report about the project. In the first paragraph, describe the project and how much of it da Vinci finished. In the next paragraph, tell why you think da Vinci didn't finish the project. Tell whether you think this habit made da Vinci less of a great man. Why or why not?

Leonardo's head always seemed to be filled with ideas. He recorded his ideas and observations in thousands of pages of notebooks. Make an idea notebook of your own. Staple at least 12 sheets of paper between two construction paper covers. Decorate the front cover. Then write in your notebook for two weeks. Fill it with sketches and notes about things you are interested in. Here are some starters to help you begin:

- I'm curious about…
- I wonder how…work.
- Today I observed…
- I've got a great idea about…

**Bonus Project:** On a large sheet of construction paper, make a poster about the life and achievements of Leonardo da Vinci. Be sure to mention a variety of his talents and include sketches of some of his works.



**Note to the teacher:** Use with "Leonardo da Vinci: Renaissance Man" on page 139. Assign the contract to individual students or small groups. Make one copy; then fill in the blanks in the student directions before making a class supply.

Names ______________________________ Reading comprehension, critical thinking

# Elizabeth I: A Renaissance Ruler

Complete the following activities to learn about one of the Renaissance's most famous rulers, Queen Elizabeth I of England.

Ruling England for 45 years was a grand adventure! What do you think it takes to rule an entire nation of people?


**Part 1:** The 12 sentences below describe the life of Queen Elizabeth I of England. Cut out the sentences. Then arrange them in order on a sheet of construction paper. When you're sure the sentences are sequenced correctly, glue them to the paper.

**Part 2:** Look at the question that Queen Elizabeth I is asking. On your own paper, write your answer.

- When she was ten, Elizabeth was being tutored in Latin, Greek, French, and Italian.
- Elizabeth died in 1603 after reigning for 45 years.
- In 1588, Elizabeth led the English navy in defeating the Spanish navy, the Armada.
- In 1547, Henry VIII died. Elizabeth's nine-year-old brother, Edward, became king.
- Elizabeth was born to King Henry VIII and Anne Boleyn on September 7, 1533.
- In 1537, Jane Seymour gave birth to Elizabeth's half-brother, Edward.
- In November of 1558, Mary died and Elizabeth was crowned queen.
- The day after Anne Boleyn was executed, Henry VIII married Jane Seymour.
- At the age of 15, King Edward VI caught tuberculosis and died.
- When Elizabeth was only three, King Henry VIII had Anne Boleyn beheaded for treason.
- As a baby, Elizabeth was moved to the country to be raised by a foster mother, Lady Bryan.
- Elizabeth's older sister, Mary, became queen of England after the death of Edward VI and a nine-day reign by Lady Jane Grey.

**Bonus Box:** On your own paper, write a definition in your own words for each of these words from the sentences you sequenced: *tutored, reigning, executed, tuberculosis, beheaded, treason*. Use a dictionary to help you.



 **Note to the teacher:** Use with "Queen Elizabeth I: A Renaissance Ruler" on page 140.

# Will Fits the Bill!

When it came to naming a favorite writer, many folks in England during the Renaissance would have voted for William Shakespeare. Not only was he England's most famous playwright, he was also a poet. One kind of poetry that Shakespeare wrote was the sonnet. He wrote over 150 sonnets, which he titled by number. Follow the steps below to help you understand one of Shakespeare's sonnets.

**Steps:**

1. Fold back the bottom of this page on the dotted line so that you can't read it.
2. Define these vocabulary words on your own paper.
   a. disgrace
   b. weep (from beweep)
   c. outcast
   d. fate
   e. scope
   f. contented
   g. despising
   h. lark
   i. sullen
   j. scorn
3. Read Sonnet 29. On your own paper, write what you think Shakespeare is trying to say in this poem. Use the definitions in Step 2 to help you.

**Sonnet 29**

When in disgrace with fortune and men's eyes,
I all alone beweep my outcast state,
And trouble deaf heaven with my bootless' cries,
And look upon myself and curse my fate.
Wishing me like to one more rich in hope,
Featured like him, like him with friends possessed,
Desiring this man's art, and that man's scope,
With what I most enjoy contented least,
Yet in these thoughts myself almost despising,
Haply I think on thee, and then my state,
(Like to the lark at break of day arising)
From sullen earth sings hymns at heaven's gate,
  For thy sweet love remembered such wealth brings,
  That then I scorn to change my state with kings.

—*William Shakespeare*

4. Unfold and read the bottom of this page. Compare what you wrote in Step 3 with this paragraph.

What might Sonnet 29 be saying?

This poem is hard to understand because it uses words and terms from the 1500s. Here is one way to interpret this sonnet. In lines 1–4, the author says he's in disgrace. This means that others are looking on him in a negative way. He is depressed and feeling sorry for himself. In lines 5–8, the author says he is jealous of others who are more hopeful or handsome ("featured"), or who have more friends ("with friends possessed"), skill ("this man's art"), or opportunities ("and that man's scope"). In lines 9–12, the author happily remembers someone he loves. In the last two lines, he says he wouldn't even trade places with a king!

**Bonus Box:** On your paper, write two to four sentences describing a plot for a great play Shakespeare could write today if he were alive.

**Note to the teacher:** Use with "William Shakespeare: Poet and Playwright" on page 140. If desired, have pairs of students complete this page together. Provide each student or student pair with a dictionary.

# A WHIRLWIND TOUR OF THE
# WONDERS OF THE WORLD

Colossal statues, awe-inspiring temples, mysterious pyramids—it's no wonder that kids love learning about the wonders of the world. Investigate these man-made and natural wonders—and learn about world geography, history, and human ingenuity—with the following "wonder-full" activities!

*ideas by Simone Lepine*

## BACKGROUND INFORMATION

This unit features activities on four different types of wonders, which are described below. For a reproducible list of the wonders in each category, see page 147.

- **Ancient Wonders:** The Seven Wonders of the Ancient World lists important objects built between 3000 B.C. and A.D. 476. These items were all made by humans and were noted for their great size or other unusual qualities. Only one of these wonders—the pyramids at Giza, Egypt—still exists today.
- **Forgotten Wonders:** Objects or structures that weren't included on the original list of ancient wonders are sometimes called forgotten wonders. Examples include the Colosseum in Rome, Italy, and the Taj Mahal in India.
- **Modern Wonders:** Wonders that were built in modern times include such structures as the Golden Gate Bridge in San Francisco and the Eiffel Tower in Paris.
- **Natural Wonders:** Wonders that occur naturally include sites such as the Grand Canyon in Arizona and Angel Falls in Venezuela.

## PASSPORT TO THE ANCIENT WONDERS

**SKILLS: COLLECTING AND INTERPRETING DATA, RESEARCHING**

Send students on a whirlwind tour of the Seven Wonders of the Ancient World with this data collection activity. First, have each student decorate the front of a file folder to resemble a passport as shown. Label seven sheets of construction paper with the names of the seven ancient wonders (see page 147). Post the signs in the room to create seven different stations. Place at least one encyclopedia or resource book (see page 146) at each station. Next, divide your class into seven groups and place each group at a station. Give each student a copy of page 148 to store inside his folder. At your signal, have each group read the information about its station's wonder and write it on the chart on page 148. After five minutes, signal groups to move to the next station. Continue until each group has visited every station. Have students use their finished charts to complete one of the following activities:

- Construct a timeline showing the dates when the wonders were created.
- Label the locations of the wonders on a map of the Mediterranean area.
- Create a scale of measurement (for example, 1 inch = 10 feet) and make a bar graph that compares the heights of the wonders.
- Write a paragraph explaining which of the seven ancient wonders you would visit if you could. Give at least three reasons for your choice.

Keep the folders for students to use to store work completed throughout the unit.

## "...AND ALL I GOT WAS THIS T-SHIRT!"

**SKILLS: RESEARCHING, PARAPHRASING**

For a research activity that will suit your students to a tee, try this! Invite students who have T-shirts from popular tourist attractions to bring them to school. Hang the shirts in your room. Ask, "If all of the Seven Wonders of the Ancient World were still standing, which would attract the most tourists?" Also, discuss the souvenirs that might be sold at the attractions. Then tell students to pretend that all seven of the wonders still exist. Their job is to design T-shirts to sell at each wonder's souvenir shop. Give each student a large sheet of white paper. Show students how to trim the paper as shown to make a T-shirt shape. Then post the guidelines shown and direct each student to choose a wonder to research. Display the finished shirts on a clothesline in your classroom or hallway. Adapt this idea to use with researching forgotten, modern, and natural wonders.

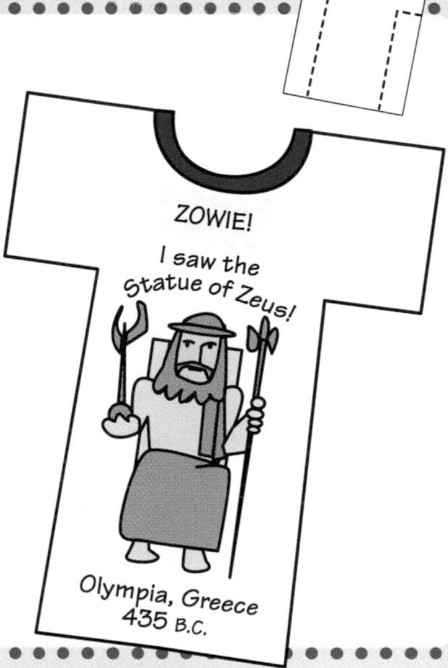


**Guidelines:**

- *Front of shirt:* catchy slogan; wonder's name, location, and date it was created; illustration
- *Back of shirt:* five fascinating facts about the wonder written in your own words

## THE FORGOTTEN WONDERS DEBATE

**SKILLS: PERSUASIVE WRITING, RESEARCHING**

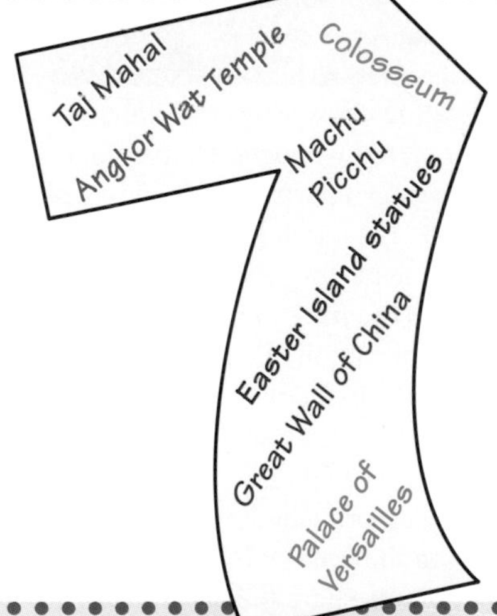


The list of forgotten wonders on page 147 features amazing man-made structures that weren't listed with the Seven Wonders of the Ancient World. Introduce this list and ask students if they are familiar with any of the structures. Then explain that the class will be creating a new list of seven wonders made entirely of forgotten wonders. Divide the class into pairs; then assign each twosome one of the forgotten wonders on page 147. After each pair researches its wonder, have the two students write a persuasive speech to convince others that it belongs on the new list.

When the speeches have been written and practiced, invite another class to listen as they are read by your students. Then ask the visiting class to vote for the top seven choices. Write the names of the winning wonders on a large cutout of the numeral 7; then post the cutout on your door.

## FOR SALE: FAB FORGOTTEN WONDER

**SKILLS: CREATIVE WRITING, RESEARCHING**

For another top-notch research activity on the forgotten wonders, have students bring in real estate ads. Have small groups of students examine the formats of several ads; then discuss the common elements together as a class. If desired, display the sample ad shown on a transparency. Point out that the ad mentions important selling points, such as the structure's size, purpose, beauty, and asking price. Then have each student or student pair choose a forgotten wonder from the list on page 147, research it, and write an ad to convince potential buyers to purchase it. Post the ads on a bulletin board titled "Wonder Want Ads." Adapt this idea to investigate ancient or modern wonders too.

Looking to buy an ancient Roman amphitheater? Does VanWormer Real Estate have a deal for you! Come see the Colosseum in Rome, a spacious structure that is 157 feet high, 620 feet long, and 510 feet wide. This amazing building will hold about 50,000 of your closest friends and family for reunions, birthday bashes, soccer games, and more. Don't forget the basement! It has lots of storage space. Needs a little TLC, but at $3 billion, it's a steal! Call real estate agent Michele VanWormer at 234-5678 if interested.

## A WONDERFUL DREAM

**SKILLS: RESEARCHING, DESCRIPTIVE WRITING**

Introduce students to some of the modern wonders of the world with a writing activity that's downright dreamy! Read aloud the picture book *Ben's Dream* by Chris Van Allsburg. In this book, a boy falls asleep as he's studying for a geography test on great landmarks of the world. The dream takes him on a mysterious journey to several of the sites. After reading the book, discuss the landmarks featured in it; then introduce the list of modern wonders on page 147. Ask students which structures in the book were forgotten wonders, modern wonders, or neither.

Next, challenge each child to write his own dreamy story that features some of the modern wonders listed on page 147. To make the book, the student researches three modern wonders and creates the pages outlined below. Then he binds his pages between two covers and illustrates the front cover. Have students meet in small groups to swap and read each other's books. For another easy-to-do project on modern wonders, see the reproducible activity on page 149.

**Outline of book:**

- Page 1: Write about what you were doing before you fell asleep. Include another character.
- Pages 2–4: On each page, feature a modern wonder in pictures only. Draw the pictures or attach copies you've made from the Internet or other resources.
- Page 5: Show a world map that indicates the route you traveled in your dream.
- Page 6: Describe the three places you visited in your dream to the other character in the story.

## IT'S ONLY NATURAL

**SKILLS: RESEARCHING, COMPARING AND CONTRASTING**

Giant rocks, erupting volcanoes, towering waterfalls—nature's full of some pretty amazing wonders. Help students get to know these natural marvels with a partner activity that sharpens research and thinking skills. Divide the class into pairs. Have each pair research one ancient, forgotten, or modern wonder and one natural wonder (use the lists on page 147). After students have gathered their information, give each twosome a large sheet of construction paper. On the paper, have the pair draw a large Venn diagram that compares and contrasts the two wonders. Then have the partners write a paragraph telling which of the two wonders they think is more wonderful and why. Have students staple the paragraph to the bottom of the diagram. Display the diagrams after students share them with the class.

## "WONDER-FULL" RESOURCES

Try the following resources to provide your students with plenty of "wonder-full" information about the wonders of the world.

**Books:**

- *Ancient Wonders* by Tim Wood
- *The Seven Wonders of the World* by Kenneth McLeish
- *Great Wonders of the World* by Russell Ash
- *Wonders of the World* (Fast Forward series) by Mark Bergin

**Web sites (current as of December 2000):**

- http://ce.eng.usf.edu/pharos/wonders/
- http://123world.com/wonders/
- http://www.cnn.com/TRAVEL/DESTINATIONS/9705/seven.wonders/

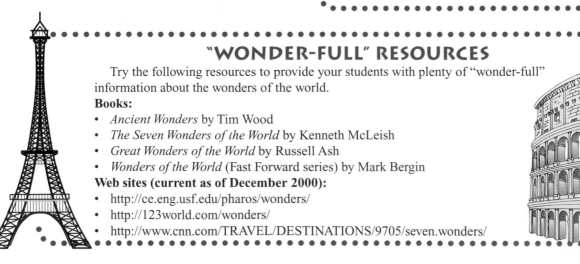

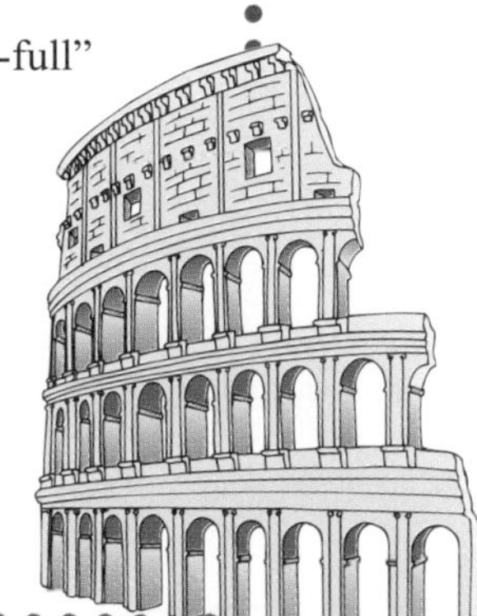

# Touring the World's Wonders

### Seven Ancient Wonders

- Pyramids of Egypt at Giza
- Hanging Gardens of Babylon
- Temple of Artemis at Ephesus
- Statue of Zeus (Olympia, Greece)
- Mausoleum at Halicarnassus
- Colossus of Rhodes
- Lighthouse of Alexandria

### Forgotten Wonders

- Temples of Abu Simbel (Egypt)
- Angkor Wat Temple (Cambodia)
- Borobudur Shrine (Java, Indonesia)
- Colosseum (Rome, Italy)
- Great Wall of China
- Machu Picchu (Peru)
- Leaning Tower of Pisa (Italy)
- Easter Island statues
- Parthenon (Athens, Greece)
- Petra (Jordan)
- Stonehenge (England)
- Taj Mahal (Agra, India)
- Great Sphinx (Egypt)
- Hagia Sophia (Istanbul, Turkey)
- Palace of Versailles (France)
- Sistine Chapel (Rome, Italy)
- Arc de Triomphe (Paris, France)
- Chichen Itza (Mexico)

### Natural Wonders

- Angel Falls (Venezuela)
- Grand Canyon (Arizona, USA)
- Great Barrier Reef (Australia)
- Mount Everest (Nepal and Tibet)
- Niagara Falls (Canada and USA)
- Victoria Falls (Africa)
- Mount Fuji (Japan)
- Kilimanjaro (Tanzania)
- Krakatau (Indonesia)
- Bay of Fundy (Canada)
- Sahara Desert (Africa)
- Ayers Rock (Australia)
- Great Salt Lake (Utah, USA)
- Meteor Crater (Arizona, USA)
- Nile River (Africa)
- Paricutin (Mexico)
- Matterhorn (Switzerland and Italy)
- Dead Sea (Asia)

### Modern Wonders

- Channel Tunnel
- Big Ben (London, England)
- Canadian National Tower (Toronto, Canada)
- Eiffel Tower (Paris, France)
- Empire State Building (New York City, New York, USA)
- Gateway Arch (St. Louis, Missouri, USA)
- Golden Gate Bridge (San Francisco, California, USA)
- Aswan High Dam (Egypt)
- Hoover Dam (Arizona and Nevada, USA)
- Mount Rushmore National Memorial (South Dakota, USA)
- Panama Canal
- Petronas Twin Towers (Kuala Lumpur, Malaysia)
- Statue of Christ the Redeemer (Rio de Janiero, Brazil)
- Statue of Liberty (New York City, New York, USA)
- Lincoln Memorial (Washington, DC, USA)



**Note to the teacher:** Use this page with the activities on pages 144–146 and page 149.

Name______________________________ Research skills

# Passport to the Ancient Wonders

Pack your bags! It's time to take a trip to visit the Seven Wonders of the Ancient World. Don't forget your toothbrush!

| Ancient Wonder | Date created | Size | Location | Description |
|---|---|---|---|---|
| Pyramids of Egypt at Giza | | | | |
| Hanging Gardens of Babylon | | | | |
| Temple of Artemis at Ephesus | | | | |
| Statue of Zeus | | | | |
| Mausoleum at Halicarnassus | | | | |
| Colossus of Rhodes | | | | |
| Lighthouse of Alexandria | | | | |



 **Note to the teacher:** Use with "Passport to the Ancient Wonders" on page 144.

Name________________



Location

## Amazing Facts & Figures

# What a Wonder!

Man-made wonders aren't just a thing of the past! There are some modern structures that are just as amazing as the ancient ones. Find out about one of them with this "wonder-full" project.

**Directions:**

1. Research a modern wonder. Write your notes in the blanks on the sides of this page.
2. Fold the two sides back on the dotted lines. Then turn this paper over and open the flaps. In the middle space, draw a picture of your modern wonder.
3. Refold the flaps so that your picture is hidden.
4. Write the date your wonder was built and its location in the boxes on the flaps.
5. To make the title, cut out a 1" x 2" piece of construction paper. Label it with the name of your modern wonder.
6. Glue the title where indicated.

picture

Attach title.

Statue of Liberty

**Bonus Box:** Create a poster that describes and illustrates the world's next great modern wonder. Answer these questions on your poster: Where will the wonder be built? What is its purpose? How big will it be? What will make it so unique? What will the wonder be called?



×

Attach title here.

Date built

## Purpose & History



**Note to the teacher:** Use with the lists of wonders on page 147. Each student will need a ruler; a small piece of construction paper; scissors; glue; and crayons, markers, or colored pencils to complete this page. Provide time for students to share their pamphlets with each other.

# Jazzin' Up Geography!

Need some new ways to teach geography skills, themes, and standards? Then try this noteworthy ensemble of cool activities and reproducibles!

*ideas by Simone Lepine, Fayetteville, NY*

## Globe-Trottin' It!

**Concept: Location**

**Skill: Latitude and longitude**

Put pizzazz into latitude and longitude practice with a game that requires a little globe-trotting! Pair students; then give each twosome a world political map labeled with latitude and longitude lines, unlined paper, a die, two different crayons, scissors, and a copy of page 153. Direct the pair to label its paper as shown and then cut the cards apart, shuffle them, and stack them in a latitude pile and a longitude pile. Guide students through the steps below.

**Steps:**

1. Player 1 draws a latitude card and rolls the die. If the roll is even, Player 1 records the latitude on his chart as degrees *north;* if odd, as degrees *south.* (No rolling of the die is needed for "0°" cards.) Then he puts the card on the bottom of the pile.
2. Player 1 repeats Step 1, this time drawing a card from the longitude pile. If the roll is even, the longitude is recorded as degrees *east;* if *odd,* as degrees *west.* If the player draws a Wild Card, he chooses any longitude desired.
3. Player 1 uses his crayon to plot a point on the map at the coordinates listed on his chart. Then he records the name of the country or body of water.
4. Player 2 takes a turn by following Steps 1–3.
5. Play continues until both players have marked ten locations on the map. Declare the player who plots more points on *different* continents and bodies of water the winner.

| Jenna | | | Kevin | | |
|---|---|---|---|---|---|
| Latitude | Longitude | Place | Latitude | Longitude | Place |
| 80°N | 40°W | Greenland | 0° | 14°E | Congo |
| 20°N | 100°W | Mexico | 20°S | 140°E | Australia |



Todd

If Vermont is east of me, Pennsylvania is south of me, Canada is north of me, and Lake Erie is west of me, who am I?

New York

## You've Met My Neighbors—Now Who Am I?

**Concept: Location**

**Skill: Cardinal directions**

Tune students in to relative location with this fast-paced game. Give each child an index card labeled with a different country or state. Have the student sign the back of his card; then have him use a map (or atlas) and cardinal directions to add clues that mention the location's neighbors. Collect the completed cards.

To play, divide students into two teams. Choose a card and read its clues to Team 1. (Explain that the clues' writer should not participate in that round.) If Team 1 identifies the location correctly, award it one point. If Team 1 is wrong, allow Team 2 to guess. Then read the next card's clues to Team 2. Continue until all the places have been guessed. Declare the team with more points the winner.

## On the Lookout for Landforms

**Concept: Place**

**Skill: Distinguishing different physical landforms**

Pack your bags and get ready to send students on a globe-spanning search for landforms! Assign each child a term from the list below. Direct her to create a poster that includes a definition and illustration of the term, plus a world map that shows several places where the landform can be found. Display the completed posters.

Next, divide students into groups of four. Give each group a reproducible political map and any four of the terms listed. Challenge each group to use the displayed posters to draw a route on its map for tourists who want to visit their four landforms. If desired, have the group include a written itinerary. As each group shares its map, have different group members point out the posters they used. Watch out—travel bugs might begin to bite!

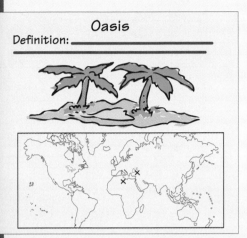

Oasis

Definition:

**Geography terms:** bay, canyon, cape, channel, delta, desert, fjord, glacier, gulf, harbor, island, isthmus, lake, mesa, mountain, mountain range, oasis, peninsula, plain, plateau, river, strait, swamp, tributary, valley, volcano

## Wish You Were Here!

**Concept: Region**

**Skill: Comparing and contrasting**

Fine-tune geography skills with an activity that lets students fantasize about a dream vacation. First, obtain several copies of four different vacation brochures from a local travel agency. Place the four sets of brochures at a center along with copies of page 154. As a classwork or free-time activity, have each student study the four brochures, complete the reproducible as directed, and then share the reasons for her choices. Extend the activity by tallying students' top getaway choices on the board. Then have each child use the data to create a graph titled "Great Getaways."

| Picture | Description | Effects on Humans | Effects on Environment |
|---|---|---|---|
|  | Golden Gate bridge | Easier to travel | Car exhaust increases air pollution |
|  | Hiking the Appalachian Trail | Relaxation, seeing the beauty of nature | Litter, possible forest fires |
|  | | | |
|  | | | |

## People + Environment

**Concept: Human-environment interaction**

**Skill: Drawing conclusions**

Help students understand the give-and-take relationship that exists between humans and the environment with this group activity. First, ask students to help you collect a class supply of pictures showing various ways—both positive and negative—in which people interact with or react to their environment. For example, hiking, farming, bulldozing, lumbering, wearing coats and hats, using air conditioners and heaters, etc. Next, divide students into groups of four. Give each group at least four different pictures, a sheet of poster board, a glue stick, and markers. Have each group discuss how the activity in each picture affects both the environment and humans. Then have the group record its conclusions on a poster similar to the one shown. After the posters have been shared with the class, display them on a bulletin board.

## The World Shopping Network

**Concept: Movement**
**Skills: Sorting, graphing**

Use this simple activity to help students understand how common it is to own items manufactured all over the world. With the class, brainstorm several products that originate in different parts of the United States or the world (apples from Washington, lobsters from Maine, televisions from Japan, cars from Germany, etc.). Next, give each child 20 index cards. For homework, have him identify items in his home that come from places other than his hometown and list each one and its place of origin on a card.

When all the cards have been returned, divide students into groups of six. Instruct group members to share their cards with one another and then sort them—by state, region, or country—according to where the items were grown or manufactured. Then have each group create a bar graph of its data to share with the class. Also have the students suggest how the products were transported to their homes.

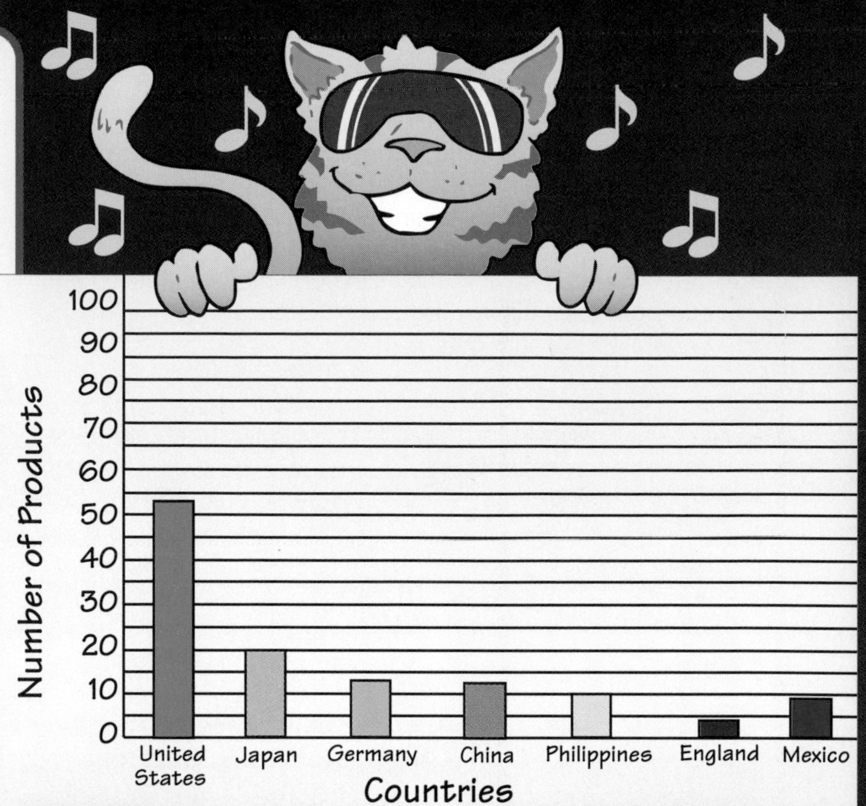

Think I'll truck on down from Cincinnati to Atlanta on I-75.

## Keep on Truckin'!

**Concept: Movement**
**Skill: Reading a map**

How *does* a Maine lobster make its way to a dinner table in Arizona? To help students get a better understanding of how goods are transported from one part of North America to another, obtain one U.S. road map for every four students. Divide students into groups of four and distribute the maps. Explain that an *interstate highway* is part of a system of roadways that connect most major cities in the United States. Have students use their map keys to find the interstate highway symbol. Then call out two major cities. Have each group find and record both the interstate highway(s) and direction(s) in which a truck would travel if it were going from city A to city B. Call on one group to share its answer. After confirming the correct route(s), call out two different cities. As an extra challenge, have students agree on an average posted speed limit for the interstates. Then have each group estimate the total distance and time it would take a truck to travel between the two cities.

Use with "Globe-Trottin' It!" on page 150.

| | | | | |
|---|---|---|---|---|
| Latitude 0° Equator | Latitude 10° (N/S) | Latitude 20° (N/S) | Latitude 30° (N/S) | Latitude 40° (N/S) |
| Latitude 50° (N/S) | Latitude 60° (N/S) | Latitude 70° (N/S) | Latitude 80° (N/S) | Latitude 90° (N/S) |
| Longitude 0° Prime Meridian | Longitude 10° (E/W) | Longitude 20° (E/W) | Longitude 30° (E/W) | Longitude 40° (E/W) |
| Longitude 50° (E/W) | Longitude 60° (E/W) | Longitude 70° (E/W) | Longitude 80° (E/W) | Longitude 90° (E/W) |
| Longitude 100° (E/W) | Longitude 110° (E/W) | Longitude 120° (E/W) | Longitude 130° (E/W) | Longitude 140° (E/W) |
| Longitude 150° (E/W) | Longitude 160° (E/W) | Longitude 170° (E/W) | Longitude 180° (E/W) | Longitude WILD CARD! |

Name ______________________________

# I'm Dreamin' of a Great Getaway!

Imagine going to places you've always dreamed of visiting! But where would you go first? Next? To help you decide, use the brochures your teacher gives you to fill in the suitcases below. Next, write a number 1–4 on each luggage tag to show the order in which you'd like to visit these places. Then complete your vacation getaway plans by answering the questions below on another sheet of paper.

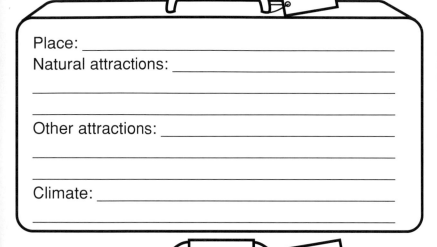

Place: ______________________
Natural attractions: ______________________
______________________
______________________
Other attractions: ______________________
______________________
______________________
Climate: ______________________
______________________

Place: ______________________
Natural attractions: ______________________
______________________
______________________
______________________
Other attractions: ______________________
______________________
______________________
______________________
Climate: ______________________
______________________

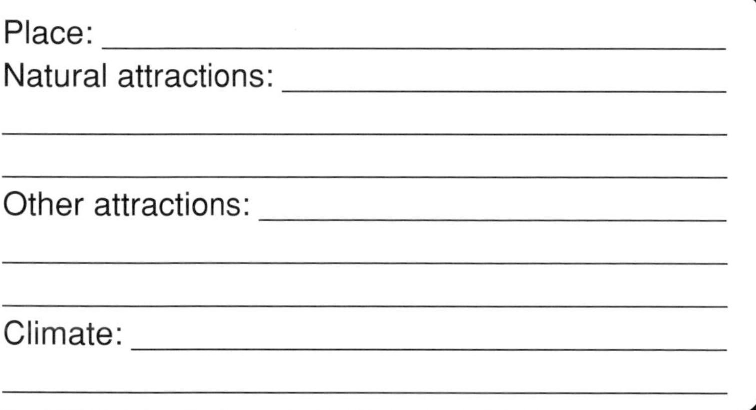
Place: ______________________
Natural attractions: ______________________
______________________
______________________
Other attractions: ______________________
______________________
______________________
Climate: ______________________
______________________

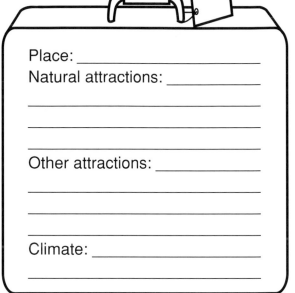

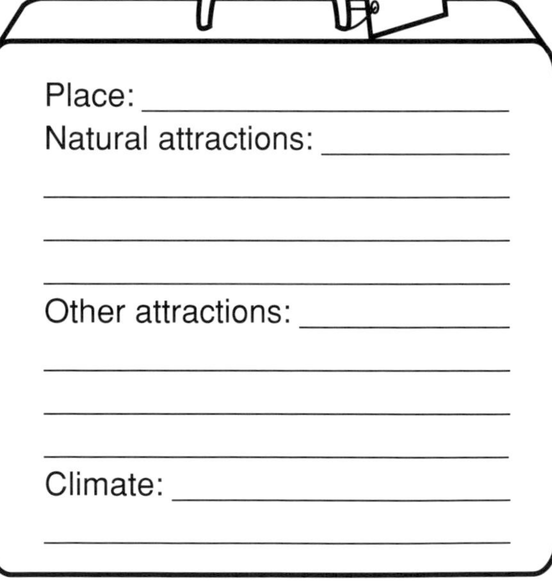
Place: ______________________
Natural attractions: ______________________
______________________
______________________
______________________
Other attractions: ______________________
______________________
______________________
______________________
Climate: ______________________
______________________

1. Look back at the numbers on the luggage tags showing the order in which you wish to visit the places above. Why do you want to visit those places in that order?
2. How is your first vacation choice *different* from the area where you live? How is it the *same?*
3. What are the major differences between your second and third vacation choices?
4. What things could you see and do at your first vacation choice that you couldn't at the fourth?

 **Note to the teacher:** Use with "Wish You Were Here!" on page 151.

# Science and Health Units

# Physics for Kids

When you hear the word *physics,* do you instantly think, "I could never teach THAT!" Bet you can! All you need are the following easy-to-do-and-understand activities that teach kids important principles about matter and energy.

*ideas by Terry Healy*

## What Is Physics, Anyway?

*Physics* is the study of matter and energy. Through performing experiments, physicists try to find laws that can describe the universe. The following activities teach some basic principles of physics. Most of the materials can be found in your classroom or home. Ask parents to help you collect any other items.

## Resources on Physics

Learn more about teaching physics or find great physics-related activities in these books and Web sites *(current as of May 2000).*

- *Mechanics Fundamentals: Funtastic Science Activities for Kids* by Robert W. Wood, McGraw-Hill, 1997
- *Magic Science: 50 Jaw-Dropping, Mind-Boggling, Head-Scratching Activities for Kids* by Jim Wiese, John Wiley & Sons, Inc.; 1998
- *How Come?* by Kathy Wollard, Workman Publishing Company, Inc.; 1993
- *365 Simple Science Experiments With Everyday Materials* by E. Richard Churchill, Louis V. Loeschnig, and Muriel Mandell; Black Dog & Leventhal Publishers, Inc.; 1997
- **Amusement Park Physics:** http://www.learner.org/exhibits/parkphysics/
- **Rader's Physics4Kids:** http://www.kapili.com/physics4kids/index.html
- **How Stuff Works:** http://howstuffworks.com/relativity.htm

## Bernoulli's Ball

**Materials: handheld blow-dryer, 3 Ping-Pong® balls**

Explore an important law of physics with a demonstration that seems to defy gravity. Hold a blow-dryer so that the nozzle points up; then turn it on. Place a Ping-Pong® ball in the middle of the air stream and release it so that the ball remains suspended in midair. Ask students why they think the ball stays suspended. Then explain that this demonstrates a law of physics called *Bernoulli's principle.* This law states that when air flows very fast, its pressure is low; when air flows slowly, its pressure is high. Because air coming from the dryer is moving very fast, the area surrounding the ball has low pressure. The air outside this low-pressure area has a higher pressure, which keeps the ball in place. The force of the air from the dryer pushes the ball up while gravity pulls it down, keeping the ball suspended. Ask students how Bernoulli's principle might be used in real life. Then explain that engineers use this law to design the wings of airplanes. For fun, challenge a student to add a second and then a third ball. But watch out—the balls may take flight!

# I'll Huff and I'll Puff...

**Materials: plastic funnel, Ping-Pong® ball**

Follow up the activity on page 156 with another easy-to-do activity that demonstrates Bernoulli's principle. Place a Ping-Pong® ball inside a plastic funnel. Ask students, "If I point this funnel up and blow into it as hard as I can, will I blow the ball out?" After tallying responses, tilt your head back and blow steadily into the funnel as shown. Surprise—you won't be able to blow the ball out! Ask students why; then explain that this demonstration illustrates Bernoulli's principle like the previous one using the blow-dryer. The flow of air rushing out of the funnel surrounds the ball and creates an area of low pressure on the ball's underside. The greater pressure of the atmosphere holds the ball in the funnel.

Next, ask students if blowing harder into the funnel will make the ball move. Then try it. Have students predict why the ball stays more firmly in place. *(The harder you blow, the more you lower the pressure on the ball's underside and the more the atmosphere's pressure will push the ball into the funnel.)*

# A "Spud-tacular" Straw

**Materials: bowl of water, paper towel, large potato, paper drinking straw**

Investigate the physics principle of *inertia* with this "spud-tacular" demonstration! Follow these steps:

1. Soak the potato in the bowl of water for 30 minutes.
2. Pat the potato dry with a paper towel. Then place it on a table.
3. Ask students, "Do you think I can pierce the potato with this paper straw without damaging the straw?" Tally their responses on the board.
4. Hold the straw about two feet above the potato. Then thrust it straight down into the potato. The straw will penetrate the potato without bending.

Explain that this demonstration illustrates a law of physics called Newton's first law of motion, or the law of inertia. It was first stated by Sir Isaac Newton, an English scientist and mathematician in the 1600s. The law states that an object at rest tends to stay at rest unless acted on by an outside force. An object in motion will tend to continue moving in a straight line at a constant speed. In this demonstration, the potato is an object at rest that remains at rest. The straw is an object in motion that keeps moving in a straight line. Explain to students that hay straws growing in fields have been driven into wooden boards during extremely strong winds such as those experienced during a tornado.

## The Balloon 500

**Materials per group: drinking straw, 12' length of string, 2 chairs, small binder clip, balloon, measuring tape, tape**

For a science lesson that your kids will talk about for days, make "vroom" for this experiment! Divide the class into groups. Then distribute the materials above, making sure to give each group the same size balloon. Guide students through these steps.

1. Run the string through the straw. Then tape one end of the string to the back of a chair as shown. Tape the other end of the string to another chair. Move the chairs apart so that the string is taut. (Make sure your chairs are aligned with those of the other groups.)
2. Put two four-inch strips of tape across the straw as shown.
3. Blow up the balloon and close it with a binder clip. Measure the balloon's circumference. Write your group's name and the circumference on the board. Then attach the balloon to the straw using the tape.
4. Gently pull the straw until the clipped end of the balloon almost touches the chair.
5. At your teacher's signal, release the binder clip. Observe which balloon wins the race.

Give each group a new balloon and repeat the race. Then ask, "Is there a relationship between the circumference of the balloon and the race results?" Examine the circumferences listed on the board and discuss the question. Then explain that this race illustrates Newton's third law of motion, which states that "for every action, there is an equal and opposite reaction." When a rocket lifts from a launchpad, it expels gas out of its engine (the action, called *thrust*). The rocket then moves in the opposite direction (the reaction). In this experiment, the balloon (rocket) with the largest circumference will expel more air (gas), giving the balloon greater thrust.

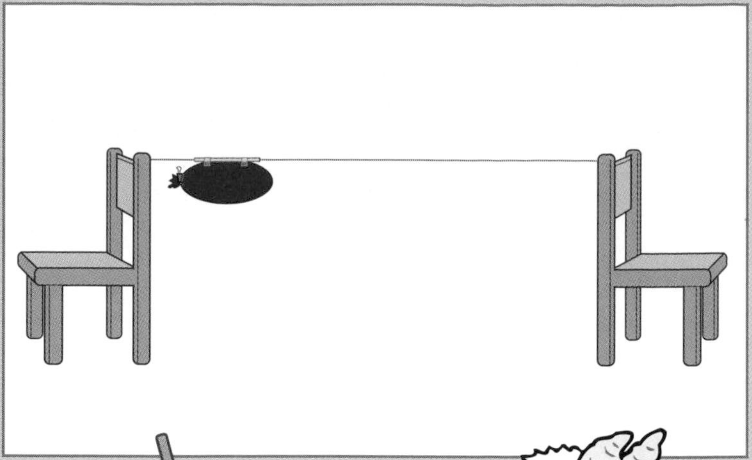

binder clip

Attention Race Fans!
The Balloon 500
Is
Today!!!

## Picturing Physics

**Materials per student: copy of page 160; crayons, markers, or colored pencils**

Examples of Newton's third law of motion are all around us! For instance, when you hit a baseball with a bat, the bat exerts a force (action) on the ball. The ball exerts an equal and opposite force on the bat—proven by the tingly feeling in your hands! Explore this principle further with the reproducible on page 160. Give each student or student pair a copy of the page and the materials listed above. Have students complete the activity as directed. Then discuss their cartoons together. If desired, have students cut out their pictures and post them on a bulletin board titled "Picturing Newton's Third Law of Motion."

## Roller Coaster Physics

**Materials per group: 6' length of 3/4" or 1" plastic tubing, 5 or 6 BBs, masking tape, ruler, copy of page 161, pencil, wall space**

What kid isn't thrilled by a speeding roller coaster? Turn that fascination into a lesson on potential and kinetic energy with the reproducible activity on page 161. Before distributing the materials, divide the class into groups. Designate a wall space for each group to use in completing the experiment. Also provide time for each group to demonstrate its coaster design.

## The Great Sipper Challenge

**Materials per student: copy of the reproducible below and the materials listed on it**

Quench your students' thirst for hands-on science with the "sip-sational" experiment below. Provide each student with the materials listed. Then have her complete the activity as directed. Discuss students' results and their answers to questions 1 and 2. Explain that when a person sucks on a straw, he creates lower pressure in his mouth. The atmosphere outside the straw exerts greater pressure—so much greater that it actually pushes the liquid up the straw. If you could reduce the pressure in your mouth and lungs to create a perfect vacuum (which you can't), you could sip water from a straw that was about 30 feet long! But since you can only lower the pressure in your mouth by a certain amount, the water can't rise more than about six feet. End the activity by having students answer and discuss question 3.

---

Name ____________________________________ Experiment: air pressure

# The Great Sipper Challenge

Thirsty? Then pucker up for this experiment that investigates the physics behind a drinking straw!

**Materials:** cup of water, 8 plastic drinking straws, ruler, scissors, tape, pencil

**Steps:**

1. Answer question 1.
2. Cut two half-inch slits into one end of a straw as shown. Repeat with another straw.
3. Connect the two straws at the slits so that they overlap. Tape the joint.
4. Try to sip water through your long straw.
5. Repeat Steps 2 and 3 to connect another straw to your long one. Repeat Step 4.
6. Continue adding straws until you can't get a sip up the long straw.
7. Answer questions 2–3 on the back of this page.

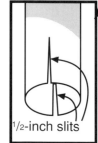

1/2-inch slits

**Answer these questions on the back of this sheet.**

1. How many straws do you think you can connect and still sip water into your mouth?
2. How many straws did you successfully use to get a sip of water?
3. How does a drinking straw work?

Name ____________________________________________

# Picturing Physics

If you've ever heard of Sir Isaac Newton, you can thank an apple. Newton was an English scientist and mathematician in the 1600s. According to a legend, the young Newton saw an apple fall from an apple tree. He thought about the accident and figured out an important scientific principle. It's known as Newton's third law of motion.

**Directions:** Read Newton's law and the examples below. In each photo, draw a cartoon that illustrates a real-life example of this principle. On the lines, explain how the picture illustrates Newton's law.

**For every action, there is an equal and opposite reaction.**

**Examples:**

- When you hit a baseball with a bat, the bat exerts a force (action) on the ball. The ball exerts an equal and opposite force on the bat—proven by the tingly feeling in your hands.
- You exert a force (action) on a trampoline when you jump on it. The trampoline exerts an equal and opposite force that causes you to bounce up.

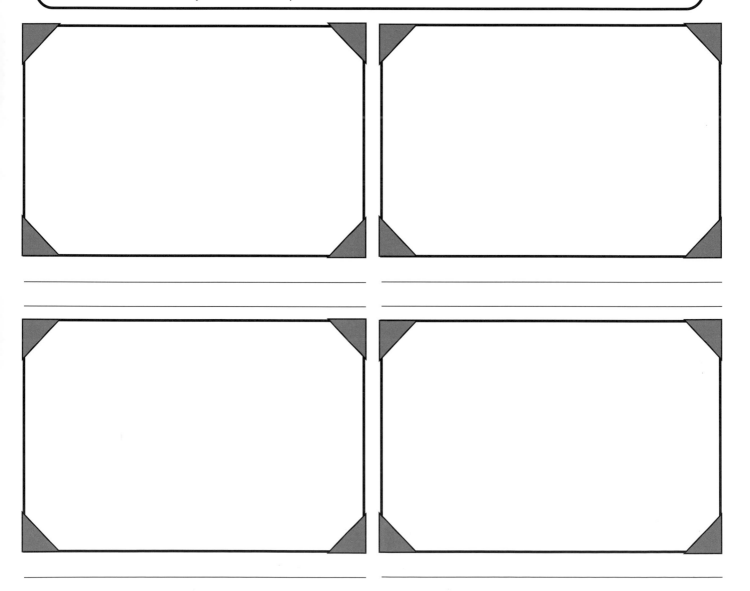

**Note to the teacher:** Use with "Picturing Physics" on page 158. Have students complete this page independently or in pairs. Provide students with crayons, markers, or colored pencils. If desired, have students cut out their photos to display on a bulletin board titled "Picturing Newton's Third Law of Motion."

Name ______________________________ 

# Roller Coaster Physics

You're riding on the world's largest roller coaster. As you race down the track, you're the perfect example of kinetic energy. *Kinetic energy* is the energy of moving objects. As you sit in your stopped car at the crest of the roller coaster's highest hill, you're an example of potential energy. *Potential energy* is stored energy that can be changed into kinetic energy.

Design your own roller coaster to experiment with potential and kinetic energy. Just follow the steps below.

**Materials:** 6' length of 3/4" or 1" plastic tubing, 5 or 6 BBs, masking tape, ruler, pencil, large wall space

**Steps:**

1. On your group's wall space, tape the tubing to make a roller coaster that has hills, valleys, and loops. (See the example.) Remember that the only power the coaster (a BB) will have is gravity and kinetic energy.
2. Release one or more BBs in the starting end of the tubing. If the BBs don't make it up a hill or get all the way through your model, revise the design. To remove a BB, untape the tubing and lower one end until the BB falls out. **Do not suck on the tube.**

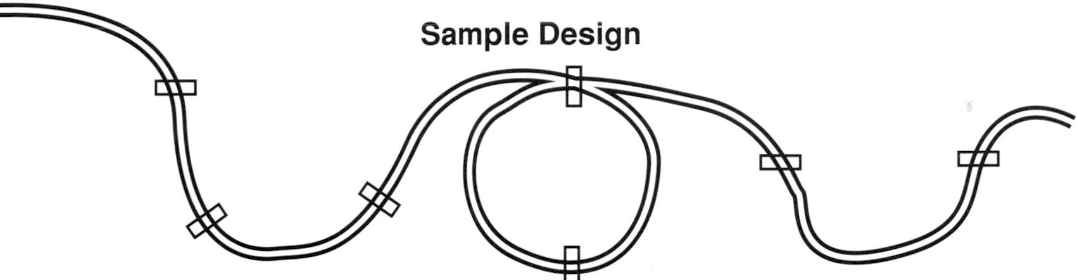

Sample Design

**Observations:**

1. What happened on your first trial? ______________________________
______________________________
2. Did you have to rework your model? ____________ What did you learn as you reworked the model? ______________________________
______________________________
3. Measure the difference between the height of your first hill and the lowest point of your first valley. What is the difference? ______________ What is the difference between the highest point of your design and the lowest point? ________
______________________________
4. Draw a diagram of your roller coaster on the back of this page. Label the following:
   - the point of the greatest potential energy
   - the point where the greatest potential energy is converted to kinetic energy
   - the point where the BBs travel the fastest
   - the point where the BBs travel the slowest

**Conclusion:** On the back of this sheet or on another sheet of paper, explain why a roller coaster car doesn't need an engine to drive it. Use the terms *potential energy* and *kinetic energy* in your explanation.



**Note to the teacher:** Use with "Roller Coaster Physics" on page 159.

# Cruisin' With the Skeletal Crew

## Activities for Teaching About the Body's Bones

Watch your students become "bone-a fide" experts on the skeletal system with the following creative ideas and reproducibles.

*by Michael Foster*

### Skeletons: Up Close and Personal

**Skills: Vocabulary, identifying bone locations**

Want your students to be on a first-name basis with their bones? Then try this fun vocabulary game! First, ask student volunteers to help you write each bone in the list shown, plus "Wild Card" and "Lose a Turn," on two index cards. Shuffle these 42 cards and stack them facedown. Divide the class into two teams, and have each team select one player to be the skeleton at the front of the room. To play:

1. The first student on Team 1 draws the top card from the deck. If he draws
   - a *bone card,* he reads it to the class and then tapes it onto his team's skeleton at that bone's location. If correct (see the key below), he sits down. If incorrect, he returns the card to the bottom of the deck.
   - a *wild card,* that card may represent any bone the player chooses. He names the bone, tells where it is located, and then attaches it to his team's skeleton.
   - a *lose-a-turn card,* he places it at the bottom of the deck.
2. The first student on Team 2 takes a turn in a similar manner.
3. If a player draws the card of a bone that has already been identified on his team's skeleton, he returns that card to the bottom of the deck. For example, each team only needs to identify the location of the patella once. The opposing team then takes a turn.
4. Play continues until a team has correctly identified and labeled all 19 bones in the list.

| bone | key |
|---|---|
| cranium | skull |
| maxilla | upper jawbone |
| mandible | lower jawbone |
| clavicle | collarbone |
| scapula | shoulder blade |
| sternum | breastbone |
| humerus | upper arm bone |
| vertebrae | bones of spinal column |
| ulna | lower arm bone |
| radius | lower arm bone |
| carpals | wrist bones |
| pelvis | hip |
| femur | upper leg |
| patella | kneecap |
| fibula | lower leg bone |
| tibia | lower leg bone |
| tarsals | ankle bones |
| ribs | ribs |
| phalanges | toe and finger bones |

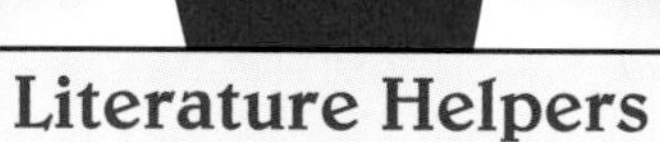

### Literature Helpers

Bone up on the skeleton with these great books.

- *Bones* (Body Books series) by Anna Sandeman (Copper Beech Books, 1995)
- *The Bones & Skeleton Gamebook* by Karen C. Anderson and Stephen Cumbaa (Workman Publishing, 1993)
- *The Skeleton and Muscular System* by Carol Ballard (Steck-Vaughn Company, 1998)
- *The Skeleton* (Look at Your Body series) by Steve Parker (Copper Beech Books, 1996)
- *Bones: Our Skeletal System* by Seymour Simon (Morrow Junior Books, 1998)

## Some Assembly Required

**Skills: Identifying bone names, creative thinking**

Use the skeleton pattern on page 165 for a variety of learning experiences for your students.

- Provide each student with a copy of page 165 and a large sheet of pastel art paper. Have the student cut out the skeleton pattern pieces and arrange them on her paper. After she glues the pieces on the paper, have her label the bones.
- Divide the class into four teams and provide each team with a copy of page 165. Have volunteers in each group cut out the 15 skeleton pieces. Then give a signal for each team to work cooperatively to put its skeleton together.
- Divide students into pairs. Provide each twosome with two copies of page 165, a die, and 15 index cards. Instruct each pair to create a learning game using only these materials. Invite students to share their games with the rest of the class.
- Divide the class into four teams. Assign a color to each team; then make one copy of page 165 on each color of paper. Cut out the pieces and hide them in your classroom. Then challenge each team to locate its colored pieces and reassemble them correctly.

GLUE

| | shoulder | elbow | hip | knee |
|---|---|---|---|---|
| Touch the floor. | | | | |

Touch the floor.
Scratch your nose.
Pick up a pencil.
Take two steps forward.
Shake hands with a classmate.
Tie your shoes.
Sit down in a chair.
Reach for the ceiling.
Take a deep breath.

## Frozen Joints

**Skill: Observing**

Help students see how important joints are to movement and activity with this…movement activity! First, explain to students that a *joint* is the place at which two or more bones meet in the skeleton. Then divide students into four groups: Shoulder, Elbow, Hip, and Knee. Have students in each group count off so that each is assigned a number.

On the chalkboard, make four columns as shown. To the left of the column headings, write an activity (see the list). Have Student 1 in each group perform that activity *without* using his team's assigned joint. After each activity, have the group decide whether or not the performer was able to do the activity well without using that group's joint. Write *yes* or *no* in each column of the chart. Continue by having Student 2 in each group do the second activity on the list, again without using his group's joint. Add your own activities to the list, as well as your students' suggestions.

## Help! I'm Shrinking!

**Skill: Measurement**

Did you know that you shrink a little bit during the course of every day? Throughout the day, the spine is compacted so that by the end of the day, we are all a little shorter than we were in the morning. To illustrate, pair up students. Have the students in each twosome measure each other's height when they first arrive in the morning. Also invite some adults into your classroom and have volunteers measure them and yourself. Provide each pair of students with a strip of adding machine tape on which to mark the measures. Encourage measurements to the nearest quarter inch or millimeter.

After the morning measurements, ask students to predict if their heights will change during the day and if a person's age or height will affect the outcome. At the end of the day, have the student pairs and adults remeasure their heights. Did anyone shrink? Who stayed the same size? What factors may have affected any changes? And before students get too worried, point out that everyone will "bounce back" to her normal size by the next morning!

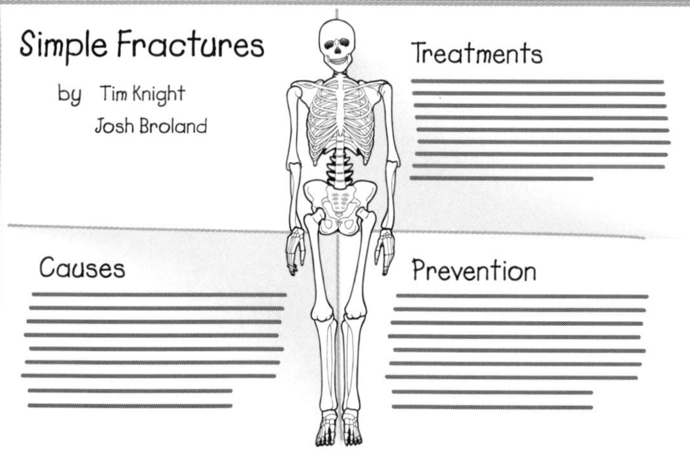


**Topics**

simple fracture
compound fracture
sprain
arthritis* (osteoarthritis, rheumatoid arthritis)
osteoporosis
gout
carpal tunnel syndrome
scoliosis

*Have students check out The Arthritis Foundation's Web site *(current as of 5-2-00)*: www.arthritis.org.

## Boning Up on Skeletal Problems

**Skills: Research, completing a group project**

Investigate the many ways in which the skeleton, joints, and tendons of the body can be damaged. Post a list of skeletal injuries, disorders, and diseases (see list shown). Divide students into pairs and assign each pair a topic. Direct students to concentrate on three areas in their research: cause, treatment, and prevention. Encourage pairs to use resource materials in your media center and from the Internet.

To display what they learn, have students in each pair create a health information poster. Give each twosome a copy of page 165 and a large sheet of art paper. Each pair folds its paper in half two times and then unfolds it to make four sections. Next, the pair cuts out the pattern pieces and glues them in the middle of the paper. To finish the poster, students follow these steps:

1. Top left: Write the topic and your names.
2. Bottom left: List the cause(s) of the injury, disease, or disorder.
3. Top right: List the treatment(s) for the injury, disease, or disorder.
4. Bottom right: Write about the prevention of the injury, disease, or disorder.
5. Label the area(s) of the skeleton that the disease or disorder affects.
6. Include any charts, diagrams, or photos that help illustrate your research.

## Patterns

Use with "Some Assembly Required" on page 163
and "Boning Up on Skeletal Problems" on page 164.

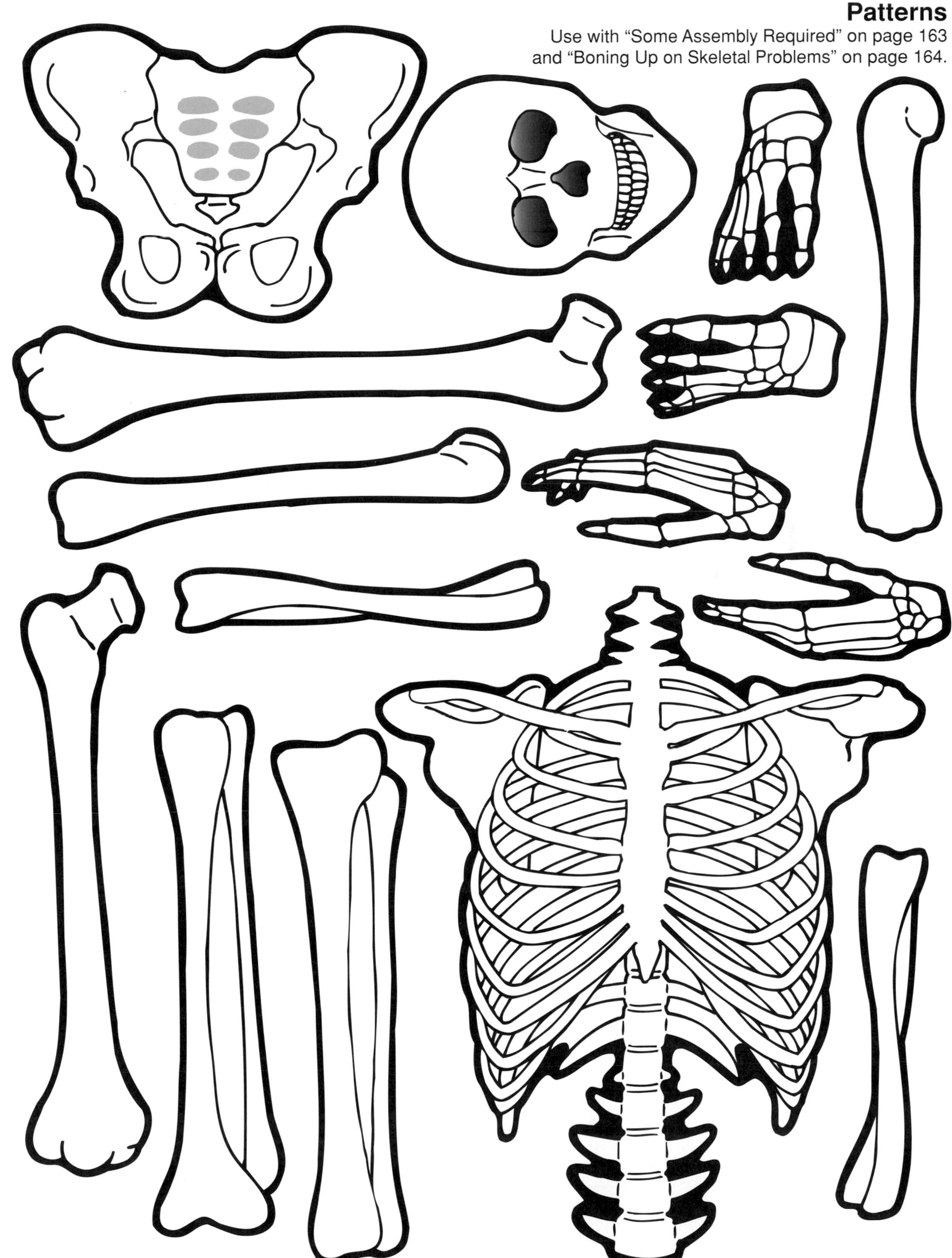

Name ________________________________ Identifying bone locations

# On a Cruise With the Skeletal Crew

Bones are well hidden behind layers of fat and muscle. But there are places on the body where bones can be seen and easily felt. People who study the human body call these places *landmarks.*

Use the captain's log below to chart the ship's progress around the human body. Fill in the label for each underlined landmark with the day the log mentions it. The first one is done for you.

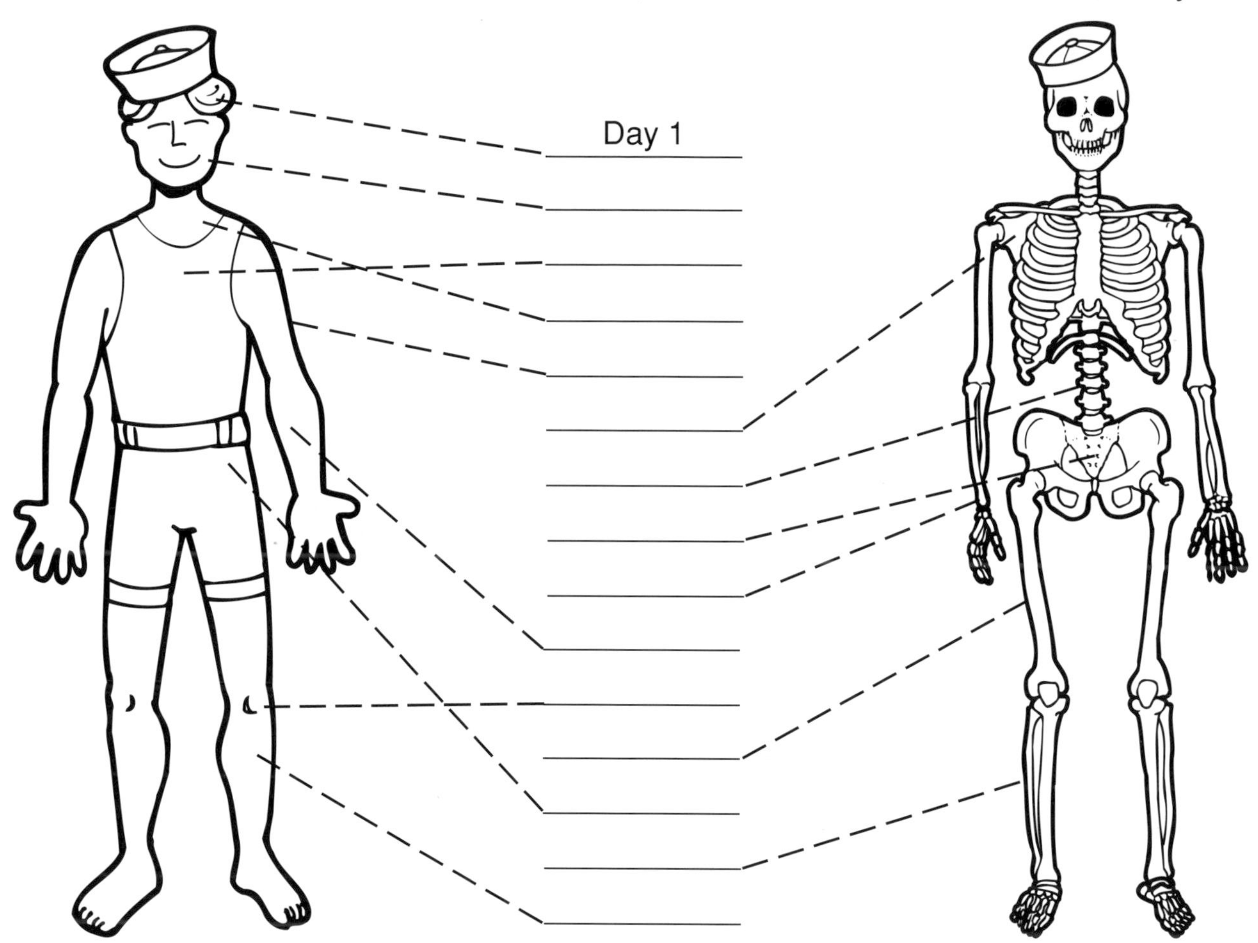


**Day 1:** Departed cranium at dawn.

**Day 2:** Sailed within a mile of mandible.

**Day 3:** Reached sternum at midday.

**Day 4:** Headed for pelvis.

**Day 5:** Encountered storm; landed at clavicle.

**Day 6:** Sighted radius in the distance.

**Day 7:** Foundered on ulna; waited for high tide.

**Day 8:** Sailed around humerus.

**Day 9:** Back on course; expect to reach patella by dusk.

**Day 10:** Sighted friendly vessel at tibia.

**Day 11:** Sailed alongside vessel to fibula.

**Day 12:** Spotted femur in the distance.

**Day 13:** On return voyage, made stop at coccyx.

**Day 14:** Followed ocean current along vertebrae.

**Day 15:** Sailed into home port at scapula.

**Bonus Box:** Pretend you are a member of the skeletal crew. Write a letter home describing some of the bones you saw on your voyage: the largest, the most unusual, the bone you wouldn't want to do without, the funniest-looking bone, the bone with the weirdest name, etc.

Name ______________________________ Problem solving

# Boning Up on Numbers

When you were born, you had about 300 bones. But when you become an adult, you will have 206 bones. Some bones grow together as you get older.

Use the bone facts in the diagram to help you solve the problems below. Show your work on another sheet of paper. You may be surprised to learn where most of your bones are located!

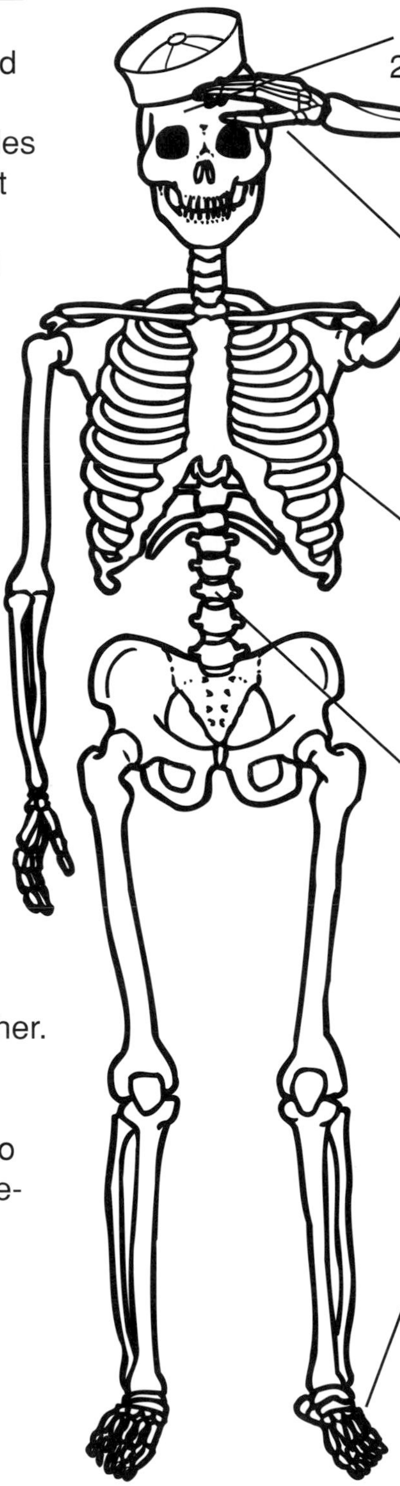

1. How many bones are in both hands? ____________
2. How many bones are in both feet? ____________
3. How many of the body's bones are in the hands and feet?____________
4. The *appendicular* skeleton has 126 bones. It includes the hands, feet, arms, and legs, plus the bones that attach them to the skeleton. How many bones in the appendicular skeleton are *not* in the hands and feet? ____________
5. There are 3 knuckles in each finger and 2 knuckles in each thumb. How many knuckles are in each hand? ____________
6. The hand bones are divided into 3 groups: the *carpals* in the wrist (8 bones), the *metacarpals* in the palm (5 bones), and the *phalanges* in the fingers and thumbs. How many bones make up the phalanges in one hand? ____________
7. Like the hand, the foot bones are divided into 3 groups: the *tarsals* in the ankle (7 bones), the *metatarsals* in the body of the foot (5 bones), and the *phalanges* in the toes. How many bones are in the toes of one foot? ____________
8. *Cranial bones* and *facial bones* make up the skull. There are 14 facial bones. How many cranial bones are there? ____________
9. Nine vertebrae are either partly or fully fused together. How many vertebrae are separate bones? ____________
10. The separate vertebrae of the spine are divided into 3 groups: the *cervical* (7 vertebrae), *lumbar* (5 vertebrae), and *thoracic.* How many thoracic vertebrae are there? ____________
11. The ribs are paired. How many pairs are there? ____________
12. One person in every 20 has an extra rib. How many people in a group of 100 have an extra rib? ____________

skull:
22 bones

hand:
27 bones

rib cage:
24 ribs

backbone:
33 vertebrae

foot:
26 bones

**BONUS BOX:** If the body has 206 bones, how many bones are *not* labeled in the diagram? List five of those bones.

# Ready, Set, Recycle!

Introduce your students to the benefits of recycling—the perfect way to celebrate Earth Day—with four environment-friendly, hands-on projects.

*ideas by Deborah Mayo, Jena, LA*

## Project 1: Can-Collection Contest

### Skill: Collecting and graphing data

Motivate students to reduce waste by involving them in a little recycling rivalry. Invite other classes in your grade level (or schoolwide) to join in a recycling contest. First, provide each participating class with a large collection box to hold its cans. Announce a place to store the overflow of cans. Also, demonstrate for each class how to use a magnet to tell whether a can is made of aluminum or another metal *(a magnet will not attract aluminum).* Then set a date for the collecting to begin. On a bulletin board in a main hallway, display a pictograph that tracks the cans each class collects. After several weeks, sell the cans to a recycling center and treat the winning class to a pizza party. Donate any remaining money to a local environmental project, or use it to purchase new equipment for your school or classroom.

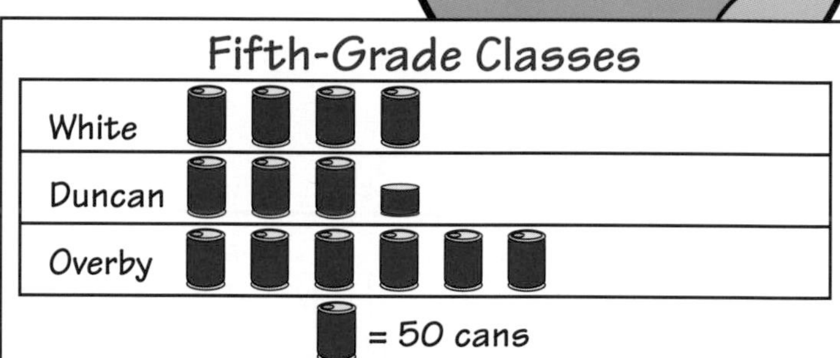


## Project 2: Landfill Logistics

### Skill: Distinguishing between biodegradable and nonbiodegradable materials

Let students discover which trash items decay faster than others by conducting a landfill-simulation project. Use the directions below to help each student construct his own mini landfill, or make a single one the whole class can study. To avoid mold-sensitivity problems, store the project(s) in an area other than the classroom. At the end of the project, have students discuss the predictions and answers on their recording sheets (page 170).

Hummpf! The food and paper scraps are decaying, but this aluminum can hasn't changed a bit!


**Materials:**

large clear plastic box with a lid
wooden craft sticks
enough soil (not commercial) to fill the box
5 trash items (aluminum can, baby food jar, plastic bottle cap, eggshells, potato peelings, piece of newspaper, piece of Styrofoam®, fabric scrap, piece of fruit, etc.)
2 to 3 cups of water
copy of page 170 for each student
ruler

**Directions:**

1. Fill the box with about two inches of soil.
2. Use a craft stick to draw lines in the soil to divide it into five equal sections. Select five items to bury. Bury one item at a time in a different section of the soil. Cover some items completely with soil. Leave others partly uncovered. Record each item on the recording sheet.
3. Add enough water to moisten the soil. Then put the lid on the box and place it in a sunny area.
4. Stir and examine the mixture with a craft stick twice each week over a period of four weeks. Record on the sheet any changes that are observed (odors, organisms, amount of decay).

# Project 3: Earth-Friendly Fact Finders

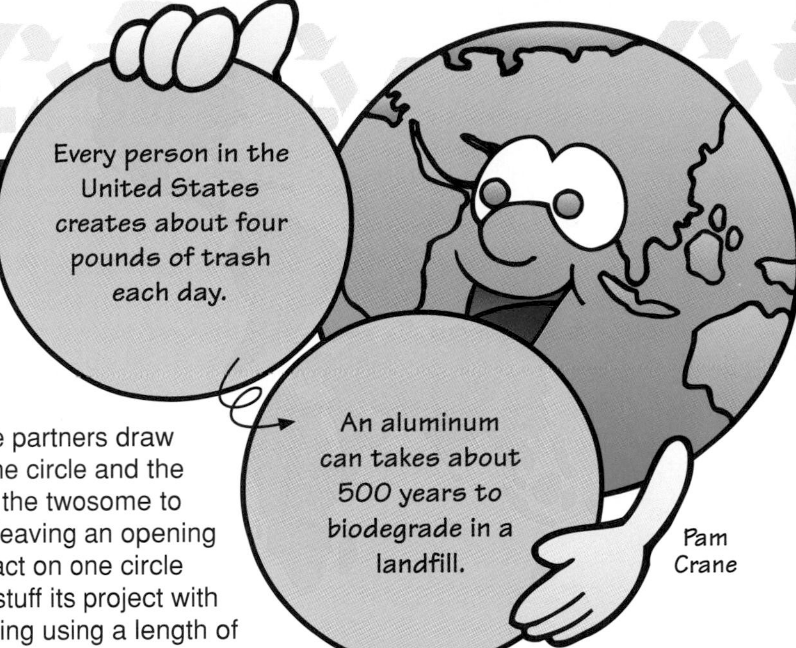

Every person in the United States creates about four pounds of trash each day.
An aluminum can takes about 500 years to biodegrade in a landfill.
Pam Crane


### Skill: Researching a topic

Want to fill your room with facts about recycling and pollution? Then try this Earth-friendly project! Pair students; then have each twosome research two facts about recycling or pollution. Next, give each pair of students two medium-sized circles cut from blue poster board. Have the partners draw and color the continents of the Western Hemisphere on one circle and the continents of the Eastern Hemisphere on the other. Direct the twosome to staple the blank sides of its circles together at the edges, leaving an opening at the top. Using a black marker, have the pair write one fact on one circle and the remaining fact on the other. Then have each pair stuff its project with paper, staple the opening closed, and hang it from the ceiling using a length of yarn.

# Project 4: Rags-to-Riches Soil

### Skills: Observing, drawing conclusions

Challenge students to transform plain dirt into fertile compost in just a matter of weeks with this "get-rich-quick" soil project. Use the directions below to help each student make his own container of compost. Or make a single one the whole class can study. To avoid mold-sensitivity problems, store the project(s) in an area other than the classroom. Have students discuss the answers written on their recording sheets (page 171) together.

**Materials:**

plastic gallon milk jug with top
ruler
craft sticks
pair of panty hose
soil (not commercial)
water
scissors
tape
9" square aluminum (or metal) pan
small pebbles
5 nonmeat food items
(potato or onion peelings,
carrot pieces, tea bags,
coffee grounds, etc.)
leaves
grass clippings
copy of page 171 for each student

**Directions:**

1. Cover the bottom of the pan with pebbles and set it aside.
2. Using scissors, poke 20 to 30 holes in the bottom of the milk jug. About an inch below the handle, cut the jug into two sections.
3. In the top section, cut out five to six small windows. Tape a small piece of panty hose material over each opening.
4. Fill the bottom section with about two inches of soil. Place the food items, leaves, and grass clippings atop this layer. Cover the materials with another layer of soil.
5. Add just enough water to dampen the soil.
6. Push the top section of the jug down into its bottom section so that the edges of one overlap the other. Put the jug in the pan atop the pebbles.
7. Each day, remove the jug's top section and stir the mixture in the bottom with a craft stick. As needed, add water to keep the soil *damp*, not wet.
8. Twice each week—once at the beginning and again at the end—measure the depth of water in the pan and observe the landfill. Record the measurement and observations on the chart.

Name________________________________________________ Recording sheet

# Landfill Logistics

Find out which landfill items decay faster than others with this cool investigation.

**Directions:** In the chart below, write the five items you buried in the soil. On the lines, predict whether items will decompose fast or slow. Then use the chart to record your observations twice each week—once at the beginning and again at the end. To complete the project, answer the questions below the chart on another sheet of paper. Use encyclopedias or other reference materials for help.

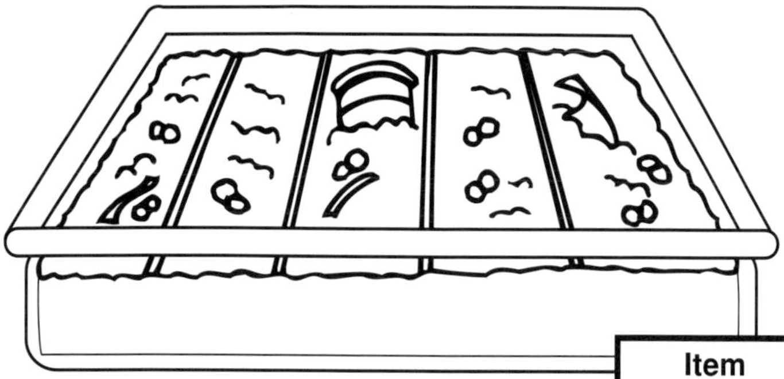

**Predictions**

| Fast Decomposers: | Slow Decomposers: |
|---|---|
| ________________ | ________________ |
| ________________ | ________________ |
| ________________ | ________________ |

| | | | Item | Item | Item | Item | Item |
|---|---|---|---|---|---|---|---|
| | | | | | | | |
| Date | Odor(s) | Presence of insects, molds, etc. | Amount of decay | Amount of decay | Amount of decay | Amount of decay | Amount of decay |
| | | | | | | | |
| | | | | | | | |
| | | | | | | | |
| | | | | | | | |
| | | | | | | | |
| | | | | | | | |
| | | | | | | | |
| | | | | | | | |

1. How is the model like a real landfill?
2. Are landfills a good thing? Why or why not?
3. How does recycling affect landfills?
4. Why do some objects decay faster than others?
5. What could happen if *leachate,* the substance formed when liquid from rotting garbage mixes with rainwater, seeps from a landfill?

**Bonus Box:** Will there be landfills 100 years from now? Explain your answer.



**Note to the teacher:** Use with "Project 2: Landfill Logistics" on page 168. Allow students to use encyclopedias and other reference materials to answer the questions.

Name ______________________________ Recording sheet

# Rags-to-Riches Soil

Recycle food scraps and other trash items to create fertile soil with this "get-rich-quick" activity!

**Directions:** In the chart below, write the name of each item you buried in the soil. Use the chart to record your observations twice each week, once at the beginning and again at the end. After making your last entry in the chart, write a paragraph on the lines summarizing what happened to the soil.

| | | | Item | Item | Item | Item | Item |
|---|---|---|---|---|---|---|---|
| | | | | | | | |
| Date | Odor(s) | Depth of water in pan | Amount of decay | Amount of decay | Amount of decay | Amount of decay | Amount of decay |
| | | | | | | | |
| | | | | | | | |
| | | | | | | | |
| | | | | | | | |
| | | | | | | | |
| | | | | | | | |
| | | | | | | | |
| | | | | | | | |

Write your rags-to-riches paragraph here.



**Note to the teacher:** Use with "Project 4: Rags-to-Riches Soil" on page 169.

# Picturing Plant and Animal Adaptations

**How adaptable plants and animals can be! Some can adjust to extreme temperatures to survive in their environments. Others rely on growth tricks and poisons. Learn more about how plants and animals accomplish these amazing feats with the following ideas and reproducibles.**

**ideas by Linda Manwiller, Boyertown, PA**

## Plantasia's Plants

**Concept: Plant adaptations**

Turn students into space-traveling botanists with this model-building and writing activity. Divide students into crews of three and share the following scenario: *You have been recruited to explore Plantasia, a planet that humans have never visited. Your assignment is to bring back a plant that could adapt to life on Earth.* Next, instruct each crew to plan a model of a plant from Plantasia. Allow students several days to collect materials. Then give each crew a sheet of poster board on which to construct and label its model. Also have the crew make a sensory chart about its plant on another piece of poster board as shown. Have the crews share their completed models and charts with the class. Follow up by having each student choose one of the prompts below and write about his crew's (or any other crew's) plant.

**Writing Prompts**

- Descriptive writing: Use the information in the sensory chart to write a detailed description of the plant. Include the plant's adaptations.
- Expository writing: Write a plan for taking care of the plant.
- Clarification writing: Compare and contrast the adaptations of the plant with a plant from your local area.
- Narrative writing: Write a story telling how you found the plant. Include the adaptations that enabled it to survive on Plantasia.
- Persuasive writing: Write a letter to persuade a group of U.S. scientists that the plant could survive on Earth. Focus on the adaptations that would enable it to live on Earth.

## Plant Hall of Fame

**Concept: Plant adaptations**

Shine the spotlight on plants with unusual adaptations by putting them in a plant Hall of Fame! Pair students; then assign each pair a different plant to research from the list below. After each pair finds its plant's special adaptations, have the twosome draw a large picture of the plant on poster board and label it with the plant's name and its special parts and adaptations. Also have the pair list several questions that could be answered by studying its poster. After students share their posters, compile the questions and make copies; then display the posters in a hallway under a banner titled "Plant Hall of Fame." Invite students from other classes to answer the questions as they walk through your Hall of Fame.

| | | |
|---|---|---|
| yucca | barrel cactus | slime mold |
| tumbleweed | rafflesia | mimosa |
| Venus's-flytrap | mistletoe | creosote bush |
| pitcher plant | dodder | orchid |
| bladderwort | lichen | saguaro cactus |
| | | mangrove |

damages its host
parasite (grows and feeds on other plants)
sticky substance on seeds
dates back hundreds of years
Mistletoe

ANIMAL KINGDOM PASSPORT

Good traveling companions:
other male and female lions in the pride

The Secretary of Zoology of the Animal Kingdom

*hereby requests that the Animal Kingdom citizen named herein be allowed passage without delay or hindrance into desired area and be given all lawful aid and protection to which it is duly entitled.*

Leo L. Lion
(signature of bearer)

NOT VALID UNTIL SIGNED

ANIMAL KINGDOM PASSPORT

Class: Mammalia
Order: Carnivora
Family: Felidae

Given Name: Lion, Leo L.
Date of Birth: 8-14-94
Habitat or Biome: Savannas and semidesert areas of Africa

ADAPTATIONS
Physical: Large canine teeth, excellent sense of smell, very muscular, hooked claws, tawny color
Behavioral: Often hunts at night or with the pride, expert stalker

## PASSPORT, PLEASE!

**Concept: Animal adaptations**

Find out more about the adaptations of animals in your local area—or those living in a place students are currently studying—with this activity. On the board, list animals that live in your area. Discuss with students the adaptations these animals have had to make to survive. Next, explain that a passport is a document used for personal identification when traveling in foreign countries. Tell students that they will be creating passports for the animals listed. Then assign each student a different animal and give her a copy of page 175. Have students use encyclopedias and other reference materials to complete the page as directed. If desired, serve animal crackers while students work. Then use the completed passports to play the game on the right.

**Steps to play Going Through Customs:**

1. Have students form two lines so that each child faces a partner.
2. Designate the students in one line as immigration agents and those in the other line as animals traveling with passports.
3. Have each agent check his partner's passport for accuracy by asking the animal to provide the proper identification (name and special adaptations).
4. Direct each agent to move one place to his right to face a new partner. (Have the agent at the right end of the line move to the opposite end of the line). Repeat Step 3.
5. Continue until each agent has questioned five different animals. Then switch the lines' roles and play again.

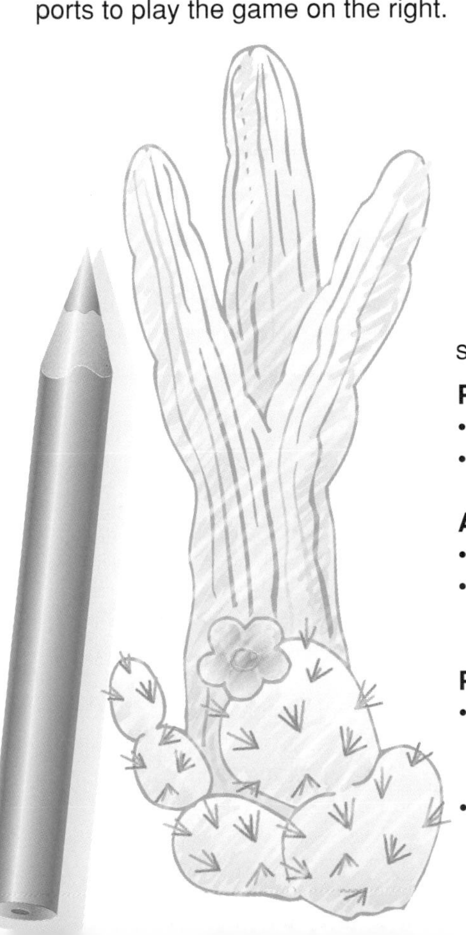

## BOOKS AND WEB SITES

Find out more about the amazing changes that some plants and animals make to survive with these great books and Web sites.

**Plant books:**
- *June 29, 1999* by David Wiesner
- *Mysteries & Marvels of Plant Life* by Barbara Cork

**Animal books:**
- *Rascal* by Sterling North
- *The Tarantula in My Purse and 172 Other Wild Pets* by Jean Craighead George

**Plant and animal books:**
- *Cactus Café: A Story of the Sonoran Desert* by Kathleen Weidner Zoehfeld
- *The Most Beautiful Roof in the World: Exploring the Rainforest Canopy* by Kathryn Lasky

**Web sites** *(current as of December 2000):*
- U.S. Fish & Wildlife Service: www.fws.gov/kids
- National Wildlife Federation: www.nwf.org/nwf/education
- Oakland Zoo (specific information about animal adaptations): www.oaklandzoo.org/atoz/atoz.html

## Suitcase Study Aids

**Concept: Plant and animal adaptations**

Help students review what they've learned about wildlife adaptations by making some handy graphic organizers. First, list types of animal adaptations on the board, such as body coverings, mouth parts, movement-related adaptations, protective coloration, protective resemblance, mimicry, migration, and hibernation. Discuss the terms with students. Repeat with types of plant adaptations, such as seed dispersal, tropisms, chemical emissions, leaves/needles/spines, and biological clocks. Then give each student a manila file folder. Have the student cut the folder on the fold and trim each half into a suitcase shape as shown. Direct the student to title one cutout "Fauna's Suitcase," divide it into six sections, and label each section with a different animal adaptation. Instruct him to label the other cutout "Flora's Suitcase," divide it into four sections, and label each section with a different plant adaptation. Finally, challenge the student to fill each section on his suitcases with two examples of animals or plants with that adaptation. After a sharing time, allow students to use their organizers to study with their buddies!

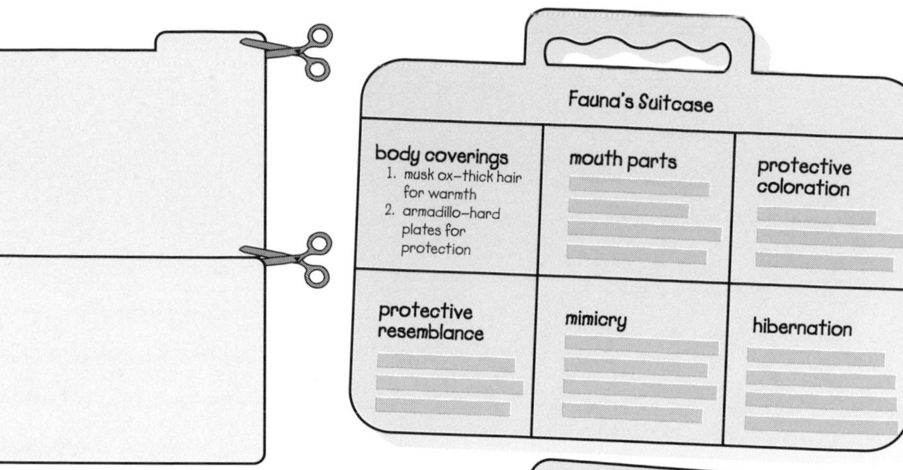

Fauna's Suitcase
body coverings
1. musk ox–thick hair for warmth
2. armadillo–hard plates for protection
mouth parts
protective coloration
protective resemblance
mimicry
hibernation


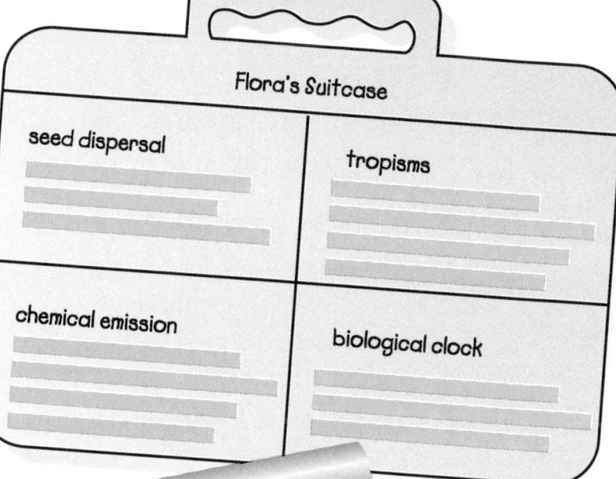

## Around the World With Animal Adaptations

**Concept: Animal adaptations within biomes**

Use this small-group activity to give students a global perspective of how animals in different parts of the world adapt to their environments. Divide students into six groups and assign each group a different biome listed below. Give each group a sheet of chart paper and a different-colored marker. Have each group research its biome; then have the group use its marker to label the chart paper with the name of its biome and a brief description.

Next, have one group at a time share the description of its biome with the class. Help students understand the adaptations that would be necessary for animals to survive in that biome. Then place the labeled charts around the room and assign each group to a different biome. Instruct each group to use its colored marker to list on the chart animals (and their specific adaptations) that might live in that biome. After three minutes, signal the groups to rotate to the next biome and repeat the process. After the groups have visited every biome, have them return to their original charts and use reference materials to check the list of animals for accuracy. Conclude by having each group share its chart with the class. If desired, post the charts in the room so students can add examples during the unit.

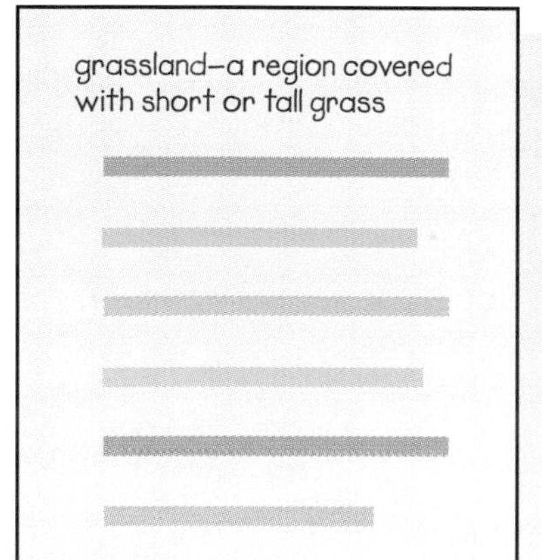

grassland–a region covered with short or tall grass


**Biomes**
deciduous forest
desert
grassland
taiga
tropical rain forest
tundra

Name ______________________________ 

# Passport, Please!

Agents in charge of admitting animals into the Animal Kingdom have an important job. They must make sure each animal that wants to live in a particular place can survive there. Help your animal get a passport into the Animal Kingdom by following the directions below.

**Directions:** Research your animal to help you fill in the information on the passport. Include a picture. Then cut out the passport along the solid lines and fold it down along the dotted line. On the front of the passport, draw a special insignia that represents the Animal Kingdom. On the back, list animals that would make good traveling companions for your animal.

## The Secretary of Zoology of the Animal Kingdom

*hereby requests that the Animal Kingdom citizen named herein be allowed passage without delay or hindrance into desired area and be given all lawful aid and protection to which it is duly entitled.*

______________________________
(signature of bearer)

**NOT VALID UNTIL SIGNED**

## ANIMAL KINGDOM PASSPORT

Class: ______________________________

Order: ______________________________

Family: ______________________________

(picture)

Given Name: ______________________________

Date of Birth: ______________________________

Habitat or Biome: ______________________________

**ADAPTATIONS**

Physical: ______________________________

______________________________

______________________________

Behavioral: ______________________________

______________________________

______________________________



**Note to the teacher:** Use with "Passport, Please!" on page 173. Students will need scissors, crayons or markers, and encyclopedias or other reference materials to complete the page.

Name ______________________ Completing a scattergram, problem solving

# Scat It!

Dr. Sigmund Charles Anthony Tuttleberry, known as Dr. Scat, is a famous ornithologist. He has collected data to see if there is a relationship between a bird's wingspan and its body length. Use the data in the box to help him make a *scattergram* (a graph that shows paired data without connecting it with a line). Then answer the questions below.

**Data Box**

| Bird | Approximate Wingspan | Approximate Body Length |
|---|---|---|
| caracara | 50 in. | 23 in. |
| golden eagle | 84 in. | 36 in. |
| magnificent frigate bird | 84 in. | 40 in. |
| gannet | 72 in. | 35 in. |
| marabou stork | 113 in. | 60 in. |
| common pigeon | 24 in. | 13 in. |
| Caspian tern | 53 in. | 20 in. |
| whooping crane | 90 in. | 60 in. |

**Comparing Birds' Wingspans and Body Lengths**

Approximate Body Length: 0, 12, 24, 36, 48, 60, 72, 84

Approximate Wingspan: 12, 24, 36, 48, 60, 72, 84, 96, 108

1. Which bird has the greatest difference between wingspan and body length? ______________
2. Which bird has the least difference between wingspan and body length? ______________
3. List two pairs of birds that have about the same difference between body length and wingspan. ______________
4. What is the difference between the longest and shortest wingspans? ______________ Longest and shortest body lengths? ______________
5. What is the average wingspan of the birds (to the nearest tenth of an inch)? ______________
6. What is the average body length of the birds (to the nearest tenth of an inch)? ______________
7. Does each column of data have a mode? __________ If so, what is it? ______________
8. What trend does this scattergram show? ______________

**Bonus Box:** Change each measurement above to feet and inches. Then order the body lengths from least to greatest. Order the wingspans from greatest to least.

Name ______________________________ Research skills

# On the Go!

The adaptations of many plants and animals are related to how they move. Each ticket below tells how a particular plant or animal gets around. Write the name of each plant or animal from the suitcase below on the correct ticket. Use reference materials to help you.

1. has a flexible backbone that helps increase the length of its stride ____________
2. has muscles that squeeze an elastic material that helps it jump high into the air ____________
3. is the fastest flier in the insect world ____________
4. has seed pods that get caught in animal fur and on human clothing ____________
5. has seeds with miniature parachutes that help them float through the air ____________
6. has seeds with wings that let them spin and drop slowly toward the earth when blown by the wind ____________
7. swoops down through the air on its prey ____________
8. cruises in the air for many hours ____________
9. rolls across the land and scatters seeds ____________
10. moves with help from microscopic structures called *cilia* ____________
11. has body segments that extend and contract ____________
12. uses a form of jet propulsion ____________

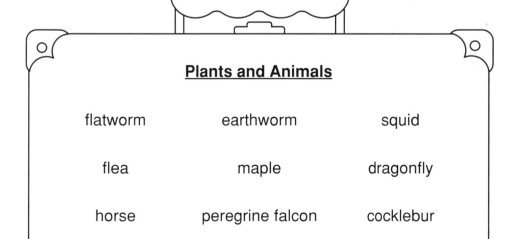

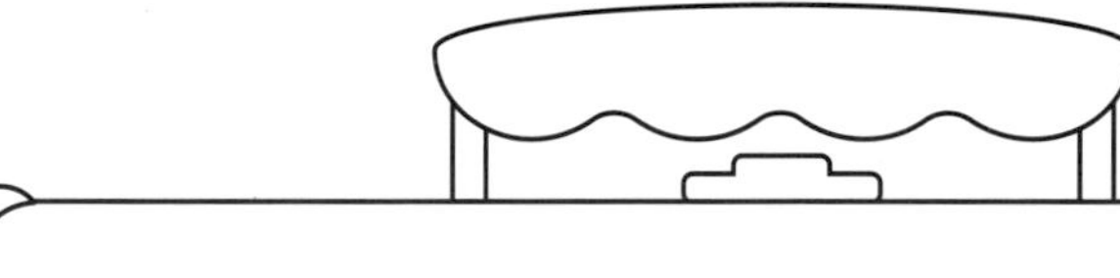

**Plants and Animals**

| | | |
|---|---|---|
| flatworm | earthworm | squid |
| flea | maple | dragonfly |
| horse | peregrine falcon | cocklebur |
| swan | dandelion | tumbleweed |

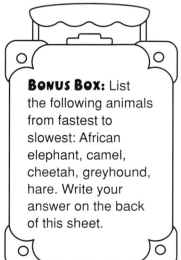

**Bonus Box:** List the following animals from fastest to slowest: African elephant, camel, cheetah, greyhound, hare. Write your answer on the back of this sheet.



**Note to the teacher:** Students will need encyclopedias or other reference materials to complete this page.

# Water, Water, Everywhere!

Whether it trickles, freezes, or evaporates, water moves and constantly changes form. Invite students to splash around in the following activities, games, and investigations to learn more about this wonderfully unique substance!

*by Daniel Kriesberg, Bayville, NY*

## Gotta Have Water!

### Concept: Importance of water

Begin your study with a relay race that helps students realize the importance of water. Label two containers—one "Yes," one "No"—for each team of students. Also, make and cut apart one copy of the cards on page 181 for each team. Arrange each team's cards on a desk next to a masking-tape starting line; then place the team's containers an equal distance away from the starting line. Finally, position each team behind its line.

On your signal, Player 1 on each team takes a card, runs with it to his team's containers, and drops it in the container that indicates whether the item needs water. Then he runs back, tags Player 2, and goes to the back of his line. Continue play until each team has played all of its cards. Announce that the team that finished first and has the most correct answers wins. Then explain that *every* card should have been dropped into a "Yes" container. Pull a card from a "No" container and discuss how it can be linked to water. (For example, the people and factories that make a stapler need water.) Continue discussing the "No" cards. Then declare the team with the most cards in its "Yes" container the winner.

## Dirty Water

### Concept: Water pollution

Is water pollution a problem that can be improved over time? Pose this question to students; then treat them to the following simulation. Place a large, clear plastic cup that's three-fourths full of water on a table. Begin reading aloud *A River Ran Wild: An Environmental History* by Lynne Cherry (Houghton Mifflin College, 1995). As you read, represent the changes that transformed a clean Nashua River into a polluted one by adding the following items to the cup:

- Add several fire-scorched twigs after reading about how the Indians set fires to clear brush from the forest floor.
- Add a handful of soil after reading about how the settlers cleared the forest.
- Add a handful of sawdust and several drops of red food coloring after reading about how paper mills dumped leftover pulp and dye into the river.

After reading about laws that were passed to stop the pollution, filter the "contaminated" water into an empty cup by pouring it through a funnel that's lined with two coffee filters. Have students compare the filtered water (the river after cleanup efforts) to a clear cup of water (the river before pollution). Help them note that the water's cleanliness improved but that some "pollutants" were difficult to remove.

## $H_2O$'s Unique Qualities
### Concept: Properties of water

All you need to demonstrate water's many properties is a glass of lemonade and the simple investigations on this page! After the experiments, let students sip lemonade as you share *A Drop Around the World* by Barbara Shaw McKinney (Dawn Publishers, 1998).

**Materials for the class:** large container of pink-lemonade-flavored powdered drink mix, tablespoon, water, 2 clear plastic cups, ruler
**For each group of four students:** 4 paper clips, 1 small plastic cup of water
**For each student:** clear plastic cup of water, plastic spoon, paper towel, ice cube

- **Water can dissolve more substances than any other liquid.** Have each student stir one tablespoon of drink mix into his cup of water and observe how it dissolves. Explain that water can dissolve more substances than any other liquid. It can even dissolve oxygen, a gas. The small amount of oxygen dissolved in water is what aquatic plants and animals breathe.

- **Water in its solid form is less dense than its liquid form.** Have each child put an ice cube in her lemonade and watch it float. Explain that if ice were heavier than water and did not float, lakes, rivers, and oceans would freeze from the bottom up and kill most aquatic life-forms.

- **Water is the only substance existing naturally in three states.** Fill two cups with one tablespoon of lemonade each. Measure and record the height of the liquid in each cup. Place one cup in a sunny place and the other in a freezer. Have students measure and record the heights of the lemonade daily for several days. Students will observe that the freezer's lemonade freezes and increases in height while the lemonade in the sun evaporates and leaves behind lemonade crystals. Explain that if water did not exist in all three states (solid, liquid, gas), there could be no water cycle.

- **Water is sticky and has capillary action.** Direct students to spill a little lemonade on their desktops; then have them soak it up with paper towels and observe how the liquid *adheres* to, or sticks to, the paper. Explain that water is easy to clean up because it can stick to other substances. Also explain that water can climb up a surface against gravity's pull. This property helps a column of water rise from a tree's roots hundreds of feet in the air to its stems.

- **Water has surface tension.** Have one student at a time in each group carefully float a paper clip in a cup of water. Explain that the water's top layer is *cohesive* (or sticky), making it strong enough to support objects heavier than itself.

## Water Cycle Circles
### Concept: The water cycle

Show students that if they can toss a ball, they can understand the water cycle! Gather a tennis ball for each group of five students. Also number and label five index cards for each group as follows: 1—Sun, 2—Evaporation, 3—Clouds, 4—Precipitation, and 5—Land, Groundwater, or Body of Water. (If you have more than 25 students, make an additional set of cards.)

Next, draw a simple diagram of the water cycle on the board such as the one shown. Review the diagram. Then give each child one labeled card. Have students circulate around the room and form teams comprised of a complete set of numbered cards. Direct each team to put down their cards and form a circle (with students standing in numerical order according to their cards); then give a tennis ball to each child who held a Sun card. Explain that the ball represents a water molecule. At your signal, team members pass the ball around the circle as quickly as possible. As a student passes a ball, she announces her role in the water cycle. Periodically call out "Stop" and a number from one to five. Have the student who held that card explain her step in the water cycle to her teammates. Conclude by asking, "How long has your team's water molecule been circulating?" Then point out to students that the same amount of water circulating in the water cycle today has been doing so since the world was formed. Amazing!

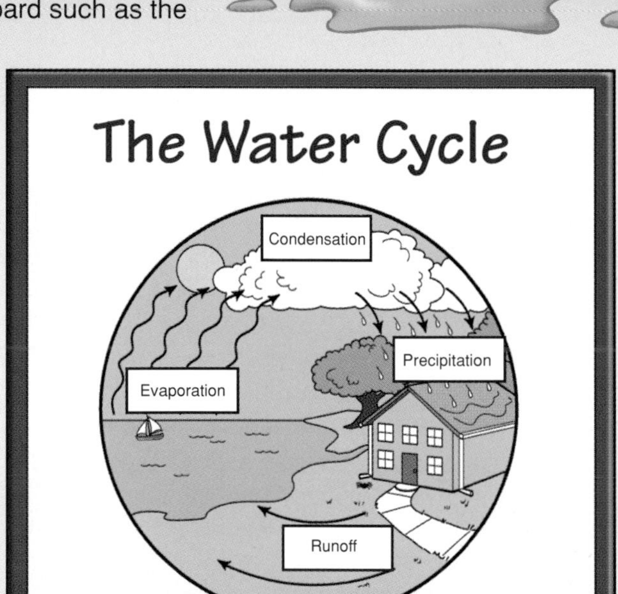

## Itty-Bitty Bits of Freshwater
### Concept: Water conservation

Use this simple demonstration to convince students of the need to conserve freshwater. Display a clear glass filled with water. Announce that the water in the glass represents all the water in the world. Pour out 97 percent of the water, explaining that it represents the salt water in the world's oceans. Announce that the remaining 3 percent represents the world's freshwater. Pour out 2 percent more, explaining that this water is unavailable because it is frozen in ice caps and other glaciers. Tell students that half of the remaining 1 percent is groundwater (found beneath the earth's surface). Only about one-fiftieth of 1 percent of the earth's water fills rivers and lakes.

Have students consider how precious this small amount of water is and how pollution can affect it. Then write these questions on the board: How can freshwater be protected from pollution? How might the water in ice caps be used without upsetting the ecological balance? How might salt be removed from ocean water? Challenge each student to research one of the questions and write a plan suggesting a solution to the drinking-water dilemma. Set aside time for students to present their plans to the class.

## Where to Absorb Interesting Water Facts

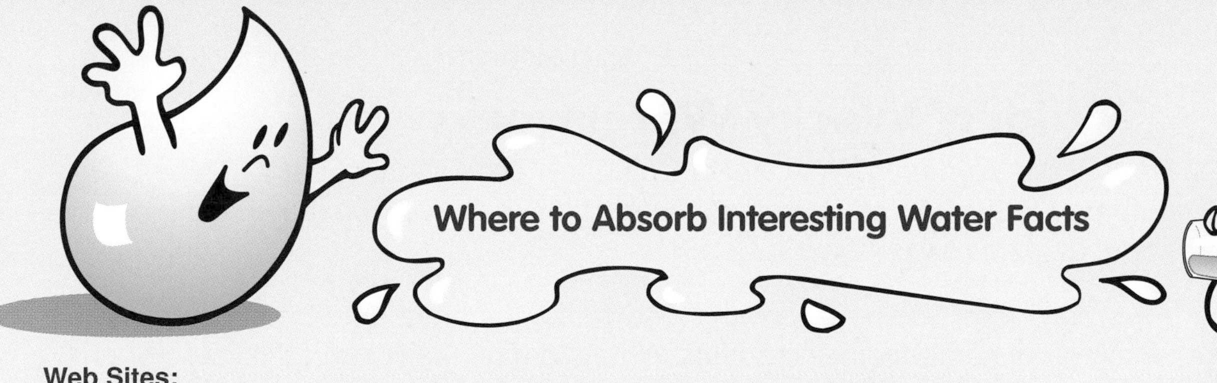

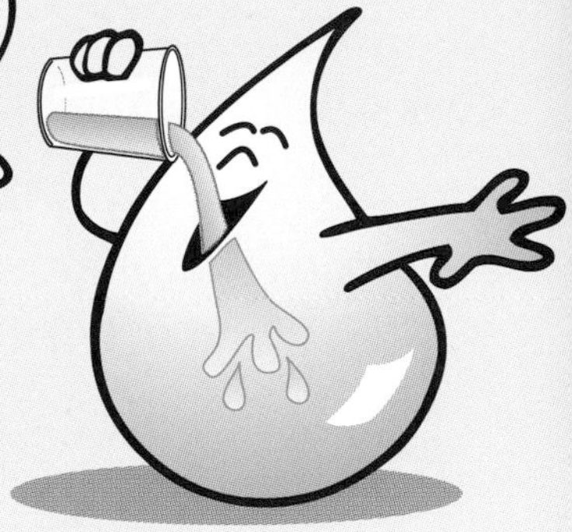

**Web Sites:**
The U.S. Geological Survey's Water Science for Schools: **ga.water.usgs.gov/edu/**
The Environmental Protection Agency's Office of Water: **www.epa.gov/ow**

**Books:**
*Drip! Drop! How Water Gets to Your Tap* by Barbara Seuling (Holiday House, Inc.; 2000)
*The Drop in My Drink: The Story of Water on Our Planet* by Meredith Hooper (Viking Children's Books, 1998)
*A Drop of Water: A Book of Science and Wonder* by Walter Wick (Scholastic Inc., 1997)
*Water Dance* by Thomas Locker (Harcourt Brace & Company, 1997)

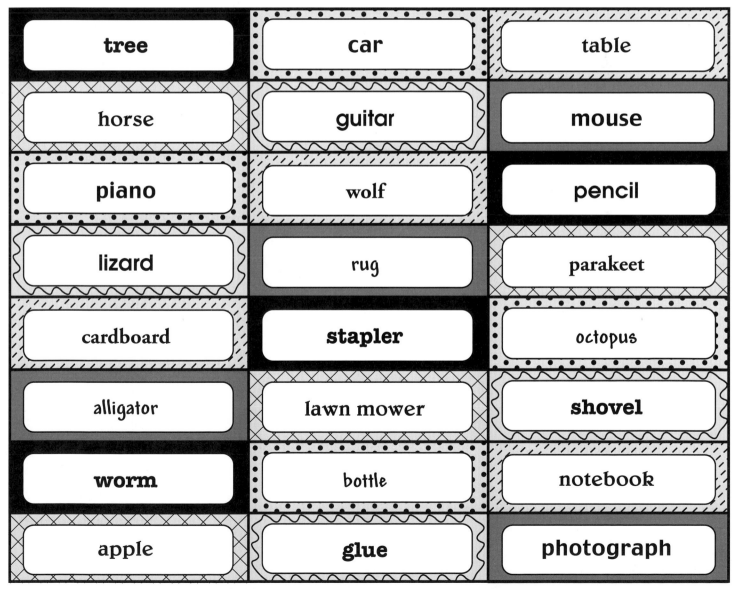

| | | |
|---|---|---|
| tree | car | table |
| horse | guitar | mouse |
| piano | wolf | pencil |
| lizard | rug | parakeet |
| cardboard | stapler | octopus |
| alligator | lawn mower | shovel |
| worm | bottle | notebook |
| apple | glue | photograph |



**Note to the teacher:** Use with "Gotta Have Water!" on page 178. Make one copy of this page for each group of students.

Name ______________________________ Reading comprehension: matching sentence parts

# Wild 'n' Wacky Waterworks

Walter and Wilma work at the Workman Waterworks Company. They connect pairs of pipes along water lines. Help them do their job by following the directions below. If you match the pipes correctly, you'll learn some amazing facts about water!

**Directions:** Match the words written on one pipe with those written on another to form a complete sentence. There are ten different sentences all together. Write them on the back of this page or on another sheet of paper.

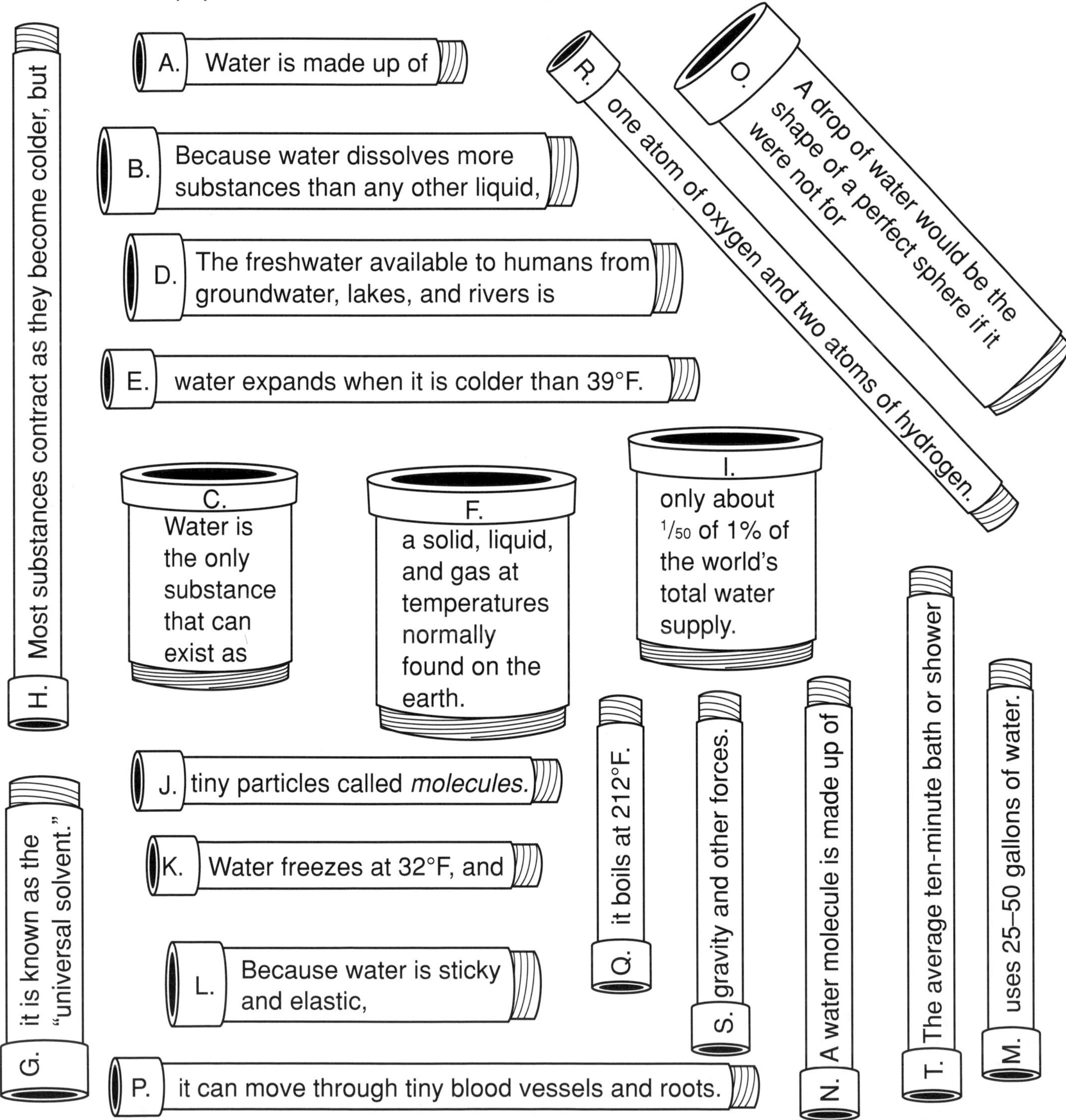

H. Most substances contract as they become colder, but
A. Water is made up of
B. Because water dissolves more substances than any other liquid,
D. The freshwater available to humans from groundwater, lakes, and rivers is
E. water expands when it is colder than 39°F.
R. one atom of oxygen and two atoms of hydrogen.
O. A drop of water would be the shape of a perfect sphere if it were not for
C. Water is the only substance that can exist as
F. a solid, liquid, and gas at temperatures normally found on the earth.
I. only about 1/50 of 1% of the world's total water supply.
G. it is known as the "universal solvent."
J. tiny particles called *molecules.*
K. Water freezes at 32°F, and
L. Because water is sticky and elastic,
Q. it boils at 212°F.
S. gravity and other forces.
N. A water molecule is made up of
T. The average ten-minute bath or shower
M. uses 25–50 gallons of water.
P. it can move through tiny blood vessels and roots.


**Bonus Box:** A tomato is about 95 percent water, an elephant about 70 percent, a human about 65 percent, and a potato about 80 percent. List these percentages on the back of this paper in greatest to least order.

# Literature

# The Phantom Tollbooth
## by Norton Juster

Milo's life seems dull and boring—that is, until the day when a tollbooth mysteriously materializes in his bedroom. Naturally, he's compelled to drive through it, especially since he has nothing better to do! With that comes the end of Milo's ho-hum life and the start of a magical journey to a land of numbers, words, illusions, reality, and lessons about life. Buckle up—the road trip of a lifetime is about to begin!

*with ideas by Lori Sammartino*

### Before Reading
**Skills: Making predictions, writing a paragraph**

Build excitement about the rollicking road trip ahead with this prereading activity. Give each student a copy of page 187. Point out that this page lists the places Milo, the book's main character, will visit during the story. Then instruct each child to complete the reproducible as directed, using a dictionary if necessary. As an extension, have each student choose one place that he predicts will be most interesting for Milo to visit. Then have him write a paragraph explaining his choice. After sharing his paragraph with the class, direct the student to staple it behind the reproducible. Collect the students' papers to use again with "After Finishing the Book" on page 186.

### During Reading
**Skill: Journal writing**

Want students to keep a journal as they travel with Milo on his incredible excursion? Then pack the half-page reproducible of journal prompts on page 188 into your lesson plans!

I'm the Mathemagician, and I say it's numbers that REALLY count!


### After Chapter 1
**Skill: Characterization**

Help students keep track of this book's colorful cast of characters with an ongoing project. First, have students help you mount 12" x 18" sheets of black paper end to end on your walls to create a giant road. Use white chalk to draw a dotted line down the middle of the road. Next, assign each student a character from the list below. After reading a chapter that includes a new character, have the appropriate student draw, color, and cut out an illustration and a speech bubble expressing the character's feelings. Have the student share her work; then attach the cutouts to the road. To periodically assess comprehension skills, make a statement about a character without mentioning his or her name; then ask students to identify the character using the display to help them.

**Characters:**

*Ch. 1:* Milo
*Ch. 2:* the Whether Man, Lethargarians, Tock
*Ch. 3:* King Azaz's advisers—the Duke of Definition, the Minister of Meaning, the Earl of Essence, the Count of Connotation, the Undersecretary of Understanding
*Ch. 4:* the letter man, the Spelling Bee, the Humbug
*Ch. 5:* Officer Shrift, Faintly Macabre
*Ch. 6:* King Azaz (also Ch. 7), Mathemagician (also Ch. 14); Princess of Sweet Rhyme, Princess of Pure Reason (also Ch. 18)
*Ch. 9:* Alec Bings
*Ch. 10:* the Giant/Midget/Fat man/Thin man, Chroma the Great
*Ch. 11:* Kakofonous A. Dischord, Dynne
*Ch. 12:* the Soundkeeper
*Ch. 13:* Canby
*Ch. 14:* the Dodecahedron
*Ch. 16:* .58 Child, the Everpresent Wordsnatcher
*Ch. 17:* the Terrible Trivium, the demon of insincerity, the Gelatinous Giant
*Ch. 18:* the Senses Taker
*Ch. 19:* the Triple Demons of Compromise, the Horrible Hopping Hindsight, the Gorgons of Hate and Malice, the Overbearing Know-it-all, the Gross Exaggeration, the Threadbare Excuse, the Dilemma

## After Chapter 4

### Skills: Vocabulary, synonyms

Superb, smashing, impressive, noteworthy, splendid—that's how King Azaz's ministers might describe this fun vocabulary activity! Tell students that King Azaz has hired them to serve as his Official Synonym Scribes. Their first job is to write a handbook of new words from the story. Have each child staple ten sheets of lined paper inside a folded piece of 18" x 24" construction paper to make a booklet. Direct him to label the cover as shown and decorate it.

After booklets have been made, display and go over the sample page shown for chapter 1. Then provide thesauruses and dictionaries so students can create pages for chapters 1–4. As you continue to read, have each student complete pages for chapters 5–20. Periodically, select a volunteer to read aloud his four synonyms for a particular chapter's vocabulary word. Challenge his classmates to skim the chapter and identify the correct word.

**Chapter:** 1

**vocabulary word:** wistfully

**synonyms:** hopefully, yearningly, wishfully, longingly

**sentences:**

1. Milo wistfully stared at the tollbooth, hoping that the trip would be worthwhile.
2. Looking hopefully at the tollbooth, Milo wished for the trip of a lifetime.
3. The child looked yearningly at the toy in the store window.
4. She wishfully watched the puppy at the pet store and hoped Mom would buy it.
5. Mom looked longingly at her friend's new ring.

## After Chapter 7

### Skill: Idioms

Serve up a fun lesson on idioms—one of the main courses in King Azaz's royal banquet—with this class book project. Make a supply of the form shown below so that you have one per pair of students. After reviewing idioms, have the class skim chapter 7 to locate examples (see the list shown) as you list them on the board. Next, divide the class into pairs. Give each twosome a blank form and assign the pair an idiom from the list. Direct each pair to fill out its form following these directions.

Section 1: Write the idiom.

Section 2: Illustrate the literal meaning of the idiom.

Section 3: Illustrate the true meaning of the idiom.

After each twosome shares its work, bind the completed pages into a class book titled "That's Not What I Meant!"

**Idioms from chapter 7:**

- how time flies
- make mountains out of molehills
- splits hairs
- makes hay while the sun shines
- leaves no stone unturned
- hangs by a thread
- a light meal
- a square meal
- eat my words
- bite off more than you can chew
- in one ear and out the other
- out of the frying pan into the fire
- bite my head off

## After Chapter 11

### Skills: Critical thinking, paragraph writing

Chapters 10 and 11 paint pictures of a world without color and a world without sound. Earlier chapters introduce students to a debate over the importance of words versus numbers. Use these scenarios and the steps that follow to set up two simplified classroom debates: Color versus Sound and Words versus Numbers.

1. Divide students into four groups: pro-color, pro-sound, pro-words, and pro-numbers.
2. Have each team write a summary of its position and a list of supporting reasons.
3. Have one pro-color group member make an initial statement, followed by a pro-sound member. Repeat with the words and numbers groups.
4. Have each team draft a rebuttal that tries to weaken the arguments made by the opposing group.
5. Have one member from each team make a closing argument summarizing the key points that support the team's position.
6. Have color and sound group members vote on the words/numbers debate; then have words and numbers students vote on the color/sound debate.
7. As a follow-up, have each student write a paragraph telling what he voted for and why. Then, as a class, discuss the persuasive techniques used by the winning teams to win votes.

## After Chapter 18

### Skills: Data collection, graphing

As they are about to be attacked by monstrous demons, Milo and Tock run into the official Senses Taker, who forces them to fill out form after form. Take a cue from this odd little man with an activity that turns a form into a great graphing exercise. Have each student complete a copy of page 189 as directed. Then poll students to find out how they answered question 20. List the data on the board. Then repeat the poll with questions 5, 11, and 21. Next, divide the class into four groups. Assign one list of data to each group. Then have the group construct a graph to illustrate its information. Hang on to the forms to use anytime you want students to grab some graphing practice.

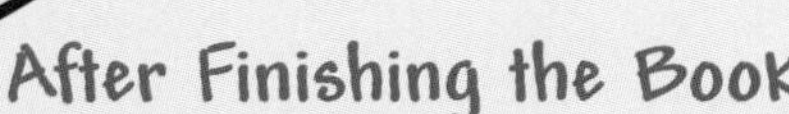

## After Finishing the Book

### Skills: Recalling details, descriptive writing

Finished? Then have each child complete a new copy of page 187 by writing a short description for each place. (For an answer key, see page 310.) After students finish the page, redistribute the copies completed in "Before Reading" on page 184. Have them compare their predictions to the descriptions and share how accurate they were.

Next, ask each child to choose her favorite place from Milo's trip and write a second paragraph explaining her choice. After a sharing time, group together students who wrote about the same place. Give each group markers and a sheet of poster board with instructions to design a travel poster advertising its place. For a display that's anything but ho-hum, have students pin their posters to a large appliance box that's been painted and decorated to resemble Milo's tollbooth.

Come Visit
DIGITOPOLIS
Countless things to see and do!
It's a vacation spot that always adds up to fun!
Learn to add, subtract, multiply, and divide!
It's the #1 place to be!

Name ________________________________



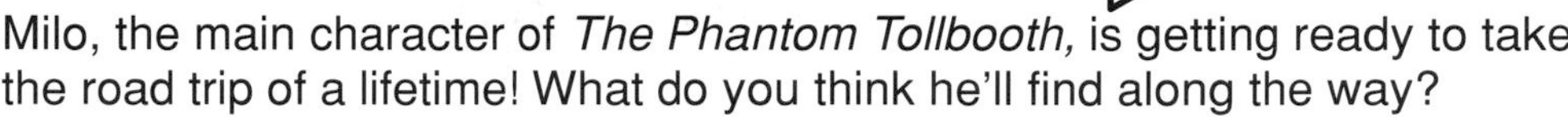

# To Destinations Unknown

Milo, the main character of *The Phantom Tollbooth,* is getting ready to take the road trip of a lifetime! What do you think he'll find along the way?

**Directions:** Below are the names of places Milo will visit on his trip. On the lines for each place, write a sentence predicting what you think this spot might be like. Use a dictionary if needed.

Expectations: ________________________________

Doldrums: ________________________________

Dictionopolis: ________________________________

Point of View: ________________________________

Illusions: ________________________________

Reality: ________________________________

Valley of Sound: ________________________________

Island of Conclusions: ________________________________

Digitopolis: ________________________________

Infinity: ________________________________

Mountains of Ignorance: ________________________________

Castle in the Air: ________________________________



**Note to the teacher:** Use with "Before Reading" on page 184 and "After Finishing the Book" on page 186.

Name ____________________ *The Phantom Tollbooth* Word order in sentences

# Sweeping Up the Sentences

When the Humbug and the Spelling Bee scuffle, they knock down all of the stalls in the word market. This mixes up all the words so that no one's sentences make any sense! Now the police officers in Dictionopolis need your help. Rearrange the words from each pile below to make a sentence about chapter 5. Write your unscrambled sentences on another sheet of paper.

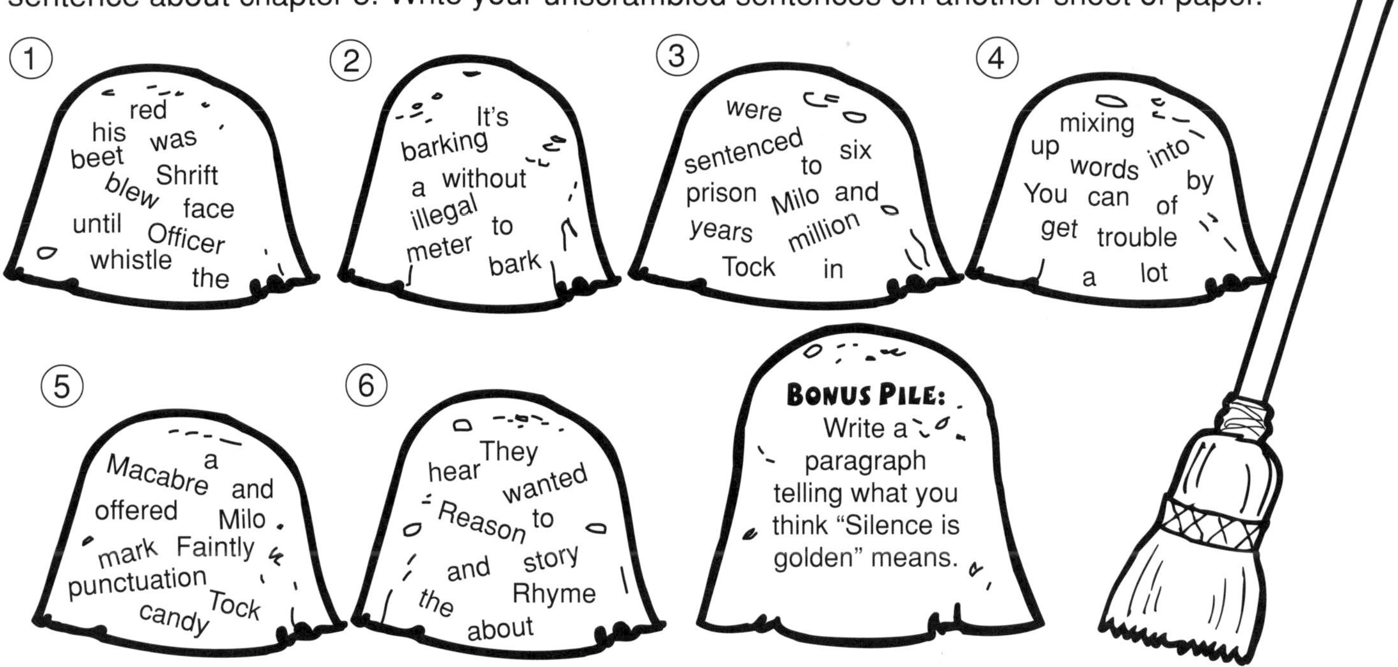

1
red his was beet Shrift blew face until Officer whistle the
2
It's barking without a illegal to meter bark
3
were sentenced six to prison Milo and years million Tock in
4
mixing up words into by You can of get trouble a lot
5
a Macabre and offered Milo mark Faintly punctuation Tock candy
6
They hear wanted Reason to and story the Rhyme about
BONUS PILE:
Write a paragraph telling what you think "Silence is golden" means.

*The Phantom Tollbooth*
Journal prompts

Name ____________________

## It's the "Write" Time!

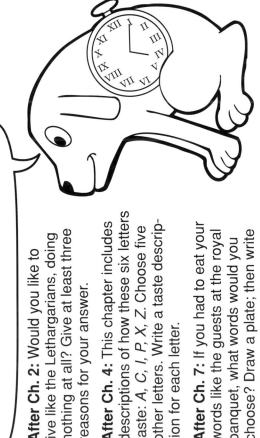

**After Ch. 2:** Would you like to live like the Lethargarians, doing nothing at all? Give at least three reasons for your answer.

**After Ch. 4:** This chapter includes descriptions of how these six letters taste: *A, C, I, P, X, Z.* Choose five other letters. Write a taste description for each letter.

**After Ch. 7:** If you had to eat your words like the guests at the royal banquet, what words would you choose? Draw a plate; then write your words atop the plate.

**After Ch. 9:** Alec Bings teaches Milo that the way things are seen depends on the point of view. For example, a bucket of water looks different to an ant than it does to an elephant. Choose an object. Describe it from an ant's point of view. Then describe it from an elephant's point of view.

**After Ch. 12:** Pretend you live in the Valley of Sound. Write a letter to the Soundkeeper telling her about some of the hardships you face living in a world without sound.

**After Ch. 14:** Pretend that you have 12 different faces, just like the Dodecahedron. Describe how each one would look. Also tell when you would use each one.

**After Ch. 16:** The Everpresent Wordsnatcher misunderstands everything Milo says because he uses words with multiple meanings. List five words that have more than one meaning. Write two sentences for each word. Make sure that each sentence uses a different meaning for the word.

**After Ch. 20:** What important lessons do you think Milo learned on his trip? Make a list of at least five.

 **Note to the teacher:** Use the top half of this page after reading chapter 5. Use the bottom half with "During Reading" on page 184.

Name ______________________________



## Beware the Senses Taker!

In Chapter 18, Milo and his travel companions meet the official Senses Taker, who puts them under a spell with things that appeal to their senses. Now it's your turn to be captivated by the Senses Taker. Complete his form below by filling in the blanks. Remember—forget even one question and he may make you do the form all over again!

1. Name: ______________________________ (First / Middle / Last)  2. Birthdate: ____/____/____ (Mo. / Day / Yr.)
3. Age: __________  4. Home telephone: (    ) ____________________
5. Number of siblings: ________  6. Shoe size: ________  7. Shirt size: ________
8. Hobbies: ______________________________
9. Height: __________  10. Eye color: __________  11. Favorite color: __________
12. Color of shirt you're wearing: __________  13. Favorite dinner food: __________
14. Number of books you read each year: ________  15. Future career: __________
16. Number of ice-cream cones you eat in a week: ______________________
17. Favorite book: ______________________________
18. Favorite movie: ______________________________
19. Number of fingers on your right hand: ______________ left hand: __________
20. Number of people that live in your house: ______________________
21. Number of times you brush your teeth in a day: ______________________
22. One place you'd like to visit: ______________________________
23. Time spent each week eating: ____________ sleeping: ____________
    playing: ____________ going to school: ____________
24. How long it takes you to get to school: ______________________
25. Signature: ______________________________
26. Date: ______________________________

**Bonus Box:** Pretend you're the Senses Taker. On the back of this page or on another sheet of paper, write five silly questions to add to this form.



**Note to the teacher:** Use with "After Chapter 18" on page 186.

# The View From Saturday

*What does the view from Saturday look like, and why is it different from the rest of the week? Perhaps it has something to do with the Saturday tea parties that The Souls hold. Or maybe it's the friendship forged by these four sixth graders as they help a teacher and win the Academic Bowl championship. Invite students to check out the view for themselves with the following activities based on E. L. Konigsburg's splendid Newbery winner.*

*with ideas by Lori Sammartino*

## During Reading

***Skills: Vocabulary development, writing sentences***

Build vocabulary and writing skills with an activity students can work on as they read the book. Each word below contains one or more smaller words as, for example, *permission* includes the shorter word *miss*. Give each child a copy of the list. Challenge her to circle a smaller word in each word; then have her write a meaningful sentence that includes both words (for example, "I'll have to *miss* the field trip if I don't turn in a *permission* slip"). See page 310 for the answer key.

**Chapter 1:** benevolently, briskets
**Chapter 2:** tendrils, incandescently
**Chapter 3:** paraplegic, chanteuse
**Chapter 4:** carafe, tamping
**Chapter 5:** quavering, enchantingly, ceremoniously
**Chapter 6:** vanquished, flanks, jubilant
**Chapter 7:** rendered, stealth, sentinels
**Chapter 8:** unison, incarnation
**Chapter 9:** publicity, precedent
**Chapter 10:** sustain, parched
**Chapter 11:** perpetual

## After Chapter 1

***Skills: Consumer math, paragraph writing***

At Margaret and Izzy's wedding, Noah must come up with five gifts. Instead of buying the presents, he ends up giving away his own prized possessions. Give students a chance to step into Noah's shoes with this math and writing activity. Photocopy a generic catalog order form for each child. Also collect a supply of old catalogs. Divide the class into groups and distribute the forms; then give each group a stack of catalogs. Direct each student to fill out his order form with five gifts that have a combined value of $100 or less. After the student has completed the form and computed the total cost (plus tax and shipping charges), have him write a paragraph explaining why each of his items would make an appropriate gift for a Century Village resident. Let students share their paragraphs; then take a poll to see how many kids would rather give away their possessions as Noah does and how many would rather purchase gifts. Work in a little graphing practice by having students graph the poll results.

## After Chapter 2

***Skill: Fact and opinion***

In chapter 1, Noah repeatedly states facts. And in chapter 2, Nadia shares facts about sea turtles. Help students practice distinguishing facts from opinions by playing Tic-Tac-Know. To prepare, have each student trace an enlarged copy of the turtle pattern on page 194 onto green paper. Direct her to cut out the tracing, divide it in half, and label the two halves as shown. Then have the student write on the cutout five facts about sea turtles from chapter 2 and five opinions.

Next, draw a giant tic-tac-toe grid on the board. Divide the class into Team X and Team O; then have each student label her cutout with an *X* or *O.* To play, a student from Team X reads one statement from her turtle to a Team O player. If the opponent correctly identifies the statement as a fact or an opinion, she tapes her turtle in one of the grid's spaces. If the opponent answers incorrectly, a Team O member then reads a statement to a Team X player. The game continues until one team makes a tic-tac-toe, scoring one point. Play several rounds before declaring the winning team.

## After Chapter 5

***Skills: Recalling story details, building character***

In this chapter and earlier ones, several characters give reasons for the "decline of Western Civilization." Mrs. Gershom thinks it has something to do with not knowing how to write a B & B letter. Tillie Nachman blames the ballpoint pen. And Mrs. Olinski wonders if it's because people no longer take afternoon tea. Discuss these reasons with students. Then guide them to conclude that kind words and acts—like those practiced by The Souls—might be one way to rebuild Western Civilization. To highlight this point, introduce the bulletin board shown and challenge students to be on the lookout for kind deeds. Each time a student observes an act of kindness, have him describe it on a teacup pattern (page 194); then have him color and cut out the pattern and add it to the left side of the board. To the right side of the board, have students add teacups labeled with examples of kindness from the book. For a three-dimensional touch, staple a few real tea bags on the board.

## After Chapter 6

***Skills: Acronyms, creative thinking***

In chapter 6, Julian challenges the advisory panel about the acronyms he has given in his answer. Use this event to introduce acronyms as mnemonic devices. First, explain to students that acronyms are words that are created by using the first letters of the main words in a title or group of words. For example, *FBI* is an acronym for the Federal Bureau of Investigation. Have students share examples of acronyms they know. Then write a spelling or vocabulary word on the board, such as *hybrid*. Beside the word, write a phrase or sentence that uses its letters, such as "Have you been rolling in dough?" Point out that this sentence might be easier to remember than the word's spelling. Then assign each student or pair of students a short list of spelling or vocabulary words. Challenge students to create a sentence or phrase that will help them remember the spelling of each word. As students share their lists, write their responses on a chart. Keep the chart up so students can add to it as they study new words.

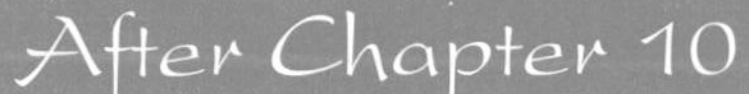

## After Chapter 10

***Skills: Characterization, critical thinking***

The Souls win the Academic Bowl state championship and bring home the trophy to prove it. Follow up chapter 10 by discussing with students which characters might deserve their own special awards. After students share their ideas, give each child a copy of page 193. While students work, label a 12" x 18" sheet of construction paper for each character listed on the page. After each child has completed the activity, have him cut out each award and glue it to the appropriate poster.

## Culminating Activity

***Skills: Critical thinking, writing a letter***

What better way to end this winning novel than with an activity that returns the kindness offered to others by The Souls? Give each student a white paper lunch bag. Then instruct students to follow these steps:

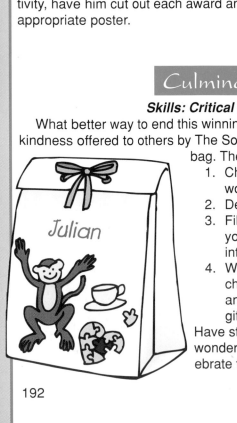

1. Choose the member of The Souls that you would most like to have as a friend.
2. Decorate the bag as a gift bag for your friend.
3. Fill the bag with items (real ones or pictures) that your friend would like, based on the traits and interests he or she exhibits in the book.
4. Write a letter to your friend explaining why you chose him or her. Also list each item in your bag and explain why you thought it would be a great gift for your friend.

Have students present their bags to the class as a wonderful way to reminisce about The Souls and celebrate their unselfish actions.

Name ____________________________________________

# The Envelope, Please!

Ethan thinks Julian deserves an award for being the strangest person to ride the bus. What unique awards do you think the characters listed below deserve? Fill in each award for a character listed on the sealed envelope. Do not give more than one award to any one character.

The
Award
Hearty congratulations
to
for
A
Star
Is Born!
Award
To
For
The
#1
Award
To
for
For
Allen Diamondstein
Homer Fairbain
Ginger
Nadia Diamondstein
Margaret Draper Diamondstein
Mrs. Olinski
Hamilton Knapp
Mr. Singh
Noah Gershom
Ethan Potter
Julian Singh
Dr. Rohmer
The
Award goes to
Champion
To
For
Hats off to
who wins the
Award for




**Note to the teacher:** Use with "After Chapter 10" on page 192.

**Patterns** Use the turtle pattern with "After Chapter 2" on page 191. Use the teacup pattern with "After Chapter 5" on page 191.

Name ____________________ Writing, reading comprehension

**Chapter 1:** Finish writing the thank-you letter Noah starts to Grandma Sadie and Grandpa Nate.

**Chapter 2:** If you had to move to a new state as Nadia does, what three things would you miss most about your old home? How would you cope with the move?

**Chapter 3:** Ethan is very embarrassed when the salesclerk assumes that the puzzle is for a girlfriend. Describe a time when you were embarrassed like Ethan.

**Chapter 5:** Do you think Julian will turn out to be a good choice for the Academic Bowl team? Explain your answer.

**Chapter 7:** Why do you think this victory is sweeter than all the others?

**Chapter 8:** Since her accident, Mrs. Olinski has had to make herself ignore people who stare at her. Why do you think she feels so comfortable with The Souls at Sillington House?

**Chapter 9:** Pretend you are a television reporter. Write one different interview question for each member of The Souls; then write an answer for each question as if you were that character.

**Chapter 10:** The author wrote this book's chapters from the perspectives of different characters. Even the time changes back and forth from the present to the past. Why do you think the author chose this style? Was it a good idea? Why or why not?

**Chapter 11:** After her team wins the championship, Mrs. Olinski feels a sense of loss. Describe an experience you've had that was great, but left you feeling sad that it was over.

**Chapter 12:** Do The Souls choose Mrs. Olinski, or does she choose The Souls? Explain your answer.

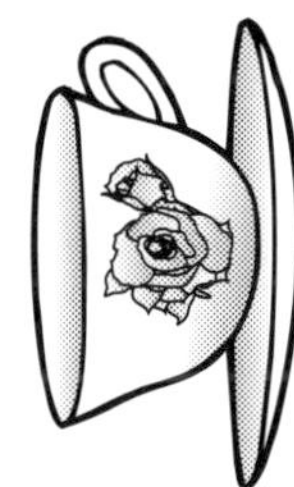



**Note to the teacher:** Make a copy of the topics above for each student to keep inside his reading journal or a file folder. Use the prompts as discussion starters or writing topics.

Name______________________________ *The View From Saturday* Student contract

# What's Your Cup of Tea?

Choose _____ of the following activities to complete by __________________. Cut out the teacup of each activity you choose and paste it on the front of a folder. Store your work for each activity in the folder.

| | | |
|---|---|---|
| Noah gives simple directions for how to fill a calligraphy pen. Write your own set of directions for completing a simple task (brushing your teeth, tying your shoes, etc.). **Chapter 1** | Draw a diagram of your family tree, showing your ancestors as far back as you are able. On a separate sheet of paper, write a paragraph explaining which family—Noah's, Ethan's, Nadia's, or Julian's—is most like yours. **Chapter 3** | Several of Mrs. Olinski's students have names that begin with *J*. List at least 30 names that begin with *J*. Then cut a large *J* from construction paper. Rewrite your list in alphabetical order on the cutout. **Chapter 4** |
| Submit a plan for holding a class tea party. Include a list of all food and supplies needed, with their estimated costs. Also design an invitation that includes all important information. **Chapter 5** | Noah names the parts of the eye in the order that light reaches them. Draw a diagram of the human eye. Below the diagram, list five new facts you have learned about the eye. **Chapter 6** | Design an Academic Bowl board game. Include directions on how to play and five questions (and answers) for each of these categories: music, math, geography, literature, and science. **Chapter 8** |
| The Souls are committed to kindness. Make a Kindness Coupon booklet that includes at least six coupons. Label each coupon with the name of the person receiving it and a small act of kindness you will do for him or her. **Chapter 10** | Pretend you are a reporter covering the 20-year reunion of Mrs. Olinski's sixth-grade class. Write an article titled "What Happened to The Souls?" **Chapter 12** | Design your own activity for chapter ______________. Get teacher's approval. ________________ ________________ ________________ ________________ ________________ Approved: ________ |



**Note to the teacher:** Before duplicating this page, fill in the blanks with the number of activities you want students to complete and a due date. To use this page, each student will need a manila file folder, scissors, and glue. Or use any of the activities as a small-group or whole-class assignment.

# The Girls' Revenge

Christmas is coming to Buckman, West Virginia, and Caroline Malloy thinks there could be no better time to seek revenge on Wally Hatford. It isn't long before her two sisters and Wally's three brothers join in the fun-filled feud. Invite students to laugh out loud with Phyllis Reynolds Naylor's book that continues her series about the ongoing pranks between the Malloy sisters and their neighbors, the Hatford boys.

*ideas by Simone Lepine*

## Before Reading the Book

**Skill: Vocabulary development**

In *The Girls' Revenge,* the Malloys and Hatfords play lots of pranks on one another. Help students recognize the difference between a playful prank and harmful ridicule with this vocabulary activity. Write the following words on the board: *prank, practical joke, ridicule.* Have students define the words and discuss the questions below; then introduce the book. Challenge students to decide as they read whether any of the characters take their pranks too far.

- What do the words have in common? How are they different? Give an example of each one.
- What holiday is famous for playing practical jokes on others? Why do you think people like to play pranks and practical jokes on others?
- Do you think pranks and practical jokes are more acceptable than ridiculing someone? Why?

## During Reading

**Skill: Cause and effect**

Almost every time Caroline and Wally plot their revenge, things get more complicated. Help students track the story's plot—and sharpen their skills at recognizing cause and effect—with this easy-to-do activity. Give each child four sheets of paper stapled together at the top. Have her fold the stack into thirds from top to bottom and label each page's sections with headings as shown. As students read about each prank, have them fill in their sheets. See page 311 for a suggested answer key.

Prank: (the cause)
Caroline plots to earn Wally's trust.

People involved:
Caroline, Wally, and Peter

Consequences: (the effects)
- Caroline picks Wally to be her partner for the December project.
- Wally lies when Caroline interviews him.
- Caroline asks Peter to steal Wally's clothes.
- Wally and Caroline fail the December project.

## After Chapter 2

**Skills: Interviewing, critical thinking**

When Caroline and Wally must interview each other for a special project, the trouble really begins! To implement your own December project, divide students into pairs. Give each student a paper clip and a copy of page 199. Then have the partners complete Part One together as directed, encouraging them *not* to act like Caroline and Wally! When students have completed Part One, have each child share his report with the class. Conclude by having students complete Part Two of the sheet independently.

## AFTER CHAPTER 8

**Skills: Vocabulary development, writing dialogue**

Writing dialogue is a challenging skill to teach, especially if your students tend to overuse the word *said.* Make this task easier by having students look in Phyllis Reynolds Naylor's book for examples of dialogue. Divide students into eight groups. Have each group spend five minutes skimming a different chapter from 1 to 8 to list synonyms the author uses in place of *said.* In turn, have each group read its list aloud; then discuss with students how the use of a single word can often change the mood of a scene in the book. As a follow-up, have each child complete a copy of the reproducible on page 200 as directed.

## AFTER CHAPTER 12

**Skills: Making a timeline, sequencing**

The Malloy girls *really* fool the Hatfords when they stage a scene that causes the boys to think Caroline is a murderess! Chapters 10–12 present this event first from the boys' point of view and then from the girls'. To help students fully understand the order in which this prank's events occurred, ask each child to pretend she is a detective. Her job is to use both the boys' and girls' stories to reconstruct the events surrounding the "murder." To do this, have each student create a timeline of the events on a 12-inch length of adding machine tape. When everyone is finished, have each child compare her timeline with a partner's.

Timeline of a "Murder"

- Eddie sees boys coming toward girls' garage.
- While boys climb ladder to loft, girls plan how Caroline will "kill" Beth.
- Caroline and Beth recite words to "Jingle Bells," while boys think they're arguing.
- Boys see Caroline appear to hit Beth on head with hammer and think a murder has been committed.
- The lights go off. The girls roll on floor laughing in dark while boys run home and call 911.

## AFTER CHAPTER 13

**Skill: Vocabulary review**

What happens when you mix the Malloys, the Hatfords, and snow? A snowball fight, of course! Let students join in the fun by having a blizzardy battle of their own! Prepare a list of vocabulary words from the book (one word per student). Have students define all the words and study their meanings. Then assign a different word to each student. Ask the student to write his word on one sheet of paper and its definition on another. Collect the papers from half the students to set aside. Ask each child who is holding two papers to give one sheet to a student without one.

Next, divide students into two teams. Position the teams so that they face each other on opposite sides of the room. (Join the fun if there is an odd number of students.) Then guide the class through the steps below. After several rounds, have students throw their papers away and play with the second batch.

**Steps:**

1. Wad the paper into a ball to represent a snowball.
2. On a count of three, throw the snowballs back and forth at each other. Aim only below your opponents' shoulders and don't throw hard.
3. Continue throwing snowballs until you hear "Freeze."
4. Find a snowball, open it, and mingle among your classmates until you find its match.

## After Chapter 14

**Skills: Point of view, letter writing**

In this chapter, Wally writes his old neighbors, the Benson brothers, to let them know about the troubles he and his brothers are having with the Malloy girls. Have students reread Wally's letter to review his perspective of what has been happening. Then have each child write a letter from Caroline to her friends back in Ohio telling them what has been happening from *her* perspective. After students share their letters, have them discuss the differences in the two characters' points of view.

## After Chapter 22

**Skills: Making inferences and predictions**

After all the crazy pranks between the Malloys and Hatfords, could it be that they are becoming friends? Challenge students to search for evidence that suggests this possibility. Give each student three to four sticky notes; then direct her to skim the last few chapters of the book and look for clues that the boys' and girls' attitudes toward each other are changing. When she finds a clue, have her place a sticky note on that page to flag it. Then divide students into groups to share their flagged sections and discuss how a friendship between the two families could be starting.

Follow up by having students make predictions about what might happen if the story continued. Will the pranks stop? Will the Bensons move back into their old house? Will the Hatfords and Malloys become friends? If students really want answers to these questions, have them read *A Traitor Among the Boys,* the next book in the series. Or if they want to know how the rivalry began, introduce them to the first three books of the series: *The Boys Start the War, The Girls Get Even,* and *Boys Against Girls.*

## Culminating Activity

**Skill: Characterization**

Have students think about what they have learned about the Malloys and Hatfords with the help of the ready-to-go activity on page 201. Give each child an $8\frac{1}{2}$" x 11" sheet of white paper, colored pencils, scissors, glue, and a copy of page 201. After discussing the directions on page 201 together, carefully model how to cut along the dotted lines to create the flaps and how to glue the sheet to the white paper. When students have completed the activity, have them share with the class what they wrote on the gift tag.

Name ________________________________________

# Part One: The Interview

**Step 1:** List everything you know about your partner on another sheet of paper. Then paper-clip the paper to the back of this sheet.

**Step 2:** Think of ten questions that could help you learn more about your partner. Write the questions on another sheet of paper, skipping three lines between each one to allow room for writing an answer. Use the guidelines below to help you word the questions. Then clip the questions to the back of this sheet.

- Word each question so that your partner has to give an explanation instead of a *yes* or *no* answer. For example, write "What did you like best about your visit to Washington, DC?" instead of "Did you like visiting Washington, DC?"
- If your partner answers a question using only one or two words, have him or her explain the response. For example, if you ask, "What is your favorite animal?" and your partner answers, "A dolphin," then ask, "*Why* is the dolphin your favorite animal?"

**Step 3:** Conduct the interview. Ask your partner one question at a time. Listen carefully to each answer. Make notes on your question sheet.

**Step 4:** Write a paragraph summarizing what you learned about your partner. Look at your notes for help. Clip the paragraph to the back of this sheet.

**Step 5:** Share what you learned about your partner with the class.

# Part Two: Reflections

Think about the interview with your partner as you answer the questions below. Write your answers on the back of this sheet or on another sheet of paper.

1. What new things have you learned about your partner?
2. Do you and your partner share a common interest? If so, what?
3. If someone wanted to buy a gift for your partner, what would you suggest this person buy? Explain why you think your partner would like this gift.
4. Caroline and Wally were not very successful with their interviews. About the only thing they learned was how much they liked to annoy each other! Compare your interview experience to theirs. What was different?
5. If you were conducting another interview, what things would you do differently? Explain.



**Note to the teacher:** Use with "After Chapter 2" on page 196.

Name ____________________________________________

*The Girls' Revenge*
Vocabulary, writing dialogue

# Say What?

Good writers tell you *what* a character says and provide clues about *how* the character says it. Those clues help a reader understand both the action and tone of what is being said. The words on the gifts below are just some of the ones used in place of *said* in *The Girls' Revenge*.

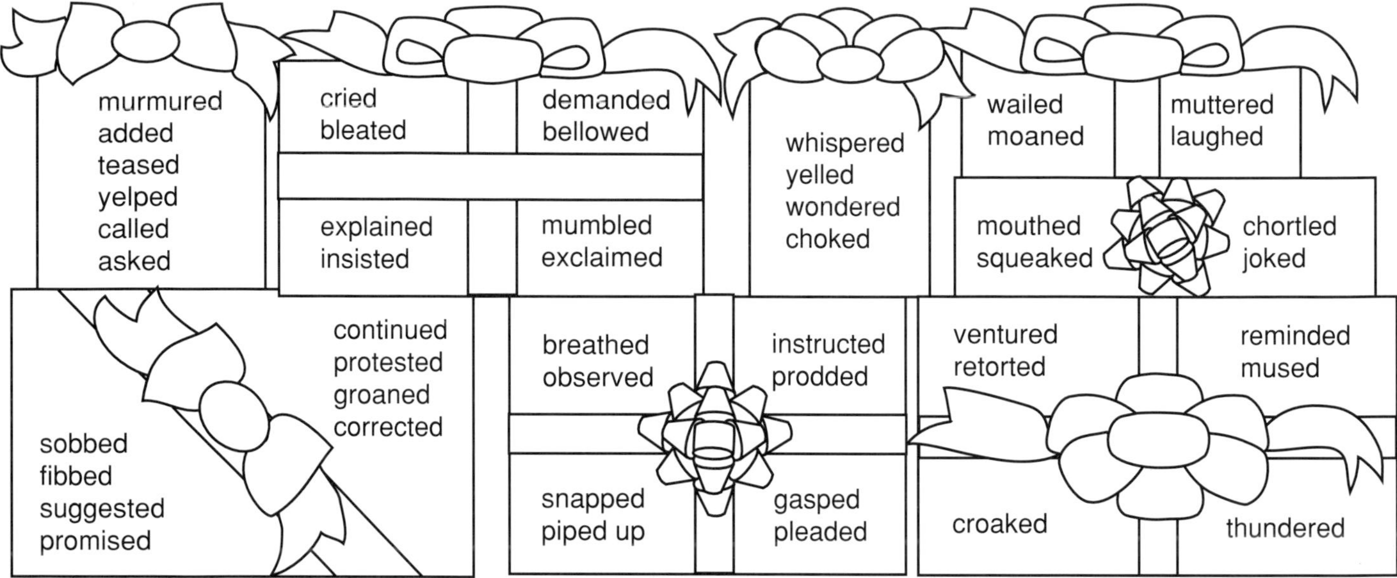


**Part One:** Read each sentence to determine the tone of the speaker. Then fill in the blank with a word above that matches the speaker's tone. There is more than one possible answer for each sentence.

1. Tammy ______________________, "Come closer. I have a secret to tell you!"
2. "Stop teasing me, or I'll tell Mom!" ______________________ Melissa.
3. "Scott, I'll help you with all your chores this morning if you'll let me borrow your skateboard this afternoon," ______________________ Jonathan.
4. Jamal ______________________, "That is the funniest book I've ever read!"
5. Marcie ______________________, "My science project won first place!"
6. "I was the one who spilled ink on the rug," ______________________ Anna.
7. "My stomach hurts from eating so much," ______________________ Rob.
8. "We'll need to leave home in an hour to get to the game on time," ____________ Grandpa.
9. "Look at the grease on my shirt," ______________________ Andy. "Wait until Mom sees it!"
10. "Mom," ______________________ Jaimie, "my gerbil's not in its cage!"
11. Casey ______________________, "You promised to return my CD today, Brad."
12. "Jenny can't go skating with us because she sprained her ankle," ____________ Taylor.

**Part Two:** Now, it's *your* turn! Use any of the words on the gifts above to help you write five of your own sentences that contain quotations. Write the sentences on the back of this sheet or on another sheet of paper. Remember to use quotation marks!



 **Note to the teacher:** Use with "After Chapter 8" on page 197. Accept all reasonable answers.

Name ______________________________

# Secret Santa Surprises

Ho! Ho! Ho! If you could be a Secret Santa to each main character in *The Girls' Revenge,* what special gift would you give each one? Of course, you'd choose a gift that matches each character's personality. Follow the directions below to surprise each character with the perfect present!

**Directions:**

1. Color and decorate each gift box.
2. Cut along the dotted lines to create a flap for each box. Fold each flap up along its top line.
3. Place the sheet with the flaps atop the paper your teacher gives you. Put a dot of glue on the back of this sheet at each holly leaf symbol. Then glue the two papers together.
4. Under each flap, write the name of the gift you would give that character. Or draw a picture of the gift.
5. Choose one character. On the gift tag below, explain why you think the gift you selected for him or her will be appreciated.

_____________, I think you'll like this gift because _____________
______________________________________________
______________________________________________
Your Secret Santa

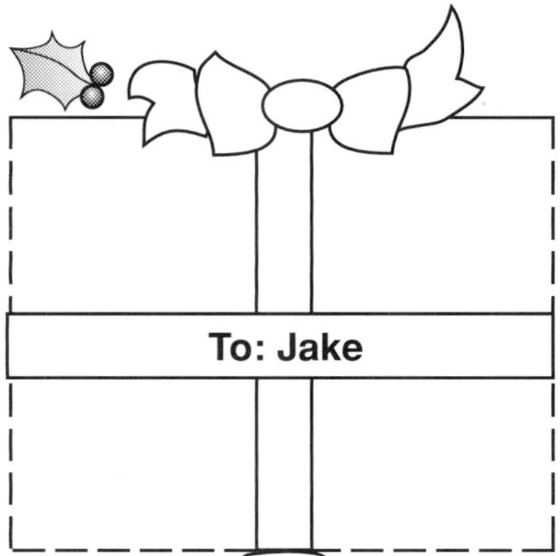

To: Jake

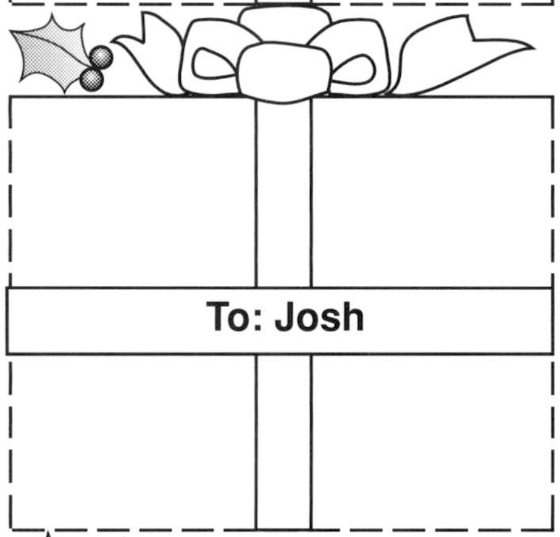

To: Josh

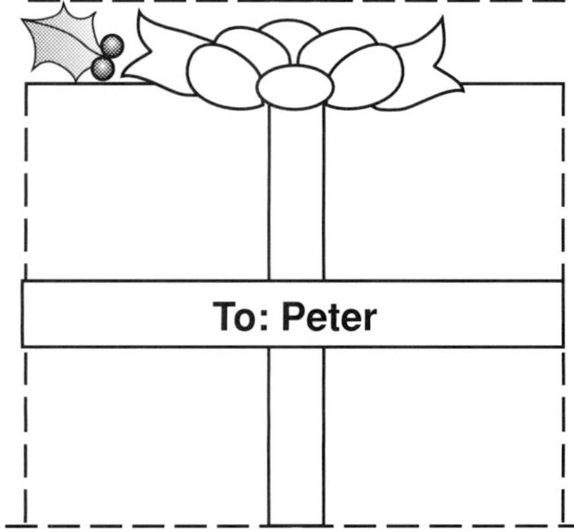

To: Peter

To: Beth

To: Eddie

To: Caroline

Surprise!

To: Wally

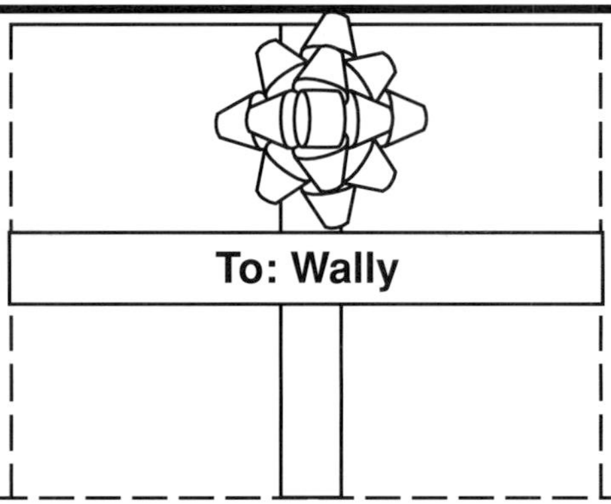

Surprise!

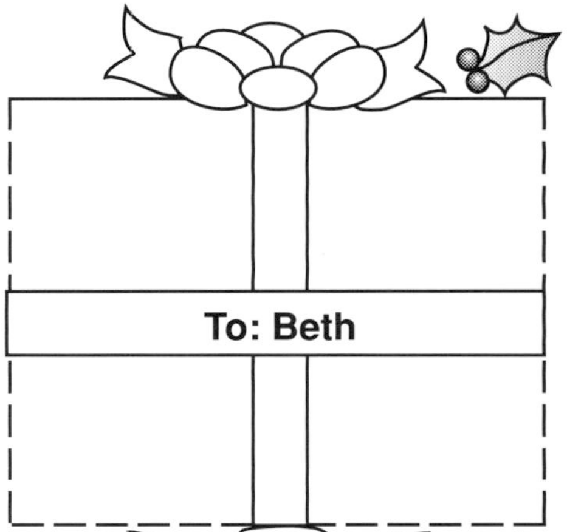

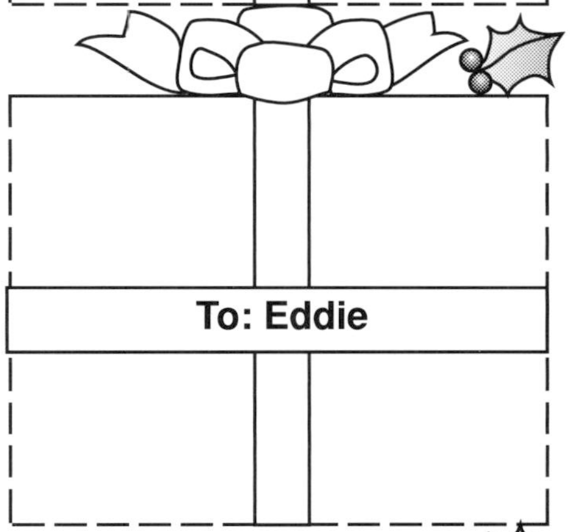

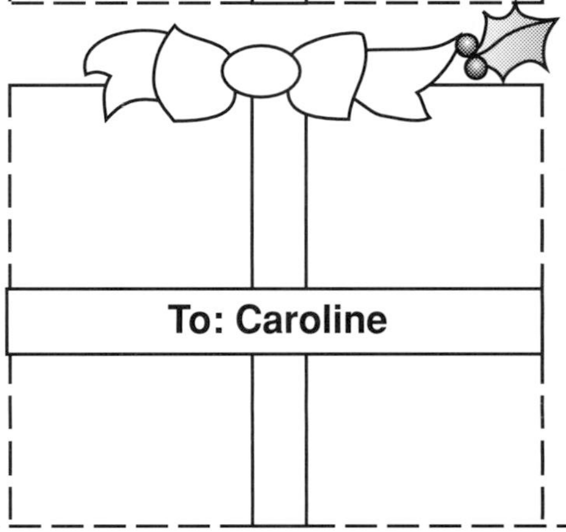

**Note to the teacher:** Use with "Culminating Activity" on page 198. Be sure students start cutting the dotted lines on Peter's, Wally's, and Caroline's gifts from the bottom edge of the page.

# The War With Grandpa

## A Literature Unit

Peter Stokes has declared war on his beloved grandpa. But what else can a fella do when his grandfather moves in with the family and takes over his bedroom? Invite your class to watch this war from the trenches by reading Robert Kimmel Smith's delightfully humorous and touching tale about family relationships.

*ideas by Terry Healy*

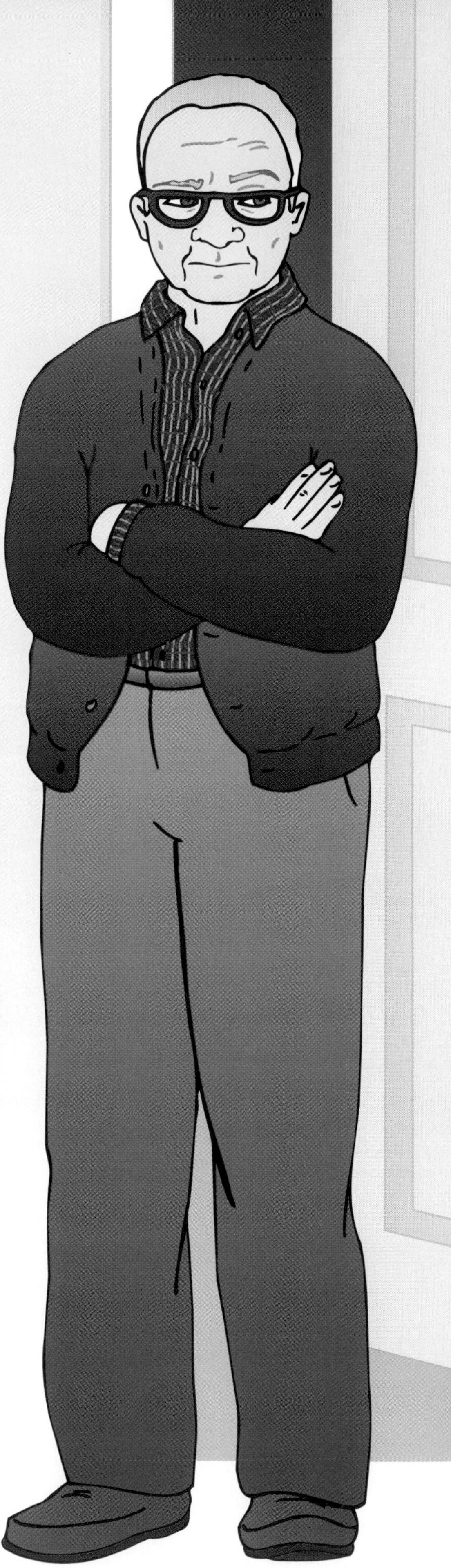

### Before Reading

**Skill: Predicting outcomes**

Introduce this novel by holding up a copy of the book (one with an illustrated cover) and asking students why a boy would go to war against his grandfather. Help students predict reasons for such a family conflict and write them on chart paper. Next, ask students how conflicts can be resolved peacefully. Record students' solutions on the chart paper next to the predicted conflicts. Then save the chart to use with "After Chapter 36" on page 204.

### While Reading

**Skill: Journal writing**

As students read *The War With Grandpa,* have them launch attacks on their writing skills by responding to the following prompts.

**Chapter 2:** Jenny has a secret that she can not keep. Describe what happened the last time you had a secret you couldn't keep.
**Chapter 6:** Reread Pete's promise to himself. Then write a set of ten rules you will follow if you ever become a parent.
**Chapter 8:** Pete is scared about sleeping in the attic. Write a paragraph describing a time when you experienced a night of fright.
**Chapter 11:** Do you agree that "only a dope will mope"? Explain your answer.
**Chapter 17:** Pete chooses the middle of the night for his first attack on Grandpa. Why do you think he does this?
**Chapter 19:** Grandpa shares with Pete how things were when he was growing up. Compare your childhood to Grandpa's.
**Chapter 23:** Pete describes Jenny's different strategies to get a new tutu. Describe an effective strategy you've used to get something from a parent.
**Chapter 27:** Grandpa and Pete have a great time fishing. Write about a time when you and another family member did something special together.
**Chapter 29:** Grandpa wages psychological warfare against Pete. Explain why you think Grandpa's actions make Pete so nervous.
**Chapter 34:** Pete announces to Grandpa that the war is over and then apologizes. Do you think the war between them did any good? Why or why not?
**Chapter 37:** Pete has finished writing his "true and real story." What do you think he has learned from the war with his grandpa?

## While Reading

**Skill: Vocabulary development**

Help develop students' understanding of the war terms in the book with this ongoing activity. Staple together several sheets of chart paper; then trim and decorate the booklet to resemble a soldier's helmet as shown. Place the book and a marker on a table. As students read, have them watch for war-related words (for example, *retaliation, truce, prisoner of war*). Each time a child finds a new word, have her write it and its definition in the booklet. By the end of the book, students will have built a battalion of new words!

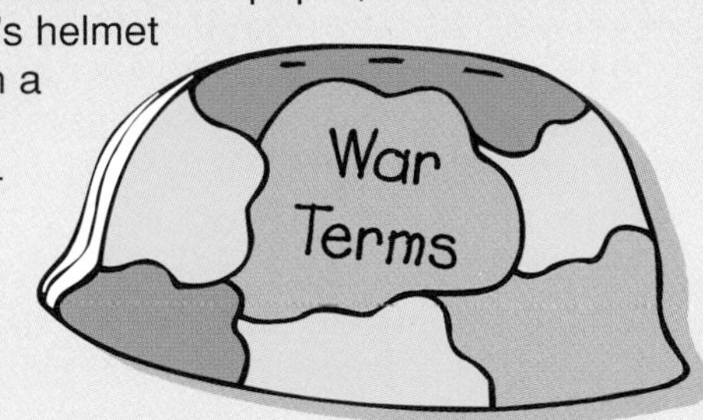


## After Chapter 3

**Skills: Following directions, writing a personal narrative**

Use this three-dimensional art project to motivate students to write personal narratives like Pete does in the story. Give each student the materials listed and guide him through the steps below to make a model of a perfect bedroom. When the models are complete, direct students to reread Peter's description of his room in chapter 3. Then have each child write a paragraph telling why his design represents a "room without gloom." Display the models and paragraphs on a bulletin board titled "Rooms Without Gloom."

**Materials:** 12" x 18" sheet of white construction paper, colorful paper scraps, crayons or markers, glue, scissors, ruler, pencil

**Steps:**

1. On the white paper, sketch a layout of a bedroom. Include items such as a window, door, closet, bed, chest of drawers, etc.
2. From the paper scraps, cut a shape for each object sketched on the layout.
3. Cut one or more flaps in several shapes as shown.
4. Glue the outer edges of the cutouts to the layout.
5. Lift each flap; then draw one or more objects that could be found there, such as socks in a drawer.
6. Color the other parts of the layout, adding details that make it a perfect bedroom.

## After Chapter 12

**Skill: Listing attributes**

Pete's buddies, Steve and Billy, are supportive and advise him on how to get his room back. Use this chapter to trigger students' thinking about the qualities of their own friends. List these words on the board: *dependable, kind, honest, loyal, fun.* Ask students if these words could describe a friend and why. Next, give each child scissors, colored pencils, and a copy of page 205. Instruct her to color one pattern so that it resembles herself and to color the other one to look like a friend. Also instruct her to leave space on each cutout to list the qualities of friendship she and her friend possess. Encourage students not to limit the qualities to those listed on the board, but to include other traits as well. After students cut out their patterns, arrange the cutouts on a wall to encircle the title "A Circle of Friends."

## Before Chapter 15

### Skill: Understanding a story's plot

Let students find out how good they are at making predictions with an activity that takes them through the book's next six chapters. First, explain that a story's plot always involves a *conflict* (a problem) that must be resolved. Next, give each child a copy of page 206. Together, read chapters 15 and 16. Ask students to identify the conflict in this portion of the book (Grandpa is ignoring Pete's declaration of war) and record it on their sheets in the space provided. Then ask them to identify what Pete did in response to this conflict (discussed strategy with Billy and Steve) and record it on their sheets along with three possible consequences of that action. To complete the sheet, have each child read the next four chapters (17–20) and follow the same procedure. As a follow-up, have students compare their predicted consequences with the actual ones described in the book.

## After Chapter 22

### Skill: Making judgments

Once the battles begin, each action taken by Pete and his grandpa has the potential of extending the war or ending it. Allow students to decide for themselves what each action could bring with this activity. Have each child label a sheet of paper as shown. As he reads chapters 23–34, have the student list each action Pete and his grandpa take. Then have him place a check mark in the column that indicates whether he thinks that action will cause the war to continue or to end. Discuss students' charts at the end of each chapter or two.

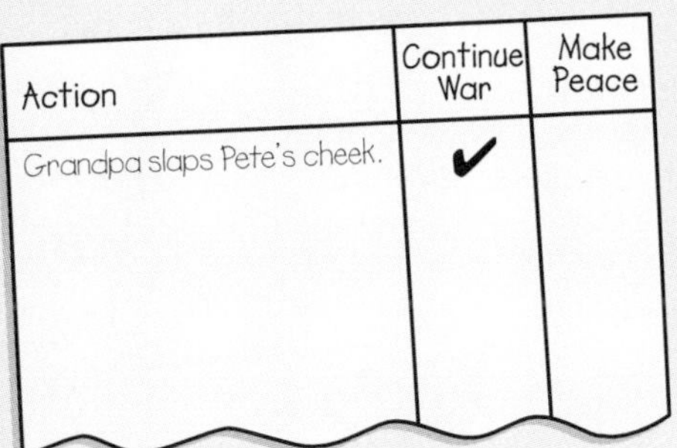

| Action | Continue War | Make Peace |
|---|---|---|
| Grandpa slaps Pete's cheek. | ✔ | |

## After Chapter 36

### Skill: Creative writing

The war has ended and Pete and his grandpa have declared peace. Review how this happened by having students discuss the events in chapters 34–36. Afterward, refer students to the chart they created in "Before Reading" on page 202. Have students decide if Pete and Grandpa ended the war by using any of their suggested strategies. Then challenge students to put the strategies into practice by writing their own peace treaties suggesting how to resolve classroom disagreements. First, divide students into groups of four. Give each group a 9" x 12" sheet of light-colored construction paper on which to record its treaty. Explain that each treaty should include one statement about working together to resolve a difference, one that explains how to resolve a difference, and one that includes a promise to avoid a future conflict. Before sharing its treaty with the class, have each group dab a wet tea bag on its document to make it appear older. If desired, have the class vote on the best treaty; then display the winning treaty next to your classroom rules.

Peace Treaty
We agree to resolve classroom disagreements in the following manner:

Use with "After Chapter 12" on page 203.

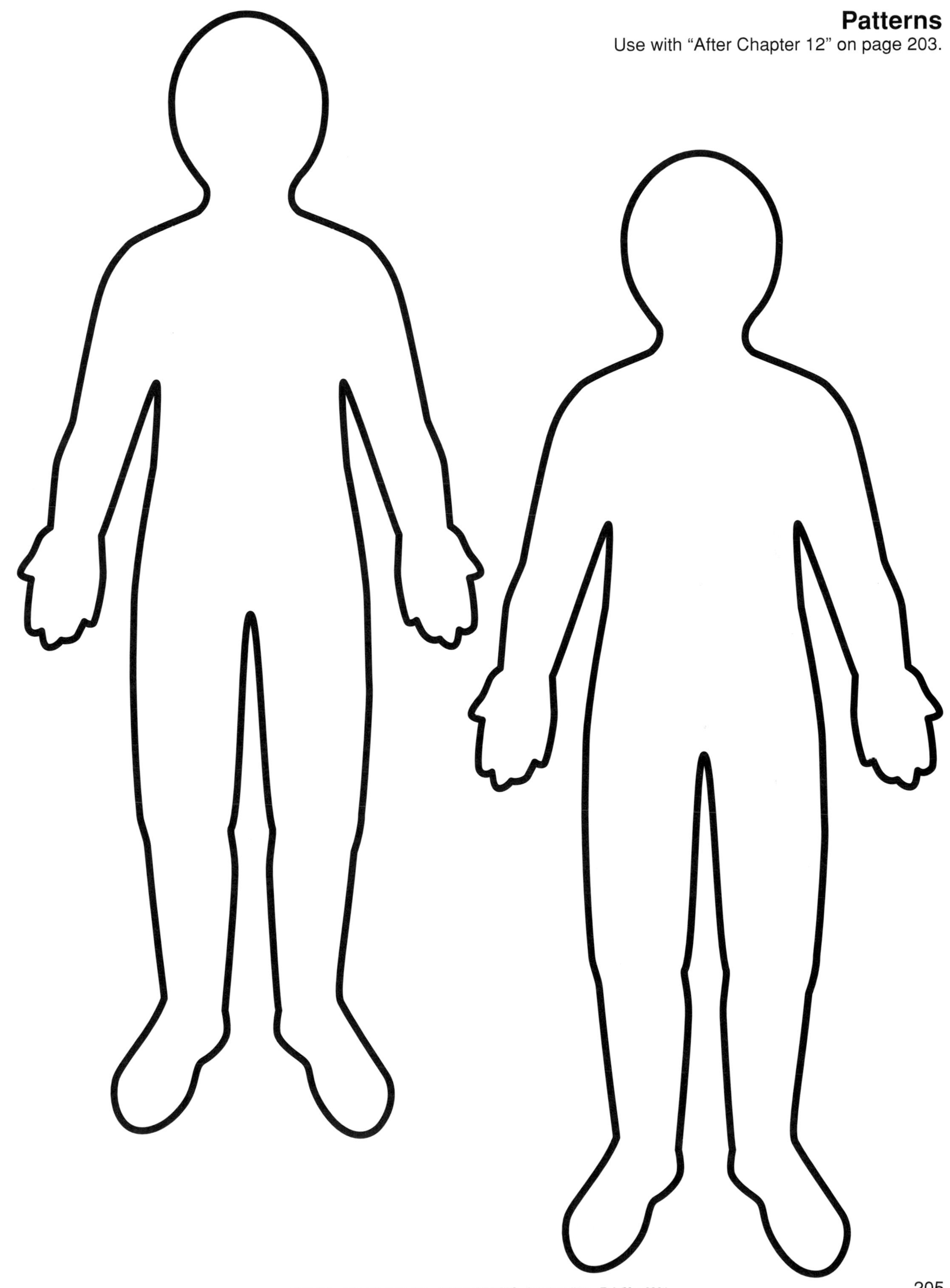

Name ______________________________



# Chain Reactions

**Directions:** First, read the chapters in the top link of each chain. Then describe the conflict described in those chapters, the action that the main characters took in response to it, and the possible consequences of that action.

**Conflict**
**Chapters 15–16**

______________________________
______________________________
______________________________
______________________________
______________________________
______________________________

**Action**

______________________________
______________________________
______________________________
______________________________
______________________________
______________________________

**Possible Consequences**

1. ______________________________
______________________________
2. ______________________________
______________________________
3. ______________________________
______________________________

**Conflict**
**Chapters 17–18**

______________________________
______________________________
______________________________
______________________________
______________________________
______________________________

**Action**

______________________________
______________________________
______________________________
______________________________
______________________________
______________________________

**Possible Consequences**

1. ______________________________
______________________________
2. ______________________________
______________________________
3. ______________________________
______________________________

**Conflict**
**Chapters 19–20**

______________________________
______________________________
______________________________
______________________________
______________________________
______________________________

**Action**

______________________________
______________________________
______________________________
______________________________
______________________________
______________________________

**Possible Consequences**

1. ______________________________
______________________________
2. ______________________________
______________________________
3. ______________________________
______________________________



 **Note to the teacher:** Use with "Before Chapter 15" on page 204.

Name ______________________________



# As the Tide Turns

Pretend that Pete and Grandpa want to go fishing again, this time in early March. To plan their fishing times, they obtain a tides table. Use the table's listings for high and low tides to solve the problems below.

| Date | Morning High Tide | Morning Low Tide | Evening High Tide | Evening Low Tide |
|---|---|---|---|---|
| March 1 | 12:23 A.M. | 6:54 A.M. | 2:07 P.M. | 6:58 P.M. |
| March 2 | 1:12 A.M. | 7:39 A.M. | 2:49 P.M. | 7:54 P.M. |
| March 3 | 2:07 A.M. | 8:23 A.M. | 3:31 P.M. | 8:56 P.M. |
| March 4 | 3:06 A.M. | 9:11 A.M. | 4:19 P.M. | 10:01 P.M. |
| March 5 | 4:11 A.M. | 10:03 A.M. | 5:07 P.M. | 11:17 P.M. |

1. Grandpa likes to fish at high tide. How much time elapses between high tides on March 3? ____________
2. How many minutes later is the evening high tide on March 3 than March 2? ____________ On March 4 than March 3? ____________
3. How many hours and minutes is it from morning high tide until evening low tide on March 3? ____________ On March 4? ____________ On March 5? ____________
4. If Pete and Grandpa want to fish at high tide on the morning of March 5, what time will they have to get up? (Hint: It will take 30 minutes to drive to the fishing spot.) Explain. ____________
5. About how many hours are there each day between high tides? ____________ Low tides? ____________
6. At which of the following times would they least prefer to fish: morning high tide, morning low tide, evening high tide, evening low tide? ____________ Why? ____________
7. How many hours later does evening high tide begin on March 5 than March 1? ____________
8. How long would Pete and his grandpa fish if they started at low tide on the morning of March 1 and stopped that evening at low tide? ____________
9. How many hours and minutes are there from evening low tide on March 2 until morning high tide on March 3? ____________
10. About what time would morning low tide occur on March 6? ____________ Explain how you got your answer. ____________

**BONUS BOX:** If Grandpa puts his boat in the water on March 5 and the water level comes to the third step on the boat's ladder, where will the water level on the ladder be at high tide? Write your answer on the back of this page.



**Note to the teacher:** Use after Chapter 27.

# Roll of Thunder, Hear My Cry

## Activities Based on Mildred D. Taylor's Newbery Winner

**The time is 1933, the place a small town in Mississippi. A black family is struggling to hold on to the land that not only represents its past but also promises hope for the future. Will the Logans be able to overcome the racism that so clearly works against them? Experience their battle through the eyes of young Cassie Logan, and learn how family pride, hard work, courage, and compassion strengthen the ties that bind the Logans to their land and each other.**

*by Lori Sammartino*

## During Reading

**Skills: Vocabulary development, writing dialogue**

Help students tackle the challenging vocabulary in this powerful novel with a cooperative activity that sharpens dialogue-writing skills. Have each student staple 12 sheets of notebook paper between two construction paper covers to make a booklet. Then have him cut out the book pattern on the top half of page 212 and glue it onto the booklet's cover. Next, divide the class into pairs. After each chapter, have each twosome work together to define the chapter's vocabulary words in its booklets. At the end of the book, challenge each pair to select at least ten words from its booklets and use them to write a dialogue between two of the novel's characters. Provide time for students to practice their dialogues before they present them to the class.

Devin's Vocabulary Booklet

## During Reading

**Skills: Writing in response to a prompt, critical thinking**

Encourage students to reflect on this thought-provoking story with the following writing prompts:

**Ch. 1:** If you had been Mrs. Logan, how would you have reacted to Miss Crocker's retelling of the book-stomping incident? Explain your answer.

**Ch. 4:** What is your reaction to Mama's punishment of the kids for going to the Wallace store? Do you think the children learned their lesson? Give evidence to support your answer.

**Ch. 5:** List the emotions you think Cassie must have felt during her trip to Strawberry. Use details from the story to support each feeling on your list.

**Ch. 6:** Mama tells Cassie that there are some things in life that you can choose and others that you have no control over. List things in your life that you have control over. Make another list of things that are out of your control. How does each list make you feel?

**Ch. 7:** Who do you think is a better friend to Stacey: Jeremy or T. J.? Explain your answer.

**Ch. 8:** Tell how you think Cassie's parents would have reacted if they had heard about her revenge on Lillian Jean.

**Ch. 11:** This chapter begins with a poem. Why do you suppose the author chose the first two lines for the title of this book?

## After Chapter 3

**Skill: Understanding an author's purpose**

In her book, Mildred D. Taylor uses the dialect of rural Southerners who lived in the 1930s. To explore this literary element, read aloud the conversation in chapter 1 between the Logan children and T. J. as they walk to school. Ask students what they notice about the conversation. When someone mentions the characters' speech, write the word *dialect* on the board. Explain that it is a form of speech spoken in a specific region by a certain group of people. Discuss with students why they think Taylor chose to use dialect in her story. Then give each child three sticky notes. Direct each student to use the notes to flag three other passages that use dialect in chapters 1–3. After students share their passages, have each child copy one of his examples on his paper and rewrite it using standard grammar and spelling. Let students share their rewritten versions. Then, as a class, compare them with Taylor's original sentences so that students can see how dialect adds authenticity and interest to a story.

## After Chapter 5

**Skills: Reading comprehension, building character**

From watching the school bus carry white children to school to her calamitous trip to Strawberry, Cassie is run down by racism many times during the first five chapters. Use her experiences as a springboard for a discussion of discrimination and its devastating effects. Ask volunteers to share about times when they were treated badly because they were different. Discuss possible solutions to the problem of discrimination, focusing students on what they can do right in their own classroom and school. Then give each child a copy of the bus pattern on page 212. On the pattern, have the student list examples of racial discrimination from chapters 1–5 (along with the corresponding page numbers). Discuss students' lists; then post the buses on black paper that has been mounted on a wall and decorated with white chalk to resemble a road. Title the display "Run off the Road by Racism."

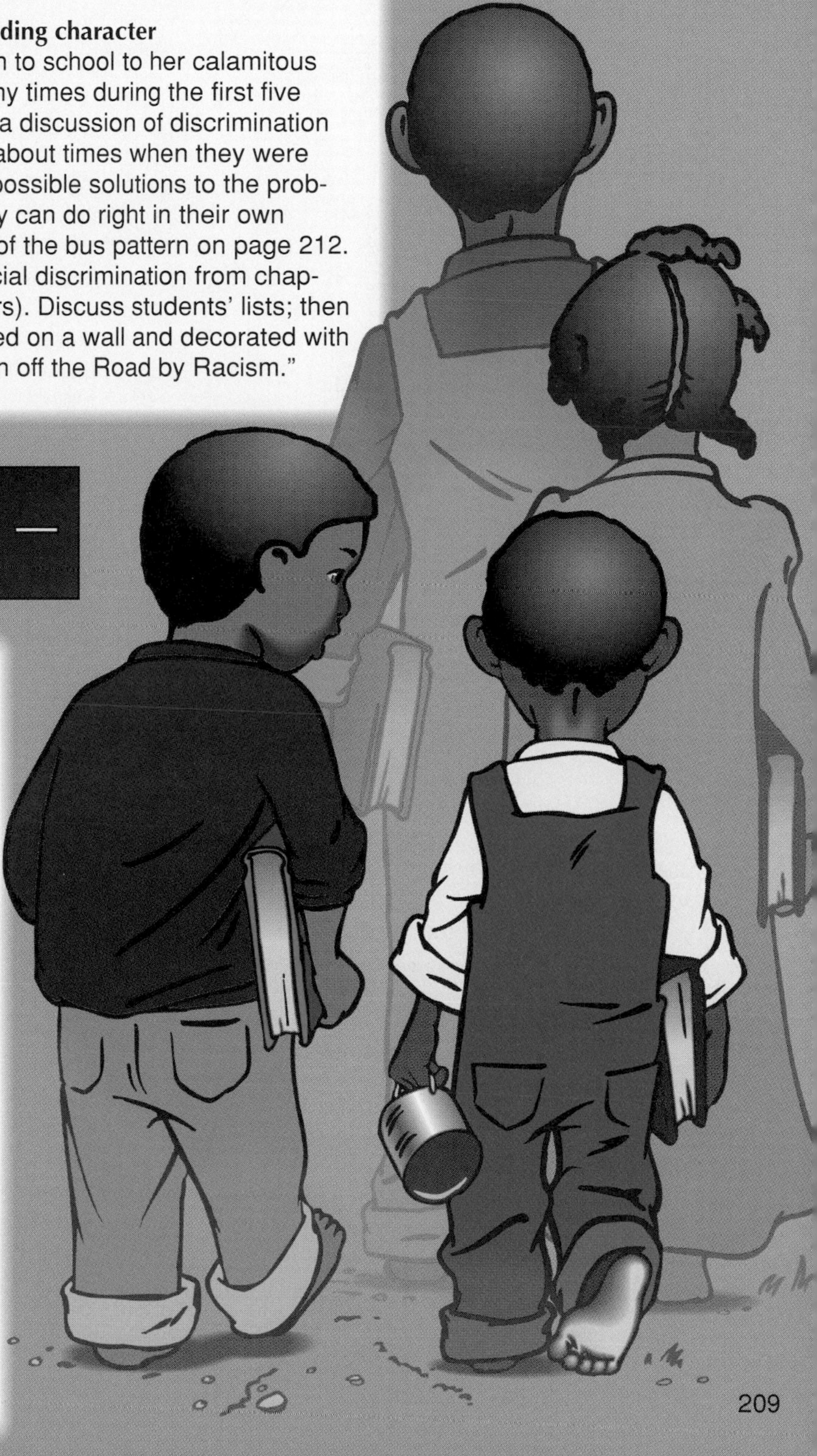

## After Chapter 7

**Skills: Listening, letter writing**

In chapter 7, Cassie and her siblings spend Christmas Day listening to the Logan grown-ups tell stories about their childhoods. Mildred Taylor shares in the author's note that her father—on whom David Logan is based—passed on his family history through masterful storytelling. To help students experience storytelling and its role in oral history, have each student ask an adult relative, friend, or teacher to tell her a story about his childhood. (Or, if desired, ask your school's principal to tell a story to the entire class.) Suggest that the student ask for a story about a favorite holiday memory, special childhood place, or school incident. After the child listens to the story, have her write a friendly letter thanking the adult for his time and describing her favorite part of the story. Review the letters; then provide students with stamped envelopes for mailing. To extend, have each student tell a story about her life to the class. Challenge students to do as the Logan adults did—"imitating the characters in voice, manner, and action"—as they tell their stories.

## After Chapter 9

**Skills: Characterization, making inferences**

Though rich in love, the Logan family daily faces the poverty often found in racism's wake. Focus on comprehension skills by having each student skim chapters 6 and 9 for examples of the Logans' financial difficulties. After students share their examples, divide the class into four groups and give each group a large sheet of construction paper. Assign each group one of the following pairs of characters: Cassie and Big Ma, Stacey and Mama, Christopher-John and Papa, Little Man and Uncle Hammer. Have each group list on its paper three or four items each of its characters might like based on what students have learned about him or her. Beside each item, have the students also write a brief explanation of why they placed it on the wish list, using inferences and details from the book. Provide time for groups to share their lists with the class.

## After Chapter 10

**Skills: Estimating and calculating costs**

In chapter 10, the Logans attend a church revival that includes a home-cooked feast. Discuss with students how favorite foods add to family traditions; then ask each child to bring to school a recipe for a favorite family food. The next day, share the recipes with the class and have students vote on one main dish, three side dishes, and a dessert. Make five copies of each selected recipe. Then divide the class into five groups and give a set of recipes to each group. After a group studies the recipes, have it estimate how much the entire meal would cost. List the groups' estimates on the board. Then provide students with grocery ads and, if possible, access to an online grocer, such as www.peapod.com or www.groceronline.com *(current as of October 2000)*. Have each group search the ads to find the costs of the ingredients and then calculate the total cost of the meal. After groups share their work, compare the students' predictions with the actual costs. If desired, ask parents to prepare each of the five recipes for your class so you can enjoy your own family feast.

## After Chapter 12

**Skills: Summarizing, using a table of contents**

Give students a chance to think like an author with this culminating activity. Point out to students that Mildred D. Taylor uses numbers rather than titles to label the chapters in her book. Then challenge each student to create an appropriate title for each of the 12 chapters as well as a new title for the book. After his list is complete, have the student construct a table of contents that lists chapter numbers, titles, and page numbers. Direct the student to glue his finished table of contents inside a folded 12" x 18" sheet of white construction paper. On the front of the folded paper, have the student write his new title for the book; then have him add an illustration. Hang the finished book jackets on a bulletin board.

If students want to read more about the Logans, introduce them to Mildred D. Taylor's other books featuring this unforgettable family: *Song of the Trees, Let the Circle Be Unbroken, The Well: David's Story, Mississippi Bridge,* and *The Road to Memphis.*

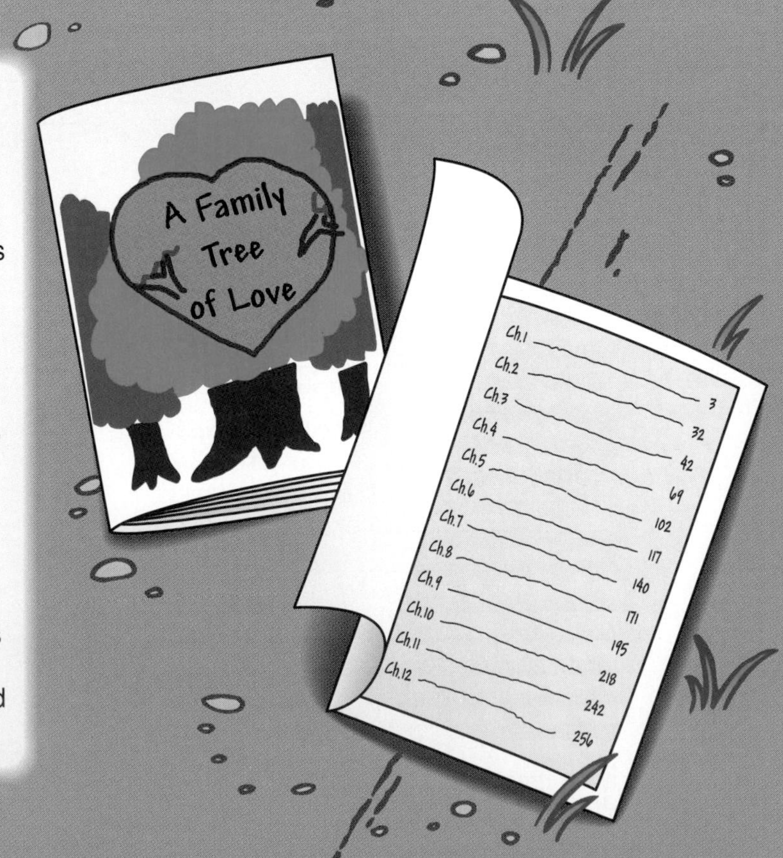

Name ____________________

*Roll of Thunder, Hear My Cry*
Reading comprehension, characterization

# Climb the Character Tree

**Directions:** Use the clues listed below to help you keep track of the many characters in *Roll of Thunder, Hear My Cry.* As you read, fill in the blanks below. Next to each character's name, try to add one or more brief clues to describe him or her. Use the back of this page if you need more space.

### The Logans

1. grandfather: Paul Edward
2. grandmother: ____________________
3. mother: ____________________
4. father: ____________________
5. uncle: ____________________
6. oldest son: ____________________
7. daughter: ____________________
8. middle son: ____________________
9. youngest son: ____________________

### The Averys

1. father: ____________________
2. mother: ____________________
3. older son: ____________________
4. younger son: ____________________

### The Simms

1. father: ____________________
2. older son: ____________________
3. older son: ____________________
4. daughter: ____________________
5. youngest son: ____________________

### Others

1. Logans' houseguest: ____________________
2. Cassie's teacher: ____________________
3. The Wallaces: ____________________
4. attorney: ____________________
5. plantation owner: ____________________
6. man who runs the Mercantile in Strawberry: ____________________

**Bonus Box:** Create a short quiz to test your classmates on the characters listed above. Also make an answer key. Then give your quiz to a friend and check it using your key.



**Note to the teacher:** Give this activity page to students before they start reading the book. After they finish the page, have students use it to help them complete the reproducible on page 213.

## Patterns

Use with "During Reading" on page 208.

**Roll of Thunder, Hear My Cry**

**Chapter 1:** admonished, billowed, barren, furrowed, indignant

**Chapter 2:** bale, sinewy, gait, formidable, chiffonier

**Chapter 3:** musty, glowered, adamantly, precariously, penetrate

**Chapter 4:** listlessly, haughtily, faltered, vex, fathom

**Chapter 5:** subdued, bellowed, malevo-lently, wryly, sullenly

**Chapter 6:** audible, aloofness, retaliated, glint, chignon

**Chapter 7:** inaudible, interminable, goaded, insolently, impaled

**Chapter 8:** feigned, sentinels, jovial, banished, fallow

**Chapter 9:** resigned, lilting, exasperation, scoffed, rasped

**Chapter 10:** mute, ambled, reproachfully, wistfully, jauntily

**Chapter 11:** grim, grimaced, vulnerability, akimbo, crescendo

**Chapter 12:** traipsing, transfixed, acrid, desolate, wan



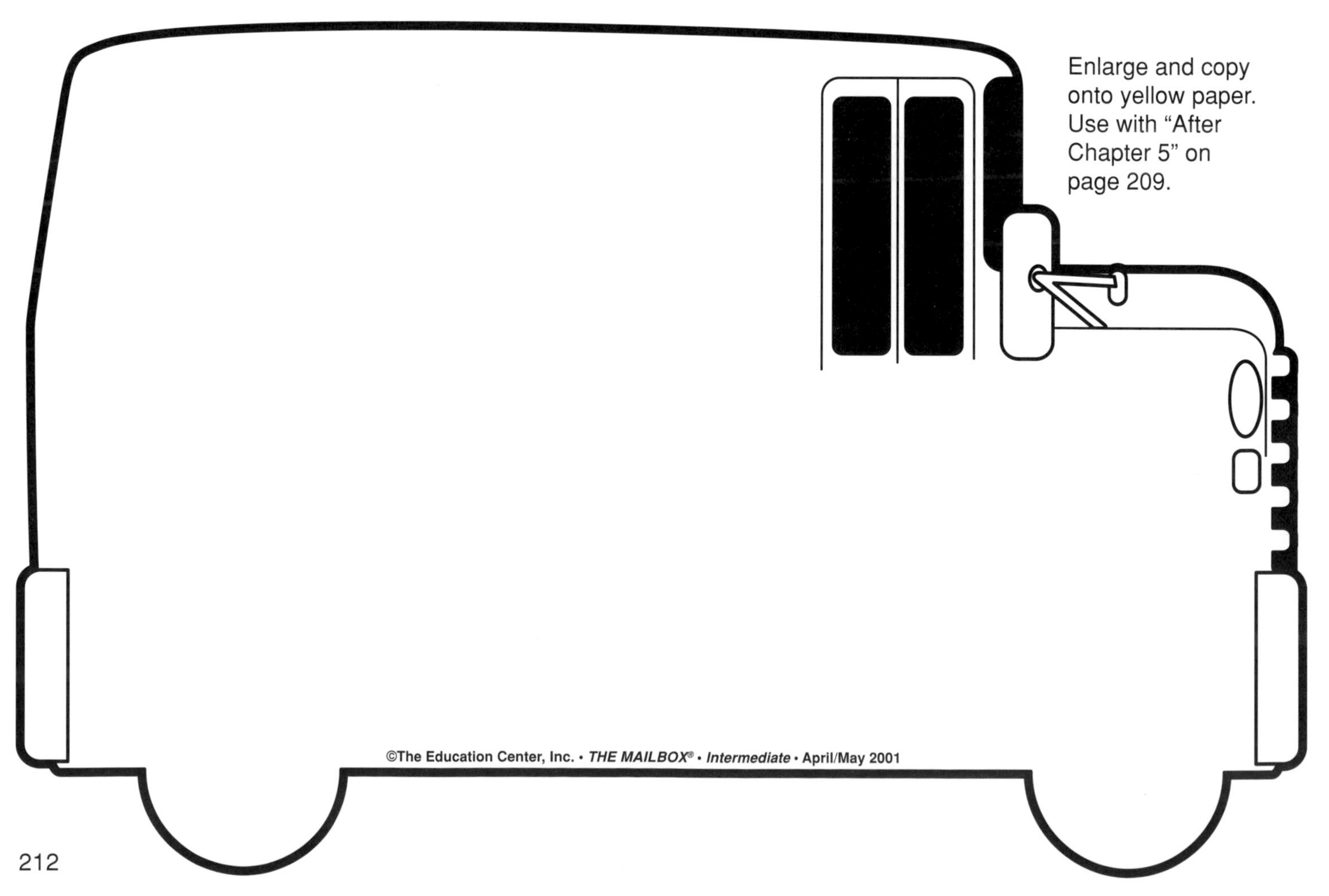

Enlarge and copy onto yellow paper. Use with "After Chapter 5" on page 209.

Name________________________________________



# The Logan Family Book of Values

In *Roll of Thunder, Hear My Cry,* Mama and Papa work to make sure their children understand the values that are important to them. Pretend that you are helping Mr. and Mrs. Logan write a record of those traits in a "Logan Family Book of Values."

**Directions:** Read through the list of traits below. Be sure you know what each word means. For each trait, write one example from the story of a time when a character demonstrated that characteristic. Include the character's name and the page number on which you found the example.

*The Logan Family Book of Values*

**Independence:** ________________________________________

________________________________________

**Courage:** ________________________________________

________________________________________

**Persistence:** ________________________________________

________________________________________

**Self-respect:** ________________________________________

________________________________________

**Responsibility:** ________________________________________

________________________________________

**Compassion:** ________________________________________

________________________________________

**Friendship:** ________________________________________

________________________________________

**Honesty:** ________________________________________

________________________________________

**Loyalty:** ________________________________________

________________________________________

**Hard work:** ________________________________________

________________________________________

**Bonus Box:** On the back of this page or on another sheet of paper, construct a character web for Cassie. In the web, show the different traits Cassie demonstrated throughout the story.



**Note to the teacher:** If desired, let students use their completed copies of the reproducible on page 211 to help them complete this page.

# Ella Enchanted

## Activities Based on Gail Carson Levine's Newbery Honor Book

Ella is not your everyday Cinderella. At birth, she was given the gift of obedience by a foolish fairy. Now Ella must obey every command given her. It's a curse that the strong-willed girl is determined to escape—even if it means fighting ogres and selfish stepsisters to do it. Fantasy, adventure, good versus evil, romance—it's all here in a rollicking tale that's guaranteed to enchant every reader!

with ideas by Lori Sammartino

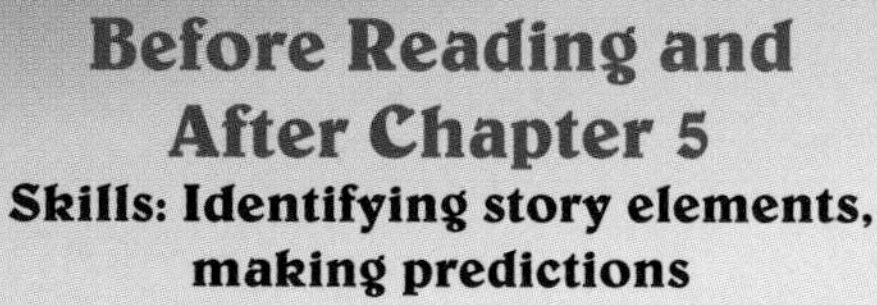

### Before Reading and After Chapter 5

#### Skills: Identifying story elements, making predictions

Before starting the book, display on chart paper a copy of the fairy-tale elements listed at the right. Explain that *Ella Enchanted* is a spin-off of the fairy tale *Cinderella.* Then read a picture-book version of this classic tale, such as *Cinderella* by Charles Perrault (North-South Books, 1999). After reading, ask students to identify the elements from the list that are included in the picture book. Then have them predict which of the elements might also be in *Ella Enchanted*.

Later, after the class has read through chapter 5, divide students into pairs. Instruct each pair to list the fairy-tale elements from the chart that they've identified in the book so far. As each twosome shares its list, draw a colorful star on the chart beside each element that is mentioned. Discuss with students whether they think the other elements will surface later in the book. As students read the rest of the story, add stars to the chart as needed.

**Fairy tales:**

- Begin with phrases like "Once upon a time…"
- Take place long ago and in faraway places
- Usually have young heroes and heroines whose virtues help them overcome obstacles
- Have a good character and a bad character
- Have characters with unusual names
- Have the good character pass several tests or overcome many trials in order to solve a problem
- Always allow the good character to win and be rewarded
- Always see that the bad character loses and is punished for his or her deeds
- Involve magic and supernatural happenings
- Don't have to include fairy characters
- Sometimes allow characters to be transformed into animals or to come under spells that only acts of kindness or love can reverse
- Often have royal characters such as kings and queens
- Use numbers such as three and seven (three wishes, seven pigs, etc.)
- Have happy endings so that the characters live "happily ever after"

## During Reading

**Skills: Responding to a prompt, critical thinking**

As students read *Ella Enchanted,* have them think and write about the story's events by responding to the following prompts.

**Ch. 2:** How would you describe Ella's father, Sir Peter?
**Ch. 4:** What would be the disadvantages of being able to see into the future?
**Ch. 8:** How do you think the fairy book might help Ella while she's at finishing school?
**Ch. 11:** Why do you think Hattie tells no one about Ella's obedience?
**Ch. 15:** How do you think Char feels about Ella? Provide evidence from the book to support your answer.
**Ch. 19:** How do you think Sir Peter describes Ella to her prospective husband, Edmund?
**Ch. 22:** Why do you think Sir Peter tells Dame Olga that he wants Ella treated with respect?
**Ch. 24:** Char misses talking to Ella while he is in Ayortha. With whom do you love talking? Why?
**Ch. 28:** Do you agree with Char that friendship can be forever? Why or why not?

## After Chapter 12

**Skills: Letter writing, reading comprehension**

Assess students' comprehension with this letter-perfect activity! In this chapter, selfish Hattie commands Ella to end her friendship with Areida. Not wanting to hurt her kind friend, Ella escapes from the finishing school at night without telling Areida. After reading this chapter, review the format of a friendly letter. Then challenge each student to pretend to be Ella and write a letter to Areida. In the letter, have the student honestly explain who she is, how she is cursed, and why she feels she must run away. Use the finished letters to assess students' comprehension of the story so far. Then post them on a bulletin board titled "My Dear Areida..."

## After Chapter 17

**Skills: Outlining, writing a personal essay**

At the giants' wedding, the bride and groom pantomime their future life together. Give each of your students a chance to plan out his own life with an activity that practices outlining skills. Have each student list the major events he would like to see happen in his future (for example, high school and college graduations, a career, etc.). Then instruct him to use his list to construct a simple outline, such as the one shown. With students, list main ideas for the outline (such as Education, Career, and Relationships) with Roman numerals. Instruct students to list examples with capital letters and supporting details with numbers. If desired, have each student use his outline to write a personal essay describing his future life. Direct him to copy his essay on paper that has been cut from a brown paper grocery bag. Have the student roll up the essay, tie it with ribbon, and present it to his parent as a keepsake to read in several years.

**My Future Life**

I. **Education**
   A. High school
      1. Graduate at the top of my class
      2. Win an award for being the top athlete in the school
   B. College
      1. Obtain an art scholarship
      2. Attend UCLA
      3. Major in art
II. **Career**
   A. Open my own art studio
      1. Find a neat building in the city for my studio
      2. Call the studio Neal's Art Cart
   B. Use my art to help kids
      1. Teach art to underprivileged kids
      2. Illustrate a picture book
III. **Relationships**
   A. Marriage
      1. Get married by the time I'm 40
      2. Have four children
   B. Family
      1. Live near my mom and dad
      2. Visit my sister at Christmas and Easter

## After Chapter 23

**Skills: Characterization, comparison and contrast**

Ella begins thinking about ways to escape the tyranny of her cruel stepmother and stepsisters. She decides to write a letter to her father asking him to come to her aid. Knowing what they already have read about Sir Peter, do your students think he will help Ella? Ask students to reflect on the personality traits of Ella's father and mother, and to compare them to Ella's. Then instruct each student to draw a chart on a large sheet of paper (see example). After the student illustrates each of the three characters, have her list personality traits in each column, along with examples and page numbers from the book to support each trait. When the chart is complete, have the student choose two of the characters; then have her compare and contrast the characters in a paragraph.

|  Ella  | Sir Peter  | Lady Eleanor |
|---|---|---|
| • a rebel: holds a bowl when asked but moves around the room so Mandy has to follow her (p. 5)<br>• smart: learns early not to tell anyone about her curse (p. 7) | • selfish: cares more about who has attended his wife's funeral than about losing her (p. 14)<br>• mean: shows Ella the beautiful porcelain castle, then tells her he is going to sell it (p. 30) | 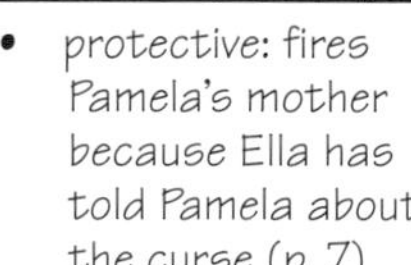 • protective: fires Pamela's mother because Ella has told Pamela about the curse (p. 7)<br>• playful: likes to slide down the banister with Ella (p. 9) |

## After Chapter 26

**Skills: Making inferences, characterization**

As Ella departs for the first ball, she leaves knowing that this gathering represents one last chance to be near her beloved Char. After reading this chapter, review the events and characters Ella has encountered so far. Ask students: "Since this ball is so important to Ella, which characters do you think she would not want to attend (because they would pose a threat to her)? Which characters would she not mind being there (because they either wouldn't pose a threat or would possibly help her)?" Instruct each student to make two lists: "Ella's Friends" and "Ella's Foes." Then have him skim chapters 1–26 to find characters to place in each list. Require that the student list a reason for including each character on the particular list. After everyone has finished, divide the class into groups so students can discuss their lists.

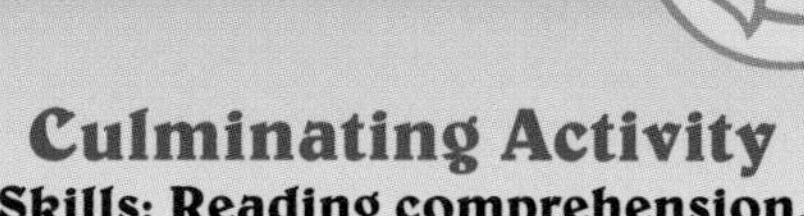

## Culminating Activity

**Skills: Reading comprehension, persuasive writing**

Prince Char and Ella are finally married in the "happily ever after" ending to this book. Challenge your students to celebrate their union by holding a wedding shower for the happy couple. First, review the main events of the story. Discuss Ella's and Char's personalities and the things students think these two characters value highly. Next, divide the class into groups. Challenge each group to list at least five appropriate wedding gifts for Ella and Char based on the earlier discussion. Then instruct each student to select a different item from her group's list and write a paragraph describing the gift and reasons why it is perfect for Char and Ella. Finally, give each student an 8" x 18" strip of white paper. Have the student fold the paper in half as shown. Then have her copy her paragraph on the top half and illustrate the gift on the bottom. Finally, have the student fold the paper where shown and decorate the front of the resulting card to resemble a package. Hold a wedding shower during which students share their gifts with the class.

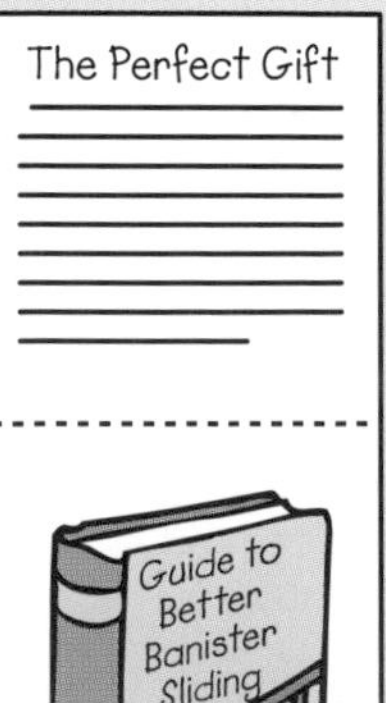

Name ____________________________________________



# Ella's Treasures

In *Ella Enchanted,* Ella acquires several objects. Some belonged to her mother; others are given to her. Each treasure is special to Ella as she tries to break free from her curse.
**Directions:** List in the carpetbag each of Ella's special treasures and the page number on which it is mentioned. Illustrate each item below its name. Then, on the back of this page, explain why each treasure is important or useful to Ella.

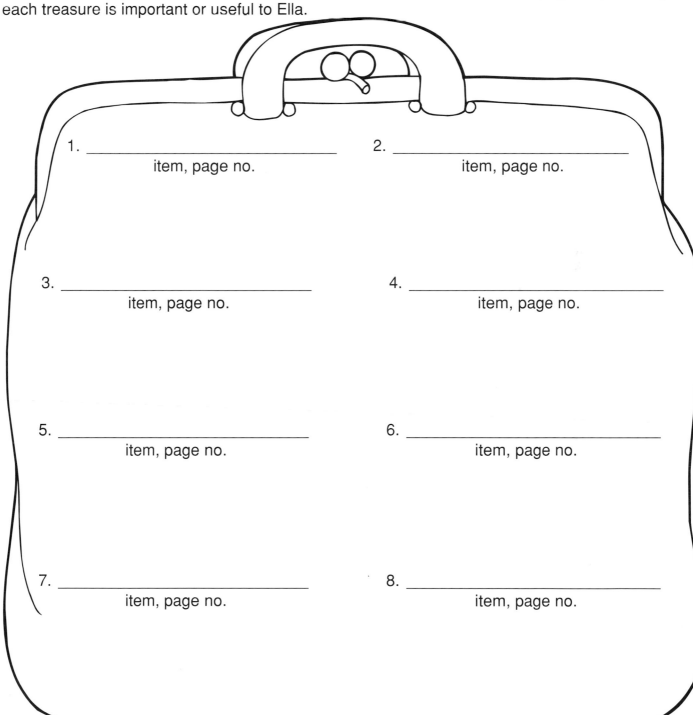

1. ______________________________
item, page no.

2. ______________________________
item, page no.

3. ______________________________
item, page no.

4. ______________________________
item, page no.

5. ______________________________
item, page no.

6. ______________________________
item, page no.

7. ______________________________
item, page no.

8. ______________________________
item, page no.

**BONUS BOX:** What special treasures do you have? On another sheet of paper, draw a picture of one of your treasures. Then write a brief paragraph that tells about the item and why it is important to you.



**Note to the teacher:** Before beginning *Ella Enchanted,* give each student a copy of this page to fill out as he reads. Or have students complete the activity at the end of the book as a way to review the story.

Name ____________________ *Ella Enchanted*
Problem solving with mixed numerals

# Ella's Enchanted Trail

Below is a map showing places that are important to Ella. Use the map to solve the following math problems. Show your work on another sheet of paper, and reduce all answers to the lowest terms. Then write the answers on the lines provided. Warning: Solving some of these enchanted problems may require more than one step!

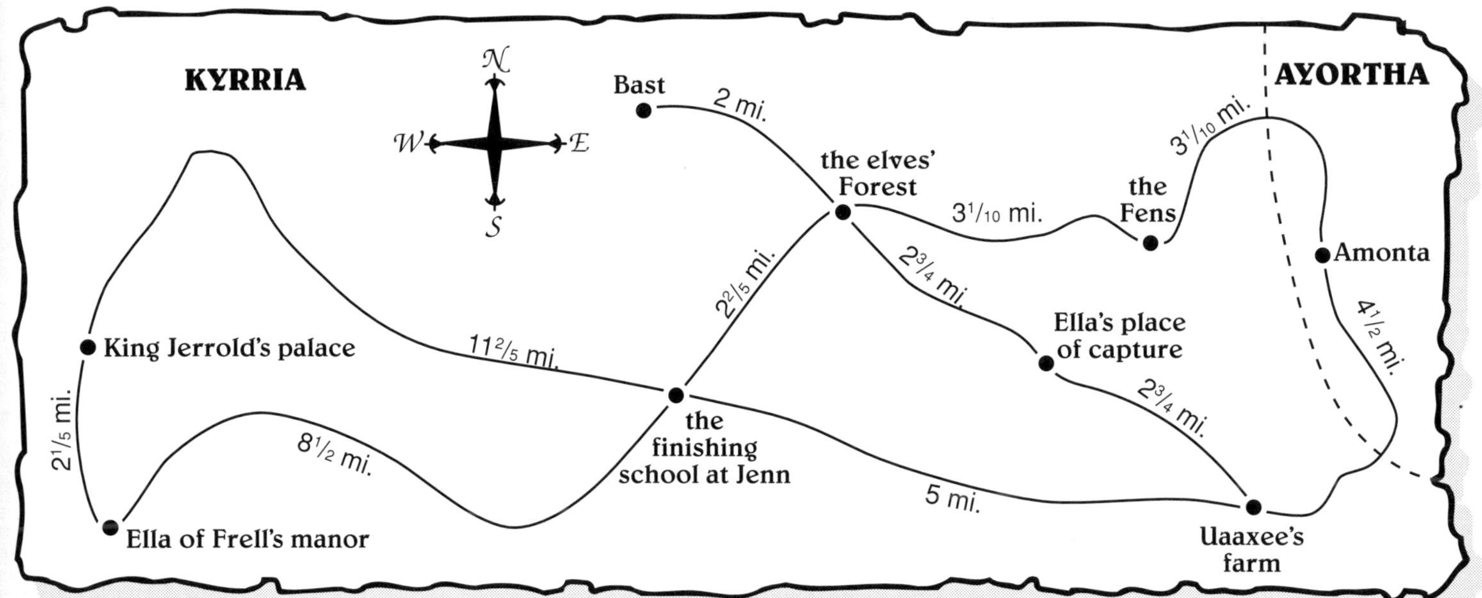


1. Ella walks from her manor to King Jerrold's palace, then back home. How far does she walk? ____________
2. When Ella leaves Jenn, she travels north through the elves' Forest, then south to Uaaxee's farm. How long is her trip? ____________
3. There is a shorter way for Ella to get from Jenn to Uaaxee's farm. How much shorter is this route than the one Ella uses in number 2? ____________
4. The ogres leave the Fens and travel through the elves' Forest to the place where they capture Ella. How far do they travel? ____________
5. The ogres leave the place where they have captured Ella and go to the elves' Forest. Char leaves Jenn and heads to the elves' Forest too. How much farther do the ogres travel than Char? ____________
6. Who lives closer to Bast: Ella or Areida from Ayortha? ________ How much closer? ________
7. If Prince Char leaves the palace to visit Ella in Jenn, he can take one of two different routes. How long is the shorter route? ________ How much shorter is it than the longer route? ________
8. If Ella had truly traveled from Bast to the ball at the palace, taking the shortest route possible, how far would she have had to travel? ________ What would be the round-trip distance? ________
9. Areida leaves Amonta and takes the shortest route to Jenn. Ella leaves her manor and takes the shortest route to Jenn too. How far does each girl travel? ____________
10. In number 9, who travels farther? ____________ How much farther? ____________



**Note to the teacher:** Have students complete this page at the end of the book. Explain to students that the map is not designed to be a completely accurate portrayal of the setting in *Ella Enchanted*.

# Other Curriculum Helpers

# Making the Most

How can a good thing get even better? By discovering nifty new ways to use it! Take a look at the following suggestions for using a word wall to help students achieve greater success in language arts and math!

*ideas by Karen S. Arnett—Gr. 5, Greenbrier Intermediate School, Chesapeake, VA*

## Tips for Planning and Using a Word Wall

- **Designate a place for the word wall.** Choose a space that will allow words to be removed and rearranged easily. Label the area with the letters of the alphabet as shown.

- **Begin with 20 words.** Select high-frequency words that follow no specific spelling pattern; words frequently misspelled by your students; easily confused words such as *to, too,* and *two;* words from a word family such as *-ake;* or other categories of words.

- **Write the words in large manuscript letters.** Color-code the words, if desired, to distinguish any categories. After writing each word, cut it out to show its shape configuration. Arrange the words alphabetically in columns under the appropriate letters. Whenever you add or remove a word, reposition the words, if necessary, to keep them in alphabetical order.

- **Use the word wall daily.** Involve students in a quick, five- to ten-minute activity each day (see the suggestions that begin below).

- **Periodically, retire words from the wall.** To make room for new words, either select certain words to use as bonus words on a spelling test, or cover them and have a special spelling quiz. Allow all words that students spell correctly to go into retirement. Make the retirement special by
  1) throwing a "retirement party" and celebrating with juice and a nutritious snack
  2) listing each retired word on an index card, alphabetizing the cards, and keeping them in a "retirement home" (card file) as a handy reference
  3) removing the words from the word wall and allowing them to "rest" at another designated place in the classroom

- **Review retired words often.** Include them in spelling lists. Bring the misspelled words out of retirement by putting them back on the word wall.

## Language Arts Activities

- **Go on a scavenger hunt.** Have students search the wall for words that fit a certain category: nouns, verbs, adjectives, adverbs, contractions, compound words, words containing certain vowel sounds, etc.

- **Write an alliterative sentence.** Challenge pairs of students to write a sentence using as many words beginning with the same letter as they can.

- **Alphabetize words.** Scramble the order of all the words listed under a particular letter. Have students write the words in the correct alphabetical order.
- **Use a game to practice webbing.** Pair students and have each child select a word. Then give each student two minutes to write words in a web format that relate to or rhyme with her chosen word. Give players one point per word. After three rounds, declare the partner having more points the winner.
- **Practice context clues.** Write a sentence on the board, leaving a blank where a wall word can be inserted. Have each child copy the sentence and use context clues to add the correct missing word.
- **Play Hangman to practice spelling the words.** Divide students into two teams. For each round, choose a different word from the wall to spell.
- **Have a sentence-writing review.** Choose one noun and one verb from the wall. Have each student use the words to write a declarative, an interrogative, an imperative, or an exclamatory sentence. Vary the activity by having students add an adjective or adverb from the wall to the sentence.
- **Review parts of speech.** Call out a part of speech. Have each student write on his paper a word from the wall that fits the category. Then have each student trade papers and write a sentence using his partner's selected word.
- **Identify prefixes and suffixes.** Use the wall to focus on words that contain prefixes and suffixes and their meanings.
- **Practice syllabication.** Point to the words one at a time. Have students clap once for each syllable to show the total number of syllables in each word.
- **Create figures of speech.** Have students use the nouns, verbs, adjectives, and adverbs on the wall to create examples of similes and metaphors.

## Math Activities

- **Make calculations.** Assign a different monetary value to each letter of the alphabet. Then have students use calculators to find any of the following:
  1) the estimated and exact values of a specific word
  2) the estimated and exact values of all the nouns (or verbs, adjectives, or adverbs)
  3) the word with the highest (or lowest) value
  4) two words with the same value
  5) three words whose added values are closest to a targeted sum
- **Practice using ordered pairs.** Announce an ordered pair, such as E5 (fifth word under the letter *E*). Have students locate and spell the word at those coordinates.

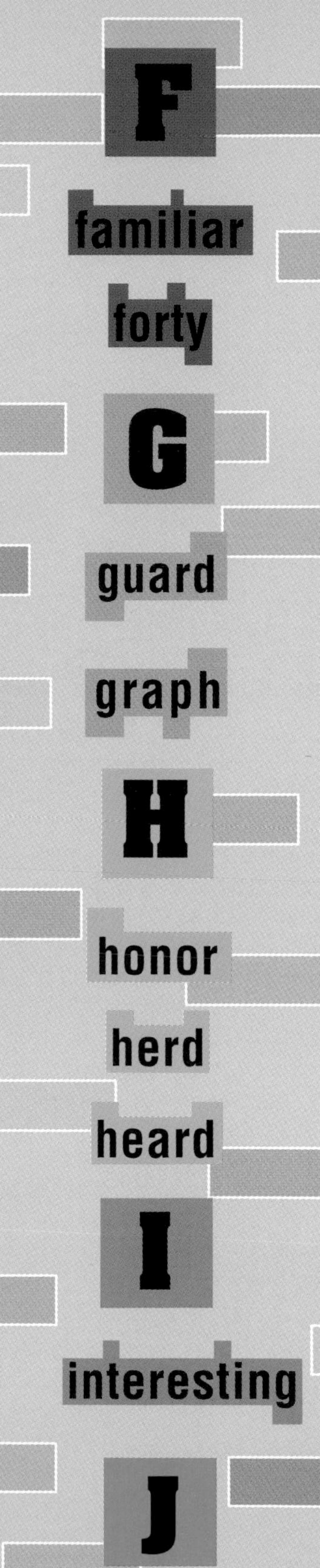

# Race for the Presidency

## Learning About the Presidential Election Process

Help your students catch election fever—and learn about the long road to the White House—with the following red, white, and new activities!

*ideas by Terry Healy and Cayce Guiliano*

### President-to-Be

**Topic: Requirements for candidates**

Who can become our nation's president? Before students answer this question, share that the Constitution requires that a presidential candidate be a "natural-born" U.S. citizen, at least 35 years old, and a resident of the United States for at least 14 years. But what about other qualifications? Help students brainstorm qualities that a person aspiring to this office should also possess, such as *honesty, dependability,* and *diligence.* List the attributes on the board. Next, give each student an index card. On the card's top line, have her copy "I can be the president because..." Then direct her to complete the sentence with positive traits she has that would make her a good president. Finally, have her illustrate the card. Display the cards on a bulletin board titled "Look at Me...President-to-Be!" Add newspaper and magazine pictures of the presidential candidates to the display.

I could be president because
I am dependable, caring, and trustworthy.


### Political "Ad-Visors"

**Topics: Political slogans, the election process**

Introduce students to important information on elections and the challenges of the campaign trail with a rollicking read-aloud, *The Kid Who Ran for President* by Dan Gutman (Scholastic Inc., 1996). In Chapter 6 of this highly entertaining novel, 12-year-old presidential candidate Judson Moon needs to write a campaign slogan to promote his political platform. Point out the three examples of past campaign slogans referred to in Chapter 6: "Keep Cool with Coolidge," "Tippecanoe and Tyler, too," and "All the way with LBJ!" Then have students brainstorm characteristics that can make a slogan memorable—such as *short, catchy, rhyming*—as you list them on the board. Challenge each student to use the characteristics to create a slogan for his own presidential campaign. Finally, let students share their slogans by making special "ad-visors" using the directions below.

**Materials for each student:** 10" square of red, white, or blue tagboard; ruler; hole puncher; two 6" lengths of thick cording (or yarn); scissors; markers

**Steps:**

1. Fold the tagboard in half and cut as shown.
2. Unfold the tagboard. Use markers to copy your slogan onto the cutout.
3. Decorate the cutout with a patriotic theme: stars, stripes, flags, etc.
4. Make a half-inch slit on the cutout's upper edge at the fold line.
5. Punch a hole in each end of the visor. Tie one length of cording in each hole.

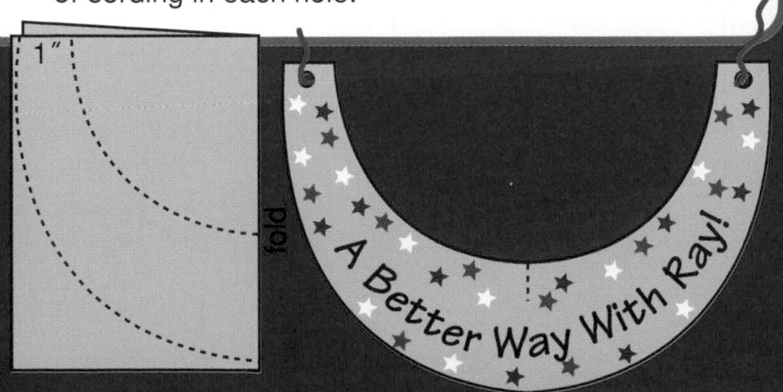

## Platforms, Planks, 'n' Posters

### Topic: Political platforms

Help students learn a little about the political platforms of today's presidential hopefuls with this literature and art activity. In advance, collect brochures and other information from local campaign offices, magazines, newspapers, and the Internet (see the Web sites listed on page 224). Then read aloud Barbara Park's *Rosie Swanson: Fourth-Grade Geek for President* (Random House Children's Publishing, 1992). This hilarious tale follows the campaign of the biggest tattletale in school as she tries to become class president. After reading the book, explain to students that a presidential *platform* is a statement of beliefs and plans written by a special committee at each party's national convention. The platform consists of *planks,* or separate parts, such as foreign policy, health care, or taxes. Next, divide students into groups (one per candidate) and distribute the materials gathered earlier. Challenge each group to identify six planks in its candidate's platform and to summarize each one in a sentence. Then guide the groups through the steps below to create patriotic posters that tout the platforms.

**Materials:**
two 6" x 9" pieces of construction paper (1 red, 1 blue)
12" x 18" sheet of white construction paper
scissors
glue
blue pen
colored markers or pencils
ruler

**Steps:**

1. Stack the red and blue paper. Starting at the shorter edge, cut four curving lines, making each resulting strip about one inch wide.
2. Turn the white paper vertically. Position the strips at the bottom half of the paper as shown, alternating colors and leaving about one inch of white space between each strip. Glue the strips to the paper.
3. From the red and blue paper scraps, cut small star shapes. Glue them to the white paper as shown.
4. Using the pen, copy one summary sentence between each colorful strip.
5. At the top of the paper, draw and color a picture of the candidate. Add the candidate's name, political party, and party symbol (if known).

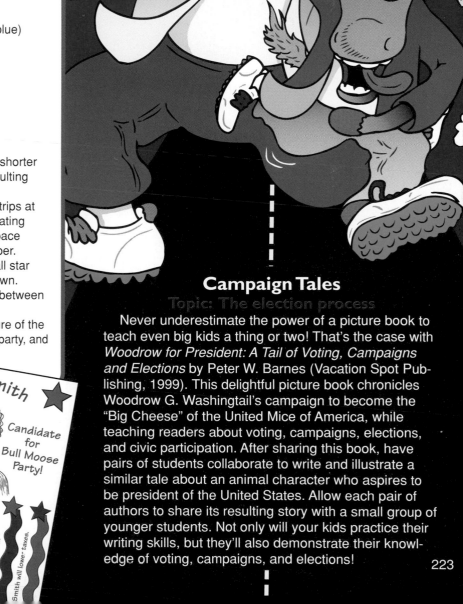

## Campaign Tales

### Topic: The election process

Never underestimate the power of a picture book to teach even big kids a thing or two! That's the case with *Woodrow for President: A Tail of Voting, Campaigns and Elections* by Peter W. Barnes (Vacation Spot Publishing, 1999). This delightful picture book chronicles Woodrow G. Washingtail's campaign to become the "Big Cheese" of the United Mice of America, while teaching readers about voting, campaigns, elections, and civic participation. After sharing this book, have pairs of students collaborate to write and illustrate a similar tale about an animal character who aspires to be president of the United States. Allow each pair of authors to share its resulting story with a small group of younger students. Not only will your kids practice their writing skills, but they'll also demonstrate their knowledge of voting, campaigns, and elections!

## And the Winner Is...

### Topic: Straw polls, popular vote

Turn students into presidential pollsters by having them conduct their own straw poll. List the names of the presidential candidates on the board. Then give each student scissors, a crayon, and a drinking straw. Instruct her to use the crayon to divide the straw into four equal parts. Point out that each section represents 25%, or one-fourth. Next, announce a candidate's name. Direct each child to cut off the part of her straw that corresponds to the fraction of the popular vote she thinks that candidate will receive. Have her label that piece "A." Repeat this process for the remaining candidates, labeling the pieces "B," "C," and so on. Then collect all the pieces for candidate A and string them together on a length of yarn. Do the same for the other candidates. Display the strings on a bulletin board. Then have students calculate which fraction of the popular vote was predicted for each candidate. After the election, have the class compare its straw poll predictions with the actual popular vote.

## Can I Vote?

### Topic: Voting rights, media's role in campaigns

As Election Day approaches, have students consider whether or not kids their age should have the right to vote. First, share with students some important historical benchmarks related to voting rights:

- Black American men were given the right to vote in 1870.
- Women were given the right to vote in 1920.
- Young Americans (18 or older) began voting in 1971.

Next, have students brainstorm media sources that provide information on presidential candidates, such as TV, radio, newspapers, magazines, and the Internet. List the sources on the board. Then poll each student about which source he thinks is most reliable and why. Discuss with students whether they think a child their age—after collecting information about the candidates—is capable of making an informed decision and should therefore be allowed to vote. After the discussion, ask each child to write a letter to one of the presidential candidates explaining his reasons for or against allowing children to vote.

## Winning Books and Web Sites

**Books:**

- *Election Night* (Politics in the United States series) by Thomas R. Raber (Lerner Publications Company, 1988)
- *Presidential Elections* (Cornerstones of Freedom series) by Miles Harvey (Children's Press, 1996)
- *Presidential Elections and Other Cool Facts* by Sylvan A. Sobel (Barron's Educational Series, Inc.; 2000)
- *The Election Book: People Pick a President* by Tamara Hanneman (Scholastic Inc., 1992)
- *The Voice of the People: American Democracy in Action* by Betsy C. Maestro (Lothrop, Lee & Shepard Books; 1996)

**Web sites** *(current as of 2-2000):*

- Yahoo: headlines.yahoo.com/Full_Coverage/Yahooligans/Presidential_Election
- The Internet Public Library: www.ipl.org/ref/POTUS/
- The Republican National Committee: www.rnc.org/
- The Democratic National Committee: www.democrats.org/index.html
- The Kids Voting USA: www.kidsvotingusa.org/introduction.html
- www.americanpresident.org/

Name ______________________________ 

# Keeping the Campaign Cash

Mona Moneybags is the campaign treasurer for presidential hopeful Pat Riotic. It is Mona's job to account for every dollar of Pat's campaign funds. Use the price list below to help Mona fill in the chart. If the activity is a contribution or donation, *credit* (or add) that amount to Pat's account. If the activity is an expense, *debit* (or subtract) that amount from the account. The first two are done for you.

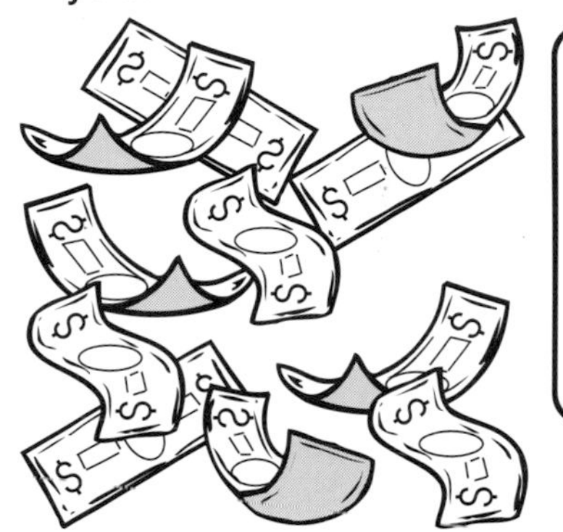

**Price List for Campaign Activities**

| | |
|---|---|
| TV ad | $5,000 |
| Radio ad | $2,500 |
| 1,500 brochures | $2,000 |
| 2,000 flyers | $1,000 |
| Political poster | $ 750 |

**Activities:**

- 9/5—opened account with $15,000 donation
- 9/6—ordered 3,000 brochures
- 9/7—ordered 10,000 flyers
- 9/8—received $5,500 donation
- 9/11—received $10,000 donation
- 9/12—ordered ten political posters
- 9/13—received $5,400 contribution
- 9/14—ordered four radio ads
- 9/15—received $1,950 contribution
- 9/18—ordered five political posters
- 9/19—ordered three radio ads
- 9/20—received $8,500 contribution
- 9/21—ordered 6,000 brochures
- 9/22—received $7,900 donation
- 9/25—ordered 4,000 flyers

| Date | Activity | Debit | Credit | Balance |
|---|---|---|---|---|
| 9/5 | opened account | | $15,000 | $15,000 |
| 9/6 | 3,000 brochures | $4,000 | | $11,000 |
| | | | | |
| | | | | |
| | | | | |
| | | | | |
| | | | | |
| | | | | |
| | | | | |
| | | | | |
| | | | | |
| | | | | |
| | | | | |
| | | | | |
| | | | | |

**BONUS BOX:** If Mona completely spends the balance left in the account on 9/25, what three things can she get for Pat?



**Note to the teacher:** If desired, allow students to use calculators to complete this activity.

# Getting the (Electoral) Vote!

Pat Riotic needs 270 of the 538 possible electoral votes to become the next president of the United States. Use the table to help Pat decide how to win the most electoral votes—and the election! Treat Washington, DC, as a state.

| State | Electoral Votes | State | Electoral Votes |
|---|---|---|---|
| AL | 9 | MT | 3 |
| AK | 3 | NE | 5 |
| AZ | 8 | NV | 4 |
| AR | 6 | NH | 4 |
| CA | 54 | NJ | 15 |
| CO | 8 | NM | 5 |
| CT | 8 | NY | 33 |
| DE | 3 | NC | 14 |
| FL | 25 | ND | 3 |
| GA | 13 | OH | 23 |
| HI | 4 | OK | 8 |
| ID | 4 | OR | 7 |
| IL | 22 | PA | 23 |
| IN | 12 | RI | 4 |
| IA | 7 | SC | 8 |
| KS | 6 | SD | 3 |
| KY | 8 | TN | 11 |
| LA | 9 | TX | 32 |
| ME | 4 | UT | 5 |
| MD | 10 | VT | 3 |
| MA | 12 | VA | 13 |
| MI | 18 | WA | 11 |
| MN | 10 | DC | 3 |
| MS | 7 | WV | 5 |
| MO | 11 | WI | 11 |
| | | WY | 3 |

(Electoral votes based on 1990 census.)

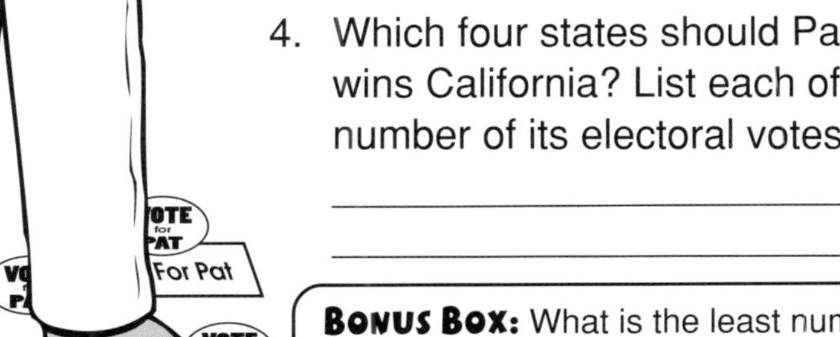

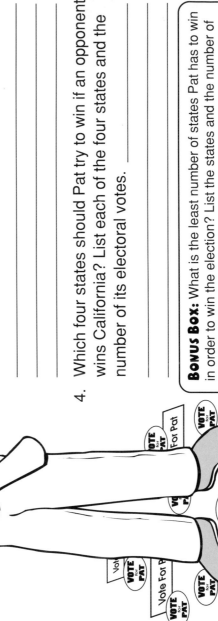

1. Name the eight states that have the smallest number of electoral votes. ______________________

2. In order from greatest to least, list the three states that have the largest number of electoral votes. What is the total number of electoral votes represented by these three states? ______________________

3. Should Pat try to win the four states with the largest number of electoral votes or the eight states that have the smallest number of electoral votes? Why?

4. Which four states should Pat try to win if an opponent wins California? List each of the four states and the number of its electoral votes. ______________________

**Bonus Box:** What is the least number of states Pat has to win in order to win the election? List the states and the number of electoral votes each one has on the back of this page or on another sheet of paper.



**Note to the teacher:** If desired, make another class set of this page to use as an Election Night homework assignment. While a student watches election returns, have him color the chart's boxes to identify the winning candidate: Democrat = blue, Republican = red, Other parties = yellow.

Name________________________________ Reading comprehension

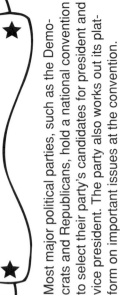

# The Road to the White House

**Directions:** Read the paragraph in each box below. Write a term from the road in the banner of the box. Then cut along the dotted lines to make two strips. Tape the left edge of Box 3 to the right edge of Box 2. Then fold the boxes along the solid lines to make a booklet about the election process.

Election Day — National Convention — The Electoral College — The Campaign — Primary Elections and Caucuses

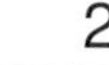

Once candidates announce their candidacy, they enter primary elections and caucuses. These are early contests to see which candidate can win the most delegates to the national convention. A candidate's goal is to win as many state delegates as possible before the convention.

1

Most major political parties, such as the Democrats and Republicans, hold a national convention to select their party's candidates for president and vice president. The party also works out its platform on important issues at the convention.

2

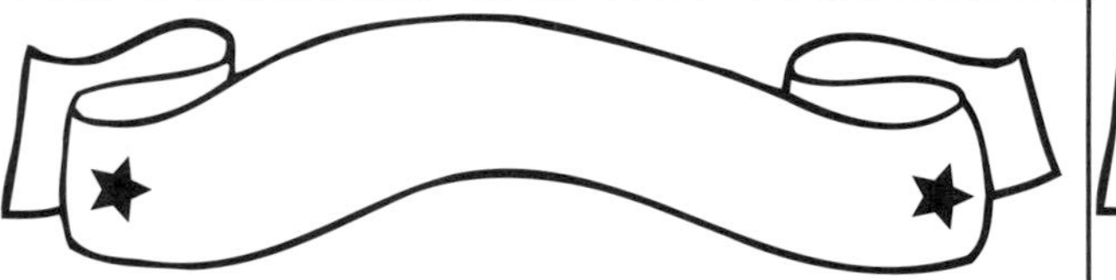

During the campaign, the candidates present their positions and try to convince people to vote for them. They fill the television, radio, magazines, and newspapers with advertising. They can also give daily news releases and schedule *whistle stops* (brief visits) in small towns across the United States.

3

Every four years, on the first Tuesday after the first Monday in November, registered voters go to the polls to vote for president. This vote is called the *popular vote*. It determines how many electoral votes each candidate receives.

4

The electoral college directly elects the president. In December, the electors in each state and the District of Columbia meet to cast their ballots. The votes are sealed and sent to Washington, DC, where they are counted. In January, the president is sworn into office.

5

**Bonus Box:** What happens when there is a tie in the electoral college and no candidate wins a majority of the electoral votes? Write your answer on the back of the last page of your booklet.





**Note to the teacher:** To complete this page, each student will need scissors and tape.

# Cooking Across the Curriculum

**Who says cooking in the classroom is only for little kids? Serve up the following cooking activities that are especially designed to add flavor to the intermediate curriculum!**

**Southern Hoecakes**

1 c. plain white cornmeal
$1\frac{1}{4}$ c. water
$\frac{1}{2}$ tsp. salt
butter
syrup or honey (optional)
vegetable oil
electric skillet

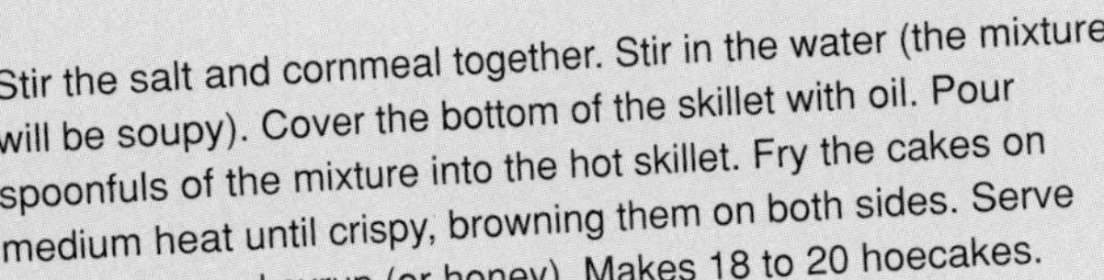

Stir the salt and cornmeal together. Stir in the water (the mixture will be soupy). Cover the bottom of the skillet with oil. Pour spoonfuls of the mixture into the hot skillet. Fry the cakes on medium heat until crispy, browning them on both sides. Serve with butter and syrup (or honey). Makes 18 to 20 hoecakes.

## Hoecake Hoedown

**Social Studies: Colonial America**

Treat students to a bread enjoyed by American colonists with this tasty version of hoecakes. *adapted from a recipe by Deborah Mayo—Gr. 5, Nebo Elementary, Jena, LA*

## Peanut Butter and "Cell-y" Sandwiches

**Science: Parts of a cell**

Introduce students to the basic parts of animal cells with this simple sandwich-making idea. Provide each child with a slice of bread, one to two tablespoons of peanut butter, a plastic knife, one round banana slice, and 12 to 14 raisins. Explain that each student will be making an edible model of an animal cell. Direct students to spread the peanut butter on the bread. Point out that the crust represents the cell membrane and the peanut butter the cytoplasm. Then have students add the remaining ingredients to the peanut butter layer as shown. Explain that the banana depicts the cell's nucleus and the raisins its mitochondria. As students munch on their models, challenge them to invent new names for the cell parts. Ever hear of a bananucleus, mitochondraisnia, and cytopeanutasm? *Joy Bennett—Gr. 5, C. B. Partee Elementary, Brinkley, AR*

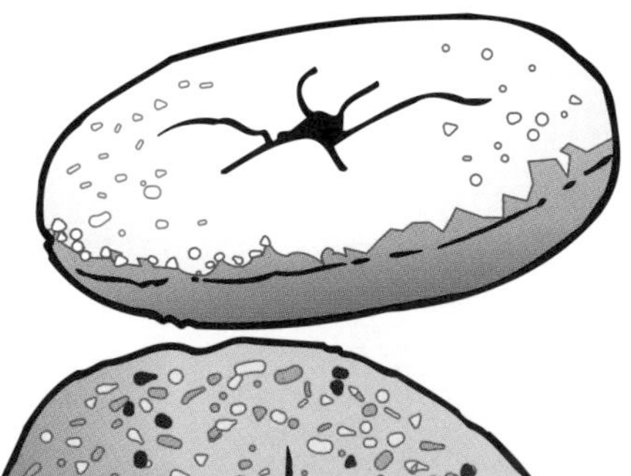

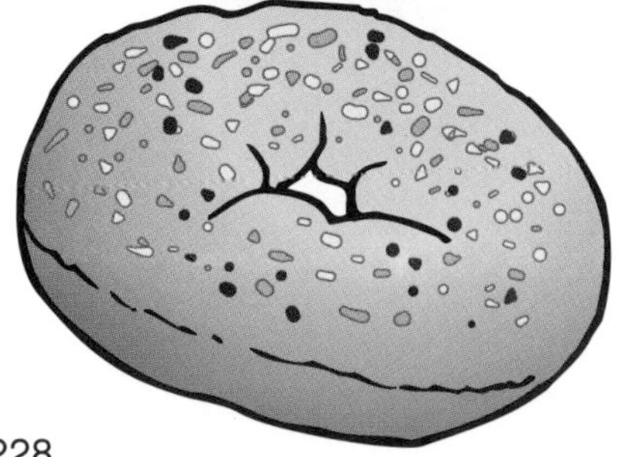

## Homer Price Day

**Literature: Creative writing, reading comprehension**

If you're looking for a great book to whet any kid's appetite for reading, there's no better place to dig than in Robert McCloskey's classic tale *Homer Price.* After students finish this fun-to-read book, have each child write a new ending to the story. Then celebrate by making delicious doughnuts—but not with a machine like Homer did! Purchase three or more eight-count cans of biscuits. After students make holes in the centers of the biscuits, drop the dough in hot oil to fry. Brown the doughnuts on both sides. Then shake them in plastic, resealable bags filled with confectioners' sugar or a cinnamon-sugar mixture. Yum! *Sr. Ann Claire Rhoads, St. Ann Catholic School, Fayetteville, NC*

# Stone Soup's On!

**Science: Matter**

What's cooking? A pot full of concepts about matter! Have students bring in the soup ingredients on the right. Next, read aloud *Stone Soup: An Old Tale* by Marcia Brown. Then place a large electric kettle (not a slow cooker) atop a large table so students can measure and add ingredients as needed. At each step, point out the scientific concept(s) being illustrated. *Joy Bennett—Gr. 5, C. B. Partee Elementary, Brinkley, AR*

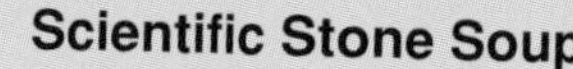

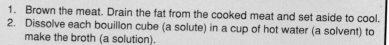

### Scientific Stone Soup

1 lb. ground beef
4 beef bouillon cubes
4 c. hot water
6 cans of vegetables (a variety of lima beans, corn, carrots, etc.), drained
2 cans whole potatoes, drained
3 cans stewed tomatoes
2 tsp. dried oregano
2 tsp. garlic powder
2 tsp. parsley flakes
2 bay leaves
4 tbsp. ketchup
salt and pepper to taste
1 small, clean stone

1. Brown the meat. Drain the fat from the cooked meat and set aside to cool.
2. Dissolve each bouillon cube (a solute) in a cup of hot water (a solvent) to make the broth (a solution).
3. Cut up the potatoes (a physical change); then add the broth, vegetables, spices, ketchup, salt (a compound), pepper, and stone to the meat.
4. As the soup simmers, point out the three states of matter: solid (meat, vegetables, and stone), liquid (broth), and gas (steam), and that the cooled fat changed from a liquid to a solid (a physical change).
5. Remove bay leaves and stone before eating.

# Spiderweb Cookies

**Language Arts: Writing directions**

Weave this oh-so-easy "spider-ific" cookie recipe into a lesson on writing directions! Bake or buy the cookies in advance; then guide students through the steps on the left. As students munch the decorated treats, have them use time-order words plus topic and concluding sentences to write paragraphs explaining how they decorated the cookies. *adapted from a recipe by Teena Andersen—Grs. 4–6, Hadar Public School, Pilger, NE*

### Spiderweb Cookies

3 dz. 3" round sugar cookies (commercial or baked from slice-and-bake cookie dough per package directions)
1–2 tubs white commercial frosting
red and yellow food coloring
plastic knives for spreading
chocolate syrup in a squeeze bottle
toothpicks

Use the food coloring to tint the frosting orange. Spread about one teaspoon of frosting on each cookie. Squeeze a spiral of chocolate syrup atop each frosted cookie. Use a toothpick to pull the syrup from the center of the spiral outward to create a web design.

# Western Roundup

**Social Studies: Westward movement**

Conclude a unit on the westward movement by preparing a roundup of hearty foods any trail-weary pioneer would appreciate! In advance, ask parents to contribute the ingredients for the dishes below and to help supervise on cooking day. When the special day arrives, divide students into four groups and have each group prepare one of the foods listed below to sample. *Vicki S. King—Gr. 5, Riverlawn School, Radford, VA*

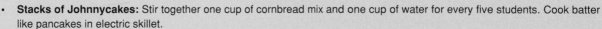

- **End-of-the-Trail Stew:** Peel and slice potatoes and carrots. Add them to about five pounds of precooked stew beef. Cover meat and vegetables with water, adding salt and pepper to taste. Cook until vegetables are tender and meat shreds easily.
- **Stacks of Johnnycakes:** Stir together one cup of cornbread mix and one cup of water for every five students. Cook batter like pancakes in electric skillet.
- **Melt-in-Your-Mouth Butter:** Shake one pint of chilled whipping cream and a pinch of salt in a chilled, tight-lidded jar until mixture thickens and forms lumps. Scoop out lumps and drain on paper towels.
- **Sweet Rocky Mountain Candy:** Cook one cup of molasses and one cup of brown sugar on medium heat until it reaches hard ball stage. Pour mixture over pan of crushed ice. When cool, break into bite-sized pieces.

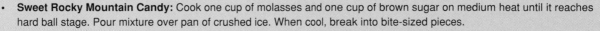

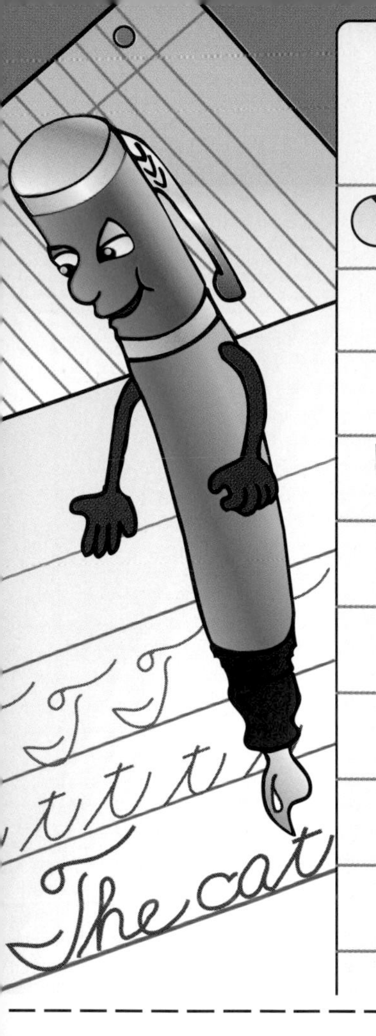

# Penmanship With a Purpose

## A Cursive Handwriting and Bookmaking Project

Start the year with a class project that refines handwriting habits *and* produces an alphabet book younger students can use to learn and practice cursive writing!

*by Kathy DeShon—Gr. 4, Tri-City Christian School, Blue Springs, MO*

### Step One: Practicing Cursive Writing

During the first few weeks of school, have students practice writing the alphabet, one letter per day, following the routine below. Specify the number of times students should write the upper- and lowercase forms of each letter and the words and sentences.

- Write the uppercase form of the letter.
- Write the lowercase form of the letter.
- Write words that begin with or contain the letter.
- Write an alliterative sentence using words that begin with the letter.

### Step Two: Publishing the Books

When all 26 letters have been practiced, give each student a copy of the checklist below. Go over each step with students. Then assign each child a different letter of the alphabet. Have the student complete the steps listed on the form. After students complete Step 3, photocopy their pages. When students have completed Step 6, bind the original layout pages in alphabetical order to make a book for your class. Bind the photocopied pages together to create an additional book to present to a class of younger students who are just learning to write in cursive.

---

Name ______________________________ Project checklist

## Cursive Project Checklist

**Directions:** Complete each step below, using the letter of the alphabet that has been assigned to you. As you complete a step, color the pencil next to it. Before going to the next step, have your teacher check your work and initial the corresponding box.

☐ 1. Do the following on scrap paper:
- List seven to ten words that begin with your assigned letter.
- Draw a star (★) next to the four or five words you plan to illustrate.
- Practice writing the words from the list.
- Write an alliterative sentence using as many of your words as you can.

☐ 2. On another sheet of paper, make a simple layout that includes the upper- and lowercase forms of your letter, the list of words, spaces for illustrating the starred words, and your sentence. Do not include actual illustrations.

☐ 3. Copy your layout onto the paper your teacher gives you. Make your writing dark and heavy. Illustrate the words you starred in Step 1 (see the example).

☐ 4. Give the layout to your teacher to photocopy.

☐ 5. Color the illustrations on your original layout and on the photocopy.

☐ 6. Give the two completed pages to your teacher.

Yy

yellow yams
yak yummy
yucky yo-yo
yell yippy

Yellow yaks ate yummy yams yesterday.



 **Note to the teacher:** Provide each student with crayons or markers and an 8½" x 11" sheet of white paper.

# Math Matters

Show students that math matters and can be loads of fun with the following easy-to-do activities!

## 292 Ways to Make a Dollar

**Skills: Problem solving, adding money**

Help students practice money concepts with this fun problem-solving contest. Challenge students to find 292 ways to make a dollar using half-dollars, quarters, dimes, nickels, and pennies. First, title a hallway bulletin board "292 Ways to Make a Dollar." Also create a set of answer keys on which you've recorded each possible combination as shown. When a student thinks she has a new combination, have her write it on a slip of paper for you to check. If the combination is correct, highlight it on your keys; then post the student's paper on the board. At the end of each day, write the total number of combinations found so far on a laminated sheet of paper posted near the display.

When your class has found all 292 combinations, list the results on chart paper. Then have students create graphs showing different combinations, such as "How many combinations include quarters compared to the number that include nickels?" Also bind the students' solutions together to make several booklets. Place the booklets in a center for students to use in original word problems, such as "If I have five pennies and three nickels, how many dimes do I need to make $1.00?" ***Lisa Laessig—Special Education, Kingswood Elementary, El Mirage, AZ***

| f-lar | quarter | dime | nickels | pennies |
|---|---|---|---|---|
| 2 | 0 | 0 | 0 | 0 |
| 1 | 2 | 0 | 0 | 0 |
| 1 | 1 | 2 | 1 | 0 |
| 1 | 1 | 2 | 0 | 5 |
| 1 | 1 | 1 | 3 | 0 |
| 1 | 1 | 1 | 2 | 5 |
| 1 | 1 | 1 | 1 | 10 |

## Rhythmic Place Value

**Skill: Place value to millions**

Practice place value like never before with an activity that calls for a little movin' and groovin'! First, write a ones-place number on the board, such as 3. Tell students that the ones place will be represented with a finger snap. Then snap three times to represent three ones. Next, write a 2 before the 3 to make 23. Inform students that the tens place will be represented by a hand clap. Then clap two times and snap three times to represent 23. Repeat this process, adding one digit and its corresponding movement at a time (see the list below). After all movements have been introduced, divide students into groups. Direct each group to choose a number to act out. Then allow the group to "perform" its number while the class tries to identify it. ***Samantha Trusty—Gr. 4, John Haley Elementary, Irving, TX***

**Ones**—snap
**Tens**—clap
**Hundreds**—stomp foot
**Thousands**—pat shoulders
**Ten thousands**—slap knees
**Hundred thousands**—click heels
**Millions**—pat stomach

## Tennis Ball Times Tables

**Skill: Multiplication**

Follow the bouncing ball to improved multiplication skills with this game! Write the numbers 1 to 9 on several tennis balls with a permanent marker. Next, take students to an outside area with a hard surface or to your school's gym.

Have students stand in circles of six to eight. Give one ball to each group. Direct one student to gently bounce the ball to a classmate. Instruct the student catching the ball to do so using *only* his thumb, index finger, and middle finger. Then have the catcher multiply the two numbers touched by his thumb and index finger. If the group agrees that the answer is correct, instruct the catcher to bounce the ball to another group member. If the answer is incorrect, have him give the ball back to the thrower and sit down. Continue until one student is left standing in each group. ***Heidi Graves—Gr. 4, Wateree Elementary, Lugoff, SC***

Show students that math matters and can be loads of fun with the following easy-to-do activities!

## "Rapping" Up Multiplication

### Skill: Multiplication facts

Have your students given multiplication facts practice a bad rap? Change their minds with this cool idea! Begin by having students call out the answers to multiplication tables three through nine in order—beginning with 12 and ending with 81—as you list them on the board *(12, 14, 15, 16, 18, 20, 21, 24, 25, 27, 28, 30, 32, 35, 36, 40, 42, 45, 48, 49, 54, 56, 63, 64, 72, 81).* After students count the products listed *(26),* ask them what they usually associate this number with *(the letters in the alphabet).* Then help them conclude that remembering 26 numbers can be as easy as remembering 26 letters. Finally, introduce the rap shown below. Students may not always remember that 43 isn't on a multiplication table, but they'll definitely dig this hip way to review! ***Linda Green—Gr. 5, Jackson Park School, University City, MO***

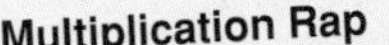

**Multiplication Rap**

They call us math rappers—we'll rap anytime!
We love to rap; we love to rhyme.
We love to rap; we love to rhyme.
We could do it all the time!

12, 14, 15, 16,
Multiplication is such a keen scene!
18, 20, 21, 24,
But learning these facts is no small chore!

25, 27, 28, 30,
Now we're gettin' pretty perky!
32, 35, 36, 40,
This factor challenge is downright sporty!

42, 45, 48, 49,
Our multiplying minds are doin' just fine!
54, 56, 63, 64,
Now there are only just a couple more.
What facts are left? 72 and 81.
We sure had some rappin' fun!

## Classified Computations

### Skills: Computing with money, writing and solving word problems

Recycle a stack of old newspapers the next time you're looking to practice money or problem-solving skills! Divide your class into pairs; then give each twosome the classified section of a newspaper and a crayon. The pair searches the classifieds to find the costs of the following items: a musical instrument, a car, a piece of furniture, a bicycle, a computer, a piece of jewelry, a pet, and two other items of their choice. Once an item is found, one child circles the ad while his partner writes the item's name and cost on a sheet of paper. Next, the pair finds the total cost of the items listed. Finally, the twosome uses its information to create five word problems that involve making change. Direct student pairs to exchange papers and solve each other's problems.

## Mental Math Day

### Skill: Mental math

Make mental math a top priority by declaring one day each week Mental Math Day. At the start of a new quarter, give each child an answer form similar to the one shown. On Mental Math Day, dictate a problem to students. After a pause, repeat the problem and have each student record an answer on her form. Then dictate four more problems in the same manner. Conclude by going over the answers together. During the first quarter, start with easier problems that require only simple addition and subtraction, such as 4 + 7 – 3 = *(8).* Gradually work up to problems that include multiplication and division. Let each student keep her form in a folder at her desk so she can monitor her weekly and quarterly progress. ***Helen D. Gromadzki—Gr. 5, Bollman Bridge Elementary, Jessup, MD***

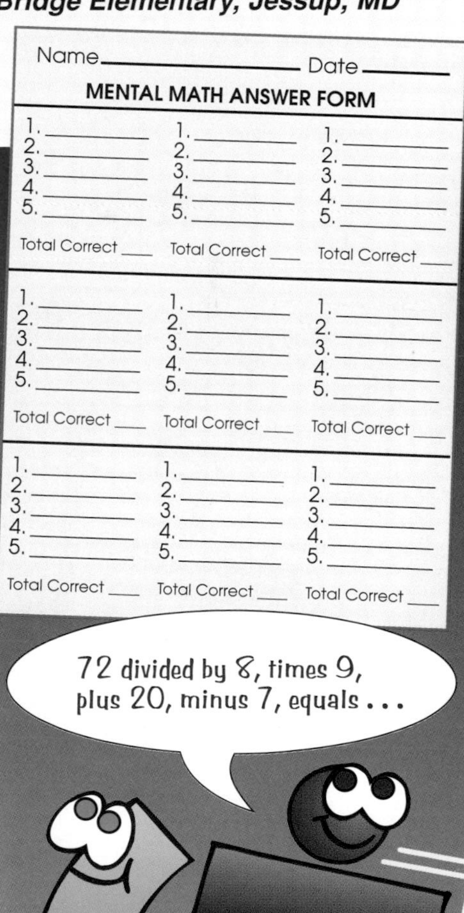

Name__________ Date______

MENTAL MATH ANSWER FORM

| | | |
|---|---|---|
| 1. ___ | 1. ___ | 1. ___ |
| 2. ___ | 2. ___ | 2. ___ |
| 3. ___ | 3. ___ | 3. ___ |
| 4. ___ | 4. ___ | 4. ___ |
| 5. ___ | 5. ___ | 5. ___ |
| Total Correct ___ | Total Correct ___ | Total Correct ___ |
| 1. ___ | 1. ___ | 1. ___ |
| 2. ___ | 2. ___ | 2. ___ |
| 3. ___ | 3. ___ | 3. ___ |
| 4. ___ | 4. ___ | 4. ___ |
| 5. ___ | 5. ___ | 5. ___ |
| Total Correct ___ | Total Correct ___ | Total Correct ___ |
| 1. ___ | 1. ___ | 1. ___ |
| 2. ___ | 2. ___ | 2. ___ |
| 3. ___ | 3. ___ | 3. ___ |
| 4. ___ | 4. ___ | 4. ___ |
| 5. ___ | 5. ___ | 5. ___ |
| Total Correct ___ | Total Correct ___ | Total Correct ___ |

72 divided by 8, times 9, plus 20, minus 7, equals . . .

Show students that math matters and can be loads of fun with the following easy-to-do activities!

## Real-World Math Posters

### Skill: Applying math concepts

Show students math's significance in the real world with a fun project that answers the question, When will I ever use this? Begin by having each student use the list below to interview an adult family member or friend. Have the student record the adult's name, job title, and telephone number on an index card. Collect the cards. Then have each child use his interview notes to design a poster about the interviewee's profession and how math is used in that job. As students share their completed posters, they will be amazed at the wide range of math skills used in the workplace. If desired, host a Real-World Math Day by inviting the people listed on the index cards to come to school and explain how they use math skills daily. ***Amy M. Pryor—Gr. 5, Parkway Elementary, Fort Worth, TX***

1. Describe your job.
2. What math skills do you use at your job?
3. Give an example of a specific math problem you have to solve at work.

**Working as an Upholsterer**

**Skills:** Exact measurement with a tape measure; customary measurement; adding, subtracting, multiplying, and dividing whole numbers and fractions

**Sample problem:** How much fabric is needed to cover a chair seat that measures $19\frac{1}{2}$" x $18\frac{1}{4}$"?

## Where Do I Belong?

### Skill: Comparing fractions

Have students put their fraction skills to the test with this simple game. Begin by dividing the chalkboard into three sections labeled as shown. Next, divide the class into two teams. Call out a fraction such as $^1/_3$, $^{12}/_7$, or $^9/_9$. Have the first player on Team 1 go to the board and write the fraction in the section in which he thinks it belongs. If correct, award his team one point; then call out a different fraction for the first player on Team 2. If incorrect, erase the fraction and give the first player on Team 2 a chance to write it where he thinks it belongs. Continue play until every player has had a turn; then declare the team with the most points the winner. Vary the game by having players write problems such as $^5/_6 + ^2/_3$, $^8/_5 - ^3/_5$, and $^3/_4 - ^1/_8$ in the correct sections. ***Julie Granchelli, Lockport, NY***

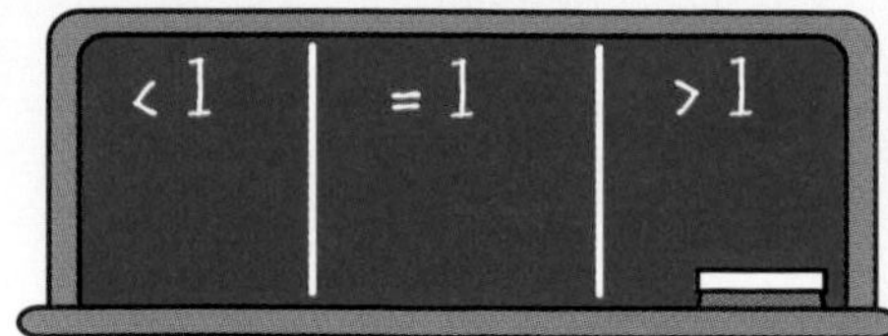


## Geo-Review Hats

### Skills: Geometry review, explanatory and descriptive writing

Conclude a geometry unit with a fashionable project that also sharpens students' writing skills. Challenge each student to design and construct a hat that incorporates examples of 15 geometric items, such as various polygons, lines, and space figures. Encourage students to use a variety of materials to create and decorate their headgear. After each student makes his hat, have him write a paragraph explaining how it was made and how he incorporated each geometry concept into its design. Then designate a day when students can model their one-of-a-kind hats. ***Shelley Graziano Swanson—Gr. 5, Ferry Farm Elementary, Fredericksburg, VA***

Show students that math matters and can be loads of fun with the following easy-to-do activities!

## Groovy Movie Graphs

### Skill: Constructing graphs

Use Hollywood flicks to trigger interest in constructing some groovy graphs! Give each child a photocopy of your area's local movie listings. Then have each student create a graph displaying the times that the movies are currently showing at one of the cinemas listed. Suggest that students use single bars for movies having only one showing and double bars for those that have two showings. Or have each student graph the number of movies showing simultaneously or that have the same ratings. Students could even graph the number of movies currently showing at more than one local cinema. If desired, have students who have actually seen the flicks rate them using a scale of one to five stars; then have them graph the results. ***Kim Bostick, Old Town Elementary, Winston-Salem, NC***

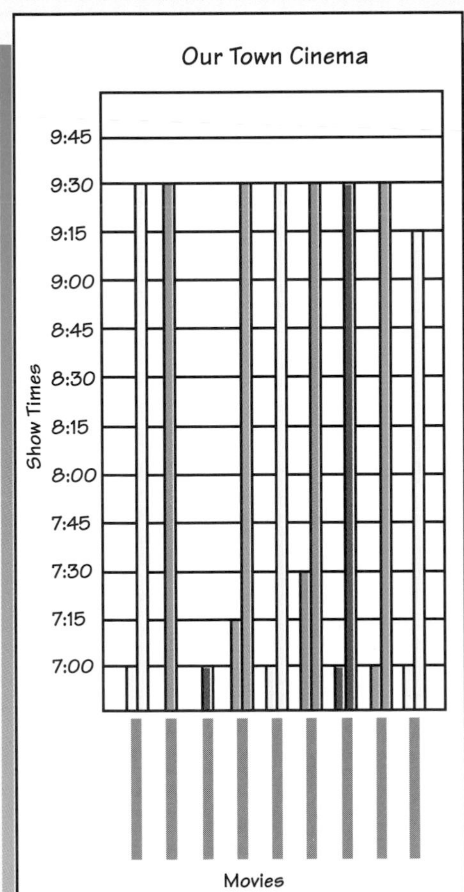


## Colorful Ratio Chains

### Skill: Writing ratios

Reinforce the concept that ratios compare two numbers with this manipulative activity. In advance, cut enough 1" x 9" construction paper strips so that each group of five students gets 50 strips in a variety of the following colors: yellow, blue, green, orange, pink, purple, and red. Review with students the four different ways of writing a ratio, such as *3 to 1, 3:1, 3/1,* and *three to one.* Next, give each group its strips and a stapler. Have each group make a paper chain with the strips, arranging the colors randomly. Then give each group a copy of page 236. Have students use their chains to help them complete the page as directed. If desired, have students also use the chains to find fractional parts of a whole, to convert fractions to decimals, or to graph the colors they used. ***Jane Scott—Gr. 5, South Mebane Elementary, Mebane, NC***

## Shoebox Rooms

### Skills: Perimeter and area

Put measurement skills into practice with a project that unleashes the talents of future interior designers! For each child, gather a shoebox (discard the lid), a metric ruler, scissors, glue, and construction paper in various colors. Also collect carpet scraps and books of wallpaper samples. Ask each child to think of a room she'd like to design, such as an ideal bedroom, a perfect kitchen, or even a psychedelic bathroom. With the shoebox lying on its side, have the student draw one or more windows on the back and side walls. Next, have her find the area of the floor and walls and the perimeter of the windows to the nearest whole centimeter. Direct her to write her calculations on a worksheet titled "Work Order for __________'s Room." Then have the student decorate the interior of her shoebox, adding details such as furniture cutouts, carpet scraps, and other math-related items, such as symmetrical or congruent objects. Display the completed projects in an area where they won't be missed! ***Sarah Harkey—Gr. 5, Ebinport Elementary, Rock Hill, SC***

**Work Order for Melissa's Room**

Area of floor: 28.5 cm x 9.5 cm = 270.75 sq. cm = 271 sq. cm

Area of wall A: 15.5 cm x 9.5 cm = 147.25 sq. cm = 147 sq. cm

Area of wall B: 15.5 cm x 28.5 cm = 441.75 sq. cm = 442 sq. cm

Area of wall C: 15.5 cm x 9.5 cm = 147.25 sq. cm = 147 sq. cm

Total area of walls: 147 sq. cm + 442 sq. cm + 147 sq. cm = 736 sq. cm

Perimeter of window: 6.5 cm + 6.5 cm + 4 cm + 4 cm = 21 cm

Names ______________________________ 

# Ratio Chains

**Directions:** Follow the steps below to write ratios that compare any two colors on your group's paper chain.

**Step 1:** Stretch out your paper chain. Count the links of each color. Record the numbers below. Then record the total links in the chain.

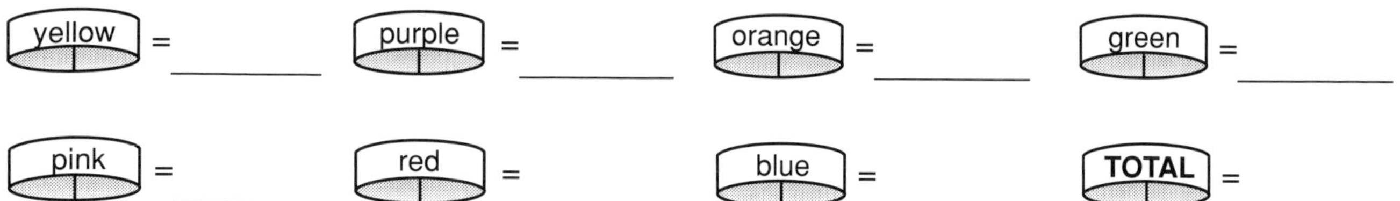


**Step 2:** Look at the chain again. Write a ratio that compares each pair of colors listed below. Record each ratio in four different ways.

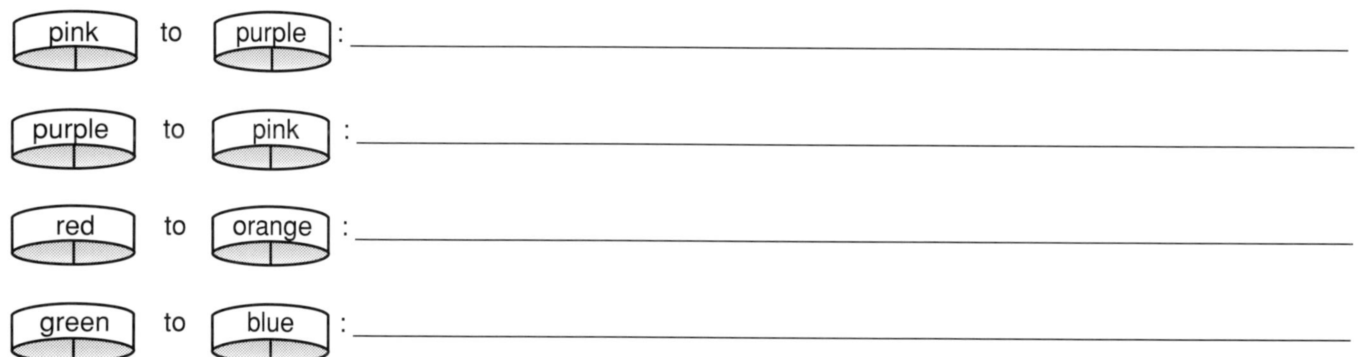


**Step 3:** In each pair of links below, write any combination of two colors **not** used in Step 2 above. Then write a ratio comparing each new pair of colors. Record each ratio in two different ways.

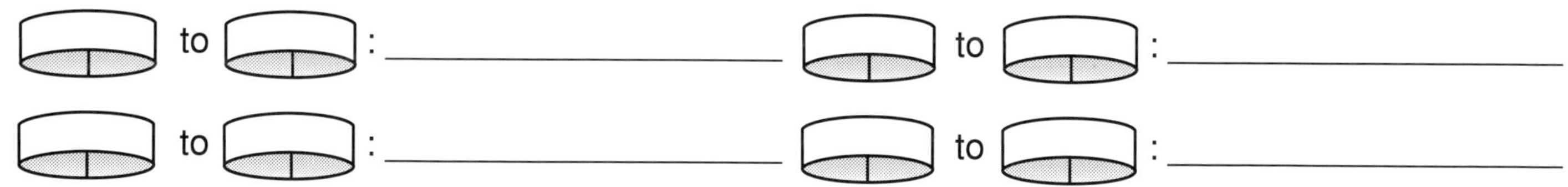


**Step 4:** Label the links below with any two colors listed in Step 1. Look at the other groups' chains and count the number of links in those colors. Add the numbers together. Remember to include the numbers from your own group's chain! Then, on the lines provided, write a ratio comparing the **total** links of color #1 to the **total** links of color #2. Record the ratio in four different ways.

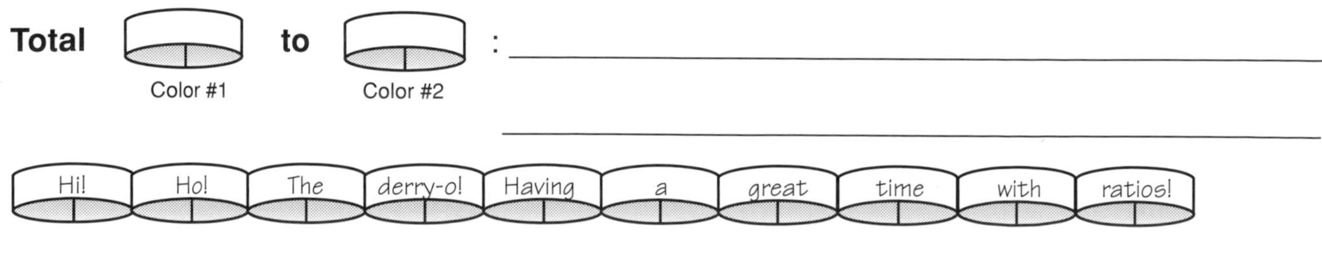




 **Note to the teacher:** Use with "Colorful Ratio Chains" on page 235.

# English Made Easy

## Verb-Filled Compliments

### Skill: Identifying verbs

Sara
Sara is a good friend to everyone.
linking verb


Review verbs with a writing activity that lets students give kudos to their peers. Write each student's name on a different slip of paper and place the slips in a container. Have each child draw a name and then write a sentence that compliments the person in a special way. Collect the sentences; then distribute them to the recipients of the compliments. Direct each child to read her compliment, underline the verb, and categorize it as action or linking. Then have her share the compliment and verb with the class. If desired, compile the sentences into a list and give each student a copy to keep. Or publish the compliments in a class newsletter. Verb practice that boosts positive feelings is hard to top!

Miriam Krauss—Gr. 4, Beth Jacob Day School, Brooklyn, NY

## "Punctu-action" Practice

### Skill: Punctuation

STAND UP when you indent a paragraph.
CLAP when you use a capital letter.
SNAP YOUR FINGERS when you use a period.
WHISTLE when you use a comma.
STOMP YOUR FEET when you use a question mark.
SAY "WOW" when you use an exclamation mark.

Energize your next writing session by having students "act out" each time they use particular punctuation marks or indent paragraphs. Copy the directions shown onto a poster. Whenever a writing activity needs some spark, display the poster and have students perform the actions as they write. Add additional punctuation marks and corresponding actions to the poster as needed. If students fail to perform certain "punctu-actions," you can quickly identify the problem areas and provide the help needed.

Judith L. Garshelis—Gr. 6, Fairfield Intermediate School, Fairfield, OH

## Adverb Headlines

### Skill: Using adverbs

Extra! Extra! Read all about how students can use newspaper headlines to practice adverbs! Write the following headings on the board: How? When? Where? Have student volunteers come to the board and list sample adverbs under the appropriate headings. Afterward, give each student a newspaper page and have her cut a headline from it. Challenge her to think of an adverb she could add to the beginning, middle, or end of the headline. Then direct her to cut the headline apart (if necessary), glue it to a colorful sheet of paper, and use a marker to add the selected adverb. Have her write the question that the adverb answers after the headline. Instruct the student to repeat the activity with five different headlines, making sure to answer each adverb question twice as shown.

Boy Courageously Saves Sister (How?)
Unemployment Slowly Falling This Month (How?)
Reds Face Braves Tomorrow (When?)
Police Release Suspect Immediately (When?)
Thunderstorms Bring Destruction Here (Where?)
Fans Everywhere Love Britney (Where?)

Joyce Hovanec—Gr. 4, Glassport Elementary, Glassport, PA

# English Made Easy

When you can't be there in person, send the next best thing:

PRONOUNS!!!

## Parts-of-Speech Pitches

### Skill: Reviewing parts of speech

Turn students into parts-of-speech pitchmen with an activity they're sure to be sold on! First, help students recall several catchy jingles and slogans of popular products. Discuss how advertisers use such tactics to help buyers remember the benefits of their products. Next, announce that an important advertising firm has hired the class to come up with clever ways to help the public distinguish one part of speech from another. Divide students into groups; then assign a different part of speech to each group. Challenge each group to create an informative and interesting television commercial, poster, jingle, and/or slogan that will help others remember its part of speech. When groups are finished, have each team present its project to the class.

Jaimie Hudson, Pace, FL

## Got a Clue?

### Skill: Reviewing grammar

Feeling a bit clueless about how to make grammar practice something students actually enjoy? Then try this exciting game that can be played over several days. Students will not only get a great preview of the grammar skills they'll cover throughout the year, but they'll also get reacquainted with a table of contents, index, and glossary.

**Before the game:**

1. Make a copy of the clues on page 240 for each group of five students. Use a different color of paper for each copy.
2. Cut each set of clues apart; then stack them in order (faceup) on a table.
3. Have students take out their grammar texts.
4. Divide students into groups of five. Assign each group a different color of clues.
5. Select a recorder and a runner for each group. Have each recorder number a sheet of paper from 1 to 29.

**To play:**

1. The runner from each group comes to you to get Clue #1 and takes it to his group.
2. Each group reads Clue #1 and searches its grammar texts for the answer. The recorder writes the group's answer next to the corresponding number on the group's paper and brings it to you to check.
3. If the answer is correct, the runner takes the next clue in his group's stack back to his teammates and repeats Step 2. Each successive clue verifies the answer to the previous one, so the group is assured of each answer before continuing.
4. If a group's answer is incorrect, the runner returns to his group and has it search again for the correct answer.
5. The game continues in this manner until one team has answered all the clues correctly.

Way to go! The plural forms are *chiefs, bunnies, donkeys, knives,* and *brushes.*

**#17:** Write the abbreviations of these words: *mister, doctor, avenue, street, before noon.*

Fantastic! The abbreviations are *Mr., Dr., ave., st.,* and A.M.

**#18:** Is the underlined part of the following sentence the simple subject, the complete subject, or the compound subject? *Her older sister is a freshman in college.*

Janelle Brinck, Leander, TX

Name ______________________________________________ 

# A "Souper" Invention

In 1642 a 19-year-old French boy created a "souper" device to make his dad's job easier. Discover the name of this device by coloring in all the letters in the soup bowl that are labeled with prepositions. Unscramble the uncolored letters to learn the name of the invention.

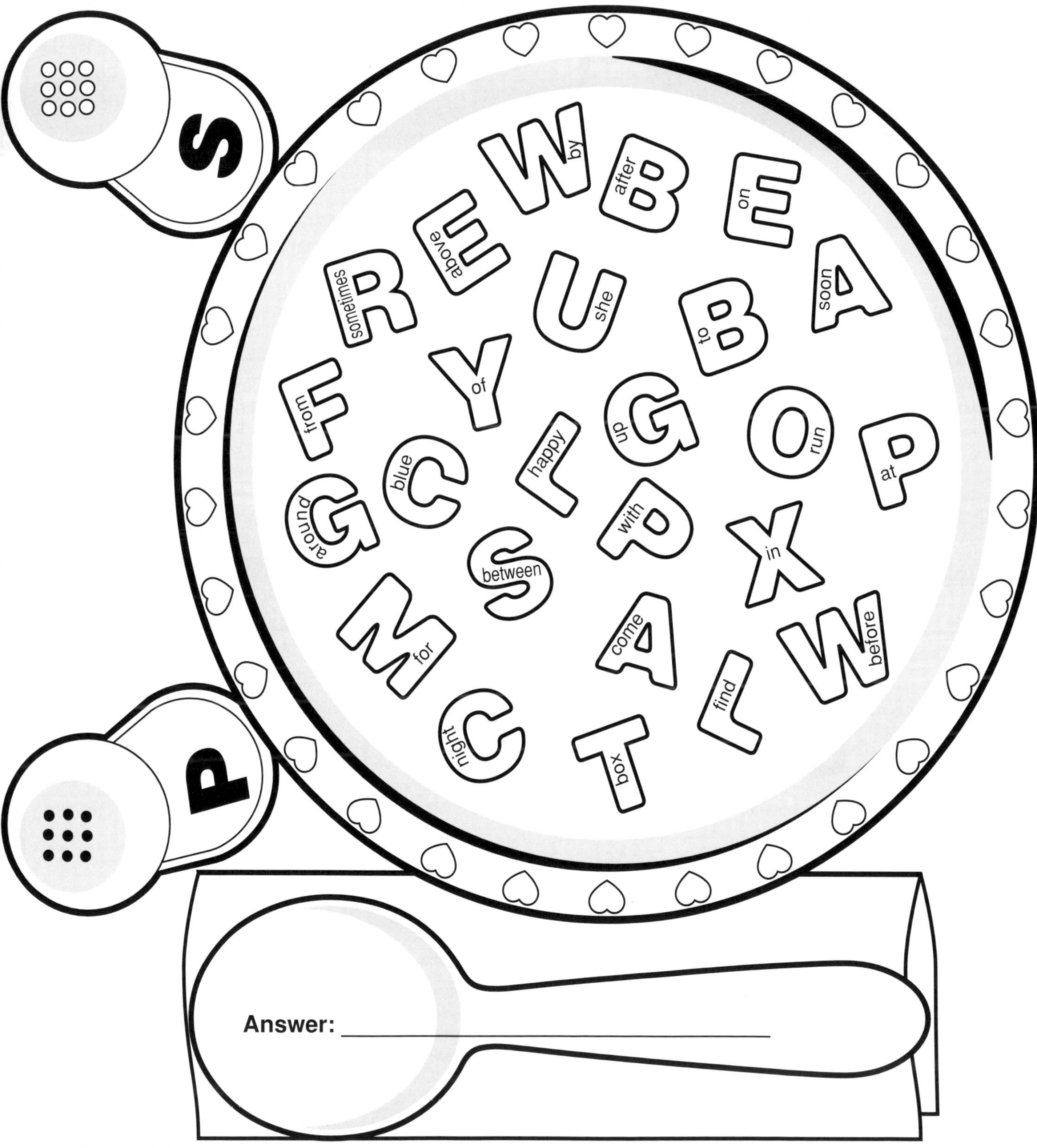


Answer: ______________________________

**Bonux Box:** Use any ten prepositions above to help you write five sentences about important classroom items you wish you had invented.

# English Made Easy

## Comic Strip Dialogue
### Skill: Writing dialogue

Turn to the comics section of your newspaper the next time you want students to practice writing dialogue. After reviewing quotation marks and how to use them in writing dialogue, ask each child to bring in a newspaper comic strip, such as *Garfield®* or *Dennis the Menace.* Direct each student to write a story about the strip. Have him include a title and an introductory paragraph that provides the story's setting. Then have him tell what happens in the strip, using the dialogue from the speech bubbles and adding descriptive phrases to indicate the characters' moods. What a fun way to practice an important skill!

Domenick C. Renzi—Gr. 5, Bells Elementary, Turnersville, NJ

A Trip to the Orthodontist

It was a cold winter afternoon. Susie entered the quiet room and put on her coat and hat. "Well, it's time for me to go to the orthodontist," Susie announced.

She turned to her brother Stedmond and said, "I don't guess you'd want to give your sister a good-bye kiss."

Stedmond, who was almost squirming at the thought of kissing his sister, looked at her and shouted, "No! I don't want to catch your crooked teeth!"

## Participial Pictures
### Skill: Identifying participial phrases

Draw attention to participial phrases with this grammar-rich version of Pictionary®! Pair students; then have each pair write three sentences, each containing a different participial phrase. For example: Begging for a bone, the dog sat up on its hind legs. When the sentences have been completed, let each pair take turns drawing a picture of one of its sentences on the board. Have the remaining pairs guess the participial phrase that is represented in the drawing. Continue in this manner until each pair has illustrated one of its sentences. Then declare the pair with the most correct guesses the winner.

Stephanie Krivan—Grs. 5–8
Austintown School District
Youngstown, OH

## Prepositional Directions
### Skill: Using prepositional phrases

Waldo's not the only thing hiding in the pages of Martin Handford's popular series of Where's Waldo? books (Candlewick Press). There's also plenty of practice with prepositional phrases! At a center, place an egg timer and books such as *Where's Waldo?, Where's Waldo Now?, Where's Waldo?: In Hollywood, Where's Waldo?: The Fantastic Journey,* and *Where's Waldo?: The Wonder Book.* Direct one partner to secretly pick an object (Waldo or anything else) from a page in one of the books. Then have her give three clues—each containing one or more prepositional phrases—to help her partner find and identify that object before time is up. After one partner guesses correctly, have the pair switch roles.

Colleen Dabney, Williamsburg-JCC Public Schools, Williamsburg, VA

The object is *near the bottom of the page.*
It is *to the left of a large wooden chair.*
The object is labeled *with musical notes.*

Turn the page for a reproducible student activity on identifying different types of phrases!

# Time to Tune In!

About how many million TV sets were there in the 1960s? Find out by using the code at the right to classify the boldfaced phrases in the sentences below. Write the correct code for each phrase in the box on the corresponding TV set. When you're finished, total the numbers in the boxes to find out about how many million televisions were around in the 1960s.

| Channel | Code |
|---|---|
| appositive | 4 |
| gerund | 6 |
| infinitive | 7 |
| prepositional | 3 |

Color telecasts began **in 1953.**

Many scientists worked **to develop television.**

In 1929, Vladimir K. Zworykin, **a Russian-born American scientist,** demonstrated the first practical TV.

"Felix the Cat," **an early cartoon,** was NBC's first experimental program.

In the early days **of television,** all national networks were based in New York City.

TV broadcasting was suspended until World War II ended **in 1945.**

**To entertain viewers,** *I Love Lucy* went on the air in 1951.

**Helping some contestants answer questions** resulted in a scandal for TV game shows in 1959.

**Holding presidential debates on TV** began in 1960 when John F. Kennedy debated Richard M. Nixon.

*Laugh-In,* **a comedy show,** was very popular in the 1960s.

*Roots* was one of the top miniseries **to watch** in the 1970s.

**Watching TV** is a popular pastime in homes today.

**Bonus Box:** Write four sentences of your own—one for each kind of phrase above—about television today. Write your sentences on the back of this sheet.

# Lifesavers...
# Management Tips for Teachers

# LIFESAVERS...

## management tips for teachers

## Big Kid Congrats

Congratulate students for a job well done with this time-saving incentive. Each month use your computer to make several sheets of labels as shown. When a student exhibits exemplary behavior or work habits, simply peel off a label and place it on his shirt. Not only will you avoid having to write out a note, but you'll also guarantee that the label will get home for parents to see. Plus the labels are small enough so that your "big kids" won't be embarrassed to wear them. Make additional labels that read "Today is my birthday!" to award on everyone's special day.

Lisa Carlson—Gr. 5
Dunbar Hill Elementary
Hamden, CT

## Class Mail System

If you never thought you'd allow note passing in class, think again! Have each student staple together the sides of a file folder and personalize the folder. Then staple the folders to a bulletin board to use as mailboxes. After establishing rules such as those listed, allow students to write and mail friendly letters to each other during free time. (If a student misuses her mail privilege, remove her mailbox from the board for a predetermined length of time.) Periodically slip a small treat into each mailbox as a reward for good behavior or for meeting an individual or class goal.

Debra Baucom—Gr. 5, New Hope Elementary, Columbus, MS

**Mail System Rules**

1. Write only positive messages.
2. Use friendly-letter format.
3. Write letters and check your mailbox <u>only</u> after you've completed your work.
4. Do not look in a classmate's mailbox.

## Recycled File Folders

Recycle file folders with this clever money-saving idea. Gather a different-colored pad of self-sticking notes for each subject area, such as pink for math, yellow for reading, etc. Then place a brightly colored note on the tab of each folder. Write the label for that folder on the note as shown. When you no longer need a folder but want to reuse it, simply remove the note and add a new one.

Barbara Kenney—Gr. 4
Colo-NESCO Elementary
McCallsburg, IA

## The Water Race

Encourage better behavior with this virtually cost-free idea that's slightly soggy but full of fun! Gather a same-sized plastic container for each cooperative group. When every member of a group completes his homework or stays on task, pour one cup of water into his group's container. (To distinguish one container from another, dye the water in each container with different-colored food coloring.) Also award a cup of water for good behavior, teamwork, or any other goal you want to reinforce. Reward the first group to fill its container with a special treat. Then empty the containers and play again.

Christine Ward—Gr. 5
East Brook Middle School
Paramus, NJ

## Grading My Project

Want students to take more ownership of the projects you assign? Then let them help create the assessment tool you'll use to grade them. Just follow these simple steps:

1. Draw a chart on the board as shown.
2. With students, discuss and determine the most important parts of the project (see the example). List their responses on the chart.
3. Work with students to determine the importance of each part. Then have students help designate a point value for each part as shown.
4. Type the completed grading chart and give a copy to each student. Direct students to use the chart as a guide for completing the project. Use the chart yourself as the project evaluation sheet.

Kelley Tijero—Gr. 6, Creighton Intermediate School, Conroe, TX

| Part | Points |
|---|---|
| island—drawn correctly; as large as possible | 10 |
| landforms—include 15 different ones on map; all labeled | 30 |
| paragraph—neatly written; describes origin of island | 25 |
| flag—colorful; includes paragraph describing symbols | 20 |
| followed all directions | 15 |
| TOTAL | 100 |

# LIFESAVERS...

## management tips for teachers

### Homework Moviefest

Motivate students to complete homework assignments with this silver screen incentive. At the start of each month, label a blank calendar page for each child. During the month, place a sticker on each day that a student turns in all homework assignments (and also on any day he is absent). At the end of the month, give each student who received a sticker every day a no-homework pass and an invitation to a special "moviefest." Also send invitations—without the homework passes—to students who have only one or two no-sticker days. During the moviefest, show a curriculum-related video and serve popcorn or other refreshments.

Kelly Fornauf—Gr. 5
Northwestern Lehigh Middle School
New Tripoli, PA

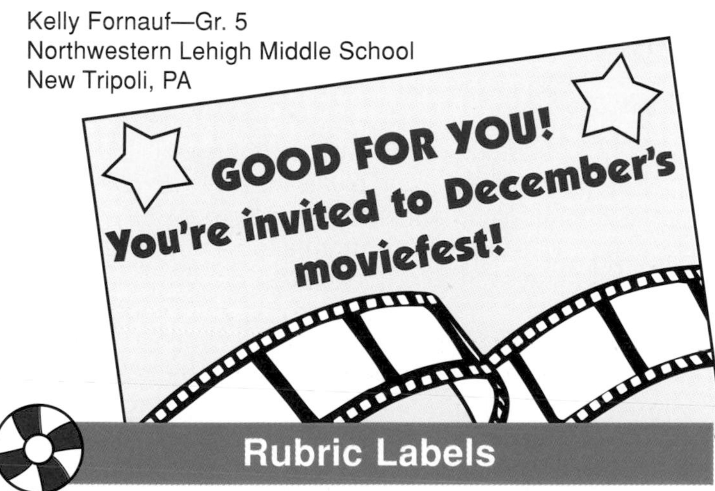

GOOD FOR YOU!
You're invited to December's moviefest!


### Rubric Labels

Who says assessing your students' writing pieces has to take a long time? It doesn't anymore with this idea. Use a word-processing program to create and print a rubric label such as the one shown. When students turn in their final copies, stick a label on each paper. Then circle a number in each row to indicate your assessment of that area (with 1 indicating mastery and 5 indicating a need for remediation). In just moments, students will be able to read your informal assessment and know how they did on the assignment. Extend this idea by creating additional rubrics for other subject areas.

Anita M. Nixon—Gr. 6
Frank J. Dugan Elementary
Marlboro, NJ

| | |
|---|---|
| **Capitalization** | **1 2 3 4 5** |
| **Punctuation** | **1 2 3 4 5** |
| **Spelling** | **1 2 3 4 5** |
| **Complete sentences** | **1 2 3 4 5** |
| **Indent new paragraph** | **1 2 3 4 5** |
| **Paragraph skills** | **1 2 3 4 5** |
| **Neatness** | **1 2 3 4 5** |

### Classroom Library Organizer

Keep your classroom library organized in a snap with this helpful tip. Use a marker to write the first letter of the author's last name on the top of each book as shown. Then shelve the books in order by author. One quick glance across the tops of the books identifies any misplaced volumes. Plus, students can reshelve books for you in no time.

Laura Eliason—Gr. 5
Woods Cross Elementary
Woods Cross, UT

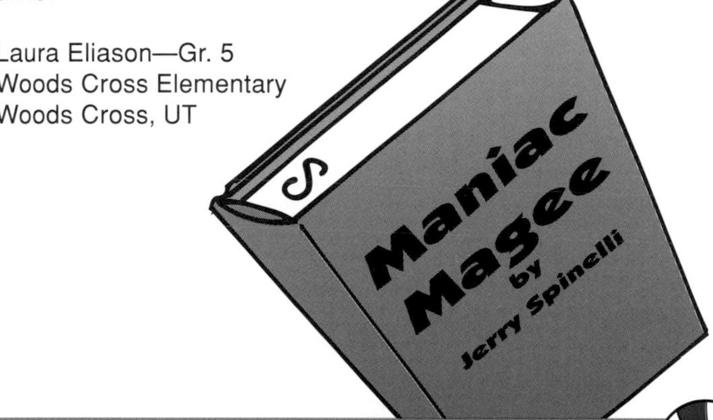


### Conference Postcards

When you want to ensure that a parent follows up on what was discussed during a conference, try this practical tip. Address a postcard to the parent as soon after the conference as possible. Thank the parent for participating in the meeting; then restate the role that you both agreed he or she would take in helping the child. End with another brief word of appreciation before dropping the postcard in the mail.

Shawn Parkhurst—Gr. 6
Canadian Academy
Kobe, Japan

### Late Assignment Solution

It's probably happened to you before: a student turns work in late only to claim later that it was submitted on time. Eliminate this problem with the help of a dated rubber stamp (like those used in most libraries). Simply stamp the date on all assignments as soon as they're turned in. Problem solved!

Judy O'Dell—Gr. 6
Caddo Middle Magnet School
Shreveport, LA

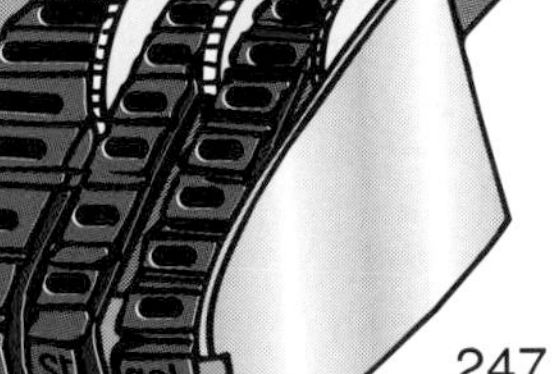

# LIFESAVERS...

## management tips for teachers

### Personalized Pencils

Even the most responsible student will sometimes ask to borrow a pencil. Instead of using valuable class time to give another lecture on being prepared, try this simple tip. At the beginning of the school year, order 100 inexpensive pencils printed with your name. Keep the pencils in a jar on your desk. Since the pencils are personalized with your name, students will be more likely to return them when they're done.

Judy O'Dell—Gr. 6
Caddo Middle Magnet School
Shreveport, LA

### Thumbs-Up!

Promote positive behavior and teamwork with an incentive that's sure to earn a big thumbs-up! Decorate a sheet of poster board with a large hand and the title "Thumbs-Up!" as shown. Laminate the poster and display it in the classroom. Also purchase an inexpensive ink pad. Explain to students that each time the class receives a compliment from another teacher or shows respect to others, you will add a thumbprint to the poster. When the class earns a predetermined number of prints, reward students with a special privilege, such as a class party or field trip. Then wipe the board clean and start the challenge over again.

Louella Nygaard—Gr. 5
Isabell Bills Elementary
Colstrip, MT

### Extra-Credit Stickers

Want to keep early finishers from frittering away their extra time? At the start of each month, copy a supply of reproducible puzzles and skill sheets (one or more for each school day). Store the activities in a file box labeled "Extra Credit." Also make a chart listing each student's name and activity. If a student successfully completes an activity, write a check mark beside his name on the chart. At the end of the month, count the marks earned by each child, divide the total by two, and write the resulting quotient on a blank peel-off sticker. Give the sticker to the student; then let him affix it to a graded test and return the paper so you can add the extra-credit points to his final grade.

Adam Fassanella—Gr. 4
Hinsdale School
Winsted, CT

### Extra Skill Sheets

If you're tired of trying to track down extra reproducibles for an absent student, this timesaver is for you! In advance, make a few copies of a variety of reproducible skill sheets. Organize the sheets by skill in labeled file folders. Then store the folders in boxes by subject area. When a student who was absent needs a copy of a reproducible assignment, just pull a sheet on the same skill from your set of extras. Also use the extra reproducibles anytime a student needs additional practice on a specific skill.

Rosemary Linden—Gr. 4
Royal Valley Elementary
Topeka, KS

### Remember!

To help students become more responsible for remembering important due dates, label a corner of the chalkboard "Remember!" In this space, list any upcoming event—but *only* if a student asks you to list the item. Then review the list at the end of the day. Students will quickly realize how helpful it is to have the reminders right in front of them. If desired, discontinue the "Remember!" list during the last quarter of the school year, and encourage each student to keep her own list at her desk.

REMEMBER!
Tues. 3-9: Science test
Wed. 3-10: Money for field trip
Fri. 3-12: Hand in book report

Gratsiela Sabangan—Grs. 4–6, Three Angels School, Wichita, KS

# LIFESAVERS...

## management tips for teachers

### Smart Choices Bucket

Looking for a way to encourage students to make smart choices? Try this easy-to-implement system. Gather two equal-sized, clear containers and label one "Smart Choices Bucket." Fill the other container with small incentives—such as candy, erasers, stickers, and bookmarks—that have been donated by parents. Each time the class makes a smart choice, such as standing quietly in line or following directions, acknowledge the students' actions by having each child select one incentive and place it in the Smart Choices bucket. After all incentives have been transferred from one container to the other, equally divide the items into goodie bags for your students. Now that's a smart choice!

Laurel Nascimento and Rebecca Worst—Gr. 4
Saint Joseph School
Marietta, GA

### Finished? Check It Off!

Use this handy tip and with one glance you'll identify which students have turned in an assignment. Make a supply of assignment forms similar to the one shown. Store the forms and a few two-pocket folders where students typically turn in their work. The first student to turn in a specific assignment fills out the top portion of a form and clips it to the front of a folder. As each student turns in her assignment, she places her work inside the folder and initials next to her name. Simple!

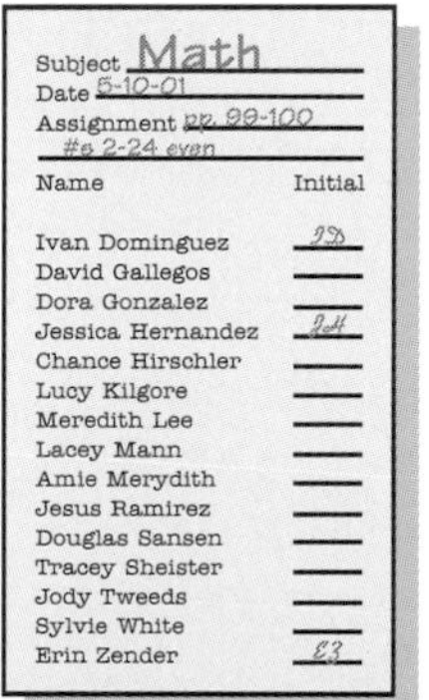

Subject Math
Date 5-10-01
Assignment pp. 99-100 #s 2-24 even

| Name | Initial |
|---|---|
| Ivan Dominguez | ID |
| David Gallegos | |
| Dora Gonzalez | |
| Jessica Hernandez | JH |
| Chance Hirschler | |
| Lucy Kilgore | |
| Meredith Lee | |
| Lacey Mann | |
| Amie Merydith | |
| Jesus Ramirez | |
| Douglas Sansen | |
| Tracey Sheister | |
| Jody Tweeds | |
| Sylvie White | |
| Erin Zender | EZ |

Lynsia Sprouse—Gr. 5
Booker Independent School District
Booker, TX

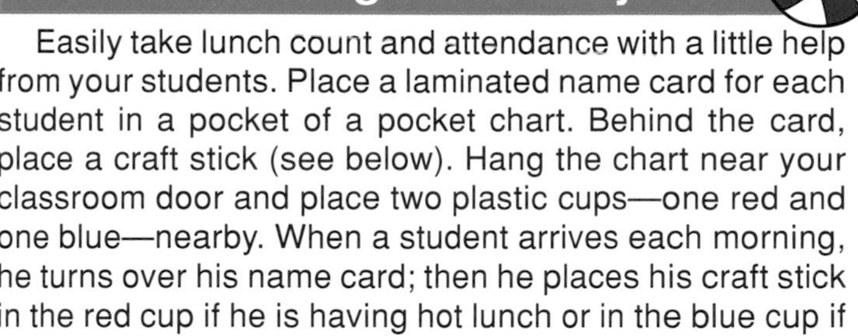

### Morning Made Easy

Easily take lunch count and attendance with a little help from your students. Place a laminated name card for each student in a pocket of a pocket chart. Behind the card, place a craft stick (see below). Hang the chart near your classroom door and place two plastic cups—one red and one blue—nearby. When a student arrives each morning, he turns over his name card; then he places his craft stick in the red cup if he is having hot lunch or in the blue cup if he brought his lunch from home. A student volunteer can easily scan the pocket chart to see the names of absent students and then count the number of hot lunch requests. What a timesaver!

Kim Smith, Meyers-Ganoung School
Tucson, AZ

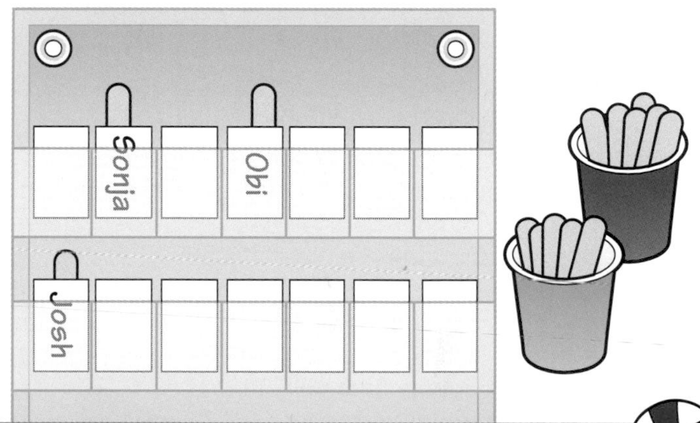


### Paper Toppers

Searching for a way to motivate students to turn in neat, legible assignments? Periodically tape a novelty pencil to the top of each neatly done assignment. Students will be thrilled to receive this reward even though their work may contain mistakes. Top that!

Patricia E. Dancho—Gr. 6
Apollo-Ridge Middle School
Spring Church, PA

### Student Book Recommendations

Try this class library tip to help students select books to read. Glue a library card pocket to the inside back cover of each class library book. Then place an index card in each pocket. After a student has finished reading a book, he writes his comments about it on the card and places the card back in the pocket. Students will love sharing their opinions and reading those written by their classmates.

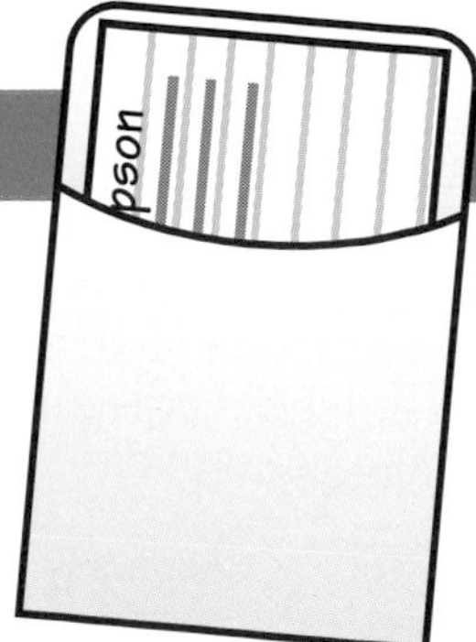

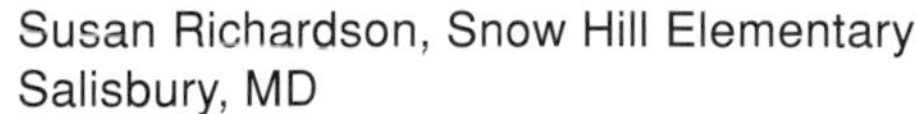

Susan Richardson, Snow Hill Elementary
Salisbury, MD

# LIFESAVERS...

## management tips for teachers

### Cooperative-Group Test Taking

If your students' desks are arranged in cooperative groups, there's no need to move them into rows on test days. Instead, provide each student with a colorful laminated file folder (a different color for each group) to stand on her desktop for privacy. After a student finishes a test and turns it facedown on her desk, have her close the folder and put it in her desk. Not only does this method give students the privacy they need while taking a test, but it also lets you know at a glance when everyone is finished.

Penny Morrison—Gr. 6
DAR Middle School
Grant, AL

### Monthly Idea Binders

How can you organize the great teaching ideas you collect from various sources so they'll be easy to use? Put them in monthly binders! Purchase a three-ring binder for each school month. Add a tab to each binder for every subject taught: language arts, math, reading, social studies, science, writing, etc. Place calendars and holiday activities in the front of each binder. Then file all remaining ideas and activities by subject for quick reference. As each new month begins, just pull out that month's binder and you're ready to go!

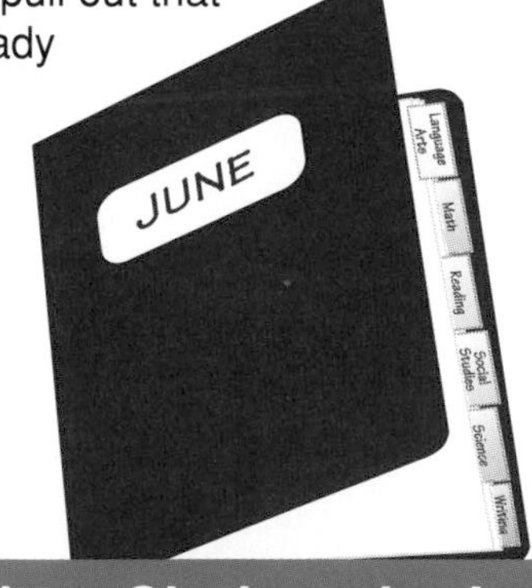


Denise Menchaca—Grs. 3–5
Eastside Elementary
Brooksville, FL

### Class-Change Organizer

Students who travel between classrooms seem bound to forget materials from time to time. Solve this problem by supplying each child with a sturdy three- to four-inch-deep plastic pan that fits inside a desk. Have students fill their pans with class essentials and then carry the pans with them from class to class. Reuse the containers each year. The benefits? Neater desks, no complaints about materials being tampered with by others, and students who are more organized and responsible!

Debra Kiley—Gr. 5
Sandymount Elementary
Finksburg, MD

### Tracking Parental Contacts

Here's a simple way to help you remember whether you've contacted a parent about a particular issue. Each time you call or send a note about a child's poor work on a particular assignment, highlight that score in your gradebook. One quick glance will confirm if the communication has taken place or not.

Goldie Eichorn—Gr. 6
Yeshiva Ateres Yisroel
Brooklyn, NY

### Call on Clothespins!

Need an easy way to keep track of who you've called on in class to answer questions, read aloud, or take turns in a game? Call on clothespins! Label both sides of each clothespin with a different child's name. Place the clothespins in a box. Draw one clothespin at a time and have that student answer the next question or perform the next task. Then clip the clothespin to the edge of the box. Continue until all names have been used. Just remove one clothespin at a time to reverse the process.

Brenda Keller—Gr. 5, Canadochly Elementary, East Prospect, PA

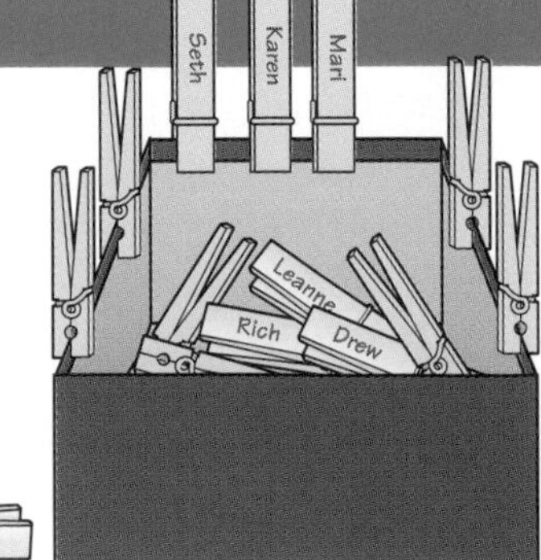


Kelly

# Write On!

# Write On!

## Ideas and Tips for Teaching Students to Write

### Writing Toolbox

Motivate students to build better writing habits with this easy-to-use activity. Have each student bring a shoebox to class. Provide each child with multicolored index cards, a large pipe cleaner, and a length of bulletin board paper. After each student covers his box with paper and decorates it, have him poke two holes (two to three inches apart) in his box lid. Next, have the student make a handle by placing his pipe cleaner through the holes and securing the ends with tape. Then have the student label the colored cards as follows:

green = synonyms for overused words, such as *said, good, big,* etc.
red = hard to spell/easily confused words
blue = story starters
yellow = metaphors and similes

Direct the student to rubber-band each different-colored set of cards together and file them in his box. Finally, have the child fill his "writing toolbox" with a pocket dictionary, favorite pencils, and a supply of erasers. There you have it—the "write" tools together in one handy carryall!

Susan Hudson Jarvis—Gr. 4, Wintergreen Intermediate School, Greenville, NC

### Bubble Trouble

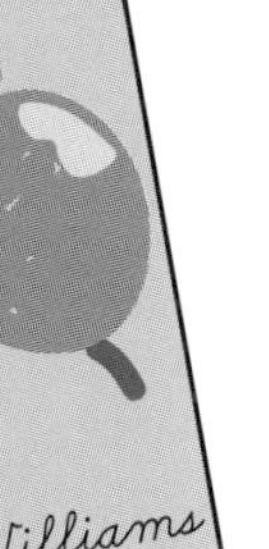

Gum in school? Sure, when it's used as a creative-writing story starter! Begin by having each student draw and color a self-portrait on a 12" x 18" sheet of construction paper. Direct the student to cut a slit between the lips; then have her stick the tied end of an inflated pink balloon through the slit, taping it to the back of the picture. Finally, instruct the student to write a story about blowing this large bubble, or have her choose from the list of topics below. Hang the stories and the bubble pictures in the classroom.

**"Bubble-licious" Writing Topics**

- Oh no! This bubble is too big!
- Gum on my shoe. Boo-hoo!
- This magic gum will __________.
- Occupation: Bubble Gum Tester

Ann Owen—Gr. 4, Wayne Center Elementary, Kendallville, IN

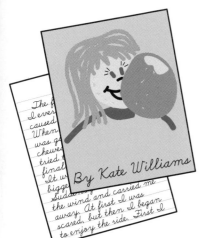

### Perfect Paragraph Practice

Help your students visualize and write good paragraphs with this hands-on idea. To begin, write each sentence of a five-sentence paragraph on a sentence strip as shown. Choose five students to line up at the front of the room facing the class; then randomly distribute the sentences to them. Remind students that a well-written paragraph begins with an introductory sentence, supplies detail sentences in the middle, and ends with a concluding sentence. Call on seated students to organize the sentences, one at a time, into a unified paragraph.

Next, divide the class into groups of five. Have each group write its own five-sentence paragraph on sentence strips. In turn, have the class arrange each group's sentences into an organized paragraph. There you have it—a practically perfect way to practice paragraph writing!

*Shopping at the mall is the best way to shop.*

*There are plenty of stores to choose from.*

*Most malls have many different places to eat.*

*Sometimes you will meet your friends there.*

*The mall is a great place to shop till you drop!*

adapted from an idea by Patrick S. McKee—Gr. 4
Morgan Elementary, Rialto, CA

# Write On!

## Ideas and Tips for Teaching Students to Write

### Details, Details!

**Skill: Elaboration**

If trying to find details in your students' writing is like one big game of hide-and-seek, try this sure-to-succeed elaboration activity. Make a class supply of a simple seven-sentence story similar to the one shown. Direct each child to read the story and choose one sentence to elaborate on. Caution the student to elaborate only on what is included and implied in his sentence, without repeating information included in the previous sentence or including anything that happens next (see the example). After practicing with this story, your students are sure to pack more sensory details, vivid verbs, dialogue, and specific examples into their writing samples.

JoAn W. Martin
Baytown, TX

Sentence 4 – Before
One day I got on the pony and stayed on.

Sentence 4 – After
I leaned to the left and almost slid off. Then I leaned to the right, but not as far this time. The saddle was slippery with sweat and the reins kept sliding out of my hands, but...

(1) I loved my new pony the minute I saw him.
(2) The first time I got on him I fell off.
(3) I was very disappointed.
(4) One day I got on the pony and stayed on.
(5) The pony took me for a ride.
(6) We saw many things together.
(7) It was almost dark when we got home.

### Stamp Collection

**Skill: Descriptive writing**

Motivate students to write descriptively with an activity they'll stick with till the end! Begin by asking friends, co-workers, students, and parents to donate old envelopes that bear interesting stamps. Clip off the stamped corners of the envelopes and store them at a center stocked with plastic cups and paper towels. Direct each student to visit the center, select a stamp, and remove it from the envelope corner by soaking it in a cup of tepid water for five to ten minutes. Next, have him place the stamp inside a folded paper towel and place the towel under a book to dry overnight. The next day have the student glue the stamp to a large index card. Then have him write on the card a paragraph describing the person, object, or event the stamp depicts. Show off this special stamp collection in a photo album displayed in your school's media center.

This stamp shows the famous Eiffel Tower. It is located in Paris, France. This 984-foot tower was built by Gustave Eiffel for a world's fair called the Universal Exposition of 1889. At that time it was the world's tallest structure. The Eiffel Tower cost more than $1 million to build. This tower is located in a park called the Champ de Mars. There are observation decks and restaurants in the tower.

Julie Granchelli
Lockport, NY

### Unresolved Mysteries

**Skill: Narrative writing**

Turn your students into crime reporters with this mysterious writing project. First, have each child make a handprint by painting her hand with tempera paint and pressing it onto paper. Have the child invent a nonviolent crime that could have been committed in the classroom (see the example) and write it at the top of her paper as shown. Next, have the student write in narrative form a crime report that answers the basic *Who? What? When? Where? Why?* and *How?* questions about her crime. Direct the student to tape the report to the bottom of her handprint. Post the completed projects on a bulletin board titled "Unresolved Mysteries." Now, where were *you* on the night of...?

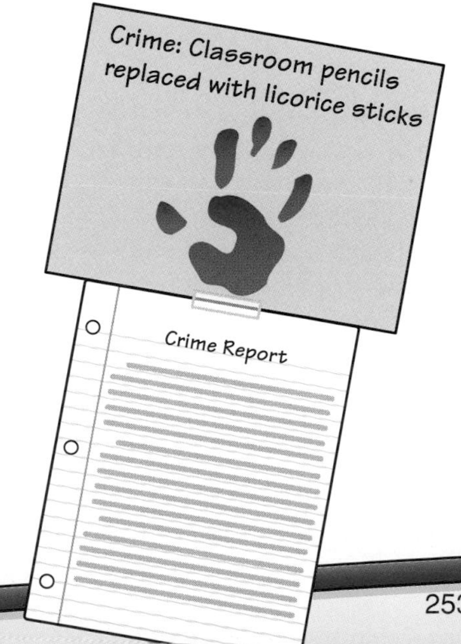
Crime: Classroom pencils replaced with licorice sticks
Crime Report

Jennifer Thiel
Lincoln Elementary
Yankton, SD

# Write On!

## Ideas and Tips for Teaching Students to Write

### Volunteer Voices

**Skill: Narrative writing**

Want to inspire your students to write their most creative stories ever? Then ask parents to volunteer their voices! First, color-code and label a supply of short-playing cassette tapes using the code shown. Send a tape home to each of your parent volunteers along with a note asking him or her to fill both sides of the tape with ideas related to the assigned literary element. In the note, also describe the types of ideas you need and direct the volunteer to pause for several seconds between ideas. Store the completed tapes in a box placed near a class tape recorder. When you need a new idea for a story starter, simply let the class listen to one idea from each of three different-colored tapes. Then write the three elements on the board (see the example). Get even more mileage out of these handy tapes by using them to provide students with storytelling ideas.

Kimberly Minafo—Gr. 4
Tooker Avenue School
West Babylon, NY

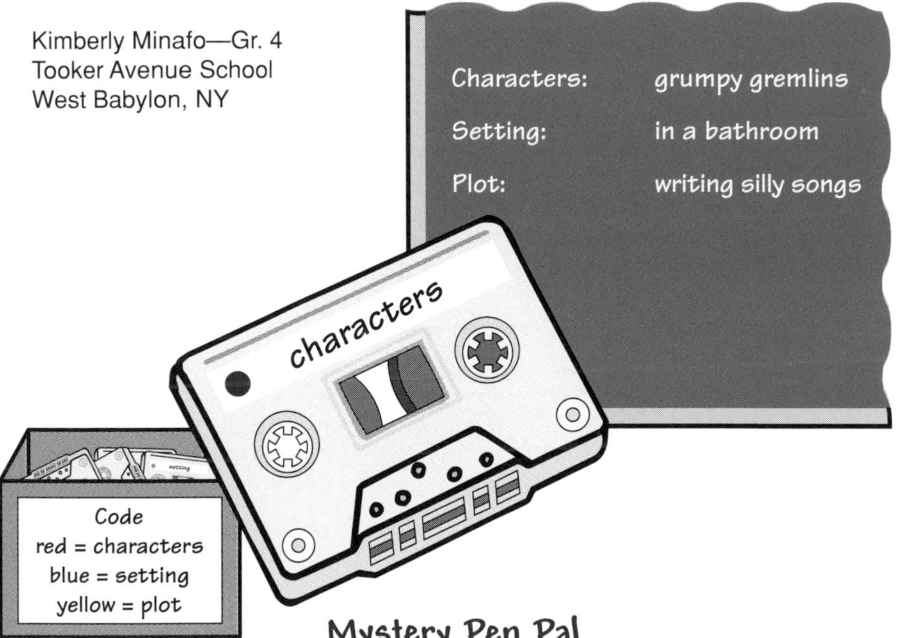


### Mystery Pen Pal

**Skills: Letter writing, descriptive writing**

Cover two important writing skills at once with this letter-perfect activity! Write each child's name on a separate slip of paper and place it in a paper bag. Have each student draw a classmate's name from the bag. Then have her write a friendly letter to that friend, describing herself in detail without revealing her identity. Direct students to sign their letters "Your Mystery Pen Pal." Then collect the finished letters and deliver them to their recipients. Challenge each student to read her letter and try to identify its author. Use this idea again by having students write letters describing their bedrooms, hobbies, or dreams for the future.

Michelle Kasmiske—Gr. 4, Monroe Elementary
Janesville, WI

### Paragraph Sandwiches

**Skill: Writing paragraphs**

Serve up a lesson on paragraph writing that students will never forget! Place the following items on a table at the front of the classroom: sliced bread, ham, cheese, tomatoes, mayonnaise, and other sandwich fixings. Explain to students that a good paragraph is just like a good sandwich. The top piece of bread is the introduction, while the bottom piece is the conclusion. Put the two pieces of bread together; then ask students whether they'd rather have a sandwich with nothing in the middle or one with lots of yummy fixings. Students are sure to agree that a sandwich without fixings isn't very appealing. Next, add some fixings to the sandwich. Point out that the "good stuff" in the middle of the bread is like the details of a paragraph. Just like a fixingless sandwich, a paragraph without details isn't very appetizing.

If desired, follow up this demonstration by asking students to bring sandwich fixings to school for a "Better Writing Buffet." Ask parent volunteers to help you set up the fixings for a lunch buffet. After each child makes and eats his own sandwich, have him write a detailed paragraph describing his scrumptious lunch.

Julie Kwoka—Gr. 5
George Southard Elementary
Lockport, NY

Angelique A. Kwabenah—Gr. 4
Matthew Henson Elementary
Landover, MD

# Write On!

## Ideas and Tips for Teaching Students to Write

A Review of High Point Bowling Center
by Tameka Owens

Families can count on having fun when they visit High Point Bowling Center on Centennial Street. Bowling is a great form of exercise, and this bowling center has 40 lanes with automatic scoring.

High Point Bowling Center is a great place for recreation. Kids can have birthday parties there and enjoy bumper bowling and arcade games. Adults can join bowling leagues. The center is open every day of the week.

One game of bowling is $2.50 before 6 P.M. and $3.50 after. Shoe rental is $2.75. There are special rates for groups. Family time on Sundays includes a laser show! Call 123-4567 for more information. The only thing that could make a trip to High Point Bowling Center more enjoyable would be having more food choices in the grill.

### Rip-Roarin' Reviews

**Skill: Writing a critical review**

Turn students into official reviewers by having them write reviews of entertainment or dining establishments right in your hometown! Begin by helping students brainstorm a list of restaurants or places of entertainment in your community, such as a bowling center, restaurant, movie theater, or video store. Next, have each student use a copy of page 256 to gather information. Then have her write a three-paragraph review of a place of her choice. Make copies of the completed reviews; then bind them into books that can become rainy-day resources for students' families.

Domenick C. Renzi—Gr. 5
Bells Elementary
Turnersville, NJ

FAME Magazine

Dahlia Lowry Breaks All-Time Baton-Twirling Record!

Dahlia Lowry became a world record holder last week when she successfully twirled her baton for 218 hours without stopping. Dahlia says the experience was a blast! She hopes to one day beat her record while riding on an elephant.

### My 15 Minutes of Fame

**Skill: Descriptive writing**

Andy Warhol once said, "In the future, everyone will be famous for 15 minutes." Borrow Warhol's statement to trigger a descriptive-writing project that turns into an instant bulletin board! First, ask students to imagine themselves becoming famous for a wacky accomplishment, such as inventing a brand-new sport, hobby, or contraption, or breaking a world's record. Next, give each student crayons or markers and a sheet of paper. Challenge the student to design a magazine cover that features herself in her newfound fame. Have her include on the cover a short paragraph describing her accomplishment. Display the completed covers and a large clock cutout on a bulletin board titled "Our 15 Minutes of Fame." To extend the activity, have students scour magazines, newspapers, or other resources for real folks who are recent achievers of their own 15 minutes of fame.

Kimberly A. Minafo—Gr. 4
Tooker Avenue School
West Babylon, NY

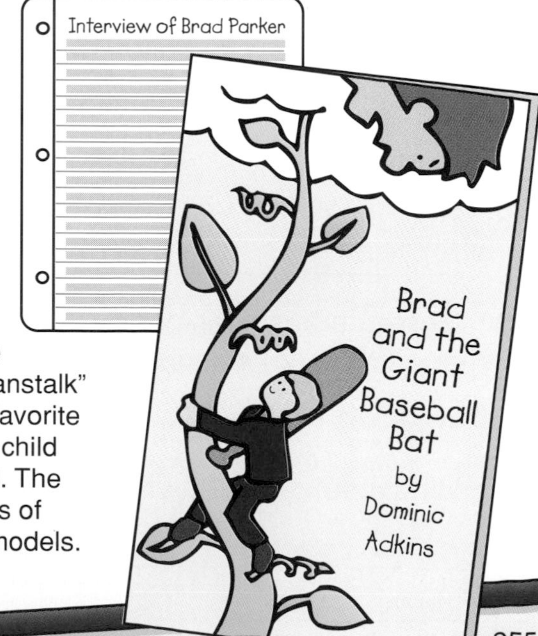

Interview of Brad Parker
Brad and the Giant Baseball Bat
by
Dominic Adkins


### Bringing Fairy Tales to Life

**Skill: Narrative writing**

Strengthen narrative-writing skills with an activity that transforms personal interviews into modern-day fairy tales! After your class reads and researches various fairy tales, arrange for each student to interview a child in a younger class. Then have each student rewrite his favorite fairy tale, incorporating the information he gathered during the interview. For example, "Jack and the Beanstalk" could become "Brad and the Giant Baseball Bat," in which Brad rescues his favorite baseball cards from the giant. After students make final revisions, have each child illustrate his tale and bind it into a book he can read aloud to his young friend. The benefits of this activity are twofold: The younger children enjoy being the stars of personalized fairy tales, while the older students bask in their status as role models.

Kelly Howell—Gr. 5, Sixes Elementary
Canton, GA

Name________________________________________ Writing a critical review

# How to Write a Rip-Roarin' Review

Wow! You've been asked to review an entertainment or dining establishment located in your hometown. How should you go about it? Don't worry! Just follow the directions below.

Turn in your review on ____________________. Make sure it is well organized, has been proofread carefully, and is written neatly. Good luck!

review—n. a critical explanation

**Directions:**

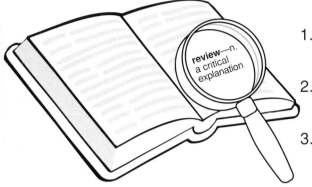

1. Select a restaurant or place of entertainment in your hometown to review.
2. Collect information about the business, such as a menu or brochure. Then answer the questions below.
3. Write a three-paragraph review. In the first paragraph, include the answers to questions 1–3. In the second paragraph, include the answers to questions 4–6. Include the answers to questions 7–10 in the third paragraph.

Menu

Brochure

Brochure

Phone Book

**Questions:**

1. What is the name of the business? ____________________
2. Where is the business located? ____________________
3. What does the business specialize in? ____________________
4. Describe the business. ____________________
5. Why will people like this business? ____________________
6. When is the business open? ____________________
7. How can someone contact this business (phone, fax, email, etc.)? ____________________
8. How much can the average customer expect to spend at this business? ____________________
9. Does the business offer any discounts to individuals or groups? Are there any special events or activities? Describe them. ____________________
10. What could make a visit to this business more enjoyable? ____________________



 **Note to the teacher:** Use with "Rip-Roarin' Reviews" on page 255. Fill in the due date blank above before making student copies.

# Seasonal Ideas & Reproducibles

# Celebrate the Season

## Holiday and Seasonal Activities for the Classroom

### Back to School: Getting-to-Know-You Poll

Use this icebreaking activity to help your students appreciate how they are alike and different. Begin by writing five yes-or-no questions on the board, such as the ones shown on the graph. (Avoid questions that would group students by gender or along racial or cultural lines.) Ask each student to number his paper from 1 to 5; then have him answer the questions. After collecting the papers, display the results of the poll in a simple double-bar graph as shown. Next, have students help you label a large sheet of chart paper with several statements based on the poll. (For example, "Most of us were born in this state. Five students don't consider pizza their favorite food.") Then have each student write a paragraph describing the benefits of having classmates who are both alike and different. ***Lisa Waller Rogers, Austin, TX***

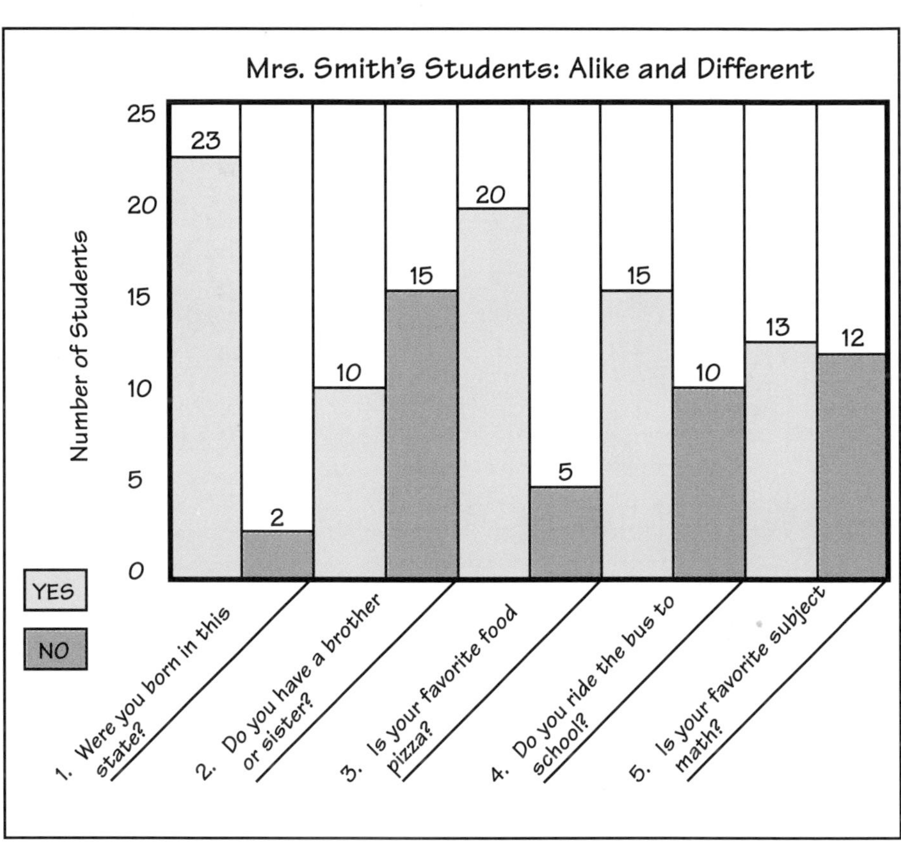


**All-About-Me Key**

**Subjects I like (body):**
Math = yellow
Social Studies = purple
Science = green
Reading = red

**Hobbies (tail):**
Computer = pink
Sports = brown
Music = blue
Art = orange

**Family (scales; one per item):**
Sister = pink triangle
Brother = blue triangle
Cat = orange circle
Dog = black circle
Other Pet = green triangle

**Food Favorites (fins):**
Pizza = red
Fries = yellow
Tacos = green
Burgers = brown

### Back to School: Into the Swim of Things

Dive into a new school year with this fishy art project! Give each student a sheet of 8½" x 11" white paper. Have the student draw a large fish shape; then have her write her name in bubble or block letters inside the outline before cutting out the fish. Post a color key as shown. Have the student use markers and crayons to personalize her fish according to her choices from the key. Display each student's fish and the key on a bulletin board that you've covered with blue paper and titled "We're Back Into the Swim of Things!" ***Joan M. Macey, Binghamton, NY***

Manners Bag

| Problem: | Polite Solution: |
| --- | --- |
| Someone cuts in line. | 1. Tell the person nicely that she is in your spot.<br>2. Give the person your spot and find another. |
| Someone takes my pencil. | 1. Calmly ask for it back.<br>2. Tell him he can borrow it but you will need it back. |

## Children's Good Manners Month: Manners Bag

As a polite reminder, did you know that September is Children's Good Manners Month? Encourage students to mind their manners every day with this role-playing activity. Begin by having each child write on a slip of paper a fictional scenario in which impolite manners are displayed. (Remind students not to name any classmates in their scenarios.) Collect the slips in a paper sack labeled "Manners Bag." Each morning during September, ask a student to choose a slip from the bag; then call on volunteers to act out the scenario in front of the class. Discuss with the class how to handle the situation using good manners. After recording their responses on the board, have students vote on the top two ways to handle the situation; then add the suggestions to a class chart like the one shown. Throughout the year, refer students to the chart and their polite solutions whenever they need a reminder.

## Fall Hat Month: Hat Stories

Tip your hat to Fall Hat Month this September with an imaginative creative-writing activity. Begin by reading aloud *Ben and Me: A New and Astonishing Life of Benjamin Franklin As Written by His Good Mouse Amos* by Robert Lawson (Little, Brown and Company; 1988). In the story, a mouse named Amos lives in Benjamin Franklin's hat and describes how he helps Mr. Franklin create his inventions. After finishing the story, set aside a day for students to bring their favorite hats to school. (Provide a few extras for students who may need them.) Then instruct each child to write a story like *Ben and Me,* in which an imaginative animal who lives in his hat describes a typical day at school. Cap this tip-top assignment by having each child read his story aloud to the class while wearing his hat.

A Day at Tom's School
by Ed Rattlesnake
Hi! My name's Ed. I'm a rattlesnake and I live in Tom's cowboy hat.
One day at Tom's school, he forgot his homework...

Name ______________________________________________ Vocabulary, wordplay

# CAPTAIN CRAYON TO THE RESCUE!

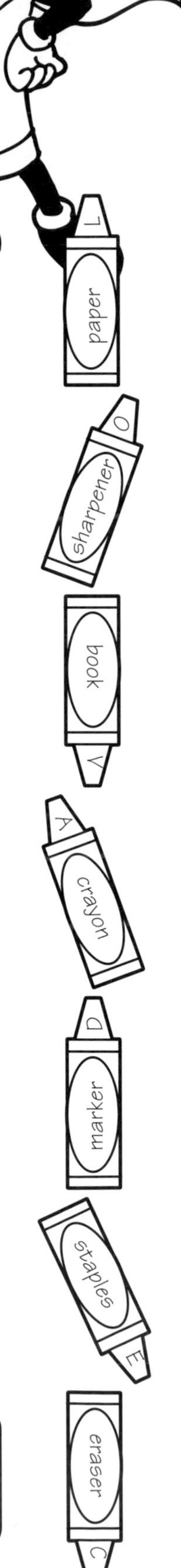


Help! Someone has hidden your teacher's supplies! The start of the school year will have to be postponed unless you and Captain Crayon can crack this mystery.

Each question below contains one of the school supplies written on the crayons. Find and circle each hidden word, and color its crayon. Then write an answer on the line to show that you understand the question. Use a dictionary to find the meanings of any unfamiliar words. Let the search begin!

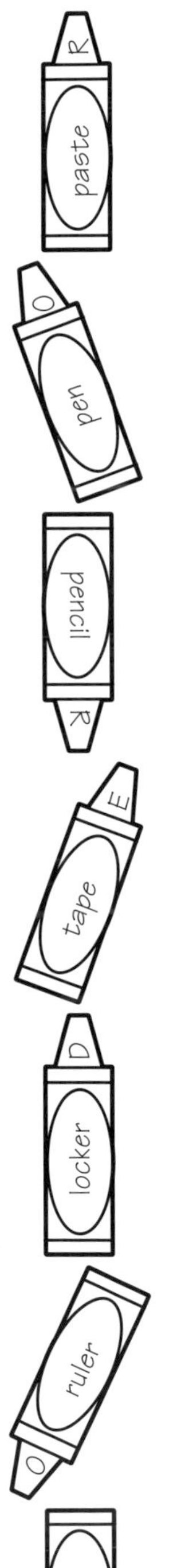


**Example:** Could a bri(de sk)ip gleefully down the aisle? (desk)
**Answer:** Yes, a bride could skip gleefully if she didn't mind looking silly.

1. Would you dampen cilantro with salad dressing or motor oil?
______________________________________________
2. Can rocks be shaped by running water as erosion occurs?
______________________________________________
3. Can a clock erratically tick and become undependable?
______________________________________________
4. Is it possible for a plastic ray on a toy starfish to break off?
______________________________________________
5. Could you catch Al King trying to make a kite ascend?
______________________________________________
6. Can a drum's tap lessen in frequency?
______________________________________________
7. Can someone's papa steadily rise out of a chair that he has been sitting in? ______________________________
8. Could a worksheet include a mark erroneously made by your teacher? ______________________________
9. Should a rule resolutely remain the same for all students in a class?
______________________________________________
10. Can music from a melodious harp energize people?
______________________________________________
11. Can a baby play peek-a-boo keenly with his mommy or daddy?
______________________________________________
12. Can a dog's rear appendage tap excitedly on the floor?
______________________________________________
13. Would a person gape nonchalantly if he were about to step on a snake? ______________________________
14. Would it be ethical for a taxi driver to dump a person in a chasm?
______________________________________________

**Bonus Box:** Rearrange the letters from the crayon tips above to spell the name of Captain Crayon's hometown and state.

__ __ __ __ __ __, __ __ __ __ __ __ __ __

# Oh, Be "Cents-ible"!

How are you going to solve the problems on this page? By being "cents-ible," that's how!
**Directions:** Pretend that each letter of the alphabet is worth $.05 more than the letter before it: A = $.05, B = $.10, and so on until Z = $1.30. Show your work on the back of this page or another sheet of paper. Then write your answers on the lines.

1. What is the total value of your school's name? ______________________________
2. Calculate the total value of your first, middle, and last names. ____________________
3. How many of your classmates have first names that are equal in value to yours?________
   List them. ______________________________________________________
   ______________________________________________________
   ______________________________________________________
4. Guess which of your classmates has the most valuable first name. _______________
   Why did you pick this person?____________________________________________
   ______________________________________________________
   Check your prediction by calculating the value of that classmate's name. Were you right?
   ______________________________________________________
   ______________________________________________________
5. Write the name of the classmate seated on your right (or left). ___________________
   Find the difference in the values of your first names. __________ Next, find the difference in your last names. __________ Then find the difference when both the first and last names are combined. __________ Which difference is greatest: first names only, last names only, or both names together? ______________________________________________
6. Which school supply below do you think has the highest value? __________________
   The lowest? ______________________ Find out by calculating the value of each item.
   a. pencil __________ e. eraser __________
   b. crayons __________ f. bookbag __________
   c. scissors __________ g. calculator __________
   d. glue __________ h. sharpener __________
7. How much would your first name be worth if you multiplied the value of each of its letters by 5? __________ By 10? __________

**BONUS BOX:** Whose name is worth more: your teacher's or your principal's?



**Note to the teacher:** To complete this activity, students may need a copy of the class roster. Use as a back-to-school activity or anytime you want students to practice computing money.

## Columbus Day:

### Charting a Course to Comprehension!

Help your students chart a course to comprehension with this story-mapping activity! First, make a transparency of page 264. Then review with students the elements of a good story and their definitions that are shown in the chart on the right. The next time you discuss a story or novel that you're currently reading, list its elements on the transparency as students describe them. Then, when you read your next story or novel, provide students with copies of page 264 to complete independently. After completing their story maps, have students color and cut them out. Post the completed ships on a bulletin board titled "Charting a Course to Comprehension!"

**Setting:** the place and time during which a story's action occurs

**Characters:** the people or animals in a story

**Plot:** the problem that needs to be solved, including the sequential events that lead to its solution

**Climax:** the event that brings about a solution to a story's problem

**Ending:** the conclusion of a story

**Theme:** the main idea of a story

### Halloween: Top Banana!

Try this "ap-peel-ing" contest as a fun and creative way for your bunch to celebrate October's top holiday. First, challenge each student to design a costume for either a real or a plastic banana. Suggest that students use a variety of materials, such as paper, cloth, paint, glue, markers, glitter, and yarn. In addition, have each student create a setting and a nameplate for his banana. Have students bring their completed projects to school on the day of your Halloween party. Invite other classes to parade by your display of costumed bananas. Also ask a few staff members to choose the five "top bananas."

For a language arts connection, have each student write a story featuring his banana as the main character. Then, during your Halloween party, have students share their stories while they enjoy banana splits—with new bananas, of course! ***Marianne Bush—Grs. 5 and 6, Our Lady of Lourdes School, Toledo, OH***

## Fall: Famous-People Pumpkins

To wrap up a study of biographies, have your students make famous-people pumpkins. Provide each child with a large sheet of orange construction paper. Have the student study a picture of the famous person she read about and then make a pumpkin to resemble him or her. Encourage students to use scrap materials and a variety of art supplies, such as pipe cleaners, ribbon, lace, and yarn. When each student shares her biography book report, be sure she shows off her pumpkin person! ***Shea Lauria, Center Street School, Williston Park, NY***

Harriet Tubman Pumpkin

Babe Ruth Pumpkin

## Sandwich Day: Picnic Pictograph

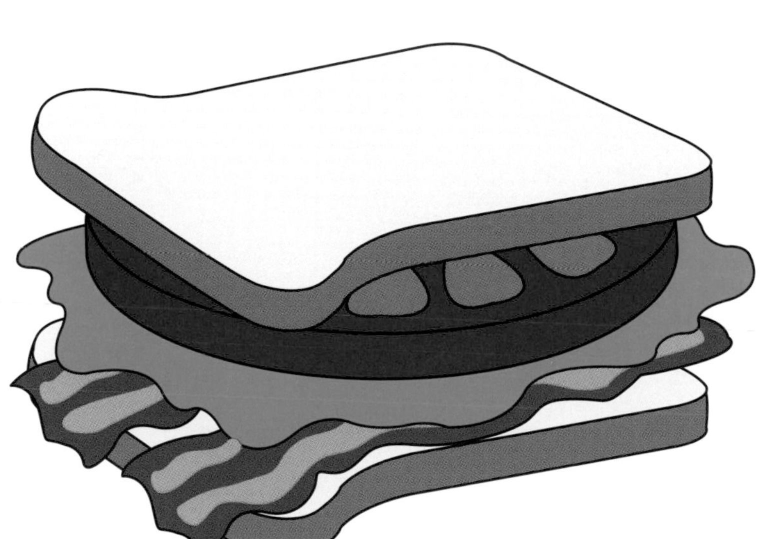

Celebrate Sandwich Day (November 3) with a graphing activity that's a real picnic for everyone! In advance, invite each student to bring his favorite sandwich to school on November 3. When the big day arrives, read aloud John Vernon Lord's *The Giant Jam Sandwich* (Houghton Mifflin Company, 1987). In this delightful picture book, a small village's citizens try to trap a mass of wasps using a giant jam sandwich. After discussing the book, have each student use art materials to make a paper version of his sandwich. Next, direct students to work together to sort their paper sandwiches into different categories; then have them pin the sandwiches to a bulletin board to create a pictograph. Help students label the graph, add a key, and draw conclusions from its data. Conclude your Sandwich Day celebration with a picnic that includes the sandwiches students brought to school. ***Leasha Segars and Lindy Hopkins—Gr. 5, Saltillo Elementary, Saltillo, MS***

## Thanksgiving: Group Shopping Spree

Want to sharpen real-life math skills? Then send students on a shopping spree to plan this year's Thanksgiving feast! Provide each group of three or four students with a copy of page 267, plus the materials listed on the page. Have the students in each group work together to budget for and plan a Thanksgiving dinner according to the directions on the page. Suggest that students make a preliminary plan on a sheet of notebook paper, check the plan with a calculator, and then complete the chart on the reproducible. Have each group glue its completed reproducible in the middle of the drawing paper and then glue the product ads around it. Post the projects on a bulletin board titled "What's Cookin'?" ***Ann Scheiblin—Gr. 6, Oak View School, Bloomfield, NJ***

# Charting a Course to Comprehension!

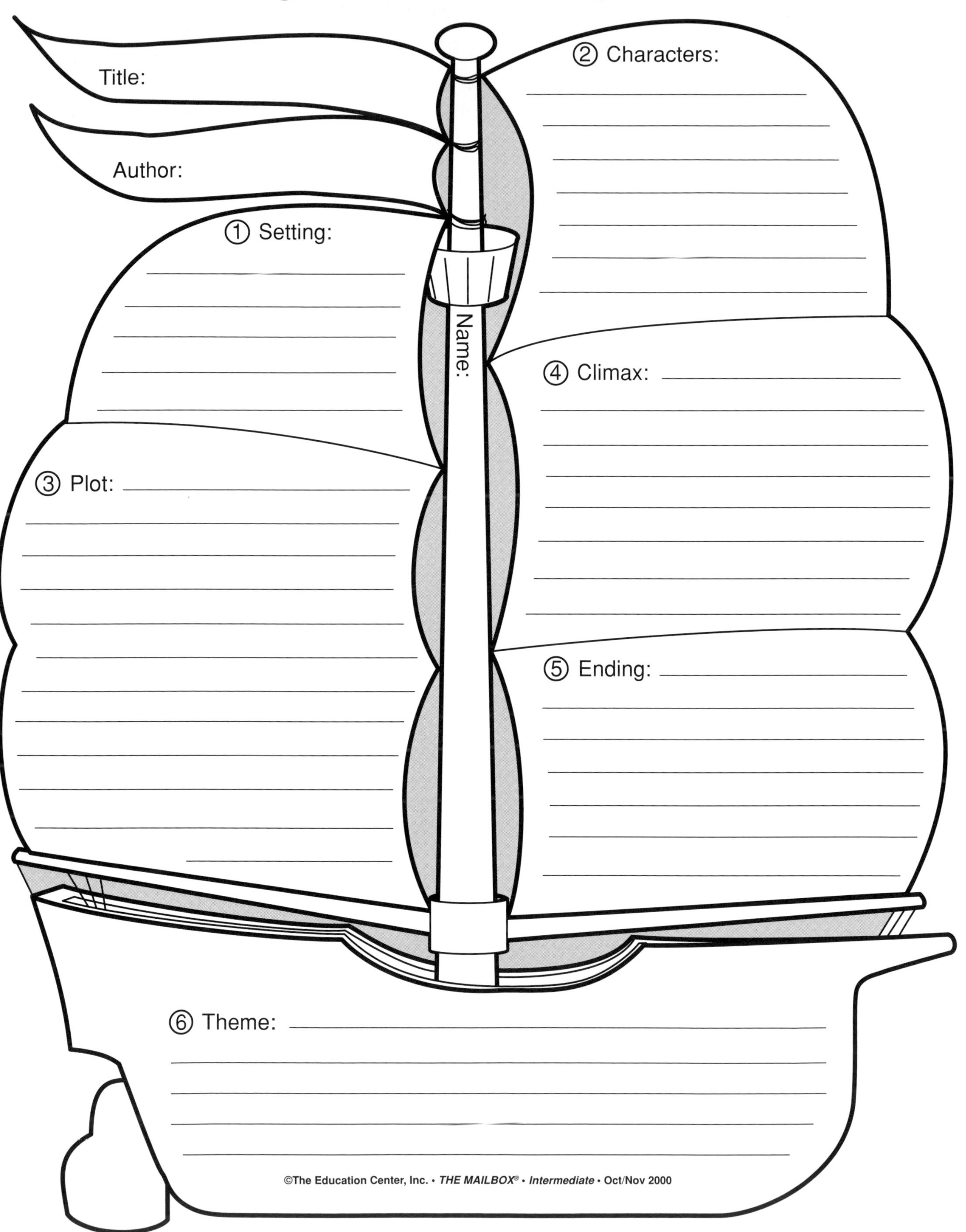




 **Note to the teacher:** Use with "Columbus Day: Charting a Course to Comprehension!" on page 262.

Name ______________________________ Rounding decimals

# Halloween Roundup

Mr. Grimly, a math teacher at Weirdly Elementary, has set up a haunted house in his classroom. In order to enter it, students must uncover a secret password. First, read Mr. Grimly's review on how to round decimals. Then follow the directions below. When you're finished, the secret password will be revealed on the ticket! Happy h(a)unting!

To round a decimal to a given place, look at the digit to the right of that place:

- If the digit is 4 or less, round *down*.
- If the digit is 5 or more, round *up*.

**Examples**

Round 1.474 to the nearest tenth.
Should 1.474 be rounded up to 1.5 or down to 1.4?
1.474 should be rounded up to 1.5.
Why? The digit to the right of the tenths place is 7.

Round 3.72 to the nearest tenth.
Should 3.72 be rounded up to 3.8 or down to 3.7?
3.72 should be rounded down to 3.7.
Why? The digit to the right of the tenths place is 2.

**Directions:** Round each decimal to the nearest tenth. Use an orange crayon or marker to color the box of each decimal that you *round up.*

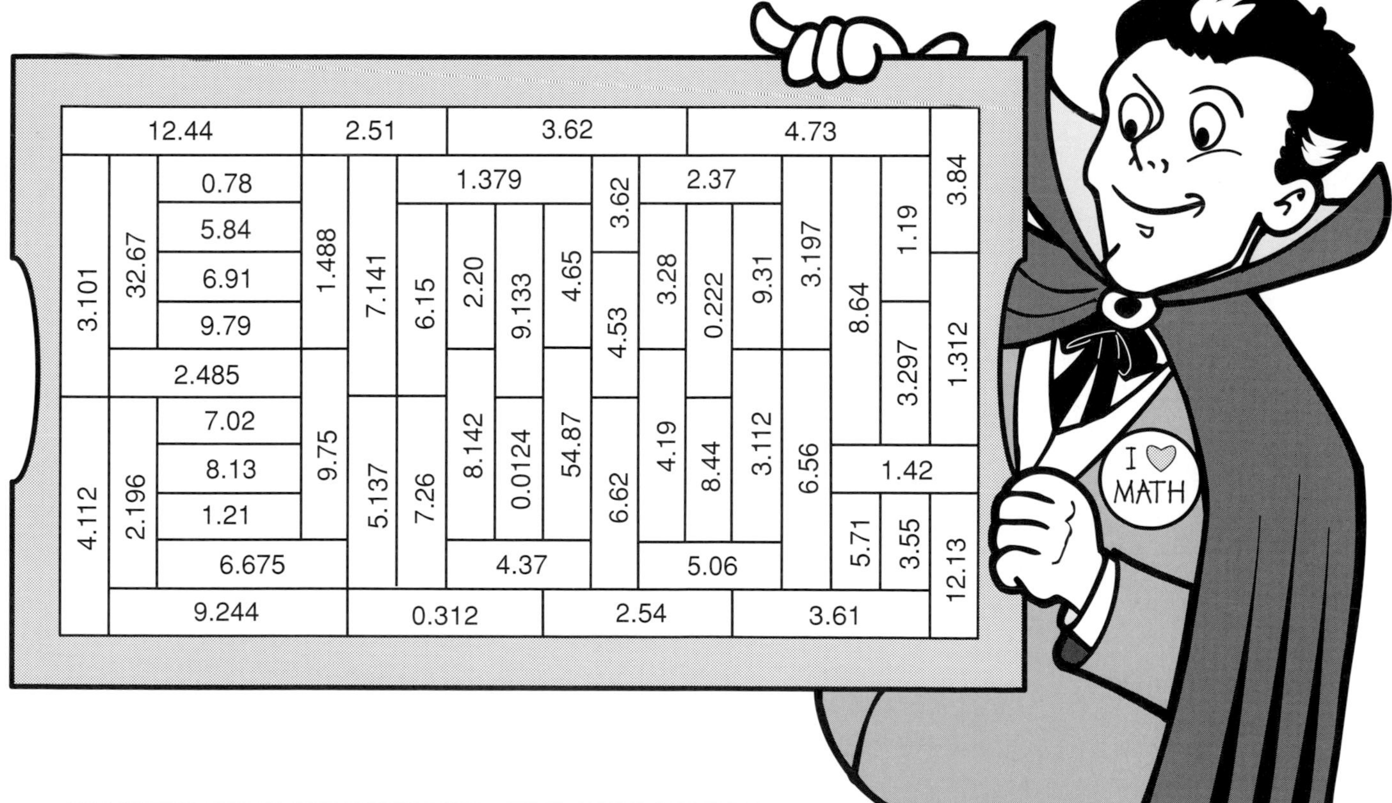


**BONUS BOX:** List the ten largest decimals (from greatest to least) that are in the boxes that you didn't color. Hint: The largest one is 12.44.

Name________________________________________________ Cloze practice

# Less is Best!

Quick…name three holidays in November! More than likely, you thought of Thanksgiving and Veterans Day. But read on to learn about another special day that's worth observing.

**Part I:** Some words have been left out of the following passage. First, read the entire passage. For each blank, choose a word from the word pile below that makes the most sense. As you write each word in a blank, color its garbage bag.

Although we recycle about 27% of our ___________, Americans still send about 150 million ____________ of trash to landfills each year. An amazing 25 million tons of this trash is thrown away in the five weeks between Thanksgiving and New Year's Day.

The clear solution to this ____________ is to throw away less trash! That's the goal of Use Less Stuff™ Day, celebrated every year on the Thursday before Thanksgiving. The ____________ of Use Less Stuff Day created the ____________ to encourage consumers to look for ways to reduce waste. Some easy ideas they suggest to ____________ your "waste-line" include taking your own shopping bag to the ____________; sending e-greetings instead of regular cards; and reusing old maps, artwork, paper bags, or comics as wrapping paper. You can also ____________ rechargeable batteries, look for ____________ that don't have much plastic and paper packaging, and donate unwanted clothes and toys to __________. These suggestions will help reduce the trash that ends up in landfills.

Using less "stuff" is the number one weapon in the war on waste. It's something ____________ can do with a little thought and ____________. Remember: *Reduce* is the first *R* in the well-known slogan "Reduce, Reuse, Recycle!"

**Part II**

How can *you* use less stuff between now and the end of the year? On another sheet of paper, write a paragraph that explains several ways you will reduce waste. Circle ten key words in your paragraph. Then copy the paragraph on the back of this sheet, replacing each circled word with a blank big enough for the word. List the missing words below your paragraph. Then challenge a friend to complete the paragraph.

**Bonus Box:** How can you reduce the amount of wrapping paper and ribbon you use when wrapping gifts? Try to think of gifts that don't have to be wrapped at all, like a plant or movie theater tickets. Can you list at least eight more?

Name(s) ______________________________________________
______________________________________________

Group project: math computation, budgeting

# What a Feast!

So, what are *you* having for Thanksgiving dinner? Here's your chance to plan and budget for a scrumptious Thanksgiving feast. Work with your group and follow the directions below. Yummmm!

**Materials needed for each group:** 1 large sheet of drawing paper, several newspaper grocery store circulars, glue, scissors, pencils, calculator

**Directions:**

1. Your group has $100 to spend. Try to spend as much as you can, but don't go over your budget! Don't add tax.
2. Everyone in the group must participate. Choose one person to be the recorder.
3. You must buy at least one, but no more than three, of each item listed below. You'll need only one turkey. Write the brand and size of each item in the "item" column.
4. You may use coupons if they are available.
5. Complete the chart below. Then glue this sheet to the middle of your drawing paper.
6. Cut out and glue your product ads on the drawing paper. Also include any coupons you used.

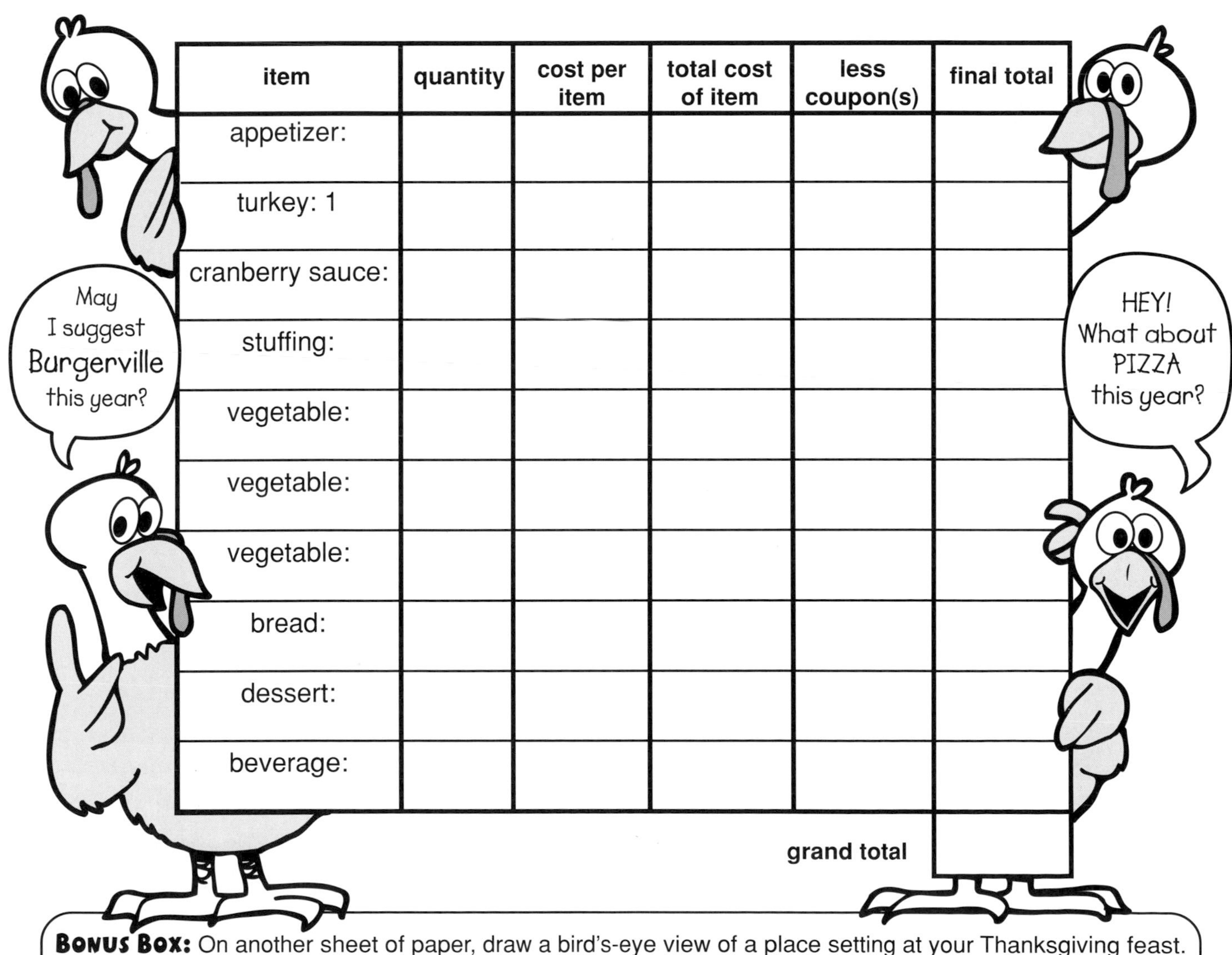

May I suggest Burgerville this year?
HEY! What about PIZZA this year?

| item | quantity | cost per item | total cost of item | less coupon(s) | final total |
|---|---|---|---|---|---|
| appetizer: | | | | | |
| turkey: 1 | | | | | |
| cranberry sauce: | | | | | |
| stuffing: | | | | | |
| vegetable: | | | | | |
| vegetable: | | | | | |
| vegetable: | | | | | |
| bread: | | | | | |
| dessert: | | | | | |
| beverage: | | | | | |
| | | | | grand total | |

**BONUS BOX:** On another sheet of paper, draw a bird's-eye view of a place setting at your Thanksgiving feast. Include a placemat, plate with food, small dessert plate, bread and butter plate, glass, napkin, silverware, and any other items you wish.

**Note to the teacher:** Use with "Thanksgiving: Group Shopping Spree" on page 263.

## December

### Hanukkah Solutions

Brighten your December science plans with this Hanukkah-related activity on solutions. Collect a class supply of shoeboxes and small juice bottles (the kind with narrow, tapered necks and metal twist-off caps). Also purchase candle/lamp oil and an inexpensive length of candlewick at a craft store. Cut the wick so that you have a six-inch piece for each student.

To begin, write "solution" on the board. Explain that a solution is a mixture of two substances in which the molecules of one substance are spread out evenly and equally between the molecules of the second substance. Demonstrate by adding 1/4 cup sugar to a cup of water. Point out that the sugar in this solution is *soluble* because it will dissolve. Next, have each student fill a bottle 3/4 full of water, mix in three drops of food coloring, and then add candle/lamp oil almost to the bottle's top. After everyone has tightly recapped his bottle, signal students to shake them. Ask, "Is the oil soluble in the colored water?" *(Students will likely say "Yes" because the oil and water will seem to mix.)* Then have students place the bottles on their desks and observe what happens. *(The oil will separate from the water and float to the top.)* Explain that the oil is *immiscible* because it does not dissolve in the water. Because the oil isn't as heavy as water, it floats to the top. Finally, have each student stick some gold foil stars on his capped bottle and then place it and a piece of wick in a shoebox lined with newspaper. Add instructions telling parents to make a small hole (using a hammer and a nail) in the center of the cap for the Hanukkah candle's wick. ***adapted from an idea by Rhona Finkel—Gr. 5, Arie Crown Hebrew Day School, Skokie, IL***

### All Wrapped Up!

Wrap up December with a narrative writing lesson that's perfect for celebrating Hanukkah, Christmas, or Kwanzaa. First, discuss with students favorite presents they've received or given in holidays past. Then have each student write a narrative titled "My Greatest Gift." To display final drafts, collect a lidded gift box for each child. Have the student wrap the lid and bottom of her box. Then have her glue her final draft inside the box. Use pushpins to attach each box to a bulletin board. During free time, let students "unwrap" their classmates' super stories by removing the box lids. ***Kimberly J. Branham—Gr. 5, Wateree Elementary, Lugoff, SC***

## Holiday "Symme-tree"

Turn a December math lesson on symmetry into a tree-trimming, door-decorating party! Fold a large piece of green bulletin board paper in half vertically; then draw half of a tree shape on the fold, as shown, and cut out the tracing. Unfold the resulting tree and mount it on your classroom door. Next, provide students with a variety of art materials, such as construction paper, gift wrap, glitter, foil, stickers, sequins, glue, scissors, etc. Challenge each student to create a pair of ornaments that are mirror images of each other. Then have him attach his decorations to the tree in such a way that it maintains its vertical line of symmetry. Totally "tree-mendous"! ***Julie Alarie—Gr. 6, Essex Middle School, Essex, VT***

## Searchin' for Santa!

Practice important map skills with the help of ol' St. Nick! First, label a class supply of index cards with the names of specific locations, such as states, countries, and cities (one per card). Announce to students that Christmas is threatened this year because Santa, who is actually a terrible navigator, is lost. Your students must help him find his way to your hometown if there's to be any hope of a merry Christmas. Next, pass out the cards. Using the maps in his social studies textbook, each student writes directions that Santa can follow to get from the location on his card to your hometown. Depending on the map skills you want to practice, require students to write instructions that include cardinal and/or intermediate directions, latitude and longitude coordinates, time zones, and mileage. Let students swap papers and check each other's directions. ***Kimberly A. Minafo—Gr. 4, Tooker Avenue Elementary, West Babylon, NY***

## Drummer Boy Ornaments

Need to drum up a great holiday gift for students to give their loved ones? Then try this can't-be-beat ornament!

**Materials:** 2 plastic caps from half-gallon milk jugs or juice cartons (the kind that screw on), one 2" x 4 3/4" piece of construction paper, one 4" pipe cleaner, 1 double-tipped cotton swab, scissors, glitter or markers, glue, tape

**Steps:**

1. With your teacher's help, use scissors to poke a hole in the center of one plastic cap.
2. Bend the pipe cleaner in half and insert both ends through the hole in the cap. Twist the pipe cleaner ends to secure the resulting hanger.
3. Decorate the construction paper with glitter or markers.
4. Apply glue on the inside rim of the hangerless cap. Roll the decorated paper to fit inside the cap. Tape the ends of the paper together. Let dry.
5. Apply glue on the inside rim of the hanger cap. Place the cap on the other end of the decorated paper. Let dry.
6. Cut the cotton swab in half to make two drumsticks. Glue the drumsticks to the top of the ornament.

***Bonnie A. Peterson, Beaverton Elementary, Beaverton, MI***

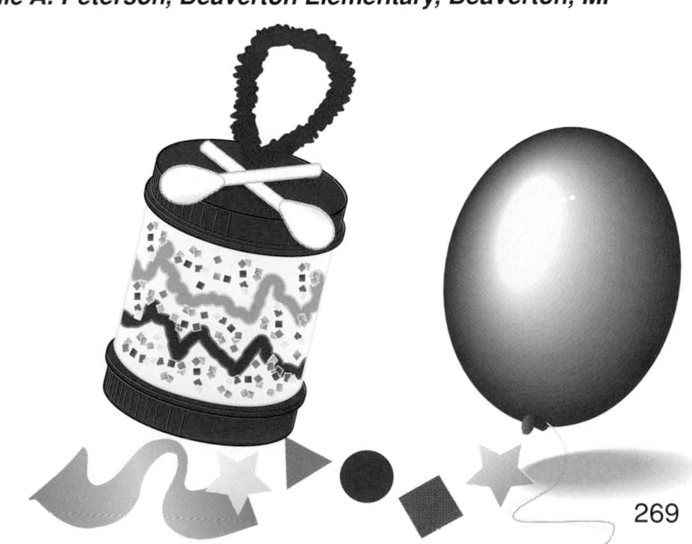

## Resolved: To Care and Share

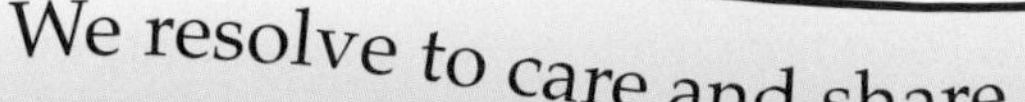
We resolve to care and share.

Make it a truly happy new year in your classroom with this great post-holidays activity. Cover a bulletin board with white paper and post a banner labeled as shown. Discuss with students the tradition of making resolutions each January 1. Then challenge students to resolve as a class to care and share for each other.

Next, have students search through old magazines and cut out pictures that show people caring and sharing with others. Have them mount each picture on construction paper and cut around it to leave a colored border. Then add the pictures to the bulletin board. Finally, have each child show her commitment to the resolution by signing the display with a glitter pen or other colorful writing instrument.

***adapted from an idea by Patricia A. Wisniewski—Gr. 4, St. Joseph School, Batavia, NY***

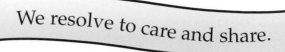

Dr. Martin Luther King Jr.

## Brave Ruby Bridges

Celebrate the birthday of Dr. Martin Luther King Jr. with an activity that helps students practice writing dialogue. Begin by explaining to students that laws were changed in 1954 to allow black children to attend the same schools as white children. The first black child to attend an all-white elementary school was six-year-old Ruby Bridges. Read aloud Robert Coles's inspiring picture book *The Story of Ruby Bridges* (Scholastic Inc.). Discuss with students Ruby's bravery and forgiveness in the face of unwarranted malice and injustice. Then have students compare Ruby's experiences with those of Dr. King. Finally, divide the class into pairs. Have each twosome write a dialogue between Ruby and the civil rights leader. Provide time for each pair to read aloud its conversation, with each child taking the role of Ruby or Dr. King. End the activity by having each student write a letter to Ruby or Dr. King in his journal. In the letter, have the student tell why he thinks the person he selected is a great role model.

Name ______________________________ Using a pronunciation key

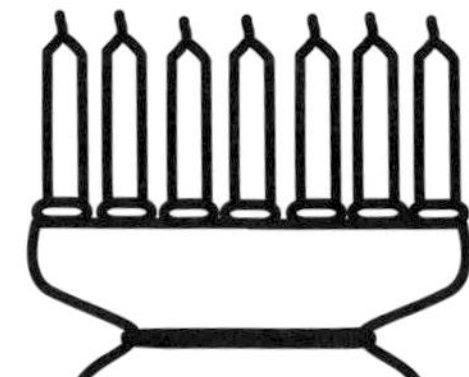

# The Heart of Kwanzaa

Each year from December 26 until January 1, many Black Americans celebrate the joyous season of Kwanzaa. *Kwanzaa* means "first fruits of the harvest." The term comes from the East African language of Swahili.

Seven candles are placed in a wooden candleholder: a black candle in the middle with three red ones on its left and three green ones on its right. They stand for the seven principles of Kwanzaa. A candle is lit during each day of Kwanzaa.

Day 1: The black candle is lit to celebrate (oo-**moe**-jah), which means "unity."
Day 2: The first red candle on the left of the black one is lit. It represents (koo-jee-cha-goo-**lee**-ah), which means "self-determination."
Day 3: The first green candle on the right of the black one is lit. It represents working together and (oo-**jee**-mah), or "responsibility."
Day 4: It's time to celebrate (oo-jah-**maah**), or "cooperative economics." The next red candle is lit.
Day 5: The fifth Kwanzaa principle is (**nee**-ah). The next green candle is lit to represent "purpose." This is a time to think about the future.
Day 6: The last red candle is lit for (ku-**oom**-bah), which means "creativity."
Day 7: The last green candle is lit for (ee-**mahn**-ee), or "faith."

**Directions:** Cut out the candle puzzle pieces below. Use the pronunciation key below and the respellings above to help you figure out the correct spellings of the seven Kwanzaa principles. Place the completed candles in order on a sheet of construction paper; then glue them to the paper. To complete the project, color each candle and add a candleholder.

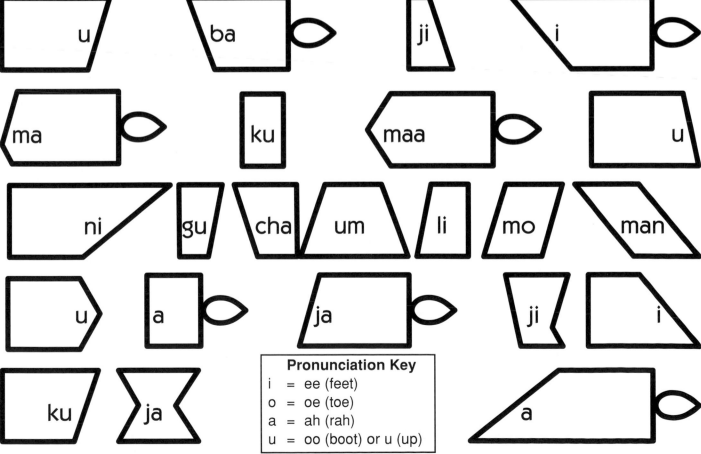

u ba ji i

ma ku maa u

ni gu cha um li mo man

u a ja ji i

ku ja a

**Pronunciation Key**

| | | |
|---|---|---|
| i | = | ee (feet) |
| o | = | oe (toe) |
| a | = | ah (rah) |
| u | = | oo (boot) or u (up) |



**Note to the teacher:** Provide each student with a 6" x 9" sheet of white construction paper, scissors, crayons or markers, and glue.

Name ______________________________ Spelling

# Santa's Not-So-Super Spellers

Santa's reindeer are busily checking over some lists before handing them over to Santa. Only one of the reindeer spelled all of the items on its list correctly; the other seven need a little help! Can you lend a hand?

Read the items in each list. Circle each item that is spelled *correctly.* Write the number of items you circled in the box at the top of the list. You will use the numbers 1–8 one time each. Make sure you don't circle any mispelled items. Oops...make that *misspelled.*

**Bonus Box:** On the back of this sheet, write the correct spelling of each item that you *did not* circle.

Name ________________________________________ Number sense, time order

# The Life and Times of Martin Luther King Jr.

Martin Luther King Jr. was one of the most important leaders of the civil rights movement in the United States during the 1950s and 1960s.

Read the following story about the life and times of Dr. King. Each blank stands for a missing number or date. From the list below the story, choose an answer that makes sense in each blank. Check off each one as you use it.

Martin Luther King Jr. was born in Atlanta, Georgia, on January 15, ______. He was the ______ oldest of ______ children in his family. His older sister was named Christine; his younger brother was A. D.

Martin was a good student. He did so well in high school that he skipped the ______ and ______ grades. At the age of 15, he entered Morehouse College in Atlanta. Martin graduated from Morehouse in 1948 at the age of ______. He was ordained as a minister just before he graduated.

Martin then attended Crozer Theological Seminary in Pennsylvania. In ______, he graduated first in his class! Martin then moved to Boston, Massachusetts, to attend Boston University's School of Theology. In Boston, he met Coretta Scott, a music student. They were married in the summer of ______. The Kings had ______ children.

In 1954, King became pastor of the Dexter Avenue Baptist Church in Montgomery, Alabama. The following year, ______, he received his doctorate degree from Boston University. He was now Dr. Martin Luther King Jr.

King's civil rights activities began in 1955 with a protest of the Montgomery bus system. It was on December ______, 1955, that Rosa Parks refused to give up her seat on a crowded Montgomery city bus. She was arrested and put in jail. Four days later on December ______, a boycott was begun. The city's buses, normally filled with ______ blacks, were almost empty. Within a year, in ______, the U.S. Supreme Court ruled that segregation on buses was illegal.

In ______, black college students across the South began sitting at lunch counters that refused service to blacks. Civil rights protests became more and more frequent.

In 1963, King gave his famous "I Have a Dream" speech in Washington, DC. More than ______ Americans gathered at the Lincoln Memorial to rally for civil rights. That year King traveled more than 275,000 miles and gave more than ______ speeches.

The January 3, ______, issue of *Time* magazine named him "Man of the Year." Later that year, King was awarded the Nobel Peace Prize. At the age of ______, he was the youngest man ever to receive it.

Sadly, on April 4, ______, King was assassinated in Memphis, Tennessee. In ______, the U.S. Congress declared the third Monday in January a federal holiday to honor King.

| | | | | | | |
|---|---|---|---|---|---|---|
| 1960 | 1 | 35 | 1968 | second | 9th | 1951 |
| 350 | 18,000 | 1929 | 5 | 1956 | 1953 | 1955 |
| three | 1983 | four | 19 | 200,000 | 12th | 1964 |

**Bonus Box:** If Dr. King were alive today, how old would he be?

# Celebrate the Season

## Holiday and Seasonal Activities for the Classroom

### Valentine's Day: That's What I Love About You

Invite your students' parents to become part of your February lesson plans with this heartwarming activity! Give each student two large heart shapes cut from construction paper. On one heart, the child writes a sentence that describes something he loves about his family. Then he takes both hearts home and asks his parent to label the blank cutout with something she loves about him. Next, the parent and child work together to decorate both hearts. The following day, display each pair of hearts on a bulletin board or in a hallway.

If a student has a difficult home situation, have him label his heart with something he loves about your class; then label another cutout with a quality you appreciate about him. Finally, set aside a few minutes for you and the student to decorate both hearts together. ***Teena Andersen—Grs. 4–6, Hadar Public School, Hadar, NE***

I love that my parents really listen to me.
Kelli


### Valentine's Day: Heartbreak!

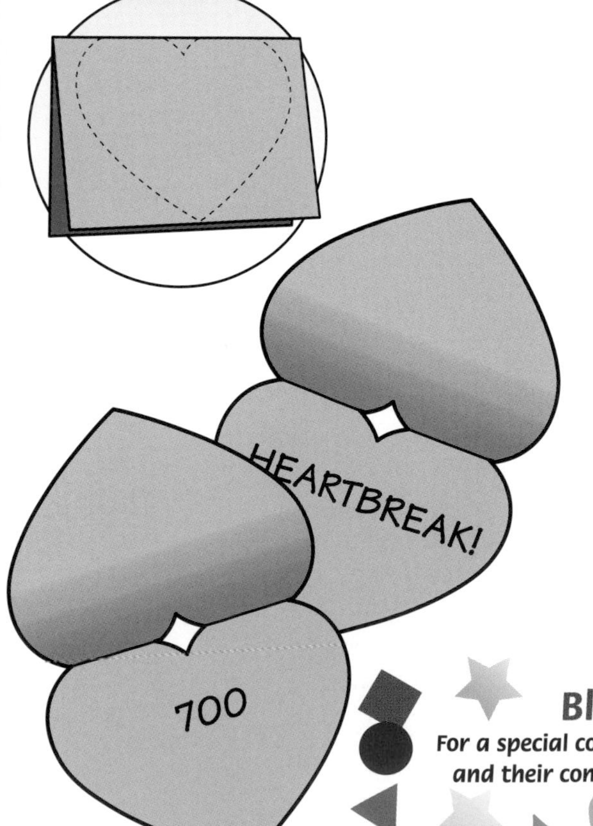


If you love an idea that's adaptable to just about any subject, then you're in luck! This fun-to-play game is easy to make and can be used to review a variety of skills. To prepare the game, cut one heart-shaped card for each student from a folded piece of construction paper as shown. Set aside two cards; then write the word "HEARTBREAK" on the inside of each one. Label the inside of each remaining card with a point value from 200 to 1,000.

To play, arrange the cards on a chalk tray or table. Divide the class into two teams. Write a math problem on the board; then have a player from each team come to the board and try to solve the problem. Let the first player to determine the correct answer choose a heart card. If the card contains a point value, add it to the player's team score. If the student selects a HEARTBREAK card, erase all points earned by her team so far. Continue playing until each student has had a turn. The team with the higher score at the end of the game wins. Make additional cards for other holidays, such as egg cards for Easter and pumpkin cards for Halloween. ***Theresa Roh Hickey—Grs. 4–5, Corpus Christi School, Mobile, AL***

### Black History Month

*For a special collection of activities on famous Black Americans and their contributions to the world, see pages 278–281!*

## Presidents' Day:
## Presidential Promises

Practice writing paragraphs this February by asking students to take a walk in the president's shoes! Give each student an index card. On his card, have the student write a paragraph describing a promise he would make to the American people if he were president of the United States. Then give each student a large red heart cut from red construction paper. Direct each student to use old magazines and other art materials to decorate his heart with a collage that illustrates his promise. After each student shares his paragraph and collage, mount the projects on a bulletin board that's covered with blue paper. ***Louella Nygaard—Gr. 5, Isabell Bills Elementary, Colstrip, MT***

As president, I promise to do
everything I can to make our
country a place where
different people get along
without fighting or prejudice.


## St. Patrick's Day:
## Somewhere Over the Rainbow I Found...

You don't have to look over the rainbow for a great poetry activity! After reviewing several different forms of poetry with students, discuss the St. Patrick's Day legend about finding a pot of gold at the end of a rainbow. Ask students, "If you traveled to the end of the rainbow, what would you want to find there?" Let students brainstorm a list of ideas; then ask each child to choose a favorite form of poetry and write a poem that describes his own special rainbow reward. While students work on their poems, let small groups color a large rainbow that you've drawn on a bulletin board. Post the finished poems on the board.
***Melissa A. McMullen—Gr. 5, Saint Patrick School, Newry, PA***

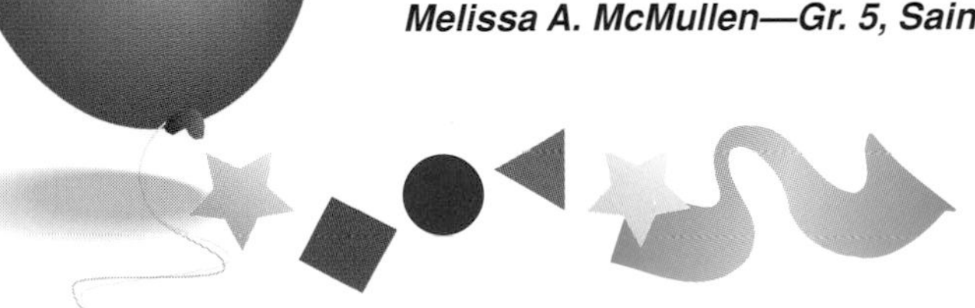

## St. Patrick's Day:
## Leprechaun Surprise

Stir up a batch of real-life math practice with this yummy activity! Gather the ingredients listed on the recipe shown and make a class supply of the "Leprechaun Surprise" reproducible on page 276. Also display a copy of the recipe. Read through the recipe as a class; then have each student (or pair of students) complete a copy of the reproducible as directed. After checking the answers together, help students make the recipe. What's the surprise? When students add the pistachio pudding (which is white), the mixture will suddenly turn a lovely shade of green! Be sure to provide small paper cups and plastic spoons so everyone can sample the surprising snack! ***Nancy Curl—Gr. 6, Olson Middle School, Tabernacle, NJ***

**Ingredients:**
20-oz. can crushed pineapple
1 c. mini marshmallows
8-oz. container Cool Whip® topping
3.4-oz. package pistachio instant pudding and pie filling mix

In a large bowl, mix together the pineapple, marshmallows, and Cool Whip. Sprinkle the pudding mix over the top; then stir the mixture thoroughly.

## Patterns

Use with "HOT Tickets" and "Homework Club Card" on page 12.

Homework Club Card
Aug.
Sept.
Oct.
Nov.
Dec.
FREE
Jan.
Feb.
Mar.
Apr.
May
name
©2001 The Education Center, Inc.


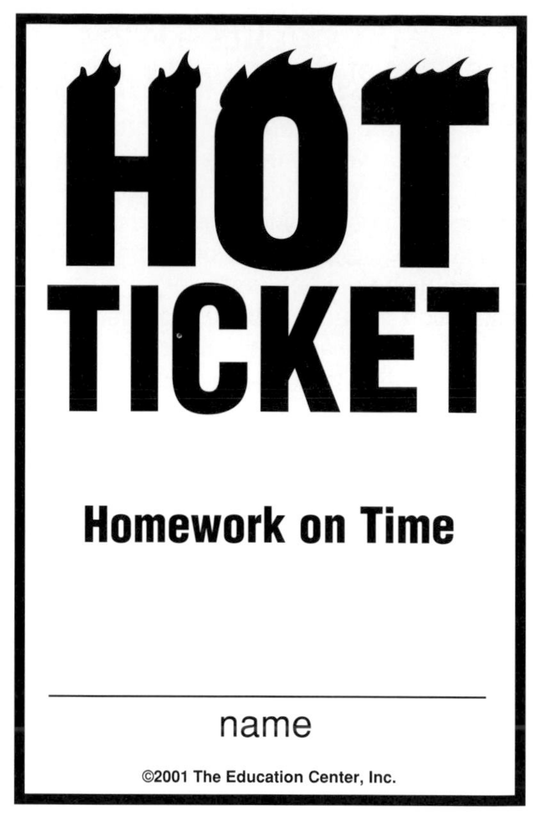


Name ______________________ Real-life math

# Leprechaun Surprise

The chart below lists the ingredients used to make a St. Patrick's Day snack called "Leprechaun Surprise." Use the chart to answer the questions.

| Ingredients | Calories | Fat Grams | Price |
|---|---|---|---|
| 20-oz. can crushed pineapple | 405 | 0 | $1.30 |
| 1 c. mini marshmallows | 200 | 0 | $1.09/bag |
| 8-oz. container Cool Whip® topping | 625 | 37.5 | $0.99 |
| 3.4-oz. box pistachio instant pudding and pie filling mix | 400 | 2 | $0.69 |

1. How many total calories are in one recipe of Leprechaun Surprise? ____________
2. How many total calories are in the recipe if you double it? ____________
3. How many total fat grams are in the recipe? ________ How many total fat grams are in the recipe if you double it? ____________
4. Write the fat grams in a container of Cool Whip as a fraction. (Don't forget to simplify the fraction.) ____________
5. If you double the recipe and give a sample to each student in a class of 20, how many calories would each person eat? (Hint: Start with your answer to question #2.) ____________
6. Could you make the recipe for under $3.00? Explain your answer. ____________
7. How much would you spend if you tripled the recipe? ____________
8. If you had a coupon for $.25 off the price of a bag of mini marsh-mallows and a half-price coupon for the pineapple, how much would the recipe cost to make? ____________
9. If the recipe serves five people, how many calories would each serving contain? (Hint: Go back to your answer in question #1.) ____________
10. Write another question that can be answered using the information in the chart. Include the answer. ____________

**Bonus Box:** Why do you think this recipe is called "Leprechaun Surprise"?



**Note to the teacher:** Use with "St. Patrick's Day: Leprechaun Surprise" on page 275. In turn, have each student share the question he wrote for #10 and challenge classmates to answer it.

Name ______________________________

# Handfuls of Candy

How many candy hearts does it take to cover the average fifth grader's hand? That's the question a group of students set out to answer. Take a look at their data in the chart; then answer the questions that follow.



**Math Words**

**data:** information
**range:** the difference between the greatest and least numbers in a group
**mean:** the average of a group of numbers
**median:** the middle number in a group of numbers arranged in numerical order
**mode:** the number in a group that occurs most often

**DATA**

| student | candy hearts needed to cover palm |
|---|---|
| Anu | 22 |
| Troy | 26 |
| Ally | 24 |
| Kyrsten | 23 |
| Andrew | 26 |
| Keisha | 26 |
| Mark | 19 |
| | 21 |
| ________ | ________ |

**PART 1**

1. Find the **range** of the group of numbers.
   a. What is the greatest number? _____ What is the least number? ______
   b. Subtract the least number from the greatest number. The range is ______.
2. Find the **mean.**
   a. Find the sum of all the numbers. _____ How many numbers are there? ______
   b. Divide the sum by how many numbers are in the group. The mean is ______.
3. What is the **median** number?
   a. Write the numbers in order from least to greatest: ____________________
   b. The number in the middle is the median. The median is ______.
4. What is the **mode** of the numbers?
   a. Does one number appear more often than any other? ______
   b. There may be more than one mode, or there may be no mode at all. The mode is ______.

**PART 2** How many hearts does it take to cover the palm of your hand?

1. Trace your hand on another sheet of paper.
2. Cut out the candy heart pattern.
3. Trace the pattern on your drawing, completely covering the palm with hearts.
4. Count the number of hearts you have traced.
5. Write your name and the number in the data chart.

pattern



**PART 3** Analyze the data again, including the new number:

range = ______ mean = ______ median = ______ mode = ______

(Hint: Since there are now two middle numbers, the median is the average of those two numbers.)

**BONUS BOX:** Ask four classmates how many hearts it took to cover each of their palms. List those four numbers, along with yours, below the drawing of your palm. Find the *range, mean, median,* and *mode* of this group of numbers.

## Ideas for Studying Famous Black Americans

Use the following activities to introduce your students to famous Black Americans who blazed a trail for others to follow.

### Pillars of Courage

**Skills: Research skills**

Honor the towering personalities in Black American history with this unique research project. In advance, ask your cafeteria staff to save a class supply of large, same-sized food cans. Have each student research a famous Black American (see the list on page 279) and write a brief report. Also direct the student to sketch or photocopy a picture of his person. After the student finishes his report, have him type it on a word processor so that it will fit (in one or several pieces) on the side of a can.

Next, measure around one can and write the measurements on the chalkboard. Give each student a ruler and a sheet of red, green, or black construction paper. Have the student measure and cut the paper to fit around his can. Then have him cut out his report and picture and glue them to his paper. Finally, have the student wrap the paper around the can and glue it in place.

After each can is finished, use hot glue to stack six or seven cans atop each other to make a pillar. At the top and bottom of each pillar, hot-glue a box that's been covered with black paper. Display the pillars in your school's lobby with a banner titled "Black History's Pillars of Courage."

Beth Patrilla—Grs. 4–5
St. Martin dePorres School
Toledo, OH



### The Interview Project

**Skills: Research skills, giving an oral presentation**

Combine a study of famous Black Americans with a book-report assignment that focuses on biographies and autobiographies. Ask your school's media coordinator to help you gather a collection of biographies and autobiographies about famous Black Americans. Have each student select a book to read; then have her fill out a copy of the form on page 280. Direct the student to be ready to answer the form's questions in a "live" interview. During the interview, the student will pose as her famous person while you ask the questions on the form. Encourage students to dress as their famous persons for the interviews and/or bring props that represent important facets of their lives. Not only will students be introduced to some of black history's major contributors, but they'll also be more motivated to pick up a biography or autobiography on their next trip to the library.

Lisa Groenendyk—Gr. 4
Pella Christian Grade School
Pella, IA

## Black History Newsletter

**Skills: Research skills, writing a newspaper story**

Want the scoop on how to work a study of black history into your already-packed curriculum? Try this activity that turns students' research on famous Black Americans into a newsworthy historical newsletter. First, have each student select a person to research from the list below. Then guide students through the following steps:

1. Collect details about your person. Start by answering these questions: *Who? What? Where? When? Why? How?* Then try to gather information that tells something important, unusual, or interesting about your person and his or her accomplishments.

2. After you've completed your research, write the first draft of your news story.
   a. Begin with a lead paragraph that gives an important or interesting detail.
   b. Write the main portion of your story.
   c. End your story by giving the reader something to think about.

3. Review and revise your story. Make sure you included all important information and that all facts are correct.

4. Edit and proofread your story for mistakes in spelling, capitalization, and punctuation.

5. Write the final copy.

Issue #1
Miss Cullum's 5th Grade Class
March 15
Black History Chronicle
Coretta Scott King Speaks Out
Jemison Blasts Off
First for Baseball
A Man of Courage


Work with your computer lab teacher to help students type their final copies and piece them together in the format of a newsletter or newspaper. Be sure to make enough copies so that the newsletter can be shared with other classes.

Amy Rzyrkowski, Gardens Elementary, St. Clair Shores, MI

### Famous Black American Achievers

**Astronauts/Explorers:** Ronald McNair, Guion Bluford, Mae Carol Jemison, Frederick Drew Gregory, Matthew Henson, James Pierson Beckwourth

**Athletes:** Jesse Owens, Jackie Robinson, Arthur Ashe, Wilma Rudolph, Althea Gibson, Jackie Joyner-Kersee

**Civil Rights Leaders:** Rosa Lee Parks, Fannie Lou Hamer, Coretta Scott King, Dr. Martin Luther King Jr., Jesse Jackson, W. E. B. Du Bois, Sojourner Truth, Harriet Tubman

**Doctors/Nurses:** Charles Richard Drew, Daniel Hale Williams, Susie King Taylor, Mary Elizabeth Mahoney

**Educators:** Mary McLeod Bethune, Booker T. Washington, Benjamin E. Mays, E. Franklin Frazier

**Film/T.V. Personalities:** Sidney Poitier, Bill Cosby, Oprah Winfrey, Lou Gossett Jr., Spike Lee, James Earl Jones

**Government Officials:** Shirley Chisholm, Ralph Bunche, Barbara C. Jordan, Thurgood Marshall, Thomas Bradley, Andrew Jackson Young Jr., Colin L. Powell

**Musicians:** Louis Armstrong, Count Basie, Dean Dixon, Duke Ellington, Dizzy Gillespie, Charlie Parker

**Poets/Playwrights:** Phillis Wheatley, Maya Angelou, Gwendolyn Brooks, Paul Laurence Dunbar, Lorraine Hansberry

**Scientists/Inventors:** Ernest Everett Just, Benjamin Banneker, George W. Carver, Garrett Morgan, Jan Ernst Matzeliger, Lewis Howard Latimer

**Singers:** Marian Anderson, Leontyne Price, Ella Fitzgerald, Lena Horne, Sarah Vaughan, Nat "King" Cole

**Writers:** Virginia Hamilton, Alice Walker, Toni Morrison, Alex Haley, Langston Hughes

Sharpen math skills during Black History Month with the **ready-to-use reproducible** on page 281.

Name ______________________________ Research skills

# An Interview With

______________________________

(name of person you read about)

Now that you've read about a famous person, it's time to share your new knowledge with the rest of the world (or at least your classmates). You will be asked to pretend to be the person you read about and give a live interview in the classroom. Below are the questions you will be asked. Fill in the blanks. Then study your answers so you'll be ready to share them during the interview.

1. What is your full name? ______________________________
2. When and where were you born? ______________________________
3. What accomplishments are you most famous for? ______________________________
4. Tell us about your family (parents, siblings, family life, etc.). ______________________________
5. Tell us about your childhood (friends, schooling, interests, etc.). ______________________________
6. What goal did you have as a young person? ______________________________
7. Tell about a favorite or noteworthy memory you have about your adult life. ______________________________
8. How did you spend the later years of your life? ______________________________
9. Why do you think you were so successful? ______________________________
10. On the back of this page, list anything else you'd like to tell the audience.

**Be prepared to answer other questions from the audience.**



**Note to the teacher:** Use with "The Interview Project" on page 278. Or use anytime you want students to research famous people, such as U.S. presidents, historical figures, authors, etc.

Name________________________________________________ Problem solving

# Famous Folks Fair

To celebrate Black History Month, Galvez School held a Black History Fair. Each booth at the fair sold an item that represented the achievements of a famous Black American. The money that was raised was used to buy books about Black Americans for the library.

Use the information on the booths to solve the problems below. In the first blank, write the equation. In the second blank, write the answer. Show your work on another sheet of paper. The first blank has been filled in for you.

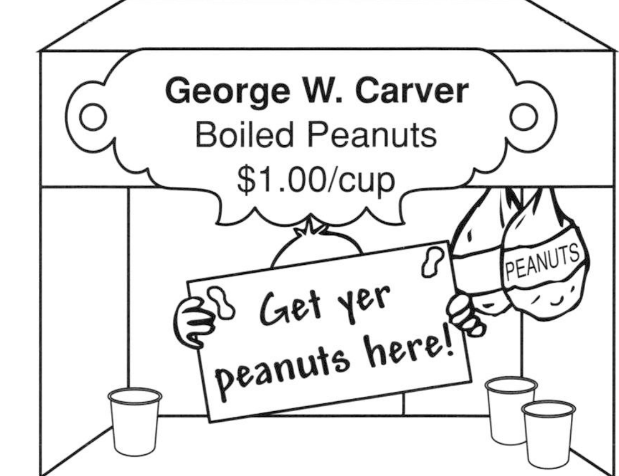

George W. Carver
Boiled Peanuts
$1.00/cup
Get yer peanuts here!
PEANUTS
Expenses: 20 pounds green peanuts at $1.89/pound
$.89 per box of salt
Sales: 98 cups of peanuts


1. How much was spent on peanuts for the booth?
   20 x $1.89 = ____________
2. For every pound of peanuts boiled, the students added 1 cup of salt to the water. If each box of salt contains 2 cups of salt, how many boxes did the students use?
   ____________ = ____________
3. How much was spent on salt? (Use the answer to #2.)
   ____________ = ____________
4. What were the total expenses for this booth?
   ____________________ = ________
5. The booth sold 98 cups of peanuts. How much money did it make (before expenses were subtracted)?
   ____________ = ____________
6. How much money was left over after expenses were paid? ____________________ = ____________
7. Each pound of peanuts filled five cups. How many cups were used? ____________ = ____________

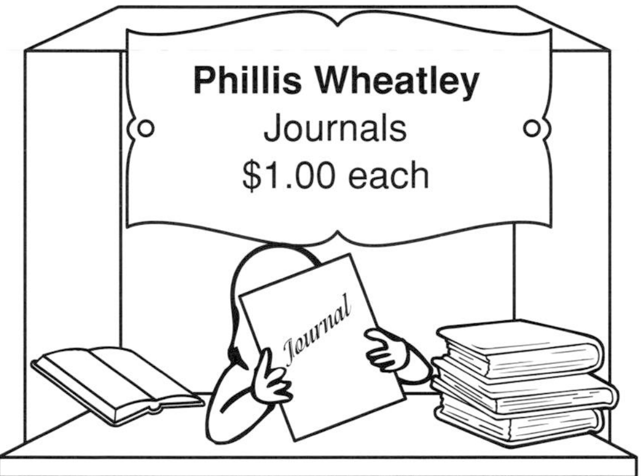

Phillis Wheatley
Journals
$1.00 each
Journal
Expenses: _____ packs of 150 sheets of lined paper for $1.50 each
2 paint pens at $2.99 each
90 front covers at $.09 each
90 back covers at $.05 each
Sales: 90 journals


8. To make each journal, students stapled 25 sheets of lined paper between a front and a back cover. How many journals did one pack of paper make?
   ____________________ = ____________
9. The students made 90 journals. How many packs of paper did they have to buy? ____________ = ____________
   (Write the answer in the blank on the booth.)
10. Find the total spent for the following supplies:
    paper: ____________ = ____________
    front covers: ____________ = ____________
    back covers: ____________ = ____________
    paint pens: ____________ = ____________
    TOTAL: ____________________________ = ____________
11. The booth sold 90 journals. How much money did it make (before expenses were subtracted)?
    ____________ = ____________
12. How much money was left over after expenses were paid? ____________________ = ____________

**BONUS BOX:** How much money did the students make on the Carver and Wheatley booths combined?

## Holiday and Seasonal Activities for the Classroom

### April

## Easter: Pop-Bottle Baskets

**Skills: Following directions, helping others**

When the hippity-hoppity time of year rolls around, have each child or student group follow the directions below to make an eye-catching Easter basket. Then donate the baskets to a local children's hospital, homeless center, or retirement facility.

**Materials for each basket:**

2-liter plastic soda pop bottle
4' length of multicolored yarn
three 3' lengths of thick light-colored yarn (3 different colors)
2 brads
scissors
pinking shears (optional)
hole puncher
ruler
Easter grass and treats

**Steps:**

1. Cut off the bottom three inches of the soda bottle. Set aside the top portion.
2. Punch holes around the top of the bottle bottom. Weave the three strands of light-colored yarn in and out of the holes; then tie the ends into a bow.
3. To make the basket handle, cut a $3/4$-inch-wide strip from the top portion of the bottle. Punch a hole in each end as shown.
4. Use scissors or pinking shears to make small notches along both long sides of the handle.
5. Tie one end of the multicolored yarn through one hole in the handle. Wrap the yarn around the handle's notches. Tie a knot when you reach the other hole in the handle.
6. Fasten the handle to the basket using two brads. Then fill the basket with Easter grass and treats. ***Rita Mulica, John Glenn School, Seven Hills, OH***

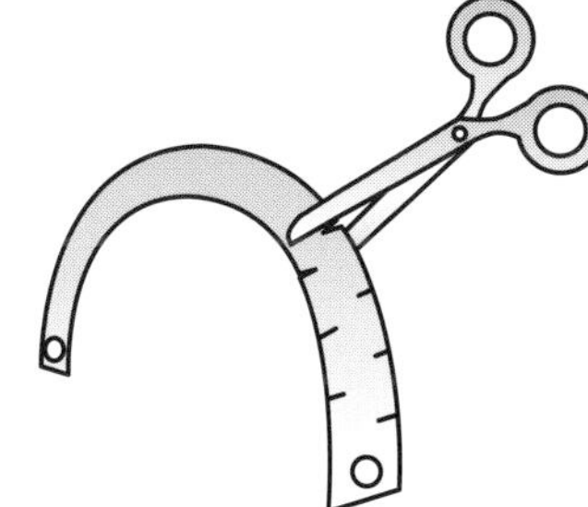

## Spring: "Egg-citing" Test Review

**Skills: Main ideas, word order in sentences**

Make reviewing for a unit test an "eggs-cellent" adventure with this idea! Divide your class into pairs. Direct each pair to review the unit's content and list the 12 most important main ideas studied. Have the students write each main idea—in scrambled order—on an egg-shaped cutout. Then have the twosome place its 12 cutouts inside an empty egg carton. Let the pair decorate its carton with the title of the unit, their names, and other illustrations that represent the unit.

Next, have student pairs swap egg cartons. Have each twosome unscramble the words on each egg in its carton, write the unscrambled sentence on a blank egg cutout, and place the answer egg in the corresponding section of the carton. When a twosome is finished, have it return the carton to its owners for checking. Swap cartons several times so that students get a thorough review of the unit's content. ***Julia Alarie—Gr. 6, Essex Middle School, Essex, VT***

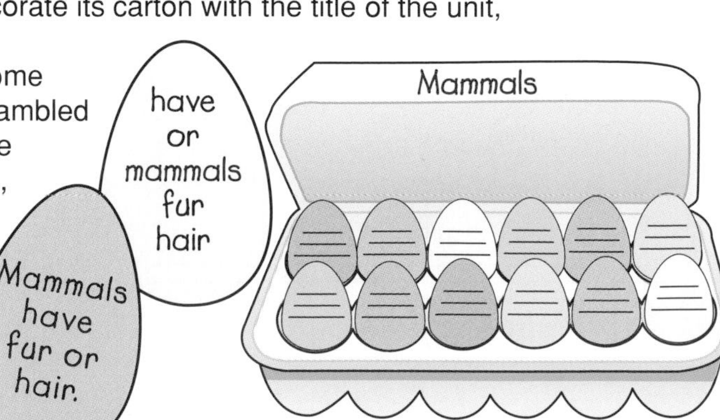

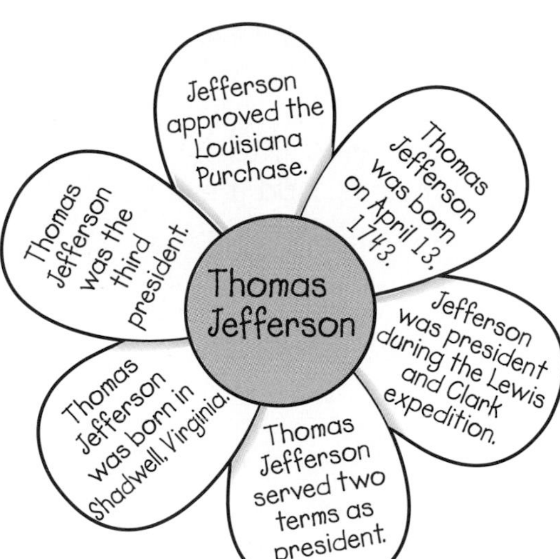


## May Day: Biography Blossoms

### Skill: Researching a topic

Watch research skills grow with an activity that blossoms into a May display! Cut out a supply of paper flower petals so that there are five to ten per student. Also cut a class supply of small circles from construction paper. Label each circle with the name of a famous person you'd like students to research.

Next, give each student five to ten flower petal cutouts, a glue stick, and a cutout circle. Direct the student to research the person on his circle; then have him glue a petal to the back of the circle and label it with a fact about his famous person. Finally, have the student pass the flower to a classmate. Continue until each flower has at least five petals. Then post the flowers on a bulletin board titled "Biography Blossoms." ***Kimberly A. Minafo—Gr. 4, Tooker Avenue Elementary, West Babylon, NY***

## Mount St. Helens Eruption: Whipped Cream Volcanoes

### Skills: Researching a topic, understanding types of volcanoes

On May 18, 1980, the world was rocked by the eruption of Mount St. Helens. Celebrate the anniversary of this milestone with a tasty minilesson on the three kinds of volcanoes. After gathering the supplies below, divide your class into groups of three. Give each student a paper plate and plastic spoon. Then challenge the groups to research the three kinds of volcanoes: *shield, cinder cone,* and *composite*. After the research is complete, place three tablespoons of whipped topping and a cherry on each child's plate. Direct each student to mold his whipped cream to show one of the three volcanoes (so that each three-member group has a model of each type). Instruct students to use the cherry as the volcano's vent and magma chamber, the chocolate syrup as lava, and the crumbled cookies as rocks and ash. After checking each group's volcanoes, let your junior geologists dig into their mouthwatering models! ***Pam Snyder—Gr. 4, Center Street Elementary, Horseheads, NY***

**Materials (enough for class of 21–25 students):**
two 12-oz. tubs of whipped topping, cool but not frozen
box of vanilla wafers, crushed with rolling pin into various sizes
28-oz. bottle of chocolate syrup
10-oz. jar of maraschino cherries with stems
1 paper plate and 1 plastic spoon per child

The Woman I Admire

Recipe for a Marvelous Mom
Ingredients:
Steps:
1.
2.
3.
4.

## Mother's Day: Now Serving...

### Skills: Expressive writing, writing a recipe

Focus on your students' favorite females with an expressive writing activity that's perfect for celebrating Mother's Day. Have each student write an expressive paragraph about her mom or another older female relative or friend. After she edits the page, have the student copy it onto the top of a sheet of paper. Next, challenge the student to write a recipe that describes her mom. Have the student write her edited recipe below the essay. Then have her add a border of colorful illustrations around the page. Combine the students' papers into a class book titled "Now Serving: Marvelous Moms, Wonderful Women!" Make a class supply of the cookbook so each student can give a copy to her mom for a Mother's Day gift. ***Dawn Castle—Gr. 6, Albany School of Humanities, Albany, NY***

Name________________________________________ Earth Day: commas, words in context

# Earth Day Bloopers

Oops! The Earth Day messages Miss Clean's class is making to promote a cleaner environment contain mistakes! Each message is missing its first letter and one or more commas. Add the missing letters and commas. Then color the symbol at the end of each message to explain the use of the comma(s). The first one has been done for you.

 = in a series  = after an introductory word  = in a compound sentence

1. E ncourage others to reduce, reuse, and recycle.
2. __ey everyone should put litter in its place.
3. __ave fuel by walking or you could try riding a bike.
4. __arious types of pollution make our air land and water dirty.
5. __et's learn ways to keep the environment clean by reading books and we can also find out by watching TV programs and videos.
6. __es each person should do his part to take care of the earth.
7. __ry to use less water when brushing teeth showering and cleaning the house.
8. __ne person alone can't solve the pollution problem but each person should do all he can.
9. __ids can you help us stop polluting our planet?
10. __ow don't you recycle?
11. __ispose of trash chemicals and wastes properly.
12. __ecycle plastic glass paper and metal.
13. __ake a commitment to clean up reduce and recycle all the trash being created.
14. __t's never too late to help and you can start today.

Miss Clean contributed a message, too. To find out what it is, fill in the blanks below by matching each first letter with its corresponding number.

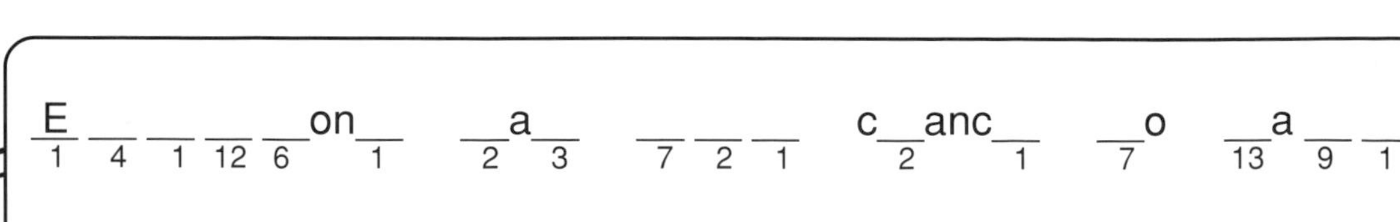

E __ __ __ __on__ __a__ __ __ __ c__anc__ __o __a__ __

1 4 1 12 6 1 2 3 7 2 1 2 1 7 13 9 1

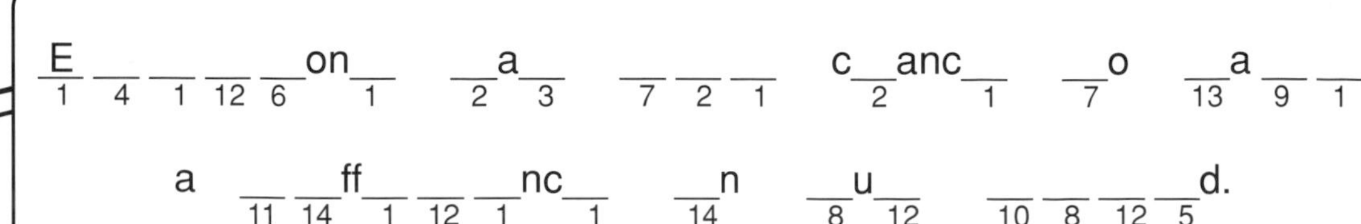

a __ __ff__ __ __nc__ __n __u__ __ __ __ __d.

11 14 1 12 1 1 14 8 12 10 8 12 5

**Bonus Box:** On the back of this page, write three Earth Day sentences of your own: one using commas in a series, one using an introductory word, and one compound sentence.



 **Note to the teacher:** If desired, have students use crayons to color the Earth Day symbols. For more recycling ideas, see pages 168–171.

Name____________________________________________

# Super Snoozing Suggestions

To celebrate Better Sleep Month in May, Nellie Nightingale is designing a quilt featuring 16 people's suggestions for getting a good night's sleep. Correct Nellie's mistakes before the public views her quilt. Add quotation marks where they belong. Draw a bed (□) around each letter that should be capitalized.

1. i like to read a good, long story, said corey.
2. plug in a small night-light, replied mr. wright.
3. a soft stuffed animal is what you need, stated mr. tweed.
4. you must, whispered mrs. willow, have a fluffy, plump pillow.
5. stretching before i go to bed, explained ramona, always puts sleepy thoughts in my head.
6. mrs. silk uttered, i like to sip on a cup of warm milk.
7. i always listen to calm, soothing music, voiced mr. busick.
8. before bed, responded jean, i never drink anything with caffeine.
9. i have to sleep in a cozy, comfortable bed, murmured fred.
10. make sure your bedroom, answered professor bold, isn't too hot or too cold.
11. never exercise late at night, suggested dependable dwight.
12. try to stick to a bedtime routine, recommended dr. eloise lean.
13. counting sheep, advised mr. leap, usually puts me to sleep.
14. take several deep, relaxing breaths, offered perky stephanie elizabeth.
15. eat spicy foods early, not late, piped in mr. slate.
16. what i suggest, declared mrs. west, is a nice, long bubble bath to relieve anyone who's stressed.

**Bonus Box:** On the back of this page, write two sentences giving your own suggestions for getting a good night's sleep. Remember to use quotation marks and capital letters correctly.

## End of the Year: "Tee-rrific" Autographs

### Skill: Class art project

Sign off on another great school year with this "tee-rrific" idea! From a craft store, obtain an inexpensive, solid-colored T-shirt (cotton/polyester blend works best), three or more bottles of colorful fabric paints, and a set of Crayola® Washable Markers. Then follow these steps to create a keepsake that's just "write"! ***Debbi Speer, Saigling Elementary, Plano, TX***

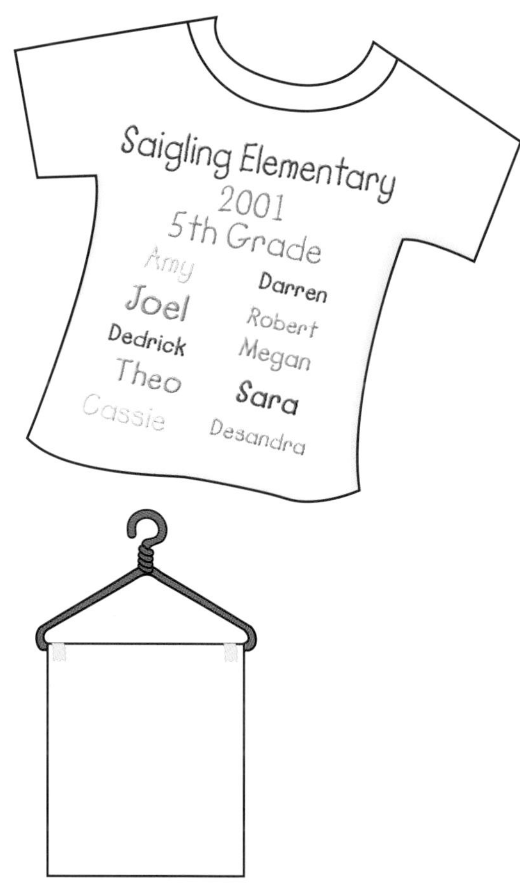


**Preparing the shirt:**

1. Wash and dry the shirt according to label directions.
2. Tape a sheet of poster board on a metal coat hanger as shown. Slip the shirt on the hanger so that the poster board falls between the shirt's front and back.
3. Tape the arms and any excess fabric to the back of the shirt.
4. Place the shirt on a hard surface. On the shirt's front, lightly pencil your school's name, the grade level, and the year. Then trace over the writing with fabric paint. Let dry for 24 hours.
5. Use chalk to draw a writing line for each student on the front of the shirt.

**Autographing the shirt:**

1. One at a time, have each child use a washable marker to write his name in big letters on a chalk line. (Start with the lines that are at the top of the shirt and move downward). Then trace over the student's name with the fabric paint of his choice.
2. After all students have autographed the shirt, hang it up to dry. If painted in the morning, the shirt should be dry by the end of the day.
3. Wash the shirt to remove the chalk lines. Then wear the shirt on the last day of school.

## End of the Year: Bulletin-Board Scramble

### Skills: Spelling, vocabulary

Time to take down your bulletin boards for the year? Turn this classroom chore into a stupendous end-of-the-year spelling game! Collect a small box for each display. Remove all cutout letters from each bulletin board; then randomly place an equal number of letters in each box (making sure that each box includes at least a few vowels). Next, divide your class into the same number of groups as boxes, and have each group sit near a blank bulletin board. Give each group a box of letters, a die, and a stapler. In turn, have a group roll its die and pull that number of letters from its box without peeking. Then challenge the group to use the letters to create the largest word possible. If the group can create a word, have it staple the appropriate letters to its bulletin board. Direct the group to save any unused letters for its next turn. As play continues, have each group try to build on words that are already on its bulletin board, like in Scrabble®. Allow a group to pass if it cannot make a new word. The game is over when time runs out or one team uses all of its letters. ***Cindy Zajac—Gr. 6, Klein Elementary, Erie, PA***

## Flag Day: It Was a Grand Ole Year!

### Skills: Creative thinking, writing a descriptive paragraph

Celebrate Flag Day (June 14) with an activity that ends the year on a flag-waving note! Brainstorm with students favorite memories of the school year. Then give each child a sheet of art paper and crayons or markers. Direct the student to design a flag that symbolizes what the school year has meant to her. Suggest that students include symbols to represent favorite activities and memories, personal accomplishments, and feelings about the year. When the student has finished the design, have her post her flag on a bulletin board. Then have her write a paragraph that explains the flag's symbols. For fun, read each paragraph aloud without identifying its writer. Then challenge students to match the paragraph with the correct flag.

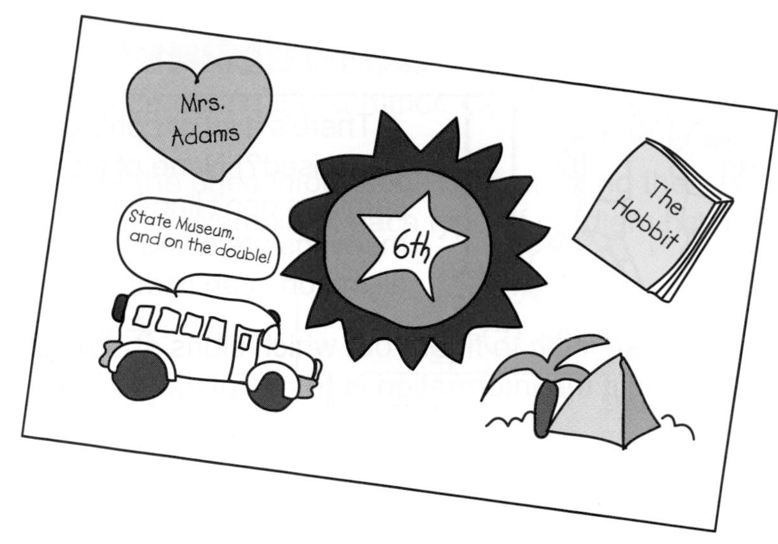


**Picture books featuring fathers:**

- *The Lost Lake* by Allen Say
- *My Ol' Man* by Patricia Polacco
- *Octopus Hug* by Laurence Pringle
- *A Perfect Father's Day* by Eve Bunting
- *The Painter* by Peter Catalanotto
- *When This World Was New* by D. H. Figueredo

Happy Father's Day

## Father's Day: Picturing Dad

### Skills: Summarizing, comparing and contrasting

Focus on fathers featured in picture books with an activity that practices several language arts skills. With your librarian's help, collect books about fathers (see the list shown). Give each of your student groups two books. Then have each group read its books and complete one or more of these activities:

- Complete a Venn diagram that compares and contrasts the fathers in the two books.
- Write a summary for each book that could be featured on an online bookstore's Web site. Include a recommendation for the book.
- Choose one book. Write a summary of a sequel your group could write for the book.
- Use inferences to write a description of the father in each book. Support each description with evidence from the story.

## International Picnic Day: Picnic Round the World

### Skills: Researching a topic, world geography

Give students a taste of world geography with an activity that celebrates International Picnic Day (June 18). Begin by dividing students into groups. Have each group choose a country and research its traditional foods. Then direct each group to plan a picnic lunch with its country's dishes. Next, have the group label and draw a picture of each food on the front of a small paper plate and write a description of the food on the back. Finally, have the group select the perfect spot in its country for a picnic and write a description of the special location. After sharing its information, have each group place its plates in a decorated basket. Display the baskets in your class or school library.

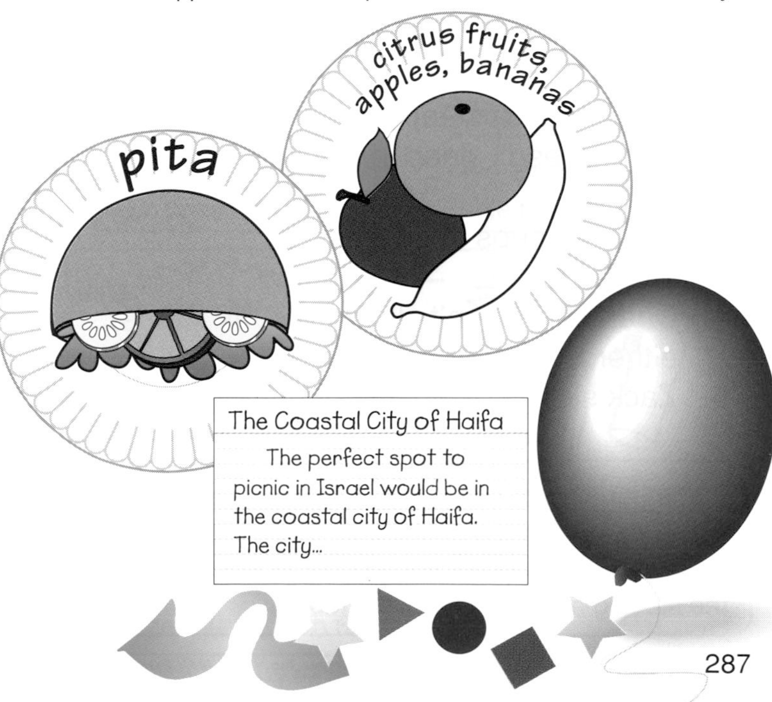

Name ______________________________________________

# You Don't Say!

You've packed a basket with summertime foods. Now you've headed to your favorite spot in the park to celebrate International Picnic Day (June 18). Or is that Inter*galactic* Picnic Day? Some uninvited (and very unusual) guests have dropped in on your picnic. What to do? Have a great time anyway! The only problem is that your guests, hard as they try, simply don't understand some of the words in your language.

To get your guests involved, you need to explain some of the activities below to them. Choose five activities. Write a three- to five-sentence paragraph explaining each one without using any of the words listed below the activity. (Hint: Use a thesaurus to help you find new words.) Write your paragraphs on another sheet of paper. Good luck and happy picnicking!

1. **How to make a sandwich**
   bread put mayo knife together
2. **How to set a picnic table**
   tablecloth on down plates place
3. **How to make a hot dog**
   bun frankfurter ketchup between roast
4. **How to roast marshmallows**
   fire stick charcoal brown hold
5. **How to play catch**
   ball mitt apart throw other
6. **How to play tag**
   it out run around player
7. **How to make and eat an ice-cream cone**
   lick melt flavor hold scoop
8. **How to prepare for a three-legged race**
   two tie legs beside pair

**BONUS BOX:** Write a paragraph about summer without using *a, an,* or *the.*

# Our Readers Write

# Our Readers Write

## Love Those Labels!

Help students keep track of their school supplies with this great tip. For each child, program two sheets of name labels with a permanent marker, or type them on your computer. Give one sheet to each student to use for labeling his personal school supplies. File the other sheet to use throughout the year for nametags, seating charts, or gift labels. Keeping track of students' supplies will no longer be a sticky issue!

Bonni Teplitz
Gordon Day School
Miami, FL

## Pocketful of 100s!

Motivate students to study their spelling words while boosting self-esteem with this "denim-ite" display. First, hang an old pair of overalls on a bulletin board. Then keep track of students who receive 100s on weekly spelling tests. When a student earns five 100s, write her name on an index card and place it in a pocket of the overalls. Then reward the student by exempting her from the following week's spelling homework. What a great way to add a pocketful of improved spellers to your classroom!

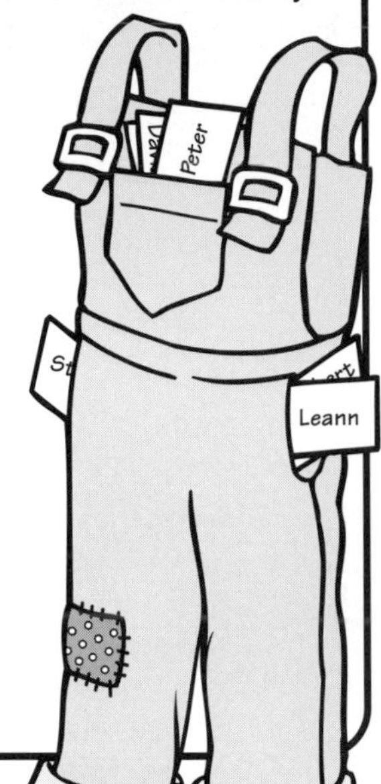


Donna DeRosa—Gr. 4
Good Shepherd Academy
Nutley, NJ

## Class Photographer

Catch every Kodak® moment as it happens by assigning the weekly job of class photographer. Bring in an old camera, or purchase several disposable ones. Direct the photographer to take the camera with him wherever he goes during school hours. Limit the pictures taken to two per day so the photographer will learn to choose his photos wisely. When the pictures have been developed, have the photographer put them into a class scrapbook and add a caption to each one. By June, you'll have a picture-perfect scrapbook of the school year—created entirely by your kids!

Tammy Brown—Gr. 6, Midway Elementary, Cleveland, MO

## Traveling Tuesdays

Send students on a journey around your state with this fun geography project. During the first week of school, have each child write a letter to the Chamber of Commerce or a travel bureau in a specific county, asking for brochures and other information. On "Traveling Tuesdays" throughout the year, have selected students share the information they've received, marking their counties with pushpins on a state map. At the end of the year, celebrate your last Traveling Tuesday with a party featuring foods and activities from different counties.

Sister Pat Madden—Gr. 4
Corpus Christi School
Lansdale, PA

## Road to Success

Start students on the road to success early in the year with this goal-setting activity. On the first day of school, hang a picture of your college or university on a bulletin board titled "Road to Success." (If you don't have a picture, ask your college alumni office for a brochure that includes a photo.) Then discuss planning for the future and goal setting with the class. Refer to your college picture and share with students the goals you set for yourself. Finally, have each child add a brief paragraph about her goals for the future to the display.

Kimberly Minafo—Gr. 4
Tooker Avenue Elementary
West Babylon, NY

## Your Work Is Monumental!

Show off your students' accomplishments with this monumental display! On a bulletin board titled "Your Work Is Monumental!" post pictures of famous monuments, such as the ones listed. Then fill the display with your students' best papers. To extend the board's use, divide the class into teams and assign one monument per group. Instruct each group to research interesting facts about its monument to share with the class. Display the facts on the board along with students' monumental papers.

**Sample Monuments**
Statue of Liberty
Eiffel Tower
Great Sphinx
Stonehenge
Great Wall of China

Stephanie Fowler, Bixby Middle School, Bixby, OK

## Seating Solution

Change your class's seating arrangement and review at the same time with this fun idea! On index cards, write questions related to a current unit (one question per card). Write the answers on another set of cards. Then tape one answer card to each desk and randomly hand out the question cards. Have each student find his new desk by locating the answer to his question. Provide additional review by discussing the questions and answers with the class. Use this idea to introduce a new unit by allowing students to use reference materials to answer the questions.

Jan Williams—Gr. 4, Hubbardston Center School, Hubbardston, MA

## Collecting Classroom Supplies

At your Back-to-School Night, mention to parents that your classroom is always in need of cups, plates, napkins, plastic utensils, etc. Then ask them to donate their extra party supplies. Remind parents that students don't mind eating off Fourth of July plates—even in August!

Lisa Borgo—Gr. 4
Gould Avenue School
North Caldwell, NJ

## Pads With Personality

Treat your students to their own personalized notepads with this noteworthy idea! Just follow these steps:

1. Have each student key her name into a word-processing program and add a small graphic as shown.
2. Copy each child's name to make four copies; then print out the page.
3. For each child, fold an 8½" x 11" sheet of paper in half two times. Unfold the paper; then cut out the copies of the child's name and paste one at the top of each of the four sections as shown. Make five copies of this page.
4. Have each student cut apart her 20 notes and staple them together.

Save each child's master copy so you can make new pads whenever they're needed.

Terry Healy—Gr. 5
Eugene Field Elementary
Manhattan, KS

Steps 1 & 2

Nicole
Nicole
Nicole
Nicole

Step 3

Nicole Nicole
Nicole Nicole

Nicole

YOU CAN DO IT!

## Star Light, Star Bright!

Brighten up the classroom for your new students with this star-studded bulletin board idea. First, cover a bulletin board with black garbage bags. Then cut out star shapes from neon paper and label them with positive phrases as shown. Title the display "Star Light, Star Bright, Let's Start the Year Off Right!"

Kathy Wolford
Galion, OH

## The "Write" Stuff

For a quick and easy source of writing prompts, look no further than a stack of old magazines. They are super sources for interesting pictures—especially science, gardening, and country life magazines. Cut out unusual pictures; then have them made into transparencies or glue them to construction paper. Use the pictures as story starters or descriptive writing prompts, for dialogue-writing practice, or to springboard any writing assignment that fits your needs.

Dana Benge—Gr. 5, Braggs School, Braggs, OK

## Weekly Word Game

Give students a chance to practice their spelling skills with this weekly word game. First, draw and laminate several charts similar to a Scrabble® board game as shown. Divide students into groups. Then display one chart for each group on a bulletin board. Instruct each student to use a different-colored wipe-off marker to add words to his group's board during free time. Give bonus points to students who use spelling or vocabulary words or who have the most words on their team's board by the end of the week. Then wipe off the boards, assign new groups, and play another round!

Isobel L. Livingstone, Rahway, NJ

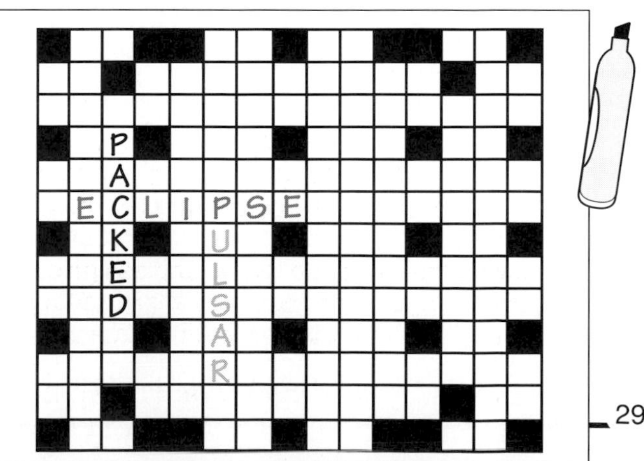

## Adjectives Made Easy

Make adjectives easier to understand with this hands-on activity. Bring to school a variety of small objects, such as stuffed animals, erasers, and toy cars. Tell students that these objects are *nouns;* then pass one item around the room and ask each child to describe how it looks and feels. As each descriptive word is given, list it on the board. Point out that these words are *adjectives* because they describe a noun. Repeat the activity with several other objects; then have students write sentences using the adjectives listed on the board. Now wasn't that easy?

Kadi Cleary—Gr. 5, Bland Elementary, Bland, VA

## Heads Above the Rest

Want each of your kids to feel like she's heads above the rest? Using an overhead projector, project the silhouette of each student's head onto construction paper and trace it. Have each child cut out magazine pictures of objects or activities she enjoys; then have her glue them collage-style within her outline. Next, have the student cut out her silhouette and glue it onto a piece of poster board. Circulate the finished posters, asking each child to write a compliment on every classmate's poster. Encourage students to be specific in their compliments, such as "I like your smile" or "You're a great soccer player." Laminate the signed posters; then display one each week before sending it home with the proud owner.

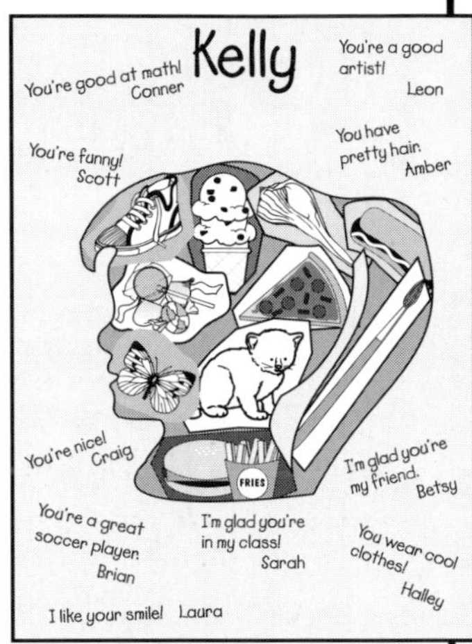


Teresa Munson—Grs. 4–5, R–9 North Elementary
Warsaw, MO

## Lost and Found

Looking for an inexpensive solution to lost or forgotten pencils? Then you'll go "fore" this idea! Keep on hand a supply of eraserless golf pencils (available at most business supply stores). The next time you hear "I forgot my pencil," you'll be prepared!

Edie Dege
John R. Downes Elementary
Newark, DE

## Classroom Menu

Serve your new students a sneak peek at the year ahead with this first-day activity! Write a menu of items such as the ones shown. Give each student a copy of the menu on the first day of school. After reading over the menu with students, discuss what they would like to add to it; then direct each child to write his ideas in the "Specialty Items" section of his menu. If desired, have each student share his list of specialty items with the class.

Kimberly Minafo—Gr. 4
Tooker Avenue Elementary
West Babylon, NY

### Minafo's Restaurant

MENU

**Main Courses**

**Melts-in-Your-Mouth Math:** A mouthwatering meal that includes such numerical niceties as Fraction Fritters, Geometry Gelatin, Measurement Meat Loaf, and a scrumptious sampler of Problem-Solving Pastries. Betcha can't eat just one!

**Scrumptious Science:** You won't be able to stop nibbling on these heavenly hands-on experiments or fabulous facts about vertebrates, earthquakes, atoms, the skeletal system, and more!

**Wonderful Writing:** A delectable blend of vocabulary, grammar, and spelling activities, topped with a creamy sauce of narrative, persuasive, expository, and descriptive writing.

**Literature à la Mode:** A savory selection of spine-tingling mysteries, tasty tall tales, appetizing historical fiction stories, fantastic fantasies, and much more! Sure to please even the pickiest reader!

**Specialty Items**

## Getting-to-Know-You Database

Get to know your students, while also giving them computer practice, with this "techno tip." Title each field in a database as shown. Then have each student fill in the information as her first computer assignment. Use this database's information to form groups, create graphing activities or story starters, and much more.

Elizabeth Spohn—Grs. 1–8, Butler Catholic School, Butler, PA

| Name | Nickname | Favorite Color | Favorite Book | Favorite Subject | Favorite Food |
|---|---|---|---|---|---|
| Rebecca | Becca | green | Shiloh | math | pizza |

# Our Readers Write

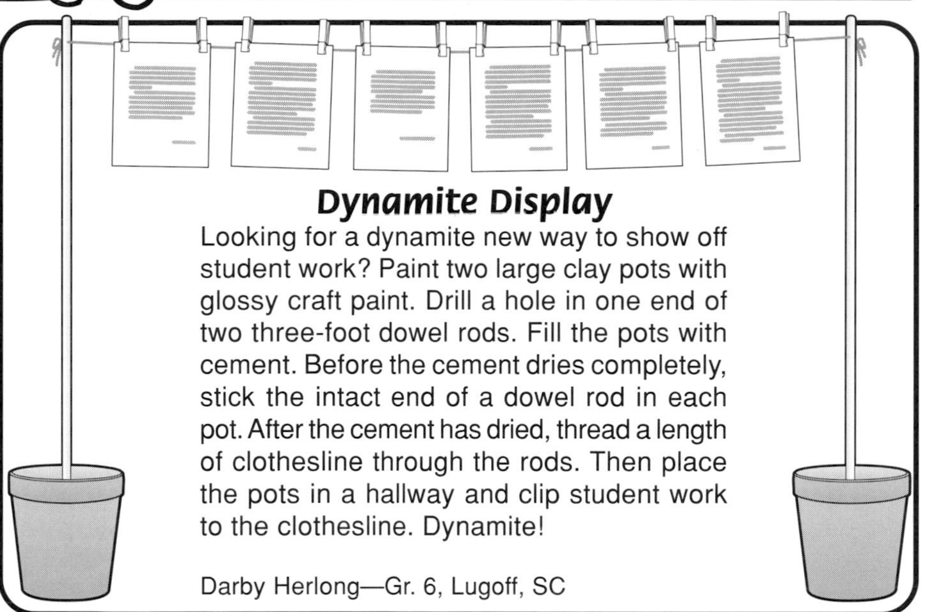

## Dynamite Display

Looking for a dynamite new way to show off student work? Paint two large clay pots with glossy craft paint. Drill a hole in one end of two three-foot dowel rods. Fill the pots with cement. Before the cement dries completely, stick the intact end of a dowel rod in each pot. After the cement has dried, thread a length of clothesline through the rods. Then place the pots in a hallway and clip student work to the clothesline. Dynamite!

Darby Herlong—Gr. 6, Lugoff, SC

## How Are We Doing?

Check student understanding anytime with this tip. During a lesson or while collecting work, ask students, "How are we doing?" If a child understands what you're teaching, he gives a thumbs-up signal. To signify "I'm totally lost," a student gives a thumbs-down. A child who thinks, "I kind of get it, but I'm not sure," shakes his thumb. This nonthreatening survey provides instant feedback that will help you adjust your lesson plans as needed.

Kimberly Minafo—Gr. 4
Tooker Avenue School
West Babylon, NY

## Positive Bookmarks

Celebrate National Children's Book Week in November with this self-esteem booster. Divide the class into groups. Have each student write her name on a large index card as shown. Collect and shuffle each group's cards before redistributing them to group members. At your signal, have each child write a positive comment on the card she is holding. After one minute, have students switch cards until everyone has written on each group member's card. Collect the cards and write a compliment on each one. Then laminate the cards and return them to students to use as bookmarks.

Keegan Smith
You've got a great smile! Natasha
I really liked your science project. Keith
You have a really mean soccer kick, man! Jason
You're always willing to help me with math. Tommy
Great team leader. Missy
You always try to be a good friend! Mrs. Mills


Kathleen Hammond—Gr. 6, Wetzel Road Elementary, Liverpool, NY

## One Letter at a Time

Build vocabulary skills one letter at a time with this fun challenge. Write a letter on the board and ask students to list words that begin with it. When time is up, have students share their words. Then ask them to list words in which the letter is second, third, and so on (see the examples using *b*). When students can no longer list any words, repeat the activity with a different letter.

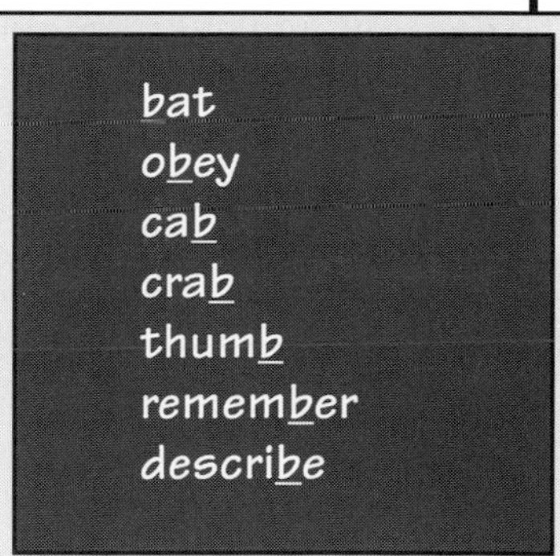


Isobel L. Livingstone
Rahway, NJ

## Regions Flash Cards

Help students memorize United States regions, states, and capitals in a flash! Post a list of regions and their states. Also give each student 50 tagboard cards. Direct the student to write each state's name on a card using a different-colored marker or crayon for each region. On the back of the card, have the student write the state's capital. Encourage students to quiz each other during free time or take the cards home to practice with family members.

Gosia Crane—Gr. 4
Our Lady of the Presentation School
St. Louis, MO

## Perfect Paper Punch Cards

For a practically perfect way to motivate good work habits, cut off the front of a greeting card for each student. Draw 10 to 15 dots on the card with a marker; then give the card to a student. Each time the student earns a perfect score, punch out one dot on her card. When all dots have been punched, reward the child with a small treat. Then give her another card. At the end of the grading period, award a prize to each student who turns in all of the completely punched cards she earned during that period of weeks.

Kris Call—Gr. 5, St. Joseph School, Decatur, IN

## Toy Toss

Turn a favorite stuffed animal into a classroom management tool! When students are having a difficult time staying on task, announce that the class can play "Save the [name of stuffed animal]" if behavior improves. To play, students sit atop their desks. The first child holds the animal, calls the name of a classmate, and throws the toy to her. If the catcher misses or drops the toy, she is out and must sit in her chair. If the thrower makes a bad throw, he is out. The winner is the last student left sitting on his desk. To vary, stipulate that a student is out if he forgets to announce the catcher's name, begs for the animal, or holds the toy for more than three seconds before throwing it.

Tammy McMaster, Mifflin County School District, Lewistown, PA

## Think Tank

Help students think in a blink with this co-operative activity. Have each student write a noun on a small index card and place it in a decorated shoebox that you've labeled "Think Tank." Next, divide the class into pairs. Have each pair draw two cards from the Think Tank, write the nouns on a sheet of paper, and then list ways that the two words are alike and different. Provide time for students to share their work with the class.

Jennifer Cook
Forest Creek Elementary
Round Rock, TX

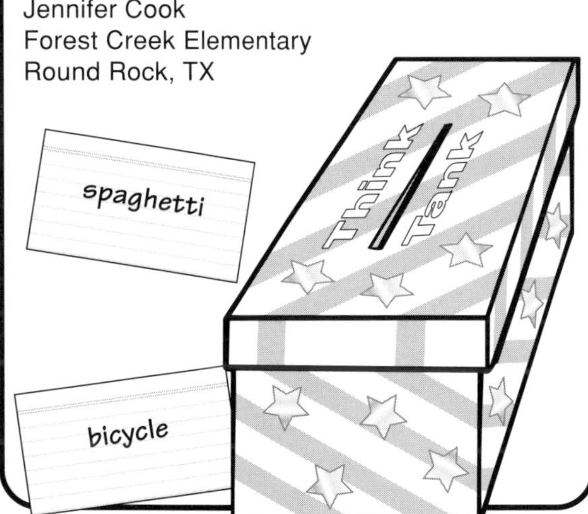
spaghetti
Think Tank
bicycle

## Chalk Tip

Do your students love using individual chalkboard slates but hate all the chalky mess? Then try this neat solution! Give each child a pencil grip to place around his piece of chalk. This simple tip will reduce chalk residue in no time!

Barbara Wilkes Delnero—Gr. 4, Tuckerton Elementary, Tuckerton, NJ

## Totally Tongue-Twisted

Follow up a lesson on alliteration with this "mask-nificent" activity! Have each child use art materials to create a colorful mask of a person, animal, or imaginary creature. Then have him attach a long paper tongue to his mask. On the tongue, have the child write an alliterative sentence about his character. Finally, direct the student to tape a pencil to the tongue's tip and roll it up. To share his project, have the student unroll the tongue and read his sentence.

Dana Mandala—Gr. 5
St. Aloysius School
Jackson, NJ

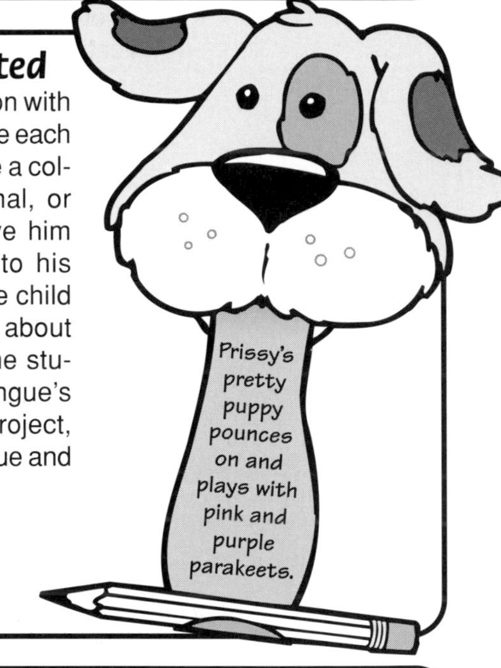
Prissy's pretty puppy pounces on and plays with pink and purple parakeets.

## Computer Reminders

Keep important computer information handy with this idea. On index cards, write step-by-step directions for computer tasks you need to remember, such as how to bookmark a Web site or set up an email address book. Arrange the cards in alphabetical order by subject. Then place the file next to your computer. The next time you need a reminder, it'll be right at your fingertips!

Sue Mechura—Gr. 4
Ebenezer Elementary
Lebanon, PA

## Science Suitcase

Pack science skills and parent involvement into one activity with this idea. Fill an old suitcase (look for one at yard sales) with safe science equipment, such as plastic beakers, goggles, graduated cylinders, lab sheets, easy-to-do experiments, etc. Allow students to check out the suitcase so they can take it home and do experiments with their families. When a student returns the suitcase, have her turn in her completed lab sheets. Encourage students who take the suitcase home to add any materials they think will be beneficial.

Pamela Murray—Grs. 5–6 Science
Boardman Glenwood Middle School
Boardman, OH

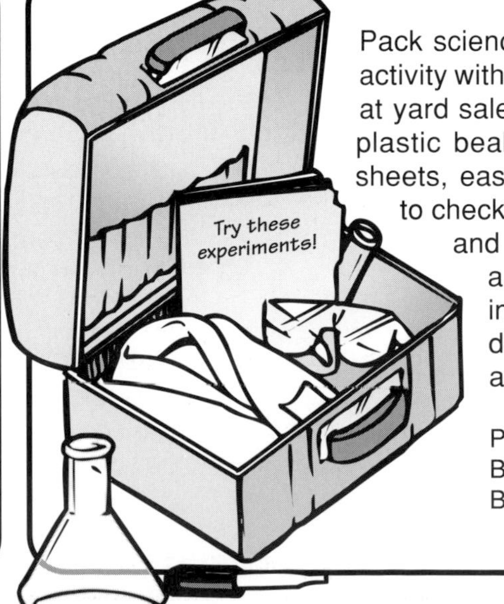
Try these experiments!

## My Family's Holiday

Kids are often more interested in gift-getting than giving. Focus on the sharing side of the holiday season with this unique activity. After Thanksgiving, send a letter home asking parents to help their child think of a family holiday tradition to share with the class. Examples might include a special food item (with samples), a favorite ornament, a holiday story, a family video, etc. Have students share their traditions on the day before the holiday break.

Karen Ruterbories—Gr. 5, Mater Dei School, Sioux City, IA

## Solar System Project

For an out-of-this-world addition to your solar system unit, tell the class that an unmanned spacecraft will soon be launched in order to look for intelligent life in outer space. Each student has been named "Chief of Communications" for the mission and must complete the following tasks:

- Make a series of drawings to be placed in the spacecraft. The drawings must inform intelligent beings about life on Earth.
- Write a paragraph explaining your pictures and why you included each one.
- Write directions on how to get to Earth. Include a map if desired.

Have students share their work during a special "Prelaunch Press Conference" in your classroom.

## Reusing Old Calendars

Does your 2000 calendar feature illustrations of famous art masterpieces? Then don't throw it away on January 1! Instead, use it to create a mini art gallery right in your classroom. Carefully clip the pictures apart and hang them in your room. Do mini units on the featured artists or hold informal art appreciation chats. Or use the photos to decorate your reading center or classroom library.

Melonie Zimmerman—Gr. 5
Lynn G. Haskin School
Sandwich, IL

## Unit Review Wreath

At the end of a unit, have the class brainstorm a list of facts and ideas they've learned. Then have each child illustrate one item from the list on a four-inch tagboard square. After each child shares his picture and summarizes the information it represents, attach his square to a Styrofoam® or cardboard wreath. Finish the wreath with a bow and a card labeled with the unit's title; then hang the wreath in your classroom. Make a new wreath for each unit you study. One glance at the colorful wreaths will remind students of all they've gotten "around" to learning this year!

Julie Alarie—Gr. 6
Essex Middle School
Essex, VT

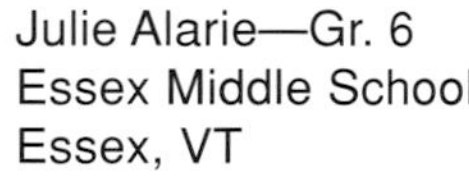

## Perky Pencil Holders

'Tis the season to recycle—your holiday greeting cards, that is! Save your holiday cards this year. Cut off the front panel from each card (be sure there's no writing on the back). Then punch two holes in the panel and insert a new pencil. Save these treats to give to next year's students in December.

Colleen Dabney, Williamsburg-JCC Public Schools
Williamsburg, VA

## Holiday Memories

For an unforgettable December display, ask each student to bring to school a photograph of herself taken during a past holiday celebration (the older the photo, the better!). Have the student attach the photo to a colorful cutout of a bell, stocking, ornament, dreidel, or other holiday decoration. Mount the decorations on a bulletin board or door with the title "Memories of Holidays Past."

Patricia Harkins—Gr. 5, Troup Magnet Academy of Science, New Haven, CT

## Removing Permanent Marker

Ever mistake a permanent marker for a water-based one? When this error happens, don't throw away your laminated materials or dry-erase board. Simply scribble over the permanent marker mistake with a dry-erase pen; then just wipe your boo-boo away!

Kim Chitwood—Gr. 4, Glade Hill Elementary, Glade Hill, VA

## Spelling Mystery Bag

If it's a mystery to you how spelling can be fun for students, try this idea! Label a gift bag "Spelling Mystery Bag." Inside, place small items that represent the week's spelling words. (For example, a letter to the editor cut from a newspaper for *persuade*.) Have a student select an item from the bag and decide on the spelling word it represents. If correct, have her spell the word while you write it on the board. If desired, save each spelling unit's items in a labeled plastic bag to use next year.

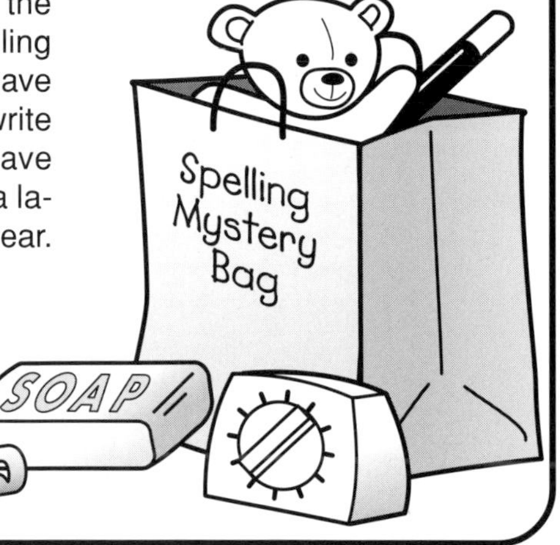


Marla Baldwin—Gr. 4
Gillis Elementary
Lake Charles, LA

## Math Hall of Fame

Fame's the name of the game with this math motivation idea! When a student masters her multiplication or division facts, scores 90% or higher on a math quiz, or meets another math-related goal, let her use a glitter pen to write her name on a cutout star. Then post the star in a hallway under a banner titled "Math Hall of Fame." Also send a certificate home with the student to recognize her bright accomplishment.

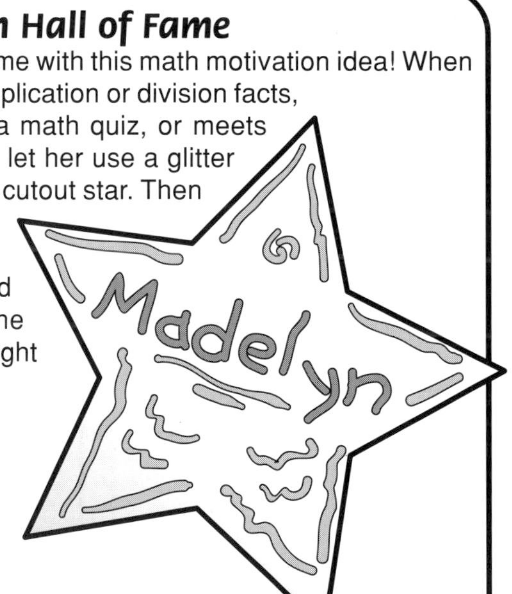


Leisa Boteler—Gr. 4
Florence Middle School
Florence, MS

Dear Becca,
The Golden Gate Bridge is in San Francisco, California. Did you know that California is known as the Golden State?
Love,
Aunt Piper
Becca Coleman
113 Hutchins Drive
Walton, NE 21200


## Family Postcard Project

Make your postcard exchange more meaningful for students with this family-friendly idea. Send home a survey asking each child (with a parent's help) to list family members who live in other states. Based on the survey results, assign a state to each student. Then have him write a letter to his relative requesting a postcard that depicts a landmark from the relative's state. Also have the student ask that a fact about the state be written on the back of the postcard. When excited students start getting responses to their letters, display the postcards on a bulletin board with a United States map.

Wendy Wanger—Gr. 5
St. Mary's School
Anderson, IN

## Yard Sale Assistance

Do you have parents who can't come to your classroom but still want to help out? Ask them to spend a few Saturdays rummaging through yard sales for inexpensive school supplies, costumes or props for school plays, and books and games for your classroom. They'll appreciate the chance to help, and you'll get some great stuff for your kids!

Patricia Glynn, Charlestown, MA

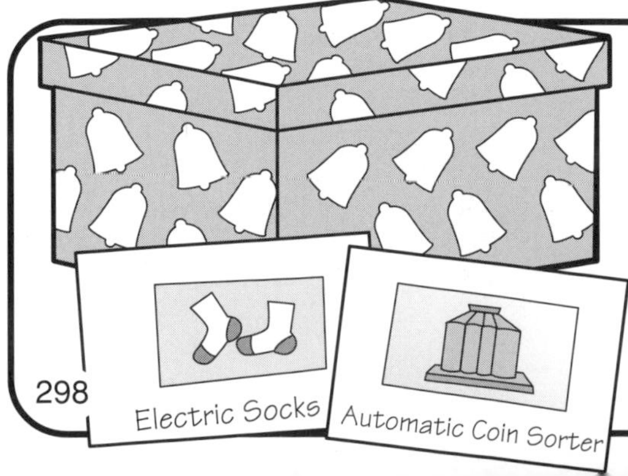


## Thanks a Lot!

Take advantage of December's focus on gift-giving with this fun activity on writing thank-you notes. Cut out pictures of unusual gifts from catalogs. Glue each picture to an index card. Then wrap a gift box and its lid with holiday paper, and place the cards inside. Ask each student to reach into the box, pull out a card, and write a note thanking you for the "gift." After the holidays, offer extra-credit points to each student who shows you a thank-you note she's written (but not yet mailed) to a relative or friend.

Kathy Moses—Gr. 4, Pocono Elementary Center, Tannersville, PA

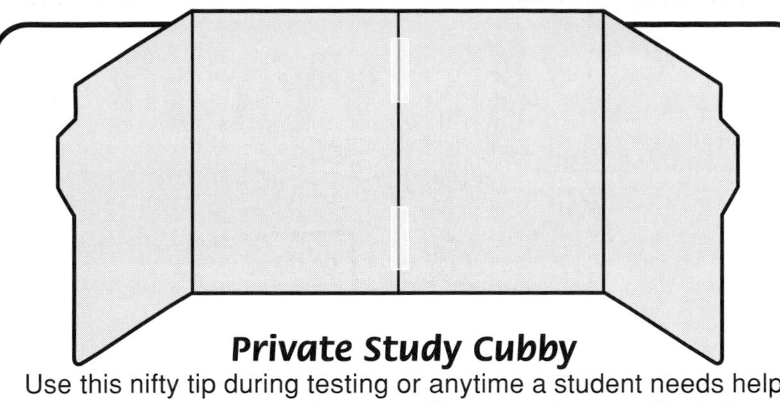

## Private Study Cubby

Use this nifty tip during testing or anytime a student needs help concentrating on an assignment. Tape together two file folders. Then stand them up on a student's desk as shown to create a private study cubby.

Angela Frazier—Gr. 6
Horace Mann Middle School
Brandon, FL

## The Most Beautiful Words

For a vocabulary lesson your kids will talk about for days, write these words on the board: *chimes, dawn, golden, hush, lullaby, melody, luminous, tranquil, mist,* and *murmuring.* Explain to students that an author selected these words as the ten most beautiful in the English language. Discuss the words together; then ask each student or small group to illustrate each one. Finally, ask each child to select ten words that he thinks are the most beautiful in the English language. Display the lists in a hallway with a blank sheet of chart paper on which schoolmates and staff members can add their own nominations.

Isobel Livingstone
Rahway, NJ

## Handy Behaviors

If building a positive classroom environment is the business at hand, have each student trace one of her hands onto colorful construction paper and cut out the tracing. Discuss with students behaviors that build a strong sense of community in the classroom. Then ask each child to write one idea on her cutout. Post the cutouts on a bulletin board titled "These Behaviors Deserve a Hand!"

I can help out my classmates when asked.
Ian


Julie Eick Granchelli—Gr. 4
Towne Elementary
Medina, NY

## Make a Better Map

If your students make relief maps, try this recipe for a dough that's both colorful and sweet-smelling! For each color of dough needed, mix one small box of fruit-flavored gelatin with two cups of flour and approximately $^{3}/_{4}$ cup of water. The dough will not only have a great consistency for molding, but it won't need to be painted to show different elevations.

Sandra Ramirez—Gr. 4
Monroe May Elementary
San Antonio, TX

## Picks of the Week

Build respect for the efforts of others with this easy-to-make display. Staple a 9" x 12" sheet of construction paper for each student on a bulletin board titled "Weekly Top [number of students in your class]." Have each student label a four-inch square of construction paper with his name; then have him decorate the square to resemble a CD cover. Attach the CDs as shown. Each week have each student select a piece of work to display on his frame. Place sticky notes nearby so students can write compliments and attach them to their classmates' papers.

Julie Eick Granchelli—Gr. 4

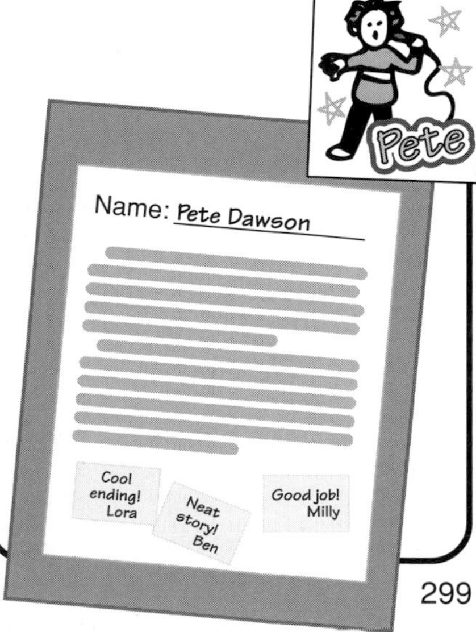


Name: Pete Dawson
Cool ending! Lora
Neat story! Ben
Good job! Milly

## Call Out!

Looking for an easy way to review vocabulary words your students learn throughout the year? When your class studies vocabulary for a new unit, ask one child to read aloud a new word's definition; then ask another student to write the definition on a large index card. Collect the card and label its back with a puzzle such as the one shown. Repeat with the other words. Then periodically play Call Out! with your ever-growing collection of word cards. To play, display the puzzle side of a card. The first student to call out the correct word earns a point. If he spells the word correctly, he earns another point. If students can't identify the word, read its definition aloud, but award only a half point for a correct answer.

Graciela Yugdar Tófalo—Gr. 6
Colegio Plaza Mayor
Buenos Aires, Argentina

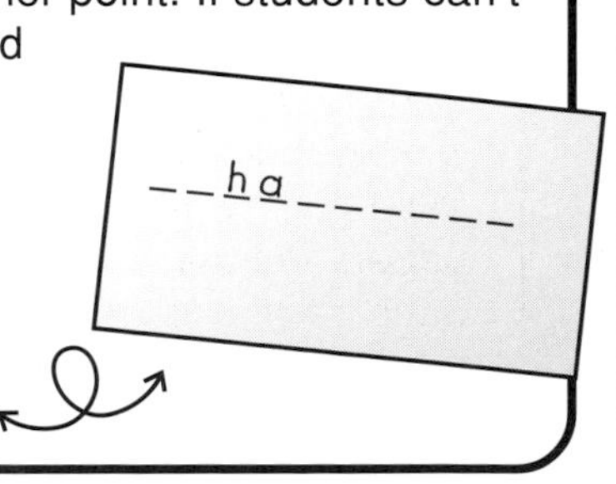

a person who lives in a particular place
(inhabitant)

# Our Readers Write

## Geography Challenge

Put your students' world geography skills on the map with this easy-to-do activity. Write the name of each continent on a separate sentence strip. Each morning give a strip to each of your student groups. During the day, point to a continent on a map or globe to indicate the group you want to line up or complete a task next. Rotate the strips so that groups are assigned different continents each day. Increase the difficulty of the challenge by labeling a new set of sentence strips with countries or bodies of water.

Cathy Butler
Shawnee Maplewood School
Lima, OH

Australia
South America

## Checkerboard Backgrounds

For bulletin boards that everyone will check out, try this simple tip. Instead of using one-color background paper, back your seasonal boards with two colors of construction paper sheets arranged in a checkerboard pattern. Use red and pink for Valentine's Day, green and white for St. Patrick's Day, orange and black for Halloween, etc. You'll be surprised at how easy it is to put up and take down this eye-catching background when you're ready to change a display.

Gosia Crane—Gr. 4
St. Kevin School
East Alton, IL

## It's About Time!

Help students determine elapsed time, stay on task, and get ready for standardized testing's time limits with this tip. Place an old, nonworking clock in your classroom. When you make an assignment, tell students how many minutes they have to complete the task. Together determine the exact time by which students should finish the assignment. Then set the nonworking clock to indicate this finishing time. Your students will love being able to compare the current time with the finishing time.

Denise Wood—Gr. 5
East Limestone Elementary
Athens, AL

## Great Lakes Reminder

Do your students use the "HOMES" mnemonic—Huron, Ontario, Michigan, Erie, Superior—to help them remember the names of the Great Lakes? Help them recall the lakes' locations from west to east with this super reminder: "Superman® helps everyone" (Superior, Michigan, Huron, Erie, Ontario).

Roberta Hite
Kokomo Christian School
Kokomo, IN

familiar

## Team Spelling Bee

Kids may love spelling bees, but teachers often hate that the number of participants dwindles as the game progresses. To solve this problem, give each child a small chalkboard slate, a piece of chalk, and an old sock (for erasing). Then divide the class into teams. Call out a word for all students to write on their slates. Then give a signal for everyone to display his slate. Award one point to each child who spells the word correctly; then total the points for each team before calling out the next word. With this variation, each student gets a chance to spell every word.

Elaine Sable—Gr. 4
Jefferson Elementary
Clairton, PA

## Amiable Adjectives

Review adjectives with a February display that boosts self-esteem while it practices parts of speech. Cut out a class supply of paper hearts. Label each heart with the name of a different student; then post the hearts on a bulletin board. Place a container of colorful fine-tipped markers near the display. Then instruct each student to write a different complimentary adjective on each classmate's heart. On Valentine's Day, let each student remove his heart from the display to take home.

Sarah Harkey—Gr. 5
Ebinport Elementary, Rock Hill, SC

## Synonym Songs

Encourage students to pick up a thesaurus or dictionary with this fun synonym activity. First, rewrite a familiar song by replacing some of the words with synonyms. For example, "Row, row, row your boat" may become "Paddle, paddle, paddle your vessel." Then share your new song with students and invite them to guess its identity. Next, have each pair of students select a different song and use a dictionary or thesaurus to rewrite it using synonyms. Students will be all grins as they try to guess each others' new songs!

Deborah West—Gr. 5
Ellicott City, MD

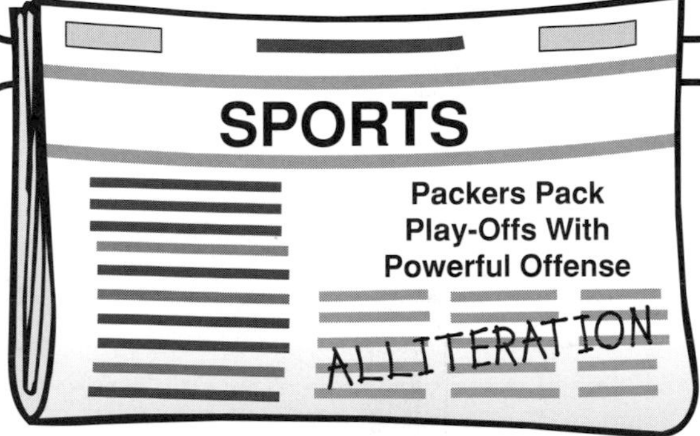

SPORTS
Packers Pack
Play-Offs With
Powerful Offense
ALLITERATION


## Hot Headlines

Don't toss those newspapers! Try using them to review figurative language. Place a stack of newspapers near a bulletin board titled "Hot Headlines." Invite students to scan the newspapers for headlines that use puns, idioms, or other types of figurative language. Have students cut out examples, label each with its form of figurative language, and post them on the display. What a scoop!

Kimberly Minafo—Gr. 4
Tooker Avenue Elementary
West Babylon, NY

## U.S. Collages

Familiarize students with the culture, landforms, and climate of the U.S. regions with this group collage project. In advance, have each student write a letter to a different state's department of tourism requesting information about the state. After the resources arrive (allow a few weeks), divide your class into five groups (Northeast, Southeast, Middle West, Southwest, West) and assign each group a different U.S. region. Have each group use the collected information on its assigned region to create a poster board collage. The displayed collages will create a terrific pictorial tour of the United States.

Domenick Renzi—Gr. 5, Bells Elementary
Turnersville, NJ

## Insect Alphabet Cards

Top off a unit on insects with this class research project. Assign each student a letter of the alphabet; then provide him with an oaktag strip, markers, and access to a variety of insect resources. Each student selects a type of insect or a fact about insects that begins with his assigned letter. Next, he draws his letter in bold type, illustrates his selected word or fact, and then writes a sentence about it. Post the finished cards in alphabetical order along a classroom wall. If desired, donate the cards to a younger class after taking them down.

Tarantula
Some tarantulas live more than 20 years.


Julie Alarie—Gr. 6
Essex Middle School
Essex, VT

## Mother's Day Keepsake Box

Transform an Altoids® mints tin into the perfect Mother's Day gift. Collect and spray-paint one tin for each student. Direct each student to decorate her tin using assorted craft items, such as ribbons, beads, and silk flowers. Next, have her write a short poem to glue inside the tin along with a picture of herself. Mom will love it!

Carry this close to your heart and we will never be far apart.


Jenny Jack—Gr. 4
Oxford Central School
Oxford, NJ

## You Bet Your Boots!

Check out this foot-stomping display for showing off your students' top-notch work. Title a bulletin board "You Bet Your Boots We're Smart!" and post a cowpoke character on the display. Also duplicate a supply of cowboy boot patterns. When grading students' work, attach a boot cutout to each exemplary paper. Then have each recipient color his boot and post it along with his assignment on the display.

Brandi Lampl—Gr. 4
Forest Park, GA

# Our Readers Write

## Picture-Perfect Work

Motivate picture-perfect work with this bulletin board alternative. Obtain a photo album containing full-size, nonpocketed pages. Label the album "Picture-Perfect Work" and decorate it as desired. Periodically select a student's outstanding writing, homework, test, or other classroom assignment to place in the album. If desired, allow each student to use permanent markers to personalize and autograph the pages containing his work. This album is ideal for sharing with visiting parents and classroom guests.

Miriam Krauss—Gr. 4
Beth Jacob Day School
Brooklyn, NY

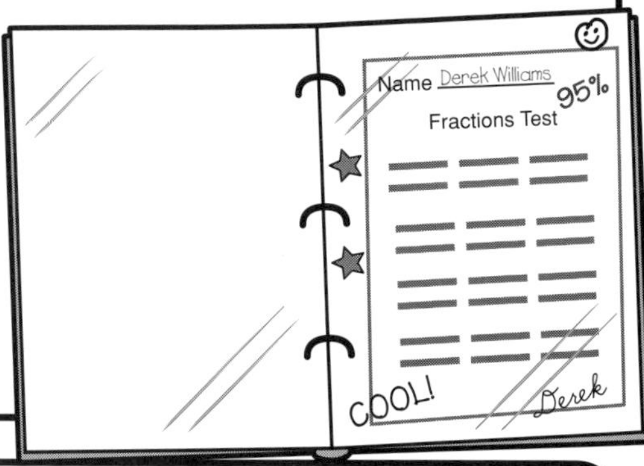
Name Derek Williams
95%
Fractions Test
COOL!
Derek

## More Than One Solution

Demonstrating that there is more than one way to solve a problem just hit the big screen! Provide each group of three or four students with an overhead transparency and transparency markers. Direct each group to work cooperatively to solve an assigned problem, showing its work on the transparency. After several minutes, invite a student volunteer from each group to present its problem-solving strategy and solution to the class using the overhead projector. Students will quickly see that one problem can be tackled in a variety of ways. Roll the credits, please!

Michelle Rosengrant—Grs. 5–6
Wingate Elementary
Wingate, PA

## Trail of Successes

For an attractive classroom display that recognizes student accomplishments, simply put one foot in front of the other! Post the words "Follow in Our Footsteps" on a classroom wall. Then duplicate a supply of different-colored construction paper footprint cutouts. Each time you want to honor a student for an individual accomplishment, have her write her name and achievement on a footprint cutout. Post each labeled footprint beside the title to form a trail of student successes. Throughout the year, your trail may snake across the walls, up the ceiling, and right out the classroom door!

Cathy Ogg
Happy Valley Elementary
Elizabethton, TN

Erik Stegall
I scored my first 100% on a science test.
Michelle Murphy
I won first place in the school spelling bee.

## Stay-Put Posters

Hang your posters using this handy tip and they'll stay on the walls, not your classroom floor. Punch one hole in the top left corner and one hole in the top right corner of the poster. Then measure between the two holes and mount two self-adhesive cup hooks (available at your local discount store) the same distance apart on the wall. To hang the poster, place each hook through a punched hole. Happy hanging!

Ellen Echols—Grs. 4–5
Crompond Elementary
Yorktown Heights, NY

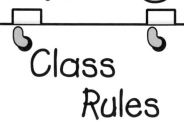

## A Cleaner Board

This easy-to-mix solution results in sparkling, clean chalkboards. Add a small amount of vinegar to a water-filled spray bottle. Then don rubber gloves, spritz your chalkboard with the solution, and wipe it clean with a sponge.

Sharon Sikes—Gr. 4, Russell Babb Elementary, Harrah, OK

I'm a great soccer player.
Andy

## Grade A Display

Take a crack at this student-made bulletin board idea for Easter. Give each student a large egg-shaped cutout. Have the student use watercolors, crayons, or markers to decorate his egg as desired, leaving an open space for writing. Next, instruct the student to write about one thing she does exceptionally well in the open space. Post each personalized egg on a bulletin board titled " 'Egg-ceptional' Students."

Theresa Roh Hickey—Grs. 4–5, Corpus Christi School, Mobile, AL

## How About a Pat on the Back?

Boost students' self-esteem with this class activity. Direct each student to trace her hand onto a sheet of unlined paper, label it with her name, and then tape the tracing on her back. Allow students 15 minutes to circulate around the room and write a compliment on or around each student's hand tracing. When time is up, each student removes her tracing from her back and mounts it on construction paper. Post the finished papers on a classroom wall. Students will be all smiles as they read the "hand-y" compliments from their peers.

Allison Beall—Gr. 4, Crawford Elementary, Eielson A.F.B., AK

## Identifying Cause and Effect

Here's a simple game for identifying cause and effect relationships. Divide your class into groups of five. Provide each group with five letter-sized envelopes and five index cards. Have each student think of a cause and effect relationship found in a story that she has recently read. Then have her write her cause on the front of an envelope and her effect on an index card. Next, have groups trade envelopes and their shuffled cards with another group. Challenge each group to match the causes with their effects by placing the correct cards in the matching envelopes. The effect? Students reinforce an important comprehension skill!

Simone Lepine—Gr. 5
Fayetteville, NY

## Wanted: Class Helpers

Searching for a class-helper chart that will really get the job done? Consider the position filled! Glue an employment page of an old newspaper to a sheet of poster board. Write each classroom job and its description on a different index card. Glue each card to a slightly larger piece of black paper; then glue each card to the poster as shown. Add the title "Help Wanted" and laminate the poster. Each week, assign jobs by using a wipe-off marker to write students' names on the cards. Wipe the cards clean at the end of the week so they can be reprogrammed with new names on Monday.

Yvonne Sturdivant—Gr. 6
Guy-Perkins Elementary
Guy, AR

## The Great State Challenge

Help students learn the locations and spellings of the U.S. states with this self-checking, interactive display. Use an overhead projector to enlarge a U.S. map to fit a hallway bulletin board. Post the map on the board and have student volunteers label the name of each state. Next, use large Post-it® Brand notes to cover each state's name. Challenge your students, as well as those from other classes, to correctly identify each state. Students simply lift up the notes to check their answers. After students have mastered the locations and spellings, label and cover each state's capital for a new challenge.

Kris Call—Gr. 5
St. Joseph School
Decatur, IN

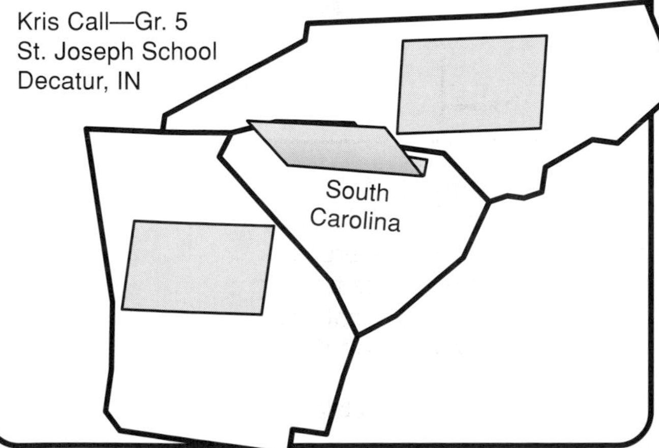


Nick

## Whale of an Incentive Program

Make a big splash with this classroom incentive program! Use a die-cutter to create a supply of whale cutouts. Each time a student exhibits exemplary behavior or work habits, present him with a cutout to recognize a whale of a good job. Direct students to sign the whales they receive and store them in a safe place. Throughout the year, ask parents to donate small incentives, such as bookmarks, magnets, stickers, and used books. Then periodically hold an auction during which students use their collected whales to buy the assorted donations.

Anne Nichol—Gr. 4
West Madison Elementary
Madison, AL

## You Oughta Be in Pictures!

Want to beat the rainy day recess blues? Play a videotape filmed from a field trip or other special event during the school year. It's a great way to reminisce, and your students will love seeing themselves on video. Didn't film any videos this year? Make a note now in your back-to-school plans to ask a parent volunteer to videotape each special event during the next school year.

Sherri McWhorter—Gr. 4
Fowler Drive Elementary, Athens, GA

## Spell Check Checkup

Do your students think using a computer's spell check is a fail-safe method of proofing their work? Perform this checkup on your spell check to help them see otherwise. Next time your class is in the computer lab, have each student type "Ewe can dew it" into the word-processing program and run the spell check. Then have each student repeat the process with "Eye no you can." Point out that the spell check returned no spelling errors because these errors are actually mistakes in word usage. After discussing other ways to proof their work, challenge students to create similar sentences to check with the spell check. What a great way to review homophones!

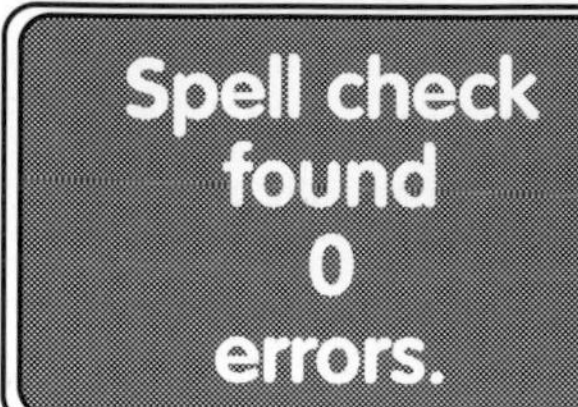

Isobel L. Livingstone, Rahway, NJ

## Fall Preview

This end-of-the-year activity gives next year's class a sneak peek at what's to come. Invite the students from your upcoming class to spend an afternoon in your classroom before the end of the year. Pair each guest with one of your students to ensure that everyone feels welcome. In addition to any special activities you may plan, allow time for students to share their tips or advice for next year with their visitors. The time these new students spend in your class now is sure to ease the transition when you meet in the fall.

Julie Maffett, Plantation, FL

## Character Report Cards

REPORT CARD

Name ____________

| Character Quality | A | B | C | D | F |
|---|---|---|---|---|---|
| 1. kindness | | | | | |
| 2. courageousness | | | | | |
| 3. patience | | | | | |
| 4. resourcefulness | | | | | |
| 5. thankfulness | | | | | |
| 6. intelligence | | | | | |
| 7. strength | | | | | |
| 8. talent | | | | | |
| 9. determination | | | | | |
| 10. contentment | | | | | |

Additional Comments:

Students will give this character-development activity high marks! After your class finishes reading a novel, give each student a character evaluation report card similar to the one shown. The student grades the book's main character by placing a check under the appropriate letter grade for each quality. These simple checklists will lead to an A+ discussion of the character as well as the book's main events.

Colleen Dabney
Williamsburg-JCC Public Schools, Williamsburg, VA

## People Posters

Help students remember important persons' names and their contributions by creating people posters. Simply label a sheet of chart paper "People Poster" and hang it in your classroom. Each time students learn about a historical person, add his or her name and contribution to the poster. If you are studying multiple topics that involve famous persons, create a separate poster for each topic. Throughout your units, students will appreciate having this important information close at hand.

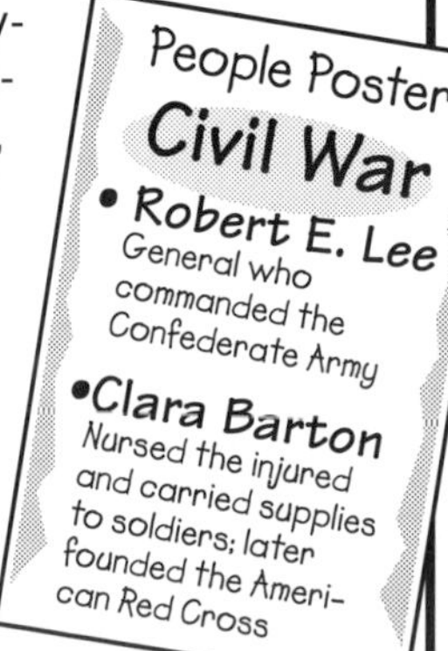

People Poster
Civil War
• Robert E. Lee
General who commanded the Confederate Army
• Clara Barton
Nursed the injured and carried supplies to soldiers; later founded the American Red Cross


Jennifer Apgar
Believers' Chapel
School Cicero, NY

## Space Suit Fashion Show

Challenge your students with an out-of-this-world activity while studying the planets. Divide your class into eight groups (one per planet excluding Earth). Each group researches its planet, noting in particular its temperature and surface conditions. The group then designs a space suit that would enable a person to explore its assigned planet. Next, the group uses household materials to create a prototype of its design and writes a script describing its features. After all eight suits have been created, invite parents and other classes to a space suit fashion show set to the music of *Star Wars*.

Brenda Keller—Gr. 5, Canadochly Elementary, Prospect, PA

## Understanding the Date Line

Try this visual aid to help students understand the International Date Line. Draw the two diagrams shown on the chalkboard. Explain that Diagram 1 reminds you that the date just to the west of the International Date Line is one day *later* (tomorrow) than the date just to the east of the line. Diagram 2 reminds you that just to the east of the International Date Line is one day *earlier* (yesterday) than the date just to the west of the line.

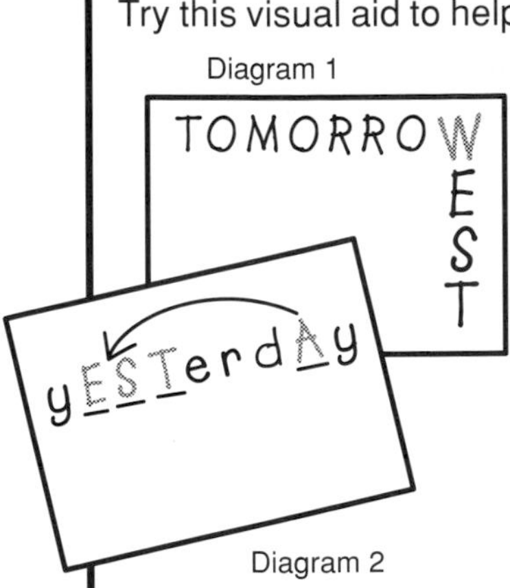


Christine Coleman, Poland, OH

## Flower Power

Use the power of flowers to work on your students' geography and language skills. Ask a local florist for donations or enlist help from parent volunteers to feature a class flower of the week. Each week bring a different flower into the classroom. Have students research the flower's native habitat, how the climate affects its growth, and the continent or region of its origin. Not only will students sharpen their research and vocabulary skills, but they'll also become more observant and learn to appreciate the beauty around them.

Zaheerah Shakir—Principal
Cedar Grove Elementary
Ellenwood, GA

## Going to the Moon!

This five-minute filler builds critical-thinking, problem-solving, and classification skills. Secretly decide on a category such as state capitals, nouns, or vertebrates. Then announce, "I'm going to the moon and I'm taking a [word that fits category]." In turn, have each student repeat the sentence, substituting a word that she thinks fits the category. (See the examples shown for the category vertebrates.) Respond to each student's guess with "Yes, you may go to the moon" if her word fits the category or "No, you may not go" if her word does not. Continue until each child has had a turn.

Sarah L. Malick—Gr. 5, L. O. Donald Elementary, Dallas, TX

**Teacher:** I'm going to the moon, and I'm taking a bird.
**Student #1:** I'm going to the moon, and I'm taking a worm.
**Teacher:** No, you may not go.
**Student #2:** I'm going to the moon, and I'm taking a cat.
**Teacher:** Yes, you may go to the moon.

## Welcome Video

Use the stars of this year's class to create the perfect welcome for next year's students. Have each child write a paragraph explaining a little about your class this year. Encourage students to include information such as books they read, field trips they took, topics they studied, and any advice for a successful school year. Videotape each student reading his paragraph; then tuck the video away until fall. On the first day of school next year, play the video for your new students. They will love hearing some survival tips from last year's gang!

Jodi Ann Filut—Gr. 4, St. Roman School, Milwaukee, WI

## End-of-the-Year Books

Send students off at the close of the school year with books they'll treasure! For each child, bind together a book containing a few of his work samples, a poem and a letter you've written for the class, and an award that reflects his personality or a funny memory of the year, such as the True Friend Award, Most Erasers Used Award, or Future Comedian Award. Present each student with his book in a just-for-fun award ceremony.

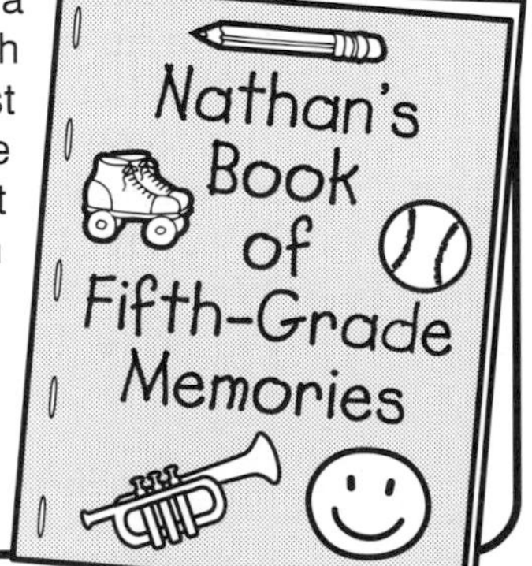


Jennifer Bruce—Gr. 5
East Sparta Elementary
East Sparta, OH

## Secrets of Success Series

Motivate your students toward success by creating your own Secrets of Success book series. First, brainstorm a list of traits or skills necessary for success, such as study skills, organization, and motivation. Label a folder for each topic. Next, discuss with students how we can learn a lot about success from other successful people. Invite each student (and former students, if possible) to write down their tips for success and place them in the appropriate folder. Also ask students and parents to help you collect stories, quotes, and cartoons that fit each topic. Place each collection of topic-related items in its own labeled magnetic photo album. Then store this special series of books on a classroom shelf so students can borrow them whenever they need some encouragement.

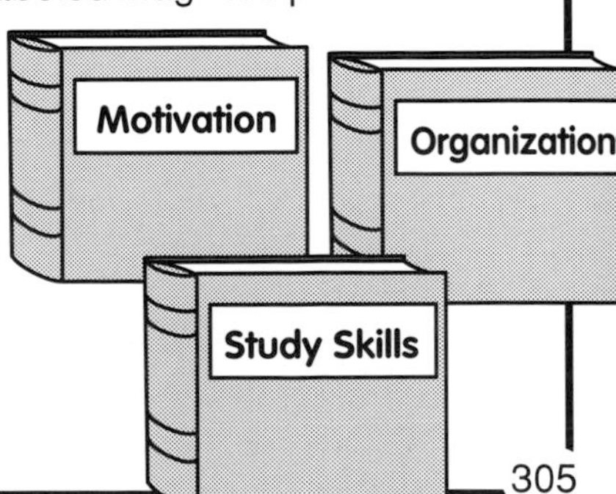


Kimberly Minafo—Gr. 4
Tooker Avenue Elementary
West Babylon, NY

# Answer Keys

**Page 55**

| | |
|---|---|
| 1. bicycles' wheels | 11. mice's cheese |
| 2. lions' cubs | 12. deer's fawns |
| 3. geese's gaggle | 13. moose's calves |
| 4. women's dresses | 14. cowboys' horses |
| 5. policemen's uniforms | 15. countries' flags |
| 6. children's toys | 16. radios' antennas |
| 7. books' pages | 17. houses' mailboxes |
| 8. teeth's enamel | 18. trout's stream |
| 9. trees' branches | 19. sheep's lambs |
| 10. songs' notes | 20. roofs' shingles |

**Page 60**

| | | | | |
|---|---|---|---|---|
| 1. ache | 6. faster | 11. kale | 16. paws | 21. use |
| 2. brief | 7. granite | 12. laces | 17. quote | 22. vase |
| 3. coins | 8. hinge | 13. meteor | 18. respect | 23. when |
| 4. denied | 9. itself | 14. night | 19. sheet | 24. yard |
| 5. edit | 10. jar | 15. ought | 20. tens | 25. zebra |

**Bonus Box answers:** bates: abets, baste, beast, beats, betas; tares: rates, stare, tears; poser: pores, prose, ropes, spore; seton: notes, onset, stone, tones

**Page 72**
Correct path: 1, 2, 3, 4, 9, 14, 13, 12, 11, 10, 15, 20, 21, 22, 23

| | | | | |
|---|---|---|---|---|
| | 1. Jason is planning to visit his friend Alan. | 2. They're going on a camping trip together. | 3. Andy and his friends ate at their favorite restaurant. | 4. Is he holding up two fingers or three? |
| 5. Put the glass down over their. | 6. Is that they're dog running down the street? | 7. There playing a soccer game at four o'clock. | 8. We want too bake five dozen cookies. | 9. Kendra will go there on her vacation. |
| 10. On Saturday, they're cleaning the garage. | 11. There are many different breeds of dogs. | 12. Their cat Snowball is completely white. | 13. Beth wants to compete in the swim meet. | 14. They're the best of friends. |
| 15. You can't help but laugh when they're telling jokes. | 16. Park your bicycle over their. | 17. We stopped at the twins' house too say hello. | 18. That team wants two win the basketball championship. | 19. They're coach is a nice guy. |
| 20. Look! There goes a shooting star! | 21. There must be at least 20 different colors in that shirt! | 22. Is it time to go? | 23. They're having tryouts for junior-league basketball next week. | You helped Bee-Bop Bing find his spaceship! |

*Corrected sentences:*

5. Put the glass down over **there.**
6. Is that **their** dog running down the street?
7. **They're** playing a soccer game at four o'clock.
8. We want **to** bake five dozen cookies.
16. Park your bicycle over **there**.
17. We stopped at the twins' house **to** say hello.
18. That team wants **to** win the basketball championship.
19. **Their** coach is a nice guy.

**Page 73**
Sentence fragments: 3, 5, 7, 10, 13, 14
Run-on sentences: 2, 4, 11, 12, 15
Rambling sentences: 1, 6, 8, 9

*Rewritten sentences may vary. Run-on sentences may also be corrected by using a comma and a conjunction.*

1. Shandra went to the basketball court. She played a game with Lianne. Then they went to Shandra's house for something to eat.
2. The dog chased his tail. He went around and around in a circle.
3. (Any person or persons) went to the bowling alley with friends.
4. Jake's class went on a field trip. They went to the aquarium.
5. (Any person or persons) knew my friend Kayla from school.
6. The football game was tied. Eric kicked a field goal during the final quarter. His field goal won the game.
7. (Any male person) ran to the store as fast as he could.
8. The computer is a good tool. It can help you get information for reports. Computers can help you make charts and graphs.
9. Lee has a guinea pig. It is cute. The guinea pig has a funny name. Lee calls it Squeaky.
10. My cousin Sharon (any sensible main verb) in my mother's chair.
11. Jon's grandmother is from Russia. She speaks Russian to him all the time.
12. The bus driver got lost. We were 20 minutes late getting to the museum.
13. (Any person) drove my brother and me to the skating rink.
14. The man on the bus (any sensible predicate).
15. Erica's sister stood in line for hours to get tickets to a rock concert. She got third-row seats.

**Page 88**
**Part One:** Students' definitions of the words they form will vary.
**Station 1:** tooth, paste, rain, coat
toothrain, toothcoat, pasterain, pastecoat, pastetooth, raintooth, rainpaste, coattooth, coatpaste, coatrain
**Station 2:** ear, drum, sun, glasses
earsun, earglasses, drumear, drumsun, drumglasses, sunear, sundrum, glassesear, glassesdrum, glassessun
**Station 3:** cup, cake, moon, light
cupmoon, cuplight, cakecup, cakemoon, cakelight, mooncup, mooncake, lightcup, lightcake, lightmoon
**Station 4:** bath, tub, air, plane
bathair, bathplane, tubbath, tubair, tubplane, airbath, airtub, planebath, planetub, planeair
**Part Two:** Students' answers will vary. Suggested compound words for each word are
**pay:** paycheck, payday, payload, pay phone, payoff, payroll, pay–TV
**tie:** necktie, tie-dye
**care:** carefree, caregiver, caretaker, day care
**color:** color-blind, colorfast
**wind:** windbag, windblown, windbreaker, windchill, windfall, windmill, windpipe, windshield, windstorm, windsurf, windswept
**sun:** sunbath, sunbathe, sunbeam, sunblock, sunburn, Sunday, sundeck, sundial, sundown, sundress, sundries, sunflower, sunglasses, sunlamp, sunlight, sunporch, sunrise, sunscreen, sunset, sunshine, sunspot, sunstroke, suntan

**Page 89**

1. Students' answers will vary.
2. a & b:
   **un-**: untie, unwind, untying, unwinding, uncaring
   **re-**: repay, retie, recolor, rewind, rewinder, repaying, recoloring, rewinding, retying
   **dis-**: discolor, discoloring
   **over-**: overpay, overwind, overpaying, overwinding
   **pre-**: prepay, prepaying
   **-ful**: careful, colorful
   **-less**: careless, colorless, sunless, tieless
   **-ing**: paying, tying, caring, coloring, winding, sunning, uncaring, unwinding, untying, repaying, retying, rewinding, recoloring, discoloring, overpaying, overwinding, prepaying
   **-er**: payer, carer, colorer, winder, rewinder
   **-y**: sunny, windy
   c. Students' conclusions will vary. Students could mention that the words have the meanings of the prefixes and suffixes in common. The meanings of the prefixes and suffixes as used in the words at the left:
   **un-:** do the opposite of; **re-:** again, back; **dis-:** opposite or absence of; **over-:** to exceed or surpass; **pre-:** in advance, beforehand; **-ful:** full of; **-less:** not having; **-ing:** action or process; **-er:** one that does or performs; **-y:** state, condition, quality
3. Students' answers and sentences may vary. Accept all reasonable responses. Suggested definitions and possible sentences:
   a. wealthy or rich; Someone who is moneyful is wealthy.
   b. without desks; If classrooms were deskless, they would have no desks.
   c. baked twice, baked again; A person would probably not want to eat a cake that has been rebaked because it might taste dry or burnt.
   d. not a cat; An uncat would be any animal that is not a cat.
   e. having to do with music; If I were feeling musicy, I could sing or hum.
   f. like a fish; If someone said I swam fishly, I'd be pleased because I'd be swimming like a fish.
   g. playing a piano; If I were pianoing, I'd be playing a piano.
   h. someone who grows, harvests, or sells pumpkins; A pumpkineer would make a living by growing, harvesting, or selling pumpkins.

**Bonus Box answer:** Students' words will vary. Possible words include *nonfat, nonfiction, coauthor, copilot, goodness, carelessness, artist, pianist,* etc.

**Page 90**

| | |
|---|---|
| 1. do + n + 't = don't; do not | 9. Se + n = Sen.; Senator |
| 2. you + 're = you're; you are | 10. M + r = Mr.; mister |
| 3. I + 'm = I'm; I am | 11. h + r = hr.; hour |
| 4. the + y + 're = they're; they are | 12. S + ep + t = Sept.; September |
| 5. he + 's = he's; he is | 13. W + ed = Wed.; Wednesday |
| 6. won + 't = won't; will not | 14. q + t = qt.; quart |
| 7. co + u + ld + n't = couldn't; could not | 15. b + l + v + d = blvd.; boulevard |
| 8. is + n + 't = isn't; is not | |

**Bonus Box answer:** Students' answers will vary.

**Page 94**

**Part 2:** The square and three rectangles are shown below. Accept two other possible rectangles as well: 10 cm x 2 cm (A = 20 sq. cm) and 11 cm x 1 cm (A = 11 sq. cm). The largest shape is the square with an area of 36 sq. cm.

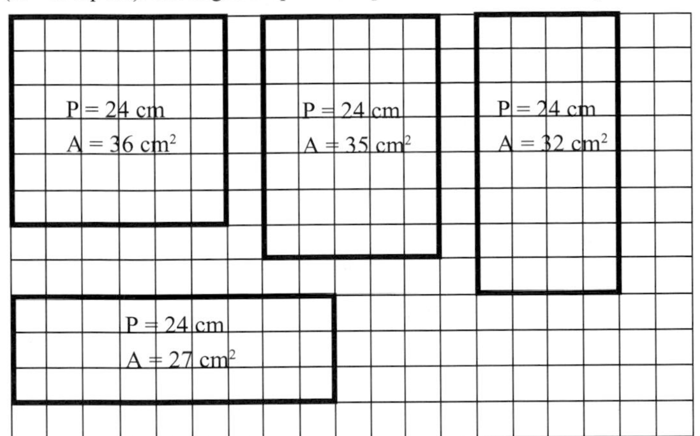


**Page 95**

The crime:

| perimeter/area | letter |
|---|---|
| 84 ft./216 ft.² | K |
| 40 ft./96 ft.² | I |
| 60 ft./216 ft.² | L |
| 108 ft./288 ft.² | L |
| 48 ft./108 ft.² | I |
| 36 ft./72 ft.² | N |
| 84 ft./432 ft.² | G |
| 84 ft./96 ft.² | |
| 72 ft./180 ft.² | T |
| 72 ft./324 ft.² | I |
| 96 ft./252 ft.² | M |
| 44 ft./120 ft.² | E |

**Bonus Box answers:**
P = **192 ft.** (4 x 48)
A = **2,304 ft.²** (48 x 48)

**Page 96**

1. **P = 48 ft.** Since the area of the rug is 80 sq. ft., the area of each section is 16 sq. ft. If the area of each small section is 16 sq. ft. and each section is a square, then each side is 4 ft. 4 ft. x 12 sides = 48 ft.
2. The largest possible garden is a 9 ft. x 9 ft. square with an area of **81 sq. ft.**
3. **72 cards:** 36 ÷ 4 = 9; 48 ÷ 6 = 8; 9 x 8 = 72 or 36 ÷ 6 = 6; 48 ÷ 4 = 12; 6 x 12 = 72
4. **P = 60 in.** Since the area of the square sheet is 400 sq. in., each side must be 20 in. Then the dimensions of each rectangle are 20 in. x 10 in. Perimeter = 20 in. + 10 in. + 20 in. + 10 in., or 60 in.
5. **A = 1,400 sq. ft.** There are several ways to solve this problem. One way is to subtract the area of the small rectangle, the pool (80 x 50 = 4,000 sq. ft.), from the area of the large rectangle (90 x 60 = 5,400 sq. ft. Ten feet is added to each dimension to include the width of the sidewalk.). Another way is to divide the sidewalk into sections and find the area of each section, as shown below.

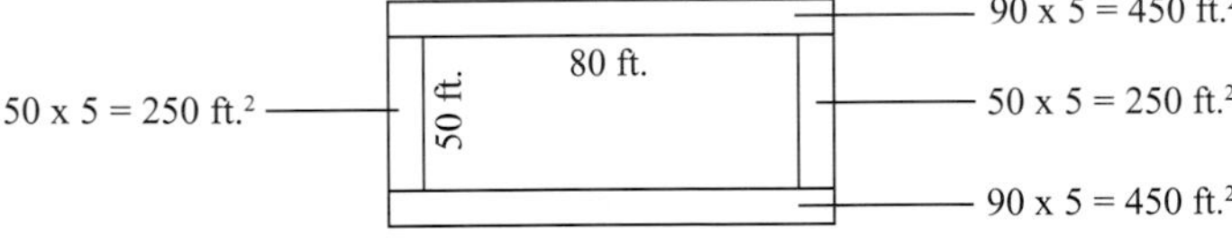


6. **P = 20 yd.** Since the area of the square is 144 sq. yd., each side is 12 yd. long. The length of each rectangle is 6 yd. (half of 12) and the width of each rectangle is 4 yd. (one-third of 12). So the perimeter of each rectangle is 2 (6 yd. + 4 yd.).
7. **A = 100 sq. ft.** By cutting out each section of the garden and placing them together, a square is formed. Since each side of the square is 10 ft., 10 ft. x 10 ft. = 100 sq. ft.
8. **P = 48 ft.; A = 108 sq. ft.**

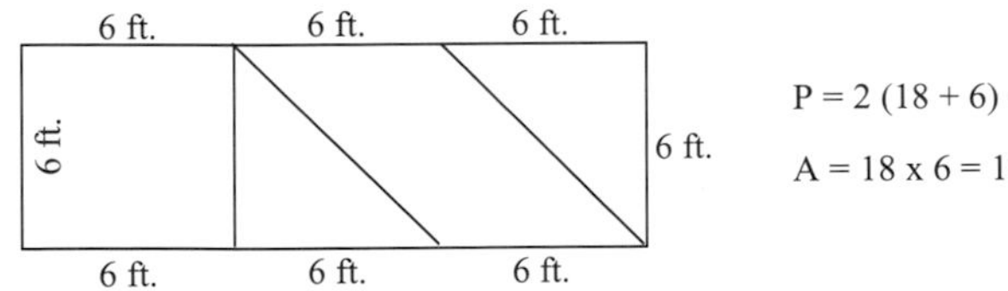


P = 2 (18 + 6) = 48 ft.

A = 18 x 6 = 108 ft.²

**Bonus Box answer:** A square whose area and perimeter are the same must have sides that are each 4 units long; then P = 4 x 4 = 16 units and A = 4 x 4 = 16 sq. units.

**Page 97**

| | | |
|---|---|---|
| Cubah: V = 729 in.³ | Punko: V = 420 cm³ | Gizmo: V = 350 cm³ |
| Lefty: V = 896 cm³ | Rubick: V = 343 ft.³ | Boxman: V = 576 mm³ |
| Righty: V = 756 in.³ | Harpo: V = 4,320 mm³ | Prizm: V = 264 ft.³ |

The crook is **Gizmo.** (Gizmo's dimensions are in centimeters, not millimeters. Also, the answers 27 in.³, 720 mm³, and 3,500 cm³ are not used.)

**Page 102**

| Pizza | Circumference | Diameter | Circumference ÷ Diameter |
|---|---|---|---|
| Pepperoni | 9.5" | 3" | 3.17 |
| Black olive | 5" | 1.5" | 3.33 |
| Cheese | 3" | 1" | 3 |
| Anchovy | 1.5" | .5" | 3 |
| Green pepper | 6.5" | 2" | 3.25 |
| Mushroom | 7.5" | 2.5" | 3 |

**Bonus Box answer:** Students' sentences will vary but should mention that the circumference is about three times the diameter.

**Page 103**

**Part 1: Answers may vary slightly.**

1. a. 33 whole squares, 10 partial squares
   b. 5 sq. units
   c. 38 sq. units
   d. 152 sq. units
2. a. 56 whole squares, 13 partial squares
   b. 7 sq. units
   c. 63 sq. units
   d. 252 sq. units

**Part 2:** Accept all reasonable estimates:
For a radius of 5 sq. units: estimated area = 76 to 84 sq. units
For a radius of 6 sq. units: estimated area = 112 to 120 sq. units
For a radius of 3 sq. units: estimated area = 24 to 32 sq. units

**Bonus Box answer:** Answers will vary. If a student didn't use the method outlined in Part 1, he might have used this method:
1. Count all of the whole squares in the circle.
2. Count the partial squares and divide by 2.
3. Add the answers to 1 and 2 together.

**Page 104**

**Part 1:**
1. sausage and extra cheese
2. 4 different combinations: pepperoni and anchovies; pepperoni and mushrooms; mushrooms and anchovies; pepperoni, mushrooms, and anchovies

**Part 2:** Students' choices of two and three toppings for the overlapping pizzas will vary.

**Page 107**

**"Looking for Gold!"**

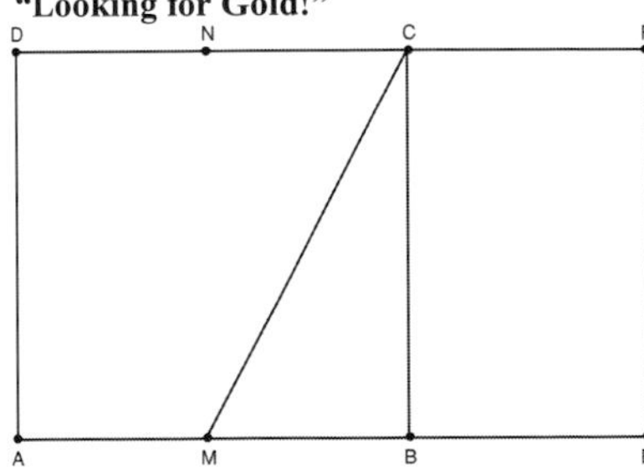


**"A Puzzling Pair"**

Puzzle 1: The checkerboard is made up of 204 squares.

| | |
|---|---|
| 1 x 1 squares: | 64 |
| 2 x 2 squares: | 49 |
| 3 x 3 squares: | 36 |
| 4 x 4 squares: | 25 |
| 5 x 5 squares: | 16 |
| 6 x 6 squares: | 9 |
| 7 x 7 squares: | 4 |
| 8 x 8 squares: | 1 |
| **total:** | 204 |

When sharing this solution with your students, have them note a pattern: the totals are equal to the squares of the numbers 1–8. Based on this pattern, ask students to determine the number of squares that would make up a checkerboard that is 5 x 5. *(55 squares)* 10 x 10? *(385 squares)*

Puzzle 2: The shape has 16 triangles: a, b, c, d, e, f, bc, ed, af, fab, abc, bcd, cde, def, efa, and abcdef.

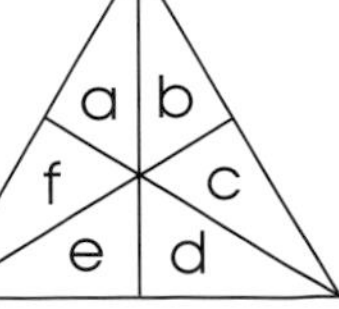

**Page 109**

**Answer Key**
Answers will vary. Many terms are illustrated several times each.

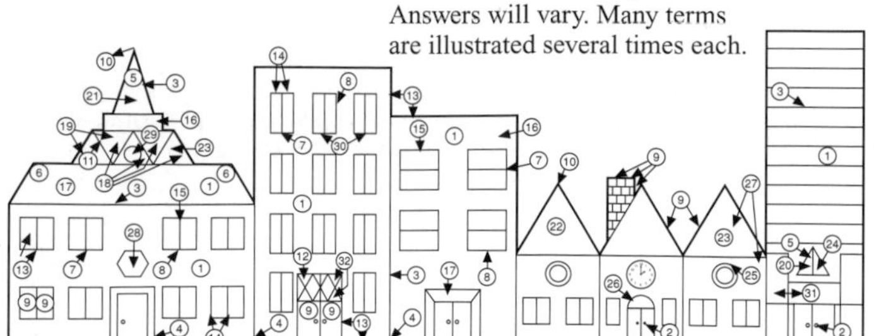

**Bonus Box answer:** Answers may vary. Suggested answers include:
- 2nd building (rectangle) is similar to 3rd building (rectangle)
- circular doorknobs are similar to clock and circle on each side of clock
- 1st building door is similar to its door frame
- 4th building roofs (three equilateral triangles) are all similar to the triangle above the 5th building's door
- 1st building windows (rectangles) are similar to rectangular front of the building

**Page 113**
Part II:
A = 7; B = 9; C = 8; D = 0; E = 6; F = 1; G = 3; H = 5; I = 4; J = 2

**Explanations**
1. F = 1 (Identity property: The only number times J that equals J is 1.)
4. J = 2 (F + F)
5. I = 4 (J + J)
6. D = 0 (If E were 1, D could represent any digit. But 1 has been used.)
7. G = 3 (I – F, or 4 – 1)
8. H = 5 (H could be 4, 5, or 6. Only 5 will work: 3 x 5 = 15.)
9. B = 9 and E = 6 (The remaining digits are 6, 7, 8, and 9. The two that work are 9 and 6: 9 – 3 = 6.)
3. C = 8 and A = 7 (C – A = 1)

**Page 114**
Input/output numbers are listed from top to bottom.
**Part I**
2. rule: + 7; I/O: 12, 17, 14
3. rule: x 4; I/O: 2, 32
4. rule: ÷ 5; I/O: 2, 4, 9

**Part II**
6. rule: + 6, ÷ 2 (or ÷ 2, + 3); I/O: 14, 7
7. rule: x 3, + 5; I/O: 5, 10
8. rule: – 4, x 2; I/O: 34, 5

**Part III**
9. rule: + 1, ÷ 3; I/O: 6, 29
10. rule: x 2, + 5; I/O: 7, 45

**Bonus Box answer:** Students' answers will vary.

**Page 115**
1. $\frac{4}{z}$
2. 5 (p – q)
3. m – 6
4. 3f
5. 16 – y + 5
6. b + 5
7. $\frac{4v}{2}$
8. 2k + 4
9. 10 + j
10. 12 – w
11. 5 (6 + u)
12. 8s
13. $\frac{n}{2}$
14. 6 (c + d)
15. 3p – 5
16. $2(\frac{3}{x})$

**Answer to riddle:** gator hole

**Page 124**
1. 4 of tile c = $^{4}/_{9}$
   4 of tile g = $^{4}/_{9}$
   1 of tile e = $^{1}/_{9}$
2. 4 of tile c = $^{4}/_{9}$
   4 of tile f = $^{4}/_{9}$
   1 of tile e = $^{1}/_{9}$
3. 4 of tile b = $^{4}/_{9}$
   4 of tile a = $^{4}/_{9}$
   1 of tile f = $^{1}/_{9}$
4. 8 of tile d = $^{8}/_{16}$ or $^{1}/_{2}$
   8 of tile g = $^{8}/_{16}$ or $^{1}/_{2}$
5. 4 of tile a = $^{4}/_{16}$ or $^{1}/_{4}$
   8 of tile b = $^{8}/_{16}$ or $^{1}/_{2}$
   4 of tile g = $^{4}/_{16}$ or $^{1}/_{4}$

**Bonus Box answer:** Tile h was not used in any of the designs.

**Page 125**
1. e ($^{10}/_{24} = {}^{5}/_{12}$; $^{14}/_{24} = {}^{7}/_{12}$)
2. d ($^{16}/_{20} = {}^{4}/_{5}$; $^{4}/_{20} = {}^{1}/_{5}$)
3. f ($^{6}/_{18} = {}^{1}/_{3}$; $^{9}/_{18} = {}^{1}/_{2}$; $^{3}/_{18} = {}^{1}/_{6}$)
4. a ($^{14}/_{28} = {}^{1}/_{2}$; $^{14}/_{28} = {}^{1}/_{2}$)
5. i ($^{20}/_{48} = {}^{5}/_{12}$; $^{16}/_{48} = {}^{1}/_{3}$; $^{12}/_{48} = {}^{1}/_{4}$)
6. c ($^{20}/_{30} = {}^{2}/_{3}$; $^{10}/_{30} = {}^{1}/_{3}$)
7. b ($^{5}/_{15} = {}^{1}/_{3}$; $^{5}/_{15} = {}^{1}/_{3}$; $^{5}/_{15} = {}^{1}/_{3}$)
8. j ($^{12}/_{32} = {}^{3}/_{8}$; $^{4}/_{32} = {}^{1}/_{8}$; $^{4}/_{32} = {}^{1}/_{8}$; $^{4}/_{32} = {}^{1}/_{8}$; $^{8}/_{32} = {}^{1}/_{4}$)
9. h ($^{3}/_{12} = {}^{1}/_{4}$; $^{3}/_{12} = {}^{1}/_{4}$; $^{4}/_{12} = {}^{1}/_{3}$; $^{2}/_{12} = {}^{1}/_{6}$)
10. g ($^{24}/_{36} = {}^{2}/_{3}$; $^{9}/_{36} = {}^{1}/_{4}$; $^{3}/_{36} = {}^{1}/_{12}$)

**Bonus Box answer:** The least common denominator of 2, 3, 4, 5, 6, 8, and 12 is 120.

**Page 126**
1. $^{3}/_{7}$, $^{4}/_{5}$, $^{9}/_{10}$
2. $^{7}/_{8}$, $^{1}/_{9}$, $^{2}/_{3}$
3. $^{3}/_{5}$, $^{17}/_{20}$, $^{4}/_{9}$
4. $^{3}/_{5}$, $^{12}/_{20}$, $^{6}/_{10}$
5. $^{3}/_{4}$, $^{12}/_{16}$, $^{6}/_{8}$
6. $^{1}/_{2}$, $^{10}/_{20}$, $^{6}/_{12}$
7. $^{4}/_{5} = {}^{12}/_{15}$, $^{20}/_{25}$, $^{8}/_{10}$
8. $^{2}/_{3} = {}^{10}/_{15}$, $^{6}/_{9}$, $^{16}/_{24}$
9. $^{5}/_{6} = {}^{10}/_{12}$, $^{25}/_{30}$, $^{15}/_{18}$
10. $^{13}/_{28}$
11. $^{10}/_{32}$
12. $^{20}/_{45}$

**Bonus Box answer:** Answers will vary. Here's one solution:

| 6 | 1 | 8 |
|---|---|---|
| 7 | 5 | 3 |
| 2 | 9 | 4 |

**Page 137**

| Park | | | Location |
|---|---|---|---|
| 9 | = | Yosemite | CA |
| 7 | = | Rocky Mountain | CO |
| 11 | = | Denali | AK |
| 2 | = | Grand Canyon | AZ |
| 10 | = | Zion | UT |
| 6 | = | Olympic | WA |
| 12 | = | Hawaii Volcanoes | HI |
| 1 | = | Acadia | ME |
| 8 | = | Yellowstone | WY, MT, ID |
| 3 | = | Grand Teton | WY |
| 5 | = | Mammoth Cave | KY |
| 4 | = | Great Smoky Mountains | NC, TN |
| 14 | = | Badlands | SD |
| 13 | = | Isle Royale | MI |

**Regions:**
Blue: MD, DE, NJ, PA, NY, CT, RI, MA, VT, NH, ME
Green: VA, WV, KY, TN, AR, LA, MS, AL, GA, FL, SC, NC
Yellow: ND, SD, NE, KS, MN, IA, MO, WI, MI, IL, IN, OH
Orange: AZ, NM, TX, OK
Red: CA, NV, UT, CO, WY, ID, OR, WA, MT, AK, HI

**Page 142**
**Part 1:**
1. Elizabeth was born to King Henry VIII and Anne Boleyn on September 7, 1533.
2. As a baby, Elizabeth was moved to the country to be raised by a foster mother, Lady Bryan.
3. When Elizabeth was only three, King Henry VIII had Anne Boleyn beheaded for treason.
4. The day after Anne Boleyn was executed, Henry VIII married Jane Seymour.
5. In 1537, Jane Seymour gave birth to Elizabeth's half-brother, Edward.
6. When she was ten, Elizabeth was being tutored in Latin, Greek, French, and Italian.
7. In 1547, Henry VIII died. Elizabeth's nine-year-old brother, Edward, became king.
8. At the age of 15, King Edward VI caught tuberculosis and died.
9. Elizabeth's older sister, Mary, became queen of England after the death of Edward VI and a nine-day reign by Lady Jane Grey.
10. In November of 1558, Mary died and Elizabeth was crowned queen.
11. In 1588, Elizabeth led the English navy in defeating the Spanish navy, the Armada.
12. Elizabeth died in 1603 after reigning for 45 years.

**Part 2:** Answers will vary.
**Bonus Box answer:** Answers will vary. Accept all reasonable answers.
- *tutored:* to be taught, especially privately
- *reigning:* ruling
- *executed:* put to death
- *tuberculosis:* a disease of the lungs
- *beheaded:* to have one's head cut off
- *treason:* an attempt to overthrow a government or hurt the ruler or the ruler's family

**Page 143**

2. Definitions may vary; accept all reasonable answers.
   a. disgrace: loss of grace, favor, or honor
   b. weep: to cry; to express deep sorrow
   c. outcast: one that is cast out or refused acceptance
   d. fate: destiny, lot
   e. scope: space or opportunity to move, act, or think freely
   f. contented: satisfied
   g. despising: regarding as worthless or distasteful
   h. lark: a type of songbird
   i. sullen: gloomily silent; dismal
   j. scorn: reject
3. Interpretations of the sonnet will vary.

**Page 148**

Descriptions may vary.

**Pyramids of Egypt at Giza**
**Date created:** 2600 to 2500 B.C.
**Size:** Great Pyramid (the largest pyramid) = about 450 ft. tall
**Location:** Giza, Egypt
**Description:** oldest of seven ancient wonders, only one of the seven ancient wonders still in existence, built as tombs for Egyptian kings, is believed that the Great Pyramid is made of almost 2.3 million limestone blocks

**Hanging Gardens of Babylon**
**Date created:** about 600 B.C.
**Size:** 400 ft. square and 75 ft. above the ground
**Location:** near present-day Baghdad in Iraq
**Description:** may only be a fable, probably built by King Nebuchadnezzar II for one of his wives, were irrigated with water from the Euphrates River

**Temple of Artemis at Ephesus**
**Date created:** about 550 B.C.
**Size:** foundation = 377 ft. by 180 ft., had 106 columns that were about 40 feet high
**Location:** city of Ephesus (west coast of present-day Turkey)
**Description:** one of the biggest and most complex temples built in ancient times, dedicated to the Greek goddess Artemis, made entirely of marble except for the tile-covered wooden roof

**Statue of Zeus**
**Date created:** about 435 B.C.
**Size:** 40 ft. tall
**Location:** Olympia, Greece
**Description:** dedicated to Zeus, the king of the gods; shows Zeus sitting on his throne holding a figure of his messenger, Nike, in his right hand and a scepter in his left hand; robe and ornaments made out of gold

**Mausoleum at Halicarnassus**
**Date created:** about 353 B.C.
**Size:** about 135 ft. high with 36 columns
**Location:** present-day southwestern Turkey
**Description:** huge white marble tomb for Persian ruler Mausolus; top part was a pyramid, probably decorated with statue of Mausolus; heavily damaged by earthquake in early 15th century

**Colossus of Rhodes**
**Date created:** early 200s B.C.
**Size:** about 120 ft. tall
**Location:** near harbor of Rhodes, an island in Aegean Sea
**Description:** huge bronze statue to honor sun god Helios, stood near harbor of Rhodes, was about same size as Statue of Liberty, destroyed by an earthquake

**Lighthouse of Alexandria**
**Date created:** about 270 B.C.
**Size:** over 400 ft. high
**Location:** on ancient island of Pharos in harbor of Alexandria, Egypt
**Description:** also called the Pharos of Alexandria, fire at top of lighthouse guided sailors, stood for about 1,500 years before being destroyed by earthquake

**Page 159**

Answers for 1–2 will vary.

3. When you sip through a straw, you lower the air pressure in your mouth. The greater air pressure of the atmosphere pushes down on the outside of the straw. The liquid is pushed up the straw by this greater pressure.

**Page 161**

Answers for 1–3 will vary.

4. Diagrams will vary.

**Conclusion:** The reason that a roller coaster car doesn't need an engine is that the car is driven by the conversion of potential energy to kinetic energy. All of the kinetic energy that the car needs to make it through the coaster is present once the car descends the first hill.

**Page 166**

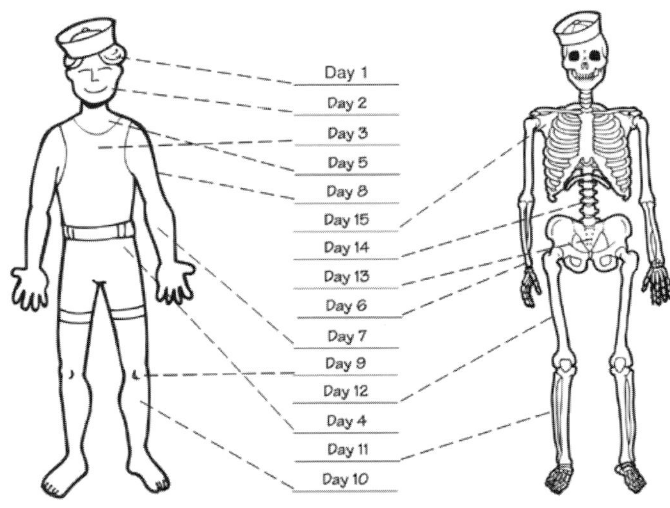


**Page 167**

| | |
|---|---|
| 1. 54 bones | 7. 14 bones |
| 2. 52 bones | 8. 8 bones |
| 3. 106 bones | 9. 24 vertebrae |
| 4. 20 bones | 10. 12 thoracic vertebrae |
| 5. 14 knuckles | 11. 12 pairs |
| 6. 14 bones | 12. 5 people |

**Bonus Box answer:** 185 bones are included in the diagram's labels, so 21 are not labeled. They include the sternum, plus two each of the following: humerus, radius, ulna, femur, tibia, fibula, patella, clavicle, scapula, and hip bones. (Note: each hip bone is actually three bones that have fused together: the ilium, pubis, and ischium.)

**Page 170**

Students' predictions and answers will vary. Suggested answers include the following:

1. The model represents how wastes are handled in a real landfill. The materials are the same types found in a real landfill: paper, plastics, cans, food scraps, yard waste, glass, etc. Some materials are covered with soil. Others are uncovered. The plastic box prevents the leaking of *leachate,* fluid that comes from garbage. Placing the box in a sunny area and adding water as needed makes it similar to the environment of a real landfill.
2. Students' options will vary.
3. When people recycle, there is less waste to put into a landfill, meaning that these areas fill at a slower rate. It also decreases the severity of the problems caused by landfills.
4. Microorganisms in the soil cause biodegradable materials like paper and food substances to decay in just a few days. Plastics and aluminum cans (which are not biodegradable) can take hundreds of years or more to decompose.
5. If leachate seeped from a landfill, it could poison the groundwater (often used as drinking water) and the surrounding soil.

**Page 176**

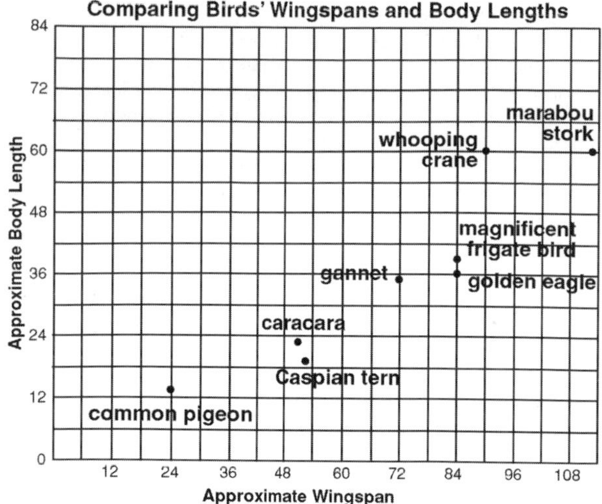


1. marabou stork
2. common pigeon
3. whooping crane and Caspian tern, magnificent frigate bird and golden eagle, caracara and whooping crane, Caspian tern and gannet
4. 89 in., 47 in.
5. 71.3 in.
6. 35.9 in.
7. yes, 60 for the body lengths and 84 for the wingspans
8. According to this set of data, a bird's wingspan increases as its body length increases.

**Bonus Box answers:** Body lengths from least to greatest: common pigeon (1 ft. 1 in.), Caspian tern (1 ft. 8 in.), caracara (1 ft. 11 in.), gannet (2 ft. 11 in.), golden eagle (3 ft.), magnificent frigate bird (3 ft. 4 in.), marabou stork and whooping crane (5 ft.). Wingspans from greatest to least: marabou stork (9 ft. 5 in.), whooping crane (7 ft. 6 in.), golden eagle and magnificent frigate bird (7 ft.), gannet (6 ft.), Caspian tern (4 ft. 5 in.), caracara (4 ft. 2 in.), common pigeon (2 ft.).

**Page 177**

| | |
|---|---|
| 1. horse | 7. peregrine falcon |
| 2. flea | 8. swan |
| 3. dragonfly | 9. tumbleweed |
| 4. cocklebur | 10. flatworm |
| 5. dandelion | 11. earthworm |
| 6. maple | 12. squid |

**Bonus Box answer:** cheetah, hare, greyhound, African elephant, camel

**Page 182**

A and J: Water is made up of tiny particles called *molecules.*

C and F: Water is the only substance that can exist as a solid, liquid, and gas at temperatures normally found on the earth.

H and E: Most substances contract as they become colder, but water expands when it is colder than 39°F.

D and I: The freshwater available to humans from groundwater, lakes, and rivers is only about 1/50 of 1% of the world's total water supply.

B and G: Because water dissolves more substances than any other liquid, it is known as the "universal solvent."

K and Q: Water freezes at 32°F, and it boils at 212°F.

T and M: The average ten-minute bath or shower uses 25–50 gallons of water.

N and R: A water molecule is made up of one atom of oxygen and two atoms of hydrogen.

O and S: A drop of water would be the shape of a perfect sphere if it were not for gravity and other forces.

L and P: Because water is sticky and elastic, it can move through tiny blood vessels and roots.

**Bonus Box answer:** tomato 95 percent, potato 80 percent, elephant 70 percent, human 65 percent

**Page 187**

Answers will vary. Possible answers may include the following details:

**Expectations** (Ch. 2): the place you must always go before you get to where you're going; home of the Whether Man, whose job is to hurry people along whether they like it or not

**Doldrums** (Ch. 2): a place where everything is gray and monotonous, where nothing ever happens or changes, and where no one is allowed to think or laugh; home of the Lethargarians; the place where people who don't pay attention often get stuck

**Dictionopolis** (Ch. 3): a happy kingdom ruled by King Azaz the Unabridged; the place where all the words in the world come from

**Point of View** (Ch. 9): located near the Forest of Sight; home of Alec Bings, a boy who is suspended three feet off the ground, giving him a unique point of view

**Illusions** (Ch. 10): a mirage in the Forest of Sight that looks like a magnificent city

**Reality** (Ch. 10): an invisible city that gradually became invisible when everyone became too busy to pay attention to how things looked

**Valley of Sound** (Ch. 12): a place that's been completely quiet ever since the people became too busy to appreciate sound

**Conclusions** (Ch. 13): a desolate island that a person arrives at whenever he or she decides something without having a good reason

**Digitopolis** (Chs. 6, 14): the city of numbers, ruled by the Mathemagician, the brother of King Azaz

**Infinity** (Ch. 15): the land where the tallest, the shortest, the biggest, the smallest, and the most and the least of everything are kept; a dreadfully poor place where they can never manage to make ends meet; a place that you know is there but can never reach

**Mountains of Ignorance** (Chs. 16–17): a dark, grimy place of shadows and evil intentions; home of the Terrible Trivium, the demon of insincerity, and other monsters; where Milo and his companions must go through to reach the Castle in the Air

**Page 188**

Answers may vary slightly. Accept any reasonable answer.

1. Officer Shrift blew the whistle until his face was beet red.
2. It's against the law to bark without a barking meter.
3. Milo and Tock were sentenced to six million years in prison.
4. You can get into a lot of trouble mixing up words.
5. Faintly Macabre offered Milo and Tock a candy punctuation mark.
6. They wanted to hear the story about Rhyme and Reason.

**Page 190: "During Reading"**

| | |
|---|---|
| Chapter 1: | benevolently = vole, lent, be |
| | briskets = risk, brisk, is |
| Chapter 2: | tendrils = ten, end, tend |
| | incandescently = in, can, descent, scent, cent, and |
| Chapter 3: | paraplegic = par, rap, leg |
| | chanteuse = chant, ant, an, us, use |
| Chapter 4: | carafe = car |
| | tamping = tamp, in, pin, tam, am |
| Chapter 5: | quavering = ring, quaver, in |
| | enchantingly = enchant, chant, tin, tingly, in, ant |
| | ceremoniously = sly, us |
| Chapter 6: | vanquished = van, vanquish, shed, an |
| | flanks = an, flan, lank |
| | jubilant = ant, an |
| Chapter 7: | rendered = render, end, red |
| | stealth = steal, teal |
| | sentinels = sent, tin, in, tine |
| Chapter 8: | unison = son, on |
| | incarnation = in, car, nation, carnation |
| Chapter 9: | publicity = pub, public, city |
| | precedent = precede, recede, cede, den, dent |
| Chapter 10: | sustain = stain, us, in |
| | parched = parch, arc, arch, arched, par |
| Chapter 11: | perpetual = pet, per |

**Page 196**
Students' answers may vary. Below are suggested pranks and consequences.
**Prank #1 (after reading chapter 1):** Caroline plots to earn Wally's trust.
**People Involved:** Caroline, Wally, and Peter
**Consequences (after reading chapter 7):**
- Caroline picks Wally to be her partner for the December project.
- Wally lies when Caroline interviews him.
- Caroline asks Peter to steal Wally's clothes.
- Wally and Caroline fail the December project.

**Prank #2 (after reading chapter 10):** The Malloy girls fake a murder scene.
**People Involved:** Malloy girls, Hatford boys
**Consequences (after reading chapter 12):**
- The Hatford boys call 911.
- The police go to the Malloy house.
- The Hatford boys get in trouble when the police go to their house.

**Prank #3 (after reading chapter 15):** The Malloy girls trap the Hatford boys in the loft.
**People Involved:** Malloy girls and Hatford boys
**Consequences (after reading chapter 17):**
- Two of the Hatford boys get paint on their clothes.
- Two of the Hatford boys have to jump out a window.
- Mr. Malloy gets paint on his sport coat.
- The Malloy girls have to apologize to the Hatford boys.
- The Malloy girls have to earn money to pay for their dad's new sport coat.

**Prank #4 (after reading chapter 19):** Caroline and Wally plot to give each other gross Christmas gifts.
**People Involved:** Caroline and Wally
**Consequences (after reading chapter 20):**
- Caroline's gift for Wally accidentally goes to her dad's secretary.
- Wally's gift for Caroline accidentally goes to Miss Applebaum, their teacher.
- Caroline helps Wally get his gift for her back from their teacher.

**Page 206**
**Conflict: Chapters 15–16:** Grandpa ignores Pete's declaration of war.
**Action:** Pete discusses his strategy with Billy and Steve.
**Possible Consequences:** Students' answers will vary.
**Conflict: Chapters 17–18:** Pete sets Grandpa's alarm clock to wake him in the middle of the night, which Grandpa doesn't appreciate.
**Action:** Pete tells Grandpa he loves him, but the war is still on; Grandpa says they'll discuss it later.
**Possible Consequences:** Students' answers will vary.
**Conflict: Chapters 19–20:** Pete steals Grandpa's slippers.
**Action:** Grandpa comes to Pete's room to get the slippers; Pete thinks he might lose the war because Grandpa is so nice.
**Possible Consequences:** Students' answers will vary.

**Page 207**
1. 13 hr. 24 min.
2. 42 min., 48 min.
3. March 3: 18 hr. 49 min., March 4: 18 hr. 55 min., March 5: 19 hr. 6 min.
4. Students' answers will vary. They should allow time for getting ready and for traveling to the fishing spot.
5. about 13 hr., about 12 hr.
6. Students' answers will vary. Students could say they would least prefer the morning high tide because those times are in the middle of the night when they would be asleep.
7. 3 hr.
8. 12 hr. 4 min.
9. 6 hr. 13 min.
10. Students' answers will vary. Accept all reasonable answers. One method for determining the time would be to look at the differences between the times of the morning low tide in the chart. Those differences are 45 minutes, 44 minutes, 48 minutes, and 52 minutes. A student could find the average of these four numbers (rounding to the nearest whole number), which is 47. The projected time for the morning low tide on March 6 would be about 10:50 A.M. using this method.

**Bonus Box answer:** It will be the same. The water level will remain at the third step because the boat will rise as the tide comes in.

**Page 211**
**The Logans**
1. grandfather: Paul Edward
2. grandmother: Big Ma/Caroline
3. mother: Mama/Mary
4. father: Papa/David
5. uncle: Uncle Hammer
6. oldest son: Stacey
7. daughter: Cassie
8. middle son: Christopher-John
9. youngest son: Little Man/ Clayton Chester

**The Averys**
1. father: Mr. Joe Avery
2. mother: Mrs. Fannie Avery
3. older son: T. J.
4. younger son: Claude

**The Simms**
1. father: Charlie
2. older son: R. W.
3. older son: Melvin
4. daughter: Lillian Jean
5. youngest son: Jeremy

**Others**
1. Logans' houseguest: Mr. L. T. Morrison
2. Cassie's teacher: Miss Daisy Crocker
3. The Wallaces: Kaleb, Dewberry, and Thurston
4. attorney: Wade Jamison
5. plantation owner: Harlan Granger
6. man who runs the Mercantile in Strawberry: Jim Lee Barnett

**Page 217**
Answers may vary.
**magical book of fairy tales:** A gift from Mandy, the book shows Ella what other characters are doing or have done.
**her mother's necklace:** Ella's mother wore it on her wedding day. It is valuable because it was made by gnomes.
**barrel of Tonic:** It makes her feel better after feeling so sad about her mother. It is the only food she gets to eat on the trip to finishing school except for one bite of bread.
**parrot from the menagerie:** It is a gift from her friend Simon, who is the bird keeper in the royal menagerie.
**centaur colt named Apple:** It is a gift from Prince Char.
**dictionary of exotic speech:** It is a gift from the Writing Mistress, who gives it to Ella after finding out that Ella wants to learn more about different languages.
**wolf cup:** It was made by the famous gnome Agulen. Ella sets it out on a table in the inn to guard her as she sleeps.
**fairy rug:** Mandy gave it to Ella's mother. It is magic.
**the best of her mother's gowns:** Ella wears them to the balls.
**pair of glass slippers:** Ella and Char find them. Ella wears them to the balls. Char makes Ella try on the lost slipper after the last ball to prove her identity.
**letters from Char:** They cheer her up while she is being treated as a servant by Dame Olga and her daughters.
**white mask:** Ella wears it at her father's wedding so Lucinda won't see her. She wears it at the balls so Char, Dame Olga, Hattie, and Olive won't know who she is.
**silver tiara and necklace:** Mandy gives them to Ella to wear to the last ball. They won't disappear at midnight.
**fairy box:** Lucinda gives it to Char and Ella as a wedding gift. It grows or shrinks to fit whatever is placed in it.

**Page 218**
1. $4\frac{2}{5}$ miles
2. $7\frac{9}{10}$ miles
3. $2\frac{9}{10}$ miles
4. $5\frac{17}{20}$ miles
5. $\frac{7}{20}$ mile
6. Areida, $4\frac{7}{10}$ miles
7. $10\frac{7}{10}$ miles, $\frac{7}{10}$ mile
8. $15\frac{1}{10}$ miles, $30\frac{1}{5}$ miles
9. Areida $8\frac{3}{5}$ miles, Ella $8\frac{1}{2}$ miles
10. Areida, $\frac{1}{10}$ mile

**Page 225**

| Date | Activity | Debit | Credit | Balance |
|---|---|---|---|---|
| 9/5 | opened account | | $15,000 | $15,000 |
| 9/6 | 3,000 brochures | $4,000 | | 11,000 |
| 9/7 | 10,000 flyers | 5,000 | | 6,000 |
| 9/8 | donation | | 5,500 | 11,500 |
| 9/11 | donation | | 10,000 | 21,500 |
| 9/12 | 10 political posters | 7,500 | | 14,000 |
| 9/13 | contribution | | 5,400 | 19,400 |
| 9/14 | 4 radio ads | 10,000 | | 9,400 |
| 9/15 | contribution | | 1,950 | 11,350 |
| 9/18 | 5 political posters | 3,750 | | 7,600 |
| 9/19 | 3 radio ads | 7,500 | | 100 |
| 9/20 | contribution | | 8,500 | 8,600 |
| 9/21 | 6,000 brochures | 8,000 | | 600 |
| 9/22 | donation | | 7,900 | 8,500 |
| 9/25 | 4,000 flyers | 2,000 | | 6,500 |

**Bonus Box answer:** With the remaining $6,500 balance, Mona can get one TV ad and two political posters.

**Page 226**

1. Each of these states has only three electoral votes: AK, DC, DE, MT, ND, SD, VT, WY.
2. CA (54), NY (33), TX (32); 119 electoral votes
3. Pat should try to win the four states with the largest number of electoral votes because they represent 144 votes, more than half of the 270 votes needed to win.
4. Pat should try to win the states with the next largest votes: NY (33), TX (32), FL (25), OH (23) or PA (23).

**Bonus Box answer:** Pat would need to win these 11 states: CA (54), NY (33), TX (32), FL (25), OH (23), PA (23), IL (22), MI (18), NJ (15), NC (14), and GA (13) or VA (13).

**Page 227**

The topics for the boxes are as follows:

*Box 1:* Primary Elections and Caucuses
*Box 2:* National Convention
*Box 3:* The Campaign
*Box 4:* Election Day
*Box 5:* The Electoral College

**Bonus Box answer:** When there is a tie, the state delegations in the House of Representatives choose the president from the three candidates having the highest number of electoral votes.

**Page 242**

calculator

**Bonus Box answer:** Students' sentences will vary.

**Page 244**

**in 1953**—prepositional phrase (3)
**to develop television**—infinitive phrase (7)
**a Russian-born American scientist**—appositive phrase (4)
**an early cartoon**—appositive phrase (4)
**of television**—prepositional phrase (3)
**in 1945**—prepositional phrase (3)
**To entertain viewers**—infinitive phrase (7)
**Helping some contestants answer questions**—gerund phrase (6)
**Holding presidential debates on TV**—gerund phrase (6)
**a comedy show**—appositive phrase (4)
**to watch**—infinitive phrase (7)
**Watching TV**—gerund phrase (6)

Total TV sets in the 1960s: about 60 million

**Page 260**

Students' answers to the questions will vary.

1. pencil (…dampen cilantro…)
   You would dampen cilantro with salad dressing instead of motor oil.
2. eraser (…water as erosion…)
   Running water can make parts of the earth wear away and change the shape of rocks.
3. locker (…clock erratically…)
   A clock with an irregular tick is not very dependable.
4. crayon (…plastic ray on…)
   An "arm" of a plastic starfish might break off.
5. chalk (…catch Al King…)
   You might be able to catch Al as he's trying to make his kite fly high.
6. staples (…drum's tap lessen…)
   The tapping of a drum could become less frequent if the drummer taps slower.
7. paste (…papa steadily…)
   A person's papa could probably rise calmly and smoothly out of a chair.
8. marker (…mark erroneously…)
   A worksheet could include a mark mistakenly made by the teacher.
9. ruler (…rule resolutely…)
   A rule should firmly remain the same for everyone.
10. sharpener (…melodious harp energize…)
    It is possible for people to feel energized and renewed by listening to pretty music played on a harp.
11. book (…peek-a-boo keenly…)
    A baby is eager to play peek-a-boo with a parent.
12. tape (…tap excitedly…)
    A dog's tail could tap excitedly on the floor when his owner comes into the room.
13. pen (…gape nonchalantly…)
    A person would not stare in a carefree manner if he were about to step on a snake.
14. paper (…dump a person…)
    It would not be acceptable for a taxi driver to dump a person into a large crack in the earth.

**Bonus Box answer:** D E N V E R, C O L O R A D O

**Page 261**

**Code for alphabet:**

| | | | |
|---|---|---|---|
| A = | $.05 | N = | $.70 |
| B = | $.10 | O = | $.75 |
| C = | $.15 | P = | $.80 |
| D = | $.20 | Q = | $.85 |
| E = | $.25 | R = | $.90 |
| F = | $.30 | S = | $.95 |
| G = | $.35 | T = | $1.00 |
| H = | $.40 | U = | $1.05 |
| I = | $.45 | V = | $1.10 |
| J = | $.50 | W = | $1.15 |
| K = | $.55 | X = | $1.20 |
| L = | $.60 | Y = | $1.25 |
| M = | $.65 | Z = | $1.30 |

Students' answers for questions 1–5, 7, and the Bonus Box will vary.

6. Students' predictions about which items are most and least expensive will vary.
   a. pencil: $2.95
   b. crayons: $4.75
   c. scissors: $6.05
   d. glue: $2.25
   e. eraser: $3.30
   f. bookbag: $2.65
   g. calculator: $5.30
   h. sharpener: $5.20

**Page 265**

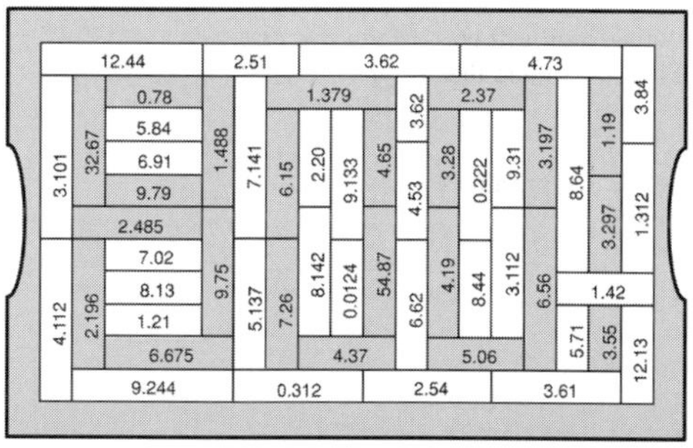

Answer: Boo!

**Bonus Box answer:**
12.44
12.13
9.31
9.244
9.133
8.64
8.44
8.142
8.13
7.141

**Page 266**

Although we recycle about 27% of our **garbage,** Americans still send about 150 million **tons** of trash to landfills each year. An amazing 25 million tons of this trash is thrown away in the five weeks between Thanksgiving and New Year's Day.

The clear solution to this **problem** is to throw away less trash! That's the goal of Use Less Stuff™ Day, celebrated every year on the Thursday before Thanksgiving. The **founders** of Use Less Stuff Day created the **holiday** to encourage consumers to look for ways to reduce waste. Some easy ideas they suggest to **reduce** your "waste-line" include taking your own shopping bag to the **mall;** sending e-greetings instead of regular cards; and reusing old maps, artwork, paper bags, or comics as wrapping paper. You can also **buy** rechargeable batteries, look for **products** that don't have much plastic and paper packaging, and donate unwanted clothes and toys to **charities.** These suggestions will help reduce the trash that ends up in landfills.

Using less "stuff" is the number one weapon in the war on waste. It's something **everyone** can do with a little thought and **effort.** Remember: *Reduce* is the first *R* in the well-known slogan "Reduce, Reuse, Recycle!"

**Page 271**

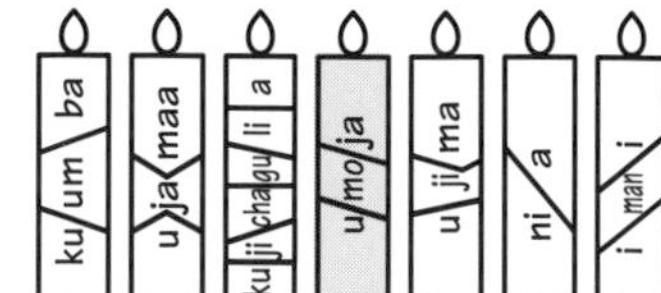

**Page 272**
**3 Book Gift Ideas**
Spelled correctly: *Treasure Island, Hatchet, Where the Sidewalk Ends*
Corrected spellings: *Maniac Magee; A Wrinkle in Time; Call It Courage; Island of the Blue Dolphins; Sarah, Plain and Tall*
**2 U.S. Cities to Visit**
Spelled correctly: Baltimore, MD; Albuquerque, NM
Corrected spellings: Cincinnati, OH; Columbia, SC; Raleigh, NC; Baton Rouge, LA; Sacramento, CA; Bismarck, ND
**4 Bodies of Water to Fly Over**
Spelled correctly: Lake Tahoe, Great Salt Lake, Gulf of Mexico, Monongahela River
Corrected spellings: Lake Michigan, Saint Lawrence River, Mississippi River, Colorado River
**6 Sports Gift Ideas**
Spelled correctly: basketball, football helmet, baseball glove, soccer ball, croquet set, roller skates
Corrected spellings: badminton set, ski equipment
**5 Foreign Countries to Visit**
Spelled correctly: Brazil, Colombia, Zaire, New Zealand, Switzerland
Corrected spellings: Pakistan, Thailand, Australia
**7 Musical Gift Ideas**
Spelled correctly: violin, trumpet, compact discs, set of drums, trombone, saxophone, stereo system
Corrected spelling: piccolo
**8 Clothing Ideas**
Spelled correctly: ski jacket, cap, blue jeans, mittens, shirt, sneakers, warm-up pants, sweater
**1 More Gift Ideas**
Spelled correctly: computer
Corrected spellings: telephone, mall gift certificate, stuffed panda bear, jewelry, camera, miniature golf passes, movie theater tickets

**Page 273**
Answers are listed in order, by paragraph.
1: 1929, second, three
2: 9th, 12th, 19
3: 1951, 1953, four
4: 1955
5: 1; 5; 18,000; 1956
6: 1960
7: 200,000; 350
8: 1964, 35
9: 1968
10: 1983
**Bonus Box answer:** In the year 2001, Dr. King would be 72 years old.

**Page 276**
1. 1,630 calories
2. 3,260 calories
3. 39.5 grams, 79 grams
4. $37\ ^{1}/_{2}$
5. 163 calories
6. No, the total cost of the ingredients is $4.07.
7. $12.21
8. $3.17
9. 326 calories
10. Answers will vary.

**Bonus Box answer:** Answers will vary.

**Page 277**
**Part 1**
1. a. 26, 19
   b. 7
2. a. 161, 7
   b. 23
3. a. 19, 21, 22, 23, 24, 26, 26
   b. 23
4. a. yes
   b. 26

**Part 2, Part 3,** and the **Bonus Box answers** will vary.

**Page 281**
1. 20 x $1.89 = $37.80
2. 20 ÷ 2 = 10 boxes
3. 10 x $.89 = $8.90
4. $37.80 + $8.90 = $46.70
5. $1.00 x 98 = $98.00
6. $98.00 – $46.70 = $51.30
7. 20 x 5 = 100 cups
8. 150 ÷ 25 = 6 journals
9. 90 ÷ 6 = 15 packs
10. paper: $1.50 x 15 = $22.50
    front covers: 90 x $.09 = $8.10
    back covers: 90 x $.05 = $4.50
    paint pens: $2.99 x 2 = $5.98
    TOTAL: $22.50 + $8.10 + $4.50 + $5.98 = $41.08
11. 90 x $1.00 = $90.00
12. $90.00 – $41.08 = $48.92

**Bonus Box answer:** $51.30 + $48.92 = $100.22

**Page 284**
1. **E**ncourage others to reduce, reuse, and recycle. *Recycling symbol*
2. **H**ey, everyone should put litter in its place. *Trash can symbol*
3. **S**ave fuel by walking, or you could try riding a bike. *Earth symbol*
4. **V**arious types of pollution make our air, land, and water dirty. *Recycling symbol*
5. **L**et's learn ways to keep the environment clean by reading books, and we can also find out by watching TV programs and videos. *Earth symbol*
6. **Y**es, each person should do his part to take care of the earth. *Trash can symbol*
7. **T**ry to use less water when brushing teeth, showering, and cleaning the house. *Recycling symbol*
8. **O**ne person alone can't solve the pollution problem, but each person should do all he can. *Earth symbol*
9. **K**ids, can you help us stop polluting our planet? *Trash can symbol*
10. **W**ow, don't you recycle? *Trash can symbol*
11. **D**ispose of trash, chemicals, and wastes properly. *Recycling symbol*
12. **R**ecycle plastic, glass, paper, and metal. *Recycling symbol*
13. **M**ake a commitment to clean up, reduce, and recycle all the trash being created. *Recycling symbol*
14. **I**t's never too late to help, and you can start today. *Earth symbol*

Miss Clean's message: *Everyone has the chance to make a difference in our world.*

**Bonus Box answer:** Students' answers will vary.

**Page 285**
1. **"I** like to read a good, long story," said **C**orey.
2. **"P**lug in a small night-light," replied **M**r. **W**right.
3. **"A** soft stuffed animal is what you need," stated **M**r. **T**weed.
4. **"Y**ou must," whispered **M**rs. **W**illow, **"**have a fluffy, plump pillow."
5. **"S**tretching before **I** go to bed," explained **R**amona, **"**always puts sleepy thoughts in my head."
6. **M**rs. **S**ilk uttered, **"I** like to sip on a cup of warm milk."
7. **"I** always listen to calm, soothing music," voiced **M**r. **B**usick.
8. **"B**efore bed," responded **J**ean, **"I** never drink anything with caffeine."
9. **"I** have to sleep in a cozy, comfortable bed," murmured **F**red.
10. **"M**ake sure your bedroom," answered **P**rofessor **B**old, **"**isn't too hot or too cold."
11. **"N**ever exercise late at night," suggested dependable **D**wight.
12. **"T**ry to stick to a bedtime routine," recommended **D**r. **E**loise **L**ean.
13. **"C**ounting sheep," advised **M**r. **L**eap, **"**usually puts me to sleep."
14. **"T**ake several deep, relaxing breaths," offered perky **S**tephanie **E**lizabeth.
15. **"E**at spicy foods early, not late," piped in **M**r. **S**late.
16. **"W**hat **I** suggest," declared **M**rs. **W**est, **"**is a nice, long bubble bath to relieve anyone who's stressed."

**Bonus Box answer:** Students' answers will vary.

**Page 288**

| | 1 | 2 | 3 | 4 | 5 | 6 |
|---|---|---|---|---|---|---|
| cafeteria | ✘ | ✘ | ✔ | ✘ | ✘ | ✘ |
| arts and crafts | ✔ | ✘ | ✘ | ✘ | ✘ | ✘ |
| showers | ✘ | ✘ | ✘ | ✘ | ✘ | ✔ |
| sleeping quarters | ✘ | ✘ | ✘ | ✘ | ✔ | ✘ |
| meeting hall | ✘ | ✔ | ✘ | ✘ | ✘ | ✘ |
| gift shop | ✘ | ✘ | ✘ | ✔ | ✘ | ✘ |

| | Bunk 1 | Bunk 2 | Bunk 3 | Bunk 4 | Bunk 5 |
|---|---|---|---|---|---|
| Chandler | ✘ | ✘ | ✘ | ✘ | ✔ |
| Mason | ✘ | ✘ | ✔ | ✘ | ✘ |
| Riley | ✘ | ✘ | ✘ | ✔ | ✘ |
| Zack | ✔ | ✘ | ✘ | ✘ | ✘ |
| Scott | ✘ | ✔ | ✘ | ✘ | ✘ |

**Page 289**
1. **sale price $11.25** (25% = .25; .25 x 15 = 3.75; 15 – 3.75 = 11.25)
2. **sale price $4,396.00** (20% = .20; .20 x 5,495 = 1,099; 5,495 – 1,099 = 4,396)
3. **35% off** (8.40 – 5.46 = 2.94; 2.94 ÷ 8.40 = .35; .35 = 35%)
4. **sale price $246.00** ($^{1}/_{3}$ x 369 = 123; 369 – 123 = 246)
5. **reg. price $35.00** (100% – 20% = 80%; 28 ÷ 80%; 28 ÷ .80 = 35)
6. **40% off** (185 – 111 = 74; 74 ÷ 185 = .4; .4 = .40 = 40%)
7. **sale price $2.85** (70% = .70; .70 x 9.50 = 6.65; 9.50 – 6.65 = 2.85)
8. **sale price $44.00** ($^{1}/_{3}$ x 66 = 22; 66 – 22 = 44)
9. **15% off** (1,385 – 1,177.25 = 207.75; 207.75 ÷ 1,385 = .15; .15 = 15%)
10. **reg. price $20.00** (1 – $^{1}/_{5}$ = $^{4}/_{5}$; 16 ÷ $^{4}/_{5}$; 16 x $^{5}/_{4}$ = 20)
11. **reg. price $1.20** (1 – $^{2}/_{3}$ = $^{1}/_{3}$; .40 ÷ $^{1}/_{3}$; .40 x $^{3}/_{1}$ = 1.20)
12. **sale price $98.45** (45% = .45; .45 x 179 = 80.55; 179 – 80.55 = 98.45)

**Bonus Box answer:** total cost $104.36 (.06 x 98.45 = 5.907; 5.907 = $5.91; $98.45 + $5.91 = $104.36)

**Index**

7 21202 04523 0